Secondary
and
Middle School
Teaching
Methods

Leonard H. Clark

Jersey City State College

Irving S. Starr

University of Hartford

FIFTH EDITION

Secondary and Middle School Teaching Methods

MACMILLAN PUBLISHING COMPANY
New York

COLLIER MACMILLAN PUBLISHERS
London

Macmillan Publishing Company
866 Third Avenue, New York, New York 10022

Collier Macmillan Canada, Inc.

Library of Congress Cataloging in Publication Data
Clark, Leonard H.
    Secondary and middle school teaching methods.
    Includes index.
    1. High school teaching.   I. Starr, Irving S.
II. Title.
LB1607.C49   1986   373.11'02   85–328
ISBN 0–02–322600–5

Printing: 1 2 3 4 5 6 7 8   Year: 6 7 8 9 0 1 2 3 4 5

ISBN 0-02-322600-5

Preface

This is the fifth edition of this book. Since the publication of the first edition, many pedagogical innovations and experiments have been launched. We have attempted to incorporate the important changes into this revision. The purpose and treatment, however, except for minor reorganization to make the book more useful and cohesive, remain the same in this edition as in the first, because the basic pedagogical principles have not changed despite innovations and experiments.

This book was written to help prospective teachers learn how to teach. It is designed as a college textbook for an introductory course in general methods of teaching in middle and secondary schools, although it might serve well as a reference work for student teachers and teachers in service. We have attempted to make the book as practical and useful as possible. To achieve this end, we have tried to write from a middle-of-the-road point of view, and to describe methods suitable for use in the types of school in which students are likely to teach when they go to their first positions. For this same reason, we have attempted to write simply and clearly, to open each chapter with an outline and overview, and to close with a summary, to use numerous examples, to point up important understandings by means of questions at appropriate places within the text itself, and to keep quotations and references to scholarly works to a minimum. To ensure that the student has the necessary

background that one needs to choose and implement suitable teaching strategies and tactics, the first three chapters are devoted to basic background information about the schools, the learner, the learning process, and the teaching process. Nevertheless, in general, discussion of educational theory has been omitted except when it seemed necessary to explain the "why" of the methods advocated. However, the emphasis is, of necessity, on principles rather than recipes. There are no surefire recipes in teaching.

Sexist expressions easily find their way into a manuscript. We have tried to avoid them and other marks of prejudice. We have at times, however, used the editorial pronoun "he" to refer to both men and women. This should not be taken as evidence of sexism, but rather as an effort to facilitate readability. The use of masculine nouns and pronouns makes the writing less awkward.

We wish to acknowledge our indebtedness to the many persons—students, teachers, and friends— who have helped us write this book. We also express our gratitude to the students, teachers, superintendents, principals, and publishing houses who allowed us to reproduce their materials, and to the colleagues and readers who have made helpful criticisms and suggestions. We are indebted to Professors Ronald Anderson, University of Colorado, John Wiles, University of South Florida, Joan Jacob, Indiana State University, Connie S. Plessman, University of Nebraska, and Lloyd Campbell, North Texas State University for their critical analyses and comments. We especially thank Maria A. Clark, who not only typed the manuscript innumerable times for each of the editions but also read the copy and made suggestions for improving the wording, and without whose help the book could never have been finished.

East Conway, N.H.   L.H.C.

Hartford, Conn.   I.S.S.

Contents

 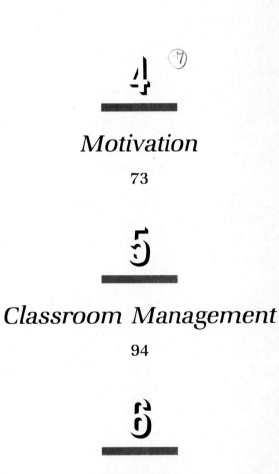

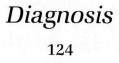

The School

Overview

In this introductory chapter we take a brief look at the middle and secondary schools as a means of orienting ourselves before we consider the teach-ing methods we may use in these schools. First, after a brief look at the history of the schools, we consider what the role of the school should be. Should it favor a well-rounded education or should it stress the purely academic and intellectual? We then look quickly at the school organization and some of its implications. What does one do about the problems of articulation and impersonality? How does one fit the teaching to the needs of a particular group of young people? What should the curriculum be like? How should it be organized? What is the place of general education, and of specialized education? How should it meet the problem of individual differences in students? Should the curriculum be subject centered or experience centered? Who should make these curriculum decisions and determine just what the curriculum will include?

Finally, we discuss the future of the schools. During the 1970s and 1980s many critics, commissions, and committees have expounded on what is wrong with our schools and what should be done to make them more excellent. In some instances, but not all by any means, their positions are well taken. We finish our chapter by discussing some of these recommendations and consider what seem to be the current trends in middle and secondary schools.

Introduction

The American school system was the first in the world dedicated to educating all the children of all the people from early childhood through adolescence. In general, this experiment has proved highly successful. In spite of alarming reports in the mass media, Americans have reason to be proud of their schools, and Americans are proud of them. In the 1984 Gallup Poll, 52 per cent of parents with children in public school rated the schools A or B.[1] In the 1982 Gallup Poll, education was rated among the top three American institutions. Only medicine and science were rated higher.[2] Even the

National Commission on Excellence in Education in its reports deploring the mediocrity of the schools' product points out that

> It is important, of course, to recognize that *the average citizen* today is better educated and more knowledgeable than the average citizen of a generation ago—more literate, and exposed to more mathematics, literature, and science. The positive impact of this fact on the well-being of our country and the lives of our people cannot be overstated.

Still, the American experiment in public education has not paid off completely. The Commission report goes on.

> Nevertheless, *the average graduate* of our schools and colleges today is not as well-educated as the average graduate of 25 or 35 years ago, when a much smaller proportion of our population completed high school and college. The negative impact of this fact likewise cannot be overstated.[3]

Evidently there is much room for improvement in our attempts to provide a quality education for all the children of all the people, through the middle and secondary grades. So let us now look briefly at the history of this noble experiment at the middle and secondary school levels.

History of Our Middle and Secondary Schools

Early American Secondary Schools

As soon as the early American settlers had established their first villages, they initiated secondary education for boys who had mastered their letters. These first American secondary schools were copies

[1] George H. Gallup, "The 16th Annual Gallup Poll of the Public's Attitudes Toward the Public Schools," *Phi Delta Kappan* (September, 1984), **66:**23–38.

[2] George H. Gallup, "The 14th Annual Gallup Poll of the Public's Attitudes Toward the Public Schools," *Phi Delta Kappan* (September, 1982), **64:**37–50.

[3] The National Commission on Excellence in Education, *A Nation at Risk: The Imperative for Educational Reform* (Washington, DC: U. S. Government Printing Office, 1983), p. 11.

> Do you feel that you received a "quality education" in your middle and high school years? In what ways did the schools serve you best? In what ways least? What would you have liked the schools to have done for you that they did not?

of the European Latin grammar schools. Although in 1647 the Legislature of Massachusetts required the towns to maintain Latin schools so that boys might prepare for college and train for the ministry, the Latin schools were never really popular. Their Ciceronian Latin curriculum did not meet the practical needs of the people. Soon independent entrepreneurs attempted to meet these needs by setting up private venture schools in which boys could learn the practical skills and knowledge required in the trades and professions of the day. Thus teachers might advertise to teach for a fee subjects such as bookkeeping, mathematics, astronomy, and navigation to boys whose parents wanted them to become merchants, navigators, surveyors, or practitioners of other businesses.

These private venture schools were successful enough to show the need for a new institution. In 1749 Benjamin Franklin proposed a plan for an academy that would provide a functional education for middle-class children. In this school's curriculum, much attention would be given to the study of English and to practical studies. As Franklin stated, since the school could not teach everything, it would teach those things likely to be "most useful and ornamental. Regard being had for the several Professions for which they are intended."

After a bit, the idea caught on and the academy became the typical secondary school of the nineteenth century.

On the whole, the academy was a successful institution.[4] Because academies were private

schools and needed students to exist, they tried to provide a suitable education for any boy or girl who could pay the cost. In many academies, the policy seemed to be that if enough students were willing to pay to study a subject, the academy would offer it.

The academy gave the students a good practical education, but parents found it too expensive. In 1821 the Boston School Committee,[5] upset because the Latin schools did not furnish "a child an education that shall fit him for an active life and serve as a foundation for eminence in his profession" and so forced parents to send their children to private academies at "heavy expense,"[6] founded the first American high school. This high school was to be a highly practical terminal institution for students who planned to enter mercantile or mechanical employment. Its curriculum was much like an academy's.

The public high school idea soon spread. After a while, the notion that the high school should be an extension of the common school system was generally accepted, although many people objected to paying taxes so that other people's children could go to high school. After considerable litigation in many communities, the right of school districts to establish public high schools was settled by numerous court decisions (notably a Pennsylvania case of 1851 and the Kalamazoo case of 1874).

Although the high schools were started as semi-vocational, terminal institutions, by the 1890s the curriculum had become largely college preparatory. This trend was reinforced by the attempts to standardize and improve secondary education, which resulted in the creation of regional accrediting associations and the College Entrance Examination Board.

---

[4] In New England, some private academies still fulfill the role of local high schools.

[5] That is, Board of Education or School Board.

[6] From subcommittee report on the basis of which the School Committee voted to establish the English Classical School. I. L. Kandel, *History of Secondary Education* (Boston: Houghton Mifflin, 1930), pp. 426–427.

A School for All American Youth

Until the turn of the century, the number of students attending high schools was small, considerably less than 10 per cent of the age group. But in the twentieth century, the school population grew rapidly. By World War I, the high schools enrolled one third of the fourteen- to seventeen year olds, and by World War II this number had risen to almost three fourths of that age group. Consequently, educational leaders tried to reorganize secondary education to make it suitable for "all the children of all the people."

So it was that the typical secondary schools in the United States became public, universal, and comprehensive. In this context *universal* means that the schools are open to all youths of the proper age group who have completed the elementary school program. Theoretically no one is denied admittance because of race, social status, wealth, intelligence, or class, although, in fact, the schools have not always lived up to this ideal. They are seldom selective in the sense of catering to an academic elite as many private and foreign schools are, however. *Public* means that the schools are financed by public funds. Theoretically students can attend without incurring any expense. Actually, in some instances, travel, materials, and incidentals make public secondary education fairly expensive. *Comprehensive* means that the school tries to provide for all the needs of all the youth in a single institution. Some school districts, however, provide specialized high schools for students with special talents or vocational goals. New York City, for instance, set up high schools for the performing arts, needle trades, science, and other academic and vocational specialties. Actually few American high schools are truly comprehensive; rather they are academic high schools with other curricula added.

To this day, the secondary schools have not learned to cope with their popularity. At first the schools tried to solve the problem by widening the curriculum to include manual training, home economics, business, art, music, and vocational programs. Later as the problems of universal secondary education became more acute, schools introduced general curricula that, all too often, turned out to be nothing but watered-down college preparatory courses, and established ability groups or curriculum tracks designed to provide different education for students with different academic abilities. At the end of World War II, many educators thought that the answer was life-adjustment education, a curriculum in citizenship, health, family living, and moral and social conduct for the 60 per cent of the students who did not want to prepare for college or enter vocational education courses. Educators and lay critics rejected this movement, which they considered a watering down of the curriculum. They insisted that the schools stress basics. Again in the 1960s and 1970s educators tried to solve the problem by attempting to make the school curricula more "relevant" to the real life of real people and more humane by introducing more and better vocational and career education courses and curricula, and by providing alternative schools and programs for students with special needs. None of these attempts has been especially successful. How

---

What should be the mission of a school whose students come from all walks of life and whose academic goals range from completion of professional graduate programs, learning a skilled trade, to becoming an unskilled laborer or machine tender? Should it have programs for all these different goals? What are the basics in such a school? How can it deal fairly with all its students?

Should the middle and high schools try to teach all youth or should there be separate institutions for students with different aspirations? Is a comprehensive high school feasible and viable?

Life-adjustment education was an attempt to provide for students with nonacademic life goals. What do you think of that solution?

to provide an effective educational program for all children at the secondary level remains unsolved.

The Junior High/Middle School Movement

At the turn of the century, junior high schools were formed to provide a school for young adolescents in which they would study a curriculum different from that of the elementary school but not as advanced as that of the high school. It was hoped that such a school would reduce the number of students dropping out of school by making the work more interesting and relevant to student needs than the elementary school work and also by enrolling students in a new school before the end of the compulsory attendance period.

It was also hoped that such a school would prepare students for their high school years by allowing them to taste the experiences and disciplines they might want to pursue, to introduce them gradually to the more formal departmentalized structure of the high school, and to provide the guidance and support students need in making the transfer from the elementary school to the high school.

In 1947 Gruhn and Douglas summed up the functions of the ideal junior high school. These functions include the following features:

1. Because the junior high school student is in a period of concept development, the student is best served by a curriculum in which subject matter is integrated; that is, correlated both within and among subject areas.
2. Because beginning adolescence is accompanied by the awakening of new interests, the beginnings of concerns about one's vocational and avocational future and a need to understand one's own interests, talents, potentials and proclivities, junior high schools should give students broad and varied programs that allow students to try, without penalty, a wide variety of experiences in order to discover their natural

bents and most suitable future courses of action.
3. Because the junior high school students are not adults, they need guidance and assistance. Junior high schools should stress individual counseling and group guidance, emphasizing educational, health, prevocational, and social-personal problems.
4. Because the growth rate is rapid and irregular in this age group, junior high school programs should differentiate learning experiences through individualized instructional programs and school activities. Differences in development make it impossible for one program to serve all students well. Provisions for individual differences must be built into the curriculum at this level.
5. Because at this age boys and girls are beginning to free themselves from the home and establish themselves as independent adults, the school, through its teachers and peer-group activities, must establish itself as a socialization agent that helps students establish their values and seek out their adult roles.
6. Because the junior high school years are transitional between the elementary and high schools, they should strive to make the change from the relative simplicity of the elementary classroom to the complexities of the departmentalized high school as smooth as possible. To carry out this function successfully, the schools must pay particular attention to articulation at all three levels.[7]

In short, junior high school should be a halfway station between elementary school and high school.

Soon after the end of World War II, some educators realized that many junior high schools were not doing the job for which they had been created. Instead of being schools for young adolescents, these schools had become simply junior editions of the high school. Furthermore, it seemed that

---

[7] William Gruhn and Harl Douglas, *The Modern Junior High School* (New York: Ronald, 1947. Rev. ed., 1956.)

boys and girls were growing up more quickly than they had in the past. Pubescence was occurring earlier. Television and radio had given adolescents at least the appearance of greater sophistication. Many ninth-grade boys and girls had become truly adolescent rather than transescent and so were more at home in the high school than in a middle school. Certainly, it was thought, seventh and eighth grade students were better off without being subjected to the domination of more mature ninth-graders who were ready for the social life of teenagers. Similarly it was thought that the sixth-graders and perhaps the fifth-graders fit in better with the seventh- and eighth-graders than with elementary school children. Besides, the beginning of grade 7 and the end of grade 9 seemed to be unpropitious times to switch into and out of the middle school. Theoretically children learned the basic skills in reading in the first four grades and were ready to move on to the study of the content areas in grade 5. Besides, high school curricula and college entrance requirements had long been built on the presumption that grade nine should be a high school grade. Consequently there developed a strong movement for the creation of schools for transescents (pubescents and young adolescents) housing grades 6–7–8, or perhaps grades 5–6–7–8. This movement came to fruition in the middle schools of the 1960s and 1970s.[8]

The Call for Excellence

Now in the 1980s the schools again see a turning toward rigorous education and stress on excellence in the academic basics. This movement has been strengthened by reports that students graduating from our high schools are not doing well on precol-

---

[8] Note that this arrangement is not a totally new idea. Intermediate schools having grades 7–8, 6–7–8, or 5–6–7–8 existed in many districts prior to World War II. Sometimes these arrangements were the result of the availability of building space rather than any pedagogical considerations, however.

It is said that the history of education consists of constant swinging from action to reaction and back again. Do you see evidence of such a pattern in this short history of the secondary school in the United States? If so, what? If not, do you spot any definite trends in American secondary education in this brief history?

lege tests such as the Scholastic Aptitude Test, that many high school graduates are functionally illiterate, and that job applicants are unable to read, write, and figure well enough to hold jobs. By the beginning of the present decade, citizens and legislators were demanding the adoption of higher standards for graduation from high school and increased emphasis on the "basics" and the academic subjects. In short, the pursuit of academic excellence in the conservative tradition was fast becoming the law of the land. To this end the nation has been swamped with a multitude of national and state commission and committee reports criticizing our schools and demanding educational reform. The gist of these reports and criticisms is discussed later in this chapter.

The Role of the Schools

In the "progressive" decades of the 1930s, 1960s, and early 1970s, attention was focused on the disadvantaged, on broadening the function of the school, and on overcoming past rigidity in the schools. In "conservative" times such as the 1890s, 1950s, and 1980s, the accent has focused on the gifted, the basics, academics, coherent curricula, and discipline. The upshot of these shifts has been very little real change. Aristotle pointed out the basic problem in his *Politics*.

That education should be regulated by law and should be an affair of state is not to be denied, but what should be the character of this public education, and how young persons should be educated, are questions which remain to be considered. For mankind are by no means agreed about the things to be taught, whether we look to virtue or the best life. Neither is it clear whether education is more concerned with intellectual or with moral virtue. The existing practice is perplexing; no one knows on what principle we should proceed—should being useful in life, or should virtue, or should the higher knowledge be the aim of our training; all three opinions have been entertained.[9]

After two millennia we still do not know what the role of the school should be. In the nineteenth century it was more or less assumed that the elementary schools would concentrate on "reading, writing, and arithmetic" and that secondary schools should concentrate on preparing students for college and various vocations. With the advent of the twentieth century and the popularization of secondary schools, scholars began to give more serious attention to the purposes of education. Many of them evidently decided that the major objective should be preparation for a "full life." At least in 1918 a national commission suggested that the secondary schools should prepare students for all areas of living: health, command of the fundamental processes, worthy home membership, vocational efficiency, civic competence, worthy use of leisure time, and ethical character. These areas were commonly called the seven cardinal principles of secondary education. In later years these goals were accepted as the goals for education at all levels of public education—elementary, middle, and secondary.[10] In short, education was to serve the needs of all the children of all the people.

Many critics of education have thought that this concept of educating for complete living was impractical. Folk wisdom tells us that people who try to do everything end up doing nothing well. Schools, it is said, should give up all the folderol and concentrate on their prime mission, intellectual education. In 1961 the Educational Policies Commission reviewed its position and announced that, although it reaffirmed its belief that the schools should educate broadly, the central purpose of American education should be to teach pupils to think independently.[11]

Although the primacy of the intellectual goal of the secondary school seems self-evident to many observers, during the early 1970s there was a great deal of pressure to place more emphasis on the affective and social aspects of life in secondary education. This type of thinking about educational goals is well illustrated by Richard Gross's 1978 reformulation of the "seven cardinal principles." In his seven cardinal principles for the 80s, Gross includes

1. Personal competence and development.
2. Family cohesiveness.
3. Skilled decision making.
4. Moral responsibility and ethical action.
5. Civic interest and participation.
6. Respect for the environment.
7. Global human concern.[12]

These principles cover the social, affective, and intellectual sides of education. Many educators would endorse them without hesitation. Nevertheless, many others who wish a return to the basics would dismiss the nontraditional portions of such lists of principles as "frills." As they see it, the schools should concentrate on teaching students academic and intellectual skills and knowledge and leave the moral, social, and affective sides of education to other institutions such as the church and home.

Other educators think that education should go

---

[9] Aristotle, *Politics VIII*.

[10] These areas represent the Seven Cardinal Principles, or Major Objectives, of the 1918 report, *The Cardinal Principles of Secondary Education,* of the Commission for Reorganization of Secondary Education.

[11] Educational Policies Commission, *The Central Purpose of American Education* (Washington, DC: National Education Association, 1961).

[12] Richard E. Gross, "Seven New Cardinal Principles," *Phi Delta Kappan* (December, 1978), **60:**291–93.

Is the notion that the secondary schools should try to serve the needs of all American youth impractical? Should the primary goal of the secondary schools be intellectual?

What stress should be placed on the affective and social aspects of students' lives?

Do you agree with Gross's seven cardinal principles for the 80s? Would you delete any? Would you add to them? What priorities would you give them? Rate them in order of importance.

In your opinion, what responsibility should the school have for teaching morals and social values?

In your opinion what implications does the role of the school have so far as the types of teaching methods to be used in the school are concerned?

much further than teaching the basic intellectual skills and knowledge. In their opinion we must teach not only for the world that is but also for the world that may be. Students must be taught to be open to change, to learn to live with and take advantage of the new. Students must not only come out of school with knowledge but they must also be able to interpret and use knowledge—particularly new knowledge that may develop after their school days. In fact they should be able to enter into the creation of new knowledge.[13]

Unfortunately, if the conclusions of *The Study of Schooling* are correct, in practice the staffs of most schools and school districts have never really thought out just what the goals of the schools should be. All too often they bumble along without much sense of direction. Even when the goals are specified, in many schools the programs seem to have little relationship to the stated goals.[14]

---

[13] Based on Allen F. Bray, "Some Considerations for Educators: The Ecology of Teaching," *NASSP Bulletin* (January, 1983), **67**:92–95.

[14] John I. Goodlad, *A Place Called School* (New York: McGraw-Hill, 1984).

Today's Schools

Perhaps the most astonishing thing about American schools is how little they have changed. The grandfather who went to school in the 1930s feels quite at home when he visits his grandchildren's school in the 1980s. Many of the changes reported to have occurred are only changes in packaging or, more likely, changes in labeling. Some of the famous so-called educational innovations of the 1920s and 1930s as well as those of the 1960s and 1970s have never been seriously implemented. Progressive education, as John Dewey visualized it, has never really been tried. Neither has such a recent innovation as team teaching.[15] In schools, as in other human institutions, the more things change the more they may stay the same.

School Organization

Presently we have middle schools (grades 6–8, or 5–8, or 7–8), junior high schools (ordinarily grades 7–9), high schools (grades 9–12), senior high schools (grades 10–12), six-year high schools or junior-senior high schools (grades 7–12), and a number of other school organizations including some schools housing grades K–12 in the same building. Most of these schools try valiantly to serve the needs of their age group. Some of them have been organized purposely to serve these groups better. Others are simply attempts to fit students into the buildings available.

The Schools in the Middle

The functions of the middle schools are basically the same as those stated for the junior high schools

---

[15] Actually this is not so terribly new an idea. A form of team teaching was used in ancient Sumer.

in 1947 by Gruhn and Douglas. Consequently, whether they are called middle schools or junior high schools, the better ones are designed to provide ten to fourteen-year-old youngsters with a school organized to provide flexibility, stability, and security as well as to ease the passage from the elementary school to the high school.

In order that middle schools be personalized and guidance oriented, it is recommended that they be kept small. If a school should enroll more than eight hundred students, it is recommended that it be divided into houses, each with its own administrative and guidance staff. It is also recommended that in order to avoid students becoming lost in large classes in fractionated, departmentalized programs, middle schools adopt block-of-time courses taught by interdisciplinary teams of teachers. These teams of teachers who would share a group of students for a multiperiod block (e.g., an English teacher, a science teacher, a mathematics teacher, and a social science teacher who share eighty to one hundred students during a four-period block of time) would be responsible for grouping and scheduling the instructional activities during the block. They might arrange for large-group multisubject activities, provide for small-group study sessions, coordinate assignments and articulate subject matter, for instance.

In addition, provisions for such subjects as art, music, home economics, and physical education would be scheduled outside the block. Particular care would be taken to give students chances to explore their interests and abilities both in the block and other courses. To this end the teachers would make much use of the techniques for individualizing. For the same reasons the school should offer a strong program of appropriate extracurricular activities. Interscholastic sports, dances, proms, and other activities more suitable for adolescents and youths than for transescents would not be offered, however.

In short, the middle school would ideally be a place where, under personalized guidance and support, a transescent could make the transition from

> Do you agree that middle schools should not offer interscholastic sports, dances, proms, and other activities?
>
> In your middle school years what did the school program do to prepare you for high school?
>
> What, if anything, did the school do to smooth boys' and girls' passage from childhood to adolescence?

being an elementary school child to becoming a high schooler.

Alternative Schools

Over the years many alternatives to the standard middle, junior, and high schools have been created. The oldest of these are the private independent schools established and maintained by and for the socially elite. Similar to these schools are the church-run boarding schools and academies. Churches also maintain parochial middle and secondary schools ostensibly to bring up boys and girls in the traditions of their faith. Other private alternative schools have sprung up because of dissatisfaction with the public schools. During the 1960s (as in the 1920s), for instance, many groups founded ultraprogressive schools designed to free students from the allegedly restrictive environments of the public schools. Other groups formed schools to circumvent laws and regulations such as those supporting school desegregation and forbidding school prayer. School districts have established alternative schools for problem youth or youth with problems, magnet schools for students with special interests or talents, vocationally oriented schools, and other special-purpose schools.

All in all, these alternative schools are not much different from the ordinary public middle and secondary schools. An elite college preparatory school may have a narrower, more academic curriculum, smaller classes, and more individualized attention than a comprehensive high school, for example, but the instruction in the schools is usually not so very different. Neither is that of the supposedly free, open alternative school.

Nevertheless each individual school does differ from every other school. It would be a mistake to judge the merits of all schools by the performance of a small sample. The quality and effectiveness of seemingly similar schools may differ tremendously.

The Problem of Articulation

Vertical Articulation

Having so many different levels and kinds of schools makes the problem of vertical articulation of the schools difficult. Vertical articulation is the fitting together of courses and units so that students can make a smooth progression up the educational ladder. Here the problem is to prevent gaps and overlaps. This problem is particularly troublesome at the break between lower and upper schools, for example, between the middle school and the high school or the elementary school and the middle school. School officials and teachers try to achieve vertical articulation by paying close attention to the sequence of courses, units, and subject matter content. This is especially difficult to do when students move from one school to another. The process requires much coordination and teamwork from the staffs of the different schools. This type of coordination is more than many school systems have been able to do successfully. It becomes extremely complicated when a school receives students from several lower schools or from schools in other districts.

The fact that schools are divided into grades also makes vertical articulation difficult. There is much repetition from grade to grade as well as many gaps in content between grades. These gaps may come about as a result of poor planning or because

the lower grade teacher was not able to complete all the content laid out in the syllabus for that grade. Another problem of vertical organization is caused by the differences in students' rate of learning. Some students keep dropping behind and at the end of the year are not ready for the next year. To solve the problem, some schools have adopted continuous progress schemes in which students move through courses at their own speed and then pick up next year where they left off the previous year. Such schemes have not been adopted widely, however.

Horizontal Articulation

Secondary schools are almost always departmentalized. Frequently, the departments go on their separate ways with little reference to each other. As a result, teachers in the various disciplines may not know what other teachers are doing. This causes problems of horizontal articulation, i.e., the correlation and coordination of what students study at the same level or grade. These problems may not be as troublesome in middle schools as in high schools because middle schools are less likely to be rigidly departmentalized and are more likely to have taken measures to promote horizontal articulation. In addition, the schools are usually smaller and more student oriented so the isolation of the various courses and their teachers is usually not so great. Unfortunately at the high school level problems of horizontal articulation are often acute. In most high schools the courses offered in the different disciplines have no relation to each other.

Attempts to articulate horizontally take many forms. First is the simple correlation of courses in which teachers point out the application or relation of the content of their courses to other courses. Another method is for teachers to plan their courses to support each other. Many junior high schools and middle schools set up interdisciplinary teaching teams in which teachers who instruct the same students plan together. Another approach is to fuse two or more courses into one. For instance, in some seventh and eighth grades English and social studies are integrated into a block. Another plan is to center all the schoolwork around problems or themes and to introduce the subject matter of the various disciplines only as it pertains to the problem or theme. For example, in the study of the city students might study literary works, history, sociology, political science, geography, the physical and biological sciences, statistics, and even the fine arts.

Impersonal Schools

Post-elementary schools are likely to be fairly large and impersonal. While the problem is not so acute in the middle school most high school teachers have to meet so many students each day that they just cannot know all of them well. Nor can they deal with them all as individuals. After all, a typical high school teacher may have 125 or more students in class each day. In large schools it is very easy for students to get lost in the crowd. Troubled boys and girls often have no one to whom to turn. As a result, they may feel unwanted and inferior. In short, they become alienated by the school. This is one reason why a quarter of the boys and girls drop out of school before completing their high school education.

The Classes

Although most boys and girls say they like school, school classes tend to be humdrum. Perhaps this is because the accent in many classes is not so much on learning as it is on order. In any case, the content and teaching procedures are not very exciting. Most of the teaching is textbook teaching that is seldom relieved by more exciting activities or more interesting readings. The lessons are most frequently lectures, recitation, questioning, workbook or detailed exercises, and quizzes largely limited to facts and information without much chance

for students to think, act, react, or enjoy. There is relatively little group work or use of audiovisual aids, demonstrations, discussions, hands-on activities, problem solving, or other pupil participatory learning activities in many classes. On the whole, the teachers are quite impersonal. They do not spend much time praising or correcting students' work, discussing their problems, showing them how to correct their mistakes, or instructing them in how to do their assignments. In fact, about 20 per cent of the senior high school students in *The Study of Schooling* did not understand what their mistakes were, how to correct them, or what the teacher was trying to get across anyway.[16]

These descriptions are true of elementary, middle, and high schools. However, classes seem to become more and more humdrum as the students get older. This is too bad, because students respond best to interesting classes in which teachers show themselves to be friendly, interested in their students, and democratic. If American education does not succeed as well as it should, it is largely because classes lack variety and power, and therefore do not keep students at a high level of involvement. When one considers the nature of so many classes, the wonder is not that schools have so many discipline problems, but that the boys and girls are so tractable.

The Curriculum

Earlier in the chapter Aristotle told us that we do not know on what principles to proceed when selecting content for school curricula. He could have gone further. Authorities do not even agree on a precise meaning for the word *curriculum.* In this book, we consider the curriculum of a school to be *the totality of the experiences that a school plans*

---

[16] Goodlad, op. cit., p. 112.

for its students. It is not restricted only to courses; the extracurricular activities and auxiliary services such as the guidance and health services are also part of the curriculum. On the other hand, the curriculum does not include everything the students learn in school. Much of that is part of a hidden agenda that influences pupil learning in spite of the school's best intentions. Many boys and girls learn to smoke at school, for instance, but smoking is not really part of the school's curriculum. Neither are many of the attitudes and values students pick up from their teachers, peers and school policies. Even the concepts about what matters and how to get by that students learn from the school organization, the school rules, the emphases on curricular and extracurricular offerings, and the physical environment, are not curriculum within our definition. Curriculum includes only the planned experiences the school provides for the education of the students.

What is actually taught in the classroom, however, is a conglomerate of what the course of study mandates, what the textbook says, what the teacher thinks is important, what the teacher is able to get across to the students, and what they pick up along the way. Much of what the school board and the curriculum experts think is in the curriculum never makes it to the classroom. Often there is just not enough time to cover everything. Sometimes teachers leave things out because they don't like them or do not see them as being relevant or important. On occasion they may not understand the content themselves. At times poor teaching keeps students from learning. Teachers may try to cover too much. They may fail to take all the steps necessary to make concepts sink in; they may fail to point out the purpose of learning, the content or its relevance to the students' lives. They may fail to show the students what is to be learned and how to go about learning it.[17]

[17] Jere E. Brophy, "How Teachers Influence What Is Taught and What Is Learned," *The Elementary School Journal* (September, 1982), **83:**1–13.

Curriculum Organization

The course offerings are set forth in the program of studies. In most elementary schools these are arranged into a single curriculum which is required of all students. In the senior high school the program is more likely to be arranged in a flexible pattern that allows students to select the sequence of courses that seems best to fit their needs and desires. Thus high school students may elect courses that will meet college entrance requirements or prepare them to become bookkeepers or mechanics. The curricula of the middle and junior high schools usually hew closer to the single curriculum pattern, although they may allow some electives. Tracking or homogeneous grouping is common in both middle and high schools. Modern thinkers find the results of these grouping or tracking practices troublesome. Students in the slower or nonacademic tracks cannot free themselves to move into more advanced tracks. Thus the tracking system tends to deny some youths the chance to be successful in secondary school and to forbid them access to important knowledge and skills. Consequently tracking and grouping may cause minority boys and girls and the less academically inclined students to become truly educationally disadvantaged.

General Education

The total curriculum is made up of both general and specialized education. General education consists of the learning that every person should have a chance to acquire. It is sometimes called common learnings. At the elementary and middle school level most of the curriculum fits into this category. Presumably everyone should have a chance to learn to read, write, and figure, for instance. At the secondary school level it is more difficult to demonstrate that any particular learning is essential for everybody. Yet there are many things that would be valuable for everyone to learn. Among them are personal relationships, home management, health, ethical values, good citizenship, and academic subject matter relevant to making one's life fuller and richer both as a citizen and as an individual. Perhaps most important of all are the various skills that enable a person to think critically. Modern critics of education tend to think that a rigorous general education focusing on basic knowledge, the use of knowledge, thinking skills, the abilities necessary for learning new knowledge and skills, plus the abilities to apply old knowledge to new situations is the best type of general education.

Specialized Education

Specialized education is ad hoc education—education designed to meet the particular needs of particular people. It provides for the differences in students by giving them opportunities to develop in ways that suit them best as individuals. It does prepare students for particular vocations or avocations. Both vocational education and college preparatory education are examples of specialized education.

Theoretically the early years of one's education should consist largely of general education. As students move toward the end of their formal schooling one would expect their education to become more and more specialized so as to prepare them for their life work and their roles as adults. The problem is to create a curriculum with an appropriate balance between general and specialized education at each academic level.

Provisions for Individual Differences

As we have already pointed out, despite strenuous efforts, the schools of the nation have never satisfactorily solved the problem of how to teach a student body that includes students from almost every intelligence level, every social and economic level, a variety of racial and ethnic backgrounds, and with a tremendous range of ambitions and interests. In their attempts to cope with the complexity of this problem, educators have invented a host of organizational, curricular and methodological strategies and techniques. Some of these are discussed in Chapter 16, "Provisions for Individual Differences," and elsewhere in the text.

The Subjects

Theoretically curricula may be classified as subject-centered or experience-centered. The subject-centered curriculum is based on formal courses and emphasizes the learning of subject matter and the study of the disciplines. The experience-centered curriculum, on the other hand, focuses on the problems and concerns of youth living in contemporary society. It accentuates the processes of learning and thinking and plays down the study of the disciplines; subject matter is introduced only as it pertains to the problems being studied. In the experience-centered curriculum students take a major role in deciding just what will be studied and how it will be studied.

Most high schools hold to the subject-centered curriculum. The faculty and administrators determine what the curriculum will be without much consultation with the students. Presumably they select the curriculum content on the basis of the students' needs, but often the courses are just blocks of more or less logically organized subject matter having little relation to the needs of anyone. At times it has seemed as if the schools were moving toward an experience-centered curriculum relevant to the needs of the students and the community, with increased student participation in curricular decision making; so far, however, most of these movements have been abortive. Middle school curricula are much more likely to be experience-centered than are those of the high school because the middle school is more concerned with the human development aspects of its transescent students than is the high school with those of its older students.

Ordinarily, then, the high school program of studies consists of separate, discrete courses in the academic disciplines. These can be classified into the following categories

• English Language Arts.
• Foreign Language.
• The Social Studies.
• The Sciences.
• Mathematics.
• The Fine Arts.
• Business Education.
• Vocational and Practical Arts.
• Health and Safety.
• Physical Education.

At the middle school level, the program may be at least partially made up of broad field or block-of-time courses, rather than discrete courses in the disciplines,[18] in order to achieve better horizontal articulation and to give coherence to the curriculum.

Balance in the Curriculum

We have already met the problem of balance between general and specialized education, but that is only one aspect of the total balance problem. Ideally the curriculum should be made up of experiences from the various fields in proportion to their importance to students' present and future lives and the needs of society. Such a nice balance has never been maintained. In the long contest between the academic studies and life-centered experiences, the academic has, on the whole, won the battle—not wholly to the benefit of the students nor of society in general. Not only should the school provide a balance in the subject matter offerings, it must also try to keep its various roles in balance, e.g., provision for the needs of the individual students vs. the needs of society, education for social change vs. education for social stability, needs of students' education for the present vs. education for future needs, education for world citizenship

Think back over your secondary school career. Was your work integrated vertically; that is, did your work in the different subjects progress in an orderly fashion straight through from grades 6 to 12? Or were there repetitions and gaps? Was your secondary school work articulated horizontally; was the content in the different subjects each year taught in such a way that the interrelationships between the content of the various fields were clear? Did the teaching and learning of the various subjects consciously support the teaching and learning in other subjects? What attempts that you know of were made to solve the problems of vertical and horizontal articulation? Can you think of anything teachers might have done to improve articulation?

Was your own school program well balanced? Was your personal program well balanced? What areas, if any, were overemphasized? What areas, if any, were neglected?

What aspects of your own teaching field are really relevant and important to the lives of youth in the last decades of the twentieth century?

vs. education for patriotism, education for diversity vs. education for unity. It should also take care that the provisions for the needs and desires of one group do not overshadow the provisions for the needs and desires of another group.

Extra-Class Activities

Part of the curriculum is not included in students' regular courses. Neither does it carry credit for graduation. This part of the curriculum is often called the extracurriculum, extracurricular activities, or cocurriculum, but it is more accurate to think of it as an elective extension of the curriculum, especially since the dividing line between the curricular and the extracurricular has become very indistinct as the result of two concurrent trends.

---

[18] For example, general science or an English-social studies block.

One is a trend for curricular activities to spread into the extracurricular (for example, French clubs, minicourses, volunteer Saturday morning laboratory classes, and field trips). The other is the trend for the extracurricular to become curricular (for example, the school newspaper published by the journalism class or the credit-bearing school chorus).

Because of their freer and informal format, extracurricular activities serve to reinforce and augment formal studies; to provide for individual interests, needs, and aspirations; to provide realistic experiences; to make the total curriculum more relevant; to aid students in life adjustment; to integrate learning; to give students experience in democratic living; and to add spice and life to the school program. Obviously, in many respects, the contribution of extracurricular activities may be fully as important and even more effective than the more formal portions of the curriculum. They deserve to be carefully planned and carried out.

The Guidance Program

The guidance program is another extension of the curriculum. It strives to help students understand themselves and the situations that face them both in and out of school so that they can make informed decisions and conduct their lives more effectively.

To accomplish these purposes the guidance personnel attempt

1. To gather pertinent information about students' abilities, potentialities, and talents.
2. To provide information about occupations and educational opportunities students can use as a basis for making career and educational decisions.
3. To help boys and girls make intelligent decisions through expert professional counselling.
4. To help place boys and girls in suitable academic curricula, institutions of higher learning, and jobs.

5. To follow up students so as to help them adjust to their post-school world and to determine whether or not their schooling has been effective.

Although schools and teachers have always provided informal educational and vocational guidance, formal guidance programs were originally conceived only for vocational guidance in the secondary school. Today educators realize that students need help in decision making at all levels. Consequently, guidance has become an integral part of the middle school as well as the high school programs. In fact, if the middle school is to carry out the role envisioned for it, the whole school program should be guidance oriented, for it is here that future adults first begin to set their life paths.

Curriculum Building

Curriculum building has always been a source of controversy. Not only are there sharp disagreements concerning curriculum content, but there is also confusion about who is responsible for curriculum building and who should make curriculum decisions. Therefore let us take a brief look at several basic questions.

- What should be taught?
- How should it be taught?
- To whom should it be taught?
- Who should decide the answers to these questions?

What to Teach?

Determining what to teach and what to leave out is a major problem. It is, of course, axiomatic that the curriculum should be relevant to both the needs of the students and the needs of society. But when in fact is a curriculum relevant? Is, as some hold, the best curriculum made up of eternal truths that everyone should learn in a common curriculum, or should the curriculum be so individualized that everyone can have a personal curriculum? Similarly, should there be different curricula for different ethnic or racial groups or for students with different vocational goals? Should, as essentialists claim, the curriculum be aimed at providing the skills, knowledge, and attitudes that youths will need when they become adults or should it, as the progressivists believe, meet the needs of students now and let the future take care of itself?

Is a relevant curriculum one that brings students face to face with the materialistic facts of society through active participation or is a curriculum that concentrates on intellectual development alone really more relevant? Is a curriculum the students select for themselves more relevant than one selected for them by knowledgeable adults who have been through the mill? Should the accent be on liberal education, or should it be on vocational education? Should the curriculum give boys and girls an opportunity to learn to be good citizens by practicing good citizenship, or should it concentrate on the intellectual?

What is the role of subject matter anyway? Should one select subject matter content because it has its own intrinsic value, or should one select it because presumably someday it will be useful to the students? Or is it possible that subject matter content does not matter at all, but that it is only important as a vehicle for teaching intellectual processes and attitudes, such as the ability to solve problems, to ferret out facts, or to view and analyze conflicting data objectively? Aristotle was right. To know what to teach and how to teach it is indeed difficult.

What does the term *relevant education* mean to you?

Did your middle and high school programs seem relevant to you? Do your present courses?

Should your middle or high school courses have been more relevant? What could have been done to make them more relevant to you?

What Methods to Use?

How one teaches is just as much part of the curriculum as what one teaches. The use of inquiry and problem-solving techniques produces learning different from that produced by the lecture or recitation. Individualized instruction generates a curriculum different from that derived from large group instruction. When teachers or curriculum committees decide on one or another strategy, they are making curriculum decisions. Unfortunately many parents and teachers have not been able to see the relationships between educational goals and teaching methods. All too often the methods they advocate for their classrooms are incompatible with the goals they say they desire.

Whom to Teach?

At the present time all youths are required to attend school until they have finished high school or reached a specified age (sixteen in many states). Some critics of education doubt whether such practice is wise.[19] Some of the students, they say, cannot benefit from a high school education and would be better off doing something else during their teens. Is it really right for secondary schools to be required to provide remedial work for students who have not met the prerequisites? Perhaps secondary education should be reserved for an academic elite who would enjoy and profit from academic secondary education. Education for only the college-bound would be cheaper and simpler to provide, they say. If, on the other hand, formal secondary education should be the right of all youth, presumably the curriculum must provide a wide choice of subjects and activities, or attending school will not be worthwhile for everyone. Furthermore, if the society at large is to benefit from its investment in secondary education, the schools must provide for the needs of all youth.

---

[19] See B. Frank Brown, *The Reform of Secondary Education* (New York: McGraw-Hill, 1973) for example.

Who Should Make the Decisions?

Teachers naturally feel that as professionals they should make, as well as implement, the important curriculum decisions. Students, the people most directly affected, feel they should have at least some part in determining what they have to learn. The contention of parents and laypeople that they should call the tune because they foot the bill is not entirely unreasonable. Finally, because local and state boards of education are charged with the responsibility for establishing and maintaining appropriate and effective curricula by law, they feel that they must control the curriculum and the curriculum-building processes.

Actually, although parents, laypeople, and the lay media are quick to blame them, teachers and school administrators make few of the really important educational decisions. The school organization, the budget, the type of staff, the broad philosophy of the school, and the general patterns of the curriculum are all decided by the community and its appointed or elected representatives. Teachers and school administrators are left with the task of supplying the nitty gritty by which to implement these big decisions.

Ultimately, however, what is actually taught in the classroom and the way it is taught is mostly decided by the classroom teacher. The real curriculum is what the teachers teach.[20]

Pressure Groups. Several groups apply great pressure to shaping the curriculum. Perhaps the most influential of these is the textbook publisher. Often curriculum building, as practiced, amounts to little more than deciding what courses to offer and then selecting textbooks. Many teachers use the textbook as a course of study. Each year they begin at the beginning of the textbook and work their way through to the end. Test publishers are

also influential. When teachers know what their students will be tested on, they teach accordingly. It is quite possible that the introduction of a national or state assessment (i.e., testing) program would dictate the exact content of future curricula. Assessment programs could very well stifle innovation and reform and harden the curriculum into an archaic mold. This, at least, seems to be the European experience.

Business and industry also influence the school curriculum—partly through the introduction of new hardware and software. Computer-assisted instruction, for instance, is a product, at least in part, of industrial initiative.

In some instances business firms have taken over the designing of curricula. Others provide workshops and training programs for teachers. Business firms also exert pressure on the school curriculum, both directly (e.g., by distributing teaching materials) and through such organizations as the Chamber of Commerce, to see to it that the schools present to youth points of view congruent with their own.

Pressure groups representing such interests as labor, political groups, patriotic organizations, and the like have influenced the adoption or dropping of books, programs, methods, and innovations. Private foundations also exert pressure by granting support to new programs and research that support their objectives and biases.

Although these pressure groups are sometimes political, self-serving, and represent biases and prejudices, they usually are motivated by a sincere desire to improve instruction in the schools. Unfortunately, in spite of good intentions, sometimes the changes pressure groups advocate stem from ignorance, naïveté, or prejudice and would do little to advance quality education. Still, many excellent programs, such as driver training programs and practical politics, are the result of the influence of pressure groups such as the American Automobile Association and the League of Women Voters.

Community Feeling. The type of programs that parents and other people of the community want

[20] Remember that the curriculum is the planned experiences even though sometimes what the students learn comes mostly from a shadow curriculum of unplanned experiences that boys and girls encounter in spite of the plans of the teacher.

is often colored by social, economic, and racial factors. A wealthy suburban community that sends more than 90 per cent of its high school graduates to college may insist on a strong college preparation program that will give students an entree to prestigious colleges and universities. On the other hand, people of the neighboring central city may be more interested in programs that develop in students marketable vocational skills.

Also, diverse interest groups seek to influence the curriculum in most communities. Often the goals of these groups are antagonistic and incompatible. The school authorities and teachers must try to reconcile differences and establish a curriculum beneficial to all the pupils. This goal is not always possible.

Higher Education.   Higher education also influences the secondary school curriculum and indirectly that of the middle school. College entrance requirements have always been an important consideration for curriculum makers. The biases of secondary school teachers toward content and method were learned in college and graduate school. Colleges and universities also influence the work of the lower schools by sponsoring research and development activities and providing consultant services, in-service education, curriculum laboratories, and experimental centers. They are also highly influential in the regional associations of colleges and secondary schools that accredit secondary schools.

Professional Organizations.   Teachers' organizations also have influence. They publish journals and newsletters that may affect local practice. They also sponsor research, commissions, and workshops designed to foster curriculum improvement. Some teachers' unions include curriculum matters in their negotiations with local school authorities.

Government Agencies.   Local school policy is determined and carried out by the local board of education and its appointed officials. In their delibera-

tions, the local curriculum builders must consider the edicts of the state education agency and the state legislature. Regulations made by these bodies have the force of law. Although states usually give the local secondary schools some freedom, legislatures at times try to dictate what should be taught and how it should be taught. Usually state dictation of anything other than broad policy is self-defeating. However, if the state did not specify standards and conduct inspections, some communities might not support their schools at all.

The state government can, of course, use both its authority and the power of the purse to enforce its mandate. Money from the federal government has had considerable impact on the schools and their curricula too. In addition, Congress has also directly influenced the content of school curricula by such legislation as "Title IX," the law that specifies equal treatment for the sexes and PL94–142 which sets forth requirements for education for the handicapped. Similarly judicial decisions of the Supreme Court and other federal and state courts have affected what we teach and how we teach it. In fact, as we have seen, if it were not for the Kalamazoo decision of 1874, we might not have any public secondary schools at all.

The Local School System.   Although the ultimate responsibility rests with the board of education, in the hierarchy of the local school system the person responsible for curriculum development is the school superintendent. In all but the smallest school systems the superintendent must delegate leadership. If the curriculum revision is to be system-wide, the leadership may actually be turned over to the curriculum director or perhaps to subject supervisors; if the curriculum revision is to be only building-wide, the key person is the building principal. Revision of single subject offerings within a school may occur under the direction of a department chairman. But no matter who is in charge or who gives the project direction, the real work is done by the teachers. It is they who are formed into committees or teams to dig out the

What role do you think that you as a teacher should have in determining the curriculum? How much freedom should you have in determining what goes into your own courses? How much influence should the parents and students have about what you teach and how you teach it? To what extent, if any, should the federal government influence local curricula and methods of teaching? What role should the local board of education have?

Should the curriculum be a matter to be decided in teacher-union-school board negotiations?

If you had your way, what role would pressure groups, community organizations, parents, and colleges have in middle and secondary school curriculum building?

To what extent do you feel the state should dictate what you teach in your courses?

necessary information, make the necessary decisions, and construct the necessary curriculum guides, resource units, and instructional materials.

Criticisms and Recommendations

During the 1970s, several groups studied the nation's secondary schools and found them wanting. The 1979 report of the Carnegie Council on Policy Studies in Higher Education, for example, says that the high schools are failing one third of American youth who leave ill-educated and ill-equipped to make their way in society.[21]

This sort of criticism of the schools and their programs continued in the 1980s.[22] Much of this criticism has been well earned, much has not. Some of the commissions' reports seem more political than educational. Moreover, what is true in some schools and some districts is not necessarily true in others, so the generalizations made in the reports do not always hold. Further, there is a tendency to blame the schools for the faults of society.

The following paragraphs are a digest of some

[21] Carnegie Council on Policy Studies in Higher Education, *Giving Youth a Better Chance: Options for Education, Work and Service* (San Francisco: Jossey-Bass, 1979). See also B. Frank Brown, ed., *Education for Responsible Citizenship* (New York: McGraw-Hill, 1977); B. Frank Brown (ed.), *The Reform of Secondary Education: A Report of the National Commission on the Reform of Secondary Education* (New York: McGraw-Hill, 1973); Philip A. Cusick, *Inside High School* (New York: Holt, 1973); *The Education of Adolescents*, The Final Report and Recommendations of the National Commission on the High School and Adolescent Education. HEW Publication No. (OE) 76–00004. (Washington, D C: U. S. Department of Health Education and Welfare, 1976); Thomas E. Gatewood, *The Education of Youth in the Middle Years*. A Joint Position Paper of the Michigan Association of Secondary School Principals and the Michigan Department of Education, January, 1976; Maurice Gibbons, *The New Secondary Education*, A Phi Delta Kappa Task Force Report (Bloomington, IN.: Phi Delta Kappa, 1976); Harry A. Passow, *Secondary Education Reform: Retrospect and Prospect* (New York: Teachers College Press, 1976); John W. Porter, chairman, *The Adolescent, or Other Citizens and Their High Schools*, The Charles F. Kettering Foundation (New York: McGraw-Hill, 1975).

[22] For example: Mortimer J. Adler, *The Paideia Proposal: An Educational Manifesto* (New York: Macmillan, 1982); Association for Supervision and Curriculum Development, *Refining General Education in the American High School* (Alexandria, VA: The Association, 1984); Ernest L. Boyer, *High School: A Report on Secondary Education in America* (New York: Harper & Row, 1983); College Board Project EQuality, *Academic Preparation for College: What Students Need to Know and Be Able to Do* (New York: The College Board, 1983); Education Commission of the States Task Force on Education for Economic Growth, *Action for Excellence: A Comprehensive Plan to Improve our Nation's Schools* (Lincoln, NE: ECS Distribution Center, 1983); John Goodlad, *A Place Called School* (New York: McGraw-Hill, 1984); National Commission for Excellence in Education, *A Nation at Risk: The Imperative for Educational Reform* (Washington DC: U. S. Government Printing Office, 1983); Theodore R. Sizer, *Horace's Compromise: The Dilemma of the American High School* (Boston: Houghton Mifflin, 1984); The National Science Board Commission on Precollege Education in Mathematics, Science and Technology, *Educating Americans for the 21st Century* (Washington, D C: National Science Foundation, 1983); Twentieth Century Fund Task Force on Federal Elementary and Secondary Education Policy, *Making the Grade* (New York: Twentieth Century Fund, 1983).

of the common criticisms and recommendations found in the literature. Most of these criticisms have been primarily aimed at the high schools.

Need for Higher Standards

Perhaps the most common criticism of education in the 1980s is that standards have been allowed to slip, that the educational product has become mediocre. This criticism is supported by the finding that although the best American students do very well on tests as compared to the best students of other countries, the scores of average American students on such tests as the Scholastic Aptitude Test have fallen considerably. The problem in the eyes of critics is that the schools do not require enough effort from their students. Our boys and girls, they say, do not spend as much time at schoolwork as they should. Other nations have longer school days and longer school years. Our teachers do not require enough homework. Too much class time is wasted on unintellectual, undemanding activities. Social promotion allows students to graduate whether they have learned anything or not. For many students the twelfth grade is a pure waste of time.

To correct these alleged deficiencies, critics insist that educational standards must be raised. In the words of the National Commission on Excellence, "Our goals must be to develop the talents of all to their fullest." All students, they maintain, should be pushed to the limit of their ability. Although not everyone should be treated alike, all students should become as excellent as possible.[23] To this end critics would make middle and secondary schools much more rigorous. Teachers would expect much more of the students. At least two hours of homework per day would be demanded of every high school student and at least one hour of home-

work of every middle school student. Classes would be more demanding. Soft pedagogy would be discarded in favor of rigorous study. The satisfactory completion of a minimum competency test would be required for admission to the middle school and high school and for high school graduation.

The critics would also upgrade textbooks. Lately, it is said, textbook publishers in their attempts to increase sales have lowered the levels of their texts to remove controversial material and make them easier to read. The result, these critics believe, is often pap—uninteresting, plodding, piddling, sketchy, and mindless. If they had their way, some textbooks would be replaced by classics and others would be replaced by well-written scholarly texts that deal forthrightly and honestly with important concepts.

Upgrading the Curriculum

Closely akin to the accusations of diminished standards are claims that the curriculum has been allowed to become diluted, frivolous, and insipid. According to these claims, rather than giving students rigorous contact with the solid disciplines—mathematics, science, English, history, and foreign languages—the curriculum has become a smorgasbord of undemanding general education courses and soft electives. Some say it has become so much so that by a judicious choice of electives a student could avoid any contact with academic work in high school.

To upgrade the curriculum and curriculum standards, many critics would reduce the number of electives and require all students to have a sound background in basic academic subjects, e.g., at the high school level

English	4 years
Mathematics	2–3 years
Science	2–3 years
Social Science	2–3 years
Computer Science	½–1 year

---

[23] National Commission on Excellence in Education, *A Nation At Risk: The Imperative for Educational Reform* (Washington, DC: U. S. Government Printing Office, 1983), p. 11.

The courses taught in these areas should be solid academic courses. In addition, some states have already set new requirements in art, music, foreign language, and vocational education. This common curriculum, it is recommended, should be required of all students, no matter what their goals in life, although some differentiation would be allowed within its framework for individual differences. Requirements for college preparatory students might be somewhat higher than those indicated here. At least two years of foreign language would be required for college entrance, according to College Board recommendations, for instance.

In such a curriculum the goal might be for

a. All students to become literate in English. They would all achieve advanced cognitive skills such as reasoning, critical analyses, ability to explain complex ideas, ability to read and understand complex ideas, ability to write clearly and correctly. All non-English speaking students would be taught to speak, read, and write English.
b. All students to have a chance to learn a second language.
c. All students to become scientifically literate. All secondary school students would have advanced training in science and mathematics.
d. All students to acquire basic understandings in the fine arts.
e. All students to become knowledgeable in the field of health education and practice in physical education.

To make such a curriculum effective, much more attention must be paid to horizontal and vertical articulation. Most critics seem to think that a carefully planned common curriculum core would solve this problem.

Accent on the Intellectual Skills

In an age of technology the real educational basics must focus on an advanced literacy that includes abilities to sort, analyze, and synthesize new information. To compete, people must be able to read and write well and know the facts, knowledge, and skills of mathematics, science, the humanities, and the other disciplines. But they must know more than these basics. The academics should be taught so as to stretch students' minds. They should be taught to use the higher mental processes, to ask questions, to think critically, to imagine, to draw inferences, to write clearly and well, and to comprehend and build on their understandings. In other words, they must learn how to learn, how to handle complex thinking procedures, how to use knowledge, and above all to understand the important questions of life.

Unfortunately in their recent efforts to concentrate on the basics, the schools have neglected these important elements. When concentrating on basic skills, facts, and information to be reproduced on tests, schools tend to neglect the higher mental processes. They bear down on rote learning, drill, and verbalizing and so do not have time to develop intellectual skills, learning skills, comprehension skills, and skill in interpreting and inferring. So the schools' minor successes may become major defeats. Evidently by pushing for minimum competency standards and tests, school authorities are falling into a trap, say educators. Minimum competency standards are liable to end up in minimum achievement. Learning the basics does not automatically lead to better reasoning and problem solving. These skills must be taught.

More Effective Efficient Teaching Methods

The teaching methods used in our classes are terribly limited. Too many classes are deadly dull. The classes neglect important skills. They do not develop ability to think, instill moral values, or promote social welfare. In a sense they are hypocritical, for although they claim to foster students' intellectual development and teach them to be good citizens, their actual impact is limited to reproducing facts on tests (by hook or crook, if the truth is to be told). Teachers should revise their classes so as to open up new horizons for the students. This they can do only if their teaching procedures focus on learning processes that will foster the academic competencies. Therefore, teachers must adopt a greater variety of teaching methods. These teaching methods should be more demanding. To bolster better development of the higher mental processes and skills, teaching methods should stress inquiry, self-expression, Socratic teaching, individual coaching, student participation in their own learning, and personalized instruction.

Stronger Discipline

According to many critics, school discipline is not what it should be. In many schools, they claim, unruly behavior is problem enough to interfere with effective teaching. Therefore some critics insist that stricter discipline codes and enforcement must be developed, that assertive discipline procedures should become the rule in all schools and classrooms, and that students should be made to realize that the teacher is boss. Other critics insist that students must be taught that they are responsible for their own behavior. In their view, the development of student self-discipline is essential. So also is the development of strong, vigorous classroom management techniques by every teacher.

The Schools and Community Cooperation

Another criticism is that the schools have become isolated from the community. Much of the instruction has little or no relevance to life outside the school. (This is not a new complaint. The Romans complained about it too.) Critics believe that this condition probably could be best rectified by establishing closer working arrangements between the school and the private sector. Business, industry,

citizen groups, and civic organizations, for instance, all have much to offer the schools. In a number of school districts businesses have adopted schools and school programs with favorable results. Citizens' groups have been instrumental in setting forth educational goals, establishing curricula, and in general helping school people in the renewing and upgrading of the schools and their school programs. According to this view, boys and girls should be encouraged to study out in the community. Action learning and similar programs in which boys and girls engage in civic activities, prevocational activities, and the like, should be encouraged.

More Personal Schools

Because high schools have become too large and impersonal, some educators believe that these schools should be broken up into several small alternative schools, minischools, or schools within schools. They feel that the school climate could be improved by decentralization and smaller student-teacher ratios. Consequently they suggest that the mammoth, all-purpose high schools should be replaced by smaller institutions with more specialized education and training purposes. According to their view, not all boys and girls should have to attend the same school or even the same kind of school, for different students may need different environments. Therefore students should be offered a choice among schools—alternative schools, magnet schools, are among the types of schools that could be provided. Middle schools should follow the personalized guidance-oriented pattern described earlier in this chapter.

Preparation for the World of Work

The role of the middle and high school in vocational education has never been settled. Presently, according to the critics, much vocational education is not productive. It neither provides students with specific skills they can use in specific jobs nor does it provide general skills that would help them in the world of work. Critics claim that too much time is spent on vocational training and not enough on general vocational education. It should be the job of the schools, they say, not to train students for specific working positions, but to focus on the skills and understandings students can use generally in whatever vocation they finally choose. In this endeavor there needs to be greater collaboration between schools and the business and industrial world. Let the workers and industry help the schools and students learn about work outside schools.

Upgrading the School Staff

Several studies maintain that teachers are not as well respected, well paid, or well trained as they might be. To improve these conditions they recommend stiffer certification requirements. Each prospective teacher should be required to demonstrate competence in subject matter and an aptitude for teaching, for example. The studies also recommend that certified teachers be continually evaluated and provided with in-service education and on-the-job training, and that school districts set up career ladders for teachers: for example, beginning teachers, experienced teachers, master teachers. Master teachers should serve as helping teachers who devise training programs and coach less experienced teachers. Teachers' pay would, of course, be adjusted to their rank and expertise. Master teachers would be eligible for other perquisites. All teachers' pay would be raised considerably and their teaching loads reduced. Further, teachers would be given extra time, perhaps a month, with pay to work on their courses, instructional techniques, and other professional matters.

What is your own position on each of the following criticisms? What has your experience been in these areas?

The schools are too soft.

Textbooks are pap.

Students do not spend enough time at their schoolwork.

Everyone should be required to take a common core of academic studies.

More attention should be paid to teaching intellectual skills.

All teachers should adopt a variety of stimulating teaching methods.

Discipline should be much stricter.

The school is too isolated from the community.

Schools are too impersonal.

Standards for certifying teachers should be raised.

Current Trends in Middle and Secondary Schools

Just what the direction education will take in the future is uncertain. The recommendations of the various commissions and studies are not always consistent and the directions of the various educational movements throughout the land are quite divergent and sometimes incompatible. The following list briefly describes some of the trends and developments in curriculum and school organization in secondary education in the United States during the 1970s and early 1980s.

1. A wave of conservatism is causing a movement "back to basics," toward higher, more rigid standards, requirements for minimum compe-

tency for school retention and graduation, and emphasis on academic learning.

2. This conservatism is accompanied by a feeling that educators should be held accountable for the school's product. Laypeople are demanding that educators guarantee learning of a specific quantity and quality as a condition for paying them and underwriting the school program.

3. In spite of this conservative shift, the movement to humanize the schools and to make them more relevant to contemporary society and to develop in students the abilities and attitudes necessary for coping with and managing the transience of our ever-changing world continues.

4. There appears to be a slight trend toward a reexamination of the worth of particular disciplines. Citizens are once again asking what benefits students derive from studying the various academic subjects. Many of them want a more functional curriculum than they have had in the past.

5. As part of the movement to functionalize the schools, there is considerably more interest in occupational, vocational, and career education.

6. There has been a renewed interest in the development of morals, ethics, and values as part of the school program.

7. Many of the progressive ideas of past years have come back in force. This can be seen not only in the return of the teaching of morals and values but also in the emphasis on learning to make decisions, independent thinking, interaction skills, human relations, and the affective side of learning in general.

8. Another progressivist idea that has returned is the movement for taking education into the community. Learning in the community programs may well be the wave of the future. Many schools are also providing more services to the community.

9. More people are becoming involved in curriculum building. Students and teachers are in the process of securing a greater voice in determin-

ing the kinds of educational experiences that are to be the requirements and electives for the completion of secondary education. Parents and the general populace are also assuming a larger role than ever before in recent times.

10. Considerable influence is being exerted upon the curriculum by minority groups. Probably this influence will continue to be felt. The great growth in bilingual and multicultural courses is powerful evidence of this influence.

11. The need for humaneness and relevance has caused a trend toward individualizing the curriculum. Laws requiring the "mainstreaming" of handicapped students will probably strengthen this movement. It may well be that the schools will actually become the continuous series of learning experiences that Harold G. Shane recommends. If it should come to pass, schools in the future would have the following characteristics:[24] (a) Since any one learner is merely progressing at a different rate than any other, there would be no failure or acceleration. (b) Much of the remedial or special education efforts or all of them would be eliminated. (c) Since each student progresses at his own rate, whether handicapped or not, all education would be "special" for the individual. Promotion and dropouts would be eliminated. (d) In this personalized program, a student could continue his education outside of school and return weeks or months later to the school experiences. (e) Other changes would involve the termination of compensatory education and report cards.

12. Recently there has been a number of organizational changes that will probably make the schools more responsive to the needs of the students. Foremost among them is the growth of the middle school concept. Others are flexi-

---

[24] Harold G. Shane, "A Curriculum Continuum: Possible Trends in the 70's," *Phi Delta Kappan* (March, 1970), **51**:389.

ble scheduling, team teaching, advance credit courses offered in the high school, the ungraded school, continuous progress schemes, teacher aides, honor study halls, differentiated staffing, team teaching, the work-study programs, a school-within-a-school, small school agreements, cultural enrichment programs, minicourses, student exchange programs, educational parks, optional class attendance, a shorter or longer school year, independent study, no-wall schools, and the accountability concept. Some of these changes are relatively recent; others were initiated years ago but have not been widely accepted until recently; some have not been tried yet; some have been tried and rejected; others have been quite successful resulting in permanent change. However, these changes have had relatively little effect on most schools.

13. The improvement in technology, both in teaching methods and in teaching tools such as the computer, is continuing and should soon make a considerable difference in the curriculum, instruction, and organization of the schools. We are only now just beginning to get the solid research base that will tell us how to make our teaching methods, curricula, and materials truly effective.

14. Many laypeople believe that the public school is an inefficient monopoly and have begun a movement to search for new agencies to educate the nation's schoolchildren and youth. These actions have caused educators to realize the need for different types of schooling. Students will probably find a variety of programs ranging from the most conservative to the most progressive in the schools of the future.

The sum total of these trends seems to be a movement toward a more humane, responsive school in which the curriculum will be much more down to earth and the needs of the community and of youth will be better and more democratically served than in the past.

Summary

To a rather large extent the American secondary school is a creature of its past. Because of tradition and inertia, ''its curriculum and organization are weighted down with considerable unnecessary baggage.'' Over the years attempts to make the curriculum more relevant, meaningful, useful, and practical have bogged down because of academic, lay, and professional reaction. Because of this academic reaction, the secondary school curriculum, public and private, has remained basically conservative. This is not so true of the middle schools that attempt to meet the needs of transescents.

The American people have never really decided what they expect of secondary and middle schools. Educational experts have proclaimed that the secondary schools should serve the needs of all American youth. Other experts have maintained that although the schools should strive for such major goals as health, command of the fundamental processes, vocational efficiency, civic competence, worthy use of leisure time, and ethical character, their primary mission was intellectual—to teach students to think. Still other writers have been calling for greater emphases on the affective and social goals of secondary education. Issues concerning the role and purpose of the schools in the United States are no more settled today than they were years ago. Although most American secondary school curricula consist of discrete academic courses, some schools have experimented with alternative programs of one sort or another. Experimentation with block or core programs and team-teaching arrangements are common in middle schools, but not in high schools.

Among the curriculum problems that face secondary school personnel are the relative roles of general and specialized education, how to best provide for individual differences, whether the curriculum should be subject- or experience-centered, how to articulate vertically and horizontally, and the question of when the curriculum is in proper balance. In addition there are such basic problems as what to teach, to whom, and by what methods. So far none of these problems has been solved.

The curriculum is the result of many influences— not the least of which is the history of secondary and middle school education. Textbook publishers, business and industry, pressure groups, professional organizations, governmental agencies, and institutions of higher learning, all have considerable input into the curriculum-making process, but it is the local teachers, administrators, and lay public that are responsible for the local curriculum. The roles of the teacher, the layman, and the students in curriculum building are growing greater. Of course, in the final analysis, what is actually taught is really determined by the teachers in the classroom. Curriculum guides and resource units provided by the school system make the teachers' work easier and serve to standardize the teaching and curriculum throughout the system.

The curriculum is not confined only to the courses taught in the school; it includes the extra-curriculum and the guidance program as well. The extracurriculum may well provide educational essentials that are impossible in the regular academic program. It should therefore be both open to and attractive to all students. The guidance program, when well organized, also provides essential services. Its purpose is to help students to understand themselves and to direct their own lives more efficiently.

It is somewhat difficult to spot trends in middle and secondary education because of the prevalence of transient fads and the constant pulling and pushing of action and reaction in educational circles. However, it appears that in spite of a movement back to basics, schools are becoming more responsive and humane and are attempting to provide curricula and methods that are really relevant and practical insofar as the wishes and needs of youth and society are concerned.

The 1980s ushered in a spate of reports recommending reform in middle and secondary education. These reports called for higher standards of scholastic achievement, more rigorous curricula, and an upgrading of the teaching personnel. They have caused considerable comment and some movement in the various states. What the outcome of these movements will be is still problematical.

Additional Reading

Brodinsky, Ben. *Defining the Basics of American Education*, Fastback 95. Bloomington, IN.: Phi Delta Kappa (Educational Foundation), 1977.

Butts, R. Freeman. *Public Education in the United States: From Revolution to Reform.* New York: Holt, 1978.

Curtis, Thomas E., and Wilma M. Bidwell. *Curriculum and Instruction for Emerging Adolescents.* Reading, MA: Addison-Wesley, 1977.

Ehlers, Henry. *Crucial Issues in Education*, 7th ed. New York: Holt, 1981.

Elam, Stanley M., ed. *The Gallup Polls of Attitudes Toward Education, 1969–1984: A Topical Summary.* Bloomington, IN: Phi Delta Kappa, 1984.

Gatewood, Thomas E., and Charles A. Dilg. *The Middle School We Need.* Washington, DC: The Association for Supervision and Curriculum Development, 1975.

Goodlad, John. *A Place Called School.* New York: McGraw-Hill, 1983.

———. *What Schools Are for.* Bloomington, IN: Phi Delta Kappa, 1979.

Gutek, Gerald L. *Basic Education: A Historical Perspective*, Fastback 167. Bloomington, IN: Phi Delta Kappa Educational Foundation, 1981.

Hampel, Robert. *American High Schools Since 1940.* Boston: Houghton Mifflin, 1984.

Jarolimek, John. *The Schools in Contemporary Society: An Analysis of Social Current Issues and Forces.* New York: Macmillan, 1981.

Kohut, Sylvester, Jr. *The Middle School: A Bridge Between Elementary and Secondary Schools.*

Washington, DC: National Education Association, 1976.

Lounsbury, John H., and Gordon E. Vars. *A Curriculum for the Middle School Years.* New York: Harper & Row, 1978.

Ravitch, Diane. *The Troubled Crusade: American Education, 1945–1980.* New York: Basic Books, 1983.

Ryan, Kevin. *Those Who Can, Teach,* 4th ed. Boston: Houghton Mifflin, 1984, Part II, III.

Sarason, Seymour B. *Schooling in America: Scapegoat and Salvation.* New York: Free Press, 1983.

Sizer, Theodore R. *Horace's Compromise: The Dilemma of the American High School.* Boston: Houghton Mifflin, 1984.

———. *A Review and Comment on the National Reports.* Reston, VA: National Association of Secondary School Principals, 1983.

Woodring, Paul. *The Persistent Problems of Education.* Bloomington, IN: Phi Delta Kappa Educational Foundation, 1983.

2

The Students and How They Learn

Overview

To teach classes effectively you must understand the characteristics of students in general and your own individual students in particular. In this chapter we first look at some of the characteristics of adolescents in general, and then examine more closely the characteristics of middle school students and high school youths. We then proceed to a discussion of how students learn, and some implications of learning theory to teaching. Finally we finish the chapter with a few comments about student rights and student-teacher relationships.

The Students

Adolescence

The characteristics of middle or high school students in general are not necessarily true for every adolescent boy or girl. Each student is unique. The set of characteristics that make up any person's physical, mental, emotional, and social being can never be duplicated exactly. Yet there are a number of generalizations true enough of youth in general to be used as a tentative guide if we remember that, when one applies these generalizations to any individual, one must be prepared for variations from the norm. Between the ages of ten and eighteen—the range of the middle and high school years—boys and girls move from childhood to young adulthood. It is no wonder that the teenagers who are our middle and high school students are full of complexities and enigmas. The business of growing up is a complicated one. Adolescents are torn by many conflicts and many moments of indecision. At one moment, they may demand complete independence; at the next moment, they may need the reassurance and protection required by young children. As they enter early adolescence, they encounter personal, social, educational, and vocational problems that they are incapable of analyzing and logically solving. Often their lives are stormy. Of course, most youngsters come through these trials relatively unscathed. Still, the teacher who understands the reasons for an adolescent's behavior can better help the student during this trying period. By getting to know and understand the students, the teacher is in a position to help them solve their problems and to adapt their programs to make the most of the situation.

It is here that you the teacher must be aware of factors that contribute to many of the changes in behavior taking place. The early adolescent, now more descriptively called a transescent, confused by the mysteries of physiological changes and concerned over the development of secondary sex char-

acteristics and new social and emotional pressures, needs strong support, not only from home but from school as well. The rebellion of the middle adolescent is understandable, too, if one is aware of the conditions of life that help create their uncertainties, confusions, and concerns. Dr. William C. Kvaraceus was probably right when he said that being a teenager is the most dangerous occupation in our society.

Growing Up

Adolescence, as we have seen, is a period of growing up. However, students do not grow up at the same speed. Some mature rapidly; some mature more slowly. For some girls puberty comes as early as age nine; for others it comes as late as age sixteen. Similarly, for boys the onset of puberty may range from age eleven to age eighteen. Therefore, you must be prepared to face classes of boys and girls who range from quite childish to very mature. Further, looks may be deceiving, for the various facets of a child's personality grow at different rates. Very mature-looking boys, for instance, may be quite childish in strength, interests, and personality. The growing-up process is also not consistent. Students who act maturely today may behave childishly tomorrow. In short, adolescence is a period of change accompanied by rapid, uneven growth.

These adolescent changes may cause many conflicts within the adolescent and the adolescent's social relationships. Consequently, adolescents tend to be emotional, moody, and flighty—a combination of naïveté and sophistication. For them schools are likely to be sources of frustration, failure, humiliation, and punishment as well as being opportunities for social growth, pleasure, learning skills and knowledge, and gaining experience in the art of becoming an adult.

Developmental Tasks

Becoming an adult is not an easy assignment. It requires boys and girls to establish themselves as young men and young women in a heterosexual world. In this process they must take on new roles and make numerous adjustments so as to fit into these new roles and to cope with the problems that accompany them. To assume these new roles successfully and to make the adjustments needed for successful growing up, each youth must accomplish a number of developmental tasks. Middle and high school youths both consciously and unconsciously strive to complete these tasks. Quite properly students give these tasks a much higher priority than their schoolwork. According to Havighurst, these developmental tasks include:

a. To learn to understand oneself, to live with and compensate for one's inadequacies, and to make the most of one's assets.
b. To learn what it is to be a young man or young woman and to act accordingly.
c. To develop a suitable moral code.
d. To learn how to act one's part in a heterosexual society.
e. To determine, prepare for, and become placed in a vocation.
f. To acquire a suitable philosophy of life.
g. To build a system of values.
h. To establish oneself as an independent individual free from parental apron strings.
i. To learn how to make reasonable decisions in serious matters without undue reliance on an older person.
j. To master the social and intellectual level and knowledge necessary for adult life.
k. To learn the skills of courtship and to establish close friendships with persons of the opposite sex as preparation for finding a suitable mate.
l. To break away from one's childhood home.
m. To learn what kind of person one is and to live with oneself.[1]

---

[1] Robert J. Havighurst, *Human Development and Education* (New York: Longmans, Green, 1953), Chap. 1, pp. 9–15, 19, 20; also *Developmental Tasks and Education*, 2nd ed. (New York: Longmans, Green, 1952).

Establishing Independence

Since part of becoming an adult is to become free from the domination of parents, teachers, and other authority figures, adolescents try to establish their independence. In the process they often become highly critical of adults and the adult world. To demonstrate their independence adolescents tend to reject adult authority, opinions, and values. Often they experiment with undesirable or unconventional behavior calculated to illustrate their independence, manliness or womanliness, and adulthood. Yet, in spite of their desire for asserting their independence, adolescents have a great need for security. They are greatly concerned about themselves—their bodies, social relations, future, image, status, and so on. This egocentrism accounts for such phenomena as going steady, early marriage, and conformity. Conformity is likely to become an obsession. Even the "nonconformists" are conformists. They tend to be ruled by the standards of the adolescent community rather than those of adults—although their long-range goals may be strongly influenced by their parents. Their need for support and security is also evident in the rapid and extreme alterations in behavior exhibited by so many adolescents.

Obviously then, since adolescents seek both independence and security, middle and high schools should try to give them plenty of opportunities to try their own wings in a supportive atmosphere.

Desire for Self-realization

Connected with the adolescents' desire for independence and adulthood is a desire for self-realization. They need to achieve, to feel important, and to be accepted by their peers and by adults. They do not want to be talked down to or to be treated like children. They need responsibility. They need the chance to be leaders sometimes. Therefore teachers should give all students a chance to shine, to show off a little, and to assume some real responsibility. Because of their desire for recognition and achievement, adolescents are likely to be sympathetic to the desires of others, particularly the disadvantaged and downtrodden in their search for civil rights, economic opportunity, freedom, and so forth. Adolescents tend to be "suckers for causes." They are also concerned about the meaning of life and self. They are concerned with vocational choice (some of them at least). They do not see much relevance or pertinence to their own lives in most of the content of the curriculum.

Cognitive Growth

Boys' and girls' cognitive skills develop greatly during adolescence. They are more ready to learn through verbal means than are younger students. They are not as dependent on demonstration, manipulation, nonverbal perception, and the like as younger students are. Although transescents are almost completely dependent on concrete thought, as adolescents they become skilled and fascinated with abstraction, theory, and higher meanings.

Middle and high school youth are self-motivating. Usually it is not so much a matter of getting them to do something as it is to directing their behavior in desirable directions. They have long attention spans when what they are doing seems to them important, adventurous, active, or novel. But their tolerance for boring lessons and curricula is minimal.

A Whole Person

Finally, each student is a whole person. Anything the student learns or does affects that individual as an entity. All activity has emotional, mental, and physical aspects. This applies to school learning as well as to other activities. Although students can be shaped, in the process they interact with the environment. They are not just wax tablets to be written on. Therefore, your teaching must give the students opportunities to participate actively in their own learning. It should involve the physical

and emotional as well as the intellectual aspects of students personalities in every lesson.

The Middle School Students

Much of the material just discussed applies to both transescents (that is, beginning adolescents and pubescents) and older adolescents. However, when thinking about middle school students, several things in particular should be borne in mind. Transescence is a period of change from childhood to adolescence. Many middle school students are still children. Moreover, those students who are already adolescents are only beginning adolescents. They need much support as they start their journey toward independent adulthood. That is why they need a transitional program like that of the middle school rather than the complexities of the high school departmentalized program. Intellectually, transescents are moving from a period of concrete knowledge to more formal abstract knowledge. During this period, they learn to work with the abstract, the theoretical, and the hypothetical. Middle school teaching should help them make this transition. They also continue, to some extent, the imaginative thinking of childhood. Middle school teachers should capitalize on these traits and encourage them. Too often we in schools tend to kill imagination and creativity. Socially, transescents are more vulnerable than at any other time in their lives. They are unsure because they are entering a new world. They are divorcing themselves slowly from their dependence on adults, so they turn to their peers for support and guidance. Sympathetic guidance at this point is most critical because it is at this point that one begins to form one's values, life view, and mode of living. Emotionally, transescents are just beginning to come to grips with the complexities of adult life. Sometimes their feelings can be overwhelming—even adults who have lived with emotions for many years sometimes find feelings difficult to handle. Middle school personnel would be wise to tone down adult-type social, sporting and other activities until boys and girls have become more ready to cope with them. When one forces children to grow up too fast, growing up becomes difficult. The same caution can be expressed about physical growth. Transescent growth is rapid and uneven, and sometimes deceptive. Boys who look like big, strong men may still be little boys whose strength or bone structure has not kept up with their growth. Middle school teachers should be very careful not to confront transescents with tasks for which they are not ready. For example, many a boy has suffered serious injury because he was urged to play football before his leg bones had finished developing.

Educators should always remember that sixth-, seventh- and eighth-graders are not high schoolers. They need time to grow up. If they can get off to a good start with positive self-images, they should do well both as youths and adults. After all, transescence is one of the most interesting and exciting times of life.

The High School Years

Now, at the risk of some repetition, we examine adolescents' high school years. The danger of repetition stems from the fact that boys and girls do

---

What implications do the characteristics of adolescents have for you?

Observe a few classes in a high school and a middle school. Which group would you prefer to work with? In what ways do they seem different?

From what you have seen of adolescents, what sorts of things should you do in your classes to attract their interest and attention?

In what ways do you think you would teach transescents differently from older adolescents? Or would you?

---

not change overnight just because they graduate from the middle school and enter high school. The transition is slow and uneven. For some students the period of transescence lingers well into their high school years. In some instances students gain adolescent or young adult characteristics and then slip back to more childish behavior. This should not be surprising, because we all may know senior citizens who have not attained fully adult status in all facets of their lives.

Many students find the transition from middle school to high school difficult because of the many adjustments they must make. In addition to the advent of sexual change with its attendant social and emotional demands, high school youth are faced by many role changes. For one, they are thrust into a new and different environment. As freshmen in the new school they have little or no status in high school society. The school structure is much less intimate and personal than what they have been used to. Often they feel lost in the crowd; some never fully find themselves in this new environment.

Under the circumstances it is not surprising to find that many high school youths are not happy in school. They feel incompetent, inferior, powerless, ignored, and rejected. They believe that they are not learning anything—at least not anything worth learning. They are bored. They have poor marks. They feel unwanted. Since, like everyone else, high school youths want to be respected, to be treated politely, to be treated fairly, to be understood, and to be listened to, when the school climate seems unfriendly they see no point in attending school. Therefore, many of them (25 per cent of black males, 22 per cent of black females, 17.7 per cent of white males, and 14.3 per cent of white females) drop out.[2]

Even so, most high school students rate schools

---

[2] Cullen Murphy, "Today's Children and Education," *The Wilson Quarterly* (Autumn, 1982), **6:**61–82. See also Charles E. Silberman, *Crisis in the Classroom* (New York: Random House, 1970); Philip Jackson, *Life in Classrooms* (New York: Holt, 1968).

fairly high. According to a Gallup Poll, 40 per cent of the students like school very much, whereas only 10 per cent say they really dislike it. Also half of the boys and girls think their schoolwork is not demanding enough; they feel that they should be required to work more.[3]

What they want from school evidently is discipline and order, plus opportunities for social contacts with their peers. In their eyes the social functions are the best part of school. They want teachers to relate to them and to respect them. The best teachers, they say, are warm, understanding, humorous, yet authoritative. Good teachers, they think, know their stuff and conduct efficient, orderly classes.[4]

Cognitive Development

Perhaps the primary concerns of high school teachers have to do with students' cognitive development. Early adolescents' thinking is likely to be largely haphazard trial and error, but older high school boys and girls can be quite systematic thinkers. As they move into the high school grades, they become more adept at thinking abstractly and generalizing from abstractions. By using formal thought they are able to think of possibilities as against realities. Preoccupation with abstractions and theories may lead to role confusion, and confusion between what might be and what is. Consequently, they tend to have high ideals and to judge the world by impossibly high standards. It may also lead to adolescent egocentrism marked by introspection, self-consciousness, overconcern with others' opinions of them, and overdependence on the practices, standards, and values of peer groups.

Since high school youths entering the formal op-

> Look at some middle school textbooks. Do they seem to match the cognitive development of transescents? Similarly examine some high school textbooks. Do these books give students opportunities to stretch their minds?

eration stage of cognitive development may be inclined to be unrealistic, teachers should quiz them about their facts, and ask them to back up their theories, hypotheses, and solutions to society's problems. Skillful teachers require students to find out what the facts are, throw facts at them, face them with any incongruities in their positions, play the devil's advocate, require them to debate the other fellow's belief and to argue against their own positions, and in other ways induce them to face the facts and consider the various sides of issues. Procedures of this type may help students to see the facts of life and possible solutions to difficult problems, and to adopt reasonable theories, hypotheses, and positions.

Their growing ability to use formal thinking processes does not limit boys and girls to systematic thinking. Adolescents can and do think originally and creatively. Their imaginations are strong and free. They are capable of cognitive leaps—and dreams. Youth is a time for dreaming. As that old Lapland song reminded Mr. Longfellow

> A boys' will is the wind's will
> And the thoughts of youth are long, long thoughts.[5]

The high school years, then, are an age of cognitive growth. Even the less promising youths can produce if given opportunities. Further, they can learn whatever they need to learn if they are given enough time and proper instruction. However, too difficult schoolwork and unreasonable demands may cause students to become disinterested and give up.

---

[3] S. M. Elam, ed., *A Decade of Gallup Polls of Attitudes Toward Education, 1969–1978* (Bloomington, IN: Phi Delta Kappa, 1978).

[4] Robert T. McNergney and Carol A. Currier, *Teacher Development* (New York: Macmillan, 1981), pp. 35–45.

[5] Henry W. Longfellow, *My Lost Youth.*

Values

Adolescents tend to see things in black and white and fail to take into account the perplexities of the real world. As they grow older and more experienced, they begin to see things in better perspective. They become aware of the varying values of rules and customs and see how the rules and customs apply in particular situations. They see the purpose of the rules and the need for rules. They understand that sometimes rules must be flexible and that the spirit of the law should override the letter of the law. As they become more understanding of the need and purpose of rules, they become desirous of participating in the forming of their own rules. In short, they gradually adopt what Piaget calls the morals of cooperation.

Some Problems of Adolescence

Most adolescent problem behavior consists of a syndrome of related behavior adopted by students in order (1) to achieve blocked goals, (2) to express opposition to adults and/or society, (3) to cope with such problems as anxiety, fear, and frustration, (4) to get solid with their peers, or (5) to demonstrate their worth.[6] It follows then that since the student is usually engaged in more than one type of problem behavior, we teachers should concentrate on preventing problems and reenforcing nonproblem behavior rather than trying to correct specific problems.

Apathy

A major problem among high school students is apathy. This is not so true of middle school students. In part, at least, student apathy is undoubt-

edly the result of a curriculum that seems to students irrelevant and meaningless, and which is no rival for the excitement of outside life, television, and the like. Some 63 per cent of twelfth-graders and 42 per cent of tenth-graders work. Their jobs take time that might otherwise be spent in schoolwork (including homework) and school activities. These working hours detract from whatever feelings of school as community the students may have. Further the world of work may seem more exciting, more real, and more important to students. So they turn their backs on what they see as unrealistic, irrelevant, boring curricula and classes.

Additionally, many high school students are apolitical and cynical. These feelings, plus parochial attitudes and beliefs that striving and schooling for the future are futile, and the resultant disinterest in other aspects of life cause the students to view schools, at best, as a waste of time.[7]

Such feelings of apathy and rejection can be combatted by involving the young people in civic community activities and by encouraging participation in school activities. Real opportunities for taking part in school governance and community affairs can be most stimulating.

Drugs and Liquor

The use of drugs and liquor creates all too many adolescent problems. Drug use inhibits short-term memory, creativity, energy, and motivation. It makes school seem unappealing and irrelevant. Teachers should refuse to teach boys and girls who are under the influence of any drugs, and make sure that the students understand that their presence while under the influence will not be tolerated. To this end you should become well aware of the symptoms of drug use. Any student exhibiting these symptoms should be referred to the proper school authorities at once.

---

[6] Richard Jessar, "Adolescent Problem Behavior and Developmental Transmission," *Education Digest* (November, 1982), **48**:47–50. Condensed from *The Journal of School Health* (May, 1982), **52**:295–300.

[7] James Mackey and Deborah Appelman, "The Growth of Adolescent Apathy," *Educational Leadership* (March, 1983), **40**:30–33.

> What steps do you think you could take in your teaching to make the school more relevant?
>
> Are there ways that you can involve students in their community? How can you make your courses part of the real world?
>
> What position will you take about student use of drugs and alcohol?
>
> What can you do to make your classes seem more humane?

Family Problems

Family problems may lead to adolescent problems. Many of today's boys and girls are the products of broken homes, single-parent homes, and poorly supervised homes. Parent self-centeredness has caused neglect and lack of supervision, guidance, and care. Boys and girls are too soon on their own. The result is that youths do not feel good about themselves. Boys and girls become less trusting, less happy with themselves and with society, and so apathetic. Schools and teachers can contribute to rebuilding feelings of worth in youths by giving them chances to be responsible.[8]

Finding One's Role

For adolescents finding one's role in life may be an ordeal. They are continually faced with such problems as: How should I behave today? How can I be popular? Should I follow the crowd or do what I think is right? What should my goals for the future be? For some, solving such puzzles may lead to identity problems. Girls, for instance, may be torn between a desire to be achievers and a longing for the traditional soft femininity our culture continues to prize. (Some girls refuse to be too smart for fear that the boys won't like them.) Sometimes identity crises caused by these confusions may lead to with-

---

[8] Gerald Grant with John Briggs, "Todays' Children Are Different," *Educational Leadership* (March, 1983), **40:**4–9.

drawal, negative identities, untoward behavior, or depression.

Role confusion is another indication of the necessity for our schools to be supportive. Since the large departmentalized high school does not lend itself to creating a supportive climate, teachers must try to make their classes as humane as possible. Students need to be recognized as people. Middle school block schedules are helpful in this regard.

How Students Learn

False Causes for Not Learning

Why is it that so often students do not learn in our classes and schools? There are many reasons, of course. But often the reasons we assume to be the causes are false ones. For instance we say

"Eileen is the silliest girl you've ever seen. She never pays attention to a thing. She can't keep her mind on anything." (But watch her at the theater. Engrossed in dreamland she sits. Seemingly no commotion in the theater could draw her attention from the plot.)

"John is the stupidest boy I've ever seen." (Yet he was able to learn to read music and become the highly successful leader of his own orchestra.)

"Joe is the laziest boy in school. He just won't do a thing. I don't think he has finished one algebra assignment this year." (But think of the hours of hard physical and mental work he has spent working on his car. His mother has a hard time getting him away from that car long enough to eat his dinner.)

Real Causes for Not Learning

Obviously these accusations do not really explain why students do not learn. If anything, they describe symptoms, not real causes. Too often such statements are only alibis by which we teachers attempt to justify to ourselves our lack of success. We can no longer fall back on such excuses. Our clients—the students, parents, and community—will no longer let us pass the buck down to the students. We must assume the responsibility ourselves when it is ours. What then are the real causes for students not learning? Let us look at a few of them.

First and most important is poor teaching. Teaching is often ineffective, because it is inadequately planned or because it violates the laws of learning. Some courses are poorly organized and lack direction. Some classes are poorly motivated. In some courses the work is too hard or too easy. Some teachers attempt to cover the subject rapidly instead of giving it time to sink in. Some teachers ignore the fact that students are individuals with varying backgrounds, talents, and interests, and attempt to teach everyone the same material at the same rate in the same way.

The curriculum itself is often a major cause of nonlearning. Too much of what is taught in the secondary school has little bearing on the lives or needs of the students. Probably half of the high school curriculum could be dropped from the school program tomorrow without anyone's noticing its passing. It is not surprising that for many students their studies seem too futile and dead-end to be worth their exerting any real effort to learn them. If we wish students to make an effort to learn, we ought to provide something for them to learn that at least seems worth learning.

Poor teaching and poor courses probably cause most failures to learn, but they are not the only causes. Students are often handicapped by poor health, fatigue, physical or mental limitations, emotional difficulties, environmental factors, family attitudes, or peer pressures. If a student's parents and friends feel that studying a Shakespearean sonnet is a waste of time and money, it probably will not be easy to convince the youth that he should devote much time to it. Or again, a young person may believe, as did the poet, in burning the candle at both ends. Although this practice may give "a lovely light," it is not helpful because fatigue hinders learning and too many interests distract students from the desired learnings.

That brings us to a major block to school learning. Few teachers and few faculties do much to make school learning seem important or attractive when compared to life's other activities. In fact, many of the things we teachers do seem to be designed so as to convince the students that learning is undesirable and unpleasant. In what other endeavor would one try to sell a product by using it as a punishment? Yet every day some teacher assigns class work as a punishment.

These, then, are some of the blocks to learning. They are also causes of student misbehavior. If we teachers are to do the job required of us—helping students learn—we must overcome these blocks. Of course, we are not always in a position in which we can do much to overcome them. But, good teachers take each youngster and try, by using the best methods and materials they know, to help the student learn in spite of any obstacles. This is a key challenge of teaching.

Learning Styles

Obviously the strategies and techniques we use in our teaching should be consistent with the best principles of learning. Let us now look at a few general principles and draw some generalizations about teaching methods from them.

In the first place, learning is an individual matter. It is the learner who does the learning—not the teacher. For this reason, as well as other reasons,

---

Evaluate the teaching to which you have been subjected. Did it stimulate interest in learning the subjects? Give examples of teaching that promoted learning and teaching that did not.

Are the courses in your field irrelevant or useless in any respect?

teaching should be centered on the students. Each individual learns differently from everyone else. Some individuals learn quickly; some more slowly. Some are verbally oriented; some more physically oriented. Some are visually oriented; some are more aurally oriented. Some like to read; others do not. Some have well-developed skills; others have poor skills. Some are active; some are passive. Some are interested in one thing; others in another. And so on and on.

These differences in orientations cause students to adopt different learning styles. These learning styles are probably the result of students' earlier learning and their emotional and physical development. Learning styles are neither good nor bad. One style may be effective in one type of situation, whereas another may be effective in another. Each learning style has its advantages and its disadvantages as the following illustrates.

Field independent persons are relatively independent from external clues. They are more intrinsically oriented, less sensitive in social or interpersonal situations, less influenced by peer pressure, and more likely to favor abstract subject matter than are field dependent persons. Researchers tell us that field independent students do better work in low structure-inductive learning situations whereas field dependent students do better in high structure-deductive classes.

Analytical persons tend to break ideas down into their component parts, but global thinkers find it difficult to do so. Some students are reflective types; others are impulsive. The impulsive are more inclined to jump to conclusions whereas the reflective types are likely to ponder over details. They are more likely than not to be narrow thinkers who are very careful, specific, and analytic, whereas the impulsive thinkers think in broad general (global) categories that sometimes may be too broad to be helpful in school learning. Some students sharpen the categories of what they learn, but levellers tend to break down distinctions. Consequently, levellers have trouble keeping track of things.

Similar dichotomies may be seen in the way indi-

Observe, if you can, differences in the way students learn. Do you and your friends have the same or different preferences for learning activities, approaches, situations, and methods of attacking learning?

viduals organize knowledge. Some use simple approaches for organizing information whereas others' approaches are quite complex. The results of these different approaches may give quite different answers. In like manner, some students are tolerant of new ideas, whereas others resist them. Some are easily distracted, whereas others concentrate. Some are more inclined to accept conventional viewpoints and practices, whereas others would rather hoe their own rows. Some are divergent thinkers, whereas others are convergent thinkers. That is to say that some people's thoughts tend to be creative, original, and far-ranging, whereas others tend to be matter of fact, prosaic, and narrow. In short, what is sauce for the goose is not necessarily sauce for the gander. Consequently, it is necessary for teachers (1) to provide different learning environments and teaching strategies for different students, or (2) to vary their teaching enough so that every student finds the learning situation compatible with his cognitive style at least part of the time, or (3) to help boys and girls develop learning styles conducive to effective learning of the content and to the teaching styles used in the school. Probably the best teachers use all three of these options. Certainly, in any case, it is imperative that students be taught how to learn if schooling is to be effective.

Learning How to Learn

One reason why students have different learning styles and abilities is that learning techniques are not entirely innate. In their earlier years, some of your students may have become very skillful in learning academic content while others of equal potential have not. Do not write off students because they do not do well in your school work. It may only be that they have *not learned how to learn academic material,* or it may be that their cognitive learning styles and your teaching style are too far apart. Perhaps by using the proper strategies and by reaiming your teaching you can help them to learn and to study effectively.

Sometimes the methods and materials we use in our schools do not help students learn how to learn. Learning via rote and memorization, lesson hearing, recitation, and the like do not help students cope with learning problems that require such intellectual skills as thinking, investigating and problem solving, for example. These strategies and techniques must be used in teaching, but you should also emphasize strategies and techniques that help students build higher-order intellectual skills. Learning how to learn transfers directly.

According to Litteri there are three types of students: students who can do it on their own, students who need some help, and students who need a lot of help, but all of them can learn how to learn.[9] The strategy is to train those who need help in the skills and controls they lack by instruction that shows them how to build concepts. These learning skills can be used in all subjects.

Learning and the Brain

To understand learning and learning styles one needs to know something of how the brain works. Recently researchers have learned much about the structure and function of the brain. This new knowledge has caused many educators and educationists to revise their views on teaching and learning. They now believe that humans are aggressive, not passive, learners. The brain is always active; it never turns itself off. Even when you are asleep your brain is working.

Learning occurs when the brain makes patterns from the stimuli it encounters. It recognizes these patterns by spotting similarities and differences— what does and what does not belong in the pattern. In this way the brain creates meaning and constructs perceptions and thought. It does not absorb them from the outside readymade. Its activity in this respect is influenced by anticipation and intention, however.

Contrary to what has been sometimes thought, the brain seems to work from the top down, from the superordinate to the subordinate. In building patterns evidently it first spots the big picture and then fills in the details. For this reason learning by logically piling up small segments of instruction seems inefficient. Evidently learning is not a particularly logical performance.

To learn best students need a lot of input in a nonthreatening environment. When a person is seriously threatened, he seems to turn off the cerebrum and downshifts to operating on the limbic brain system—the old prehuman mammalian brain. This means that as long as the threat seems serious or frightening the person cannot use the higher mental processes well. Probably the only learning that occurs in such circumstances is rote learning. Therefore for effective learning to occur, the environment needs to be both nonthreatening and rich.

For this rich positive environment to be most effective for learning, students must do things. They must talk. They must be active. Sitting still and silent in the traditional classroom setting is counterproductive. Learning situations should be active as well as supportive.

The Two Hemispheres

Recently much has been made of the differences in the left and right cerebral hemispheres of the brain. Verbal learning, logical thinking, and the like are supposedly lodged in the left hemisphere, and spatial, emotional, affective aspects are lodged in the right. And to some extent that is true. A child

---

[9] Charles A. Litteri, lecture, University of Southern Maine, 1983.

who prefers the use of the left hemisphere may learn to read more readily by the phonetic analysis approach whereas the child who prefers the right hemisphere may do better by the sight method. In introducing the child to reading it may pay to take advantage of these preferences at first, but as soon as possible one should get the whole brain into the act, for all learning in all subject matter is a synthesis of both left hemisphere and right hemisphere activity. So in your teaching you should combine the verbal of the left hemisphere with the nonverbal of the right hemisphere. This is important because brain organization is largely a matter of training. Just because a youth favors one hemisphere over the other is no reason for catering to that hemisphere. In fact, catering to one hemisphere may cause poor development in the other.

Actually, approaches that call for the use of both sides of the brain are most useful in class. By using both types of approaches you can help students develop different cognitive learning styles. Further, the use of both types of approaches helps to develop the whole brain of all students. As it stands, in most schools and classes left-hemispheric approaches dominate instruction too much. We need to develop whole brains and total personalities. Therefore our classes should combine intellectual, emotional, affective, and physical elements.

Problems and the Brain

Evidently, as John Dewey believed, people are naturally problem solvers. They need problems to solve in order to develop intellectually. A brain without problems does not work up to capacity.[10] It follows then that to be what Hart calls "brain compatible," curricula and teaching should be problem centered. Classroom activities should be free from threats, of course, but they should also be challenging, of real importance to the learners,

and to some extent student directed although carefully supervised and guided by the teacher. In ideal teaching, rote learning would be used only to achieve mastery after the students have established the basic skills and knowledge, according to Hart.[11]

A key word in this description of problem solving teaching is "challenging." The brain was built to solve problems. It does so from the moment of birth and thrives on it throughout all the three score and ten plus years allotted to us. The human ability to cope with problems is amazing. Given the opportunity, most high school youth are good problem solvers who need opportunities to whet their talents on challenging problems.

Consequently, secondary school students should have opportunities to do high-level thinking. They need curricula that are not fettered by facts, prescriptions, and preconceptions of what is right and wrong. Rather, they need opportunities to think creatively—to make imaginative leaps—in order to develop intellectually and emotionally and to enrich the meaningfulness of their lives.[12]

Verbalism versus Knowing

One reason teachers sometimes pick inappropriate teaching strategies and techniques is that they have not thought through what it is they are trying to do and do not comprehend what understanding and knowing entail.

To understand something one must have clear concepts. Many times we think we know something when actually we have only a vague notion. When we try to explain the meaning of a word and find that we cannot do it, we say "I know what it means, but I just can't explain it." More often than not, the truth is that we really have only a fuzzy idea

---

[10] Based on Ralph Tyler's comment in Jeri Ridings Nowakowski, "On Educational Evaluation: A Conversation with Ralph Tyler," *Educational Leadership* (May, 1983), **40**:26.

[11] Leslie A. Hart, *Human Brain and Human Learning* (New York: Longmans, 1983).

[12] Based on John Barell, "Reflections on Critical Thinking in Secondary Schools," *Educational Leadership* (March, 1983), **40**:45–49.

> What sort of learning techniques does a student need to learn in order to cope with the learning tasks common in your field?
>
> What implications do the findings in brain research have for you as a teacher?
>
> What classroom activities could you use to harness the brain's proclivity for problem solving? List a half dozen specific problem-solving type activities that call for a high level of creative thinking.
>
> What type of problem-solving activity would seem best suited for middle school transescents?

and do not really understand what the word means. If we do not know clearly enough to use the knowledge, we do not really know at all.

There are several types of knowing: we can know *about;* we can know *that;* and we can know *how.* Learning about something is not the same as learning it, nor learning how to do it. The boy who only reads about how to swim may drown when thrown into the water. Neither does one learning product guarantee another. The girl who learns the rules of grammar and can do all the exercises in her grammar workbook perfectly may not be able to write a clear, idiomatic sentence. Or again, a

graduate student may find that studying technical French has not helped him a bit when trying to order a dinner in Paris. Neither does studying American history necessarily produce good citizens. To learn something we must study *it*—not about it or something like it. To learn to do something we must study and practice how to do it.

An example of this confusion is the common error of mistaking memorizing for understanding. We confuse the word with the deed, the name with the object. Children are often asked to learn words and phrases which mean nothing to them. It is quite possible to repeat that in a right triangle the square of the hypotenuse is equal to the sum of the squares of the opposite sides and yet not have the slightest idea of the meaning of square, hypotenuse, opposite sides, or right triangle. Thousands of persons can glibly recite that a noun is the name of a person, place, or thing, and yet not be able to pick a single noun out of a sentence. The cartoon of Miss Peach's class illustrates how well some elementary school children understand the pledge of allegiance to the flag. This parroting is called verbalism. One of the banes of both the elementary and secondary school, it is an example of what can result when one uses the wrong strategies and techniques. To really know something we must know it well enough to use the knowledge.

FIGURE 2–1.
Miss Peach's Pupils Recite the Pledge of Allegiance to the Flag. (Copyright, 1957, New York Herald Tribune, Inc. Reproduced with permission.)

Need for Both Vicarious and Direct Learning

In some instances verbalism is the result of an overuse of vicarious learning. Much of our best learning comes through direct experience like that of the burned child who learned to fear the fire. Fortunately, it is not necessary to get burned. We can learn vicariously, through the experiences of others. Not everyone can go to see the pyramids, but anyone can learn about them from descriptions and pictures. Direct experience usually results in more vivid learning, but it is not always efficient. Sometimes it is quite inefficient, time-consuming, and costly, as in the case of the burned child. "Learning the hard way," we call it. For this reason we must rely on vicarious experience for much of our schoolwork. To do so is quite proper. It saves time, money, and effort. Used correctly it can be quite effective. In many instances it is the only type of experience possible. However, many teachers rely too much on vicarious learning. Everything else being equal, direct learning is usually more effective than vicarious learning.

Need for Realistic Learning

Realistic learning situations help make the learning meaningful to the student and thus help to avoid verbalism. Only meaningful material can be learned efficiently. In the first place, if the learning is meaningless to the learner it is useless. In the second place, meaningless material is much more difficult to learn than meaningful material. Yet many youngsters are required to learn things meaningless to them every day. How many youngsters have strived to learn:

> Once upon a midnight dreary, as I pondered, weak
> and weary,
> Over many a quaint and curious volume of forgotten
> lore,
> As I nodded, nearly napping, suddenly there came a
> tapping
> As of someone gently rapping, rapping at my chamber
> door.

even though they had not the slightest idea of what it was all about and could not translate "midnight dreary," "quaint and curious volume," "forgotten lore," or even "chamber door."

In order to avoid mere verbalism and inefficient learning among students, you should see to it that all learning situations in your classes are meaningful. Eliminate meaningless material either by omitting it altogether or preparing the students for it so that it will be meaningful when they study it. In the foregoing example you might substitute a less difficult poem for Poe's *The Raven,* or you might prepare the students by studying the poem, its message, and its vocabulary before the students attempt to learn it.

Building Understanding

One reason for the prevalence of verbalism in our schools is that it has become a general practice to teach (1) isolated facts or bits of information, (2) generalizations presented as isolated facts or bits of information, or (3) a combination of facts and generalizations stated as isolated facts or bits of information. This is not the way to build understanding. To build understanding effectively one must give pupils opportunities to examine the information, to establish the relationships among the facts, and to draw conclusions.

In this process, since concept building is a matter of categorization, one must see to it that students understand what is included in the concept and what is not. To that end, research suggests teachers should present pupils with distinct examples of both positive and negative instances of the concept. It seems to help if students meet several positive cases at once, if the examples of positive instances are uniform, if positive instances are shown side by side with negative ones, if irrelevant attributes are kept to a minimum, and if students' attention is focused on the relevant attributes. Evidently, concept teaching is especially effective when teachers provide pupils a framework on which to build their concept. For instance, definitions followed by examples seems to work well. Since it is also helpful to teach concepts in related groups it usually pays to examine the structure of one's subject matter before teaching it.

Mixed methods, as a rule, work best for teaching concepts. Learning via a variety of instances and examples seems to aid understanding and transfer. Thus looking at and handling things and talking to oneself about their attributes as one studies them tends to make concepts clearer. So does feedback. Students should learn why such and such is right and so and so is wrong.

All of this takes time. Students need time to digest the various factors. If they are rushed through concept learning, they do not have time to assimilate the concepts properly. Therefore, the atmosphere of the class should not be too pressing. Neither should it be threatening. Although anxiety may aid in the learning of simple concepts, to learn complex concepts requires a supportive, anxiety-free climate.

Building Skills

Skills must be learned directly by actually performing the skill. Of course, one can, and probably must, learn a lot about the skill in other ways, but the only way to master a skill is to practice it. As Comenius pointed out in 1657,

> What is to be done must be learned by practice. Artisans do not detain their apprentices with theories, but set them to do practical work at an early stage; thus they learn to forge by forging, to carve by carving, to paint by painting, and to dance by dancing. In schools, therefore, let the students learn to write by writing, to talk by talking, to sing by singing, and to reason by reasoning.

All too often teachers forget this obvious, long-known fact. And so they make the mistake of trying to teach students how to write by teaching them grammar, and how to reason by memorizing rules and facts.

Teaching Attitudes, Appreciations, and Ideals

To develop in your students an attitude, appreciation, or ideal, you must provide them with experiences that foster that attitude, appreciation, or ideal. You cannot develop critical attitudes suitable for scholarly study by requiring students to regurgitate the wisdom given out in your lectures. Neither can you teach the ideals of scientific investigation by drilling students on scientific facts. Nor can you instill a love of music by making students memorize composers' dates. Rather you must try to provide an atmosphere conducive to the attitudes you seek, give the students many chances to emulate suitable models and to practice the attitudes, appreciations, or ideal desired, and then reinforce these attitudes, appreciations, and ideals at every opportunity. Exhortations and lectures seldom bring about the affective learning one desires.

Can you give examples of different types of knowing? What implications do these different ways of knowing have for the teacher?

Can you cite examples of verbalism from your own school experience?

Can you cite examples from your own school experience of methods that seemed to bring out the wrong learning?

Can you think of tactics in your own field of teaching you think would be effective for teaching such objectives as

1. A deep understanding.
2. An appreciation.
3. A change in attitude.
4. An intellectual skill.
5. A physical skill.
6. Memorization.

Readiness

Learning is usually developmental. That is to say, *new learning builds upon previous learning*. Students need to understand simple multiplication before they can succeed with long division. A student who does not know the principles of solving simple equations will probably have a difficult time with quadratics. Since this is so, learning should follow an orderly sequence with new learning building upon past learning.

Moreover, learning is not merely the accumulation of new concepts, skills, ideals, attitudes, and appreciations. Rather it is the integration of these new learnings and the concepts, skills, ideals, attitudes, and appreciations already present. The new learning becomes interwoven into one's personality. The result is really a personality change. This takes time. Although many students learn many things rapidly, thorough learning is apt to be a relatively slow process.

Since learning is developmental, it follows that one learns better when one is ready to learn. The principle of readiness has confused both teachers and laypeople. Psychologically it can have many ramifications, but for our classroom purposes it can be defined quite simply. Readiness is a combination of maturity, ability, prior instruction, and motivation. Individuals are ready to learn something when they have matured enough to learn it efficiently; when they have acquired the skills, knowledge, and strengths prerequisite to learning it; and when they are sufficiently motivated. When students have reached such a state of readiness, the teacher's job is relatively easy; when they have not, the teacher's job is more difficult and sometimes absolutely impossible. No one would attempt to teach a toddler classic ballet: one must learn to walk before one can learn to run. Therefore it is essential to pick strategies, techniques, and subject matter for which the students are ready. Sometimes when students are not ready, you may be able, by adopting suitable methods and approaches, to make them ready. Otherwise all you can do is to wait for the child to grow older, stronger, and wiser.

Transfer and Retention

Planning for Transfer and Retention

Courses are not very productive unless they bring about transfer and retention of learning. By transfer we mean using the outcome of learning in another situation. Thus, when students use in a history class skills they originally learned in English, transfer has taken place. If such transfer does not take place, the learning is of little value.

As you might expect, students do not transfer and remember extrinsically motivated learning as well as intrinsically motivated learning. When we want to learn something because we want to learn it, we are more likely to use the learning in other situations and to remember it. This is another argument for the use of intrinsic motivation whenever feasible.

Learning of unmeaningful material does not transfer either. Therefore transfer is more likely to result when the application of the learning to other situations is pointed out. When that is not done, transfer may not take place because the learner does not make the necessary connections. Transfer also takes place when components common to the original learning situation are present in the situation in which the learning is to be used. In other words, the more the learning situation is like the using situation, the greater chance there is that the learning will transfer.

Another aid to transfer is thorough learning. One can transfer what one knows and understands thoroughly much more readily than something less well known. Thorough knowledge also helps us retain our learning, but the best way to retain what we learn is to use it. What we do not use we tend to forget. Of course, we remember extremely vivid happenings well and we have learned some things so well that it seems we can never forget them.

Still, in spite of exceptions, the rule holds. Even one's native tongue becomes rusty if one does not use it. The key to retention is renewal through frequent use.

Both transfer and retention are encouraged by the mastering and use of generalizations for, as a rule, generalizations can be remembered and used better than detail. The best remembered generalizations (and therefore the generalizations most available for use) seem to be the ones the student derives for himself from specifics. Predigested generalizations worked out by the teacher and handed to the student are liable not to take at all, or to remain at the level of mere verbalism. (When you do present generalizations to students, you should probably support them by much "forgettable detail," in order to make the generalization stick. Ordinarily, however, it is probably more effective to give the students the details and encourage them to draw their own generalizations, or let them encounter details and applications that will make their generalization clear.) The more opportunities one has for applying principles, the clearer the generalization becomes.

Need for Reinforcement

If any learning is to be successfully retained and transferred, it must be reinforced. In teaching, the word *reinforce* is used in two ways. In one sense, reinforce refers to psychological reinforcement wherein a behavior is strengthened by providing some sort of reward when a learner does the behavior, for example, awarding a lollipop to the good boy who sits quietly without making a big fuss when the barber trims his hair. The other type of reinforcement is the strengthening of behavior that accompanies repeating the behavior. Behavior that is not reinforced or renewed by practice, drill, or some other form of repetition soon drops out. Thus in selecting your teaching strategies and techniques you should provide for the rewarding of desirable behavior and for frequent reuse and re-

newal of what the students have learned so that they will not forget.

Time on Task

As we have already hinted, all of this takes time. The more time one spends actually learning something, the more likely one is to learn it successfully. In fact, probably students can learn almost anything if they work at it long enough.[13] Therefore to be most effective, teachers should manage their classes so that students actually spend their time on the learning task—not on side trips.

Teaching Styles and Teacher Goals

One implication of all this is that we must adjust our teaching methods to meet our goals. Direct expository teaching seems to be effective for teaching young students the fundamentals, while indirect inductive styles, discussion, independent study, and the like are more successful for teaching the higher mental processes and academic skills to older, more sophisticated and talented students. Individualized study plans that are most successful with college students do not seem to work well with young middle school students.

Student Rights

The U. S. Constitution, state constitutions, laws, and legal decisions have given students certain rights. All teachers should make it a point to become familiar with these rights and to conduct themselves so that these student rights will not be violated.

---

[13] John B. Carroll, "A Model of School Learning," *Teachers College Record* (1963), **64**:723–732.

Not to do so is illegal and leaves one open to unpleasant consequences.

Perhaps the first right of students is the right to an education. This right guarantees that the schools must be open to every child; no boy and girl may be excluded (e.g., suspended or expelled) except for sufficient cause established by suitable due process. Further it implies that without exception the schooling provided all boys and girls must be of high quality. In short, schools may not discriminate against any student or group of students, or favor one type of student over another. When students have been the victims of discrimination, they have the right to special treatment to counteract and alleviate their mistreatment.

The U. S. Constitution gives all students the right to be let alone except for good and sufficient reasons. Therefore, except for reasons of misbehavior, or other actions prejudicial to the welfare of the school, the class, the other students, or the student himself, teachers and administrators must respect students' privacy and their right to be free of harassment.

Students all have the right to religious freedom. They may not be bothered because of any religious belief or nonbelief. They may not be forced to take part in any religious exercise or be embarrassed because of nonparticipation in religious activities. Students may not be subjected to semi- or quasi-religious teaching. All teaching of values, morals, and ethics must be free from any religious bias. Neither may students be required to recite prayers, pledges of allegiance, creeds, or similar statements that conflict with their beliefs.

The constitutional rights of free speech, expression of ideas, and the press extend to students also. These rights, however, do not include the use of obscenity or practices that may be injurious to others. Neither may they be used in a manner, time, or place that would interfere with normal educational activities and school decorum. Publications may be censored by school officials only if subsidized by the school.

Punishment of students is also limited and regulated by constitutions and other laws. Students have the right to know what the rules and regulations are. Therefore, school and class rules and regulations should be published clearly so that students will know what is permitted and what is not. When students do transgress, punishment may not be arbitrary or capricious; rather it should follow the course of due process. The rules must be enforced fairly. Persons enforcing school rules and regulations must be careful to avoid cruel punishments and to follow reasonable procedures for establishing guilt. Students have the right to be presumed innocent until they are proven guilty. They also have the right to remain silent; certainly this is true in legal cases and presumably is true in schools, for no one is obligated to convict himself. Likewise search and seizures should be conducted only under controlled conditions, for everyone has the right to be secure from improper searches and seizures. Lastly, all accused have the right to defend themselves. To this end they have the right not to be branded for past misbehavior or mistakes. School officials must ensure that permanent records do not include ill-based, deleterious information. To protect students from incorrect prejudicial entries, parents have the right to review their children's records when they think it advisable. For similar reasons students' transcripts must be limited to their academic record. Comments on attitudes and behaviors are not permitted.[14]

Summary

Adolescence is a time of growing up. During this period youths attempt to complete certain developmental tasks, to become independent persons, and to realize their dreams and potentials. To many

---

[14] Based on Edward T. Ladd (with John C. Walden), *Students' Rights and Discipline* (Arlington, VA.: National Association of Elementary School Principals, 1975), pp. 9–17, Chap. 1.

of them school seems a hindrance rather than a help toward achieving their most important, most personal goals. In their middle school years they move from childhood to adolescence. This period called transescence is marked by the beginning of change from concrete thinking to abstract thinking, from childhood to sexual maturity, and from total dependence on adults to comparative independence and to physical maturity. But they are not grown-ups.

High school youth carry on these transitions toward more complete fulfillment. Although many high schoolers are unhappy in school, most of them give school fairly high marks. They appreciate its social functions most and would be happier if teachers would treat them with more respect, run classes more efficiently, and demand higher standards. As they enter the formal operation stage of mental development, high schoolers need opportunities to think systematically and creatively.

Among the major problems of high school youths are apathy, drugs and liquor, family problems, and role confusion. Usually students who have problems are faced with a combination of problems. Therefore, adults wishing to help young people should concentrate on preventive approaches rather than on attempts to cure specific difficulties.

Schools are for learning. More often than not, nonlearning in school is the fault of the school and the system rather than the students. These problems would not be so great if we teachers gave more attention to adapting methods to students learning styles, to teaching them how to learn and how to study, and to using teaching approaches compatible with the working of the brain. It is particularly important that instruction be aimed at real learning—not mere verbalism. The methods used should be those best suited to building clear, full concepts, thoroughly developed skills, and appropriate attitudes. Consequently teachers must pay attention to student readiness and plan for transfer and retention of the knowledge to be learned. To do so they must see to it that there is plenty of reenforcement of the important learnings and that sufficient time is spent on the important things to be learned.

The Constitution of the United States provides students with certain inalienable rights. These rights include the right to an education, the right to religious freedom, the right to be let alone except for cause, the right of free speech and expression, and the right to fair treatment. These rights have the force of law and all teachers are required by law to respect them.

Additional Reading

Bugelski, B. R. *Some Practical Laws of Learning,* Fastback 9. Bloomington, IN: Phi Delta Kappa Educational Foundation, 1977.

Charles, C. M. *Educational Psychology,* 3rd ed. St. Louis, MO: C. V. Mosby Co., 1982.

Gage, N. L. and David C. Berliner, *Educational Psychology,* 3rd ed. Boston: Houghton Mifflin, 1983.

Gander, Mary J., and Harry W. Gander. *Child and Adolescent Development.* Boston: Little, Brown and Co., 1981.

George, Paul, and Gordon Lawrence. *Handbook for Middle School Teaching.* Glenview, IL: Scott Foresman, 1982, Part I.

Hart, Leslie A. *Human Brain and Human Learning.* New York: Longmans, 1983.

Hill, Winfred F. *Learning: A Survey of Psychological Interpretation,* 3rd ed. San Francisco: Chandler, 1977.

Hudgins, Bryce B., *et. al. Educational Psychology.* Itasca, IL: F. E. Peacock, 1983.

Ingersoll, Gary M. *Adolescents in School and Society.* Lexington, MA: D. C. Heath, 1982.

Karmel, Marilyn O., and Louis J. Karmel. *Growing and Becoming: Development from Conception through Adolescence.* New York: Macmillan, 1984.

Ladd, Edward T. (with John C. Walden). *Student's Rights and Discipline.* Arlington, VA: National Association of Elementary School Principals, 1975.

LeFrancois, Guy R. *Psychology for Teaching.* 4th ed. Belmont, CA: Wadsworth, 1982.

Lipsitz, Joan, ed. *Barriers, A New Look at the Needs of Young Adolescents.* New York: Ford Foundation, 1979.

McCarthy, Martha M., and Nelda H. Cambrow. *Public School Law: Teachers' and Students' Rights.* Boston: Allyn and Bacon, 1981.

Meier, Blanche Garner. *Changing: The Psychology of Adolescence.* St. Louis, MO: C.V. Mosby Co., 1982.

Novak, Joseph, and D. Bob Gowen. *Learning How to Learn.* New York: Cambridge University Press, 1984.

Reilly, Robert, and Ernest Lewis. *Educational Psychology: Applications for Classroom Learning and Instruction.* New York: Macmillan, 1983, Part I.

Ripple, Richard E., Robert F. Biehler, and Gail A. Jaquish. *Human Development.* Boston: Houghton Mifflin, 1982, Parts 5 and 6.

Sahakian, William S. *An Introduction to the Psychology of Learning.* Itasca, IL: F. E. Peacock, 1984.

3

Introduction to Teaching Methods

Overview

Teaching is exciting, rewarding work, but, like all other professions, it is demanding. It requires that its practitioners clearly understand what should be done to bring about the most desirable learning in students and be highly proficient in the skills necessary to carry out these tasks. These skills and understanding make up teaching method which includes a sound knowledge of the strategies and techniques available, the ability to select and use subject matter, familiarity with the nature of the learner, and an understanding of learning theory and its application.

In this chapter, we take a quick look at the nature of the communications and management problems we teachers face and some of the factors that bear upon the solution of these problems. We hope that it will make clear the absolute necessity of creating a positive climate and feeling of cohesiveness in your class; of having clear-cut objectives; of selecting and using teaching strategies and techniques consonant with those objectives in view of the nature of the subject to be taught, and the strategies and techniques available. Finally we hope you will be persuaded of the need for following the five-step process we conceive as the basic one to all effective teaching—diagnosis, preparation, guiding learning, evaluation, and follow up.

The Task

Some Definitions

Teaching Methods

Teaching methods are the means by which the teacher attempts to bring about the desired learning. Basically, method in teaching concerns the way teachers organize and use techniques of teaching, subject matter, teaching tools, and teaching materials to meet teaching objectives. It consists of formulating the goals and objectives for teaching, selecting the subject matter and the teaching procedures that will best achieve those objectives, carrying out the procedures, evaluating the success of the learning activities, and following up their successes and failures. Because teaching method includes selecting content and instructional materials as well as teaching procedures, it determines to a large extent what students actually learn. The understandings students gain of the political process in a political practicum or a community involvement project are likely to be much different from those derived from lesson hearing recitations in a civics course. *The way we teach a subject is as much subject content as the information we include!*

Strategies and Tactics

Methods are made of strategies and techniques. A strategy is really a plan of attack. It outlines the approach you intend to take in order to achieve your objective. Thus you might decide that in a certain lesson you will try to develop a certain concept by using Socratic questioning. That is your strategy. The means that you use to carry out the strategy, in this case the asking of specific questions and handling of answers, are variously known as tactics, operations, or techniques. Technically these words deviate somewhat in meaning, but in this book we use them indiscriminately. The important thing to remember is that (1) your strategies must be aimed at your objective and must be appropriate for achieving it, and (2) that the techniques you use must be suitable to your strategy—otherwise your teaching will result in fiasco.

Another phrase you will encounter frequently is learning activities or teaching-learning activities. By learning activities we mean the things students do, or are supposed to do, in their lessons and units. Reading a selection from a textbook is an activity, as is taking a test, or even listening to a lecture. Any learning activity that a teacher incorpo-

```
    List all the learning activities you can think
of.
a. Individual Learning Activities
    1.              6.
    2.              7.
    3.              8.
    4.              9.
    5.             10.
b. Group Learning Activities
    1.              6.
    2.              7.
    3.              8.
    4.              9.
    5.             10.
```

rates into a lesson is part of that teacher's strategy. Learning activities are always specific for specific teaching-learning situations; they are never general.

The Communications Problem

Teaching is not, as some critics and teachers seem to think, a simple matter of presenting one's message. It is a complicated communications problem.

The Receivers

In the first place, there are so many receivers— perhaps two dozen or more in a class—and each receiver presents a different problem. Take the cases of two tenth-graders, Joe and Billy.[1]

Joe is slightly under middle height. In class he is very quiet. He never causes disciplinary disturbances. Neither does he do any work. In fact, one would hardly know he was in the class at all. He just sits there. When the teacher cajoles him, he says that he is "dumb and can't do it, so there's

---

[1] The names are fictitious, the descriptions are not.

no use trying." But this is not true. Test scores show him to be well within the normal range. His other activities do not indicate lack of ability. He cannot read well, but he is one of the best soccer and basketball players in the school. On the field his playing is marked by its aggressiveness. As a matter of fact, his aggressiveness largely makes up for his lack of height in basketball. The coach says that he is one of the "smartest" forwards he has seen on the soccer field in the last few years.

Joe has never been known to pick up a book voluntarily. It has been a long time since he has turned in an acceptable paper. He knows that his failures will make him ineligible for varsity athletics, but he sees no reason for working because he believes that he will fail anyway. If he should pass, he will say that it is only because the teacher is "giving him a break." Seemingly, he has no interest other than athletics.

Difficult cases like Joe's challenge the ingenuity, the resources, and the skill of the teacher. The unskilled teacher might be overwhelmed by Joe's lack of enthusiasm and decide to give up. Not so the professional teacher. He knows that he must teach Joe—whether Joe wants to learn or not—and he has the knowledge and the resources with which to undertake this task.

Joe poses a difficult problem, but even cases like that of Billy need skillful teaching. Billy is an average eighth-grader with average intelligence. Usually a happy person, he gets along well with his teachers and his peers. Billy's mother is a homemaker and his father is a mechanic. There are two other children at home, one younger and one older than Billy. Home is the focal point of life in the family. Billy seems to have no great problems. Yet he does have trouble with some of his schoolwork. All normal students do, and Billy is normal, not brilliant. Although he is a willing worker and as cooperative as he can be, he finds many of his assignments too much for him. It will take plenty of skillful teaching if Billy is to get the most out of his mathematics, for instance.

Joe and Billy are different, but not more different

than the other individuals in the class. The media and methods most effective for one student may not be the best for others.

The Media

Secondly, teaching is complicated by the number of media used in presenting its messages. Among these media are the *spoken word* in the forms of lectures, informal talks, and discussions; the *written word* in books, magazines, pamphlets, and newspapers; *dramatic media* such as films and television; *pictorial* or *graphic media* such as illustrations, graphs, charts, and maps; *inquiry, questioning, questing media,* and more. With such a variety of media available, deciding just which approach will be best in any given teaching situation becomes difficult. Unfortunately some of the less sensitive teachers are unaware of this problem.

The Messages

A third complicating factor in teaching is the number of different messages that we must transmit to our pupils. Among them are information, concepts, intellectual skills, physical skills, habits, attitudes, appreciations, and ideals—all of which require different teaching strategies and techniques, and some of which may not be highly valued by the potential receivers.

The Group Dynamics

A fourth complicating factor is the dynamics of the group. Each class soon develops its own dynamics. It has its own leaders and followers, its own tensions and friendships, and even its own goals and aspirations that are not always compatible with those of the teacher.

The Competition

A fifth complicating factor is the outside competition. Not only do we teachers have to compete with the inducements of radio, television, and social life for the attention and time of our students, we also have to compete with highly skilled media personalities who are selling messages quite different from those we want our students to accept. Winning students' attention in a world filled with so many competing attractions faces us with a real challenge.

The Complex Learning Process

Another complication, already hinted at, is the complexity of the learning process. Not everyone learns in the same way, nor does any individual learn in the same way all the time. Many a skillful teacher has found that the approach that worked so well with our tenth-grader, Billy, gets absolutely nowhere with his buddy, Joe, or that the plan that was such a howling success in period four, bombed in period seven, or that the approach that resulted in such impressive results on the civics assessment test seems to have had no discernible effect on students' attitudes toward citizenship. To accommodate these differences, we teachers must learn to teach in ways compatible with individual learning styles and to adopt teaching strategies and techniques suitable to our different teaching objectives and the groups being taught.

The Possible Strategies

A final complication is that there are so many different strategies and techniques that one might use—none of which is suitable for every teaching-learning situation. Because teaching is such a complex problem, teachers should, as Bernays insists, adopt the approaches of the social engineer. As adapted for teaching, the steps in this approach are

- Define your objectives.
- Study the students.
- Modify the objectives in view of the study of the students.
- Decide on a strategy.
- Set up motivational machinery.

- Organize your plan.
- Carry out the plan.[2]

The Management Problem

Teaching is more than just a communications problem. For classes to be productive, they must be smoothly running, distraction-free, efficient operations in which students can learn effectively. This calls for skillful classroom management. Managing a classroom is not just a matter of managing learning activities, but of managing everything that goes on in the classroom in such a way as to create a climate favorable to learning and to provide the means of learning. For this purpose it involves organizing the physical elements of the classroom, classroom logistics, the materials and tools of instruction, classroom interpersonal relationships, and instruction itself. In addition to designing and carrying out effective teaching strategies and tactics, it includes building students' knowledge; creating and sustaining their enthusiasm; enriching their abilities to think and reason; helping students meet their need for belonging, self-esteem, and fulfillment; and developing wholesome interpersonal relationships among the students.

Time on Task

What boys and girls do with their time makes a difference in learning! If they are actively doing real learning tasks (e.g., listening actively, paying attention, and the like), they tend to learn more than if they are not. Therefore one of the most important steps one can take to make teaching effective is to see to it that all the students are working at profitable learning activities. Too much time is wasted in too many classes. In all content areas

Discuss the phrase: "There is no teaching unless there is learning." Is it true or partially true? What implications does it have for the teacher?

Do you agree that it is the teacher's job to teach Joe whether Joe wishes to learn or not? Should the teacher's competency be judged on the basis of Joe's success or failure?

If the pupils do not learn well in your class, does that mean that you are a poor teacher?

the most productive classes are ones in which students actually work on academic learning tasks which are well organized; free from interruptions, misbehavior, time-killing dead spots, and other interferences; and focused on the teaching-learning objectives. The only exception to this principle may be in creative learning, which seems to depend on insight, creative expression, and mulling things over rather than intense academic engagement. Too much pressure can interfere with thinking and creativity.

Mastery Learning

Theories concerning the effectiveness of time on task are based on Carroll's hypothesis[3] that the amount of learning is a function of the time spent learning. Carried to the ultimate, this hypothesis implies that one can teach anything to anyone if only one takes the time. This thinking has led to the theory of mastery teaching developed by Bloom and others.[4] We discuss mastery teaching more fully in Chapter 16. Basically, however, the idea behind mastery teaching is to give each person enough engaged time to master the objectives of each unit before moving on to the next one. In

---

[2] Adapted from Edward L. Bernays, *The Engineering of Consent* (Norman, OK: University of Oklahoma Press, 1955). Quoted in Harold W. Bernard, *Psychology of Learning and Teaching*, 2nd ed. (New York: McGraw-Hill, 1965), pp. 9–11.

[3] John B. Carroll, "A Model of School Learning," *Teachers' College Record* (1963), **64**:723–732.

[4] See for instance Benjamin S. Bloom, "Learning for Mastery," in Benjamin S. Bloom, J. Thomas Hastings, and George D. Madaus, *Handbook on Formative and Summative Evaluation of Student Learning* (New York: McGraw-Hill, 1971), Chap. 3.

general, mastery teaching seems to be successful although some research does not bear out this generalization.[5]

Teaching As an Art Form

The teacher's task is to bring about desirable learning in students. Some authorities say that as far as school classes are concerned, if the students have not learned anything, the teacher has not taught anything. This statement is perhaps too harsh, but it does introduce an important point: since the goal of teaching is to bring about the desired learning in the students, the only way to tell whether or not one's teaching has been successful is to determine whether or not the learners have actually learned what one intended they learn. It follows then that to succeed at your job you must know (1) what the students ought to learn, and (2) how to bring about this learning. To carry out these requirements calls for considerable artistry.

For many years teachers and scholars have been trying to create a science of teaching, but teaching still is, and ought to be, an art rather than a science. It requires a large stock of skills, but more, it requires teachers to be able to put these skills together in new forms at the spur of the moment as new situations arise. All good teachers improvise; they must. Classes do not fall into set patterns. No one educational environment or approach serves all students equally well, just as no one environment or approach serves all educational goals equally well. To be effective, the teaching must be adjusted to the nature of the task. Depending on tried-and-true formulas will surely backfire. Good strategies become counterproductive when they are overused. The trick is to select old tactics and create

new tactics that are right for the teaching-learning task and circumstances at hand.

In a sense then, as Donmeyer reminds us, teaching is similar to the theatrical improvisations of the past centuries. The teacher, like the old-time actors, takes a basic outline and shapes and ornaments it to meet the needs of the moment.[6] Every time a student answers a question, the teacher must improvise a comment. Every time the student does a problem, the teacher must improvise feedback. Every time a student misbehaves, the teacher must improvise corrective procedures. Through these improvisations the teachers build the learnings that are the instructional objectives. In this way they create teaching strategies that are not scientific, but works of art.

Teaching As Decision Making

The heart of the art of teaching, therefore, is decision making. *There is no best method of teaching or any method that will suit all occasions.* In almost every instance, to be maximally successful, the teaching method used should be tailored for the specific teaching-learning situation. In each one of these situations you, as teacher, must decide what objectives you should strive for, what content you should include (and exclude), what procedures you should use, how best to evaluate what you have accomplished, how to capitalize on what you have accomplished, and how to repair any errors and omissions in the students' learning. In doing so you should consider such factors as

- the goals, aims, and objectives of the curriculum.
- the nature of the subject.
- the strategies and techniques available.
- the materials and equipment available.
- the students.
- how students learn.

[5] Theodore A. Chandler, "Mastery Learning: Pros and Cons," *NASSP Bulletin* (May, 1982), **66**:9–15.
   Robert L. Bargert, James A. Kulik, and Chen-Lin C. Kulik, "Individualized Systems of Instruction in Secondary Schools," *Review of Educational Research* (Summer, 1983), **53**:143–158.

[6] Robert Donmeyer, "Pedagogical Improvisation," *Educational Leadership* (January, 1983), **40**:39–43.

- the nature of the group.
- your own skills and inclinations.

Obviously there are alternatives galore to choose from. The important thing is to be able to select and use the strategies and tactics appropriate for obtaining the results you desire. Therefore the more techniques you can handle well and the more you understand your subject matter, the better your teaching will be.

> Observe a class. What did the teacher have to do to teach the class? What preparations were necessary? What was done to keep the class moving smoothly and effectively? What follow-up would be necessary? How much of the give and take in the class had to be impromptu? Did the strategies, tactics, and techniques used seem to fit the nature of the learning? What decisions did the teacher have to make before and during the class?

The Elements of Teaching Methods

Objectives

For every school program, curriculum, course, unit, or lesson, the planner should decide just what learning should result. These objectives are all important. In planning courses, units, and lessons they should be the basis for the selection of the content and the instructional approaches and teaching activities (that is, strategies and techniques). For instruction can be effective only when the teaching methods and content are aimed directly at objectives. These objectives and the behavior they describe fall into a number of categories. In this section we discuss these various types of objectives. As we do so, remember that the categories are not necessarily mutually exclusive.

FIGURE 3–1
General to Specific Objective Continuum.

General and Specific Objectives

Some learning products are extremely broad and general; others are very narrow and specific. The central purpose of education in the United States according to the Educational Policies Commission, for instance, is to teach students to think independently.[7] Nothing could be much broader than that. On the other hand, an objective for a science lesson might be for the pupils to learn by heart the chemical formula $NaSO_4$. Nothing could be much narrower.

Objectives, then, vary from the broadest statements which may be used to describe the general aims of the entire American educational system to the extremely narrow objective of a specific drill exercise. As Figure 3–1 shows they may also fall at any level between these two extremes. In other words, while there are general objectives and specific objectives, some objectives are more general or more specific than others. In theory, and in the best practice, specific objectives are subordinate to and contain the basic ingredients of the more general objectives (as in Figure 3–2). In general, the broadest objectives are those for all education, followed by (in descending order) those for specific schools, those for specific curricula in schools, those for specific units, and finally, the least broad, those for specific lessons and exercises. If lessons, courses, and curricula are well built, the specific objectives of the lessons contribute directly to the more general objectives of the course, which in turn are the ingredients that make up the more

---

[7] Educational Policies Commission, *The Central Purpose of American Education* (Washington, DC: National Education Association, 1961).

FIGURE 3-2
Pyramid of General and Specific Objectives. Note that the pyramid extends from the very specific to the very general and that the specific objectives at each level make up the components of the general objective in the next level above it.

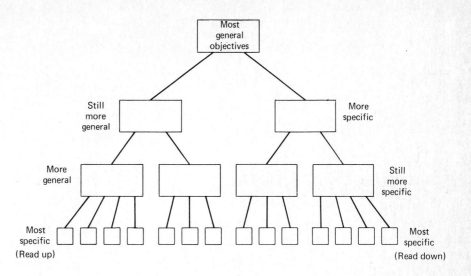

general objectives of the curriculum. Similarly each unit, course, and lesson may contain a number of specific objectives which combine to form a more general objective. For instance, the teacher may set the learning of the formula $NaSO_4$ as a beginning step toward his more general, although still rather specific, objective of learning the properties of sulfuric acid.[8] (See Figure 3–3.)

Overt and Covert Objectives

Sometimes learning results in overt (i.e., observable) behavior. If the pupil learns to conjugate the

Latin verb *amare* in the present tense, he learns to say or write

Amo	I love
Amas	You love
Amat	He, she, it loves
Amamus	We love
Amatis	You love
Amant	They love

Similarly if the goal were for the student to be able to translate the simple Latin sentence *Nauta puellam amat* (The sailor loves the girl), the student would be able to tell what the sentence means and distinguish it from the equally simple Latin sentence *Puella nautam amat* (The girl loves the sailor). We can tell when the student has reached these goals because we can easily observe the behavior.

On the other hand, many objectives are covert, that is to say, the learning products are not easily or directly observable. *Understandings, appreciations, attitudes,* and *ideals* all fall into the category of covert objectives. If the object of our instruction is that students will appreciate the beauty of a Van Gogh painting, it is pretty hard to tell whether or not that objective has really been achieved. The observable behavior of the students may or may not give a true indication of appreciation. Students

---

[8] Writers on educational topics have developed a nomenclature that differentiates between the kinds of general and specific objectives. Unfortunately there is little agreement about the terminology. The terms *educational goals, educational aims,* and *educational objectives* are often used to denote the broad general goals of education in the United States or in a school system or school. The term *general objective* is most often used to describe the major goals of a unit or course. The terms *specific objective* or *instructional objective* are used to describe subsidiary objectives that go to make up general objectives. They are usually used to denote specific learnings to be taught in units or lessons.

In general these definitions hold true, but in the literature the words are sometimes used indiscriminately and even intermixed. It is wise, therefore, to check an author's definition to be sure that you are speaking the same language.

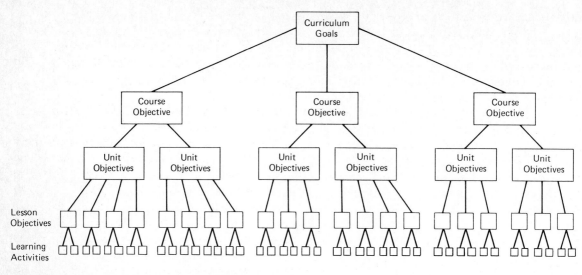

FIGURE 3–3
Lesson, Unit, Course, Curriculum Pyramid.

may be able to recite the right words and simulate the proper actions without having any real feeling or appreciation or understanding.

The Cognitive, Affective, and Psychomotor Domains

According to Bloom and his associates, objectives fall into three domains:

The cognitive domain: "Objectives which emphasize remembering or reproducing something which has presumably been learned, as well as objectives which involve the solving of some intellective task for which the individual has to determine the essential problem and then reorder given material or combine it with ideas, methods, or procedures previously learned. Cognitive objectives vary from simple recall of material learned to highly original and creative ways of combining and synthesizing new ideas and materials."[9]

The affective domain: "Objectives which emphasize a feeling tone, an emotion, or a degree of acceptance or rejection."[10] Interests, attitudes, ideals, appreciations, and values are included in the affective domain.

The psychomotor domain: "Objectives which emphasize some muscular or motor skill, some manipulation of materials and objectives or some act which requires a neuromuscular co-ordination."[11]

Objectives in these domains have been arranged into hierarchies or taxonomies. In the following paragraphs we try to explain the significance of these hierarchies.

A Hierarchy of Cognitive Domain Objectives. When inventing their taxonomies of educational objectives, Bloom and his associates tried to classify educational goals in the cognitive domain into categories according to their complexity—from simple remembering, the lowest of the cognitive processes,

---

[9] David R. Krathwohl, Benjamin S. Bloom, and Bertram B. Masia, *Taxonomy of Educational Objectives, Handbook II: Affective Domain* (New York: McKay, 1964), pp. 6–7.

[10] Ibid.

[11] Ibid.

to evaluation, supposedly the highest type of thinking. The classifications they arrive at are:

1.00 Knowledge.

In this taxonomy, to know something is simply to have sufficient mastery of the information to remember it. It does not imply understanding what one remembers. Among the subcategories included in this general category are remembering specific information; remembering generalizations, principles, and theories; and remembering the ways and means of dealing with specifics.

2.00 Comprehension.

Comprehension refers to low-level understanding. At this level, one understands well enough to be able to translate an idea into different words, to interpret the meaning of the information or notion, and to extrapolate the implications or consequences that may follow from it.

3.00 Application.

Application refers to a somewhat higher level of understanding. At this level, one can apply abstract knowledge for use in real life.

4.00 Analysis.

At this level, thinking begins to be a really higher mental process. Here one breaks down complex ideas, principles, theories and information into component parts to see relationships—for example, cause and effect, or subordinate and coordinate elements—and so derive a more complete, clearer understanding. Analysis includes analysis of elements, analysis of relationships and the analysis of organizational principles.

5.00 Synthesis.

At the level of synthesis one puts together things so as to make new wholes. This is the basic process in creativity. It is the process one uses in writing a poem, evolving a theory, or inventing a new machine. It requires very high mental processes.

6.00 Evaluation.

In Bloom's taxonomy, evaluation is the top of the cognitive ladder. It consists of placing considered objective judgment on something. It is the highest of all mental processes.[12]

Whether or not these categories really progress from the least complex to the most complex in all instances is doubtful. However, there is no doubt that synthesis and evaluation are considerably more complex than just remembering. It is the objectives in these categories that develop higher cognitive powers in students. While it is, of course, necessary to be sure that students do acquire knowledge and remember it, unless we aim at least some of our teaching at application, analysis, synthesis, and evaluation, our teaching will not help students develop their cognitive powers fully. To make teaching most effective, it should include objectives from all levels.

A Hierarchy of Affective Domain Objectives. To create a taxonomy of objectives in the affective domain, Kratwohl, Bloom, and Masia arranged the affective domain into categories according to the degree of internalization they represent. By internalization the researchers mean the degree to which one has assimilated an affective behavior into one's personality. As set forth in the taxonomy, this behavior ranges from the lowest level of simply being aware of the affective stimulus without reacting to it in any way, to, at the highest level, total acceptance of the affective stimuli and incorporation of them into one's personality as determiners of one's overall pattern of behavior. In the following paragraphs we try to give you a notion of the main orientation of each category and some idea of the range of subcategories it includes.

1.00 Receiving.

The lowest category, receiving, ranges from 1.1, a simple state of awareness of the affective stimulus

---

[12] Ibid.

without any reaction or feeling about it pro or con, through 1.2, a feeling of tolerance toward the stimulus, to finally 1.3, a tilting toward a preference for this affective stimulus. At the lowest levels the behavior is really not affective at all because the person has no feeling about the stimulus one way or another. At the highest of the three levels, however, the person seems to begin to have feelings favoring it.

2.00 Responding.

At this the second level in the taxonomy the person responds to the stimulus. In the beginning of the responding level, the person (2.1) starts to take an interest in the stimulus, then at a higher level the person (2.2) begins to respond to it favorably, and voluntarily and finally (2.3) comes to enjoy it.

3.00 Valuing.

In valuing, the third category of this taxonomy, the person becomes committed to the affective behavior. The lowest level (3.1) starts off with a sort of tentative belief in the value of the affective behavior, but at higher levels (3.2) this belief becomes strengthened to the point that one prefers it and (3.3) at last becomes committed to it.

4.00 Organization.

After having become committed to the value, the person organizes personal values into a value system. Finding that more than one value may apply to a situation and that sometimes values conflict, the person finds it necessary, first (4.1) to gain better understanding of the values and then (4.2), to organize them into a system of dominant and subordinate values, values the individual holds precious and values less highly prized.

5.00 Characterized by a value or value complex.

At the highest level of the taxonomy, the values already internalized become so much of the person that they (5.1) form a hierarchical cluster of attitudes that rules the individual's general behavior and determines personal opinions. Finally by shap-

ing the person's attitudes, ideas, and behaviors, this generalized set becomes an integral portion of the person's general character and the person's philosophy of life (5.2).[13]

Actually these categories and levels of affective behavior are not as precise as we have made them seem. As one might expect of behavior that develops over a period of time and where the higher levels develop out of the lower levels, the signs of the higher levels of behavior can be found at the lower levels and elements of lower level behavior continue to persist at the higher levels. Also the common subdivisions of affective behavior—attitudes, appreciations, adjustment, interests and values—overlap the various categories. Figure 3–4 graphically shows the degree of overlap among categories and subdivisions of the affective behavior.

It is not usual for teachers consciously to aim their teaching at categories in the affective domain, notwithstanding pious statements about the teaching of appreciation, interest, values, and attitudes. Nevertheless, it seems self-evident that teachers should attempt to achieve goals on the higher side of the affective domain taxonomy. No doubt these objectives are difficult to achieve, but, because they represent a high degree of internalization, achieving them is essential if there are to be real changes in students' affective behavior.

A Hierarchy of Psychomotor Domain Objectives. It may well be that a taxonomy of objectives for the psychomotor is really superfluous, because in skill development the goal is the degree of proficiency in the skill, and the enabling objectives are, on the whole, simply steps from unskillful to most skillful. However, the following hierarchy may be helpful for forming educational objectives.

1. Familiarization

The first level in this set of objectives is familiarization. At this level the learners find out what the

---

[13] Ibid.

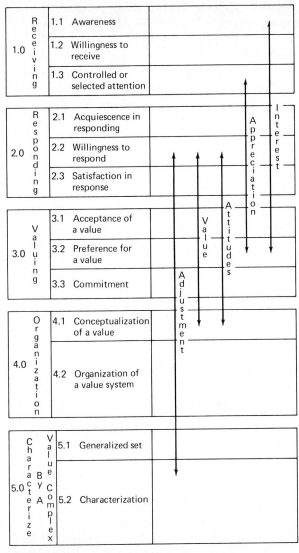

FIGURE 3–4
Objectives in the Affective Domain. (David R. Krathwohl, Benjamin S. Bloom, and Bertram B. Masia, *Taxonomy of Educational Objectives. Handbook II: Affective Domain* [New York: McKay, 1964], p. 37.)

skill is all about. They may read up on what to do and how to do it, they may see someone demonstrate it, they may handle the tools or equipment or run through the motions. All of these activities

give them knowledge about the skill, but not the skill itself.

2. Fundamentals

The second level is to develop fundamental skills. At this level the learners may learn such basics as how to hold the ball, grasp the racquet, finger the typewriter keyboard, swing the club, or put spin on the ball so that it goes into the court instead of over the fence. The learners practice the skills in an attempt to learn the basic procedures without developing imperfections in style and technique that they would have to unlearn at a later stage.

3. Development

The third level is to develop the skill by guided practice. The goal is to eliminate errors, master the techniques and perhaps develop speed. At this level, one's performance at first requires continuous conscious thought and guidance, but as the skill develops the behavior becomes automatic, until finally one can perform the acts smoothly and skillfully without conscious thought, and habit takes over.

4. Adjusting and Adapting

When the skill has reached the level of habituation, it is still subject to adjustment to suit the situation and to allow the learner to become more proficient. The pianist adapts his technique to play loud or soft, fast or slow, smoothly romantic or staccato. The tennis player learns to lob, chop, and drive and to adjust these strokes to her position in the court, the speed and direction of the approaching ball, and so on. In the hurly-burly of a soccer match, the player who decides to try to head the ball forward, or to the right, or to the left, must have learned to adjust his actions to the situation and his objective automatically.

5. Perfection and Maintenance

The last stage is that of perfecting and maintaining the skill. As we all know, skills that are not maintained soon become creaky even though not

Consider a course you might teach. What overall objectives would you like to achieve in such a course? Would you want to achieve general affective and psychomotor objectives as well as cognitive ones?

List several general cognitive objectives and then list specific unit objectives that would help you attain the general objectives. List objectives at each level of Bloom's taxonomy suitable for a unit in your subject.

Examine the general objectives of a school. List specific objectives suitable to a course you might teach that would contribute to the school's various general objectives.

forgotten. Skillful performers must continue to practice if they wish to maintain their skill. If they wish to become better, they must work at their performance, varying their techniques a little here or there in continual search for improvement, just as the world-famous concert pianist who tells us he practices five hours a day in order to keep up his skills, maintain his dexterity and perfect his renditions.[14]

Implications of the Taxonomies for Teaching

There are at least two principal implications of the teaching taxonomies for the teacher. One is that one must learn to flap one's wings before one can fly. Before one can judge something one must know it; before one can create a values system one must have values; before one can play Beethoven at a Carnegie Hall recital one must learn to play the scales. The other implication is that we teachers should be trying to lead our pupils to higher levels than we usually do. We should help students to evaluate carefully and objectively; we should help

them to integrate an exemplary set of values into their characters; we should help them develop at least some of their skills to high levels of proficiency and to encourage them to perfect and maintain these skills at the high level. Of course no one can reach the highest levels in everything. There is not enough time or ability in all creation. Yet everyone should have a chance to reach the highest level in something.

Subject Matter

The Importance of Content

Nothing we have stated minimizes the importance of content. Command of the subject matter is absolutely essential in secondary and middle school teaching. Teachers who are not knowledgeable and comfortable in their content are usually dull, boring, and ineffective.

In this connection, we should emphasize that the content of one's subject includes more than just information. In fact, as a rule, the information in a course should primarily be a means to ideas, understandings, thought, attitudes, and skills. Thus, for instance, appreciation is essential content for literature courses, and objectivity for science courses. Such intellectual skills as critical thinking, problem solving, and writing are essential content for any course. In many cases, these skills and appreciations are much more important than the informational content. So much so, in some instances, that the only real value of the informational subject matter in the course is as a medium by which to teach essential skills and attitudes. *Knowing how is as much part of curriculum content as knowing what.*

The Role of Subject Matter

Thus when selecting strategies and techniques, one should consider the subject matter to be taught. And there seem to be three ways to think of subject

---

[14] For a more formal and erudite taxonomy of the psychomotor domain see Anita J. Harrow, *A Taxonomy of the Psychomotor Domain* (New York: McKay, 1972.)

matter. One is to consider it something valuable in and of itself. According to this position, one should learn the subject matter, whatever it is, not for any contingent values that may come from knowing it, but because to know it is good. The second position is to think of subject matter as having some utilitarian value. According to this position one should learn the content, whatever it is, because one can use that particular knowledge for some practical purpose, for example, to earn a living or to get into college. The third position is to think of subject matter as a means of teaching process, methods, or structure. According to this way of thinking it is not so much the content that has value, as the skills, attitudes, and generalizations we gain by means of learning the content. Thus if the real object of learning history is to learn historical method or to think historically, then it does not matter particularly what history we learn as long as we learn it in such a way that we learn

---

Which of the three positions do you favor? Are you sure? What approach to teaching do you think you ought to follow in order to teach properly and well?

What are your positions on each of the following:

1. What is education?
2. What is the relationship of schools to society?
3. Why should children go to school?
4. How, why, and where do students learn?
5. How and in what way or ways do teachers teach most effectively?
6. What should be in the school curriculum and who should determine it?
7. Is teaching an art, skill, or profession?
8. Are schools now doing an acceptable job of educating American youth?
9. In what ways can schools be improved?
10. What is the reason for your decision to teach?

---

the method. In this view content is only a vehicle to use to teach process.

Even though many teachers have never considered their own views about subject matter, all teachers, consciously or unconsciously, lean toward one of the three positions mentioned. Although they may not be aware of it, their inclinations determine, to a large extent, the content emphases in their courses and the way they teach. *Your own philosophical orientation then will be a determiner of the educational methods you will use.*

The Structure of Subject Matter

Another consideration is the structure of subject matter. By structure we mean the interrelationships or organization of parts. Therefore the structure of subject matter includes its scope and sequence, the vertical and horizontal organization of its content, the interrelationships among its major principles and concepts and the modes of investigation used to determine its truths. These all differ in some degree from subject to subject. These differences in structure have, or should have, considerable impact on the methods we use in teaching various subjects. It is therefore most alarming, as Schwab points out,[15] to find that teachers tend to teach everything in the school curriculum in the same way. For instance, poetry that is meant to be enjoyed, savored, and reacted to is frequently taught as though it were fact to be learned. This is malpractice.

Every day knowledge changes faster and faster. Consequently teaching centered on facts alone leads to dissatisfaction when people learn that new discoveries have proved that the "facts" they learned are facts no longer. Students need to know how to cope with new knowledge. Therefore they need familiarity with the structures of the disci-

---

[15] Joseph J. Schwab, "Structure of the Disciplines: Meanings and Significances," in G. W. Ford and Lawrence Pugno, *The Structure of Knowledge and the Curriculum* (Chicago: Rand McNally, 1964), p. 17.

plines and knowledge of the mechanisms by which knowledge in the disciplines is created. Above all, they need to master the intellectual skills and attitudes that allow them to keep well informed and well educated no matter what new knowledge appears. To meet these needs, you should adopt teaching strategies that will teach students to seek out rather than to accept knowledge.

The Futility of Subject Covering

You should also find strategies that provide depth rather than superficiality. In the modern world, attempting to cover the subject is futile. We should limit ourselves to the content that seems the most desirable in view of our goals. Again, as with the revisionist nature of knowledge, the situation calls for an emphasis on the teaching of process and structure. What criteria to use for the selection of subject matter depends somewhat on one's philosophy. But no matter what that may be, we have come to the point where it is more important to select carefully rather than to try to include everything. Let your motto be, *Teach more effectively and thoroughly by concentrating on the most useful and ornamental and eliminating the less important.*

How can we teach so that what the students learn will not be soon out of date?

According to one educationist any high school teacher who believes that he must cover the subject is incompetent. What then should the teacher be doing?

In what way is the teaching strategy one uses likely to determine the nature of the subject matter students learn?

To what extent and in what ways does method determine content? and content method? Think of some examples.

The basic problem of method is said to be selection. Do you agree? Explain.

Teaching Strategies and Tactics

As we reiterate, strategies and techniques that lead to one objective, for example, the learning of fact, will not necessarily lead to another objective, for example, learning to appreciate. *Remember that once you have decided on your objective, if you do not utilize strategies and techniques that will lead to that objective, you will never achieve your goal.*

As you select your learning activities, you will find many strategies and techniques from which to choose. Among them are ones most suitable for

- building concepts
- clarifying students' ideas
- showing students how to do things
- affecting or changing attitudes, ideals, and appreciations
- giving security
- motivating and set-inducing
- evaluating or measuring
- guiding or directing students' work
- arousing, directing, or assuaging emotions
- kindling critical and creative thinking.[16]

Try to think of an example of a teaching strategy or technique that could be suitable in teaching each of the types of learning listed here.

Other examples include strategies and techniques one can use to direct, request, explain, suggest, praise, point out possibilities and alternatives, create problem situations and show materials, methods, and tactics by which teachers try to motivate students, tactics in which teachers compare and judge correctness, tactics in which the teachers praise or condemn student behavior, tactics in which they present an attitude or behavior in a

---

[16] This list is, in part, based on Louis Raths' *What Is Teaching,* undated, mimeographed.

favorable light, or reinforce it with emotion or emotionally toned behavior; and the pointing out of suitable models for students to follow.

Clarifying Tactics

Some tactics help students make their ideas clear. No one can clarify understandings for anyone else. Neither can he have insights for anyone else, nor do anyone else's thinking. Each person must do these things for himself. But it is possible for a teacher to help and guide a student to clearer understandings and insights. The clarifying tactics are the tactics the teacher can use to accomplish this purpose. Some of them are described in the following paragraph. Note that almost all the operations described are based on questions and are examples of what Flanders calls indirect teaching.[17]

A typical clarifying tactic is to ask the student to define what he means in his own terms. Another is to ask him to illustrate or demonstrate his meanings. Yet another is to ask him where he got his idea—what is its basis and is this basis a tenable one? Still another would be to throw back the student's idea to him, perhaps rephrased, and to ask him whether that is what he means. If it is what he means, then another tactic would be to ask him to forecast the implications or logical consequences of this idea. In other words, if so, then what? Still another tactic is to ask the student to summarize what he means or to organize his meaning into the logical outline. Another is to question his basis for belief—is he dealing with fact or opinion, fact or feeling, fact or emotion? Questioning the student about what causes his difficulty in order to help him solve it is still another example of a clarifying tactic.

Show-How Tactics

The show-how tactics are mostly concerned with skills. They include such operations as demon-

---
[17] See the following section.

strations using visual and audiovisual aids, and helping students to perform the task, perhaps by showing them alternate or better methods to use, or by analyzing the students' present techniques to see where they are at fault. Telling students how to do something and taking them through the task step by step can also be included among the show-how tactics even though such tactics are often not so much "show-how" as "tell-how." So can correcting faults in techniques or form during practice, as when the golf instructor tells the student to hold the club like this and not like that.

Security-Giving Tactics

The security-giving tactics are the operations that make it possible for students to feel free to learn. For many students school is a challenging and frightening experience full of many strong pressures. Teachers need to help students gain the confidence they need to meet the pressures and to cope with the challenges. The tactics that provide these qualities are the ones by which the teacher lets students know that they are welcome in the class and that the teacher respects their individualities and will support them in their efforts to learn, even when they make mistakes.

One of the most important aids to security giving is consistency in the teacher's behavior and in the types of operations one uses in teaching. Although one should use many different types of teaching activities, variety should not be confused with in-

> Perhaps you would like to arrange the various strategies and techniques into a set of categories of your own.
> How can a teacher determine which strategy and technique to use in any specific situation?
> What differences in strategy and techniques would be called for in teaching situations in which the main objective was (a) an appreciation; (b) a skill; (c) an attitude; (d) information?

consistency. The teacher who is authoritarian one day and permissive the next, or one who swings from using very conservative to very progressive procedures without adequately preparing the students for the change, adds not interest but insecurity, confusion, and chaos.

Direct and Indirect Approaches

Some tactics influence students directly and some indirectly. In their analyses of verbal teaching tactics, Amidon and Flanders report four categories of teacher talk operations that influence students indirectly. These include accepting students' feelings, praising or encouraging them, accepting their ideas, and asking questions. In addition, two student-talk categories, student responses and student-initiated talk, presumably also represent indirect teacher influence. Teacher talk operations that Amidon and Flanders say influence students directly include lecturing, telling, giving facts or opinions, asking rhetorical questions, giving directions, scolding, and justifying class procedures. When so defined, indirect teaching seems to be more efficient than direct teaching.[18]

More recently Rosenshine[19] and others in their studies of elementary school teaching have defined direct teaching differently. To them direct teaching is "academically focused, teacher-directed instruction using sequenced and structured materials." It combines large group teaching with highly teacher-directed comments, questions, and goals. In direct teaching there is little student choice of activity or individual work. Emphasis is on large-group instruction rather than on small-group instruction, single-answer, factual low-order questions rather than high-order questions, and controlled practice.

Rosenshine has found this type of teaching effective. It involves students in active work much of the time. There is little wasted motion. In indirect teaching as he defines it, there is more likely to be dead time, fooling around, lost time because of not knowing what to do, and so on. In other words, direct teaching is likely to produce more time on task.

However, time on task and direct teaching may not always be the best routes to teacher effectiveness. The intensiveness of the contact between the student and the learning may be more important. Direct instruction seems to be effective for teaching basic skills, but not so effective for high-order skills and understandings. Indirect, less structured, more open methods seem to work better for concept development, creativity, and high-order thinking. Direct instruction seems to be more effective in mathematics instruction and indirect methods in teaching English. Low socioeconomic and young students seem to benefit more from direct teaching, whereas higher socioeconomic, older students do better in indirect classes. Cognitive learning style is also a factor.[20] Evidently, then, direct teaching styles should be more useful in middle schools, and indirect teaching more useful in high schools.

Individualized Instruction

For many years teachers and theorists have advocated the use of individualized instruction to allow for the differences in students' talents, abilities, interests, goals, attitudes, values, and learning styles. Some of the techniques used for individualized instruction called for self-pacing programs, some for individualized learning activity packages, some for independent study within units, and some for mastery learning. A number of individualized systems of instructing in which students work through un-

[18] Allan C. Ornstein, "How Good Are Teachers in Effecting Student Outcome?" *NASSP Bulletin* (December, 1982), **66:**61–70.

[19] See, for instance, Barak V. Rosenshine, "Content, Time, and Direct Instruction," in Penelope L. Peterson and Herbert J. Walberg, eds., *Research on Teaching* (Berkeley, CA: McCutchan, 1979).

[20] Shirley A. McFaul, "An Examination of Direct Instruction," *Educational Leadership* (April, 1983), **40:**67–69.

Has the instruction you have received been direct or indirect, or both? Have teachers changed their style for various instructional purposes? How has the teaching style affected you personally? Do certain styles turn you off? Do certain styles turn you on? Which does which and why?

How much has instruction been individualized in your classes? In what ways have your teachers individualized instruction? What advantages do you see in individualizing instruction? What disadvantages? Were your individual needs and tastes considered in your classes? If not, could they have been? What did teachers do to meet your needs?

its at their own rates have been developed. At the college level some of these systems seem to be spectacularly effective. Their success has not been so great at the middle school and high school levels, however. It seems that a certain amount of socialization and group support, rather than complete individualization or independence, may be necessary for students of this age. Probably more mature high school students can benefit from doing much work independently, but, evidently, most secondary and middle school students should do considerable amounts of their school work in group situations. Seemingly they need "more stimulation, guidance, support, and constraint than the individualized systems ordinarily provide." Tactics that provide greater support such as peer and cross-age tutoring and computer supported instruction seem to be quite useful.[21] Perhaps in the middle and high school grades there should be a mix of individualized and group methods with the accent on methods having social support elements.

---

[21] Bargert, Kulik, and Kulik, op. cit.

Working with Groups

Although students learn as individuals, we teachers must teach these individuals in groups. Consequently, we should try to use teaching strategies and techniques that will produce effective learning in classroom groups. To do so it is necessary to understand something of the nature of groups and how they work.

Necessity for a Positive Climate

Most authorities seem to agree that a positive climate is one of the conditions necessary for maximum school learning. In other words, they believe that school learning is enhanced in classrooms in which students know and accept each other and are accepted by the teacher, work well together, understand the group goals, know and accept what their own roles and responsibilities are in working toward the group goals and take satisfaction in their roles. In such classrooms, students develop the feeling of personal worth, belonging, and security that supports learning.

Other Group Characteristics

Not only is the social climate within a group important in determining the group's effectiveness, other characteristics of the group—its leadership, attraction of the members for each other, its norms, its communication patterns, the amount and kind of its cohesiveness—are also important. Classes lacking in leadership, mutual attraction, suitable norms, student-centered communication patterns, and cohesiveness do not function well. Fortunately it is within the power of the teacher, who is aware of these characteristics and the processes that affect them, to influence what the characteristics of any group class will be. The teacher's influence is limited, however. You should not expect to make great changes in group structure overnight; rather you should expect to make progress slowly.

Group Leadership

Leadership is a process. People become group leaders because of what they do and how they do it, rather than because of what they are. This process involves both interpersonal relationships and leadership skills. Students are more likely to perform well for persons they like than for persons they dislike or for whom they have no feeling. Students also respond more readily to persons who have acquired skill in the functions of leadership. These functions include the task-oriented ones, such as the initiating and selling of ideas that get things done, and the social, emotional ones, such as the encouraging, harmonizing, and compromising that smooth over interpersonal relationships and maintain a congenial, productive atmosphere.

You cannot depend upon your position of authority to make you the true leader of the class. Although students are influenced by coercion and the authority of one's position, they respond more readily to the leadership of someone they accept as an acknowledged expert (someone with expert power) or someone they consider charismatic and with whom they identify (someone with referent power). Although teachers are leaders by virtue of their position, students who exert expert power or referent power are apt to be as influential— sometimes more influential.

Similarly democratic leadership is much more likely to be productive than authoritarian leadership. (Laissez-faire leadership in which the leader lets students do as they please is quite useless.) Although the authoritarian leader may get things done, the democratic leader usually gets better quality work in a much more positive climate. Authoritarianism tends to cause, or at least aggravate, hostility, high dependency, friction, and other negative qualities. The more students feel that they have some influence on the decisions that are being made, the better things are for the group. Consequently it helps to involve students in decision making as much as possible. Chapter 8 describes cooperative group planning techniques suitable for this purpose.

Some students are natural leaders. Their feelings toward teachers and classes have great impact on the other students. Other students have no influence at all. On the whole, the group is not much affected by teacher relationships with low-status students, but relationships with the natural leaders cause a ripple effect that carries over to the rest of the students. Consequently you would do well to seek the cooperation of high-status students. If they are on your side, all of the students will perform better. In the long run you will find it very advantageous to involve these high-status students in decision making.

Obviously you would be wise to try to spot the natural leaders as soon as you can. Although sociometric tools may be useful, probably the best technique for spotting the high-status student is careful observation. If you take pains to set aside part of each day for observation, you should soon be able to find who the leaders are. Put the students to work in small groups or a laboratory type study situation and watch to see whom the other students turn to for help, guidance or ideas.

To encourage optimal performance you should distribute leadership roles to as many students as possible. Try to arrange it so that everyone feels that he has influence and responsibility. Your goal should be not to make leaders out of the low-status students, but to raise everyone's participation in leadership roles. You can further this objective by providing students with many opportunities to lead in small ways. Small-group work, for instance, makes a natural setting for a large number of students to take part in leadership and decision making. So does entrusting some planning and decision making to a class steering committee whose personnel change from time to time. Small success in leadership and decision-making roles of this type may lead to success in larger roles in the future.

Attraction and the Group Process

Obviously, to create an environment favorable to learning you must demonstrate that you like the students and you must also foster an atmosphere of mutual liking among the students. In short, you should try to make your class into a diffusely structured group.

Diffusely structured groups differ from centrally structured groups in that there is no in-group or out-group. In diffusely structured groups, most of the students like each other equally well. There is no group of high-status favorites. In fact, differences in status are pretty well obscured by a democratic atmosphere in which most pupils have a fairly high sense of self-esteem.

Centrally structured groups make up the type of classes in which the teacher asks all the questions of a small group of students who do all the reciting and garner all the teacher's praise. In the centrally oriented group, difference in status stands out. A relatively few students make up the in-group; the rest of the class makes up an out-group, which feels neglected, unwanted, and disliked. Students are well aware of these differences in status and feel its effects. To the students who do not make the high status in-group, the centrally structured class is a threatening, hateful place. Therefore they do not learn well.

Evidently students tend to live up to what is expected of them. In centrally structured groups little is expected of all except the accepted few. Consequently, large numbers of students do not perform well, because they do not feel that they are expected to perform well. In diffusely structured groups where self-esteem is spread more evenly around the group, students respond much better. Since self-esteem tends to foster good performance, and good performance seems to reinforce self-esteem, diffusely structured groups provide the positive social climate that encourages learning. You, therefore, ought to concentrate on building self-esteem, attractiveness, and good feeling in your classes. Opportunities for establishing relationships of mutual respect and liking are easier in diffusely structured groups than in centrally structured groups.

To develop the wide range of friendships and mutual liking that are basic to the diffusely structured class, the teacher can use teaching techniques that force students to know each other and to asso-ciate with different students from time to time. Almost all student-centered teaching strategies help make the class structure more diffuse. Teacher-centered strategies will not. The more evenly the teacher can spread responsibilities and leadership roles, the more diffuse the class structure will be. Therefore, you should find small-group and committee work productive, especially if the committee membership is changed occasionally. A group should never be allowed to form itself into a permanent committee. Other techniques that you might use include games in which students mix with each other, exercises in which students compile biographies of other students, or radio or TV interviews in which students interact with each other. Some teachers have had considerable success with role-playing activities in which students act out roles different from those they normally take in the class.

Norms and Group Behavior

Norms are expectations common to most of the students in the group. In a large measure, they determine the behavior of the group members. Thus, if the students expect teachers to be dictators, as they usually do, they will be suspicious of teachers who say that they want open class participation. Similarly, if students expect teachers to give them information, they may resist or rebel against teaching methods that require them to dig up information and think for themselves. Educational goals

---

Are your college classes centrally structured or diffusely structured? If there are some of both types, which type seems to be the more effective? What does the teacher do to create the atmosphere found in these classes?

Visit some middle or high school classes. Are they centrally structured or diffusely structured? How does the structure seem to effect the classroom atmosphere? the effectiveness of the class?

and curricula that do not harmonize with students' notions of what is valuable and relevant may backfire.

If the class social climate is to be positive, the group norms should allow for a wide range of behavior and individual differences. When norms are flexible, allowing for differences in individual behavior, they create an atmosphere of tolerance, encouragement, good feeling, and support. Narrow, rigid norms cause an atmosphere of restraint, threat, and anxiety.

With luck you can change group norms so as to make them more favorable. If, for instance, you continually encourage and support students who participate openly, the students may come to accept open participation as the norm. You can also use group discussion to change group norms. Discussion allows students to examine the norm closely. It may turn out that the assumed norm does not really represent the true feeling of the group members. Adolescents, like adults, often have incorrect notions about what other people think and believe. Discussion also seems to bring out feelings of group solidarity so that the group members support the norm once the group has accepted it. For that reason cooperative teacher-student planning is useful for fostering desirable norms. When students work together to make the rules or to plan the units they will study, they are more likely to incorporate these norms into their behavior.

Communication within the Group

To facilitate a positive social climate, communication—both verbal and nonverbal—should be free, open, and supportive. Although there must be plenty of interaction, dialogue, and feedback among teacher and students, basically the communication pattern should be student-centered. Optimum communication does not occur in a highly teacher-centered class (Figure 3–5).

You can establish better communication in the classroom by teaching students such communication skills as

- Paraphrasing.
- Behavior descriptions.
- Descriptions of one's feelings.
- Perception checking.
- Feedback.

Practice these skills (for many teachers are less than proficient in using them). You might also use a combination of direct teaching and observation of class discussion. The observation techniques described in Chapter 12 would also be useful as a guide for observing communication skills. Role-playing activities in which the spectator analyzes the communication process can also be used.

Group Cohesiveness

Groups are most effective when they are cohesive; in other words, closely knit, purposive, and well organized. In a cohesive group, the students have high morale and positive feelings toward the group. Because the students know where they stand, what they are supposed to be doing and are doing it, they produce. In short, a cohesive group works together.

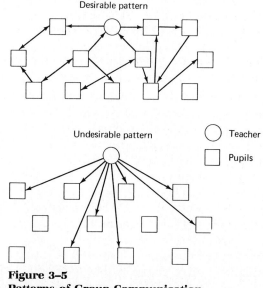

**Figure 3–5
Patterns of Group Communication.**

How do the characteristics of effective instructional groups differ from ineffective ones? In what ways can you as a teacher influence each of these group characteristics so as to make your teaching more effective?

You can build classroom cohesiveness by creating a diffusely structured classroom in which student participation and involvement are encouraged. Building self-esteem by supporting the students and involving them in the decision-making process also helps establish cohesiveness, as does anything one can do to make students feel important and influential. Try to create cohesiveness by fostering an atmosphere of liking in which students have many opportunities to become involved with each other, by keeping classes student-centered and by involving students in planning and evaluating their class activities. Diffused structure plus clear goals produce a cohesive group.[22]

A Model for Teaching

In general, the procedure in most good teaching follows a five-step pattern. The steps in this model for teaching are

1. Diagnosing the learning situation.
2. Preparing the setting for learning.
3. Guiding learning activities.
4. Evaluating the students' learning.
5. Following through.

These steps are, or should be, the basis for all teaching strategies. (See Figure 3–6.)

---

[22] This section, Working with Groups, has been based largely on Richard A. Schmuck and Patricia A. Schmuck's excellent *Group Processes in the Classroom* (Dubuque, IA: Brown, 1971).

Diagnosing the Learning Situation

The first of these procedures is to diagnose the teaching-learning situation. Somehow you must find out the needs of the students so that you can plan experiences that will help them satisfy their needs. This entails knowing every youth as well as possible. The more you know about your students' abilities and aptitudes, strengths and weaknesses, likes and dislikes, aspirations and anxieties, competencies and deficiencies and the like, the easier it will be to devise ways to help them learn the things they ought to learn. Use the tools of diagnosis to find whether students have already learned what you intend to teach, whether they are ready to move on, whether they ought to take more time to strengthen, reinforce, deepen and clinch their learning, or whether you ought to go back and reteach something that has been missed, as well as important leads about students' personalities, interests, and nonacademic life.

Preparing the Setting for Learning

The job of a theatrical producer is to provide a setting in which the action of the play can take place. So it is with the teacher. As a teacher, you must provide a setting for learning. This setting for learning includes many things. It includes both creating a pleasant physical environment that will invite the students to learn and providing the materials for learning. More than that, it includes providing an intellectual setting that will cause boys and girls to want to learn and an emotional setting that will provide the security and support that fosters learning. Set induction, that is attempting to produce favorable mental sets in the students, is an essential step in any teaching-learning situation.

To this end some teachers present students with advance organizers, directional questions, or study guides to alert them to what is coming and to direct their energies in proper paths. But most important, preparing for learning consists of planning (1) what

Figure 3–6
Complete Teaching-Learning Cycle.

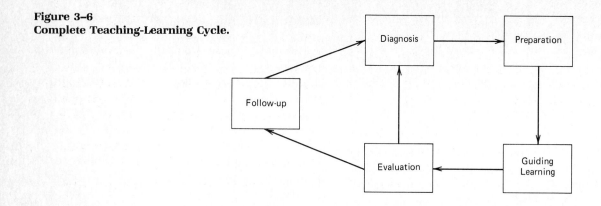

should be accomplished (that is, your objective) and (2) how to accomplish it (that is, your strategy) in view of what you have learned about your students in the diagnostic stage.

Guiding Learning Activities

Once the stage has been set and the students are ready to work, you must guide their learning. This can be done in many ways, e.g., explain to students what they are supposed to be doing and why, show students how to do things, present new facts and concepts and explain old ones through such techniques as asking questions, giving vivid examples and using audiovisual aids. You can also guide students by pointing out their errors. Show them where they have taken the wrong approach, where they have gone off on a tangent or where their thinking has gone awry. Praising good work and encouraging successful and profitable lines of endeavor are also among the effective techniques in guiding learning.

Evaluating the Students' Learning

Guiding students' learning is also a continuous process of evaluation and reevaluation. In order to ensure that learning proceeds on its proper course, you must assess the progress of the learning. From the feedback this evaluation gives, you

can tell what has been missed and what must be retaught, and what to emphasize in succeeding classes. Evaluation also tells the students where they have hit or missed the mark. It is essential to diagnosis and necessary to good instruction. It gives the basis for determining what steps to take next. After a course gets rolling, the evaluation phase of one unit can often be used as the diagnostic phase of the next one.

Following Through

Much teaching is not truly effective because teachers often forget the final step of the pattern— the follow-through or follow-up. Without it teaching all too often becomes a case of "so near and yet so far," for it is the follow-through which drives home and clinches the learning. The follow-through can take any of many forms. At times a simple summary will do. Other times one must repeat a point week after week, or apply the learning in new practice situations. But in every case try to make the learning a little more thorough than in the original teaching-learning situation.

In many instances this extra effort must consist of reteaching those things that the evaluation tells us the students have not learned, for the follow-through is not only an opportunity to clinch students' learning but also a chance for correcting mistakes and filling in gaps. Thus, any good mathematics teacher who, upon checking the students' work, finds that they have not mastered one of the principles of the latest unit should stop to go over the principle again to be sure the students understand it before moving on to the new unit. The teacher's failure to clinch basic learnings is an all too frequent cause of students' failure at more advanced levels. Whatever is worth teaching is worth teaching well, and, if students miss it the first time around, the follow-up gives them a chance to make up the loss. A little additional effort can make the difference between half-baked learning and real understanding.

Frequently, when the evaluation tells you that the objectives of a unit are pretty well mastered, your follow up should be to move on to a new unit. Use the information you have learned about the students and their learning in this unit not only as a basis for building new learning in the next unit but also as a signpost indicating the need for individual help and filling in the gaps as the new unit proceeds.

The Model's Fluidity

An interesting characteristic of this teaching model is that it is not fixed. As we have seen, the evaluative phase in a unit may serve as the diagnosis phase of the next one. The follow up for one unit may be preparing and guiding the learning activities in the next one. Frequently a unit's evaluation and teaching activities run side by side. Still, even though the steps may not always follow each other in strict order and may sometimes change places with each other, to be truly effective you must make use of all of them in all your teaching.

Summary

The role of teaching method is to bring about learning. It includes both content and techniques, strategies and tactics. The key to method is to bring about the desired learning in students by selecting the proper strategies and tactics and consequently the proper content and techniques. This is complicated by the difficulty of the communications and management problems in teaching, and by the abundance of possible alternative strategies and tactics. This abundance of possible procedures and the need for making many spur-of-the-moment decisions makes teaching an art, not a science. Teachers must select or create teaching objectives most suited to the needs of the students, and then pick content and teaching strategies and tactics that will bring about these objectives.

Subject matter is not all the same and so all subjects should not be taught in the same way. Rather, the teaching approach should vary according to the structure and methods of the disciplines concerned. No longer can teachers be content to teach students information and to cover the subject. The modern world contains too much information to cover and the facts are changing too swiftly. Modern teaching must concentrate on organization, method, process, structure, skills, and attitudes so that young people can cope with the new and different knowledge that will be discovered before they get the old knowledge well digested. It is for these reasons that the teacher must teach more by covering less.

The strategies and tactics available include clarif-

Is the fact that a student has successfully passed the prerequisites to a course any guarantee that he is ready for it? How might one tell if the student is ready?

Without continuous evaluation teaching is seldom efficient. Why?

Can you think of any teaching-learning situation in which any of the five steps of the general pattern of teaching strategies should be omitted?

Evaluation usually shows that not all students have reached the same point. What implications does this have for the guiding of learning activities?

ying operations, show-how operations, and security-giving operations. Their approach may be direct or indirect and they may be individualized. Which strategy or tactic is best depends on the circumstances. Sometimes it is better to teach directly; sometimes indirectly. Much teaching should be individualized, but almost all our common teaching methods involve working with groups. Consequently, teachers should understand the characteristics of groups, which include leadership, attraction, norms, communications, and cohesiveness as well as how one can influence those group characteristics. Evidently teaching is most effective when leadership is democratic and groups are diffusely structured.

Whatever the teaching situation, good teaching requires that teachers follow a teaching model such as the following.

1. Diagnose the situation.
2. Prepare for the learning.
3. Guide the activities.
4. Evaluate the learning.
5. Follow up.

Additional Reading

Biehler, Robert F., and Jack Snowman. *Psychology Applied to Teaching.* Boston: Houghton Mifflin, 1982, Chap. 7.

Blue, Terry W. *The Teaching and Learning Process.* Washington, DC: National Education Association, 1981.

Crabtree, June. *Basic Principles of Effective Teaching.* Cincinnati, OH: Standard Publishing, 1982.

Dock, Lloyd. *Teaching with Charisma.* Boston: Allyn and Bacon, 1981.

Frymier, Jack R. *The Nature of Educational Method.* Columbus, OH: Merrill, 1965.

Gage, N.L. *The Scientific Basis of the Art of Teaching.* New York: Teachers College Press, 1978.

Gage, N.L., ed. *The Psychology of Teaching Methods,* The Seventy-fifth Yearbook of the National Society for the Study of Education, Part I. Chicago: University of Chicago Press, 1976.

Joyce, Bruce, et. al. *Flexibility in Teaching: An Excursion Into the Nature of Teaching and Training.* New York: Longman, 1980.

Levin, Tamar with Ruth Long. *Effective Instruction.* Alexandria, VA: The Association for Supervision and Curriculum Development, 1981.

Orlich, Donald C., et. al. *Teaching Strategies: A Guide to Better Instruction.* Lexington, MA: D. C. Heath, 1980, I–IV.

Peterson, Penelope L., and Herbert J. Walberg, eds. *Research on Teaching.* Berkeley, CA: McCutchan, 1979.

Pierce, Walter D., and Michael A. Lorber. *Objectives and Methods for Secondary Teaching.* Englewood Cliffs, NJ: Prentice-Hall, 1977.

Schmuck, Richard A., and Patricia A., Schmuck. *Group Processes in the Classroom.* Dubuque, IA: Brown, 1971.

Seltzer, Leigh, and Joanna Banthin. *Teachers Have Rights Too: What Educators Should Know About School Law.* Boulder, CO: Social Science Educational Consortium, 1981.

Silvernail, David L. *Teaching Styles As Related to Student Achievement.* Washington, DC: National Education Association, 1981.

Sprinthall, Norman A. *Adolescent Psychology: A Developmental View.* Reading, MA: Addison-Wesley, 1983.

Student Learning Styles and Brain Behavior. Reston, VA: National Association of Secondary School Principals, 1982, Part III.

Troisi, Nicholas F. *Effective Teaching and Student Achievement.* Reston, VA: National Association of Secondary School Principals, 1983.

Walberg, Herbert J., ed. *Improving Educational Standards and Productivity.* Berkeley, CA: McCutchan, 1982.

Wragg, E. C., ed. *Classroom Teaching Skills.* New York: Nichols, 1984.

4

Motivation

Overview

In this chapter we discuss motivation, the back-bone of all student behavior. To have well-run classes in which students learn, you must see that students' motivation is favorable toward learning. High school principals evidently feel that student apathy and lack of motivation are about the most troublesome of all the problems they face.[1] This lack of motivation is responsible for classroom

[1] David R. Byrne, Susan A. Hines, and Lloyd E. McCleary, *The Senior High School Principalship*, Vol. 1 (Reston, VA: National Association of Secondary School Principals, 1978).

See also Vernon Smith and George H. Gallup, *What the People Think About Their Schools: Gallup's Findings*, Fastback 94. (Bloomington, IN: Phi Delta Kappa Educational Foundation, 1977); and Gallup Polls on schools reported in the *Phi Delta Kappan* annually. (e.g., Sept., 1984, pp. 23–38.)

management, discipline, and control problems as well as deficiencies in student learning. To learn, students must do the work and engage in the learning activities. If teaching and learning are to occur, students and teachers must be orderly, well behaved, disciplined, and courteous. None of these conditions is likely to occur in your classroom if your students are not well motivated. To secure such motivation must be one of your highest priorities. Of course you realize that in spite of what the principals' report says, the difficulty is not really so much lack of motivation as the incompatibility of the students' motivation with classroom learning and discipline. Your problem is to somehow steer their motivation so that it will support your instructional goals.

Therefore when you teach, it is important that you do your best to build up students' feeling of self-esteem and utilize the motives that the students already have. To this end you should do your best to make the learning seem worthwhile and encourage students to establish suitable objectives. This can be done by taking particular care when making assignments. If you can keep the class moving along in a lively fashion in a pleasant, supportive atmosphere in which you reinforce desirable behavior and provide the students with desirable models, the students' motivation should make your teaching pleasurable. Although there is no royal road to student learning, there is no reason why it should be completely frustrating. Let us make learning attractive. Motivation is not only the key to learning, it is also the key to good discipline.

The Nature of Motivation

Learning results from one's interactions with the environment—both what one does to the environment, and one's reactions to what the environment does to one.

The teacher's job is somehow to get the students to engage in activities that will result in the desired learnings. This process is the essential ingredient in both instruction and discipline.[2] We call this process motivation. By definition, motivation is whatever it is that arouses people to do whatever it is they do.

Aversive Motivation

It is, therefore, strange that teachers do so many things to turn students away from learning. All too often classes are so dull and dreary that they alienate students. In these classes boys and girls encounter a hidden curriculum that teaches them to despise schoolwork, if not to hate it. From this hidden curriculum the students learn that

a. working hard, trying hard, and going beyond the minimum requirements do not pay off;
b. the extrinsic rewards of schooling may be obtained more easily by other methods than by academic endeavor. For instance, soft soaping the teacher or throwing the bull may bring a student more and better results than diligent study;
c. it does not pay to be too successful. Excellence in schoolwork may cause the student to be pilloried by other students as a violator of the peer culture or as a greasy grind, or to be singled out for extra work by the teacher;
d. "conformity is rewarded"; originality and creativity are not. It does not pay to think for oneself, to be enterprising, or to have original ideas. Imagination, creativity, and thinking are not acceptable classroom occupations;
e. "curiosity is irrelevant." What one is supposed to do is to learn the prescribed lessons. To be curious about the subject matter and to try to find out more about it upsets the teacher.[3]

---

[2] In a sense instruction and discipline, or control, are really synonymous. One cannot have good instruction without good discipline.

[3] Melvin H. Marx and Tom N. Tombaugh, *Motivation* (San Francisco: Chandler, 1967), pp. 206–207.

So it is that although elementary and middle school students may study to learn, high school students have learned to be more interested in what schooling will get them than in the learning itself.

The Complexity of Motivation

Motivation is extremely complicated. In a strict sense no one can motivate anyone else. In the first place, everyone is already motivated. When we say that a person is not motivated, we mean that that person is not motivated in the way we would like him to be. In the second place, everyone's motivation is personal. No one can give a motive to another person. Of course, it may be possible to frighten someone into action, or persuade someone to do something. But, in truth, in these instances, as in all others, all one really does is to influence the other person's motivation.

Influencing another person's motivation is not a simple task. For one thing the person is already a tangle of different and perhaps conflicting motives. Some of these motives are innate. Among these are need for security, avoidance of hunger, dread of pain, need for activity, craving for stimulation, and sex. Other motives are learned. Learned motives include desire for certainty, need to achieve, craving for companionship, desire to reduce anxiety, requirement for independence or dependence, and many more. Innate motives are very powerful comprising, as they do, basic human needs. When innate motives are aroused they are likely to take over. Then the higher learned needs must usually stay on the back burner until the innate motives have been quieted. The learned motives themselves vary in intensity. Some may be very strong and some very weak. However, the strength of these motives may change, for circumstances do alter cases. Motives, both basic and otherwise, tend to compete with each other. For another thing, when students walk into your classroom, each one brings a hierarchy of motives that range from very strong to very weak. These hierarchies are personal; they differ from individual to individual. One girl's need to achieve may be much stronger than her need for peer approval, whereas her sister may be much more influenced by peer pressure than by a desire to achieve. Further, the priorities within an individual's hierarchy of motives change with time and circumstances. At times everyone suppresses certain desires; at other times circumstances make certain motives almost uncontrollably powerful. Still, on the whole, most motives retain their relative positions within one's hierarchy of motives even though circumstances modify motives and alter their importance.

For a third consideration, motives are affected by many factors. In classroom situations, for instance, student motivation depends not only on the power of the student's competing personal emotions but also on the impact of attitudes toward the subject matter to be learned, past experience and such other considerations as the learner's feeling tones, the learner's interests, the difficulty of the learning task, knowledge of results, the relationship of the activity to the reward for learning, the student's learning style, the teacher's teaching style, the classroom atmosphere, the student's attitude toward the content, and the student's previous experience with the subject.

What is motivation? What are its implications for teaching?

"Learning takes place only through activity." What does this mean? What are the implications for teaching?

What causes people to do things? List the reasons why you have done the more important things you have done today.

Do you recall what your teachers did in your high school classes that made you wish to study and work in their courses? What did they do that caused you to dislike schoolwork in general and the assignments in their courses in particular? What types of teacher actions particularly turn students off? What turns them on?

How to Motivate Students

How, then, does one motivate students? Unfortunately it is not easy. Techniques that work well in one situation may be useless in another. Incentives that create enthusiasm in some individuals in a class leave others completely indifferent. However, general approaches that seem to apply to the development of positive motivation toward school learning include,

1. Try to build up students' feelings of self-esteem.
2. Take advantage of the students' present motives.
3. Make the potential learnings seem worthwhile.
4. Help students establish suitable tasks and objectives.
5. Keep up the pace.
6. Develop a receptive mood in the learners.
7. Provide a pleasant environment.
8. Cultivate in the learners ideals and attitudes conducive to learning.
9. Utilize reinforcement theory as much as feasible.
10. Provide good models for students to fashion themselves after.

The *best motivational devices and techniques are positive* in nature. In the past teachers have placed too much emphasis on negative, aversive punishment measures in attempting to motivate and discipline. It is time for us to turn from negative motivation to positive motivation. Success breeds success.

Cultivating Self-esteem

Just as success breeds success, feelings of high self-esteem lead to successful academic performance. Everyone wants to feel important and respected by friends and associates. No one wants to be a failure. For this reason competent teachers give students plenty of opportunity to preen their feathers. They do their best to help even the least successful students find something of which to be proud.

Recognition of one's success by others is most enjoyable. When this recognition takes a tangible form, it is usually even more enjoyable. In addition, just the feeling of having succeeded, whether anyone praises you or not, can be motivating. Teachers should see to it that students have many successes in their schoolwork. They can do so by differentiating the work to be done and seeing to it that students are assigned tasks commensurate with their abilities. Repeated failure soon puts an end to the desire to try.

The accompanying diagram (Figure 4–1) gives some indication of how self-esteem and praise lead to good motivation. In this diagram you see that good feelings of self-esteem lead to a higher level of aspiration that in turn leads to an enhanced need for achievement, which leads to stronger efforts to reach the learning goal. Teachers can promote these feelings by showing that they expect students to do well by giving positive feedback, and by using praise judiciously.

Levels of Aspiration

As a rule, after success students raise their goals; after failure they lower them. One's level of aspiration then, is generally a compromise between one's fear of failure and one's hope for success. Success-oriented students set themselves reasonable goals that they can reach, but students accustomed to failure tend to set either impossibly high goals or unnecessarily low ones so as to avoid the stigma of defeat. Because of their fear of failure, low achievers are liable not to try; students who experience success, being more confident, are more likely to exert real effort.

Because these feelings of self-esteem are engendered by success, it is wise to "accentuate the positive." This approach is more profitable because negative motivation tends to inhibit and retard learning and may be accompanied by other unwelcome side effects. Positive approaches build positive student

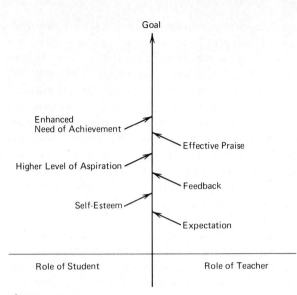

Goal

Enhanced
Need of Achievement

Effective Praise

Higher Level of Aspiration

Feedback

Self-Esteem

Expectation

Role of Student   Role of Teacher

Figure 4–1
Self-esteem, Praise, and Motivation.

attitudes and self-esteem. Challenging reasonable objectives and assignments, plus positive feedback, promote self-direction, and self-confidence. Such feelings arouse in students the will to try to do well.

There will be times when even the highest achievers fail; this cannot be avoided. Perhaps this is a good thing if you treat failure positively. Students can learn from mistakes. Teachers should use student failures as a step toward success. If students correct their errors and learn to avoid mistakes, the failures will not have been in vain.

In middle and high school grades, to raise students' levels of aspiration may be difficult, but a positive empathetic class climate, plus plenty of experience with legitimate success, teacher encouragement, and social approval should help. Teachers who encourage the students to take over their own learning may develop in students feelings of confidence in their own ability. This is especially true if they teach students to do things well, for doing things well is a powerful ego booster.

Great Expectations

Teachers who show students that they confidently expect them to do well raise their aspiration levels and self-esteem. This may be partly because teachers with high expectations act more positively than other teachers do. Since these teachers expect much of their students, they are inclined to give the students more time to answer, to wait longer for answers, to help with more clues, to utilize more extended questions, and to offer more praise and encouragement. In short, they tend to create a more motivating climate.

It is important, then, that you encourage students by arranging your classes so that students have experiences of success, encouragement, and support.

Providing a Favorable Climate

The school and classroom atmosphere can make the difference between an enthusiastic learner and a hater of the subject. Evidently the ideal classroom climate is that of an active partnership in which the teacher demonstrates that she likes teaching the subjects and the students. It includes five conditions, according to Riordan.

1. Communication is open and active, featuring dialogue rather than monologue.
2. High levels of attraction exist for the group as a whole and among its members.
3. Norms are supportive for getting work done, as well as for optimizing individual opportunities to be different.
4. Members share high amounts of potential and actual influence both with one another and with the leader.
5. The processes of working and developing together as a group are important in themselves and open to examination and change.[4]

---

[4] Richard J. Riordan, "Educational Climate: Discussion," in Herbert J. Walberg, ed., *Improving Educational Standards and Productivity* (Berkeley, CA: McCutchan, 1982), p. 309.

Teachers who are punitive, righteous, and power bent get negative results.[5] Harsh discipline raises resentment that is transferred to the subject matter. Therefore, for the sake of good motivation, avoid harsh, restrictive, disciplinary measures, unpleasant teaching methods, and anything else that may cause dislike and antagonism. Remember that you are trying to sell a valuable commodity. People who dislike you, your product, and your store will not buy from you. Punishment can also motivate, but it should seldom be used for classroom motivation because it tends to create an atmosphere of surly, sullen repression. In such an atmosphere students' work is usually halfhearted. Since the object of teaching is learning, you need more efficient motivating devices than punishment. Still, boys and girls must learn that if they misbehave or neglect their work they must suffer the consequences. Occasionally, you will have to use negative measures to make these points clear. Poor papers should be redone. Neglected responsibilities should lead to loss of privileges. Undone work should be made up—perhaps in after school hours or detention periods, or even, on occasion, next term as a repeater. Such treatment should always be fair, just, reasonable, and preceded by fair warning.

That a customer must be put in a receptive mood is almost axiomatic among salesmen. So it is with teaching. What we are after is to get learning across to the students. To make the learning or the learner disagreeable is unrealistic. Perhaps making your subject pleasant may seem to be sugarcoating it. If so, remember that it is the learning that counts. *Any method or device, within reason, that you can use to expedite learning is legitimate.* If to expedite learning one must sugarcoat the subject, do not spare the sugar.

A "Pleasant House"

It is also axiomatic that boys and girls (and for that matter men and women) work better in pleas-

ant surroundings. A dark, dirty, repressive atmosphere seems to hold back the average person. In a bright, cheerful atmosphere students are more likely to become interested in their schoolwork and perform it conscientiously. Therefore, you should strive for a pleasant classroom. It may be that you can do little about the classroom's decor, although you can usually help that considerably, but you can do something about the social setting. The social setting has much to do with motivating. For instance, the more personal social climate in a small school where everyone is known seems to enhance motivation, probably because everyone is known.[6] Although teachers in larger schools cannot replicate all the virtues of the small school, they can take steps to make their classes warm and intimate with a personal touch. You can also do much for the spirit of the students by eliminating overseriousness in the classroom. Learning is not necessarily solemn. People learn better in a happy frame of mind. Laughter, fun, humor, cooperation, pleasantness, and politeness all go to make the classroom a happy place. Vittorino da Feltre, the great Renaissance schoolmaster, called his school "The Pleasant House." As part of our motivational technique we should strive to make our schools "Pleasant Houses."

Creature Comforts

Finally, one must not forget the creature comforts. As we have seen, innate motives and basic needs are very powerful. Therefore you should be careful to take care of the students' creature comforts. Students who are sleepy, thirsty, hungry, hot, tired, or craving physical activity do not learn academic material with optimum efficiency. They need breaks, physical activity, comfortable classroom conditions, relief from physical stress, and opportunities to socialize. In addition, they need an occa-

---

[5] Ibid., p. 310.

[6] Willard Duckett, "Student Motivation: Finding the 'Missing Link'," *Practical Applications of Research* (September, 1982), **5:**1–4.

> What does psychology tell us about the effect of praise, reproof, rewards, and punishment upon learning? What are the implications for teaching?
>
> Should emulation, competition, and rivalry be used to motivate classroom learning? What are the advantages and disadvantages of each?
>
> Evaluate sarcasm, ridicule, and fear as motivating techniques.
>
> What will you do to raise the level of aspiration in your classes?

sional change of pace. Students cannot keep going at top level continuously. They need opportunities to relax, and to consolidate their learning. On the other hand, students cannot stand continuous, low-activity levels either. They work best when periods of strong stimulation are interspersed with periods of rest, relaxation, and rehabilitation.

Making Learning Seem Worthwhile

Unless students think that what they are about to learn is valuable to them personally, they will participate grudgingly, no matter how important the learning really is. Of course, sometimes the students are right: the subject matter has no real meaning to them. In such cases the only answer is to change the curriculum. There is no point in doing something well if it is not worth doing in the first place. But when the content is worth learning, you should take every possible reasonable step to make it seem worthwhile to the students, for when something seems worth learning, then learning is its own reward.

One way to convince students of the worth of your subject matter is to show by your behavior that you think it important. Teachers who are enthusiastic about their subject are much better salespeople than teachers who find it a bore. Real enthu-

siasm is hard to resist. Before the students realize it, they may begin to catch the teacher's spirit—perhaps in spite of themselves. Of course, enthusiasm alone will not fire up every member of a class, but it helps. If you do not like a subject, you have no business teaching it.

Immediately Useful Learning

Students are more likely to be motivated if they see that what is to be learned is useful *now*. Therefore, whenever possible, you should try to make the students aware of the immediate values in their lessons. You can do so by centering classwork around everyday concerns of students, by including current issues in the school and community, by pointing out how the classroom learning may be used in other classes and activities, and by consciously attempting to tie the lessons to the present attitudes and interests of students. For example, in a mathematics class one might use graphs to illustrate problems being studied in the social studies class, or the study of percentages might be related to the standings of the major-league baseball teams. Such techniques are much more likely to succeed in setting students to work than exhortations to "study because you will need to know it in college."

Applying the Learning

Using what one has learned is one of the best ways to show that the learning is worthwhile. As Torrance asserts

many children and young people not now motivated to learn in school will become excited about learning and will achieve in line with their potentialities, if given a chance to use what is learned, if given a chance to communicate what is learned, if we show an interest in what is learned rather than in grades, if learning tasks are not too easy or too difficult, if there is a chance to use their best abilities and preferred ways of learning, if we reward a variety of kinds of excel-

Select a course you probably will teach. Why should students study it?

Can you justify teaching your major fields?

Go through a textbook you might use in your teaching. How can you make this material seem worthwhile to a group of teenagers? Why is it worthwhile? In what ways can students immediately apply the subject matter learned in units of this text?

lence, and if learning experiences are given purposefulness.[7]

Utilizing Present Motives

Intrinsic and Extrinsic Motivation

Ordinarily learning proceeds best when it is intrinsically motivated, that is to say, when students learn what they learn because they want to learn it. An example of intrinsic motivation is learning to drive a car. Most young people learn to drive because knowing how to drive has intrinsic value to them.

When the things students should learn in their classes seem to have no intrinsic value to them, we must turn to extrinsic motivation. To do so we try to provide the students with a reason that will stimulate them to learn even though they do not see value in the learning. An example of this type of motivation may be the case of the girl who learns geometric theorems because she wishes to earn an A in the course or because her father has promised her a prize if she learns them. Here the goal is not the learning itself, but something that can be

obtained through the learning. Such goals are called incentives. They are really ulterior motives for undertaking activities otherwise considered not worth doing. Ordinarily, we should prefer that boys and girls do their schoolwork because of its intrinsic value to them. When this proves impossible or impractical, you should use incentives that will create the desired response. In either case you should take advantage of the students' natural motives.

Harnessing the Natural Motives

As we have seen, every boy and girl comes to school with certain basic drives. These natural motives are often more powerful than any incentive you can invent. Be alert to these drives and use them in your teaching whenever you can. If you cannot utilize them, at least strive to adapt your classwork so that it does not conflict directly with natural motivation. For instance, in a social studies class one morning the juniors were all upset because they had had a most interesting and exciting speaker from Russia at assembly. However, because some faculty members dominated the discussion, the students had not had a chance to ask the speaker their questions. So, rather than go on with her prepared lesson, the teacher took time to discuss their questions, in this way easing their frustration and taking advantage of their interest.

Perhaps you can think of examples of natural motives interfering with the normal course of learning. Have there been any instances in your college classes when the teaching has been hampered by the natural motivation of the students? What, if anything, did the instructor do? What might he have done?

Let us now look at some of the natural motives that you might capitalize on.

[7] E. P. Torrance, ''Are There Open Tops to the Cages?: Using Educational Resources,'' in E. P. Torrance and R. S. Strom, eds., *Mental Health and Achievement* (New York: Wiley, 1965), p. 260. Quoted by Lita Linzer Schwartz, *Educational Psychology*, 2nd ed. (Boston: Holbrook Press, Inc., 1977), p. 111.

Capitalizing on Student Curiosity. People are naturally curious. Watch children examine things. Listen to them asking questions: Why? Why? Why? This curiosity abides in adults also, and it is probably just as strong. Witness the crowds that gather whenever there is an accident. When people are not naturally curious about a certain thing, it is usually fairly easy to arouse their curiosity. One way of doing so is to puzzle them a little so that they ask themselves what will happen next, or what will this result in. Another is to make use of suspense. If you can capitalize on the curiosity of youth, the youngsters will do their schoolwork more eagerly because they will want to find out. This is an important type of motivation.

Using Students Attitudes and Ideals. Among the motives students bring to school are their ideals and attitudes. Insofar as you can, you should try to harness such attitudes as cooperativeness, neatness, industry, fairness, courtesy, patriotism, and honesty, and utilize them in your teaching. Often students will willingly carry out group-project roles they do not particularly like because the teacher has appealed to their attitude of cooperation. Undoubtedly you can think of examples in your own school life in which you have performed downright distasteful tasks simply because an attitude or ideal told you that this was the thing to do under the circumstances. Frequently this type of experience leads us to our most useful and valuable learning. Sometimes, in spite of our prejudice, the experience itself turns out to be extremely rewarding. Many older students find great enjoyment in academic activities they thought to be distasteful when they first encountered them. Adults have had a lifetime of happy fulfillment in careers stemming from academic tasks they had to do against their will.

Need for Certainty. Among the learned motives is the need for certainty. Sometimes people like to be surprised, but most of the time we like to know the score. Where do we stand? What is expected? What is acceptable? What is the routine?

By giving classes structure, teachers can meet this need for certainty. Routinization of daily classroom procedures, carefully presented assignments, clear directions, definite standards of behavior, precise delineation of requirements, well-organized orderly classes, and explicit feedback give one's teaching the structure necessary for students to understand where they stand and what they must do. Without this structure both students and classes tend to drift. With it the students (and the teacher) feel more secure.

Need for Security. Any threat to a young person's security makes learning a more difficult problem. For this reason one should probably avoid the use of fear as a classroom motivational device even though fear is one of the most powerful of motives.

As Chapter 2 points out frightened persons cannot think well. When intensely afraid they may become completely disorganized. Constant worry, a milder form of fear, may lead to mental and emotional idiosyncrasies if not to actual illness. A little anxiety can be motivating, but too much anxiety is debilitating. Adolescents have fears and worries enough without our creating more. Fear should be saved for such important things as life-and-death situations, for example preventing young people from driving too fast or little children from crossing the highway alone.

It is for these reasons that overemphasis on tests and marks should be discouraged. Also to be avoided are class recitations in which students are shamed if they answer incorrectly. Ignorance is not a crime to be punished. Overharshness keeps students from trying their best and tends to make students who do try rigid so that they cannot think their best. Students learn better in a more relaxed atmosphere. Classes become more profitable when teachers find good ways to reduce anxiety to reasonable levels.

Desire for Adventure and Action. Paradoxically, the need for security is accompanied by a desire for action, adventure, and excitement. This often causes youngsters to take chances that seem to belie their desire for security. Often they find security by seeking adventure in groups and by soliciting the approval and admiration of their peers for their adventuresomeness. You would do well to feature activities and materials that have plenty of excitement and action at least part of the time. Use competitive games to give excitement to practice and drill lessons. Stimulate English classes with stories of adventures. Employ puzzles to spice up mathematics classes. Harness the exploits of such men and women as George Washington, Lewis and Clark, Chief Joseph, Andrew Jackson, Peggy O'Neill Eaton, Sacajawea, Frederick Douglass, Amelia Earhart, and Martin Luther King, Jr., to give history courses excitement and adventure.

Desire to Play and Have Fun.   Enjoying oneself is a prominent goal in every person's life. We all need to play and amuse ourselves—even the hypochondriac who enjoys poor health. This motive is closely akin to the need for action, adventure, and excitement. The ordinary class abounds with opportunities to use games—an example is the use of pseudobaseball games in drill activities. At least one New Jersey high school teacher adds fun to tests by including silly questions such as "In ten words or less explain why this is the best course you ever heard of."

The Need for Friendships.   Youths are gregarious. One of the most powerful natural drives is the desire for friendship. Any attempt to keep boys and girls quietly working by themselves in a crowded classroom for long periods of time is against the laws of nature. Capable teachers will usually refrain from making quiet periods overly long and will not be too harsh on boys and girls who feel the need for conversing with their friends. Youth's gregariousness and friendships can be of considerable help to the able teacher—especially in grouping and in conducting group activities.

To have friends is exceedingly important for adolescents but most important of all perhaps are the

> What student attitudes and ideals would be desirable aids to classroom motivation? How might you use them? How might you develop them?
>
> What could you do to encourage an attitude favorable to the subject you hope to teach?

heterosexual friendships that begin to form at this stage of life. Sex and the desire for one's own home are basic drives. Their power and importance should not be underestimated.

In transescence the need for friendship creates strong peer pressures. As beginning adolescents start to free themselves from parental domination, they turn to their peers for support and approval. Consequently, transescents tend to conform with the norms of their peer group, although in the long run they may hold to the standards taught them by their parents and other adults. For a transescent to be branded as different may be anathema. A middle school boy singled out by the teacher for praise or conspicuous recognition may find his social status ruined. Both boys and girls would usually rather be regular fellows than special cases. Peer pressures continue to be powerful in adolescence and youth. However, as people get older and more sophisticated, their need to conform lessens.

Utilizing and Building Interests

The Importance of Interest.   Students undoubtedly learn more efficiently those things that interest them. Therefore, that teachers should try harnessing student interest as a means to effective teaching seems to be self-evident. This doctrine of interest does not imply that the whims of students should determine the curriculum. It does imply that when possible you should use student interests already established or, if suitable student interests are not established, you should somehow create interest.

As we grow older most of us find it increasingly difficult to know and understand the interests of young people. The goals of youth are not the same as the goals of adults. Adults are sometimes shocked to find that what they feel ought to be of the utmost intrinsic value to all youth seems to be quite worthless to young eyes. Even young adults find that what is intensely interesting and exciting to them at twenty-two may not find a single response in a group of fifteen-year-olds. For this reason you should make a point to find out the interests, attitudes, ideals, and goals of your students. Once you know what your students think is important, you can adapt your motivational techniques accordingly. This information can be gathered by using the devices and techniques given in Chapter 7.

Students who have strong college or vocational goals may plug on through lackluster lessons and courses. But most students who find their coursework drab and uninteresting reject it. It may help if you talk over possible benefits of studying the course or unit with your students. In doing so you should remember that exhortations to study are not nearly as productive as actually showing students how they may make use of the learning. If you can encourage students to relate the learning to their own interests, so much the better. Using student ideas may convince them that the subject has interest to them. An English teacher, for instance, who encouraged her students to develop their own ideas, found that their interest in literature increased greatly.

Participating in One's Own Learning. It seems that increasing student involvement in learning through democratic participatory approaches may well stimulate student interest, cause them to accept more responsibility, and expend greater effort. Learning may be its own reward. Learning is always emotionally tinged and usually quite gratifying to the learner. The opening up of new vistas and the excitement of new ideas and skills and the sheer involvement in the learning process can catch a young person up in the excitement of intellectual attainment. For many of us the intellectual experience alone is enough to keep us working diligently

all the rest of our lives. It is important that we teachers give the students opportunities to really participate in true learning experiences. When we do, we give the students a chance to share the emotional experience that Keats had "On First Looking into Chapman's Homer."

Then felt I like some watcher of the skies
  When a new planet swims into his ken;
Or like stout Cortez[8] when with eagle eyes
  He stared at the Pacific—and all his men
Look'd at each other with a wild surmise—
  Silent, upon a peak in Darien.

Such experiences make learning worthwhile; for the person who has a real chance "to participate in his own learning" these experiences are rather frequent occurrences. Many scholars derive their greatest motivation from their involvement in the learning. Fresh ideas and fresh insights really make life exciting. In addition they help students realize they are responsible for their own learning. The assumption of such responsibility is one of the strongest of motivating factors.

What people elect to do themselves usually interests them more than something imposed by someone else. At least, they are likely to think it is more interesting and are, therefore, more willing to start it. Consequently, boys and girls who plan their own activities may begin them more willingly than the students who do not. If you allow the students to pick what they will read, or which of the activities they will do, or in which order they will do them, or to discuss what is important to learn in the new unit or topic, this may engender a favorable attitude in the students toward the work to be done. It also gives you a considerable advantage. If you can capitalize on this start, quite often the students' enthusiasm will carry throughout the study of the topic or activity. Try to encourage student participation in the selection of topics and activities in order to capitalize on their motivational value.

---

[8] Keats was mixed up. It was really Balboa who stared at the Pacific from a peak in Darien.

Involving students in such decision making is discussed in Chapter 8, "Planning for Teaching."

Problems and Problem Solving.   Often you can create interest by utilizing problems and problem-solving techniques. Problem solving is particularly useful in challenging the interests of boys and girls. Humans have always loved to try to solve problems. Challenging problems appeal to the natural drives of activity, success, and curiosity. They should not be too hard, neither should they be too easy. Although you should be ready to help and guide, you should beware of helping too much. Most people prefer to solve their problems themselves, free from kibitzing.

Something Suitable for Everyone.   What we know about individual differences tells us that boys and girls are not all interested in the same things. This complicates the motivating of a class of adolescents. We want our classes to seem worthwhile to the students in order that the students will work at high levels. But what one student finds worthwhile another may find a waste of time. What is the answer? Obviously one way out is to provide enough types of activities and materials so that everyone finds something interesting and worthwhile. Consequently you should try to arrange stu-

dents' activities so that they have opportunities to pursue individual interests. To find out what these interests are, one might use diagnostic observation as described in Chapter 7.

Getting Set

Set Induction

When student interest in your subject may be minimal or when you and the students are encountering something new, interest may be stimulated by set induction activities. For instance, a student teacher in a junior high school general science class performed an experiment in which he attempted to demonstrate the power of air pressure by creating a vacuum in a large can. He first talked to the students telling them what he intended to do, and asked them what they thought would happen when he created the vacuum. Several theories were proposed, among them the theory that the pressure of the atmosphere would "smash the can." "All right," he said, "let's see if the atmosphere can smash the can." He then heated some water in the can filling it full of steam. Capping the steam-filled can he said, "O.K., now let us see what happens." An air of intense expectancy hung over the classroom as the eighth-graders stared at the can. Suddenly one yelled, "There it goes," as the can slowly started to crumble. In a few minutes the class was off on a lively discussion of what had "smashed the can." By harnessing the natural appeal of curiosity, through the medium of suspense and a simple experiment, the student teacher had aroused the class to productive activity.

This type of activity is often called set induction. A set is, psychologically speaking, a predisposition to respond or act, as in "get ready, get set, go!" In most cases starting off a new lesson or activity with an interesting, exciting opener will catch the students' attention so that they will get set for the new activity. Such techniques are useful for launching units, lessons, and all sorts of classroom activi-

It has been suggested that students could well participate in determining which short story or novel the class should read, or deciding in what order units should be taken up, or discussing what should be emphasized in a particular unit. Give specific examples of matters students could decide in teacher-student planning in your own field.

Pick a unit from a middle or high school text for a course you might teach. What would you do to make this topic exciting? How could you involve the students in democratic participatory approaches in this area?

ties, assignments, and learning tasks. Techniques that will arouse students' interest, tickle their curiosity, point out relationships between the new learning and past learning, and establish the worth of the new endeavor are effective for this purpose. In any case the introduction should set the proper mood, give the students adequate directions so that they can get on with the task, and so orient them that they will act and react properly as they proceed with the learning task.

Setting Directions

Both long-term and short-term goals are necessary to keep students moving in the way they should go. Long-term goals are necessary for giving overall direction, but it is the short-term goals that move us through the daily tasks and keep us going forward. For this reason, if classes are to be worthwhile, you must have a definite goal for each lesson. Furthermore, the students should know approximately what this goal is and why it is important and adapt the goal for themselves.

As a matter of fact, students always participate in the selection of their own objectives. That is to say, they establish tasks. The tasks are their objectives even though they may be considerably different from what you had in mind. Your role is to provide situations in which the students will select, or accept, tasks that will help them toward the learning desired. You can do so through the use of directions, advance organizers, study guides, assignments, and learning packets. The most important of these is the assignment.

The assignment is your best chance to start students off in the right direction. When making the assignment, either classwork or homework assignment, you have a chance to show the students what to do, how to do it, why to do it, the value of doing it, and to tie the work to be done to their needs and interests as individuals and as a group. Well-executed assignments may make the students want to work. They can, and often do, make the difference between successful and unsuccessful

---

Describe a set induction activity you might use to get students aroused concerning a topic you expect to teach.

Do your college assignments perform the functions assignments should perform? If they fail, in what ways do they fail? Give examples of how they might be improved.

A student teacher's assignment to his United States history class was, "Read pages 184–297 for tomorrow." In what way is this assignment deficient?

---

teaching. Assignments and making assignments are discussed in detail in Chapter 15, "Guiding Student Learning."

Combating Boredom

People must have stimulation. Lack of stimulation causes boredom—perhaps the greatest cause of discipline problems and nonlearning in our schools.

To combat boredom, try to add life to classes by introducing interesting, stimulating materials and teaching techniques. You can also attack this problem by talking things over with the students in order to make them aware of constructive activities they might undertake so as to make studying more interesting. In the course of conversations with individuals, teachers can bring up such questions as,

Question 1: Are you *aware* of what you are doing?
Question 2: What are the *consequences* of what you are doing?
Question 3: Is what you are doing *useful* to you as a student?
Question 4: If not, what *constructive plan* can you make for dealing with your boredom?[9]

---

[9] Joseph S. Karmos and Ann H. Karmos, "A Closer Look at Classroom Boredom," *Action in Teacher Education* (Spring–Summer, 1983), **5**:51.

Such questioning should not be inquisitorial. It should come from the natural flow of the conversation. Aim it at helping students understand themselves and their options.

Keeping Classes Lively

Students are naturally active. They do not relish sitting still all day. Because they enjoy doing things, activities in which they can actively participate interest them. Moreover, once they are actively participating, their interest is much more easily kept at a high level. Witness the difference between the lecture and a workshop or laboratory. Quite often, the very persons who anxiously wait for the bell in lecture classes do not know when to stop in a workshop or laboratory situation. To keep motivation high, teachers should use such activities to the optimum. Active, lively lessons may make even rather uninteresting subject matter seem interesting.

Once a class is started, keep constantly alert to keep the class free from dead spots. Dull classes lead to wool gathering and switching of attention and interests to other less desirable activities and goals. In every meeting of every class the students should feel that the class is going somewhere important. They should also feel a certain amount of pressure, however light, to exert themselves to go along too.

Challenging But Not Discouraging Work

One way to reduce boredom is to see that the work is challenging but not discouraging. Some adolescents do not do their schoolwork well because it does not challenge them. This is particularly true of the bright students. Youth wants to test itself. It wants to fly high. Boys and girls do not want baby work. An industrial arts teacher, for instance, was having trouble with discipline. This was not surprising because the class consisted largely of discontented boys, who were impatiently awaiting their sixteenth birthdays. Yet the problem was largely teacher-caused. In an attempt to make the instruction fit the needs of these boys, the teacher had devised a course in home mechanics. The activities of this course consisted of such things as puttying windows, changing fuses, and the like. These activities were not interesting and provided no challenge. When the teacher switched to assigning more challenging activities, his discipline problems abated considerably. On the other hand, work that is too difficult can be frustrating. When people see little hope of succeeding, they usually do not try very hard.

Varying the Stimulus

Although too much variety in method or activities may be confusing to some learners, in order to keep motivation high, effective teachers vary their strategies and tactics from time to time. They liven up their classes with such interest-catching tactics as the use of vivid illustrations, audiovisual aids, and demonstrations. Even such a simple technique as moving around the classroom can help. Too much movement on the part of the teacher can be distracting perhaps, but a moderate amount of changing teaching positions (e.g., the side, middle, or back of the room) can aid both control and motivation. Similarly, skilled teachers use head, body, arm, and hand movements effectively. They also take care to point up important content by such tactics as the use of verbal emphases, stress on key words, or gestures (e.g., pointing or pounding on the desk).

Changing the tempo of instruction is also a valuable technique. Pauses in lectures and discussions can be effective. Use them to call student attention to important points, to give an opportunity for ideas to sink in or gel, or to give students a chance to think. Shifting the sensory pattern (e.g., from oral stimuli to visual ones by changing from a lecture to an audiovisual) may give the class a lift. So may switching the interaction from teacher-group activities (e.g., lectures) to teacher-student activities (e.g., making a point with one student), or to student-student activities (e.g., small group projects, interstudent explanations, and discussions).

Almost any type of change of activity can relieve humdrum classes. However, do not overdo it. Too much change may deprive students of the security gained from an accepted pattern or framework. This is particularly true for low-ability students.

Providing Feedback

Students need to know how they are progressing. Knowledge of one's progress makes it possible to reform one's goals and take further strides ahead. The knowledge that one has accomplished a certain amount is often sufficient cause to go further—with renewed vigor. To make the most of this phenomenon you should try to see that students understand and appreciate their own achievement. For this knowledge to be really effective the students need to know "how they did" almost immediately. If, for instance, you take a couple of weeks to read and evaluate papers, their motivational value may have pretty well evaporated by the time you hand back the papers to the students. Feedback should also be quite specific. A simple mark on the paper does not really help the students' motivation much. If your students are going to understand "how they did," you must provide some analysis of each paper's strengths and weaknesses. A checklist or comments written in the margin would serve the purpose. Students can improve only if they understand where they hit and where they missed the mark.[10]

Teachers who expect high performance should utilize class comments, group corrective comments, private conversations, and detailed written comments to make sure that students know what standards are expected of them, what they are doing well, and what they should do to do better.[11]

[10] See Chapter 13 for further explanation of this.
[11] Howard Kirschenbaum and James Bellanca, "Grades—Help or Hindrance," *The Practitioner* (January, 1983), **9:**4–5.

As always in teaching, the accent should be on the positive.

Effective teachers find positive reinforcement techniques useful in discussions and recitations. Reinforcement of this sort can increase student participation, which in turn causes students to become involved with the material to be learned, and to pay better attention. Examples of positive reinforcers include,

1. the use of verbal clues (e.g., that's right, go ahead, yes, O.K.);
2. the use of facial expressions (e.g., smiles);
3. the use of gestures (e.g., nods);
4. the use of tangible rewards;
5. writing the response on the board.

Negative reinforcers may also be used. Examples of negative reinforcers are,

1. the use of words expressing disapproval (e.g., No, That's not right);
2. the use of facial expressions (e.g., scowls, frowns);
3. the use of negative gestures (e.g., shaking the head);
4. silence, moving away from students.

Praise

The judicious use of praise can be a super motivating force. But used indiscriminately, praise can lose its impact and even backfire. Beware of using

What does psychology tell us about the effect of praise, reproof, rewards, and punishment upon learning? What are the implications for teaching?

Should emulation, competition, and rivalry be used to motivate classroom learning? What are the advantages and disadvantages of each?

Evaluate the following as motivating techniques: sarcasm, ridicule, fear.

it too profusely. To be effective praise should be sincere, deserved, and immediate. Praise that is un-earned is soon recognized as empty flattery. Praise should also be specific. Tell students exactly what about their work is praiseworthy and why. Inform-ing the students of the frame of reference you use in making your judgment not only helps direct the students' efforts but also provides them with a goal at which to aim.

Marks and Grades

The incentive most used in our schools is the school mark or grade. That it should have become so important is most unfortunate because in many classes the real learning and understanding tend to be lost in the race for marks. When this happens, too much stress on the incentive defeats the pur-pose of education. One result is cheating. Another is the transient learning that results so often from cramming for tests. Here today but gone tomorrow.

The mark has equally failed as a motivating force for the nonacademic, non-college-bound students. Our grading practices are very discouraging to them. Only in schools is it necessary to compete with everyone in the total population. Because they know they will not do well and because they sus-pect that their marks will never really have much influence on their lives, many of these young people could not possibly care less about school marks. To them good marks are unattainable and not very desirable. Even to the average student they are not a very sharp goad. Their only effect seems to be to arouse spasmodic bursts of effort to cram in as much knowledge as possible during certain periods of stress. So we find that the typical classroom re-ward structure is effective with only the top students.[12] If one promises good grades for hard work, 25 per cent of the students will respond posi-tively, 75 per cent will not, and if one threatens

It has been stated that marks, prizes, and pun-ishment are poor motivating devices for school use. Why do some authorities take this position? Do you agree? Defend your position.

What techniques might a teacher use to induce students to adopt goals that will lead to the learn-ings desired by the teacher? Consider such things as

teacher talks and lectures	demonstrations suspense
field trips	problem raising
moving pictures	quizzes and tests
stories	study guides
dramatizations	organizers

poor grades for poor work, about 25 per cent will respond and 75 per cent will not.[13]

Actually it seems that marks or grades give the least incentive to those who need it most—the low-ability student. Rather than to depend overmuch on grades for motivation, it would ordinarily be more profitable to adjust the lessons and curricu-lum so that they would appeal to students' intrinsic motives, and to use such techniques as computer-assisted instruction or continuous promotion.

Behavior Modification Techniques

Earlier in the chapter an attempt was made to show how one might harness the students' attitudes and ideals. Fortunately for the teacher, attitudes and ideals are acquired, or learned, characteristics. Since this is so, it is possible to teach students new attitudes and ideals and change old ones. Therefore,

[12] James W. Michaels, "Classroom Reward Structure and Aca-demic Performances," *Review of Educational Research* (Winter, 1977), **47**:87–98.

[13] Duckett, op. cit.

you should do your best to create and cultivate attitudes and ideals that foster learning. Behavior modification techniques have proved quite successful for this purpose. Among these techniques are shaping, modeling, token economics, contingency contracts, mastery approaches, and Grandma's rule. They are all useful but dangerous. You should be on guard against using behavior modification to manipulate young people.

Reinforcement Techniques

Reinforcement Theory

Basic to reinforcement theory is the belief that people tend to behave only in ways that pay off with some sort of reward valuable to them. That is to say, when a behavior results in some sort of reward it is reinforced and so more likely to be repeated. Therefore, in order to encourage students to engage in a certain action one should reward them when they engage in that action, and when we wish to discourage students from certain misbehavior, we should reward them when they engage in behavior incompatible with the misbehavior. In teaching, the theory tells us that the basic principle to follow is to give praise and attention to student behavior that facilitates learning and to avoid rewarding behavior that hinders learning.

Neglect of this principle is a primary cause of discipline problems in the school. Very frequently we teachers reinforce the behavior we wish to eliminate, e.g., we encourage "the negativistic student by arguing with him, the aggressive student by paying attention to him, the dependent student by doing things for him, or the whiny student by eventually giving in to him."[14] On the other hand, most teachers neglect to reward or to recognize "the talkative child when he is quiet, the hyperactive

child when he is in his seat, or the impossible student when he turns in an assignment."[15] All too often good behavior does not pay off, whereas misbehavior is rewarded because it commands attention from the teacher and establishes the student's prestige and status among his peers.

Reinforcement Principles

The following list of reinforcement principles should be a useful guide to teachers in their attempts to change student behavior. They are based on the behavior modification theory of shaping.

1. Try to reinforce new behavior by rewarding it every time it occurs.
2. Then, when the behavior has been established fairly consistently, gradually reduce the frequency of reinforcement until finally the reinforcement occurs only occasionally at haphazard intervals. Such intermittent reinforcement is much more effective for maintaining an established behavior than frequent or regular reinforcement.
3. At first, reward the behavior as soon as it occurs. Then, as the student becomes more confident, you may delay the reward somewhat.
4. Try to use rewards suitable for the students. Remember that what is rewarding for one student may be punishing to another. (Conversely, what may be a punishment for one student, or what you may think to be a punishment, may be rewarding to another.) Remember also that performing the act, or improving one's competency, may be its own reward. Probably a mix of tangible rewards, social rewards, rewarding activities and feedback, and success activities will be the most satisfactory. If possible, try to see to it that the performance itself is rewarding. Verbal reinforcement seems to be more effective than tangible rewards. Tangible rewards are likely to create interest in the rewards, not learning. In fact,

---

[14] Harvey F. Clarizio, *Toward Positive Classroom Discipline* (New York: Wiley, 1971), p. 15.

[15] Ibid.

accent on tangible rewards may deter learning for its own sake.[16] It is advantageous if the students can select their own rewards. For this purpose the reinforcement menus described in a later section of this chapter can be very helpful.

5. In using rewards with recalcitrant students it is wise to start small. Sometimes it is very hard to find anything really commendable in a student's work at first. Therefore you should reward such students when they do better and keep rewarding small improvements until the student achieves the behavior desired. This process may take a long time, as the following steps from a sequence worked out by Clarizio for a student who refuses to do his arithmetic illustrate.[17] In this sequence Clarizio recommends that the teacher reward such improvements as
   - Being in his seat even though he is not working.
   - Taking out his book.
   - Opening the book to the assignment.
   - Looking at it.
   - Doing one problem.
   - Doing two or three problems.
   - Completing the assignment.
   These steps are only a portion of the entire sequence Clarizio recommends.
6. Utilize contingency contracts and reinforcement menus.

Contingency Contracts

   Contingency contracts are particularly effective at the secondary school level, according to Clarizio.[18] They are based upon the common practice L. E. Homme calls Grandma's law: that is "If first you do this, then you can do that (or have that)." Most of us probably remember this law in

the form of "If you first eat your vegetables, then you can have some dessert." To be effective the contingency contract must lead to an extremely desirable reward that the student cannot attain outside of the contract. These contracts are best worked out by the teacher and the students together before the term of the contract begins. Occasionally teachers may set up the details of the contract unilaterally and get the students to agree to its terms but this procedure is usually not really satisfactory. Sometimes students may work out the terms of the contract and present them to the teacher. Figure 4–2 is an example of a contingency contract.

Reinforcement Menu

   A reinforcement menu is similar to the contingency contract. It consists of a list of highly desirable activities that students can do once they have completed a set assignment. Ordinarily these activities should be congruent with one's educational goals, but not always so. Sometimes activities that are pure fun or relief from class activities may be more effective. An example of a reinforcement menu appears as Figure 4–3.

Modeling

   Much of what we learn we learn by imitating a model. It is imperative then to try to provide students with good models to copy. To be effective, these models should be highly esteemed by the students. Models whom students do not respect or identify with are usually of little value. Nevertheless, students will model themselves after the behavior of a person whom they do not regard especially highly if they know that they will be expected to demonstrate that they can reproduce that person's behavior and that they will be rewarded if they can do so.

   A model may be almost anyone students admire and can identify with. You should seek out models

---

[16] Duckett, op. cit.

[17] Clarizio, op. cit.

[18] Ibid., p. 41.

FIGURE 4–2
Educational Contract
(Harvey F. Clarizio,
Toward Positive Class-
room Discipline
[New York: Wiley,
1971], p. 15.)

Between (Student's name) and (Teacher's name)

Student agrees to
  1. Complete assigned homework—   5 points
     if well done and accurate   2 extra points
  2. Hand in assignments on date due—   5 points
     if handed in before due date   2 extra points

Teacher agrees to
  1. Check homework and give appropriate number of points to the student (as indicated
     above).
  2. Not reprimand or comment when homework is not completed or handed in.
     (a) If two consecutive assignments are not handed in—3 points are subtracted from
         accumulated total.
     (b) If three consecutive assignments are not completed and handed in the contract is
         considered void.

Student can exchange his points for
  (1) Free period time during class (5 points per 5 minutes).
  (2) Access to the driving range (10 points per 15 minutes).
  (3) Excuse from the weekly social studies quiz (30 points each week).
  (4) Being helper to shop teacher (10 points per 15 minutes).
  (5) Credits for purchase of pocket book (5 points per credit—10 credits for free book).
  (6) Being a student referee for a varsity game (30 points per game).
  (7) Access to student lounge during free period (study hall) (30 points per period).

Signed _____
                              STUDENT

Signed _____
                              TEACHER

among the students' peer group and in the community. Admired personalities such as the stars of
stage, screen, sports, and television, and other public figures in the news are natural models that some
youths imitate. Oftentimes you yourself may be a
model. Teachers who are carefully organized, well
planned, enthusiastic, and knowledgeable may well
influence students in scholarly ways.

Students also look to certain of their peers as
role models. In this respect there seems to be a
"ripple effect"[19] which causes students to learn

from the experiences of others in their classes. Thus
if students see a certain behavior in Student A, they
are likely to adopt that same behavior themselves.
Consequently, it seems desirable to utilize methods
by which students can learn from one another, i.e.,
from each other's example and from the effects of
their behavior on others.

Unfortunately live models are not always predict-
able. They sometimes act in ways one would rather
students did not imitate. Consequently, it is often
necessary to resort to symbolic models—films,
tapes, stories, drama, simulations, role playing, and
the like—in which students can see the behavior
to be imitated at the appropriate time and place
and in the proper sequence.

[19] J. Kounin, *Discipline and Group Management in Classrooms*
(New York: Holt, 1970).

FIGURE 4–3
Reinforcement Menu:
High School Geometry
Class. (Harvey F.
Clarizio, *Toward*
Positive Classroom
Discipline [New York:
Wiley, 1971], p. 30.

1. Challenging teacher or another student to a game of chess.
2. Using the portable computer.
3. Doing extra credit problems and seeing how they can raise his grade.
4. Making up a geometry quiz and then giving it to the class.
5. Sitting at the teacher's desk while doing homework problems.
6. Preparing the bulletin board using a display of the student's choice.
7. Writing letters.
8. Playing chess.
9. Reading.
10. Playing charades.
11. Talking over past or forthcoming athletic or social events.
12. Having a creative exhibit period (a grown-up version of show-and-tell).
13. Comparing a 1902 Sears-Roebuck catalogue with the current one, discussing changes in style, price, and the like, and trying to discover why the changes occurred.

Daily Specials
   Monday. Appear as guest lecturer in the other math classes.
   Tuesday. Do the special crossword puzzles involving geometry concepts learned.
   Wednesday. Time in which you can play a math game with another student.
   Thursday. Construction of special paper models using geometrical figures to complete.
   Friday. Do mystery problems involving mathematical solutions.

A certain teacher says that it is impossible to teach her students anything because of the no-failure policy of the school. The supervisor says that the teacher is merely excusing her inability to make her teaching interesting. React to these statements.

Prepare a list of motivational devices for possible use in a class you expect to teach.

Show how you could use a contingency contract in a class you expect to teach. What would you use as point-getting devices? What for rewards?

What rewards could you include in a reinforcement menu?

Summary

Motivation is too important in the teaching-learning process to be left to chance. It is the key both to good learning and to good discipline. Only students who are well motivated learn well. When students fail to learn, the chances are great that the basic cause of the trouble has to do with motivation. The fault lies with the teacher and the school as often as it does with the students, for they have not taken steps necessary to motivate students to work and study. Fortunately all kids can be motivated.

Since each of us has a valuable commodity to sell to sometimes unwilling clients, it is important that we find a way to motivate them. If we can do so by positive means, the chances of successfully teaching our students will be greatly enhanced. Unfortunately, positive motivation does not always come naturally. More frequently than not, we must convince reluctant students of the value of our wares and create in students an inclination to buy. Fortunately for this purpose, we have many tools and techniques at our command. One of them is to harness as far as possible students' natural motives, such as curiosity, attitudes and ideals, desire for success, self-esteem and security, love of fun, adventure and action, and need for friendship. Another method is to try to make the subject matter seem valuable to the student. Perhaps the best way to do this is to really believe in the material's importance yourself. In this connection one should remember that students are more likely to be moved by immediate rather than deferred and intrinsic rather than extrinsic values. Because people respond differently to things, individual motivation may be fostered by making adequate provisions for individual differences. Marks have not proved to be adequate motivating devices for most boys and girls; teacher-student planning has been somewhat more successful.

New ammunition for the development of techniques and strategies that can be helpful in the motivating of students can be found in reinforcement theory. Basically this theory holds that one should reward students when they behave in the way one desires, but not when they behave in undesirable ways. Unfortunately many of our present disciplinary procedures tend to reward untoward behavior. As we develop and use teaching methods that utilize reinforcement techniques properly, we should find our students becoming better motivated and better behaved. Among the techniques recommended are judicious use of rewards and the use of contingency contracts, reinforcement menus, and modeling.

Additional Reading

Ball, Samuel, ed. *Motivation in Education.* Orlando, FL: Academic Press, 1977.

Biehler, Robert F., and Jack Snowman. *Psychology Applied to Teaching,* 4th ed. Boston: Houghton Mifflin, 1982, Chap. 8.

Emmers, Amy Pyett. *After the Lesson Plan: Realities of High School Teaching.* New York: Teachers College Press, 1981, Part II.

Frymier, Jack. *Motivation and Learning* in School, Fastback 43. Bloomington, IN: Phi Delta Kappa Educational Foundation, 1974.

Gage, N. L., and David C. Berliner. *Educational Psychology,* 3rd ed. Boston: Houghton Mifflin, 1984, Chap. 16–18.

Paris, Scott G., and Gary M. Alson, eds. *Learning and Motivation in the Classroom.* Hillsdale, NJ: Lawrence Erlbaum Associates, 1983.

Presbie, Robert J., and Paul L. Brown. *Behavior Modification, What Research Says to the Teacher.* Washington, DC: National Education Association, 1976.

Reilly, Robert R., and Ernest L. Lewis. *Educational Psychology.* Macmillan, 1983, Chap. 8.

Schwartz, Lita Linzer. *Educational Psychology,* 2nd ed. Boston: Holbrook Press, 1981, Chap. 4.

Silvernail, David L. *Developing Positive Student Self Concept.* Washington, DC: National Education Association, 1981.

Sloane, Howard N., Jr., and Donald Jackson. *Guide to Motivating Learners.* Englewood Cliffs, NJ: Educational Technology Publications, 1974.

Wlodkowski, Raymond J. *Motivation, What Research Says to the Teacher.* Washington, DC: National Education Association, 1977.

———. *Motivation and Teaching: A Practical Guide.* Washington, DC: National Education Association, 1978.

5

Classroom Management

Overview

Classroom management is the process of organizing and conducting the class so that it runs smoothly. Well done, it reduces wasted time and wasted motion. Since it aims the efforts of both teachers and students at the important goals and tasks of schooling, it makes it possible for students to spend their time on learning tasks rather than on nonessentials. Classroom management reduces problems of discipline and control. It ensures that students know what to do and have the time and materials with which to do it. Without it classes are neither efficient nor effective. Successful management is achieved by careful planning, attention to business, explicit instructions, and thorough follow up.

In this chapter we consider principles and procedures that should help you to manage your classes well.

Classroom Management Defined

According to Johnson and Bany, classroom management can be defined as the "process of establishing and maintaining the internal environment of the

94

group and the classroom conditions for the attainment of educational goals."[1] It consists of all "the provisions and procedures necessary to maintain an environment in which instruction and learning can occur."[2]

Among these provisions and procedures are such tasks as

- Planning, organizing, coordinating, directing, controlling, communicating, and housekeeping.
- Manipulation of time, space, personnel, materials, authority and responsibility, rewards and punishment.
- Resolving conflicts between school and society, between roles and personalities, between the group and individuals, between immediate and long-term goals, among personalities, and among roles.

These tasks are influenced by such situational factors as

- Group size.
- Age and background of students.
- Solidarity of groups.
- Organizational content.
- Space, facilities, and resources.

They are also affected by the ideological stances of both the school and the teacher: e.g., task-oriented, individual-oriented, or group-oriented.[3] Figure 5–1 illustrates these features and their relationships.

Obviously classroom management is both difficult and complicated, but well done it is worth the effort. It sets the tone for the class. It allows teaching strategies to move smoothly. It improves class morale, group cohesiveness, and student motivation. It directs student effort toward learning. When classes are well managed, students work more thoroughly, make fewer mistakes, and, in general, become more productive. *Remember! The purpose of classroom management is to ensure that class time is concentrated on teaching and learning, not on side issues.*

Building the Classroom Climate

Teacher Personality and Classroom Atmosphere

Classroom management is dependent on the students' respect. This can be won only by treating students "fairly and compassionately over a sustained period of time."[4] Teachers who rub students the wrong way, who do not like adolescents, who are more interested in the subject than in their students, who are inconsiderate, unhappy, and lack a sense of humor, are not likely to command the respect or cooperation of their students. Students are much more likely to cooperate with teachers who show themselves to be empathetic, warm, and genuine.[5] In other words, you should be friendly, cheerful, fair, consistent, interested, honest, interesting, and helpful. If you can create a feeling of rapport with your students, you will probably have little difficulty with discipline.

For this reason as soon as possible you need to get to know your students as individuals. Most particularly, from the very first learn each student's name and use it in class. This practice is not only good for the student's ego but also serves to notify the students that their behavior will not be anony-

---

[1] Lois V. Johnson and Mary A. Bany, *Classroom Management* (New York: Macmillan, 1970), p. 24.

[2] Daniel L. Duke, "Editor's Preface," in Daniel L. Duke, ed., *Classroom Management*, The Seventy-eighth Yearbook of the National Society for the Study of Education, Part II (Chicago: University of Chicago Press, 1979), p. xii.

[3] Based on Mauritz Johnson and Harry Brooks, "Conceptualizing Classroom Management," in Daniel L. Duke, ed., Ibid. Figure 1. A Conceptual Model of Classroom Management, p. 41.

[4] William G. Spady, "Authority, Conflict, and Teacher Effectiveness," *Educational Researcher* (January, 1973), **2**:4–10.

[5] Duane Brown, *Changing Student Behavior: A New Approach to Discipline* (Dubuque, IA: Brown, 1971), p. 12.

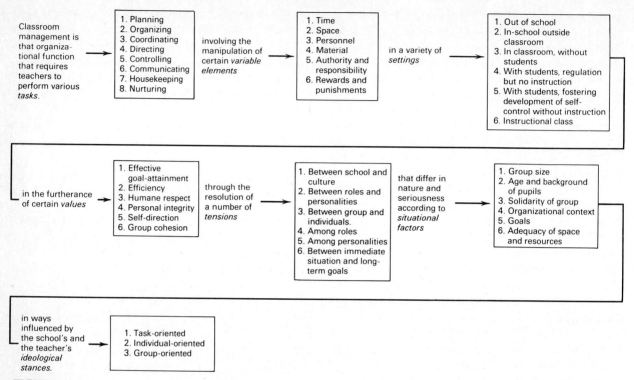

FIGURE 5–1

A Conceptual Model of Classroom Management. Mauritz Johnson and Harry Brooks, "Conceptualizing Classroom Management," in Daniel L. Duke, ed., *Classroom Management,* The Seventy-eighth Yearbook of the National Society for the Study of Education, Part II (Chicago: The University of Chicago Press, 1979), p. 41.

mous. In addition, if you know something of the student's background and interests, you can use this knowledge to cement friendly relations and to direct student interests in desirable directions.

As the chapter on motivation points out teachers' attitudes tend to spread to the class. Tense teachers usually convey their tenseness to their students, and teachers who expect misbehavior usually get it. By acting on the assumption that everything is going to be all right, and by concentrating on the main job, i.e., teaching, you may eliminate a good share of the potential difficulties. In securing and maintaining good classroom relationships a businesslike, matter-of-fact bearing can be very persuasive.

Nevertheless, even in the best-regulated classes and schools, youngsters do misbehave. When this happens try to take it in stride. This calls for keeping a tight rein on your own emotions—not always an easy thing to do.

Achieving the Proper Perspective

One of the best techniques for keeping on an even keel is not to take oneself too seriously. Teachers are human, too. They do not know everything, and they do make mistakes. What is more, the students know it. No amount of dissembling can keep this truth from them. The sooner you realize this and relax, the better off you will be.

Many young teachers seem to think that every incident of student misbehavior is a personal insult.

This is not so. Actually most teachers are not important enough in the students' scheme of things to be acted against personally unless provoked. They do not ordinarily misbehave or neglect their work or fail to follow routines in order to hurt you. You should not be upset by students' misconduct any more than you should be upset by students' lack of knowledge. This is the way youngsters are; your job is to help them achieve the highest goals they can. If you view student misdemeanors as personal insults, you may soon find that they have become just that.

In other words, try to combine a sense of humor with a sense of proportion. When you get to the point where you can laugh at your own failings, you will be well on the way to developing a pleasant classroom atmosphere and good classroom control. Clowning in the classroom should not be encouraged, but when something is funny, laugh at it and then turn the good feeling toward the work of the day. Laughing with students clears the atmosphere. It is always easier to learn in a pleasant class than in a repressive one, and after all, student learning is what you are after. You need a sense of perspective too. Try to put first things first. You are not the police. You are a teacher. Your primary job is not to enforce rules, but to draw out learning. Do not let little things upset you.

Creating a Friendly Atmosphere

The well-managed classroom is a friendly place. By your actions, rather than by words, let students know that you would like to be a friend. This does not mean that you should attempt to be a buddy. In such cases familiarity may breed contempt. No one can be a boon companion to everyone, and teachers must avoid creating favorites. Besides, adolescents prefer that adults act their age.

Setting a Good Example

Perhaps the best summary of what we have tried to say is that the teacher should set a good example. Remember, you, the teacher, are "one source of

reinforcement for both positive and negative behavior patterns."[6] If your behavior is truly considerate, patient, pleasant, and sympathetic, and shows that you care for the students as individuals and are truly trying to teach them well, then the class will probably respond favorably to your teaching. But what sort of behavior can you expect of your students if you run a sloppy, unpleasant class? Without self-discipline teachers make little progress.

Diffusely Structuring the Class

In your planning you should try to take advantage of the nature of the group. Try to utilize student leadership potentials, to build positive social climate, to establish suitable group norms, to construct student-centered communications patterns, and to foster group cohesiveness. You can usually further your goals by creating diffusely structured classrooms in which you encourage students' participation and involvement and exhibit democratic leadership. These strategies are discussed in Chapter 3.

> What is your philosophy of classroom management? What sort of atmosphere do you hope to have in your classes? How do you hope to achieve this atmosphere?

Organizing for Classroom Management

Planning

"Our teacher is funny," a small boy reported to his mother. "She wants you to keep at work all

---

[6] Ibid., p. 74.

the time whether you have anything to do or not.''[7] This anecdote is as true today as it was in 1892. Dead spots in which students have nothing to do ruin many classes. If you plan carefully, you can eliminate most of these empty spots. In your planning you must be sure that everyone has plenty of worthwhile work to do. You should also avoid teaching in which you do all the work and the students just sit and vegetate. This is one reason why you should be wary of the beginner's tendency to overuse the lecture. You should also plan to be sure that the learning activities proceed in a logical sequence.

Not only should the students have plenty of worthwhile activities to do, but you should be sure that the students know how to carry out the activities. Many learning problems are caused because students do not know what they are supposed to do or how to go about doing it. A little instruction in how to study, or how to use the tools of learning, or how to carry out the assignments may pay off in more profitable classes.

Another essential of good planning is to provide plenty of good materials for students to work with. Failure to provide enough of the right materials can cause the worst dead spots of all. In order to eliminate mischief-breeding periods of waiting, in your lesson planning make sure that the materials needed for the lesson are on hand and that you have included procedures for rapid delivery and collection of materials.

Arranging the Setting

If you can arrange the classroom so that it is attractive and easy for the students to work in, your classes are likely to progress more easily than in the dull drabness of an old-fashioned classroom. Many modern methods and techniques do not work as well in traditional formal classroom setups as they do in more relaxed environments.

---

[7] Sarah L. Arnold, ''Waymarks,'' *Journal of Education* (February 4, 1892).

Most modern schools are equipped with movable chairs rather than fixed furniture. This being so, you should resist the temptation to position the furniture in serried ranks, as was done with the old fixed furniture. Although arranging chairs in rows has some advantages from a control and convenience point of view, no classroom seating arrangement is perfectly satisfactory for all activities and all classes. Arrange the class according to the classwork the students are to do. For watching a movie, or listening to a lecture, some variations of the ordinary row setup may be desirable; for committee work, small circles of chairs may be best; for a discussion, a circle or some segment of a circle may be suitable. Move the chairs to suit the activity. After all that is why the school board bought movable furniture.

Some teachers like to seat the students in alphabetical order or with the larger students in the back. In the traditional class these practices may make the routine easier, but if one uses flexible methods, such plans are pointless. To let the students select their own seats is probably as good a plan as any. However, for at least the first few days, the students should keep the same seats so that you can identify them by means of a seating chart and learn their names.

Some examples of possible class arrangements are shown in Figure 5–2.

Some teachers recommend breaking up boon companions, cliques, and troublemakers by seating them so that they can not talk to each other easily. Others say this is a useless procedure and creates more harm than good. What is your opinion on this problem?

Setting Up Routines

Usually middle and high school classes will make better progress if the more usual tasks are routinized. Routines make it possible for boys and girls

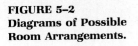

FIGURE 5–2
Diagrams of Possible Room Arrangements.

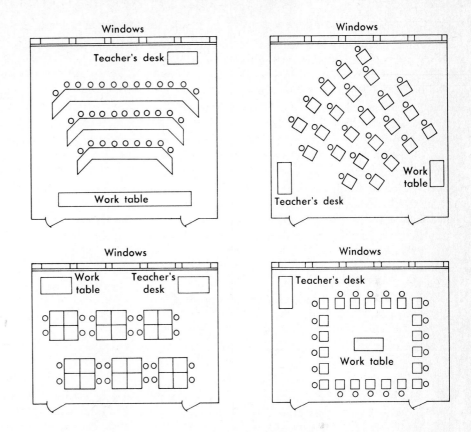

to know what to do without being told over and over again. For instance, there should be no question about whether to write on both sides of a paper, or whether to give one's oral report from one's desk or from the front of the room, for we *always* write on only one side of a sheet and we *always* give oral reports from the front of the classroom.

Time is critical in any class. Routinization of housekeeping activities is an effective way to save time. The more time we can save for active instruction the better. However, too much routinizing can lead to boredom and loss of interest. A good rule is to routinize as many of the administrative and managerial aspects of the classroom as possible but to leave the instructional activities free from unnecessary routine.

Routinization can be applied to such administrative matters as attendance, tardy slips, and excuses. In handling these, the teacher must, of course, carry out the school regulations. However, in order to save time and interruptions, all of this work should be completed before the class starts. Attendance should be taken by some quick method such as noting the unfilled chairs. Calling the roll is a time-wasting procedure.[8] In order to take attendance quickly it is usually a good practice to have students start off at the beginning of the class in their assigned stations, even though they move to other work stations later.

In order to start your classes with a minimum of confusion, routinize the issuing of equipment and materials. The issuing of papers and books can often be delegated to students. Before the class starts, materials to be used during the period should

---

[8] Except when used as a means for learning who the students are.

be ready for instant distribution. A good way to minimize confusion is to list on the board those things that will be needed during the various periods. Thus the students can equip themselves with the necessary materials without asking a single question. A similar routine can be set up for putting things away at the end of the period. In some classes you will want to routinize the collection and distribution of student papers. This is usually done by passing the papers to, or from, the ends of rows, or to the head of the table. However, in a classroom laboratory perhaps a better way is to circulate unobtrusively about the class and to collect or distribute the papers without interrupting the students' work.

One should never become a slave to routine, but if certain tasks must be done again and again, a properly used routine can make the class more efficient and pleasant.

If you were to begin teaching next week, how would you plan to learn the students' names speedily? What sort of lesson would you use to get the course off to a good start? What procedures would you use to make the passing out and collecting of papers, the taking of attendance and so on occur speedily and smoothly? What about such details as sharpening pencils, use of reference works and the like?

Establishing Rules

One of the maxims of our country's forefathers was that the government which governs least governs best. This maxim seems to apply, to some extent, to the modern classroom. Every class needs some rules; no class needs many. Too many rules confuse students. A few definite rules that make sense to students and teachers alike will prove to be the most successful. Perhaps just a few general principles such as "You must not interfere with the learning of others by being rowdy" may work just as well.

In any case, rules should not be too rigid. Rigid sets of rules tend to encourage rule breaking. Furthermore they are likely to inflict you with the necessity of enforcing rules you do not wish to enforce. Keeping to a few general rules or principles of conduct will give you room to maneuver. These rules should give the students considerable freedom, but let them know exactly what the limits are.

A rule can be considered a good rule when it clearly spells out what it is the students must do, seems reasonable, and can be enforced. Such rules are usually more effective when they are stated as standard operating procedures spelling out what is expected rather than what is forbidden. Emphasis on the positive is almost always more fruitful than negative statements or threats.

The following are some sample room standards for a ninth-grade class.

Sample Room Standards, Ninth Grade

1. Have books, paper, and pencil ready. Begin work immediately.
2. Participate and help in class planning.
3. Maintain an atmosphere that helps everyone to study.
4. Contribute to the class and help fellow students.
5. Always do your own assignments—never "crib" from others.
6. Get all work in on time and in acceptable form.
7. Help keep the room clean, neat, and orderly.
8. Keep an individual progress record and try to keep improving it.
9. Never bring gum, toys, animals (except on assignment), or other distracting materials into the classroom.
10. Take pride in clean speech, appropriate dress, and courteous manners.
11. Protect desks, books, and other school supplies and equipment.[9]

---

[9] Emery Stoops and Joyce King Stoops, *Discipline or Disaster*, Fastback 8 (Bloomington, IN.: Phi Delta Kappa Educational Foundation, 1972), p. 36.

When establishing classroom rules try to use a method that will develop positive behavior in the students. One way to do this is to have the students participate in developing their own standards of behavior. For instance, one teacher had great success with the following technique. For many years at the beginning of the term he addressed his class in the following manner: "We are going to have to spend the rest of the year here together. In order to keep out of each other's hair we need some rules. Let's talk the situation over and see if we can figure out what rules we want to have in this class." Then the class set to work to discuss why they needed rules and what kind of rules they needed. Finally, they drew up a set of rules which a committee put in final form for class adoption. During the discussion the teacher presided and made suggestions. Most of his comments were questions such as, "Is that what you really want to do? Do you need that? Aren't you being a little strict?" The resulting rules were usually a workable code that the students could follow quite well. The teacher's greatest difficulty was to keep the rules from becoming unworkably strict and too detailed. Some-

times, after a few weeks, the teacher had to suggest that the rules be reviewed and revised.

A procedure of this type tends to take the onus of rule making and enforcement off the teacher. Arbitrary imposition of rules on students is an invitation to rebellion; however students tend to abide by their own rules quite willingly.

The technique just described worked for this social studies teacher for more than twenty years, but it may be unsuitable for other teachers in different situations. Teachers must suit their methods to their classes and their own personalities. The important thing is to develop for each class standards of conduct the students will accept as reasonable and worthwhile. Extra time spent on this important task at the beginning of the year may result in much greater class progress throughout the rest of the year.

Managing the Class

Getting Off to a Good Start

Since classroom management sets the tone of the class, you should give careful attention to its details from the very first day of class. This means you need not only to plan carefully your management strategies, but that you should also be fairly strict and keep student movement at a minimum during the beginning of a course. After patterns of suitable classroom behavior have been established, it may then be profitable to loosen the reins. To make sure that their early lessons move effectively and create the type of atmosphere they wish, some teachers arm themselves with alternate plans in case their first plans fail. In any case your lessons should always start the moment the period begins. Neophytes, a little unsure of themselves perhaps, are sometimes tempted to give themselves a little respite by stalling a minute or two at the opening of the class. To do so is dangerous; the class that has time to fool around before the lesson starts may

---

What rules or standards for behavior are appropriate for a high school class? A middle school class? Prepare a list of rules you think would be suitable for a class you might teach at the high school level. Prepare a similar list for a middle school class.

Should a set of rules for classroom behavior be provided? (Some texts say yes; some say no.) If so, who should make it and how should it be enforced? Be prepared to defend your position.

Do you agree with the practice of having the students develop their own rules for behavior? How would you go about developing such rules?

Lay out the strategies you think you should use to set up an excellent, orderly, supportive learning environment in your classes.

never find time to get down to business before the period ends.

Keeping the Class Moving

To keep the class moving smoothly, to avoid dead spots, and to evade confusion you should become adept at what Kounin[10] calls "movement management," that is, the technique of guiding the class smoothly through its activities and from one activity to another. To attain smooth movement, you must be careful to avoid interrupting the progress of the class yourself.

- Be sure that students are ready to hear you before you make an announcement, issue orders, or make statements. Particularly avoid interrupting them with your instructions or statements when they are busy doing something else. Otherwise you may interrupt the progress of ongoing work, or your remarks may fall on deaf ears.
- Finish one activity before you start on the next. Don't leave students dangling. Don't allow yourself to get off the topic even if you do come back to it later.
- Don't let yourself start another topic or activity and then find you must jump back to the unfinished previous one.
- Avoid letting yourself be distracted by irrelevant happenings or thoughts. Don't interrupt yourself to harp on inconsequential matters not pertinent to the activity at hand.
- When you have said what you have to say, quit. Don't hold up progress by talking it to death.
- Avoid going into too much detail. Don't break things down into a zillion steps when a few would do. If you need to call up a group, then call them all up at once, not one by one.

Other techniques that one should develop in order to manage classes well include the ability to

keep an eye on the entire class at once, making the class aware that you are alert. Kounin calls this technique "withitness." We used to call it "eyes in the back of your head." In any case, it calls for a "roving eye" and resisting the tendency of so many beginning teachers to concentrate their attention on just a few members of the class. Another technique allied to "withitness" is "overlapping," the ability to do two things at once, for example, listening to one student at his desk while keeping tabs on the progress of another group in a different part of the room. Such procedures help keep students on their toes. To accomplish your tasks, refrain from getting overinvolved with any one student or group, look around the room frequently and avoid getting nailed down to one spot in the room. Other techniques that keep students alert are calling out names after asking questions, calling on students randomly, involving everyone in the lesson, and frequently checking on student progress and activity.[11] Keeping up a high level of classroom management requires continual monitoring.

Allow for students' predispositions, however. Any class procedure that violates the natural inclinations of boys and girls creates a situation that can lead to misconduct. Adolescents are naturally gregarious, social creatures. A class that is all keyed up cannot easily settle down to a placid routine. By adjusting the material and tempo of the instruction to the predispositions and mood of the class, the predispositions of students may be made an aid to learning rather than a threat to peace. Switching from a lecture or recitation to a discussion, snap quiz, or written assignment when a class is restless is a most effective example of this principle. This is the reason some teachers make a point to plan unusually interesting, sprightly lessons or activities on Friday afternoons.

Above all try to keep the class highly motivated. In your planning try to keep the students busy doing things that appeal to them or that they know

---

[10] Jacob S. Kounin, *Discipline and Group Management in Classroom* (New York: Holt, 1970), pp. 102–8.

[11] Ibid.

On Friday afternoon students may be feeling the need to ventilate a little early. What other periods are likely to be stressful? Think out and note down activities you think might relieve such occasions and make for invigorating classes.

In a Vermont intermediate school it has become the practice to show movies every Friday afternoon to relieve classroom tedium. What do you think of this practice?

will pay off in a gratifying way. To this end you should avoid letting your classes fall into the same routine day after day.

Some Specific Suggestions

Before the School Year Starts

Managing the class starts well before the first day of school. As soon as you receive your teaching assignment you should become as familiar as you can with your school, your students, and your classes.

1. *Climate:* What is the overall climate in the school?

2. *Policies and Routines:* What are the standard operation procedures and routines *re* reporting attendance, requisitioning equipment and supplies, and the like? Who is responsible for what? To whom do you report what? What are the school policies? To find out consult the school handbook and talk to other teachers, your department head, the assistant principal, and other school personnel.

3. *The Students:* Find out as much as you can about your students. At what levels are they? What prior experience have they had? If feasible, look through their permanent record folders for clues about their hearing, eyesight, interests, outside activities, and so on.

4. *The Classroom:* What facilities are at your disposal? What can you do to make the environment optimally attractive and efficient? If you are to share facilities, what arrangements can you make with the other teachers *re* the organization and use of common facilities and equipment?

5. *The Courses:* Become familiar with the courses you are to teach. What is the level of each course? What is its place in the curriculum? What are its course goals and instructional objectives? Is there a syllabus or guide? What resources (e.g., texts, supplementary readings, instructional aids, materials of instruction, equipment, and supplies) are available?

6. *You:* Clarify to yourself what you believe about teaching and how it should be carried out. What are your overall teaching goals? I.e., What do you really want boys and girls to get out of your courses? What type of class climate do you wish in your classes? What do you consider appropriate behavior? How loose or how tight do you want to run your classes? To what extent do you think your classes should be teacher centered or student centered? What steps must you take to run the type of classes that you want?

Once you have gathered this information about the school, the students, your courses, and yourself, you must make some decisions. You must decide on how you will organize your class. What rules, routines, and procedures will govern the conduct of the class? What incentives, penalties, rewards, and punishments will you use? As soon as you have made these decisions, you should write down what the rules, procedures, and routines will be. Before the beginning of the first class, post the rules where all can see them. Routines and procedures such as passing out materials, checking work, turning in papers, and checking attendance may be explained later as the occasion arises.

The most important decisions have to do with the conduct of your courses. Block out a course outline for each of them. Set up your course objectives. Prepare your first lessons. It is very important that you appear to be well prepared and well organized in the first days of the courses. The impression you make on the students in the first days may make the difference between a successful and an unsuccessful year.

For this reason try to make sure your classroom is well organized. Try to make it as attractive as possible. Set up work and seating arrangements, bulletin boards, display areas, and so on. Decorate the room. Obtain your supplies, equipment, and materials of instruction. Check them for adequacy. Are there enough, are they in good condition? Do they work? Organize and store them so that they are readily available and usable. Be sure that all the forms, gradebooks, passes, tardy slips, paper, and the like are readily available and ready for use, and that any pertinent notices, rules, regulations, pictures, and so on have been posted.

On the First Day

Your first class should be impressive. It should demonstrate to the students that you are in charge—well organized, and well prepared.

Begin by starting the class on the stroke of the bell. Introduce yourself, and take care of the necessary administrative tasks. Then briefly introduce the course. Tell them what the course is about and what you hope to accomplish. Explain the rules and what you expect of the students. Start the course with some short, easy, academic activity. About a half minute before the end of the period stop for a short cleanup session. Then when you are ready, dismiss the class. Remember! *You* dismiss the class; the bell does not. The students should understand this from the very first day.

Sometime in the first class you should present and explain the rules (which you have already written out and posted). Be sure the students understand them and understand the reasons for them. After the class has progressed a few weeks, you may wish to have the students review the rules and to participate in their adjustment, but the time for such student participation is not during the first class. Rather, on the first day teach them the

> If you were going to teach next September, what would you need to review and study? What could you do in the summer to make your work easier in the fall?
>
> Plan a first day for a course you may teach. What introductory activities would you try? How might you work in administrative tasks? What would you do to motivate the students?

rules just as though they were subject content to be learned. The success of your teaching depends in a large part on students' understanding and complying with the rules.[12]

If possible it helps if one can prepare a seating plan during the first period. One method is to write the students names on slips of paper before the period starts, or in a pinch let the students write their names on the slips. When they have chosen their seats (do not assign seats at the middle or high school level), call the roll and insert the slips in the appropriate slots in a pocket-type seating chart. (See Figure 5–3.) Then as soon as you possibly can, associate the names of the students with their faces. When the students know that you know who they are, it is much easier to establish rapport with them.

Begin the course with a lively, worthwhile lesson. At this point students are often in a mood to learn. They have hopes that the new course and new teacher may have something worthwhile for them. So your first lesson should be one of your best. If you can possibly do so, use an interesting experiment, a demonstration, an exciting story, an intriguing problem, or something equally appealing. Some teachers devote the first day to a discussion of what one might study in the course. Others introduce

[12] Edmund T. Emmers et al., *Organizing and Managing the Junior High Classroom* (Austin, TX: The Research and Development Center for Teacher Education, University of Texas, n.d.), pp. 75–84.

FIGURE 5–3
A Seating Chart.

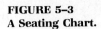

	Kiesman Walter		Costa Beverly	
Jones William	Regan Pauline	Martin John	Bassett Charlotte	Reynolds Barbara
Edgerton Ronald	McNeill Margaret	Williams Henry	Beyer George	Parsons Russell
Eastman Louise	Hill Caroline	Graves James	Faust Paul	MacArthur Carole
Wasserman Joseph	Swanson Kathleen	King Andrew	Bonham Robert	Bell Albert
Donahue Donald	Werbach Walter	Meehan Nancy	Armstrong Susan	Perry Lloyd

Room No. _____2_____   Period _____3rd_____

Teacher _____H. Lewis_____   Subject _____General Math._____

an interesting problem. Then, while their students search for the solution, the teacher records the book numbers and performs other necessary administrative duties. Another possibility is to conduct a review in the form of a game or a television quiz program.

The Second Day and Thereafter

Ordinarily you should start introducing your classroom routines and procedures on the second day of the course. Usually it is best to introduce these as they come up (e.g., if now is the time for students to pass in their papers, now is the time to explain the routine for handing in papers). Take time to explain thoroughly, but do not overdo it. Explanations that slow down class progress may be as bad as no explanation at all. In any case you

should plan the explanation and how you intend to put it across just as carefully as you would introduce important academic course content. Write out instructions for complicated standard procedures and pass them out or post them so that the students will have the instructions for reference. The point, of course, is to have the students learn the routines and procedures so that they will carry them out automatically as the class gets rolling along. For that reason you should review the procedures and routines from time to time until they become second nature.

You should also use the content activities as a medium for setting standards. Ordinarily it is best if the learning activities in the first few weeks are short, relatively easy, whole class activities at which the students can succeed. (Individualization, small group activities, and the like can come later.) Use these whole group activities to show the students what you expect of them, what the work procedures will be, and what you consider acceptable in addition to showing them that the course will be interesting, worthwhile, and important. These early activities should demonstrate to the students that you expect them to be productive and do well. They should also give the pupils opportunities to firm up their understanding of the rules and how they work.

In order to inculcate desirable habits, understandings, knowledge, and attitudes from the very first you must monitor, monitor, and monitor. First make sure that the students understand each assignment and have the tools necessary for completing it. Routinizing the procedure for giving assignments is very helpful. So is clarifying your standards for marking and grading. Then, check the students' work to be sure they really do understand what they are supposed to be doing and have the basic understandings necessary for doing it. At this stage you should provide feedback so that the students will know what they are doing correctly and what incorrectly. If students are acting inappropriately, correct them. Make sure they know why what they are doing wrong is wrong, and what they should do to make it right.

To carry out this monitoring move around the classroom to see what the students are doing. Learn to scan the class frequently for signs of misunderstanding, confusion, and other difficulties. Check the students' work often. If you can catch and correct mistakes, wrong procedures, misunderstandings, inappropriate behaviors, and misbehaviors before they develop into major problems, you will do much to smooth out the students' rocky road to learning.

In this connection it is essential to curb any misbehavior before it gets out of hand. Do not overreact, however. If you take misbehavior in stride it probably will not become a big thing.

In sum, your teaching should be clear, logical, and smooth. Your lesson objectives should be set forth clearly. It may be helpful to list them on the chalkboard. The use of an advance organizer, a study guide, study questions, or a unit outline may help the students focus on the understandings or skills to be learned. Certainly your presentation should be clear and logical. Usually it helps to follow an outline. Presenting the outline on a transparency or the chalkboard ordinarily makes the presentation easier for students to follow. You can also make the presentation easier to follow by concentrating on one thought at a time. Finish each thought and nail it down before you move on to the next. To avoid confusion be sure to let the students know when you stop presenting one idea and start on the next one. Assure clarity of expression by using complete sentences, a vocabulary level appropriate to your students' sophistication, and uncomplicated sentence structure. Use plenty of examples to make things clear, repeat major points, be specific, speak directly to the students, and keep the content and examples as concrete and precise as feasible. In short, your lessons should be a smooth, orderly, direct sequence to the learnings that are your instructional objectives.[13] You should always be in charge and the students should always be aware of their tasks and doing them.

To accomplish this you should not only monitor your students, you must monitor yourself. Unless you carefully carry out your classroom management duties, all else may be for naught.

Building Self-discipline

A major goal of effective classroom management is student self-discipline. Self-discipline is a necessity for success in one's studies and in later life; however, it does not come naturally. It must be learned and learning it takes time. You should con-

---

[13] Kounin, op. cit., pp. 111–112.

sciously try to help students develop self-discipline, but in doing so you should expect to proceed slowly. In doing so you should help students learn the importance of accepting responsibility for working diligently, for being dependable, and for carrying out what they have agreed to do. This can be done by running well-organized, efficient classes in which students learn what appropriate behavior is and that behaving appropriately is rewarded. Depend on the reasonableness and workability of your standards rather than on authority alone. Without preaching, show youths how many people make their lives more satisfying by following good codes. Also let the students know how teachers and other people feel about proper conduct. In this way you may be able to convince students that these standards will make life better for them and induce them to adopt suitable patterns of behavior voluntarily.

Summary

Classroom management refers to the process of organizing and carrying out classes so that learning occurs smoothly and efficiently. Its major purpose is to focus classes on learning. The attainment of this purpose is dependent on the establishment of a suitable classroom climate. For this reason you should strive to treat students fairly, reasonably, and pleasantly. It will help if you do not take yourself too seriously and try by your own actions to exemplify the type of behavior you expect of students. Creating a diffusely structured class will facilitate the type of classroom climate you need.

To organize classroom management requires careful planning. You must arrange a physical setting for learning, set up suitable routines, and establish a few carefully chosen rules. Managing the class is largely dependent on getting off to a good start, and then keeping the class moving smoothly. To do this you need to develop skill in movement management and "withitness." Perhaps most important is checking on both your own and the students' work and behavior. Specifically you should concentrate on becoming well prepared before the first day of school starts. Then on the first day you should conduct an interesting, well-organized class to set the tone for the course. After that you should take care to keep things rolling smoothly. Introduce routines and procedures as necessary. Take care of details. Be sure students understand what is expected of them. And, finally, monitor, monitor, monitor! If in the process you can teach the students to discipline themselves, your classroom management will prosper. Developing self-discipline is a slow process, but one that is essential for good learning.

Additional Reading

Duke, Daniel L., ed. *Classroom Management,* The Seventy-eighth Yearbook of the National Society for the Study of Education, Part II. Chicago: University of Chicago Press, 1979.

———. *Helping Teachers Manage Classrooms.* Alexandria, VA: Association for Supervision and Curriculum Development, 1982.

———, and Adrienne Maravich Mickel. *Teacher's Guide to Classroom Management.* New York: Random House, 1984.

Emmers, Edmund T. et. al. *Organizing and Managing the Junior High Classroom.* Austin, TX: The Research and Development Center for Teacher Education, The University of Texas, n.d.

Harvey, Karen. *Classroom Management.* Glenview, IL: Scott Foresman, 1985.

Laslett, Robert, and Colin Smith. *Effective Classroom Management.* New York: Nichols Publishing, 1984.

Lemlech, J. D. *Classroom Management.* New York: Harper & Row, 1979.

Orlich, Donald C. et al. *Teaching Strategies: A Guide to Better Instruction,* 2nd ed. Lexington, MA: D. C. Heath, 1985, Chap. 10.

Wallen, Carl J., and LaDonna L. Wallen. *Effective Classroom Management.* Boston: Allyn and Bacon, 1978.

Weber, Wilford A., et al. *Classroom Management: Reviews of the Teacher Education and Research Literature.* Princeton, NJ: Educational Testing Service, 1983.

6

Discipline

Overview

In this chapter we discuss ways of establishing and maintaining classroom discipline. Modern school discipline is democratic discipline, not dictatorship. In classrooms the law requires you to treat students as citizens, not subjects. However, you are expected to maintain reasonable control and discipline. In this endeavor you should depend largely on preventive measures and good classroom management. Rules must be enforced. To enforce them, accentuate the positive whenever possible. Use punishment sparingly, but consistently. Negative approaches such as harsh punishment, nagging, and verbal abuse do more harm than good. Minor disturbances should be kept minor. More serious incidents and major offenses require more drastic action. Fortunately in cases of emergency help is available in the "office." In dealing with chronically disruptive students your major responsibility is to teach—not to treat the students' mental, emotional, or social problems. However, talking out the problem and using such techniques as negative reenforcement, incompatible alternatives, and other behavior-modification techniques may reduce the students' misbehavior. In the following pages we discuss these matters in some detail.

109

Modern Discipline

In 1915 Ellwood P. Cubberly wrote:

> So long as boys are boys and girls are girls and teachers not perfect in training and insight teach, the problem of discipline will continually recur in the administration of our schools. In the whole field of school and classroom management probably no other school problem causes teachers and principals so much perplexity, and all kinds of devices have been tried with a view of minimizing the amount of trouble from this source.[1]

Today's notion of what constitutes a well-ordered class differs from that of yesteryear's. Modern thinking is quietly making totalitarian classrooms and martinet teachers obsolete. In today's ideal classroom, teachers are expected to emphasize courtesy, cooperation, and self-control. In classes both teachers and students alike ideally practice the freedoms of democracy. The students are supposedly free from fear, for they are citizens of the class, not subjects of the teacher. As citizens their job is to cooperate for the common good, to obey the laws of their classroom democracy and to respect and obey proper authority.

Reasonable Control

There are a number of reasons for this change of philosophy. First, dictatorship does not seem to pay off in long-range educational results. Secondly, it is out of tune with the times and modern theories of government. Thirdly, it does not square with the legal role of the teacher. Boys and girls, young men and women, are United States citizens. They do not shed their rights (nor their responsibilities) as citizens when they enter the school door.

The Supreme Court has been quite blunt about this fact. In the words of Mr. Justice Fortas,

> In our system, state-operated schools may not be enclaves of totalitarianism. School officials do not possess absolute authority over their students. Students in school as well as out of school are "persons" under our Constitution. They are possessed of fundamental rights which the State must respect, just as they themselves must respect their obligations to the State.[2]

The courts, however, strongly support teachers and the teaching profession in reasonable attempts to enforce reasonable rules and to provide a reasonable climate for education in our schools. The key word in dealing with discipline and control from the legal, and probably any other standpoint, is "reasonable." If teachers make it a point to become familiar with the laws and regulations applying to their school district and to carry out their responsibilities in a reasonable fashion in view of these laws and regulations, the courts will support them even in this litigious age. Every school should have a statement of it's rules and regulations printed in a student handbook which all students should be required to read. You should follow these rules faithfully.

Discipline and Mental Health

Some beginning teachers are under a misapprehension about discipline, permissiveness, and mental health. They are afraid that any thwarting of students' desires and impulses may ruin the students' mental health. Not so. In fact, strict control in itself can be a virtue leading to the development of worthwhile learning for the future and desirable behavior in the present. An orderly no-nonsense atmosphere is probably more healthful than a laissez-faire, overpermissive atmosphere. Teachers may not hide behind the shibboleths of permissive-

---

[1] Ellwood P. Cubberly, "Editor's Introduction," in Arthur C. Perry, Jr., *Discipline As a School Problem* (Boston: Houghton-Mifflin, 1915), p. 1.

[2] *Tinker* vs. *Des Moines Independent Community School District* 309 U. S. 508–9 (1969).

ness and mental health. Classes should be permissive only to the extent that they are supportive. The mental health of the students will be fostered best in an orderly, democratic class. Your job is to create, enforce, and teach discipline. Discipline comes with the territory. You cannot avoid it. You must set up and enforce rules. You must make your classes orderly and distraction free. You must induce students to work diligently on appropriate tasks.

Much has been written and will continue to be written about control and discipline, and most of it will be disappointing to the neophyte. The truth of the matter is that no one can tell anyone what techniques to use for any particular situation. We can, however, share some general principles and a few specific techniques which may give some overall help.

> What is good discipline? How can you tell a well-ordered classroom?
> How much freedom should there be in a classroom?

Disciplinary Techniques

Preventive Discipline

Seldom is any misbehavior the result of a single motive. Rather it is the result of the confluence of many factors triggered by some immediate happenstance. According to Feldhusen

> . . . it is clear that the causes of disciplinary problems, violence, and delinquency in high schools are multifarious. They include weakened home and family structure, the heavy dose of crime and violence modeled by TV, school experiences that precipitate a failure-frustration-aggression sequence, and school and societal conditions that make it easy and rewarding

for youth to engage in violence and crime as an effective mechanism for adaptation or coping.[3]

In addition, much student restlessness in class may be related to a simple need to work off energy and to the problems inherent in finding and adjusting to adolescents' new roles in society aggravated by poor curricula and methods of teaching.

What you can do to alleviate the problems caused by society and the advent of adolescence is minimal, but you can and should take steps to prevent your teaching and your classes from being the cause of discipline problems. You can do so by focusing on preventive discipline in your planning and teaching.

First, try to make sure that you yourself are not part of the problem. Some teachers act as though they want to create misbehavior. They are martinets, bullies, inefficient incompetents, or bores. They come to class late or start class late. They waste time. (Did you ever think of how much time students spend just waiting?) Their work habits are sloppy, and so is their class organization. They abuse their students by being sarcastic, calling them names, making fun of them and their mistakes, giving them injudicious tongue lashings, and generally treating them like dirt. Other teachers are unconsciously discourteous, brusque, and unsympathetic. They are unfair and inconsistent in their demands. Some act as though they disliked students. It is difficult to get cooperation from people who feel you dislike them.

Second, try to make sure that your classes are not part of the problem. Often the curriculum and teaching methods cause problems. Lesson planning is the key to good teaching. Yet many teachers never seem to plan well. Their classes never seem to go anywhere because they have no real objective. There are no provisions for motivating the students.

---

[3] John Feldhusen, "Problems of Student Behavior in Secondary Schools" in Daniel L. Duke, ed., *Classroom Management*, The Seventy-eighth Yearbook of the National Society for the Study of Education, Part II (Chicago: University of Chicago Press, 1979), p. 229.

> Think back over the classes you have attended in which there have been disciplinary incidents. What seemed to be the cause? What were the causes of disciplinary incidents involving you or your friends when you were in secondary school?
>
> Why do students misbehave? List all the possible causes for misbehavior that you can name. How might knowledge of the causes of misbehavior influence the teacher's action?
>
> Many (some say most) behavior problems are teacher-created. Can you think of some examples? How can the teacher avoid creating such situations?

There is no variety; every day the classes repeat the same monotonous grind. Boring classes are always invitations to misbehavior. Sometimes the classes contain dead spots in which students have really nothing to do. The assignments are vague; students are not sure what they are supposed to do and how they are supposed to do it. Such assignments are frustrating. Also frustrating are lessons that are too hard or too easy, too fast or too slow.

Third, teach students how to behave. Discipline must be taught. It does not come naturally. Teaching discipline is "the most basic of the basics."[4] The steps in this process are,

1. Establish self-discipline in yourself.
2. See to it that students know what is expected of them and why.
3. See to it that the students live up to these expectations. (In the realm of school behavior, as in other areas, practice tends to make perfect.)

As you can see these steps are simply those of good classroom management. Other techniques for

---

[4] William W. Wayson et al., Phi Delta Kappa Commission on Discipline. *Handbook for Developing Schools with Good Discipline* (Bloomington, IN: Phi Delta Kappa, 1982).

"teaching" discipline are discussed in the section on behavior modification.

Enforcing Rules

Classroom rules must be enforced. The students should have no doubt that these rules are operative and that breaking them will not be countenanced and that living up to them pays off in some worthwhile reward. Laxity in the enforcement of rules makes them worthless. The students lose respect for them and resent subsequent attempts to enforce them. By your enforcement of the rules, you quickly establish what behavior you will accept and what you will not tolerate. Although it is possible to be too rigid, one characteristic of the teacher with good control is consistent enforcement of the class rules. Boys and girls like to know where they stand. The teacher whose rules are sacrosanct today and of no importance tomorrow is anathema to them. Also, since getting away with mischief may be possible, the students will be tempted to try their luck.

In this connection firmness pays off because of its "ripple effect." The way you handle one case of misbehavior has considerable effect on other students who see or hear of the incident. Thus if students find that you are consistently firm in the handling of a few cases initially, they will assume that you are strict and will act accordingly. The ripple effect is particularly strong when high-status students are involved. Consequently you should work hard to control these students. If the high-status students are brought into line, the other students will follow along. Obviously the ripple effect can make a great difference in your relationship with students. If students find you to be fair, just, pleasant, and empathetic in your dealings with others they will tend to respond to you in the same way.

Along with consistency goes fairness. Teachers should treat all students alike. Any teacher who has favorites or who treats some students preferentially may be creating behavior problems. Playing favorites will lose you the respect of your students and create dislike in the students not so favored. This, of course, does not mean that you should never make an exception to a rule. As long as students have different personalities, they must be treated differently from one another. For instance, the punishment that one student might find devastating another might take as a lark. To this extent the punishment must suit the offender. Nevertheless, the enforcement of the rules must remain consistent even if the means of enforcement may vary. Exceptions should be made only for extraordinarily good reasons. It helps considerably if the reasons and their merits are evident to the class as a whole. Otherwise the students may accuse the teacher of favoritism and unfairness.

Avoiding Poor Enforcement Techniques

Especially guard against nagging, for it disturbs the lesson and may cause additional student misbehavior. At times you would do better to disregard minor infractions than to attempt ceaselessly to correct the students. Criticizing or scolding a student too much will result only in arousing the support and sympathy of the other students. Besides, it slows down the lesson.

Instead of scolding, try the basic technique of Teacher Effectiveness Training.

Start describing BEHAVIOR instead of judging, evaluating, or making inferences about it. Want to transform your classes Monday morning? Then stop telling students what is going on in terms of assumptions you have made ABOUT their behavior. Start telling them what you see, what you hear . . . without blame, judgment or evaluation. A student who is late to class is not irresponsible, he or she is LATE TO CLASS. Get it? A kid can deal with being late to class. Irresponsibility is tough. Besides that, you have ABSOLUTELY NO IDEA WHETHER THE KID IS IRRESPONSIBLE OR NOT. The only thing you know is that here is a kid coming in after the class has begun.

When you get used to doing that, you are well on your way to being ready to take the next step, defining conflicts (continuing unacceptable student behavior)

not as fights to be won or lost, but as problems to be solved.

The key to doing this is to define the conflict in terms of unmet needs. If a kid is behaving in an unacceptable way, some need of yours as the teacher must be unmet. You have a right to get your teacher (read human) needs met. But that unacceptable behavior! What is that about? Well, it is about the kid's way of getting some need of his or hers met. Once you get it that there is no such thing as "good" or "bad" behavior, just behavior, then you can begin to find all sorts of ways to see that both you *and* the kid get your respective needs met. This way you both win. Therefore, there is no need for either you or the kid to form coping mechanisms to handle each other.[5]

Nagging often results from insistence on unnecessarily high standards of student behavior and from poor organization of classes. If you find it necessary to keep admonishing a student, you should check to see whether the student has something worthwhile and appropriate to do. Sometimes a good remedy is to direct a question to the youth whose mind seems to be wandering or to start the restless student off on a new activity. Often just a reproving glance, a gesture, or moving in the direction of an incipient behavior problem will bring the potential culprit back in line before anything really untoward has had a chance to happen. Such techniques distract youths from mischief. The teacher who keeps alert can often head off cases of misbehavior before they start. This is what Kounin means by "withitness."

Besides nagging, other poor methods of enforcing rules also cause misconduct. Harsh punishment, for example, often brings about resentment and revolt. In spite of the number of people who believe in force as the supreme disciplinary agent, harshness has never been really successful. According to Quintilian, the great Roman teacher, harsh punishment did not work in ancient Rome. It still

---

[5] Noel Burch, "What You Already Know About Discipline," *NJEA Review* (October, 1978), **52**:22. Reprinted with permission from the October 1978 (Vol 52, p. 22) *NJEA Review,* copyright New Jersey Education Association.

doesn't, according to modern researchers. As we pointed out earlier, it may make students hate their studies and often causes them to rebel or to stop trying. Besides, it may lead to more trouble because of the resentment it builds up. A good teacher can do better without it.

When enforcing rules, try to avoid making big scenes out of insignificant acts. To do so is utterly pointless. Most little things can be brushed off lightly. Often a look or a pleasant word will suffice. Teachers who make major issues of minor transgressions soon find that they do not remain minor. It is better to save your fire for something important. You should also shun threats and ultimatums. These create scenes and, if a student misbehaves, fetter your course of action, since you must carry out your threats if you are to keep the students' respect.

Punishment

Sooner or later, no matter how sensible the rules and how careful the planning, some student will commit an offense for which he must be punished. The Mikado probably meant well when he sang

My object all sublime
I shall achieve in time—
To let the punishment fit the crime—
The punishment fit the crime;
And make each prisoner pent
Unwillingly represent
A source of innocent merriment,
Of innocent merriment![6]

But his scheme would not have worked well. Punishment should never be used as a source of "innocent merriment." But it should be appropriate and, whenever possible, constructive. If a student smashes a window willfully or carelessly, that student should clean up the mess and make proper restitution for it. In general, if your punishment

---

[6] W. S. Gilbert and Arthur Sullivan, *The Mikado*, Act II.

is the logical result of misconduct, students are likely to accept it without resentment and may learn not to offend in the same way again. For that matter, any punishment is more likely to be effective when students see its reasonableness.

You should use punishment sparingly because its overuse creates the repressive atmosphere you should avoid. Furthermore, overusing punishment takes the force out of it. Sometimes it causes lying, cheating, truancy, and rebellious behavior. Punishment should be held as a reserve for specific important offenses. It should never be used as a general disciplinary measure. If you commit your reserves too soon, or too often, or on too wide a front, you will find yourself with nothing to fall back on in real crises. Rewarding alternative behavior and negative reinforcement are much more useful techniques.

When you do use punishment, it should be swift, sure, and impressive. Never punish on impulse; think twice before you act; but act at once. Should you become emotional, however, it would be wise to calm down before prescribing the punishment, for punishing students in anger can be disastrous. It requires a cool head to ascertain without the shadow of a doubt that one has correctly identified the guilty one and to select a punishment appropriate for both the offense and the offender. To make punishment effective, combine it with positive measures. It is important to be sure that the students know just what behavior is expected from them. Positive reinforcement techniques, modeling, and direct instruction in how to behave will give point to the punishment and lead to the behavior desired when punishment alone will not.

A Word About Corporal Punishment. Some teachers, clergymen, and newspaper editors blame all the ills of modern civilization on the schools because they no longer beat out the tune with a hickory stick. That anyone should have so much faith in corporal punishment is astonishing in view of its centuries-long history of little success. David Ausubel, for instance, found that behavior in "Spare the rod, spoil the child" New Zealand schools was no better than in American schools.[7]

It is almost always wiser to use some other method in punishing secondary school students. Students of this age are too nearly grown up for corporal punishment. High school girls are young ladies and fall under the taboo against striking women. High school boys are young men who may not accept such punishment graciously. Under no circumstances should you ever use corporal punishment except in a formal situation with suitable witnesses according to the laws of your state and school district. Otherwise you may lay yourself open to accusations and legal difficulties. All in all, if such drastic measures as corporal punishment must ever be used, discretion tells us to turn the matter over to the principal. Never ever use it yourself.

Detention. Detention, or staying after school, is one of the most frequently used punishments. In general, there are two types of detention periods. One is the sort common in large schools in which the students must report to a detention hall. The other is a do-it-yourself arrangement whereby each teacher looks after his own detainees. In spite of its widespread use, detention is not very effective. Further, detention periods are a waste of time unless they are used constructively. Their force as a deterrent is not strong enough to warrant keeping the student sitting doing nothing. When one uses detention it would be better to combine it with a conference or some educationally valuable activity.

Verbal Punishment. The reprimand is probably the commonest and most poorly used kind of punishment. Like many other measures its effect soon dissipates when it is overused. Then it becomes mere nagging, the futility of which we have already discussed. Loud, frequent reprimands are ineffec-

tive. They only add to the turmoil. Calm, firm reprimands are much more effective. As a rule, reprimands should be given in private. Frequent public reprimands tend to reinforce misbehavior. The class may either sympathize with the student being reprimanded or make him a folk hero. However a quiet, calm, firm reprimand describing the fault given when needed by a teacher who is fair and gives plenty of honest praise for what the student does well, will be effective and have no deleterious side effects. From time to time, however, a whole class may need to be told the hard facts of life. Whenever such explanations are in order, they should be businesslike and matter-of-fact. It is not a time for emotionalism.

Sarcasm and ridicule are two other common types of verbal punishments. Although in faculty lounges one is likely to be regaled with stories of the Mr. Chips type who ruled his classes with a tongue of acid and so endeared himself to the hearts of generations of students, on the whole, such weapons should not be used. They hurt people's feelings, cause resentment, destroy students' self-esteem, and in general break down the classroom atmosphere. Avoid them.

Isolation. Changing seats to break up seating arrangements that permit cliques and friends too much opportunity for social visiting is a common practice. This procedure has much to recommend it as long as the teacher does not create a situation in which the students who formerly whispered to each other now shout and pass notes. Another similar plan is to change the seat of a chronic offender so that he is isolated from the rest of the class all alone somewhere in the back of the room. Other teachers like to put their behavior problems up front in the first row next to the teacher's desk or podium. Placing the student up front may be objectionable for two reasons: (1) It places the student where he is assured of an audience if he wants to show off, and (2) it seems to assume that the teacher will work entirely from his desk at the front of the room, a practice not generally recommended.

---

[7] David P. Ausubel, "A New Look at Classroom Discipline," *Phi Delta Kappan* (October, 1961), **43**:25–30.

In the case of an extraordinarily bad incident one can send the student out of the classroom. One should do this sparingly—only when faced with a major problem with which, for one reason or another, one cannot cope at the time.

Assigning Extra Work.   At one time the most common method of punishing secondary school students was to assign them a number of lines of Latin verse to translate. Today the assignment of extra work continues to be a common punishment, but really it is a silly practice. Associating schoolwork with punishment creates a prejudice against the subjects in the minds of the students. If you want to create dislike for the subject you teach, this is the way to do it. However, there should be no objection to making students redo sloppy work again and again—in fact, the teacher who accepts papers that have been carelessly prepared encourages poor work habits. Likewise, there should be no objection to keeping students busy at class assignments during detention periods.

Deprivation of Privileges.   One of the few punishments that seems to be both effective and acceptable to experts in pedagogy is to take away privileges from students who misbehave. In general, this practice is a good one. Unfortunately all too many students do not have many privileges the loss of which would greatly concern them. In poor schools and for chronic offenders it may carry no weight at all. One can capitalize on this type of punishment by combining it with a system in which the teacher rewards good behavior by granting the students desirable privileges.

Deducting from Academic Marks.   Punishing students by lowering their marks in the course is a tempting technique which should be avoided. Academic marks, if they are to have any validity at all, must be based upon students' achievement. To lower course marks because of misbehavior is unfair to the students, their parents, and prospec-

Why should the teacher avoid use of the following?

> sarcasm
> threats
> nagging
> yelling
> constant vocal correction
> arguments with students
> corporal punishment

Are any of the above ever permissible? If so, when? Justify your reply.

What techniques do you propose to use to enforce your rules?

tive employers or college admission officers. Under no circumstances can such punishments be tolerated.

Positive Approaches

After reading such a devastating description of the punishments at your disposal, you may be somewhat discouraged. Is there nothing that can be done? Yes, of course there is. The answer lies almost entirely in preventive approaches and positive corrective measures.

Using positive measures is not only productive, but relatively easy if you establish the rules and standards, rewards, and penalties in advance. Think of rule enforcement as a way of teaching students to behave properly rather than as retribution for academic crimes. In the long run it will probably be more effective to pay more attention to rewards than to penalties. Try to recognize every individual who does something well. Display their good work or congratulate them on their successes, for instance. Take care to spread rewards and praise to all the deserving—not just the brightest. Every student does something worth recognizing at one time or another.

Dealing with Minor Disturbances

On occasion minor disciplinary problems will arise. Often they are not really anyone's fault, but rather the result of human boys and girls being herded together in schools and classes. Often, if the behavior is not outrageous or dangerous, it may be wise to simply ignore it. Almost always, however, you must take some action. If students are noisy, merely asking for quiet and moving on to the next item may be all that is necessary. If a student is distracting other students' attention, simply standing next to him may quiet him down. Finding other work for troublemakers so as to get them out of the public view may solve the problem. Actually many disciplinary situations may be avoided if you talk out problems with the students concerned and have the class help you draw up rules for procedures and standards of behavior that they accept as fair and reasonable, before the incidents happen.

When Chaos Threatens

Sometimes classes get out of control, or threaten to. Then you must do something fast. Steps that teachers take in such situations may not always be helpful in the long run. But if they quell the immediate incipient or actual disturbance, they are worthwhile. The late Edward T. Ladd suggested the following tactics for such emergencies.

1. Find a means to catch the attention of the majority of the children, shouting if—but only if—you must.

2. Aim for two things, in this order: everyone in a seat, or standing still and looking at you; and everyone essentially quiet. Keep working insistently but calmly to achieve these two things, even though it seems to take an hour.

3. If things don't go as you would like, try cajoling, giving very specific instructions, and calling on individuals ("You in the red sweater, please come over here now and sit down.").

4. If chaos persists, show slight impatience or slight irritation, but no more.

5. Don't say anything unfriendly or humiliating to anyone.

6. Try to avoid threats; if you feel you must threaten, make your threat ambiguous ("I'd hate to have to get anyone into trouble," "None of you wants to be punished, do you?" or "See me after school.").

7. Whatever happens, don't blow your cool. If you feel panicky, just freeze; say nothing for a while.

8. If a situation gets dangerous, seek help.

9. Be ready to move into the next phase—acting affirmatively—as soon as you can.[8]

Sending Students to the Office

Sometimes behavior is of the sort that makes it necessary for the teacher to send the miscreant to the office. As a general rule, principals and vice-principals are not overjoyed by the visits of these young people. A certain vice-principal was discussing an important matter with a visitor when a surly faced girl of fifteen arrived in his office with a note from her teacher. He looked at it and then sent her into an outer office to wait. As soon as she had left he exclaimed to his guest, "Now what am I supposed to do with her? I don't mind having them come up here once in a while, but you'd think that woman could handle some of her own discipline!"

Take the responsibility for your own discipline. Sending the student to the office should be reserved for really serious offenses. Principals and assistant principals are not in a good position to deal with routine cases. They are handicapped by not knowing exactly what has happened, and their special disciplinary powers are best suited for dealing with

---

[8] Adapted from Edward T. Ladd (with John C. Walden), *Student Rights and Discipline* (Arlington, VA: National Association of Elementary School Principals, 1975), pp. 47–48.

major offenses. Sometimes their sympathies may lie with the student. Furthermore, sending the student to the office may be taken as a sign of weakness and lower your prestige among the students. Doubtless there will be crises when you must cast students into outer darkness, but these occasions should be kept to a minimum. If you handle your own discipline problems, you will usually rise in the esteem of your students and of your principal as well.

In spite of these warnings, do not hesitate to send bad actors to the office for correction when it is necessary—for example, when dealing with the students would disrupt or interfere with the progress of the class lesson, or when the offense is beyond the scope of your power and authority. In no case should the misbehavior of one student be allowed to break up a class.

When sending students out of class be sure to inform them just where they are to go and what they are supposed to do, and also to inform the official to whom the students report just exactly why the students are coming, either by a note or by the intercommunications system.

Dealing with Major Offenses

Occasionally you may be faced with a major offense. Carrying weapons, stealing, use of drugs, arson, vandalism, defiance, and leaving the room without authorization are examples of such offenses. Your major responsibility in such cases is to try to stop the behavior and see to it that it does not occur again. This is not always possible, of course. If the case is really serious, you should report it to the principal immediately. Administrative personnel have greater resources at their disposal than you do. Besides, they are responsible for major problems. Further, it helps them to know of these problems before they are confronted by irate parents, concerned central administrative personnel, or the police. If an incident merits calling in the police, it is the principal's job to do so.

Helping the Students with Problems

Every school has difficult students who for some reason or other do not seem able to adapt to the school program. This inability to adjust to a school situation may be caused by problems at home, the social environment in the community, or personality defects. Frequently such students seek release from their problems in undesirable ways.

Teachers are usually well aware of the obstreperous student. However, a behavior problem that is fully as dangerous is presented by the quiet, withdrawn student. Such students often develop severe emotional problems. These students need to be helped. They should be treated with sympathy and understanding. In most cases, they should be referred to guidance counselors for help. In the meantime you should try to find out as much as possible about these students and treat them accordingly.

Direct Instruction

In some school systems the most difficult cases are removed from the regular classes to attend alternative schools or in-house suspensions. In most systems you will be expected to carry on on your own. When you must do the job yourself, you should focus on attempting to improve the overt behavior of the student rather than finding and correcting the underlying causes. After all, your job is to teach; you cannot allow one student, even a student with problems, to upset the entire class. Besides, you are not trained to treat mental or emotional problems. Even if you could identify the underlying problems, you are not in a position to do anything about them, and if you were, the behavior might continue to exist after the causes have been treated. (They often continue after the student returns from the specialist.) So there is little you can do except to deal directly with the behavior. Fortunately, direct instruction in how to behave using the motivational and disciplinary techniques at your command can and frequently does change misbehavior to acceptable behavior. There is no excuse for allowing students to continue to misbehave just because they have problems.

Special Techniques

Psychologists of the behavioristic persuasion recommend the following principles to help correct the undesirable behavior of individuals. These principles are:

1. Satiation: Forcing the miscreant to continue the misbehavior until he gets sick of it.
2. Extinction: Arranging it so that the student gets no reward for misbehavior.
3. Incompatible Alternative: Rewarding behavior incompatible with bad behavior.
4. Negative Reenforcement: Setting up an aversive situation that the student can end only by improving his behavior.
5. Punishment: Making the misbehavior yield a result so distasteful or unpleasant that the miscreant will not behave in that fashion again. (This fifth method may be considered a form of negative reinforcement.)

Only occasionally can one use the satiation principle in middle and secondary schools. Although there may be occasions when one can force a student to continue a misbehavior to the point at which he never wants to do it again, such opportunities are rare. Extinction is also difficult to use in middle and secondary schools, partly because the teacher does not always have full control of all the reinforcing agents. Nevertheless, as Clarizio wisely states, "The teacher, even though he might initially feel uncomfortable, will do a more adequate job of managing classroom behavior if he can learn to avoid responding to certain misbehavior. Remember that teacher disapproval can strengthen deviant behavior, whereas ignoring it

can weaken such behavior by removing the payoff. The student has to learn that unacceptable behavior is worth nothing.[9] The incompatible alternative principle can be useful. The idea is to set up a desirable alternative behavior which would result in a reward so great that the student would choose it above the misbehavior. To be effective, the reward for the alternative behavior must be really powerful—powerful enough to offset the reward gained from the deviant behavior.

The negative reinforcement principle consists of setting up a mildly aversive situation which you terminate as soon as the student's behavior improves. Thus every time the student misbehaves he gets into trouble which ceases as soon as he starts behaving. The difference between negative reinforcement and punishment is that in negative reinforcement the aversive situation ends just as soon as the student's behavior improves. Thus it is more effective than punishment. Sometimes punishment is necessary, however, to shock students into trying the alternative behavior.[10]

Reality Therapy

Recently there have been several training programs designed to reduce and correct misbehavior. One is the Teacher Effectiveness program mentioned earlier. Another is the Reality Therapy program recommended by William Glasser. Glasser's ten-step approach to good discipline is:

1. Choose a student who is a discipline problem (but not a hopeless one). List what you are doing to cope with the student's disruptions.
2. Analyze the list. Are these measures working? If not, discard them.
3. "Plan a better tomorrow for your student." Do something that says "you are special, I care for you," e.g., send the student on a special errand.

---

[9] Harvey F. Clarizio, *Toward Positive Classroom Discipline* (New York: Wiley, 1971), p. 65.
[10] Ibid., pp. 182–186.

By treating disrupters well you influence them to better behavior.

4. When the student is disruptive, ask "What are you doing?" Then ask the student to please stop it.

5. If problem incidents continue, carry out a short conference. Ask, "What are you doing?" Next ask, "Is it against the rules?" Then ask, "What should you be doing?" The implication being that you expect the student to start doing what is proper.

6. If the short conferences do not work, repeat step 5 but instead of asking "What should you be doing?" say, "We have to work this out. What kind of plan can you make to follow out the rules?" The result should be a short-term, specific, simple plan worked out by the two of you, but acceptable to the student. The more the plan is the student's, the better.

7. If disruptions continue, isolate the student by placing him somewhere away from the rest of the class and barring him from participation in any class activities until he is ready to reform.

8. 9. 10. If disruptive behavior continues, administrative authority must be called in to carry out step 8, in-school suspension; step 9, out-of-school suspension and showdown with parents; and step 10, permanent exclusion from the school.[11]

Life-Space Interview

Another somewhat similar approach is the life-space interview as worked out by William C. Morse. The steps in life-space interviewing are:

1. In a non-threatening way, ask the pupil to tell what happened. The purpose of this first step is two-fold: to find out the pupil's own perceptions of the event and to be an empathetic listener so that trust is established. (If more than one pupil is involved, attention must be given to balanced listening.)

2. Try to determine if the problem is really the central issue. Are there other related problems? As we have seen, learning problems often lie at the heart of behavior problems. Some pupils are so confused and frustrated about their work that they strike out in anger through fighting and hitting.

3. Ask the pupil "Well, what do you think should be done about this?" Often, the pupil will make a self-commitment for change. Some pupils will suggest that they make restitution for destruction that they have caused. As Morse points out, reasonable discussion, in which the factors bearing on the problem are brought into the open, often leads to resolution of the problem at this stage. If not, the teacher must go on to step four.

4. Discuss the realities of what will happen should the behavior continue. Here it is imperative that the teacher know the policies and resources of his or her school. One does not, for example, say to the pupil that he will be suspended if no one is ever suspended from that school.

5. Elicit from the pupil how the pupil thinks she might be helped and what the teacher might be able to do to help the pupil control the behavior impulse in question.

6. Develop a follow-through plan with the pupil. What will we have to do if this happens again? The point made in step 4 must be repeated here: any plan must be conceived within the limitations of school resources.[12]

Such an approach tends to redirect behavior to more desirable channels. Other techniques that tend to redirect student behavior are reinforcing the positive and giving students opportunities for positive socialization, such as helping young children, participating in text selection, teaching minicourses, producing plays, working with senior citizens and various types of action learning, and learning in the community activities.

[11] William Glasser, "10 Steps to Discipline," *Today's Education* (November–December, 1977), **66**:60–63.

[12] William C. Morse, "Working Paper: Training Teachers in Life Space Interviewing." *American Journal of Orthopsychiatry* (July, 1963), **33**:727–730. Quoted by Laurel N. Tanner, *Classroom Discipline for Effective Teaching and Learning* (New York: Holt, 1978), p. 168.

Criticize the following rules for discipline:

1. Watch carefully for the first small signs of trouble and squelch them at once *with no exceptions.*
2. Hold your group to very high standards at first. You can relax later if the situation warrants it.
3. Be a real friend to the children.
4. Employ self-government only if you are sure the class is ready for it.
5. Be fair.
6. Be consistent.

Criticize the following practice reported by a national wire service: "The Boston School Committee recently directed that the following commandments be read bi-weekly to students in grades 7 through 12.

1. Don't let your parents down; they've brought you up.
2. Be smart, obey. You'll give orders yourself some day.
3. Stop and think before you drink.
4. Ditch dirty thoughts fast or they'll ditch you.
5. Show-off driving is juvenile. Don't act your age.
6. Pick the right friends to be picked for a friend.
7. Choose a date fit for a mate.
8. Don't go steady unless you're ready.
9. Love God and neighbor.
10. Live carefully. The soul you save may be your own."

What can you do about the student whose behavior problems arise from the home? From emotional difficulties? From social problems?

Think back to your high school days. Try to picture the teacher who had the most trouble with discipline and the teacher who had the least difficulty. What was it about those teachers that made the difference in their relations with students?

The No Lose Method

In his Teacher Effectiveness Training (TET) approach Gordon recommends what he calls the "No Lose Method of Resolving Conflicts." This method utilizes the six-step Deweyan problem-solving process to resolve conflicts between individuals and groups. These steps are

1. Defining the problem.
2. Generating possible solutions.
3. Evaluating the solutions.
4. Deciding which solution is best.
5. Determining how to implement the solution.
6. Assessing how well the solution solved the problem.

The problems are, according to Gordon, of three types: student owned problems, i.e., problems that frustrate the student's needs; teacher owned problems, i.e., problems that frustrate the teacher's needs; and shared problems, i.e., problems in which teachers and students are frustrating each other's needs. The method makes considerable use of active listening and "I messages" by the teacher. The idea is that if the student owns the problem, the teacher should listen carefully to the student, and try to understand the student's point of view. In this process the teacher should also listen for the student's feelings and reflect them back to the student so that the student will know that the teacher knows and understands both the point of view and the feeling. If the teacher owns the problem, the teacher should let the student know what the teacher's problem (i.e., the student's misbehavior) is and how the teacher feels about it. If the process works, the student will realize what the misbehavior is, what harm it does, and how it affects the teacher without raising anger or blame.[13]

---

[13] Thomas Gordon, *T.E.T. Teacher Effectiveness Training* (New York: David McKay Company, 1974), Chap. VIII.

Summary

There are really two keys to good discipline. One is good motivation, the other is good classroom management. A well-managed class is ordinarily a well-disciplined class. So it would seem that the following rules that combine principles of motivation and classroom management should help any teacher achieve and maintain good classroom control.

Preventive Measures

Set a good example.
 Don't take yourself too seriously.
 Develop a sense of humor.
 Do as you would be done by.
 Be friendly, but not too friendly.
 Control your own temper.
 Let sleeping dogs lie: do not go looking for trouble. Expect good conduct.
 Remember, you are an authority figure. Act that way.

Stand on your own feet; assume the responsibility for your own classroom control.
 Take a personal interest in your students.
 Be businesslike.
 Assume everything will be all right.
 Act like an adult.

Develop good relationships with students.
 Promote democratic atmosphere.
 Respect students' feelings and feelings of self-esteem.
 Do not demean the students either by your rules or by your enforcement of them.
 Avoid laissez-faire techniques. Students need to know where they stand.
 Create a friendly atmosphere.

Get off to a good start.
 Start with a bang on the first day.
 Start each class at the stroke of the bell.
 Be strict at first.
 Learn students' names as quickly as you can.
 Prepare a seating plan.

Pay attention to classroom management.
 Be sure the materials and equipment are ready.
 Demand quiet before you speak.
 Adapt your techniques to the situation and the mood of the class.
 Utilize all means of support available.
 Set up routines for the more usual tasks such as passing out of papers, attendance, etc.

Plan classes well.
 Eliminate lags and dead spots.
 Provide for individual differences.
 Vary classroom activities.
 Make classes interesting.
 Make classes seem worthwhile.
 Help students feel important.
 Adjust teaching to students. Avoid too much student failure and frustration.
 Be sure your classes are relevant.
 Be sure everyone has plenty of worthwhile things to do.

Set up a few rules.
 Be sure the rules are reasonable—not too strict.
 Do not make the rules too rigid. Leave yourself room to maneuver.
 Be sure everyone understands the rules.
 Let students help make the rules.

Try to develop self-discipline.

Corrective Measures

Enforce the rules firmly, fairly and consistently.
 Don't make mountains out of molehills.
 Avoid scenes.
 Avoid ultimatums.
 Avoid threats.
 Do not nag.
 Take it easy. Don't get excited.
 Utilize the ripple effect.
 Be reasonable.
 Do not scold. Try describing behavior instead.
 Avoid harsh punishment.

Utilize positive approaches to correct and redirect behavior.

Utilize the incompatible alternative principle and negative reinforcement principle.

Utilize the life-space interview approach.

Utilize such techniques as those of reality therapy.

Try to redirect behavior via positive reinforcement and socialization techniques.

Punishment should be rare but, when necessary, swift and certain.

Never use sarcasm, ridicule, or harsh or humiliating punishments.

Never embarrass students.

Do not use corporal punishment—ever! If it must be used, let one of your superiors do it.

Don't punish the entire class for the faults of a few.

Be sure that your punishments are reasonable.

Use soft reprimands. Avoid shouting, scolding, and roughness.

Utilize isolation techniques with care.

Never assign schoolwork as a punishment.

Never use academic marks as punishment.

Utilize the help of specialists when necessary.

Refer serious cases of student problems to the guidance staff.

Refer really serious disciplinary cases to the principal or the assistant in charge of discipline.

Handle your own discipline problems. Call in the principal or assistant principal only in extraordinary circumstances.

Additional Reading

Alschuler, Alfred S. *School Discipline.* New York: McGraw-Hill, 1980.

Canter, Lee, and Marlene Canter. *Assertive Discipline: A Take Charge Approach for Today's Education.* Los Angeles, CA: Canter and Associates, 1979.

Charles, C. M. *Building Classroom Discipline.* New York: Longman, 1981.

Connors, Eugene T. *Student Discipline and the Law,* Fastback 121. Bloomington, IN: Phi Delta Kappa Educational Foundation, 1979.

Discipline in the Classroom, 2nd rev. ed. Washington, DC: National Education Association, 1980.

Duke, Daniel L. *Managing Student Behavior Problems.* New York: Teachers College Press, 1981.

Faust, Naomi F. *Discipline and the Classroom Teacher.* Port Washington, NY: Kennikat Press, 1977.

Gnagey, William J. *Motivating Classroom Discipline.* New York: Macmillan, 1981.

Kohut, Sylvester, Jr., and Dale D. Range. *Classroom Discipline: Case Studies and Viewpoints.* Washington, DC: National Education Association, 1979.

Ladd, Edward T. (with John C. Walden) *Student Rights and Discipline.* Arlington, VA: National Association of Elementary School Principals, 1975.

Madsen, Charles H., Jr., and Clifford K. Madsen. *Teaching Discipline.* Boston: Allyn and Bacon, 1974.

Mann, Lester. *Discipline and Behavioral Management.* Aspen, CO: Aspen Publications, 1983.

Sevich, Kevin J. *Disruptive Student Behavior in the Classroom.* Washington, DC: National Education Association, 1980.

Tanner, Laurel N. *Classroom Discipline for Effective Teaching and Learning.* New York: Holt, 1978.

Wayson, William W. et al. *Handbook for Developing Schools with Good Discipline,* Phi Delta Kappa Commission on Discipline. Bloomington, IN: Phi Delta Kappa, 1982.

Wolfgang, Charles H., and Carl D. Gluckman. *Solving Discipline Problems: Strategies for Teachers.* Boston: Allyn and Bacon, 1980.

7

Diagnosis

Overview

According to the model of teaching we set forth in Chapter 3, the first step in effective teaching is diagnosis. By diagnosis we mean the sizing up of a situation so as to understand it fully and to find clues for deciding what to do. Successful diagnosis tells you

1. what level of learning your students have reached;
2. where your students are weak and strong;

3. what your students' aptitudes, aspirations, backgrounds, problems, and needs are.

All these data are, of course, approximations. Yet they make it possible to understand the various factors that influence the teaching-learning situation you face. They put you in a position to capitalize on students' strengths and intrinsic motivation, to correct their deficiencies, to take advantage of the plusses in the situation and to avoid its pitfalls. They can give you a basis for placing students in the proper group, module, unit, section, course, curriculum or track, for selecting remedial procedures, for preventing and solving discipline problems, for adjusting assignments to individual needs, for stimulating interest and cooperation, and for adapting the level and pace of instruction as well as selecting course content and instructional strategies.

In short, diagnosis gives you the information necessary for intelligent teaching. Without it you will be teaching in the dark!

In this chapter, we introduce some procedures and instruments to use in the diagnosis process. We pay particular attention to standardized tests and diagnostic tests. We also consider the use of cumulative records, observation, analysis of classwork, and conversations with the students.

The Process of Diagnosis

Basically the process of diagnosis is to see what the situation is and what should be done next.

In teaching, diagnosis includes an assessment of the students' abilities and resources and your teaching resources in order to decide how best to conduct your instruction.

Although our model of teaching treats diagnosis as the first of five steps, diagnosis is really a continuous process of evaluation and assessment. In order to establish a firm basis for your teaching, you should make a general diagnosis of the status of each student's learning and associated traits as early as you can and continue with similar diagnoses as the course goes on. In fact, the evaluation phase of each succeeding unit should become, in effect, the diagnosis phase for the next one. (The planning and teaching of the next unit thus becomes the follow-up phase of the preceding one.) In effect, then, in any course or sequence, one would expect to find an initial diagnosis at the beginning of a course or sequence and then continuing diagnosis and reassessment as the course, or sequence, proceeds. In any case, as we see it, the

process for both initial and continuing diagnosis should conform to a pattern something like the following.

1. Assess the situation.
2. Determine if there is any difficulty.
3. In case there is a difficulty,
   a. Identify just what the difficulty is.
   b. Having pinpointed the difficulty, if there is one, determine just what the cause of the difficulty is.
   c. Search for factors in the situation that would help you to make your teaching more effective and, if there is a difficulty, eliminate the difficulty and its cause.
4. Make a final estimate of the situation in view of the information obtained in the earlier steps.
5. Make decisions on the basis of the final estimate of the situation. (See Figure 7–1.)

Initial Diagnosis

Initial diagnosis provides a basis for placing students in appropriate curricula, tracks, courses, and units. Of course, most of the decisions about placing students in courses and curricula have been made before the students arrive at your classroom. Sometimes, however, initial diagnosis will show the need for reassigning students. Perhaps the girl who did so well on the achievement test probably should be allowed to drop from the course and take a more advanced one. Frequently students are placed in courses, sections and units on the basis of their marks in previous ones. Such procedures are dangerous. Single grades may hide more than they show. They give you little basis for judging what is best for the students in the new situation. Further, they tend to be self-fulfilling. Boys and girls who have not done well in last year's course tend not to do well in this year's course even though they have plenty of aptitude and ability. You would be wise to make as careful an analysis as you can of all your students. In modular courses your analysis should determine where each student should

FIGURE 7–1
**Model of the Process
of Diagnosis.**

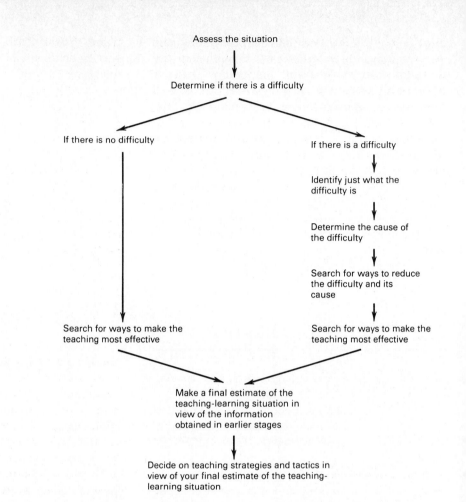

be placed in the sequence of units. In other courses it can be used as the basis for providing for individual differences in students, remedial work, review, and selection of other instructional strategies.

For the initial diagnosis, one might give a test to ascertain each student's position in relation to the goals and demands of the course. Norm-referenced, standardized tests may be useful for giving a general picture of how students stand. Students who score low on standardized achievement tests may not have the prerequisites for the course; students who score very high may already know everything that the course has to offer. Some commercial tests give charts that describe what the students'

weaknesses may be and suggest possible remedies. Usually, however, these tests are not sensitive enough to give you anything more than a general indication that a difficulty exists. To pinpoint the difficulty and its magnitude, you will most likely have to use other kinds of diagnostic techniques.

Teacher-made instruments may be just as satisfactory, (perhaps more so) as standardized tests for finding each student's initial position in relation to the goals of the course. In many courses an objective paper-and-pencil test would be a good device to show how each student stands, while in others another type of test would be more desirable. Paper-and-pencil tests are usually not the best device for measuring skills, attitudes, appreciations, and ideals. To get at these learnings, you might do better with checklists, observation, analysis of papers, rating of skills, rating of products, questionnaires, and reports of previous teachers.

In addition more general information such as the following may help to give you a clearer picture of the student and suggest steps that you might take to make learning more thorough and efficient.

a. Vital Statistics
  (1) Name, grade, course, and so on
  (2) Health record—mental and physical (defects?)
  (3) Any standard test results (reading grade level, aptitude and ability, and so on)
  (4) Attendance record
b. Home Situation
  (1) Family background
  (2) Intrafamily relationships
  (3) Social contacts with community (club membership, and so on)
  (4) Religious attitudes and affiliations
  (5) Economic status
c. Social Outlook
  (1) Friends
  (2) Social activities
      Spare time
      School extracurricular
  (3) Group acceptance
d. Personal Qualities
  (1) Ethical standards and attitudes
  (2) Talents and capabilities
  (3) Goals and ambitions (immediate and future)
  (4) Interests and hobbies (in or out of school)
  (5) Antisocial traits causing discipline problems.

Thus a careful examination of the students' cumulative records is usually well worth the effort.

Continuing Diagnosis

After the initial diagnosis, you should continue to diagnose, revising your assessment as new evidence comes up. At the very least you should at-tempt to take stock at the end of each unit. One way to do this is to give the students a formative unit test to see where they stand in relation to the goals of the unit. For this purpose, a criterion-referenced mastery test would be most in order. In addition you should consider the information you have gleaned from observing your students and analyzing their oral and written work during the unit. Preassessment tests before a unit begins may also give you essential information, particularly if your course is modularized. Sometimes, however, the post-test for one unit can and should serve as the pretest for the next one.[1] In any case, you should perform some sort of preassessment before each and every unit.

A Basis for Remedial Procedures

At times it will become evident that some students are falling behind. Their difficulties may be more serious than their inability to reach the goal of a unit—in some cases much more serious. For these persons other techniques are necessary. Some students may need the specialized help of remedial classes and teachers, if available. Others can be best helped by the classroom teacher.

For example, John is doing very badly in algebra. A check of his papers shows that one cause of his trouble seems to be his arithmetic. Consequently, the next step would be to try to find what about his arithmetic is faulty and why it is so. Perhaps a diagnostic arithmetic test can find the answers to these questions. If no such test is available, perhaps one can find out the trouble in a conference, or by a more minute study of the student's papers, or by giving him specific work in arithmetic and checking to see just what type of errors he makes. In any case, a painstaking search for the exact trouble is imperative if the remedial teaching is to be of any value at all. An item analysis of the student's

---

[1] For information on building diagnostic, formative, preassessment and post-assessment mastery tests see Chapter 17.

test responses may be particularly helpful at this point.

The Tools of Diagnosis

As you have seen, diagnosis depends upon a sufficient supply of accurate information. The more you know about the students, the better chance you have for making an accurate diagnosis. Fortunately the grist for diagnoses is never really in short supply—although you may find it difficult to get it to your mill. Therefore you should be well acquainted with the tools for gathering information about students, and their use. These tools are, of course, the tools of assessment and evaluation. They make it possible to become fairly well acquainted with your students even though you have five sections of thirty students each. Among the tools you will find useful are

a. Records
   (1) Cumulative record folder (Permanent Record Card)
   (2) Test results (vocational, interest, aptitude, ability, intelligence, achievement, and so on)
   (3) Anecdotal records
   (4) Physical examinations (dental, visual, auditory, and so on)
b. Indirect Contacts
   (1) Home visits
   (2) Reliable members of community (Boy Scout leaders, priests or ministers, police, and so on)
   (3) Contacts with parents
   (4) Guidance nurse or guidance counselor
   (5) Other dependable teachers
c. Direct Contacts
   (1) Personal observations during
       informal discussions
       conferences
       special help periods
       nonschool activities

   (2) Conclusions drawn from
       autobiographies
       questionnaires
       sociograms and other sociometric devices
   (3) Diagnostic, formative, and summative evaluation—tests and quizzes, written and oral classwork, homework.

Cumulative Record

Well used, the cumulative record can be very helpful in diagnosis. This record is a compendium of data concerning the student's life both in school and out, gathered over the years. Most cumulative records contain a permanent record of such things as vital statistics, student's personal goals, significant experiences, conferences, test data, health records, family history, academic progress, extra curricular activity, personality rating and descriptions, questionnaires and administrative information. In addition they may contain copies of documents and reports, such as anecdotal reports, behavior logs and conference reports.

When using cumulative records, you must be very careful not to let the information in the records lead you to unwarranted prejudgment. Just because a girl did poorly last year does not mean she does not have the capacity to do well this year. To eliminate the possibility of prejudging students and to allow for honest judgments about students, some

---

An example of a cumulative record form is shown in Figures 7–2, 7–3, 7–4 and 7–5. What information of value might you find in it? In what ways might the information in this cumulative record help the teacher in his teaching? What physical and health data would be helpful? Is there any information omitted from the printed form?

How might each of the records suggested in the list above be used by a teacher?

1 [A]	LAST NAME	FIRST	MIDDLE	RELIGION	PLACE OF BIRTH	DATE OF BIRTH	M F W C
2	YEAR AND AGE						
3	ADDRESS — HOME						
4	ADDRESS — TELEPHONE						
5	ADDRESS — SCHOOL						
6	PHYSICAL DISABILITIES						
7	HEALTH PHYSICAL						
8	HEALTH MENTAL						
9	SOCIAL ADJUSTMENT HOME CONDITIONS						
10	STUDY CONDITIONS AND HOURS STUDY PER WEEK						
11	COMMUTING HOURS PER WEEK						
12	INTERESTS REPORTED						
13	VOCATIONAL PREFERENCE						
14	EDUCATIONAL PLANS						
15	EDUCATIONAL SUGGESTIONS						
16	LOANS OR SCHOLARSHIPS						
17	SUPPORT OF SELF OR DEPENDENTS						
18	PERSONALITY RATINGS	+2					
19		+1					
20		N					
21		−1					
22		−2					
23	PERSONALITY TESTS USED						

	NAME OF	HEALTH	RELIGION	DIED	BIRTHPLACE - NATIONALITY	ARRIVED U S A	EDUCATION-WHERE-KIND-DEGREE	OCCUPATION	ADDRESS (IN PENCIL) TELEPHONE
24	FATHER								
25	MOTHER								
26	STEP PARENT OR GUARDIAN								

	HOW MANY	NOW ATTENDING WHAT COLLEGE	GRADUATED FROM WHAT COLLEGE	AUTHORITY OF BIRTH CERTIFICATION		HOME	BEFORE 10 YRS OLD	AFTER 10 YRS OLD
27	OLDER BROTHERS			31 PASSPORT	35 CHURCH RECORD	38 LANGUAGE SPOKEN IN THE HOME		
28	YOUNGER BROTHERS			32 OATH	36 HOSPITAL RECORD	39 TYPE OF HOME COMMUNITY		
29	OLDER SISTERS			33 BIRTH CERTIFICATE	37	40 IF PARENTS ARE SEPARATED GIVE DATE		
30	YOUNGER SISTERS			34 OTHER EVIDENCE				

K. P. 14196

FIGURE 7–2   A Sample Cumulative Record Folder (First Page).

teachers recommend that one not consult the cumulative record until a month or so after school begins. This procedure seems to be overcautious; besides, it deprives teachers of an important diagnostic tool. If one is careful, it seems unnecessary.

Interpreting Test Scores

You will note that part of the cumulative record (Figures 7–4, 7–5) reports test scores. Usually the tests reported are standardized tests of the norma-tive type. These scores can be an excellent source of information concerning students' aptitudes and achievement. However, interpreting the scores takes some skill.

Normative tests give one only a general impression of a person's standing in relation to a group. They do not give specific information concerning the achievement of individual goals or the attainment of particular skills or knowledge. Thus, for instance, a standardized test score might indicate how well a student is progressing in an area, but it would not indicate what specific skills, abilities,

1	**B**	YEAR AND AGE						
2	COUNSELLORS							
3	DISCIPLINE							
4	NUMBER OF DAYS ABSENT							
5	NAME AND TYPE OF SCHOOL							
6	DATE AND REASON FOR LEAVING							
7	NOTABLE ACCOMPLISHMENTS OR UNUSUAL EXPERIENCES							
8	CLUBS AND OFFICES							
9	EXTRA CURRICULUM EXPERIENCES	ATHLETIC						
10		HRS A WEEK						
11		NON ATHLETIC						
12		HRS A WEEK						
13	VOCATIONAL EXPERIENCES	TYPE AND DURATION						
14		WEEKLY PAY						
15		HRS A WEEK						
16	SUMMER EXPERIENCES							
17								
18								
19								
20	OBJECTIVE TEST SCORES							
21								
22								
23								
24								
25								
26								

FIGURE 7–3   A Sample Cumulative Record Folder (Second Page).

or knowledge the student had or had not learned in that area.

As a rule standardized tests provide norms that permit the comparison of one group with other groups. Norms should not be confused with standards. A standard is a level of achievement or ability required for some purpose. A norm is quite a different thing. It is an average. Usually we deal with grade norms or age norms. A ninth-grade norm, for instance, is simply the average or mean score of the sampling of ninth-graders on whom the test was standardized. It is a theoretical point at which the average of the scores of all the ninth-graders falls. Similarly, an age norm is the theoretical average of the scores of all the students at that age. This means that in an average group at any particular level, half of the students should be higher, and half of the students lower, than the norm. Thus any student who is reading at the tenth-grade level is reading as well as the average tenth-grader. Without further information one cannot tell whether this is good or bad.[2]

_____

[2] Information about test scores is usually taught in courses in educational psychology. It is recommended that you take such a course before you begin to teach.

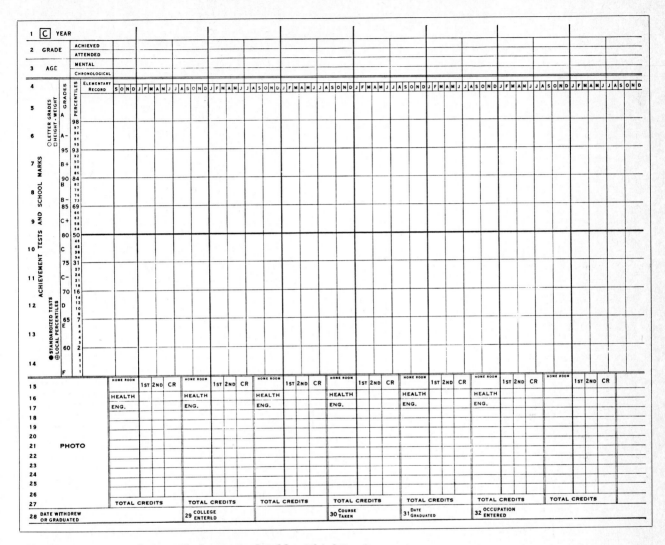

FIGURE 7–4   A Sample Cumulative Record Folder (Third Page).

Test Norms

Norms are useful in that they provide a basis for comparing students from different school systems. They are valuable in evaluating school programs, and they can also tell the approximate standing of students with respect to their peers. Thus they can be useful in developing individual programs for students and in providing for individual differences. For instance, if you find that an eighth-grade girl seems to have ability at the tenth-grade level, you should investigate the feasibility of giving her work that would be challenging at that level.

One of your ninth-graders is reading exactly at grade level according to the tests. Other tests and your observation of the girl indicate that she is very bright. Is her reading ability good or bad, assuming the test score is accurate?

SUBJECT SELECTIONS

NAME_____   YEAR OF GRADUATION_____

GRADE 9	Points	GRADE 10	Points	GRADE 11	Points	GRADE 12	Points
1. Phys. Ed. & Health	1	1. Phys. Ed. & Health	1	1. Phys. Ed. & Driver Ed. & Health	1	1. Phys. Ed. & Health	1
2. English I	5	2. English II	5	2. English III	5	2. English IV	5
3.		3.		3. U.S. History I	5	3. U.S. History II	5
4.		4.		4.		4.	
5.		5.		5.		5.	
6.		6.		6.		6.	
7.		7.		7.		7.	
Total Points		Total Points		Total Points		Total Points	

IOWA TESTS	GRADE 7	8	9
Vocabulary			
Reading Comprehension			
Language Skills			
Work Study Skills			
Arithmetic			
Total			
DIFFERENTIAL APTITUDE TESTS			
Verbal			
Numerical			
Abstract			
Spatial			
Mechanical			
Clerical			
Spelling			
Sentences			

COOPERATIVE TESTS	GRADE 9	10	11
(Vocabulary)			
Reading Comprehension			
Mechanics of Expression			
Social Studies			
Mathematics			
Science			
Foreign Language			
OTHER TESTS:			

	GRADE 8	9	10	11
Vocational Plans				
Educational Plans				
Rank in Class				
Scholastic Aptitude				
Interest Inventory	Grade 8 — California 1. 2. 3.		Grade 11 — Kuder 1. 2. 3.	
Counselor's Approval				
Parent's Signature				

FIGURE 7–5   A Sample Cumulative Record Folder (Course Selection Insert).

Standard Scores

Standard test scores are often expressed in standard deviations above or below the mean. Thus a score falling one standard deviation below the mean would be recorded as a standard score (or z score) of −1. To avoid the use of negative numbers these standard scores are usually changed to converted z scores, Z scores or T scores, as Figure 7–6 shows. Note that these scores all say the same thing although in slightly different dialects: a z score of −1 is the same as a converted z score 90, or a T score of 40 or a Z score of 40. Similarly a score one half a standard deviation above the mean could

Percentiles	0.1	2.3	15.9	50.0	84.1	97.7	99.9
Standard deviations	−3	−2	−1	0	1	2	3
z scores	−3.0	−2.0	−1.0	0	1.0	2.0	3.0
Converted z scores	70	80	90	100	110	120	130
T scores	20	30	40	50	60	70	80
Z scores	20	30	40	50	60	70	80
Deviation IQ's	52	68	84	100	116	132	148
Stanines		1	2	3	4	5	6	7	8	9	

FIGURE 7–6
Comparison of Various Derived Scores. (*Note:* Deviation IQs are computed with a standard deviation of 16; stanine scores represent ranges or bands rather than points.)

be reported as a z score of 0.5, a converted z score of 105, a T score of 55, or a Z score of 55.[3]

In interpreting standard scores, it may help you to think of a score of from +1 to −1 as falling within the middle two thirds of the population, and a score of +1 or above as falling in the upper 15 per cent, while a score of +2 or above falls in the topmost 3 per cent. Similarly think of a score of below −1 as falling in the lower 15 per cent and a score of −2 or below in the lowest 3 per cent.[4]

---

[3] In T scores the mean is designated by 50 and the standard deviation has the value of 10. Some writers use the term T scores only when dealing with normal distributions. When the distribution is not normal, they call the scores Z scores. The z score itself has been varied to eliminate signs by taking 5 or 10 or 100 as the mean and expressing the deviation from the mean as a multiple of the standard deviation. Thus a score of +0.5 might be indicated by 5.5 or 55, or 110, depending on the values used.

[4] Note that these numbers are approximations. Figure 7–6 indicates the actual percentages of the total these scores represent.

Stanine Scores

Another useful score based on the normal curve is the stanine score. This is a nine-point score in which each unit represents a band equal to one half a standard deviation and the mean is equal to 5 and the standard deviation, 2.

Comparison of Scores

Figure 7–6 shows the equivalent weight of each of these types of scores. From this table we see that a T score of 70 can be interpreted to mean that the student is rated at two standard deviations above the mean or within the top 3 per cent of those taking the test and so would have a z score of +2.0 or a Z score of 70 and a stanine score of 9. If this were an Intelligence Test the student's deviation IQ would be 132. Presumably this is a very good score indeed, but until one knows more about the student and the test situation, one cannot be sure. We repeat, to make decisions on the basis of test scores alone can be very dangerous.

In a certain seventh grade a test indicated that 25 per cent of the students were reading below the seventh-grade level. The teacher claimed that there was no cause to worry. Would you agree? Why, or why not? Do you need more information on which to decide?

The parents of a brilliant boy have just been informed that their youngster has achieved his grade norm in all areas and is slightly above norm in one area. They are well pleased. Should they be?

The IQ

Norms of standardized tests are really derived scores provided by the test makers to aid the user in the interpretation of the test. Grade norms and age norms, however, are not the only types of derived scores that may be used. One of the most familiar types is the intelligence quotient. This score is, in effect, a refinement of the age norm. Although in older tests IQ was computed as a ratio between the mental age and chronological age, i.e.

$$\frac{MA}{CA} \times 100,$$

newer tests usually represent the IQ as a standardized score having, for most intelligence tests, a mean of 100 and a standard deviation of 16 (or sometimes 15). In other words, the IQ of a person of average intelligence would be 100, while a person whose intelligence was a standard deviation above normal would be 116.

In either case, these IQ scores should be viewed with caution. Estimating an individual's intelligence is too complicated a matter to be based on a single test score. Different tests of intelligence do not yield the same scores. Also, scores from the same tests vary considerably. IQs may be accepted as general indexes of brightness, but they cannot be accepted at their face value. A good rule might be to assume that the chances are good that the

actual index of brightness would fall within a range of five points above or below the IQ derived from the test. To judge how bright a particular youngster is requires the use of other criteria in addition to the IQ.

Percentile Scores

Another type of derived score is the centile or percentile norm. The percentile score indicates the per cent of the sample population whose scores fall at or below that score. For example, if a boy receives a percentile score of 10, 10 per cent of the group did less well than or as well as he, and 90 per cent did better. The fiftieth percentile, of course, is average.

Some schools segregate boys and girls into homogeneous groups on the basis of an IQ score alone. After reading this short discussion do you think this practice is proper? Why, or why not?

Diagnostic Tests

Criterion-Referenced Standardized Tests

Recently educators have been turning to the use of criterion-referenced tests instead of norm-based tests. Well-made, criterion-referenced tests are excellent diagnostic instruments. So far test builders have had relatively little experience with these tests at the formal level. At the present state of the art, procedures for developing standardized criterion-referenced tests and criteria for excellence for tests of this type have not been fully determined and so it may be difficult to find a published criterion-referenced test suitable for your needs.[5]

---

[5] See W. James Popham, *Criterion-Referenced Measurement* (Englewood Cliffs, N J: Prentice-Hall, 1978), Chap. 8, for guidance in selecting criterion-referenced tests.

Listings of diagnostic tests available commercially may be found in such references as Buros' Mental Measurement Yearbooks. Before selecting a commercial diagnostic test for any particular mission, you should examine several and compare them carefully. Not all of the tests are equally good. In fact, some are downright bad. Moreover, not all of the good tests do each job equally well. When in search of a diagnostic test you should consult the references and apply the criteria for commercial-test selection found later in the chapter.

When selecting a diagnostic test, the most important criterion to check is whether or not the test items actually test the presence or absence of the specific skills, understandings, and attitudes that you wish to find out about. You can obtain this information by examining the test manual furnished by the publisher and by inspecting the instrument itself and comparing it with your teaching objectives.

Teacher–Built Diagnostic Tests

A well-made, teacher-built criterion-referenced test may better suit your purposes in diagnosing students' academic strengths and weaknesses.

To make up your own diagnostic tests, use the procedures for building criterion-referenced tests outlined in Chapter 17. After giving and scoring the diagnostic test, an item analysis such as that shown in Chapter 17, in which you check to see what item (and hence objectives) students have succeeded in, will reveal the strengths and weaknesses of individual pupils. However, the analysis of test scores does not always have to be quite so formal.

Actually, except for end of the year or end of the term tests, probably all of your tests should be diagnostic mastery tests. If well made, such tests show what the students have mastered, and what they have not. Just looking at the students' answers carefully should give you a fairly firm impression of what the students have learned and what they have missed. With this information you can go on to plan future classes so as to take advantage of students' strengths and to correct weaknesses either as individuals or as a group. The formal item analysis described in Chapter 17 will give you more dependable data, but in the hurly-burly of teaching you may find it expedient to rely on inspection. In either case the key to this type of testing is to aim specific test items at specific learnings—understandings, skills, facts or what you will. If you aim your quiz and test items at specific learnings, you can frequently locate trouble spots, misapprehensions, and the like, as well as indications of strength and talent, by a rather quick inspection of students' responses to the items.

Observation

You can gather a lot of data for your diagnoses by observing your students as they work in class and relax in moments of leisure. Often the information you collect from your observations, particularly when combined with what you have learned from conversations with your students and others, will reveal glimpses of the causes of their behavior. Sometimes you can use these clues to help students solve problems—both academic and personal.

One example of an observational device you might employ is the following scheme, which is sometimes used to determine whether or not a book is beyond a certain student's reading ability. The technique is amazingly simple. One just gives to the student a portion of the book to read and then questions the student on what has been read. If the student can answer the questions, the work is probably not too difficult; if the student stumbles, perhaps you should try something less difficult.

Diagnosis of this sort is very useful. Many students have been shortchanged in life and their earlier schooling and are quite unprepared for what we expect of them. One reason so much teaching fails in secondary schools is because it makes no contact with the realities of student knowledge, skills, interests and aspirations. It is not very effective, for instance, to pile reading assignment on top of reading assignment when the students can-not read. Nor is it effective to force them to read selections that have no relation to their interests, aspirations, or experiences. Watching students at work and at play should indicate to you what would be more attuned to their lives and needs.

Following is a sampling of some of the things you might look for when observing.

- Does the student seem bored?
- Does the student appear to like or dislike the subject?
- Does the student understand the content?
- Does the student understand what to do?
- Does the student know how to proceed?
- Does the student have the necessary background and skills?
- Is the student uncomfortable?
- Has the student given up trying because of past failures?
- Is the student afraid of failing?
- Is the student distracted by other interests, goals, and so on?
- What is the student good at?
- What type of things does the student like or en-joy?
- What are the student's goals and aspirations?
- What problems does the student seem to have?
- Where does the student need help or encourage-ment?
- To what does the student react well?

Your observations will probably be more effective if you make them systematically. Each day select three or four persons to observe on a regular sched-ule until you have completed observing the whole class. Also set aside certain periods of time to watch the entire class for certain symbolic behavior—does anyone have vision problems, for instance. By using such devices as checklists and rating scales, you can make your observation more objective and ac-curate. However, you may learn as much by being alert and concerned about students when observing them informally.

Analysis of Classwork

Other useful techniques that complement obser-vation include analysis of written work, analysis of oral work, analysis of records and conferences. For instance, questioning a boy about his mathe-matics paper might disclose that he does not know how to marshal his facts in order to attack a prob-lem. In mathematics again, and in other subjects as well, analysis of the students' papers might show errors in their thinking, poor problem-solving tech-niques, or a lack of understanding of the fundamen-tal processes.

Conversations

Perhaps the best way to find out about the stu-dents is to talk to them. Informal, *friendly* conversa-tions are probably more productive than most other techniques. At times it helps to have the stu-dent in to discuss a problem or talk things over, but it is surprising how much you can learn about students from casual questions asked in passing. Take time to talk to students between classes, dur-ing breaks, after school, and at extracurricular and

Arrange to spend an hour or two observing a class in a subject you hope to teach. Make a list of the things you would look for to help you understand the students better. As you ob-serve the class, apply your list to various individ-ual students and the class as a whole.

Examine some homework or classwork of the students. What does it tell you of their strengths and weaknesses? Do you see evidence of any need for help?

Talk to some of the students. What can you learn about students' attitudes, likes and dislikes, understanding of their subject, and ability to handle their learning tasks?

social functions. Pleasant chitchat may not bring about great learning but it does improve the atmosphere and may incidentally give one leads for improving teaching and learning. Short exchanges about students' work can be very productive. Let students tell you what they are doing, what troubles them, how they plan to proceed, what they think of the subject at hand, what they would like to do, and how you can help. Such exchanges are especially useful during work sessions, and laboratory classes and at other times when students are busy working individually. Conversations that follow up on your examining students' work can be productive, particularly if they show students how they are doing and how to do better. Remember that studies have found that fully a fifth of high school students do not know what they are doing or how to do it. Short conversations may clear up some of these confusions for the individual student.

Conferences with Parents and Other Teachers

Many times you can understand a student's problem better after observing and talking with the parents. Other teachers are also an excellent source of information. Objective discussions with one's colleagues can reveal much. These discussions, however, ought to be planned. Even though sometimes greatly illuminating, chance conversations with other teachers are liable to be unproductive. On the other hand, planned conferences of all the teachers and guidance counselors concerned are often extremely helpful in bringing about an understanding of the personality and problems of a particular boy or girl. It is almost always profitable to arrange a serious talk with other teachers who have or have had your students in their classes—particularly in cases in which your students are having difficulties.

Anecdotal Reports

Significant information gained from your observation of behavior can be recorded in a behavior log or anecdotal report. A behavior log consists of a page on which one notes information about the student as it is gathered. An anecdotal report is a brief description of significant incidents. In it one records what happened when, where, and under what circumstances. Sample behavior log entries, and an anecdotal record appear as Figures 7–7 and 7–8.

FIGURE 7–7
A Behavior Log Page.

Matthew McGuire

Date	Entry
9/27	Matthew requested permission to build a model of the solar system.
9/30	M. was involved in an argument with John at the end of the laboratory period. Cause of the argument was not determined. M. said J. was picking on him.
10/5	Conference with M. concerning his project. So far he has done nothing constructive. He says he would like to do something else.
10/6	M. was elected class treasurer at the sophomore class meeting.
10/7	M. has decided to go ahead with his project after all. He has finished his plans with working drawings. They were quite acceptable.

FIGURE 7–8
Anecdotal Report Form

Name of Student: Date:

Description of incident:

                                             Reported by:

                                             Position:

Summary

Diagnosis provides a basis for planning instruction that fulfills the needs of students. The process of diagnosis is a continuing one in which one first attempts to find the facts of the case, then from time to time rechecks to see if these facts are correct and still hold, and, as the occasion demands, makes decisions about appropriate instructional approaches and content. Among the resources one can use in diagnosis are the cumulative record, diagnostic tests, observation techniques, analysis of the students' classwork, conversations, and conferences. Perhaps the most useful tools for classroom diagnosis are teacher-built, criterion-referenced tests. They should be used for preassessment of the students' knowledge and abilities in all units, and as a source of information for effective follow-up. The cumulative record includes useful information about such things as the students' vital statistics, past academic experiences, health records, family histories, extracurricular activities, and test data. In interpreting standardized scores it should be remembered that most of them are norm-based.

So far test experts have not settled on procedures for standardizing criterion-referenced tests. Most modern standardized tests are scored on the basis of percentile or standard scores of a norm group. Versions of the standard score commonly used are z score, T score, Z score, deviation IQs, and stanines. Grade and age norms are obtained by averaging the scores of all the students in the norm group of a particular age or grade. Test users should remember that these norms are not standards but averages. For most diagnostic purposes diagnostic mastery or criterion-referenced tests are more useful than standardized instruments for they compare the state of the student's progress with the specific goals to be mastered. In the classroom context, teachers will ordinarily find it imperative, because of time and logistics, to depend on observation, analysis of classwork, and conversations with students. These techniques make it possible to get a handle on a student's actual knowledge, skills, and attitudes more easily than do more formal methods. When desired, these observations can be recorded in anecdotal reports, behavior logs, or just plain notes.

Additional Reading

Biehler, Robert F., and Jack Snowman. *Psychology Applied to Teaching*, 4th ed. Boston: Houghton Mifflin, 1982, Chap. 10.

Bloom, Benjamin S., George F. Madaus, and J. Thomas Hastings. *Evaluation to Improve Learning*. New York: McGraw-Hill, 1981.

Ebel, Robert L. *Essentials of Educational Measurement*, 3rd ed., Englewood Cliffs, NJ: Prentice-Hall, 1979, Chaps. 11, 16–19.

_____. *The Uses of Standardized Testing*, Fastback 93. Bloomington, IN: Phi Delta Kappa Educational Foundation, 1977.

Emmers, Amy Puett. *After the Lesson Plan: Realities of High School Teaching*. New York: Teachers College Press, 1981, Part II.

Fox, Robert, Margaret B. Luszki, and Richard Schmuck. *Diagnosing Classroom Learning*. Chicago: Science Research Associates, 1966.

Fremont, Theodore S., David M. Seifert, and John J. Wilson. *Informal Diagnostic Assessment of Children*. Springfield, IL: Thomas, 1977.

Gronlund, Norman E. *Measurement and Evaluation in Teaching*, 5th ed. New York: Macmillan, 1985.

Perrone, Vito. *The Abuses of Standardized Testing*, Fastback 92. Bloomington, IN: Phi Delta Kappa Educational Foundation, 1977.

Tuckman, Bruce W. *Measuring Educational Outcomes: Fundamentals of Testing*. New York: Harcourt, 1975, Chaps. 12–13.

"Understanding Student Behavior." *NASSP Bulletin* (September, 1979), **63**:1–87.

8

Planning for Teaching

Overview

Planning is a part of the step in our pattern of teaching called preparing a setting for learning. There is no substitute for good planning. It helps create correct discipline, a pleasant atmosphere in the class and purposeful teaching-learning activity free from dead spots and waste motion—in short, good planning promotes worthwhile learning. No one can teach well for long without planning well.

Basically planning consists of deciding what to accomplish, how to accomplish it, and how to tell what has been accomplished. We hope that this

chapter will give you a general idea of how to carry out these steps. We pay particular attention to selecting objectives and learning activities by which to achieve those objectives. We also consider team planning, teacher-student cooperative planning, and the resources one can use in planning. As you study, pay particular attention to the role of the objectives and the ways in which different kinds of activities can aid students in attaining those objectives. Also note the need for adjusting your choices of learning activities to the learning situation, the students, and to your own strengths and inclinations.

140

Who Does the Planning?

Planning is done at many levels. Commissions, committees, and state departments of education set up the overall educational goals and outline curriculum requirements. At the local district level, local school authorities and committees of teachers and supervisors set up goals and map out the programs of studies for the local school curricula. Recently, in an effort to make schooling more thorough and efficient, some state and local authorities have taken a much more active part in setting up specific objectives and standards of achievement. The idea in back of their effort is that (1) schooling should develop certain competencies in the students; (2) the state and local school authorities should take steps to determine what these competencies should be, and (3) the students should actually achieve these competencies.

At the most important level, the persons responsible for planning the courses, units, and lessons are the teachers. They determine the actual objectives, content, and procedures in the lessons, units, and courses. In some cases, in order to facilitate cooperation and correlation, teachers plan together as teams.

To what extent students participate in the planning of their own learning activities varies greatly from school to school and class to class, the range being from almost no participation in conservative traditional classrooms to (rarely) students' making almost all the decisions in progressive alternative schools and advanced college seminars. In almost every course, however, students do some planning, if only to select and carry out their own projects, reports, outside readings, and similar activities even when the teachers do the major planning activities.

Nevertheless, even when the course plan is largely prescribed by school officials, or when the planning is shared by colleagues, or when students cooperate in establishing the goals and activities, the responsibility for determining the objectives and procedures of the courses, units and lessons falls squarely on the teacher.

What the Planners Do

All good teachers plan. In the long run the success of any course depends upon the excellence of the plan, and the skill with which the plan is carried out. Almost literally, then, in the classroom situation good planning is half the battle.

Sometimes experienced teachers disparage planning. Some of them claim that they never make lesson plans or course plans. Be not deceived. A lesson plan is only a decision concerning what one intends to do and how one intends to do it. When the world-famous university professor decides that tomorrow he will tell the students what really caused the French Revolution, and, to accomplish this purpose, he will trot out his old reliable lecture for the edification of the scholars, he is planning. As a rule, young, inexperienced teachers and capable, creative teachers with years of experience find that they need to plan much more carefully.

Basically, as we have noted, planning consists of deciding (1) what one wishes to accomplish, and (2) how one wishes to accomplish it. It requires one to consider for each plan the questions:

- What is to be accomplished?
- How is it to be done?
- Who is to do what?
- When, and in what order, shall things be done?
- Where shall it be done?
- Why do we want to accomplish this, and why do we plan to do it this way?
- How will we know how well we have succeeded?

Therefore, the task you, the teacher, face in planning is to set up, on the basis of your best estimate of the situation (that is, your diagnosis),

1. the teaching objectives,
2. teaching-learning activities designed to attain these objectives,
3. a plan for evaluating the success of the teaching and the progress of the students toward objectives.

Setting Up the Objectives

The first step in lesson, course, or unit planning is to set up objectives. In other words, you must decide what you hope the students will learn as a result of your teaching. These learning products may include

1. What the learner will know (concepts);
2. What the learner will be able to do (skills);
3. What the learner will feel (attitudes, appreciations, or ideals).

They should be selected on the basis of such considerations as the following.

- The nature and structure of the subject.
- The needs of the students.
- The readiness of the students.
- The interests, abilities, attitudes, and other characteristics of the students.
- The larger educational goals and general objectives.
- Your own philosophy, inclinations, and capabilities.
- Community expectations.
- The feasibility of the objectives, for example, the facilities, equipment, supplies, and time available.
- Other elements of the curriculum.

Do this before you proceed further in your planning. Remember, much teaching fails because teachers do not really understand what they are trying to accomplish.

Writing the Objectives

Ordinarily in planning for instruction it is best to write out your objectives. Doing so

- ensures that you have acquired the learning yourself (If you cannot describe the learning you probably never learned it thoroughly yourself);
- gives you a definite goal for which to aim;
- gives you a standard by which to evaluate student achievement;

- helps to eliminate fuzzy thinking about the learning and thus helps to avoid soft pedagogy—i.e., pedagogy that results in no learning or little learning.

Descriptive or Behavioral Objectives

You may choose to write out your objectives either as descriptive or behavioral objectives. In writing out a descriptive objective, all one does is to describe the learning product desired as in the following examples.

Descriptive Cognitive Domain Objectives

A theme in music, or musical sentence, expresses a musical idea or feeling.

No modern society has invented more than a small fraction of its present culture—all owe tremendous debt to cultural inventors of other places and other times.

The works of the Romantic poets illustrate the eloquent beauty of the language of lyrics and point out universal feelings and emotions.

Descriptive Affective Domain Objectives

No nation can depend entirely on itself.

Cooperation is more desirable than warfare.

One should respect the rights and feelings of others.

The study of international politics can be exciting.

Descriptive Psychomotor Domain Objectives

The ability to write the vowel-inside curve, as in *ail* ℮ and *ray* ℒ. (shorthand)

The ability to play a single paradiddle—both open and closed—on the drums.

The ability to run the 100-yard dash in 12 seconds flat.

Behavioral objectives are somewhat more complicated. Here the essential element is a description of what the student will be able to do as a result of the learning. They may be written in terms of covert, i.e., not observable behavior, as in this example. "Upon completion of the unit the student will understand the forces that caused the United States and the British Empire, now called the Commonwealth, to develop a real friendship." In this objective the key word is "understand," an action that is not readily observable. Or objectives may be stated as overt behavior, as in this example. "Upon completion of the unit the student will be able to explain in his own words the significance of at least three of the principal reasons why the United States and the British Empire, now called the Commonwealth, developed a real friendship." In this objective the key action is "to explain" which is readily observable.

As a rule, "covert" behavioral objectives should be used only for broad, general objectives or course goals. In such objectives the verbs that delineate the behavior are words such as *know, understand, appreciate, feel, enjoy,* and *comprehend,* as in the following examples. "At the completion of the unit the students will know the basic properties of simple geometric figures." "At the completion of the unit the students will appreciate the beauties of Shakespearian poetry."

Often, however, general objectives of both the cognitive and affective domains are more useful when expressed as overt behavior, as the following example from the affective domain illustrates. "At the completion of the course students will read Shakespearian poetry for recreation." General objectives in the psychomotor domain should always be written in terms of overt behavior.

Specific behavioral objectives probably should be written only in terms of observable behavior in all of the domains. In other words, at the level of specific behavioral objectives the objectives should be what Tyler calls performance objectives, i.e., objectives that describe the performance of the students. For example, "At the end of the lesson each student will be able to describe the procedure for constructing a map profile step by step without error." In this example the overt behavior is "describing." It can be easily observed and evaluated by the teacher.

Specific behavioral objectives of this type are valuable because they give one specific targets at which to aim one's teaching, and specific behavior to use as criteria for evaluating teaching and learning. In writing these objectives, one should always use action verbs such as *identify, describe, list, explain, display, define, demonstrate, execute, state, tell, construct, organize, select, write, present, interpret, locate, compare, pronounce, perform, draw* and so forth. Examples of specific behavioral objectives follow. "At the completion of the lesson the students will be able to draw a trapezoid." "At the completion of the lesson the students will be able to identify a *non sequitur.*"

Simple or Criterion-Referenced Behavioral Objectives. Behavioral objectives may be either simple or criterion referenced. Simple behavioral objectives tell only what the learner will do at the end of the instruction, as in the preceding examples. Criterion-referenced behavioral objectives go one step further and specify the level of performance the student will have to achieve to meet the objectives. For example, the criterion-referenced or performance objective: "At the end of the lesson each student will be able to describe the procedure for constructing a map profile step by step without error," sets errorless performance as the criterion for achievement of the objective.

Thus, you see, simple behavioral objectives consist of three elements

a. an introductory phase,

b. who,

c. does what,

while the criterion-referenced behavioral objectives, when written out completely, contain four or five elements.

a. The introductory phase

b. Who (i.e., the learner);

c. Does what (i.e., the behavior required);

d. How well (i.e., the level of performance required or, in other words, the "criterion of acceptable performance"), and when desirable

e. Under what conditions (i.e., the givens and/or

restrictions or limitations that govern an acceptable performance).[1]

Following are examples of both simple and criterion-referenced objectives and analyses of their elements.

In the simple behavioral objective "The student can cite three evidences of the friendship of the United States and Great Britain in the first half of the twentieth century," the elements are

a. At the conclusion of the unit (understood)
b. The student (who)
c. Can cite three evidences of the friendship of the United States and Great Britain in the first half of the twentieth century (does what).

The action verb in this instance is *cite*.

Similarly in the simple behavior objective "The student can demonstrate how the Hague Court, the World Court and the United Nations were evidences of the role of the English-speaking nations as a force for keeping the peace," the elements are

a. At the conclusion of the unit (understood)
b. The student (who)
c. Can demonstrate how The Hague Court, the World Court, and the United Nations were evidences of the role of the English-speaking nations as a force for keeping the peace (does what).

In this objective the action verb is *demonstrate*.

When describing an objective in the affective domain, it is usually helpful to include a notation telling what affect is being described. Thus in the objective "The student shows enjoyment of classical music by purchasing and playing classical records," the elements are

a. At the end of the instruction (understood)
b. the student (who)
c. shows enjoyment (the affect)
d. by purchasing and playing classical records (does what).

The action verb is *purchase*.

[1] Robert F. Mager, *Preparing Instructional Objectives* (Palo Alto, CA: Fearon, 1962), p. 43.

Following are examples of simple behavioral objectives in the affective and psychomotor domains. Point out the elements in each:

As a result of the instruction in scientific thinking, the students demonstrate the scientific attitude by searching out and examining evidence before making decisions.

At the completion of the unit, the student will be able to play a closed paradiddle on the drums.

In the following sample criterion-referenced behavioral objective in the cognitive domain "Given examples of the type X^5/X^3, students will be able to solve the examples by subtracting the exponents in at least nine out of ten cases," the elements are

a. At the completion of instruction (understood)
b. the students (who)
c. will be able to solve the examples by subtracting exponents (does what)
d. in at least nine of ten cases (how well)
e. given examples of the type X^5/X^3 (under what conditions).

The action verb in this objective is *"solve."*

In another example of a criterion-referenced objective in the cognitive domain "The student will be able to pick out proper and common nouns from a page of his textbook with 90 per cent accuracy," the elements are

a. At the completion of instruction (understood)
b. the student (who)
c. will be able to pick out proper and common nouns (does what)
d. with 90 per cent accuracy (how well)
e. from a page of his textbook (under what conditions).

The action verb here is *pick*.

In the following example of a criterion-referenced objective from the psychomotor domain "The student will be able to run the 100-yard dash in 12 seconds," the elements are

a. At the completion of training (understood)

b. the student (who)

c. will run the 100-yard dash (does what)

d. in twelve seconds (how well)

e. (under what conditions, not stated).

Here the action verb is *run*.

Note that criterion-referenced objectives must always be "overt." They are best suited for use as specific objectives in the cognitive and psychomotor domains. Because of the difficulties in judging affective behavior, we do not recommend their use for the affective domain in ordinary classroom instruction.

Because criterion-referenced specific behavioral objectives are more precise than simple specific behavioral objectives, they usually provide (1) better targets for the instructor, and (2) more definite standards by which to judge the success of the teaching and learning than other types of objectives do.

Point out the elements in the following criterion referenced objective.

Given a quadratic equation in one unknown, the student will solve the equation in eight out of ten instances.

Tips for Writing Cognitive Behavioral Objectives. Although behavioral objectives are not difficult to prepare, there are some cautions you should bear in mind to make your objectives effective.

Express behavioral objectives as statements that begin "At the completion of the lesson (or unit, or course) the student. . . ." For purposes of brevity some or all of the beginning portion of the behavioral objective may be omitted so that the behavioral objective as written begins with a verb, e.g., "Types at the rate of forty words per minute without making more than one error per minute." When it is written this way, it is understood that the beginning words "At the completion of the instruction the student" have been omitted and that the objective in full would read "At the completion

of the instruction the student will type at the rate of forty words per minute without making more than one error per minute."

Be sure each behavioral objective describes potential student behavior. Sometimes the behavioral objectives teachers write are not behavioral objectives at all. Behavioral objectives must describe the student behavior expected. The objective "to discuss the picaresque novel" is not a behavioral objective because it does not describe the students' terminal behavior. Rather it describes the learning procedure. Similarly the phrase "the picaresque novel" is not a behavioral objective because it merely names a topic and describes no behavior at all. "In this class I will demonstrate the cause-and-effect principle" is also not a behavioral objective because it describes teacher behavior rather than student behavior. We repeat, *if it does not describe the students' terminal behavior, it is not a behavioral objective at all.* The following is an example of a behavioral objective because it tells us what the student can do, i.e., identify the best painting. "From a group of three paintings the student will be able to identify the one painting that most closely adheres to the principles of quality set forth in the course."

Be sure that each behavioral objective includes one and only one learning product. The objective "At the end of the unit the students will understand the principles underlying the problem-solving methods and apply them rigorously in their daily work" is not really satisfactory because it calls for two different learning products requiring different types of evidence. A student may understand the principles but because of an attitude or lack of skillfullness not use them.

When you write criterion-referenced objectives, be sure that the criteria you list are really indices of the learning you seek. Objectives such as the following beg the question. They do not give us any honest criteria by which to judge the student's achievement: "When you finish this packet you will be able to answer with reasonable accuracy questions on ions, isotopes and static electricity."

Beware of trivia. To write objectives that measure the higher mental levels is difficult, particularly when we limit ourselves to overt behavior. Consequently the behavioral objectives listed for many courses, units, and lessons largely concern memory work, simple skills, isolated facts and other low-level learning. This is unfortunate. Even though to write objectives sampling the higher mental processes may become frustrating, one should not give up trying. They are the important objectives that make education worthwhile. Following is an example of an objective at synthesis level: "Given an unknown, the student will be able to construct a reasonable procedure for determining the chemical consistency of the unknown."

Criticize the following objectives showing why they do not qualify as behavioral objectives. Rewrite each of them as a viable specific objective suitable for a single lesson.

1. My goal in this lesson plan is to teach a geography course. I will attempt to show regions of Anglo-America as to its original occupants—the American Indians. I will attempt to show how these people in their specific regions developed specific cultures in relation to their surroundings.

2. Aim: To review the four major parts of speech.

3. Purpose: To reaffirm the definition, recognition, and the use of the parts of speech.

4. What are the effects of a volunteer army on military security?

Student Objectives

So far we have discussed only the teacher's objectives: the objectives set forth by the teachers for the students to accomplish. These objectives will be futile unless the students adopt them, or compatible objectives, as their own. It is the student's ob-

jectives that cause him to act. It is excellent policy to inform students early in the lesson, unit, or course just what it is they are supposed to gain from the instruction and convince them that the learning is worthwhile. If the students think your objectives are desirable and adopt them as their own, the learning process is well on its way. If they do not, you must resort to some other motivational scheme, or fail. One technique that has good motivational effect is to ask students to choose their own objectives from among alternative objectives.

The following set of objectives was designed for a unit on *Organizing for an Emergency.* Evaluate them. Do you find them clear? Would they be better stated as descriptive objectives than as behavioral objectives? Why or why not? Do the specific objectives sufficiently support the general objective? Would they be more useful if criterion-referenced? Why or why not? How could you criterion reference them? What steps would you take to ensure that the students set for themselves objectives consonant with the stated teaching objectives?

General Objectives:

Through a simulated disaster situation, the students will develop a change in attitude and behavior leading to planned and rational action in any community disaster.

Specific Objectives:

When presented with the simulated disaster situation, the students will demonstrate ability to make decisions.

The students will be able to interpret through discussion the decisions they made and how they affected them, their families, and their community.

The students will be able to compare their experiences in the simulation to the responsibilities and decisions of citizens in their community.

The students will be able to define the responsibility of civil defense to their community.

Another is to encourage students to set up objectives as part of a teacher- student planning activity. Knowledge of the goals and feedback concerning one's progress are among the best motivators of student learning. More often than not, if students know what it is they are supposed to learn, they will try to learn it. When teachers state their specific objectives as learning products, students are quite likely to accept them as legitimate objectives and work to achieve them.

Selecting the Learning Activities

Matching Activities to Instructional Needs

Once you have selected and described your objective, it is time to decide upon the learning activities and upon the way you will organize and conduct these activities. When planning the learning activities, you should be guided by several considerations.

First, there are many different methods or techniques that may fit the bill. Bruce Joyce and Marsha Weil have identified more than eighty different "models of teaching," each of which is slightly different from the other models and useful for a slightly different purpose.[2] Presumably the learning resulting from each of these models will be somewhat different from that resulting from any of the others, for teaching strategies do make a difference in what students learn and how well they learn it. In fact, how one learns may have as much impact on one's final understanding, attitude, or skill as the subject content. To a certain extent teaching

strategies are, for practical purposes, a part of the content. Thus if a teacher uses a method that encourages creative thought, the chances are that that teaching will kindle not only a fuller understanding, but also a greater inclination to think creatively than if another method had been used. Therefore take care to choose the type of learning activity that fits your objectives.

This is not to say that only one specific method can achieve your objective or that one method is necessarily the best for your purpose. No learning activity guarantees the attainment of any particular objective (most learning activities can be used for several types of objectives). Neither can you depend on any method to stand long alone. One should always try to support it by other strategies and techniques that will combine their impact to produce the learnings you desire. Nevertheless some strategies are likely to be much more useful than others for your purposes. For instance, if the goal is to teach information or basic skills, try direct telling and showing, mastery learning procedures, questions directed toward specific contents or skills, practical constant checking, and immediate feedback. These strategies will probably be most effective if the content is offered in small incremental steps. In any case the teacher should point out what is to be learned and why.

If the goal is to develop social attitudes, try case studies, guided questions, laboratory procedures, action learning, independent investigation, group investigation, and problem solving or other strategies that feature inquiry, practice of social analyses, and observation of oneself and other people.

If the goal is self-development, try nondirective, nonthreatening student-centered activities concerning "practical problems, social problems, ethical and philosophical problems, personal issues and research problems, moral dilemmas, and moral problems." Group discussion seems to be an effective technique for executing such strategies.

If the goal is to develop information and problem-solving skills, try inquiry, problem solving, advance organizers, and inductive questioning, and follow

---

[2] Bruce Joyce and Marsha Weil, *Models for Teaching* (Englewood Cliffs, NJ: Prentice-Hall, 1972). See also the introduction to their *Personal Models of Teaching, Information Processing Models of Teaching,* or *Social Models of Teaching* (Englewood Cliffs, NJ: Prentice-Hall, 1978). (The same introduction is repeated in each of these books.) Also Bruce R. Joyce, *Selecting Learning Experiences: Linking Theory and Practice* (Alexandria, VA: Association for Supervision and Curriculum Development, 1978).

inductive techniques and the methods of the discipline.[3]

One concern is to pick an approach that will bring about your most desired objectives without interfering with other desirable learning. However, that problem is not as bothersome as it may seem since most learning activities can be used for more than one type of objective. If you concentrate on selecting methods that will further your principal objective, you will probably also attain your secondary goals.

Second, learning activities, as we have seen, can carry out different roles in the teaching process. Some are excellent for motivating; some for clarifying; some for skill development; some for clinching the learning (closure) and so on. Try to pick learning activities that will maximize the effects you are seeking.

At the beginning of a unit or lesson, for instance, try to use an activity that will catch the students' attention or attract their interest. Telling a simple anecdote may do the trick; so may facing them with a problem situation, or a lively discussion on a relevant issue. The use of an advance organizer, or a description of what the unit or lesson will cover and why, and what will be expected of the students, may help the students set their directions. Involving the students in planning and conducting activities may spark student interest and stimulate their willing effort and cooperation.

In the development portion of your class you might act as a manager of instruction, or as a coach, or as an inquiry trainer. You might help students develop concepts and intellectual skills by such operations as problem solving, Socratic discussion, practice in logical decision making, drawing of inferences, and determining facts. Or you might fill in students' background and widen their horizons

by the skillful use of lectures, demonstrations, audiovisual media, careful questioning, and other clarifying operations. To develop skills you might use show-how activities and practice. Review, practice, reenforcement activities, role playing, discussing points and issues, and tests may serve to drive home the desired knowledge and skills and to tie the learning together. Security-giving operations are particularly necessary for promoting a supportive classroom climate.[4]

The methods one uses should be adapted to the classroom situation. When it seems desirable one should change one's technique so as to add to the class structure; other times it may be better to make the class looser. More often than not decisions of this sort must be made according to your feel for the situation. Your choice of techniques does not have to follow any rigid pattern.

Third, individual students react differently to various methods. In a sense, as Bruce Joyce points out, the students are really part of the method for it is they who do the learning. What they do, their attitudes, their abilities, and so on determine what is learned. The method influences the outcome in any learning situation, but does not determine it. Therefore the learning activities selected should be compatible with the students' abilities, style of learning, and background.[5] Students who have not learned the prerequisite for an activity should not be expected to attempt the activity until they have the necessary background, knowledge, or skill. On the other hand, students who have excellent background and skills should not be sentenced to relearn things they already know or can do. Similarly, students should not be forced on a steady diet of activities that are incompatible with their learning styles. Students who are not very flexible need structured activities, whereas flexible students will be more productive in less structured classes. Similarly sociable students will fit into social group

[3] Based on Doris T. Gow and Tommye W. Casey, "Selecting Learning Activities," in Fenwick W. English, ed., *Fundamental Curriculum Decisions, ASCD Yearbook 1983* (Alexandria, VA: Association for Supervision and Curriculum Development, 1983), Chap. 9.

[4] See Chapter 3.

[5] Joyce, *Selecting Learning Experiences,* op. cit.

types of activities more readily than do less social students, whereas creative youngsters react more favorably to methods calling for divergent thinking and originality than do less creative types. Perhaps the most reasonable way to match students' capabilities and attitudes would be to individualize your teaching in some fashion. Another approach would be to use a variety of activities so that all students would have compatible learning experiences at least part of the time.

Fourth, insofar as is feasible, the activities should be appealing to the students. Although philosophers tell us there is no royal road to learning and that much of school learning must consist of hard work that students must do willy-nilly, you will get a lot more mileage out of your plans if they contain learning activities that are appealing to the students. Teachers who push hard at mastery teaching, for instance, find that after a while students get sick of striving so that it pays to introduce a change of pace at times. There is always a place for exciting content in every course. Films, dramas, simulations, discussions, games, real problems, field trips, and the like can add interest and student involvement to classes. Although you do not want your classes to become slack, an occasional relaxed class may make your total effort more effective. A little fun and excitement never hurt anyone.

Fifth, you should also consider your own abilities, aptitudes and preferences. We all have methods and techniques with which we are more comfortable. Ordinarily we are more effective when we use them. Too many teachers, however, have only a small repertory. If you limit yourself to only a few approaches, you soon become dull, repetitive, and ineffective. Besides you need to have a number of methods and techniques at your fingertips to cope with the different teaching goals and learners, to create the type of climate you wish, and to give variety and depth to your teaching.

Sixth, you should bear in mind such practical factors as the time and space available, supplies and equipment needed, expense and health and safety.

Seventh, subject matter is an integral part of the learning activity. Without subject matter there can be no learning activity. When appropriate, the learning activity should include high level cognitive, affective, and psychomotor subject matter rather than being restricted to simple information and low level skills. Be sure that the subject matter you select contributes to the objective. Remember that subject matter content is a means to an end and not an end in itself. The end is to attain your teaching objectives.

Eighth, the teaching strategies and techniques that make up your learning activities must be suited to the subject matter to be taught.

Ninth, each of the learning activities you use should be aimed at at least one of your teaching objectives, and every teaching objective should have at least one learning activity aimed at it.

Finally, once selected, the learning activities must be arranged into a sequence or an organization for learning. This organization is, in effect, the body of the course, unit or lesson.

Evaluation Activities

You should plan for evaluating the students' progress and the success of your course, unit or lesson before you begin to teach it. Some experts of the competency-based education persuasion say that you should do so before planning your learning activities. This does not mean that every lesson plan should have a section entitled *evaluation*. It does mean that you should consider how you are going to assess student learning for each one of your objectives, determine the procedures you will use, decide the weighting of the various elements in your evaluation, and build the instruments before you start to teach. Hence, for instance, the unit test for a unit, if there is to be one, should be written before instruction in the unit begins.[6]

---

[6] See Chapter 17 for a discussion of the evaluation plan or table of specifications.

Implications

At this point, you should note several implications of the preceding sections.

1. Any teaching-learning activity that is not aimed at one or more of your objectives is useless and should be discarded.
2. Any teaching-learning activity that is not of a kind suitable for bringing about the learning desired is useless and should be discarded.
3. Any evaluation plan that does not assess the attainment of the teaching objectives fully and evenly is incomplete and should be discarded, rebuilt or supplemented.
4. Any evaluation item that does not assess the attainment of one or more of your teaching objectives is useless and should be discarded.

Make up two or three instructional objectives for a lesson you might teach. Give a half dozen learning activities you might use to achieve each of these objectives.

Team Planning

School district curricula, programs of study and course syllabi are generally planned by committees of teachers and supervisory or administrative personnel, or by central district office staffs. We shall not concern ourselves with this sort of planning. Planning for what actually happens in classes is the work of individual teachers who sit down with themselves and figure out what it is they want to do and how they want to do it. Presumably this is as it ought to be, if it is not overdone. Sometimes, however, courses, units, and even individual lessons are carried on as teacher team projects. This type of planning may be part of a formal teaching team arrangement or simply an informal ad hoc arrangement between colleagues. An example of such a flexible arrangement is that in which a social studies teacher and an English teacher finding that they by chance shared the same group of ninth-graders decided to collaborate on thier assignments. Another more formal arrangement is that in which the social studies, science, and English teachers agreed to cooperate on the assigning and reading of major research papers. Another more formal type of team planning arrangement in a middle school involves multidisciplinary teams which share the same students in their classes. The members of a team meet regularly to coordinate the planning in the various courses. In such planning the team members might agree to share assignments, or agree not to give long, difficult homework assignments or tests on the same day, or discuss the strengths and weaknesses of various students and work out special assignments and activities for them. Still another type of team planning is that of the formal teaching team of the so-called Trump Plan in which different teachers play different roles, some conducting large groups, some small groups, and so on. Teams of this sort require careful planning. To allow sufficient time for such planning, team-planning sessions may be incorporated into the daily schedule.

Except for the fact that it is done cooperatively by the team, team planning is not so very different from other planning. The problems of what, how, when, and where bear the same importance in cooperative efforts as in individual planning. The real difference is that the planning is complicated by the need to merge the varying notions and inclinations of several teachers into one unified, workable whole. Bringing about such harmony requires team members who are well versed in group process and careful attention to details so that each member knows what to do and how and when to do it. It also requires an infinite amount of following through and checking to ensure that the plans are properly executed.

Team planning does not necessarily imply teaching teams of any sort. Teachers who teach the same or similar courses may collaborate on the planning of course sequences and course content. Such planning can be instrumental in making a harmonious, well-articulated curriculum.

Teacher-Pupil Planning

In a social studies classroom a group of junior high school students were conducting a lesson. This lesson consisted of a series of committee reports on research projects just completed and a class discussion of the implications and significance of each of the reports under the quite capable direction of the young lady in charge.

The young lady was a ninth-grader. The lesson, the culmination of several weeks' work, had been organized and conducted by the students under her chairmanship. Three or four weeks before, the students had selected their topic from a short list of alternatives suggested by the teacher as one naturally following from their previous unit. In a group discussion they had decided the various facets of the topic they thought ought to be the most important to investigate. Then they formed committees to look into the various aspects of the topic to be investigated and to report to the group what they had learned. But before letting the committees start their work, the class as a whole had set up a set of standards to guide them in their research and to use in evaluating their success. Now they had come to the last step.

Almost every activity in this unit had been planned by the students themselves under the surveillance of the teacher. At no time had the teacher dictated to them just what they must or must not do. Neither had she ever left them without support or guidance. She was always there to remind them of the essentials, to suggest alternatives, to point out untapped resources, to correct errors, to question unwise decisions. This sort of teaching is teacher-pupil planning at its best. To do it well

requires great skill, much forebearance, and the careful training of one's students.

As you can see, cooperative teacher-pupil planning is an excellent method for involving students in the learning process. It is particularly effective in long-term planning (for example, unit planning) and the planning of individual projects. Furthermore, involving students in planning can also aid motivation. No one knows what students find interesting and important better than the students themselves. In addition, once the group has planned an activity, if the planning has been really successful, it becomes a group concern. Students who fail to do their part not only face the displeasure of the teacher, but let down the group. But, probably most important of all, teacher-pupil planning *offers one a laboratory in thinking, in making choices, in planning and in learning to work with others—in short, in democratic citizenship!*

Yet, in spite of its many virtues, teacher-pupil planning is not suited to every course and every teacher. To ask students to plan the topics in a course whose sequence is largely determined by the nature of the subject matter—as in mathematics—seems pointless. Besides, the students may not have enough information about the subject at hand to know what can be learned, its potential values or how to proceed. In order to plan well, one needs information.

Cooperative teacher-pupil planning is not student planning. It does not relieve you from your responsibilities and role as mentor. You must guide and limit; seldom, if ever, should you turn the students completely free. The amount of freedom the students should have depends upon many things, such as the students' maturity, their ability level, the subject, and their previous experience in cooperative planning. Students who have not learned how to plan will be overwhelmed if suddenly allowed to direct themselves. You either should explain to them potential directions they can take, or direct them to activities that will give them the knowledge they need, even if you must assume the major role in the planning and make most or even all of the decisions. Obviously teacher-pupil planning should not be used in the same way with all students, nor with all subjects.

Neither is teacher-pupil planning suited to all teachers. It requires teachers who do not need to be the center of the picture, who are not afraid of making errors, who can command respect without demanding it, who are relatively sure of their control and who are not afraid to subordinate themselves to the group.

Sometimes teachers are tempted to utilize teacher-pupil planning as a device for tricking students to do what they have already planned for their student to do. Such planning is not teacher-pupil planning. It is fakery. Do not do it. In all things you should be honest with your students. If you plan for them to choose within limits, prescribe the limits in advance. If you do not, you should go along with the students' decisions even though they be poor ones. To allow the students to plan and then to veto or revoke the plan is dishonest and it destroys the students' faith in your integrity. So do attempts to manipulate students' decisions. If you are not ready to accept students' decisions, you are not ready for teacher-pupil planning.

Introducing Teacher-Pupil Planning to a Class

The natural way to start on the road to teacher-pupil planning is to encourage students to plan their own individual activities. Once their objectives are firmly fixed and they know what activities they may choose from, or what activities may help them learn what they want to learn, then individuals can do much of their own planning without your doing much more than approve their plans. Of course, you will usually need to suggest a few changes of plan, recommended sources of materials and references, and guide the students as they work along. Using this procedure will relieve you of much of the detail, so that you can spend more

time working with individuals. In addition, the students learn how to do their own planning. It is unfortunate that many students have been deprived of this type of learning by overzealous teachers.

After starting with the planning of their individual activities, students can move up to planning small group activities. Again, you must expect the students to make mistakes and be ready to help them. The use of guide sheets can be quite helpful for students attempting to plan their own individual or group activities.

As they develop more maturity and skill in working as groups, the students can proceed to the more difficult task of planning class activities. Later, when they have become more sophisticated, they can move on to such difficult tasks as planning what to include in a topic, and, finally, what topics to include in a course. With inexperienced students one should not expect great success initially. The secret of success is to give them small responsibilities at first and gradually to increase these responsibilities as the students show they are ready. This principle of moving from a small beginning shows up in other techniques recommended for introducing teacher-pupil planning. One of these is to present alternative plans and to allow the students to select the plans they prefer. Thus, in a general mathematics class which is studying how to prepare a budget, you might ask the class whether they would prefer to make up a personal budget or to set up an organizational budget. In a music class you might ask the group to choose between preparing "The Soldiers' Chorus" or "When the Foeman Bares His Steel." In an English class the students might decide whether to study the short story or the drama next. Similarly students, as individuals or as a class, might choose their own goals from a list of behavioral objectives. Another way to involve students in the teacher-pupil planning is for the teacher to propose a plan of action and then ask for their suggestions and approval. In business education, for example, the teacher might ask the students if they would like to go to a bank and see how a bank operates. If they agree that this idea has possibilities, then they might discuss ways and means of making the visit and things they might wish to see when they get there.

Discussion Techniques in Teacher-Pupil Planning

As groups become skillful in using teacher-pupil planning techniques, they can do much of their planning in group discussion. *Discussion techniques are especially useful in deciding what to include in a topic.* If you were about to begin the study of insects, you might ask, "What do you think we should learn about insects?" During the discussion the students might propose such things as

- What do insects eat?
- How do they reproduce?
- What are insects anyway?
- How do you make an insect board? And so on.

Undoubtedly you will have to suggest some things yourself. For instance, somewhere in the discussion you might ask: "Don't you think we ought to know something about the insect's life cycle?" Perhaps the students will not know what a life cycle is. Probably when they do know, they will want to include it. If they do not, you should indicate the importance of the life cycle and point out the necessity for including it in the study.

Discussion techniques can also be used to plan learning activities. For example, as the class decides what it wants to study, you or the student leader should ask, "How do we go about it?" Thus, through class discussion, committees can be formed, readings can be suggested, dramatic roles can be cast, and field trips can be projected. Sometimes the class may ask a student or group to investigate and report on the feasibility of a project. Included in these plans should also be plans for evaluating what has been learned.

The same group discussion techniques can be used by a relatively mature group to select a topic for study. A good way to launch such discussion

is to ask the students to suggest possible plans for consideration. Perhaps you might ask the students to skim a chapter or a book to find topics in it they would like to learn about. Perhaps their curiosity may be piqued by a movie, a story, a teacher talk, or a discussion of some current event.

If discussion techniques are used in teacher-pupil planning, someone should keep a record of the decisions as they are made. If this record is kept on the chalkboard where everyone can see it, it makes the planning easier. As soon as the group has finished its planning, the final plan should be reduced to writing and given to the students, or posted on the bulletin board or the chalkboard, so that the students will have it for ready reference.

In making group decisions, straw votes are usually helpful. The technique seems to be to avoid putting the question to a formal vote, but frequently to seek an expression of opinion. This allows easy elimination of unpopular alternatives and avoids foundering on difficult decisions. When the straw vote shows a split decision, further discussion can often bring the students to agreement. If no agreement is reached, the students will usually be willing to compromise, e.g., "first your topic, then ours." If necessary, one can resort to a formal vote, but doing so may defeat the purpose of teacher-pupil planning and is liable to split the group.

Teacher-pupil planning is usually more satisfactory when the group has some criteria on which to base its decisions. These criteria can be made

What are the advantages of teacher-pupil planning? What are its dangers? When and where would you use it? How would you set about to use it?

Is teacher-pupil planning really better suited to certain subjects and courses than to others? Explain your answer.

How would you introduce teacher-pupil planning to a high school class that had never had experience in planning?

jointly or by the teacher with class approval. During the planning session the teacher may often have to remind the class of the criteria. "Is this the sort of thing you really wanted to do? Is this really pertinent to our problem?" By so doing you can usually improve the quality of group decisions without seeming to impose your own will on the students.

Resources for the Planner

Many resources are available to help you in your planning. Among them are textbooks, commercially developed courses and curriculum materials, curriculum guides and syllabi issued by local school authorities, curriculum bulletins from state and federal school agencies, and resource units. In some districts curriculum guides specify in great detail what should be taught and how it should be taught, but usually these materials are suggestive only. When this is true, how closely you should follow the text or the school curriculum guide is up to you. Perhaps at first, at least until you feel at ease with teaching and the course, it is wise to follow their suggestions rather closely.

You may find considerable help from the curriculum guides published by other school districts. A typical New York City curriculum bulletin for a social studies course, for instance, includes—in addition to such general background matter as the nature and structure of history, placement of social studies skills in the curriculum, and the scope and sequence of the New York City social studies curriculum—an outline of the course, suggested learning products for each of the various units or themes, a great sampling of suggested learning activities, and a list of recommended learning materials. Curriculum bulletins published by state departments of education and teachers' professional organizations are also helpful. So are such professional journals as *The English Journal, The Mathematics Teacher,* and *Social Education.* Many of these list

suggestions that can be particularly helpful for specific lessons.

Resource units can be especially valuable when planning units and lessons. They usually include such helpful information as

- An overview.
- A list of desired outcomes divided according to
    Understandings.
    Attitudes.
    Skills.
- An outline of content.
- A list of activities divided according to
    Initiatory activities.
    Developmental activities.
    Culminating activities.
- An annotated bibliography.
- An annotated list of films.
- An annotated list of filmstrips.

Teachers who utilize sources such as this usually find it easier to prepare good lessons than when they go on unassisted.

If they are not available in your school, look for curriculum guides, resource units, bulletins, textbooks, and other materials in teacher centers maintained by local county and state education agencies and colleges. In addition, ERIC Clearing Houses have multitudes of inexpensive resources available in microfiche. Collections of suggested teaching objectives are available from such organizations as IOX Assessment Associates, and in books such as Westinghouse Learning Press's *Mathematics Behavioral Objectives.*[7] Finally, you should always remember that other teachers and supervisors have hoards of information collected over the years. Teachers should share their ideas. Most teachers would be flattered to be asked to do so.

---

[7] IOX Assessment Associates, P.O. Box 24095W, Los Angeles, CA 90024-0095.

John C. Flanagan, Robert F. Mager, and William M. Shanner, *Mathematics Behavioral Objectives* (Palo Alto, CA.: Westinghouse Learning Press, 1971).

Examine the collection of curriculum bulletins, resource units, and the like, available in the teacher centers or curriculum libraries of your college and the local county or area school systems.

Check out several curriculum bulletins and resource units in your subject field. What do they contain? How could you use them in your work? How would they help you?

Examine the activities recommended for units in curriculum guides and resource units. Do they seem to you to be suited to the objectives and subject matter to be taught?

Make up a list of learning activities that would be suitable for teaching the content of a text in your own field.

Summary

Planning is absolutely essential if you are to make full use of your knowledge and skill. Poor planning has ruined many classes. In fact, it has been described as the most common cause of students' not learning.

The basic ingredients of a good teaching plan map out (1) what one plans for the students to learn, and (2) how one plans to bring about this learning. In addition, the planning must provide for evaluation, for without evaluation the two basic ingredients will not work. Good planning must be based on adequate diagnosis. Also helpful as a basis of planning are such instructional and curricular aids as textbooks, curriculum programs, curriculum guides and bulletins, and resource units. Teachers would do well to consult these resources carefully before they commit themselves to any particular plan.

Determining one's objectives is perhaps the most crucial part of planning for teaching. Many teachers neglect this aspect of planning, and as a result, their teaching is pointless and ineffective.

Since teaching objectives are potential learning products, they should be stated as learning products. They should be stated clearly and precisely as descriptions of the skill, understanding, or attitude one is seeking to develop or of the behavior by which one can judge the presence or absence of the desired skill, understanding, or appreciation. Perhaps the more useful type of instructional objective is the behavioral objective. Behavioral objectives may be either overt or covert, simple or criterion-referenced. Criterion-referenced behavioral objectives consist of five elements: The introductory phase, who (i.e., the learner); does what (i.e., the level of performance); how well (i.e., the behavior required); and under what conditions (i.e., the givens and/or restrictions or limitations that govern an acceptable performance). In any case, when writing behavioral objectives one should

1. Be sure that each general behavioral objective is written as a statement describing the behavior sought in general terms covert or overt, such as *understands, comprehends, knows,* or *appreciates.*
2. Be sure that each behavioral objective, general or specific, describes student performance rather than teacher performance.
3. Be sure each behavioral objective, general or specific, describes the terminal behavior of the student rather than subject matter, learning process, or teaching procedure.
4. Be sure that each behavioral objective is stated at the proper level of generality.
5. Be sure that each general behavioral objective is defined by a sampling of specific behavioral objectives that describe terminal behavior which will show when the objective has been reached.
6. Be sure that there is a sufficient sampling of relevant specific behavioral objectives to demonstrate that each of the more general objectives has been achieved.
7. Be sure that the behavioral objectives include

the complex high-level cognitive and affective goals that are so frequently omitted because they are so difficult to write.

8. Be sure that each specific behavioral objective includes only one learning product rather than a combination of learning products.

The learning activities in the plan should always be aimed at learning objectives. Therefore, you should take care to pick the types of activities that will further your goals. You should also consider such caveats as the abilities, interests, and learning styles of the students, the classroom situation, the materials available, the subject matter to be taught, and your own abilities and inclinations. No one method will meet all the requirements, so you should be prepared to use a variety of methods as the occasions demand.

Although the responsibility always rests on the teacher's shoulders, the students can often cooperate with the teacher in planning. If such planning is to be successful, students must be taught to plan. Usually the teacher and the students should start by designing class activities together. For a class to decide what it hopes to learn from a topic and what the topics of a course should be requires considerably more sophistication. With inexperienced students one should not expect great success initially. The secret is to give them small responsibilities at first and then increase the responsibilities as the students show they are ready.

Additional Reading

Alcorn, Marvin D., James M. Kinder, and Jim R. Schunert. *Better Teaching in Secondary Schools*, 3rd ed. New York: Holt, 1970.

Clark, D. Cecil. *Using Instructional Objectives in Teaching*. Glenview, IL: Scott Foresman, 1972.

Grambs, Jean Dresden, and John C. Carr. *Modern Methods in Secondary Education*, 4th ed. New York: Holt, 1979, Chap. 7.

Gronlund, Norman E. *Stating Objectives for Classroom Instruction*, 3rd ed. New York: Macmillan, 1985.

Hoover, Kenneth H. *The Professional Teacher's Handbook*, abridged, 2nd ed. Boston: Allyn and Bacon, 1976, Chap. 3.

Kibler, Robert J., Donald J. Cegala, Larry L. Barker, and David T. Miles. *Objectives for Instruction and Evaluation*. Boston: Allyn and Bacon, 1974.

Parrish, Louise, and Yvonne Waskin. *Teacher-Pupil Planning*. New York: Harper & Row, 1958.

Pierce, Walter D., and Michael A. Lorber. *Objectives and Methods for Secondary Teaching*. Englewood Cliffs, NJ: Prentice-Hall, 1977, Chaps. 2–4.

Popham, W. James, and Eva L. Baker. *Establishing Instructional Objectives*. Englewood Cliffs, NJ: Prentice-Hall, 1970.

Tanner, Daniel. *Using Behavioral Objectives in the Classroom*. New York: Macmillan, 1972.

Thompson, Duane G. *Writing Long-Term and Short-Term Objectives, A Painless Approach*. Champaign, IL: Research Press, 1977.

Zapf, Rosalind M. *Democratic Processes in the Secondary Classroom*. Englewood Cliffs, NJ: Prentice-Hall, 1959, Chaps. 4–6.

9

Course and Unit Planning

Overview

In this chapter we show you how to apply the general principles of planning to the planning of courses and units. By the end of the chapter you should have the basic information you need to write course and unit plans. In each case it is a simple matter of setting objectives, selecting the content and learning activities, planning the sequence and timing, providing for materials of instruction, and deciding how to evaluate one's success. This process is theoretically simple, but complex and difficult to execute.

Course Planning

As we have seen, many school agencies publish curriculum guides and course outlines in which they describe course objectives, unit objectives, content, teaching strategies and learning activities, materials of instruction, and evaluative procedures and instruments. Sometimes these are merely suggestions, but in this era of accountability some of these materials are highly prescriptive. When this is the case, wise teachers stick quite closely to the course outline. Your success as a teacher may be measured by how well your students meet the objectives set forth by the education agency. Even when the course outline is only suggestive, it is wise to follow it, making only minor adjustments to deal with specific conditions. The chances of a new teacher's improving on the suggested course are not great.

Three Steps in Course Planning

Whatever one uses as a basis for planning, the procedure for planning a course is relatively simple. You may enlist the aid of the students in carrying out the procedure, or you may do it all yourself. In either case, the responsibility for all the decisions made is yours. The procedure consists of the following steps.

1. Decide what it is that the students are to learn from the course. These are the course objectives which should determine the nature of all later procedures. This step may require considerable evaluation and diagnosis before it can be completed.
2. Decide what course content will bring about the desired objectives. This course content consists of two parts: (a) the subject matter of the course, i.e., the sequence of topics, and (b) the approach or strategy to be used in teaching the topics.
3. Decide the amount of time to be spent on the various topics in the sequence. This step is essential to ensure that the various portions of the course receive the attention they deserve. Neglect of this step is one cause of the all too common practice of proceeding slowly in the beginning of the course and then rushing through the last weeks of the course because of lack of time.

Some Principles of Course Planning

These steps are quite simple, but they should be done carefully to provide a course of maximum benefit to the students. When executing them you should keep the following principles in mind.

1. In general, knowledge of subject matter has very little value in and of itself. Rather, its value lies in its availability for use. Ordinarily the course objectives should consist of things that are useful now and appear most likely to be useful in the future in view of the goals, potentialities, and opportunities of the students, and the needs and expectancies of the nation—not just a mere accumulation of knowledge. This doctrine is sometimes called the *doctrine of contingent value.* To an extent this value is dependent upon the nature and structure of the subject matter or discipline concerned. Therefore, in setting up your objectives you must make your decisions in relation to the nature of the discipline and the probable usefulness of the subject matter. Once you have clearly established the course objectives, you should constantly keep them in mind. The objectives should be the touchstones you use in making decisions in later steps.
2. The subject matter and procedures that make up the content of the course should be such that they will contribute toward achieving the objectives of the course. Subject matter and procedures that are not consistent with the objectives should be discarded.
3. The course should be psychologically organized; that is to say, it should be organized around the students rather than around the subject matter. To that end the content and activities should
   a. be suitable to the students' abilities and interests;
   b. allow for differences in students;
   c. be a judicious mix of vicarious and direct experiences;
   d. seem to be of value to the students;
   e. provide an optimum amount of usable learning and opportunities to learn that learning;
   f. be selective, making important omissions in subject matter rather than attempting to cover everything;
   g. encourage logical memory and problem solving rather than overemphasizing rote learning and verbalism.
4. The course content should be so selected and

so organized that it gives the maximum amount of transfer and retention.

These principles apply to all course planning. At first glance they seem so axiomatic that they do not need repeating. Yet more teachers ignore them than follow them. One reason so much teaching is ineffective and irrelevant is that teachers neglect these four simple, but basic, principles.

The Objectives

With these principles in mind, you are now ready to decide what you wish to achieve in the course. In theory, you should be able to determine the course objectives from your study of the subject and your knowledge of the students. In practice, many teachers find this task demanding and very time-consuming. That is why the objectives listed in the curriculum guides and courses of study can be so helpful.

If no curriculum guides are available, you can determine what goals to pick for your course by studying the textbook or books commonly used in courses of this sort. The content of the texts will show what others have thought the course should contain. After studying these books you can decide how much of their thinking to accept, how much to reject, what you wish to add, and what you wish to emphasize. Then, once your decisions have been made, you can write down your objectives as the understandings, skills, and attitudes, i.e., terminal behavior, you hope the students will achieve.

The Content

Once the objectives have been selected, you must select a sequence of topics and approaches for teaching that will bring out these objectives. Too often planners forget this necessity. To reduce the argument to absurdity, if in French I your primary object is to teach students how to speak French, then the bulk of your coursework in Level I should consist of exercises in speaking French, not in translating written French or written English or in learning rules of grammar. *In some courses the subject matter and the manner of teaching it seem to have absolutely no relationship to the objectives the teachers claim to have.*

Planning the Sequence

With all these principles in mind, you can set up the sequence of topics or units for the course. This sequence should consist of broad topics that can be expected to take two to four weeks of class time to accomplish. At this time it is not advisable to map out the course in great detail day by day, because, at this stage, no one can forecast just how the course will develop. Save your detailed planning for your unit and lesson plans.

At this time you should also consider the general approach for the various topics and any major assignments such as research papers and projects. These items need to be considered because they will to some extent affect the time allotments of the various topics, and also, they need to be scheduled as to be integral parts of the course.

Courses of Study and Curriculum Guides

In deciding the sequence of topics, a course of study or curriculum guide can be a great help. Many courses of study or curriculum guides outline in great detail suggested topics, sequences and time allotments, as in the following example.

1. Air. Introduction to Physical Science. The Scientific Method (4 weeks)
2. Water (2 weeks)
3. Fuels (3 weeks)
4. Forces (3 weeks)
5. Chemicals (5 weeks)
6. Metals (2 weeks)
7. Plastics (2 weeks)
8. Textiles (2 weeks)

9. Food and Drugs (2 weeks)
10. Sound (1 week)
11. Light (2 weeks)
12. Electricity (2 weeks)
13. Vacuum Tubes (1 week)
14. Atomic energy (1 week)
15. Earth Science (8 days)
16. Astronomy (8 days)
    Review (2 weeks)

Other courses of study and curriculum guides, although they do not suggest the topics to be studied, do suggest what content should be covered. If your school system provides curriculum guides and courses of study of either type, make use of them. Not to do so may introduce confusion into a carefully planned school program. At times however, courses of study are suggestive and allow for considerable variation. Even when courses are rigidly laid out, teachers find they must vary them to suit the interests, needs, and abilities of the students. You can do so by such procedures as changing the course sequence, modifying the time spent on various topics, determining which topics should receive most emphasis, and varying the methods of teaching.

The Textbook and Course Planning

If your school system does not provide a curriculum guide, syllabus, or course of study, the most common method of selecting the content of a course is to follow a basic textbook. The chief merit of this plan is that it gives the beginning teacher an organized outline of the subject content to follow. However, you should recognize that all chapters are not of equal importance, and the text sequence is not always the best for every class. Slavishly following a textbook may cut one off from many opportunities for creativeness, from new ideas, from flexibility of approach, and from variety of method. It often leads to merely covering the subject rather than to significant learning.

Covering the Subject

In laying out the sequence of topics one should remember the principles of psychological organization of courses that were mentioned earlier in the chapter. Not only should we be sure that the sequence of topics follows a proper order psychologically, e.g., earlier units should lay a firm foundation for later units, but also we should guard against violating the principle of psychological organization in other ways. Perhaps the greatest danger to guard against in planning a course is the temptation to include too much. One of the worst diseases in American education is the belief of so many secondary school teachers that they must "cover the subject" by which they mean that they feel that they must squeeze into the course everything alluded to in the textbook or, perhaps, even all the topics in the field. When they attempt to "cover the subject," teachers often try to cover too much content for the time allotted. Consequently they whiz through a multitude of topics superficially. As a result, students may end up learning very little about anything. It would be much more satisfactory for them to gain clear concepts and skills in a smaller area. One cannot teach students everything on any subject. Better to teach more by attempting less than to attempt more and teach nothing.

The Course Calendar

Once you have decided on the topics to be discussed, you should map out a calendar for the course year. As you pick topics and arrange them in order, estimate the amount of time to be spent on each topic. Again the decisions should be approximate—in weeks and fractions of weeks rather than days. You should, however, base the course calendar on the days available in the school year. In making this estimate remember to allow for assemblies, examinations, storms, and other contingencies that cause class periods to be cancelled. Ten days is a reasonable allowance for missed periods. If at the end of the year you find that this allowance is too great, you can use the extra time for review or for a special topic at the end of the term.

Continuous-Progress Modulated Courses

Planning individualized modulated curricula or courses is little different from planning ordinary courses. About the only difference is that one must divide the course into modules (i.e., units) and provide the students with instructional or learning-activity packets.

As a rule, students work through the modules according to the sequence set up by the instructor. However, in many courses it may be better if the modules are built so that the students can choose their own sequence of units on the basis of their interests and abilities rather than to follow a set sequence of modules in courses in which a set sequence is not essential.

Discussion of the planning and conducting of continuous progress curricula may be found in Chapter 16, "Provisions for Individual Differences."

Of what value are textbooks, curriculum guides, and courses of study in the planning of a course? How should each of them be used? How rigidly should they be followed?

Examine a text for a course you might teach. What would you stress? What, if anything, would you omit?

Study a course guide for a course you might teach. Compare it with a text. In what ways would it help you with your planning?

One author says that one should not follow a text in planning a course. Do you agree? Why, or why not?

Unit Planning

Courses are divided into units. A unit is a planned sequence of learning activities or lessons covering a period of several weeks and centered around some major concept, theme, or topic. It may be made up of a series of mainly expository, content-oriented lessons or semiindividualized laboratory-oriented, experience-centered unit assignments or any of a variety of combinations or variations of either of these extremes. Learning activity packets, learning modules, and learning contracts are all examples of variations on the unit idea.

To Plan an Ordinary Unit

An ordinary unit is simply a sequence of daily lesson plans that present a topic, a chapter, or portion of a course. To plan such a unit, one simply devises a sequence of daily plans that will present the contents and objectives of the topic, chapter, or section of the course outline. In any case, planning an ordinary unit is a relatively simple matter. In general, it can be reduced to the following steps.

1. Select the topic. Presumably the topic will be one suggested by the course outline or the textbook outline. In any case it should

---

How can a teacher determine whether a particular topic is worth the time and effort?

It has been stated that the basic criteria for judging a topic are the nature of the student and the nature of the society in which he lives. Is this a valid statement? Why, or why not?

Where might one turn to find suggestions for suitable topics?

a. Center around some major understanding, problem, issue, or theme.

b. Fit the course objectives and further the course plan.

c. Be relevant to students' lives and to the society in which they live.

d. Be manageable—not too difficult, too big, or too demanding on time and resources.

e. Be suitable to students' abilities and interests.

2. Prepare the goals or objectives. Again these may be set forth in the local course outline, curriculum guide, resource unit, or curriculum bulletin. If not, you may wish to consult curriculum materials published by other schools. Or you may wish to decide yourself what you want the students to get out of the unit from a study of the textbook or from your own expertise. In any case, you should decide and note down what your general objectives will be. These should correspond to the course outline. Then you should decide what learnings are necessary to meet these objectives. These learnings will be your specific objectives and to some extent your content. The point is to pick objectives that are worthwhile and which contribute to the achievement of course and unit goals. Then write them down as descriptive or behavioral objectives. If these have been spelled out in the course outline, so much the better. If the district has set them up as performance objectives (criterion-referenced behavioral objectives), it is usually imperative that you use these specific objectives as your specific objectives.

3. Outline the content if it seems desirable. If the specific objectives delineate the unit content sufficiently, a content outline may be superfluous. Otherwise preparing an outline may clarify the subject matter to be covered and help you give organization to your unit. Again, if an outline of the unit content is provided in the district's curriculum guide, bulletin, or course outline you should adopt (rarely adapt) the suggested outline. Following is an example of a content outline for a unit in a junior high school block-of-time course specified by a local school district.

AMERICAN EDUCATION

Outline of Content

A. Why do we have public schools?
  1. History of public education in America.
  2. Comparison of education in the United States with other countries, both free and totalitarian.
  3. Value of private and parochial schools in American life.
  4. Purposes of the public schools:
    a. Health.
    b. Command of fundamental processes.
    c. Worthy home membership.
    d. Vocational preparation.
    e. Civic education.
    f. Worthy use of leisure time.
    g. Ethical and moral character.
  5. Achievements of our public schools in America.
    a. Americanization of 30,000,000 immigrants in the past (assimilation).
    b. Helped unite American people (promoted nationalism).
    c. Promotion of ethical and moral values, tolerance, respect for groups, etcetera.
    d. Promoted equality of opportunity for all.
    e. Provided leaders and skilled workers to promote the miracle of American economic production.
    f. Promoted loyalty to America.

B. What is our local school organization like?
  1. Levels of schools:
    a. Elementary.
    b. Junior High.
    c. Senior High.
    d. Possible local college.
  2. Purposes of various levels:
    a. Elementary:
      (1) Development of basic skills.
      (2) Social competencies.
      (3) Good citizenship.
      (4) Security through the self-contained classroom.

b. Junior High
   (1) Continuation of basic skills.
   (2) Beginning of departmentalization in some areas.
   (3) The core (block-of-time) program of integration of subject matter.
   (4) The junior high as a transition between elementary and senior high.
   (5) The junior high designed for early adolescents and their problems.
   (6) Improved guidance services.
   (7) More school activities.
c. Senior High
   (1) Continuation of basic skills.
   (2) More departmentalization.
   (3) More emphasis on vocational training or college preparation.
   (4) Special courses such as typing, driver training.

C. What do we need to carry out our school program?
  1. Personnel: What are the functions of the following?
    a. Board of Education.
    b. Superintendent.
    c. Assistant Superintendents.
    d. Principal.
    e. Vice-Principal.
    f. Teachers.
    g. Counselors.
    h. Psychologist.
    i. Nurse.
    j. Librarian.
    k. Custodians.
    l. Matron.
    m. Maintenance workers.
    n. Cafeteria workers.
    o. Curriculum coordinator.
    p. Secretaries.
    q. Lay committees.
    r. P.T.A.
  2. School Plant
    a. School buildings old and new.
    b. Functional design of our building.
  3. School Materials. Summary of books, supplies, equipment and furnishings we use, and the cost of each.

D. What is the cost of public education and how do we pay for it?
  1. Cost.
    a. of buildings.
    b. of current expenses.
  2. Sources of funds
    a. Local.
    b. State.
    c. Federal.
  3. The school budget
    a. What it is.
    b. How it is made up.
    c. What this year's budget looks like.
    d. Analysis of items.

E. Our program at Thomas Jefferson J.H.S.
  1. Basic subjects offered.
  2. Extra-class activities.
  3. Special things our school offers, such as foreign language, advanced curriculum, and block-of-time programs.

4. Set up the learning activities. At this point it may not be necessary to plan each activity in detail as long as they are specific enough to be organized into a plan. In setting up these activities consider what activities you wish to use to introduce the unit (introductory activities), what activities to develop the unit (developmental activities), and what activities to use to clinch the learning, assess the success of the teaching and learning, and generally bring things to a satisfactory conclusion (culminating activities).

5. Arrange the activities into a series of lessons and set up a schedule or calendar for the lessons. These lessons can be listed as a calendar, e.g., First week
    Monday: Introductory lecture, discussion;
    Tuesday: Movie; American Revolution, and so on;
or the layout sheets of a lesson plan book (see Chap. 10).

6. Plan the unit's logistics: i.e., gathering and preparation of the materials of instruction. This includes the preparation of study guides, bibliographies, lists of materials, dittos, and the like, plus the collection of audiovisual materials, reading material, supplies and equipment for group and individual projects, and so forth. You should also prepare for your own guidance lists of materials, equipment, audiovisual aids and readings pertaining to the unit. Here you indicate the materials and equipment that will be needed and references one should read to be properly prepared.

7. Plan and prepare the tests and other evaluative exercises.

Pick a topic from a text for a course you might teach. Outline what you would include in the unit on that topic.

What introductory activities might you use?

What developmental activities might you use?

What culminating activities might you use?

Arrange these activities into a sequence of lessons.

Laboratory-Type Units

Mr. Jones's Unit

The unit just described is simply a series of lesson plans focused around a certain topic or central idea. The author of such a unit plan blocks out tentative plans for each day and provides for additional optional activities such as projects, writing assignments and the like.

Mr. Jones's unit on minority groups at Quinbost High School is quite different. Mr. Jones always tries to make his course interesting and challenging so that it will stimulate and motivate students. For this unit he decided that in order to induce in students a proper set for the beginning of this unit, he would play the devil's advocate. Therefore, on the day he was to begin the unit, he came to the classroom seemingly in an angry mood, tossed his books on the desk, and glared at the class. He then began a tirade on a particular minority group, telling the class about something a member of this group had done to him the day before, and concluded by saying that all members of that particular group were alike.

Immediately his class began to challenge him, disagreeing and telling him that he was unfair to generalize from one incident and that he shouldn't talk like that. Seizing upon this reaction, Mr. Jones then asked the class whether or not they had ever expressed such feelings toward any group. As the animated discussion continued, the class members began to see what the teacher was doing. Almost as one body they said that they wanted to discuss minority groups as a class topic.

The stage had been set! The teacher had fired their interest; the desire to study the topic was evident[1] He, then, set the class to talking about what subject matter they felt should be discussed and what outcomes there should be. This led to general teacher-pupil planning. Soon students were choosing committees and projects on which to work. Then, with the aid of study guides and their committee and project assignments, individual students completed tentative plans for their role in the unit.

The study guide they used consisted of three parts. The first part noted questions and problems everyone was to find answers for and suggested where the students might look to find these answers. The second part listed a number of readings and activities that the students might find interesting. All students were expected to do some of these, but no one had to do any particular one. In none of these optional activities or the required problems and questions were the students held to any prescribed reading or procedure. All they were asked to do was carry out the activity, solve the problem, or find the information; they had free choice of ways and means. The third part of the study guide was a bibliography.

---

[1] You, of course, recognize this tactic of Mr. Jones's as a form of set induction.

Once the teacher and students had finished the planning, they began to work. Except for two periods that Mr. Jones used for motion pictures, the next two weeks were devoted to laboratory work. The committees met; the researchers researched; the pupils carried out their plans.

Then the committees began to report. Some of the groups presented a panel. One did a play. Another conducted a question-and-answer game. In all of these activities students tried to bring out what they had learned. In between these reports, Mr. Jones and the students discussed the implications of the findings and other points they thought pertinent and important.

Finally the unit ended with all the students setting down their ideas concerning the treatment of minority groups and with a short objective test based on the teacher's objectives as shown in the questions of the study guide.

Thus, after a little over three weeks, the unit was finished.

What do you think of Mr. Jones's method of set induction? Do you see any dangers in using such an approach?

What advantages does this type of unit have over a unit made up of a series of lesson plans?

Planning a Classroom Laboratory-Type Unit

Mr. Jones's unit was carried out as a classroom laboratory. Planning the classroom laboratory-type unit is similar to the planning of an ordinary unit except for the following embellishments.

After you have set up the unit objectives and decided on the unit learning activities, you should prepare a unit assignment. This unit assignment should include both required and optional activities.

The Basic Activities.   The basic required activites should be prepared so that all the students may have experiences suitable to their own levels. At least some of the activities should be appealing to the nonacademically minded youngsters. Sometimes teachers reserve all the interesting projectlike activities for optional activities or extracredit work after the required work has been finished. This is poor practice. The youngster who needs stimulation most may never have a chance to do anything stimulating.

The students should be able to reach all of the teacher's specific objectives by way of the basic activities. To be sure that the activities really do contribute to all of these learnings, you should note just what learning product or products each activity is supposed to produce. This practice will help ensure that each activity does contribute to some objective and that all the objectives are provided for.

The Optional Activities.   Optional related activities are activities that students may do if they wish. They should be truly optional. No student should be required to do any of them, although an effort may be made to interest particular students in whichever of these activities might be especially beneficial to them. Students' marks should not depend upon their completing any of them. You should allow students to drop optional activities that prove to be distasteful, if it seems desirable. In a sense the optional activities are projects. The students should be encouraged to suggest other activities not yet included in the unit assignment. Often student-suggested activities are the best of all.

Phases in the Laboratory Unit.   As in other units, the activities in the unit assignment should be arranged into introductory, developmental, and culminating phases. In addition to introducing the unit, arousing students' interest and showing the relationship of this unit with other units, the introductory phase is used by students to plan their individual assignments, especially if, as in Mr. Jones's unit, students are to do individual or small group work. A good procedure is to distribute study guides and let the students, under guidance, prepare their own plans. A sample form for a student plan follows. The students should not be held closely to their plans; they should be permitted to change and amplify them throughout later phases of the unit.

Work Plan

NAME _____ CLASS _____
UNIT _____ DATE _____

Activities I plan to do.

Committees I plan to work with.

Materials I plan to read.

Things I plan to make.

Select a unit for a course you hope to teach. What specifically might you do to challenge and motivate the students during the introductory phase of the unit?

What are the merits of using a pretest as an introductory activity? Under what circumstances would you recommend using a pretest?

The following were suggested as possible interest-catching introductory activities. What do you think of them?
1. Example One is a demonstration.
   To get things moving quickly, one chemistry teacher makes a practice of starting his unit on oxidation with a *bang*. As he starts his introductory talk, he casually mixes together the ingredients for a demonstration that, he says, is yet to come. Suddenly an explosion nearly rocks the students off their seats. The teacher and students quickly follow the explosion with questions and discussion. What happened? Why? And so on.
2. Example Two is a laboratory procedure. The directions for it are
   a. Select five substances with characteristic odors, such as an onion, orange, fish, mint,

or peanut. Place them in small corked bottles.
   b. Blindfold your companion and be sure he holds his nose so he cannot smell. Let him taste each substance separately and describe it to you. Record each description carefully. Make two trials.
   c. Keep your companion blindfolded, but do not hold his nose. This time let him smell each substance and describe it. Make two trials.
   d. Compare the descriptions of the taste and smell of each substance as he gives them to you. How do they differ? Can you draw any conclusions about a person's relative ability to taste and smell? Do you think a cold in the nose makes any difference in the enjoyment of food? Why?
   Are these examples really good interest-catching introductory activities? Why, or why not? If not suitable as is, how might you adapt them?

In the developmental phase, one jumps off from the springboards set up in the introductory phase to accomplish the nitty-gritty of the learning process. You might, for instance, set up a series of lessons—teacher talks, discussions, investigative assignments, small group work, composition, reading, oral reports, evaluation and research as well as optional activities—or you might decide to use a laboratory class approach[2] as Mr. Jones did in his unit on minority groups. Although this approach may be somewhat difficult to organize and control, the use of the laboratory class and unit assignment has the advantage of making it easier to organize teaching techniques and teaching devices so as to facilitate individualization of instruction, motivation, student planning and student responsibility for their own learning, and place

---

[2] See Chapter 16, "Provisions for Individual Differences."

teaching emphasis on the higher levels of cognitive and affective learning.

In the laboratory unit assignment the students should find a wide selection of both required and optional activities from which they may choose. Usually these activities are best presented to the students in a mimeographed study guide. This gives the students a basis for planning their own activities and allows them to begin new activities without waiting for other members of the class. It also frees you to work with individuals and small groups who need help, guidance, and counseling.

Logically, the laboratory unit assignment approach should culminate in the sharing of the interesting things learned during the laboratory experience. Ordinarily, the students should do the programming themselves, but the teacher must guide them carefully to ensure variety and sparkle. Some devices that you may use are

1. Panels.
2. Oral talks.
3. Dramatizations.
4. Writing up the activities for publication.
5. Debate.
6. Group discussions.
7. Meetings of the class.
8. Exhibits.
9. Demonstrations.
10. Preparing an anthology of student work.
11. Presenting and defending a position.
12. Recordings and tapes.
13. Audiovisual materials.
14. Moving pictures.
15. British style debate.
16. Mock trials.
17. Student-conducted summaries.
18. Teacher-conducted summaries.

A laboratory unit assignment type of unit plan can succeed only if it is kept flexible. It does not always roll forward relentlessly. Not everyone spends Monday and Tuesday working on individual projects and Wednesday and Thursday sharing what they have learned with each other, although

sometimes this makes an excellent plan. Instead, progress in the unit's developmental phase may vary from student to student. For some it speeds; for others it dawdles. For many students it starts, stops, turns back, and then starts again. If one group has finished the preparation of a dramatization and is ready to present it to the class early in the unit long before any other group is ready to share the experience, a good unit plan must be flexible enough to allow this group to present its dramatization then and there. Later the students may go to some other activities. Thus the unit has passed from the laboratory activities to the sharing of experiences and back again. In fact, in units that emphasize individualization, different students may be working on each of the phases at the same time. Furthermore, the developmental activities may be interspersed with evaluative activities from time to time. In a good unit the process of evaluation is continuous. Both laboratory and sharing of experience activities give the teacher excellent opportunities to assess students' progress and needs. The unit assignment laboratory class approach is especially adaptable for student self-evaluation.

How can a teacher provide for individual differences if he prepares a unit assignment in advance?

Should optional related activities be done only by the brilliant students who finish early?

Would it be good practice for a teacher to suggest a number of activities and then insist that every student freely select and do at least one of these activities whether interested in any of them or not?

It is sometimes said that the unit assignment should consist largely of a series of problems. Do you agree? What would the advantages be? the limitations?

At what point and how much should the students plan the unit assignment or their part in it?

Study and Activity Guides. After selecting the basic required and optional activities, the teacher should prepare a study guide containing instructions for carrying out basic activities and assignments, problems to be solved, suggestions for optional activities, and so on.

Some theorists decry the use of study guides on the basis that study guides may limit the creativity and originality of the student. To some extent this may be true, but good study guides seem to have advantages that outweigh the disadvantages.

1. They give the student a *source* to which they can refer if they forget the assignment.
2. They give the students a *picture* of possible activities so that they can pick the activities they wish to do and the order in which they wish to do them.
3. They give the students a *definite assignment* so that they can go ahead to new activites on their own without waiting for a new assignment from the teacher.
4. They give *definite instructions* which should eliminate misunderstandings about assignments and many excuses for incomplete or unattempted assignments.

The following is an example of a study and activity guide developed for a unit on race relations in a twelfth-grade class in Problems of Democracy.

General Study and Activity Guide

1. What are the various groups that make up the population of the United States? 2:42–45[3]
2. Make a classification of the different groups and give numbers. 14:521–527.
3. What is the composition of our population in Middletown?

---

[3] These numbers refer to readings that the student may consult to find the answers to a particular problem.

4. What are the various sects (religious) in the United States? 1:101.
5. Give the names and numbers of the ten largest. 1:101.
6. How many of these religions are represented in Middletown? In Middletown High School?
7. How have these various groups affected the growth and development of the United States? Name the contributions of these groups. 14:512–517, 521–524.
8. What are some of the problems of harmonious relationships between different races and groups? 14:498–502.
9. When is a group regarded as a minority? 6:582.
10. How does prejudice destroy harmony between groups? 6:586–587.
11. What is prejudice ? 26:Ch. 1.
12. How do we get our prejudices? 26:16; 22:29–33.
13. What are the principal races in the world? 6:84–89.
14. What is the meaning of discrimination? 6:89.
15. Give one example of political, social, and economic discrimination from your own experience.
16. How can we improve on the existing efforts to destroy prejudice and discrimination?
17. What is the work of the Commonwealth Fair Employment Practices Commission?
18. What can you do to prevent discrimination?
19. Name four types of groups often regarded as minorities. 6:582–606.
20. What is the dominant group in America? 6:582–606.
21. What constitutes the differences between groups? 6:606.
22. Name the effects of prejudice on the person who practices it. 27.
23. Discuss the relationship of prejudice to Democracy. 27.
24. Is there such a thing as "racial superiority"? Explain your answer. 6:84–95.
25. Make a full report in writing on social adjustment involving the immigrant.

26. Read the Roll of Honor in your neighborhood for World War II. Copy ten names at random and try to determine their ancestry. Conclusion.

The study guide should also include a list of any materials needed by the students and a bibliography. (These have been omitted from the sample study and activity guide to save space.) The bibliography should consist largely of materials at the reading level of the students. However, there should be books difficult enough to challenge the brightest students, as well as others for the slow learners. References in the text may be keyed into this bibliography by a system similar to that illustrated in the sample study and activity guide.

Lists of materials required for specific activities should be part of the description of the activity. If including the list makes the description of the activity too long, the detailed description may be filed on 4 × 6 or 5 × 8 cards or placed on the bulletin board, thus keeping the size of the study guide reasonable.

Special Study and Activity Guides. Usually the optional activities should be described by title and perhaps a brief notice in the study and activity guide or on a bulletin board. This serves to make the students aware of optional activities which might interest them. Detailed instructions for such activities can be kept on 5 × 8 or 4 × 6 file cards. Upon spotting a likely optional activity in the general activity and study guide, the student can go to the file, examine the card and, if the activity seems worthwhile, proceed to carry it out with the teacher's permission. This means, of course, that several cards must be available for each activity. If this seems impossible, the student can himself copy the instructions.

Another type of special study guide is that which is prepared to help the students get more out of such activities as field trips and moving pictures. Such special activity and study guides are used to point out the things that one should observe and the things one should investigate in such activities.

The following is an example of a special guide for an optional activity in Mr. Jones's unit on Race Relations.

Special Activity Guide

Report on Americanization Work in Middletown
1. Interview Mr. Rand in Room 310. Mr. Rand is head of the evening school in Middletown. Ask him questions along this line and take notes on his answers.
   a. What is the work of the Americanization classes?
   b. Who teaches these classes? What are their qualifications?
   c. What people are eligible for these classes?
   d. Why are the classes necessary?
   e. What subjects are taught and why?
   f. When a person completes the course what happens?
   g. How long does this course last?
   h. Who pays for it?
   i. What is the attitude of the people in the class toward America?
   j. How many people in Middletown have completed the course in the last ten years?
   k. Where do these people come from?
2. Write up the answers in the form of a report and submit it to the teacher for approval. Indicate whether you would be willing to give the report to some other class if called upon to do so.

The Daily Lesson Plan in the Unit Assignment

The unit plan does not eliminate daily planning. Before each class you should think through what is to be done that day and jot down the agenda for the day. This plan will include such things as announcements, programs of activities, reminders to work with certain students or groups, notes for teacher talks, and the like. When the major part of the planning has been taken care of by the unit assignment the daily plan may be quite sketchy and informal. At times it may be as simple and brief as "continue laboratory session"; at other times it may be simply a list of the committee and individual reports or activities to be presented that period. Sometimes, however, it will be necessary to work out detailed lesson plans for carrying out what the unit plan outlines.

> What part of the unit assignment should be placed on cards or on the bulletin board? Why?
>
> What is the use of a study guide? Some authorities do not approve of using study guides. Do you?
>
> What is the use of a special study guide?
>
> Should all students begin at the beginning of a unit assignment and proceed with the suggested activities in order? Why, or why not? If not, how should they proceed?

Learning Activity Packets

Learning modules (sometimes called instructional learning packets, learning activity packets, instructional modules, instructional packets, or learning packets) are really a variation of the unit plan. They are especially useful for individualizing instruction. Basically the procedure for planning and building a learning module is the same as that for any other unit. The differences lie in the provisions for individualization and continuous progress.

1. The general objective is written as an overview that includes not only a description of the terminal behavior expected, but also reasons for studying the module and acquiring this learning.
2. The specific objectives are written as behavioral objectives, either simple or criterion-referenced, that tell the students what they are supposed to know, do or feel at the end of the module. Usually these should be written in the second person.

3. The activities are so designed that the students can work on their own without having to depend on the teacher for direction. The idea behind the learning module approach is for the learner to be largely self-directing and the teacher to be a guide rather than a master.
4. The evaluation plan should include some sort of self-correcting pretest which will show students where their strengths and deficiencies lie. In individualized programs probably there should be some means for capable students to "test out" of a module by demonstrating that they have achieved its objectives. Teacher-administered pretest schemes can be used for this purpose. Self-correcting progress tests will also be useful for helping the students evaluate their own work as they progress through the module. In addition some sort of posttesting device should be used to measure the students' final progress. Probably this should be some sort of teacher-corrected criterion-referenced post-test or performance instrument.
5. The instruction is centered around the study guide or learning packet. This is the document students will use to guide themselves through the module. Since it is the basis of individual study and self-guidance, it should be prepared very carefully. In it students will find
   a. Topic.
   b. Rationale, including the general objectives and reasons why the learning is worthwhile.
   c. The specific objectives stated as specific behavioral objectives—and addressed to the student, e.g., "At the end of this mod you should be able to locate the principal oceanic streams on the globe." Sometimes provisions are made for students to check off each of these behavioral objectives upon mastering the behavior called for.
   d. Directions for the student to follow while completing the module. These directions should include
      (1) General directions: agenda, time limits (if any), and options.

(2) Specific directions: that is, the directions and explanations for specific activities. For example,

   (a) Problems to be solved: What the problem is, what the background of the problem is, what requirements must be met to solve the problem successfully.

   (b) Reading: Purpose of the reading, what information is to be learned, what is to be done with the information, questions on the reading, exact citations.

   (c) Information to be learned: possible sources of the information.

(3) Where to go for materials and information.

e. Bibliography.

f. Instructional materials that you have prepared for the module. (These may be included with the study guide or distributed separately.)

g. Self-correcting and other testing and evaluating materials. These should include both pre-test and post-test material and perhaps intermediate progress tests. These may be included with the study guide or distributed separately. Note, however, that teacher-corrected mastery tests should be distributed separately as needed—not included in the original packet. Mastery tests should be administered separately under supervision and corrected by the teacher. Progress tests, on the other hand, are more useful when they are self-correcting.

An example of a learning module may be found in the Appendix.

The Contract Plan

The contract plan is a variation of the unit plan, in which the student agrees to do a certain amount of work during a time period.

Procedure for a Typical Contract. In preparing contracts you might follow a procedure something like the following:

1. Set up objectives and activities whereby students may achieve the objectives.
2. Decide which activities will be required.
3. Decide which activities will be optional.
4. Provide these to the student in writing so he can study them.
5. Let the student decide how he will meet the requirements and what optional work he will do.
6. On the basis of the decision have the student make out a contract in writing. Each contract may be different from every other contract.
7. An example of a contract is:

CONTRACT

John Jones   To be completed by May 1.

During the period of April 10 to May 1, I will

1. Read Chapters X–XIII of book A.
2. Do problems and exercises #1, 2, 4, 7, 8, 9, 11 of the study guide.
3. Participate on the map committee with Mike Smith, John Walsh, and Ted Burke.
4. Prepare a report on the topography of the area.
5. X X X X
(Remaining activities omitted to save space)

Signed _____
                    Student

Approved _____
                    Teacher

Another type of contract calls for setting up certain requirements for the various grade levels. For example,

To pass with a D you must complete activities 1–12 and pass the post-test.

To receive a C you must complete activities 1–12, receive at least a C on the post-test, and do two (2) of the optional activities satisfactorily.

To receive a grade of B, you must complete activities 1–12, receive at least a grade of B on the post-test, and satisfactorily complete at least four of the optional activities very well.

To receive a grade of A you must complete activities 1–12, do four of the optional activities excellently, complete at least one major optional activity very well, and receive at least a B+ on the post-test.

Summary

The responsibility for planning is the teacher's. You must plan your own courses and units, although you may have curriculum guides, courses of study, resource units, textbooks, and other materials to draw from. When planning courses, you can find these devices greatly helpful. In some school systems you may be expected to follow them exactly. Often, however, they are intended to be suggestive rather then prescriptive. In either case the course planner should select subject matter that has contingent value, clear, reasonable objectives, and content and procedures that will build these objectives. To lay out the course, the planner should set up a sequence of broad topics or units and suggest a timetable for the completion of the topics. Care should be taken not to overload the course, for attempting to cover too much may result in nothing's being done well. Many teachers use the textbook as the course outline. This is good practice, but one should not become a slave to the text. Usually teachers find that they must adapt the text or a suggested course outline to exigencies of the teacher's situation.

One prepares continuous modulated courses just as any other course, except that in addition to laying out the topics or units one must prepare learning activity or instructional packets for the students as well. In such courses the course timetable is allowed to vary from student to student. When a student finishes one packet satisfactorily, he then goes on to another one.

In planning an ordinary unit, one, in effect, assembles a group of lessons around a topic. Basically the procedure consists of
1. Selecting teaching objectives.
2. Building a series of lessons by which to reach these objectives.
3. Arranging the lessons into a sequence consisting of
   a. Introductory lessons.
   b. Developmental lessons.
   c. Culminating lessons (including unit tests).

Variations on the unit plan include classroom-laboratory type units, learning-activity packets, and contracts.

The following is an outline of the type of classroom laboratory unit plan suggested in this chapter.

1. An overview that describes the nature and scope of the unit.
2. The teacher's specific objectives that are the understandings, skills, attitudes, ideals, and appreciations he hopes the students will get from the unit.
3. The unit assignment that includes activities in which the class will participate during the teaching of the unit. The activities will be of two types: (1) the basic activities to be done by all students to some extent in some time, and (2) the optional related activities.
4. The study and activity guide that will contain the instructions for carrying out the core activities to be done individually and in small groups.
5. The special study and activity guides that contain the instructions for carrying out the optional activities.

6. A list of materials and readings the boys and girls may use in their study.
7. A short bibliography and list of materials for the use of the teacher alone.
8. Testing or other devices to be used in evaluating the success of the unit. These devices should test adequately each of the learning products described in 1 and 2 of this outline.

As in the ordinary unit the unit assignment should be introduced by introductory activities that will catch the students' interest and help the teacher know the students. Following the introductory phase comes individual and small-group work interspersed by class activities and opportunities for the students to share their experiences and learning. Finally the unit of work ends in some sort of culminating exercise.

Learning modules are really special types of units. The procedure for planning them is essentially the same as for other units. In carrying out the modules and packets, you will find that they are most successful when you use the laboratory approach.

Contracts are simply units in which the student agrees to do certain things. The contract may or may not specify the grade the student can expect for completing the work contracted for satisfactorily.

Additional Reading

Alcorn, Marvin D., James W. Kinder, and Jim R. Schunert. *Better Teaching in Secondary Schools,* 3rd ed. New York: Holt, 1970.

Gayles, Anne Richardson. *Instructional Planning in the Secondary Schools.* New York: McKay, 1973, Part IX.

Grambs, Jean D., and John C. Carr. *Modern Methods in Secondary Education,* 4th ed. New York: Holt, 1979, Chap. 7.

Hoover, Kenneth H. *The Professional Teacher's Handbook,* abridged 2nd ed. Boston: Allyn and Bacon, 1976, Chap. 3.

Meyen, Edward L. *Developing Instructional Units: For the Regular and Special Teacher,* 3rd ed. Dubuque, IA: Brown, 1980.

Pierce, Walter D., and Michael A. Lorber. *Objectives and Methods for Secondary Teaching.* Englewood Cliffs, NJ: Prentice-Hall, 1977, Chaps. 9–11.

Stewart, William J. *Transforming Traditional Unit Teaching.* Boston: American Press, 1982.

————. *Unit Teaching Perspectives and Prospects.* Boston: American Press, 1983.

Zapf, Rosalind M. *Democratic Processes in the Secondary Classroom.* Englewood Cliffs, NJ: Prentice-Hall, 1959, Chaps. 4–6.

10

Lesson Planning

Overview

Lessons are the atoms that make up units, courses, and curricula. They usually last for a single period although sometimes they may be continued for several days. On their success depends the effectiveness of the unit, course, or curriculum. Therefore the daily lesson plan is a key element in successful teaching.

Ordinarily teachers are best served by carefully thought out, written lesson plans. In this chapter we examine in some detail the writing of lesson plans according to one format. We also present several alternative formats. The type of plan one adopts is not so very important as long as it is clear, logical, and easy to follow. We also present several sample lesson plans. It is hoped that by the time you get through with this chapter you will have some understanding of the need for careful lesson plans, and of the essential elements in lesson planning.

The Need for Planning

Every lesson should be planned. Sometimes the daily lesson plan should be minimal. For instance, one may be carrying on a unit in a laboratory fashion. In such a case the procedure may be simply to help and guide students' endeavors as they do their laboratory work. Other unstructured classes include certain kinds of problem-solving and discussion classes. Nevertheless, no teacher can face a class for long without having carefully thought out what the students are to learn from the lesson and how they are to learn it. In short, you need to know what the lesson's objectives are, what the content is, what the procedures will be, and how they will be executed. It is, perhaps, not always necessary that the plan be carefully written out. Experienced teachers may know the content well enough and be so skilled in the strategies and tactics that much of their teaching can be both intuitive and successful. Some teachers are convinced that the best classes are unstructured; they believe that classes find their way to true learning best in such an atmosphere. Whether or not they are right is doubtful, but, right or wrong, as a beginner you will do well to avoid such approaches. They are too likely to end in mere drifting and, all too often, sheer chaos—another waste of time and taxpayers' money. You will be wise to learn to plan and conduct a tight, closely structured, well-knit lesson before you venture off into the unmapped unknown of unstructured classes.

Even the most experienced teachers must give careful thought to their lesson plans, if they are to be successful for long. Careful planning ensures that one is familiar with the content. It helps give one the confidence that comes from knowing what one is doing. It shows the students that one is prepared. It gives the lesson structure, organization, and sequence and helps ensure optimum time on task.

Preparing the Lesson Plan

No matter what approach you take to lesson planning, the general principles of planning apply. So in planning your lessons be sure that

- The objectives contribute directly to your unit and course objectives.
- The objectives are clear in your own mind.
- Each objective is a learning product or terminal behavior so definite and specific that you can aim directly at it.
- Your lesson is feasible. To try to teach something that is too difficult or cannot be completed is pointless. Avoid attempting to cover too much subject matter. *It is better to do a little well than a lot badly.*
- The teaching-learning activities will yield the objectives you desire, and are aimed at those objectives.
- You are prepared to carry out the activities you have selected, that is, you know what to do and how to do it, and have the materials to do it with.
- You have provided for a suitable introduction and a culminating clinching activity.
- You have allotted a suitable amount of time for each activity.

The Lesson Plan Format

In writing up a lesson plan there are a number of formats you might follow. Which format you use is not particularly important. Use the one that seems easiest and most comfortable to you. We prefer an outline based on the following six elements, but you may find some other format more congenial. Examples of other formats can be found later in this chapter.

The six elements of the format we prefer are

1. The objective.
2. The subject matter or content.
3. The procedure (teaching strategies and tactics and learning activities).
4. The materials of instruction.
5. Special notes.
6. The new assignment.

7= EVALUATION

Let us now look at these elements.

The Objective

As we have seen, the lesson objective should describe precisely what is to be learned in the lesson. This objective may be in the form of behavioral or descriptive objectives just as long as it points out clearly what the students are expected to learn. At this level the objective should be quite specific and aimed at furthering a more general unit or tropical objective.

The Subject Matter

Here one should indicate the subject content of the lesson. Often it is helpful to outline the content as a separate part of the plan. In other circumstances it may be more suitable to write out the content outline on a separate sheet of paper (for use in a lecture, for instance). Sometimes it is best to incorporate it into the procedure.

The Step-by-Step Procedure

You should list the activities by which you hope to attain your objectives in sufficient detail for you to follow them easily. List the key questions, exercises, and other learning activities in the order you plan to use them. Include introductory set-inducing motivational activities to get the lesson started, developmental activities to keep the lesson going, and culminating, clinching activities to bring the lesson to a conclusion. Evaluation activities should also be included as needed or desired.

The lesson plan by Harry Lewis, a teacher of some forty years of classroom experience and the author of successful secondary school mathematics texts, illustrates the planning of these activities (see Figure 10–1). Notice how meticulously Dr. Lewis has mapped out the activities in this plan for a lesson demonstrating the discovery approach in mathematics.

Introductory Activities (*Getting Set*).   The introductory activities set the stage for the developmental activities to follow. You may use these activities to tie the new lesson to past lessons and to make sure the students have sufficient understanding on which to build the new learning. Review and recapitulation exercises may be useful for these purposes. You may also use introductory activities to set forth the direction and objectives of the new lesson and for other motivational purposes. For instance, you might plan a set induction tactic that will induce in the students a favorable attitude or mental set toward the lesson. It is difficult to teach when you do not have students' attention, and set-induction activities are intended to be attention grabbers. Or you might incorporate activities that point out the worth of what is to be learned. Although exhortations on the part of the teacher do not usually aid much in creating student interest and energy, attempts to point out the usefulness or relevancy of the work may bear fruit. More effective are sprightly activities, interesting content, student planning and decision, and other techniques that catch the students' interest and convince them that the learning is worthwhile. If such attention-catching activities come early in the lesson, they may catch and hold otherwise apathetic students through to the end. Items 1a. b. c. d. of Dr. Lewis' plan (Figure 10–1) are introductory activities.

Developmental Activities.   In building your lesson procedure do not make the mistake of skimping the planning for the developmental activities. It is not enough to say "Lecture on the amoeba—fifteen minutes"; you should plan what will be in the lecture. It is not enough to state that there will be a discussion on the civil rights law; you should plan the direction the discussion will take, the main points it will bring out, and the questions you will use. It is not enough to state that we shall have some problems done at the chalkboard; you should plan which problems and work out the answers. Therefore:

- If you plan to use questions, decide what questions to ask and note down the wording and the answers you expect to the most important ones.

(continued on p. 180)

▶*Plane geometry*

FIGURE 10–1
An Illustrative Lesson Plan

Objective: The student will be able to prove:
1. A ray to be the bisector of an angle.
2. A point to the midpoint of a line segment.
3. A line to be the bisector of a line segment.
4. Similar conclusions that are an outgrowth of the congruence of triangles.

Text: Geometry— A Contemporary Course, pages 222–224.

Procedure:
1. Ask the following questions to point up the information that the students already have that is a prerequisite for understanding the topic that is to be developed in this lesson.
   a. *Teacher:* "I wonder if one of you would summarize the nature of the material we have been exploring over the past few days?" [*Ans.:* "We have been proving line segments congruent, and we have been proving angles congruent."][1]
   b. *Teacher:* "Just what have we been using as a basis to conclude that a pair of angles are congruent?" [*Ans.:* "We have been showing that these angles are corresponding parts of congruent triangles."]
   c. *Teacher:* "Why are we in a position to say that two angles will be congruent if they are corresponding parts of congruent triangles?" [*Ans.:* "The reverse of the definition of congruent polygons permits us to draw this conclusion."]
   d. *Teacher:* "Hence, in general then, if we are asked to prove that a pair of line segments are congruent or a pair of angles are congruent, what will probably be our method of attack?" [*Ans.:* "We will find a pair of triangles that contain these parts as corresponding parts and then try to prove those triangles to be congruent."]
2. *Teacher:* "I would like to explore something with you today that is just a bit different from what we have been doing over the past few days. For instance, consider this situation in which we are asked to prove that *AD* is the bisection of ∠ *BAC.*" With the aid of a straightedge draw the accompanying figure and write the following Given Data and Conclusion.

---

[1] Because this is a demonstration lesson, Dr. Lewis has, he says, included student answers in order to illustrate the type of answers he would expect. Ordinarily he would leave them out, but perhaps a beginning teacher should include them in order to be sure to know what the students' answers should be. It is quite embarrassing when you cannot remember the answers to your own questions or how to solve you own problems. In any case, you should provide yourself with good notes, because it is almost impossible to remember every-thing in the hurly-burly of an active class. It is better to plan too carefully than not to plan carefully enough.

   Notice also that the lesson procedure begins with initiatory activities, continues with devel-opmental activities, and ends with culminating activities.

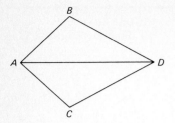

Given: $\overrightarrow{DA}$ bisects $\angle BCD$

$DB = DC$

Conclusion: $\overrightarrow{AD}$ bisects $\angle BAC$

a. *Teacher:* "In searching for the proof to a problem such as this, what should be the *very first thing* we must examine?" [*Ans.:* "The conclusion."]

b. *Teacher:* "From what standpoint do we examine the conclusion?" [*Ans.:* "We mentally try to come up with all the ways we have for proving a ray to be the bisector of an angle."]

c. *Teacher:* "Well, how many ways do we have at our disposal for proving a ray to be the bisector of an angle?" [*Ans.:* "Just one, the reverse of the definition of the bisector of an angle."]

d. *Teacher:* "What does this imply we will have to prove before we can show that a ray is the bisector of an angle?" [*Ans.:* "That the ray forms two congruent angles with the sides of the angle."]

e. *Teacher:* "Then, in terms of the letters in our diagram, exactly what will have to be shown to be true before we can conclude that $\overrightarrow{AD}$ is the bisector of $\angle BAC$?" [*Ans.:* "That $\angle BAD$ is congruent to $\angle CAD$."]

f. *Teacher:* "Just what would you suggest we do in order to prove that these two angles are congruent?" [*Ans.:* "Try to prove that $\triangle BAD$ is congruent to $\triangle CAD$."]

g. (Now attempt to reverse the direction of the thinking of the students.) "Assuming that the two triangles can be shown to be congruent, what will follow?" [*Ans.:* $\angle BAD$ will be congruent to $\angle CAD$."]

h. *Teacher:* "And on this information, what conclusion will we be able to draw?" [*Ans.:* "That $\overrightarrow{AD}$ is the bisector of $\angle BAC$."]

i. *Teacher:* "In view of our analysis, basically, what does the proof of this problem depend upon?" [*Ans.:* "Proving two triangles to be congruent."] *Teacher:* "And this we have done many times over during the past few weeks!"

j. *Teacher:* "Incidentally, why is is that we do not merely prove the triangles to be congruent and then simply say that $\overrightarrow{AD}$ is the bisector of $\angle BAC$ as a consequence of this?" [*Ans.:* "The information that triangles are congruent merely leads to pairs of congruent angles or pairs of congruent line segments and nothing else. The fact that triangles are congruent does not immediately imply that a ray is the bisector of an angle."]

3. Ask one of the brighter students in the class to go to the board to give a formal proof of the problem.
4. At the completion of the proof ask the following questions, calling on only the average or below average students in the class for the answers.
  a. "In developing her proof, Dorothy stated that $\overline{DB}$ is congruent to $\overline{DC}$. How did she know this?"
  b. "I notice that she has marked the diagram in such a way as to imply that $\angle BDA$ is congruent to $\angle CDA$. What enables her to do this?"
  c. "What remaining parts of the two triangles did she have to prove congruent before she could conclude that the two triangles were congruent? What theorem, postulate, or definition permitted her to conlude that $\overline{AD}$ is a congruent to $\overline{AD}$? Is the statement you have just given a definition, a postulate, or a theorem?"
  d. "Why did Dorothy want to prove these two triangles to be congruent?"
  e. "Now that the triangles are congruent, what will follow?"
  f. "And where does the fact that $\angle BAD$ is congruent to $\angle CAD$ lead us?"
5. *Teacher:* "There are other situations that are very much the same as the one we have just examined. As an illustration, consider the situation here (at this point make a freehand drawing of the figure). Suppose we are called upon to prove that B is the midpoint of $\overline{AC}$, how would you suggest proceeding?" [*Ans.:* "Prove that $\overline{AB}$ is congruent to $\overline{CB}$."]

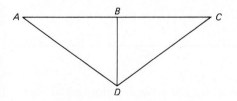

  a. *Teacher:* "What would you probably have to do in order to arrive at this conclusion?" [*Ans.:* "We would probably have to prove $\triangle$ DBC congruent to $\triangle$ DBA."]
  b. *Teacher:* "Hence, here again, what seems to be our method of attack?" [*Ans.:* "Prove a pair of triangles to be congruent. This leads to a pair of line segments being congruent and, in turn, this leads to a point as the midpoint of a line segment."]
  c. *Teacher:* "Let's consider that the conclusion we are asked to reach is that $\overleftrightarrow{DB}$ is the bisector of $\overline{AC}$ rather than that B is the midpoint of $\overline{AC}$. In what way will the attack just outlined have to be altered?" [*Ans.:* "It would not have to be altered at all."] *Teacher:* "Justify that." [*Ans.:* "Well, to prove a point to be the midpoint of a line

segment we have to prove two line segments to be congruent and to prove a line to be the bisector of a line segment we have to do the same."] *Teacher:* "Is there any part of the write-up of the proof that will have to be altered?" [*Ans.:* "Yes, the last 'Reason.' Rather than being the reverse of the definition of the midpoint of a line segment, it will be the reverse of the definition of the bisector of a line segment."]

6. *Teacher:* "Let's all of us open our texts to page 223 and examine Exercise 1."

   a. Now call upon only the average or below average members of the class to answer the following questions:

   (1) What is the first thing you will examine in Exercise 1, [John]?[2] In order to prove that $\overrightarrow{DB}$ bisects $\angle ADC$, what will you have to show to be true. [Mary]? How would you suggest that $\angle ABD$ is congruent to $\angle CDB$, [James]? What ways do we have for proving triangles congruent, [Bill]? Let's look at the Given Data for a moment. Which of the two ways of proving triangles will probably be applied in this situation, [Eleanor]? What makes you think that this is so? Once the triangles are proved to be congruent, what will follow, [Henry]? What reason would you write for that conclusion, [Paul]? What follows from the fact that those are congruent, [Judith]? And, finally, why can this conclusion be drawn, [Ann]?

   b. Exercise 3 is examined in exactly the same manner as Exercise 1 has been.

Homework: If at all possible, this should be begun in class. Pages 223 and 224: Exercises 1, 2, 3, 7, and 9.

- If you plan to use demonstrations or films, gather the necessary materials and equipment beforehand and check them carefully to be sure that everything is in working order.
- If you plan to use any experiment or demonstration, try it first to make sure of the apparatus and technique. Nothing is flatter than a demonstration that does not work.
- If you plan to use a problem or exercise, check to see that it is solvable and that you can solve it.

---

[2] Ordinarily one would not include the names of specific students in one's plan.

In other words, lay out your developmental activities in detail. Items 2–5 of Dr. Lewis' plan (Figure 10–1) are developmental activities.

Culminating Activities (Closure). Every objective needs to be driven home. Many teachers fail—when they fail—because they neglect to make the little extra effort that would clinch the learning that is their objective. Again, how to do this clinching depends upon the situation. In many lessons the clincher may be a summary at the end of the session. In others it may be a review or drill. In still others it may be a student summation to the question: "What was the main point that we were trying to get at in this discussion, John?" At times it might even be a short quiz. Even though sometimes lessons must carry over to the next class, one can take it as axiomatic that any lesson plan that does not make provision for a clincher is not a complete plan. This is what we mean by following through. Item 6 of Dr. Lewis' plan (Figure 10–1) gives examples of culminating activities.

> Go over Lewis' mathematics lesson carefully. How does Dr. Lewis try to launch the lesson? What does he do to create interest? What does he do to get students thinking? What does he do to allow for differences in student ability? What does he do to tie together and clinch the learning in the lessons? How does he prepare the students for the homework assignment?

The Problem of Time. When listing the activities in the procedure of the lesson plan you should estimate how much time the class will spend on each activity. Beginning teachers find this estimate so difficult to make that they often ask for ways of determining just how long to allow for each activity. Unfortunately no one can give them this help, because there is really no way to tell how people will react. An activity that can be done in five minutes in one class may take fifteen minutes in another. All this notwithstanding, we shall attempt to provide a few rules of thumb to use as guides.

1. The first of these is to make your procedure too long at first. By doing so you may prevent the embarrassment of running dry with the period half over. Beginning teachers tend to talk fast and move swiftly, because of the tenseness caused by the newness of the classroom situation. As a rule this tendency wears off with experience. New teachers are often troubled because they do not have enough material; experienced teachers are more likely to be troubled because they do not have enough time.

2. The second rule of thumb is to provide a few minutes at the beginning of the period for taking attendance and the making of announcements, and five or more minutes at the end of the period for clinching the lesson. One also needs to provide, at some point, time enough to make an adequate homework assignment. It is this need to provide for classroom and teaching chores that accounts for the astonishing fact that a forty-minute moving picture may be too long for a fifty-minute period.

3. A third rule of thumb is to mark in your procedure by an asterisk or by underlining (some teachers use red ink) the activities that really must be covered during the period in case time starts to run out. This procedure can save you from such situations as never getting around to showing students how to do their homework assignments, and so on.

4. A fourth rule of thumb is to give students time to learn. Don't rush. Points have to be made and remade. The fact that one of your bright students grasps the answer in a flash is no sign that everyone else does. Take time to be sure by asking others about the same point in different ways. One makes concepts clear by turning them over and over in one's mind. Give the students a chance to do that. Introduce your points and follow them up.

5. Finally, if you do run out of material, don't panic. Use the time for a review of what has gone on before, or for a chance to let the students start their homework under supervision. For a while at least, you would be wise to have some extra activities planned just for such a contingency.

These rules of thumb are based on the principle that the lesson should be completed in a single period. There are several reasons for advocating that lessons be single daily lessons, the primary one being that lessons seem to be more effective when one can finish the period with a clinching experience. Lesson closure of this type at the end of the period seems to fix the learning in the students' minds and to lead to a good jumping off place for the next day's lesson. Without such closure it is more difficult to work in a proper introductory activity that will key up the students in the next day's class, although a quick review of what had been done the day before and a quick résumé of what is to come now may suffice.

These generalizations probably hold true for all expository-type teaching. Longer expository lessons should undoubtedly be divided into shorter daily plans. However, other types of lessons, e.g., research, inquiry, problem solving, group work and so on, may be more fruitful if they run on for several periods. In such lessons the work may naturally flow on from one period to the next. Although you may need to stop the lesson from time to time to sum up, reorient, and regroup, the clinching may better be saved for the culmination of several days' work.

The Materials of Instruction

Lessons will not go well unless arrangements have been made for suitable instructional materials. You must find what materials and equipment are available before you firm up your lesson plan. This may mean arranging for audiovisual machines and software, running off ditto or mimeograph sheets, assembling auxiliary readings, procuring maps or charts, setting up displays, gathering materials for laboratory or seat work, and so on. Lesson planning also includes making decisions about the classroom environment and preparing the classroom for the lesson, e.g., rearranging the chairs for a discussion. Notes in your lesson plan concerning these matters may keep you from forgetting to make provisions for details in your preparations for your classroom activities or reminders of things that need to be taken care of for the lesson later in the week.

The Special Notes

The special notes section of the plan provides for reminders of anything that might be forgotten. Here one usually includes matters that are out of the ordinary. Announcements, special work for individuals, and reminders to speak to particular students about their assignments are examples of the type of thing that may be included here.

The New Assignment

In this section one prepares students for the new assignment. It may be only a brief note concerning tonight's homework and preparation for tomorrow, or it may be a detailed explication of what is to be done. The point is to set forth the assignment in sufficient detail so that you can present it clearly. Unless the assignment is presented well, you cannot be sure that the students understand exactly what they are to do and how they are to do it. The making of assignments is discussed in some detail in Chapter 15.

Prepare several lesson plans for a course you hope to teach. Evaluate the plans according to the following criteria:

Are your objectives clear?

Are your objectives reasonable?

Will your learning activities lead to the objectives?

Do the lessons have a beginning, middle, and end (i.e., initiatory, developmental, and culminating activities)?

Are the learning activities worth doing?

Assuming a fifty-minute period, have you allowed enough time?

Observe a lesson in a middle or high school. Does the lesson seem well planned? Does it have a beginning, a middle, and an end? Does it seem well organized? Does it make its point?

Alternative Lesson Plan Formats

Although the authors prefer the lesson plan format just described, you may prefer another format or your school system may prescribe a specific different format. Of course, if your school system prescribes a specific format, you must follow the mandated format although you may find it necessary to supplement the prescribed format with additional details of your own for your own use.

Alternative Lesson Plan Format 1

This lesson plan format (Figure 10–2) is prescribed by a suburban school district. In addition to the identifying data at the top of the plan, it provides spaces for the lesson objectives, content, procedure, instructional material, and evaluation. In this plan format the evaluation section is for the planning of test items, classroom questions, and exercises to be used for evaluating student progress.

Alternative Lesson Plan Format 2

Alternative Lesson Plan Format 2 (Figure 10–3) is also used by a city school district. Basically it is similar to Alternative Lesson Plan Format 1, except that a section for the assignment has been added and provisions have been made for notes concerning the content. The identifying data at the beginning of the plan are quite specific, because these plans may be inspected by supervisors from time to time.

Alternative Lesson Plan Format 3

Alternative Lesson Plan Format 3 (Figure 10–4) follows an outline advocated by William Meisner. In addition to the identifying data, this outline provides a place for the general objective of the unit of which this lesson is to be a part and the specific objective for the lesson. These objectives may be stated descriptively or behaviorally. The plan format also provides sections for the content and the procedure. Included in these are places for describing the lesson introduction, the content of the lesson development, the instructional methods and activities, key points, and the conclusion. It ends with an evaluation section that should be used after the lesson to indicate how successful the plan was and how it could be improved, if it is ever used again.

Lesson Topic	Date
Unit	Grade

1. Lesson Objective

2. Content

3. Procedure

4. Instructional Materials

5. Evaluation

FIGURE 10–2
Alternative Lesson Plan Format 1

Teacher: Course Topic: Date:

Unit:

Objectives

Content   Notes

Procedures

Evaluation and Questions

Assignment

Materials of Instruction

FIGURE 10–3
Alternative Lesson Plan Format 2

1. Name of course and grade level.
2. Name of unit.
3. Topic to be considered within the unit.
4. General objective for the lesson (may be the same for the entire unit).
5. Specific objective for the lesson (daily).
6. Content to be included.
   a. New material to be included.
   b. Questions for discussion.
7. Introduction
   Review of preceding lesson
   Old vocabulary
   New vocabulary
   Old concepts.
8. Key points or point.
9. Conclusion.
10. Method or methods to be used.
11. Materials of instruction.
12. Assignment.
13. Evaluation.

FIGURE 10–4
Alternative Lesson Plan Format 3

Many experienced teachers keep a file of lesson plans with notes about the success of the plans. In that case a plan format such as Meisner's is helpful. Other teachers find this not to be helpful. They never really repeat their lesson plans.

Alternative Lesson Plan Formats 4 and 5

Alternative Lesson Plan Formats 4 and 5 differ from the other formats in that they present the procedure in two columns. Alternative Lesson Plan Format 4 (Figure 10–5) lists the content in one column and the key questions to be asked about the various items on the same line in a second column. Alternative Lesson Plan Format 5 (Figure 10–6) lists the objectives in one column and the specific learning activities to be used to teach those objectives in an opposing column. These formats have the advantage of tieing the methods to be used to the content or objectives they are supposed to teach.

Unit	Course	Date

Lesson Topic

Objective

Introduction

	Content	Key Questions

Summary

Materials

Assignment

FIGURE 10–5
Alternative Lesson Plan Format 4

Alternative Lesson Plan Format 6

This format (Figure 10–7) is adapted from the format used in a large metropolitan school district. It provides for the listing of the understandings, skills, and attitudes that the lesson will focus on, reminders, and student assignments for the next day or so. Then, in a three-column format, it shows the time sequence, the content, and the teaching methods, techniques, and instructional materials. This format is designed to supply the class with a detailed organization and to promote smooth classroom management.

Sample Lesson Plans

On the following pages you will find examples of lesson plans prepared according to various formats. (Figs. 10–8 to 10–13). Most of these plans were prepared by college students. *None of them is perfect.* As you read them criticize them. Consider such questions as these:

1. Are the objectives clear and precise?
2. Are they attainable?
3. Could you write test items that would tell whether the objectives were actually achieved?
4. Will the procedure outlined lead to the attainment of the objectives?
5. Are the procedures detailed enough so that you feel the teacher really knows what he intends to do? Could you follow the plan if you were a substitute?
6. Are the procedures likely to encourage learning? Or will they be boring?
7. Do the activities allow for differences in the students in any way?
8. Does the plan note exactly what material and equipment the teacher needs to have ready so that he will not forget?
9. If you were a student would you enjoy the class?

10. If you were a student would you learn from the class?

Note that lesson plans are not always written in perfectly logical form—nor in finished prose. They are the teacher's notes, and so quite personal. Consequently they frequently contain abbreviations and shorthand expressions. The important thing is that they be clear to the user. To make it easy to follow the plans, many teachers make ample use of underlining, capitals, asterisks, and other signposts. You will find examples of personal shorthand devices and signposts in these lessons. Do they help or hinder?

Look at the various sample lesson plans and formats.

Do you have any preferences as far as formats are concerned? Which of the formats described seem to you the easiest to follow?

Using Plan Books

School officials often provide teachers with plan books with which to plan their lessons. These are valuable for planning the long-term sequence for the school year. Unfortunately, some of the commercial plan books do not allow enough space for one to enter an entire plan. They are merely layout sheets for indicating the general nature of the work projected for various days and periods. Since this is the case, you may want to prepare your daily plans on sheets of composition paper or in a notebook kept for that purpose.

Even though you keep more detailed plans elsewhere, you need to keep at least skeleton plans in your plan book for at least a week ahead. Here you should record the lessons to be studied, the assignments, and a word about the approach. Keeping these plans up to date is important because (continued on p. 195)

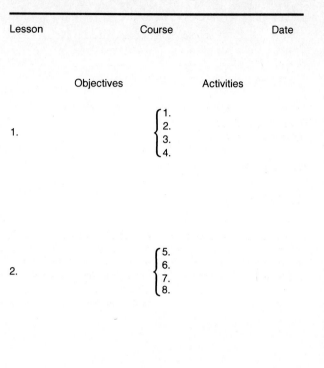

FIGURE 10–6
Alternative Lesson Plan Format 5

Class _____ Grade _____

School _____

Period(s) or Mod(s) _____   Room(s) _____

Date _____ Day _____

Week Ending _____

Daily Lesson Plan

Day's Aims & Objectives
  Major Understandings:

Skills to be Developed:

Attitudes:

Routines (General Housekeeping Reminders)

Student Assignment(s) (For one or more days)

Chronological Time Sequence (Minute by minute or number of minutes to be used in each part of outline)	*Outline of Content to Focus Upon in Order to Achieve Aims & Objectives.* Content should be arranged so as to begin with *Initiatory Activities:* interest getters, previews, or previous unit work; move to *Developmental Activities* (those which expand understanding of what is known); and end with *Culminating Activities* which can include summary, review, and evaluation.	*Teaching Methods Techniques* (and needed materials). Student involvement is prime consideration for choice of method.
	(continue on additional paper if needed)	

FIGURE 10–7
Alternative Lesson Plan Format 6

▶*Senior English*

FIGURE 10–8.
Lesson Plan 1

Objective: At the end of the lesson the pupils will
1. Perceive the mood of melancholy and retreat in Byron's *The Ocean.*
2. React to the emotional tone of the poem.
3. Realize that Romanticism was sentimental.

Procedure:

2 min.   **1.** Take attendance.

4 min.   **2.** Read the poem to the students without their books.

4 min.   **3.** Now read it to them with their books. They should attempt to find the main meaning of the poem.

5 min.   **4.** Have the class list in their notebooks some of the attributes the poet gives to the human race, e.g.,

         Man marks the earth with ruin
         Man's ravage
         The vile strength he wields for Earth's destruction
         Men's empires have all disappeared yet ocean lives on
           unchanged.

5 min.   **5.** Discuss the different attributes

5 min.   **6.** Is the picture of man created by the poet a happy or unhappy one?

         Do you think that this is a true picture of man? Or is it too one-sided?

5 min.
shore.   **7.** List the attributes of the ocean, e.g., rapture on the lonely

         Time writes no wrinkle on thine azure brow—
         Such as Creation's dawn beheld, thou rollest on.

         The ocean is seen as great and powerful.
         Does it have any qualities of kindness and sympathy with
           the human race or is it simply a blank force?

5 min.   **8.** Ask this question:

         The poet says in the first stanza that he loves "not Man
           the less."
         Later he urges the ocean to leave man lying dashed upon
           the earth.
         Do you find that this poem seems to be a personal lashing
           out at man by the poet rather than an expression of a
           universal truth or an insight into man's condition?

5 min.   **9.** Give a quick lecture on the Romantic melancholy prevalent in Byron's time. The turning to nature for a source of strength.
         a. Sentimental contemplations of nature.

        b. For the Romantic, nature becomes a great restorative and spiritual guide.

        c. Nature is to be untouched by human hand. Celebration of nature in the ruin.

5 min.   **10.** Ask these questions:

        Do you feel that this poem is applicable to modern-day life?

        Are we marking the earth with ruin?

        Do we have no control over the sea today?

Materials: Textbooks

5 min.   Assignment—Read "The Grave Digger" by Bliss Carmen.

        Does his view of life vary from or resemble Byron's?

        How does Carmen view man and ocean?

▶ *Biology*
INTRODUCTION TO PLANT REPRODUCTION

FIGURE 10–9.
Lesson Plan 2

Objectives: At the completion of the lesson the pupils will be able to
1. Identify corolla, sepals, calyx, perianth, stamens, pistil (stigma, style, and ovary), filament, and pollen grains.
2. Explain the purpose of each of the above.

Subject Content:

Text Reference: pages 370–373, covering topics: petals, corolla, sepals, calyx, perianth, stamens, pistil (stigma, style, and ovary), filament, and pollen grains.

Class Procedure:

2 min.   **1.** Initiate class by forming four groups of five pupils each (out of a class of 20).

or   Then distribute four orchids, one to each group.

3 min.   **2.** In each group have the third student from the end or the middle student hold the flower so that all may see the interior.

20 min. **3.** With each group referring to the distributed flower, I will construct an artificial flower with the use of homemade (paper or cardboard) parts and a flannel board.

20 min. **4.** Go over each part again, this time telling the use of the part.

        a. Petals (1) arranged in a circle to collect pollen grains in the bottom (2) are brightly colored to attract insects, (3) protect the reproduction organs of the flower against wind and the like.

        b. Sepals—are green (make food).

             c. Stamens—have a stem called a filament and an anther (sack which contains pollen).

             d. Pistil—usually one, but some flowers have more, composed of a stigma (sticky), which pollen attaches itself to; a style, which supports the stigma and transfers the pollen to the ovary; and an ovary, where pollenization takes place and where seed is produced.

5 min.   **5.** Terms:

             a. Corolla—all petals together

             b. Calyx—all sepals together

             c. Perianth—corolla and calyx together

         6. Without the pistils and stamens of flowers there would be no seeds and without seeds the human race would not survive.

Instructional Materials:

1. Text—Biology—Kroeber, Wolff, and Weaver

2. Four orchids (real)

3. Flannel board—Homemade flower

Assignment:

3 min.   Think about growing either lima beans or peas, collecting growth data, and reporting in a small paper a summary of root, leaf, and stem growth.

▶ *Economics*

FIGURE 10–10.
Lesson Plan 3

Objective: At the completion of the lesson the pupils will understand that the corporation became the dominant form of business organization.

Specific Objectives: At the completion of this lesson the pupils will be able to

1. Give a valid operational definition of corporations in their own words.

2. Describe how a corporation is formed.

3. Describe the factors that caused the growth of corporations in the United States after 1865.

Procedure:

1. What is a corporation?

Ans.: *working definition*—a form of business organization in which the small savings of many investors are combined to provide the necessary funds for operating a business.

2. Prior to 1860 what forms of business organization were prevalent in the United States?

    a. *partnership*—owned by two or more individuals.

    b. *proprietorship*—owned by a single individual.

3. The corporation offers several advantages over the partnership and proprietorship. What are they?

    a. It can raise sizable amounts of money by selling stock.

    b. Stockholders risk only the money they invest. (Compare with partnership and proprietorship where owners may be sued for debts.)

    c. Ownership can change hands more readily.

    d. A corporation continues indefinitely.

4. How could we, as a class, form a corporation? (Class discussion) *Put terms on blackboard.*

    a. *charter*—from state—legal right to conduct a certain type of business.

    b. *capital*—raising of funds for business purposes.

    c. *stock*—certificates of ownership.

    d. *directors* and *officers*—run corporation for stockholders—are elected by stockholders.

    e. *bonds*—means of borrowing money—fixed rate of interest.

    f. *dividends*—a share of the profits (if there are any) given to the stockholders.

5. Corporations grew rapidly after 1865.

    a. Outburst of manufacturing after 1865. Production on a large scale for a larger national market seemed to offer the best hopes of a good profit.

    b. The new labor-saving machines and technological processes lowered production costs, but these machines were too expensive for the small local businessman to buy.

    c. By the 1890s corporations produced nearly three fourths of the total value of manufactured products in the United States.

Materials:

Text—*The Making of Modern America.*

Assignment: for tomorrow answer:

1. What are the chief features of the corporation? What are its advantages over other forms of business organizations?

2. How does the ownership of a corporation differ from its control and management?

3. Why did corporations grow rapidly after 1865? What happened to many small businesses? Why did the number of companies manufacturing a particular product decrease?

Answers can be found in todays' notes and in text (pp. 368–372)

Ask students to begin thinking on a choice of an industrial tycoon (e.g., Carnegie, Rockefeller, and so on) or an industry (its development) for group reports.

▶ *Chemistry*

FIGURE 10–11.
Lesson Plan 4

1. **Objectives**

    A molecule is the smallest possible division of a substance which can be made without destroying its properties.

    Energy is the ability of matter to move other matter, or to affect the motion of other matter.

    The two kinds of energy are: active or kinetic, and stored or potential.

    Matter and energy are related since matter cannot be moved without some force to cause the movement.

2. **Subject Content**

    Text reference: pages 34–39, covering topics: molecules, elements and compounds, matter and energy, and two kinds of energy.

3. **Class Procedure**

    a. Initiate lesson with brief review of matter, and introduce its composition;

    b. Read pages 34–39 orally and then go over the sections slowly, explaining the more difficult passages;

    c. Display a picture of an atom and list the elements;

    d. Have a discussion on energy and its kinds;

    e. Have each student write examples of some form of matter having a particular kind of energy;

    f. Have some of these examples contributed to the class.

4. **Instructional Materials**

    Text—*Our Environment;* general chemistry textbook.

5. **Assignments**

    Memorize the definition of energy and its two kinds: potential and kinetic.

▶ *Geography*

FIGURE 10–12.
Lesson Plan 5

Objective: (Concept to Be Learned)
The earth's grid is used for locating places on maps.

Procedure:

1. Distribute globes.
2. **a.** What is a *grid?* Some examples?

    Ans.: Anything marked with *parallel* lines (draw grid on board).

    b. What does parallel mean?

    Ans.: Anything equally distant, as one line to another.

    c. Examples:

        Football field.

        Patterns.

        Lined paper, graph paper.

        Crossing zone.

    d. Point out something in the classroom that is a grid.

3. Can a grid be used in relation to the earth: How?

    Ans.: Yes, it can be used to locate positions on the earth's surface.

4. What constitutes the earth's grid? Four things. How are they represented on a globe or map?

    Write on board

    a. *North and South Poles*—starting points, ends of axis on which the earth rotates (have students locate these and the following on their globes).

    b. *Equator*—great circle considered to pass around the earth halfway between the poles.

    c. *Parallels of Latitude*—smaller circles which are parallel to equator and mark off the *angular* distance in degrees north and between the poles and the equator.

    d. *Meridians of Longitude*—treat circles *perpendicular* to the equator and parallels which intersect each other at the poles. Measure distances east or west of an arbitrarily chosen starting line. (Demonstrate on board a perpendicular line and intersecting lines.)

5. Review all terms by having students relate them from globes to wall map.

6. We said that the earth's grid is used to locate positions on the earth's surface. How is this done?

    Ans.: through units of measurement called *degrees:*

    a. 1 = 1/360 of a circle.

    b. Equator = 0.

    c. North Pole = 90 N.

    d. South Pole = 90 S.

    e. Prime Meridian = Greenwich.

    f. 180th Meridian = Pacific Ocean.

    (Demonstrate all on board.)

7. Locate longitude and latitude of places in text, p. 86.

Materials:

Globes.

World map—wall.

Pointer.

Text, manual.

Notes: None.

Assignment:
Complete unfinished longitude and latitude problems on page 86 in text. Also prepare a grid for tomorrow's lesson on maps. Do this on white construction paper and make parallel lines 1″ apart from each other (give example on board). If any questions tonight, see sample grid on page 89 in text. Be sure to bring rulers and pencils to class tomorrow.

▶ English III

FIGURE 10–13.
Lesson Plan 6

OBJECTIVE   ACTIVITIES

Objective: Proper punctuation, proper word choice, and proper construction help make sentences clear.

1. Return compositions.
2. Explain marking system (Two grades: one for comp., one for mechanics).
3. Review theme. Point out that the story must carry out the premise in order to be successful.
4. Go over the following sentences selected from the composition. *Note:* Exercise should be considered a help. First correct sentences on paper, then discuss them. Rewrite, if necessary.

   What is wrong with each of these sentences:
   a. The body of the dead wolf loomed up before him. (*loomed up* is inappropriate, perhaps *lay, appeared*)
   b. Coming into the room Mother asked What is the matter? (dangling phrase, quotation marks)
   c. Now I've really tried it, he'll be on my back the rest of the week were Johnny's thoughts. (quotes, half sentences)
   (*Five other sentences have been omitted to conserve space. In actuality the teacher had listed*

*these on a separate sheet of pa-
per.*)
Summary questions: Why punctuate? Why good sentence structure?
Why be careful of words?

Assignment: Read *The Spectre Bridegroom.* What do you think the premise to be in this story?

Note: Period cut to 10:14 because of grade reports.

Remember to show Allan how to develop premise. He missed original
explanation. He should rewrite the composition.

(continued from p. 186)
they may be used as the index for an estimate of
the adequacy of the course by supervisors and as
a basis for teaching the class if a substitute has
to take over. The plan books are particularly important for substitutes. Without the layouts of your
weekly plans, a substitute, having nothing to build
his teaching around, will be completely at a loss
and so will be your class. A sample layout sheet
appears in Figure 10–14.

Following the Plan

On the whole, you would do well to follow your
plan fairly closely. Doing so is about the only way
you can be sure to do what you have intended to
do. Otherwise, in an active classroom situation you
can easily get sidetracked and lose sight of your
objective. Nevertheless, you should not let your
plan handcuff you. At least two types of situations
require you to leave your plan: (1) when the lesson
planned is going so badly that something must be
done to save it, and (2) when something happens
before or during the class to indicate that the students would benefit more from a different attack.

As a rule it is foolish to stick by a lesson plan
that is obviously not succeeding. Of course it should
be only seldom that such a contretemps occurs,

yet you would be wise always to have an alternate
approach ready to use in case of emergency.

Often a change of pace is needed to cut off an
incipient behavior problem. Students who are
growing restless in a lecture or recitation may be
ripe for a discussion or a problem-solving activity.
Sometimes a written assignment can be quite effective for channeling energies that seem about to
break the bonds of propriety. At other times you
can see by the looks on students' faces that what
you are trying to teach is not getting through to
them. In such cases a few well-directed questions
may tell what the difficulty is so that you can reorient yourself and start off with a different approach or perhaps switch to a different, more elementary lesson.

At times students raise questions during the lesson that are sufficiently important to warrant immediate followup. Sometimes the point or problem
is worth pursuing in detail. In such circumstances
perhaps you should discard your lesson plan completely and devote the class's attention to this new
point. More often, the students' questions warrant
only a short diversion from the planned procedure.

Sometimes events of importance may occur
within or outside the class to make your plan obsolete. In the case of an event of national importance
or of great importance to the school or community,
it may be desirable to interrupt the class to talk
about the event even though it has no visible rela-

Period Subject Grade	Subject_____ Week Beginning_____19__		LESSON PLAN	Teacher's Name_____ Home Room_____	
	Monday	Tuesday	Wednesday	Thursday	Friday

FIGURE 10–14
Lesson Plan Layout Sheet.

tionship to the course or subject concerned. In the case of an exciting school event, it may be wise to let students talk about it for a few minutes at the beginning of class so as to let them blow off steam a little before they settle down to work.

No one can tell you when to stick to your plan and when to depart from it. What you do must be decided on the basis of what seems best at the time. The criteria on which to base your decision are simple: (1) What will benefit the students most? (2) What will advance the cause of learning most? (3) How relevant and significant to the course is the change? Remember that, after all, the plan is only a means to an end. If something better comes along feel free to use it.

On the other hand, do not change plans capriciously. Usually, if you are inspired by a "better" idea during a lesson it is wise to resist it and stick to your original plan. Good inspirations are hard to find. The chances are that your original plan will serve you better than any spur of the moment idea. Only rarely does it pay to be daring and discard your plans.

> One day a supervisor visited a beginning teacher who was having difficulty. This young person had taken on a job which was almost too much for him. He was teaching material difficult for him and was having considerable trouble keeping up with the class. When the supervisor asked him for his plans, he replied, "I am so busy I have not been able to make any lesson plans yet." What would your answer be to this beginning teacher?

Summary

Every lesson needs a plan. The essentials of a daily lesson plan are the objectives, the subject matter, the activities, the list of materials needed, the assignment, and any special notes. These essentials tell us what to do and how to do it. The format one uses for a lesson plan is not so very important as long as the plan is clear and easy to follow. Sometimes daily lesson plans used in conjunction with units need not be very detailed. The important thing is to know what it is we wish to teach in the lesson and to provide activities that lead to these goals. One test of a lesson plan is to ask how each activity in the procedure will help to bring about the desired goal. Once you have decided on a plan of action, you would be wise to keep to that plan unless there seem to be very important reasons for changing course.

Additional Reading

Berenson, David H., Sally R. Berenson, and Robert R. Carkhuff. *The Skills of Teaching: Lesson Planning Skills.* Amherst, MA: Human Resources Development Press, 1978.

Grambs, Jean Dresden, and John C. Carr. *Modern Methods in Secondary Education,* 4th ed. New York: Holt, 1979, Chap. 7.

Henak, Richard M. *Lesson Planning for Meaningful Variety.* Washington, DC: National Education Association, 1980.

Hoover, Kenneth H. *The Professional Teacher's Handbook,* abridged 2nd ed. Boston: Allyn and Bacon, 1976, Chap. 3.

Kim, Eugene C., and Richard D. Kellough. *A Resource Guide for Secondary School Teaching,* 3rd ed. New York: Macmillan, 1983, Part II.

Orlich, Donald C. *et al. Teaching Strategies: A Guide to Better Instruction,* 2nd ed. Lexington, MA: D.C. Heath, 1985, Chap. 5.

Pierce, Walter D., and Michael A. Lorber. *Objectives and Methods for Secondary Teaching.* Englewood Cliffs, NJ: Prentice-Hall, 1977.

Lectures, Questions, and Practice

Overview

In this chapter we discuss some of the more formal and traditional teaching approaches: lecture and teacher talks, the recitation, questioning, practice and review. They are all strategies with which you have had much experience. Yet, perhaps there is more to them than has met your eye. In any case, as you read the chapter, try to think how you would use these techniques in your teaching and student teaching. For what purposes would you use formal lectures? formal talks? Of what advantage are open-text recitation techniques? Most teachers use many questions, but limit themselves almost entirely to memory questions. What advantages do you find in each of the various kinds of questions? How can you use questions to make students think and to help them understand? How can you use questions to proble without nagging? As you study, try to form questions that will do more than just check knowledge. Similarly try to think of ways in which you can introduce into your courses the repetition necessary for implanting knowledge and skills deeply enough to ensure recall and transfer without boring the students unnecessarily.

Student-Teacher Interaction

Balancing Teacher-Student Participation

Before we begin our study of the various teaching methods or strategies, let us first consider the matter of student-teacher interaction in the classroom. In the United States most of the teaching is done by teachers telling things to students. This is unfortunate for, as P. J. Phillips tells us, experience seems to show that pupils generally remember

10 per cent of what they READ.
20 per cent of what they HEAR.
30 per cent of what they SEE.
50 per cent of what they HEAR and SEE.
70 per cent of what they SAY.
90 per cent of what they SAY as they DO a thing.[1]

If this observation is accurate, it does not augur well for the effectiveness of lectures and teacher talks as teaching strategies. Just the same, teachers must tell students things. Teaching is not telling, but telling is an important ingredient in teaching. No teacher can get along without it.

Interaction Criteria

Still, teachers should guard against talking too much and overdominating classroom activities. Without an optimum amount of student-student and teacher-student interaction, classes tend to become stifling. Although in any particular lesson the objectives and design of the lesson plan plus other factors in the specific situation determine what types and amounts of interaction are desirable, certain criteria apply to most lessons in general:

- Students should be actively participating at least half of the time. (If you find yourself to be talking more than half of the time, you should check your procedures.)
- As far as possible, every student should participate in some way. (Classes that are dominated by only a few students are hardly satisfactory.)
- A good share of the classtime should be given to thoughtful, creative activity rather than to mere recitation of information by either teacher or students.

Interaction Analysis

Interaction analysis will give you an indication of whether or not you are meeting these criteria. Most interaction-analysis techniqes are easy to use. You can do it yourself if you tape (audio or video) one of your classes. Otherwise the basic data gathering can be done by an observer, for example, a cooperating teacher, supervisor or classmate, during an actual class session.

Simple Interaction-Analysis Techniques

The simplest method of gathering interaction-analysis data is for an observer to record T every time the teacher talks and S every time a student talks. This technique gives some idea of the number of times students talk as compared to the teacher.

A more useful refinement of this same technique is for the observer to mark down who is talking

[1] Marvin D. Alcorn, James S. Kinder, and Jim R. Schunert, *Better Teaching in Secondary Schools*, 3rd ed. (New York: Holt, 1970), p. 216. According to Alcorn, Kinder, and Schunert these figures, which were originally developed by P. J. Philips at the University of Texas, Industrial Education Department, are only approximations and should be taken as such, but experience indicates that they are reasonably accurate.

at regular intervals, e.g., three seconds. Again the observer uses the symbol T to indicate that the teacher is talking and S to indicate that a student is talking. Thus for one minute period the observer's record might take the following form: T S T T T S T T T T T S S T T T T T S S T T T. Such an analysis would show the amount of time that is given to teacher talk as compared to student talk.

A more complex refinement of the technique is for the observer to sit at the back of the class with a seating chart and to tally the number of times each person speaks. (Figure 11–1.)

In another version, as in the earlier example, the observer could record who was talking at stated intervals, e.g., every five seconds. This type of analysis has the advantage of showing just which persons were interacting, how much, and how often. The chart shown in Figure 11–1 would be suitable for recording such analysis. In discussions, flow charts of the type discussed in Chapter 12 can be used for the same purpose.

The Flanders System

Several writers and researchers have devised much more sophisticated interaction-analysis techniques. Because these procedures provide means for indicating the kind of interaction going on at any moment, they give a much more complete picture of what has happened in a class.

One of the best known of these techniques is the Flanders Interaction Analysis System. In this system, classroom interaction is divided into the categories listed in Figure 11–2. To conduct the analysis, every three seconds an observer records the category of action in progress and then at the conclusion of the observation arranges the observations into a matrix from which one can read not only what happened in the class, but also the class atmosphere.[2]

Lectures and Teacher Talks

The Formal Lecture

There are three basic types of teaching telling activities: (1) the formal lecture, (2) the short informal teacher talk, and (3) teacher comment and reaction. Each one has its place. Unfortunately many teachers lean too heavily on the lecture.

In the formal lecture the teacher presents the lesson by what amounts to making a speech. There is a minimum amount of give and take in this type of teaching. This one-way formula is partly a result of the history of teaching, particularly as it was done in the medieval universities. In those days the professor was the only person who had access

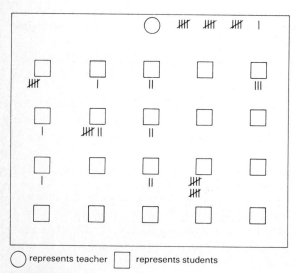

○ represents teacher   ☐ represents students

FIGURE 11–1
Form of Interaction Analysis.

[2] Edmund J. Amidon and Ned A. Flanders. *The Role of the Teacher in the Classroom* (Minneapolis, MN.: Paul S. Amidon and Associates, 1963). Edmund Amidon and Elizabeth Hunter recommend a refined version of the Flanders system that they call the Verbal Interaction Analysis System in their *Improving Teaching* (New York: Holt, 1966).

FIGURE 11-2
Summary of Categories for Interaction Analysis (Edmund J. Amidon and Ned A. Flanders, *The Role of the Teacher in the Classroom.* [Minneapolis, MN.: Paul S. Amidon and Associates, 1963].)

Teacher Talk

Indirect Influence

1. ACCEPTS FEELING: accepts and clarifies the feeling tone of the students in a nonthreatening manner. Feelings may be positive or negative. Predicting and recalling feelings are included.
2. PRAISES OR ENCOURAGES: praises or encourages student action or behavior. Jokes that release tension, not at the expense of another individual, nodding head or saying "uhhuh?" or "go on" are included.
3. ACCEPTS OR USES IDEAS OF STUDENT: clarifying, building, or developing ideas or suggestions by a student. As teacher brings more of his own ideas into play, shift to category five.
4. ASKS QUESTIONS: asking a question about content or procedure with the intent that a student answer.

Direct Influence

5. LECTURES: giving facts or opinions about content or procedure; expressing his own ideas; asking rhetorical questions.
6. GIVES DIRECTIONS: directions, commands, or orders with which a student is expected to comply.
7. CRITICIZES OR JUSTIFIES AUTHORITY: statements intended to change student behavior from nonacceptable to acceptable pattern; bawling someone out; stating why the teacher is doing what he is doing, extreme self-reference.

Student Talk

8. STUDENT TALK-RESPONSE: talk by students in response to teacher. Teacher initiates the contact or solicits student statement.
9. STUDENT TALK-INITIATION: talk by students, which they initiate. If "calling on" student is only to indicate who may talk next, observers must decide whether student wanted to talk. If he did, use this category.

10. SILENCE OR CONFUSION: pauses, short periods of silence, and periods of confusion in which communication cannot be understood by the observer.

to the text, so he read it to the students with appropriate commentary.[3]

Lately, largely because of a reaction against its long years of misuse and overuse, it has been fashionable in some circles to downgrade the lecture, but the lecture has been used with success in the past, is being used with success at the present, and no doubt will be used with success in the future. As a matter of fact, most teachers find lectures al-

most indispensable for certain purposes. They use them

- To introduce activities or units.
- To motivate students.
- To sum up.
- To explain difficult points.
- To bridge gaps between units or topics.
- To establish a general point of view.
- To point out a different point of view.
- To provide information otherwise not readily available.
- To provide additional information.
- To propose a theory.

[3] The word *lecture* is derived from the Latin *legere* (*lectus*) to read. In England some college instructors are called readers.

Moreover, as long as the lecture remains the predominant form of teaching in our colleges, college-bound boys and girls should have considerable experience with lectures in the last stages of their high school careers. It goes without saying that this experience with lectures should be accompanied by instruction in how to profit from lectures, most particularly in the art of taking notes.

Just the same, in spite of its values, the formal lecture is ordinarily a rather ineffective method of teaching middle and secondary school students. Because learning from lectures is relatively passive learning, it is often relatively sterile learning. Lectures do not give students opportunity to explore, to think, or to interact. They are not conducive to study in depth, but rather tend to make students receivers of knowledge. They do not allow for differing responses or the exercising of one's curiosity. They are seldom useful for changing attitudes or imparting the higher cognitive skills. Except in unusual cases, very little of the lecture sticks in the students' minds. Students seem to learn better when they put themselves into the learning. Unless the students do something with the information presented in a lecture, their learning and retention may be rather thin. The lecture format gives very little opportunity for reinforcement to take place or for one to assess the progress in learning of either the group or individuals. Sometimes they are a waste of time. It might be better to mimeograph or ditto the information to be presented and use the class time for other purposes.

The lecture technique may also cause discipline problems. Adolescent attention spans for the typical lecture are notoriously short. This statement does not mean that secondary school boys and girls cannot pay careful attention to a good lecture for a long time. Rather, it means that it takes a really good lecturer to hold any audience's interested attention for an hour. In the secondary school a stimulating lecturer, skillful enough to hold the students' attention and really teach them by his lecturing, is indeed a rare bird. Besides, to make lectures exciting four or five times a day, week after week, is beyond the capabilities of most mortals. New teachers who place great faith in their continuous use of the lecture day after day are foolhardy. Remember: Adolescents have a low tolerance for boredom.

Preparing the Lecture

Most middle and secondary school lectures should be short. A twenty-minute lecture is quite often more than a middle school class can abide. Short talks of about ten minutes duration are likely to be more acceptable. Senior high school classes may be able to stand lectures that are much longer. However, it takes a really good lecturer to hold the interest of even adult groups for more than half an hour. In university graduate lectures students really have to battle to keep from daydreaming or falling asleep.

One reason that many secondary school lectures are not more stimulating is that good lectures require more preparation than most teachers have time to give them. Very seldom can a teacher lecture effectively on the spur of the moment. If you want to have a high degre of effectiveness in your lectures, you must plan them meticulously. Not only must you plan what you wish to say, but you should also plan how you intend to say it.

Why is the lecture considered to be a poor technique for use in middle schools? In secondary schools?

You have been assigned a ninth-grade general science class. This class consists largely of slow learners. It has a reputation of being hard to handle. The youngsters are restless and not much interested. How much would you plan to lecture to such a group? What might you be able to do to hold the attention of such a group when you lecture?

Presenting the Lecture

Making the Lecture Clear. If they are to be effective, lectures must be both clear and persuasive. With this goal in mind, the teacher planning a classroom lecture must guard against attempting too much. Because of its one-way format it is very easy for the teacher who lectures to present ideas quickly and then move on to new ones before the students have caught the first ones. Neither secondary school students nor adults are likely to learn much from ideas skimmed over lightly.

Expert lecturers claim that the way to put your points across in a lecture is to

- Tell them what you are going to tell them.
- Tell them.
- Tell them what you have told them.

This formula is a good one. It has served the best lecturers well over the years. It calls for a logical, well-ordered presentation, well aimed at only a few salient points, which the lecturer hits at least several times. (Repetition and the use of visuals are about the only ways one can reinforce learning during a lecture.)

To carry out this procedure, state clearly what each point is and support it with illustrations, examples and other details which, in themselves, may not be important, but which do tend to make the point stand out. And then, after all this has been done, come back to your point again, restating it clearly, in order to drive it home and clinch it as firmly as possible in a final summation. As a rule, this type of procedure will carry your ideas across to your audience, whereas attempting to cover many points may only confuse the listeners. As you develop your points, try to adjust your ideas and sequence of ideas to your audience. In general the content should move from the concrete to the abstract, and back again to the concrete so as not to leave things hanging in midair. Try to be sure the lecture develops logically enough so that students have the background necessary for understanding new material. The content should be new, however. There is no excuse for lectures that parrot the textbook. The whole idea of lecturing is to give students new, fresh ideas or information that is not otherwise readily available.

Clarity also depends on the use of language. Beginning teachers and student teachers are inclined to talk over the heads of their students. Concepts and words familiar to college seniors and recent graduates may be foreign to sixth-graders and even high school students. Although you should avoid talking down to your students, be careful to talk to them in language they understand.

The language used should be good English, of course. Some teachers attempt to reach the students' level by introducing slang expressions and street language into their talks. This is usually a poor policy. Slang and overinformality are more likey to muddy a lecture than clarify it. Furthermore, whether you like it or not, you are a model whenever you speak. If your influence on the students is to be a good one, you must see to it that your language is the type that you wish the students to imitate.

The use of illustrations and figures of speech often makes lectures clearer and livelier, but their injudicious use can at times defeat their purpose. Particularly treacherous in this respect is the metaphor, which can truly be a two-edged sword. With middle school students particularly, a teacher should call things by their proper names and use fights of poetic fancy to others. If you must use such figures of speech, at least take steps to make sure that the students understand what you really mean. Not doing so may make the entire lecture meaningless.

In addition, illustrations, audiovisual aids, and demonstrations in lectures help to clarify and point up desired concepts. Frequently, visual representations can give meaning to what would otherwise remain just a mass of words. Even when the lecture is clear and interesting without them, the use of visual aids can reinforce the learning by adding the impact of another sense. Teacher lecturers who depend solely on their voices are being unfair to themselves and their students.

As you lecture try to help the students learn from the lectures. The need for the use of repetition and other rhetorical devices has already been mentioned. Another strategy is to help students learn to take good notes. For this purpose an outline of the lecture on the chalkboard or overhead projector can be most helpful. The common practice of providing a skeleton outline for the students to fill in as the lecture goes on has much to recommend it. So does the even more common practice among good teachers of stopping to point out to the students that what has just been explained, or is about to be explained, should be put in their notes. Once students have become skilled in note taking these practices should no longer be necessary.

Making the Lecture Interesting.   Lectures should also attract students' interest and attention. One way to arouse attention and interest is to open the lecture with a challenging question, a problem, or a perplexing fact. If at the beginning of the lecture you can puzzle the students a little, they may be anxious to listen in order to solve the puzzlement. It will also help if you show the students what it is you intend to do and reason for doing it. If you can establish a purpose that relates directly to the students' purposes and concerns, so much the better. Certainly you should point out how the information in the lecture relates to past and future content and to what they already know and like. Real and rhetorical questions, the use of humor, and above all lots of illustrations and examples will help maintain interest and make points clear. Demonstrations, pictures, exhibits, projectuals, and other instructional aids all seem to spice up the lecture and to hold students' attention when their minds begin to wander.

Informal Teacher Talks

Much, if not most, of the average teacher's group instruction is done through informal talks to groups or to the entire class. These talks differ from the formal lecture in that they are usually short, extempore discourses rising out of the needs of the moment. Often they stem from class discussion or students' questions. Because these talks are short, teachers do not need to prepare for them as they do for the formal lecture. Usually they are most effective when interspersed with questions and discussions both from and to the teacher in what is sometimes called the lecture-discussion.

Because this technique will probably be one of your mainstays, you should become proficient in its use. You should also be aware of its dangers and shortcomings.

All of the comments about clarity of language in the lecture are applicable to the short informal talk as well. So too are comments about utilizing aids to make the instruction clearer and more effective. The greatest danger is that the teacher will talk too much. When teachers talk, all too often students stop thinking. Oftentimes teachers must explain, but *they should try to turn many of their teacher talks into indirect teaching by asking questions, posing problems, seeking comments, and entertaining questions.* Also, beware of the danger of thinking that students have learned something just because you have told it to them. Whenever it is possible to do so, students will misunderstand, misinterpret, or miss altogether what the teacher tells them. Therefore make it a habit of following up your explanations, and other short talks, with questions designed to check the students' understanding. If you try to limit your talks to a minimum

For what purposes would you plan to use lectures in your secondary school teaching? What kinds of lectures are there? How can they be used?

How does one plan a lecture or informal talk? Consider objectives, outline, illustrations, motivations, length, aids, clarity, interest.

How does one tell whether a lecture or talk has been successful?

and substitute instead questions, discussions, Socratic techniques, and other tactics and strategies which call for the students to carry the load of the thinking, you will probably be more effective.

Recitations

Several decades ago V. T. Thayer wrote a well-known book entitled *The Passing of the Recitation*. That title was somewhat premature. Today the recitation still remains a common teaching strategy.

The method in this strategy is simple. Teachers assign students content to study in their textbooks and then orally quiz the students on what they have learned in the assignment. Although this technique is not very satisfactory for teaching high level learning, it does have advantages for teaching basic information. It reinforces knowledge students have already acquired and gives immediate feedback concerning the accuracy of one's answers. It also gives students the opportunity to learn from the replies of other students. The fact that the students will be questioned on what they have studied is a motivating factor. Many a student has read the homework text assignment solely because he is afraid he may be called on to recite in the next class.

Still, the recitation yields little besides the rote learning of information. It does not encourage true understanding of the information learned, to say nothing of encouraging the application of knowledge, the solving of problems, or thinking of any sort. It actually discourages the development of listening and discussion skills; not only that, it creates an unfriendly, inquisitorial class atmosphere that is really antisocial and works against the development of class cohesiveness and cooperativeness. All in all, it would be difficult to find a more antiintellectual, antisocial pedagogical method than the recitation as it is ordinarily used.

To make the recitation more productive of full understanding, as soon as the students seem to understand the basic information, try to build the recitation around thought questions. Key thought-provoking questions should be carefully planned in advance both as to purpose and as to sequence and wording. The answering should emphasize thinking rather than remembering. That is why the open-text type of recitation is likely to be more advantageous than the ordinary recitation particularly at the secondary school level.

Open-Text Recitation

The open-text recitation differs from the ordinary recitation in that it is really a discussion in which students can refer to their books and other materials as the discussion progresses. It can be used effectively as part of either controlled or open discussions.

This open-text recitation has many merits. It frees students from the rote memorization of facts. It shows students that facts are not so much ends in themselves as they are means for understanding and for thinking. On the other hand by stressing the use of facts and the necessity for factual accuracy, the open-text recitation stragegy emphasizes the need for factual information and getting the facts straight. The strategy also helps students master the intellectual skills needed to seek out and check facts and to determine which facts are important and which immaterial. All in all, the open-text method is an effective and efficient strategy.

Briefly, the procedure for conducting an open-text recitation is

1. Assign reading and study or some other information-gathering activity.
2. In the assignment include suggestions and questions that cause the students to read in an inquiring manner and to think and draw inferences from what they read or study (or otherwise gain information).

3. Use Socratic or open-ended thought-provoking questioning. If possible, encourage various interpretations, inferences, and conclusions from various students. Encourage students to react to and challenge each other's ideas. During the discussion allow students to consult their books, notes, or other material, in order to justify their views and substantiate their opinions. In this type of recitation it is not remembering the facts but using them in the higher mental processes that matters.

4. Sum up (or have a student sum up). No final conclusion or agreement is necessary. At times it may be better if no common conclusions are made.

> V. T. Thayer, in his *The Passing of the Recitation*, advocated the elimination of the recitation from the teacher's arsenal of teaching strategies. Do you agree that the recitation should be eliminated? What would you do to make a recitation more than a meaningless repetition of inconsequential details? Develop a plan for conducting an open-text recitation that would further the higher mental processes and result in clear concepts and full understandings.

Questions

Use of Questions

Throughout the course of educational history, questioning has been one of the most common of teaching techniques. It continues to be so in spite of modern changes in educational theory and technology for it is a fine tool. Use it

1. To find out something one did not know.
2. To find out whether someone knows something.
3. To develop the ability to think.

4. To motivate student learning.
5. To provide drill or practice.
6. To help students organize materials.
7. To help students interpret materials.
8. To emphasize important points.
9. To show relationships, such as cause and effect.
10. To discover student interests.
11. To develop appreciation.
12. To provide review.
13. To give practice in expression.
14. To reveal mental processes.
15. To show agreement or disagreement.
16. To establish rapport with students.
17. To diagnose.
18. To evaluate.
19. To obtain the attention of wandering minds.

> Can you think of a question to illustrate each one of the purposes mentioned above? After you have formed the questions, test them against the criteria in the following section. How well did you do?
>
> Attend a class in a school or college classroom. Observe the teacher's use of questions. What techniques were used? Were they successful? Why, or why not?

The Right Question

According to Gallagher and Aschner's analysis, there are four basic categories of questions.

1. Cognitive memory questions: questions that call for simple recall of information. For example, Who discovered penicillin? or What is the formula for prussic acid?
2. Convergent questions: thought questions for which there is a single correct answer. For example, Study the route of the Oregon Trail on the map. What advantages does the circuitous route via South Pass have over the much more direct route used by Lewis and Clark?
3. Divergent questions: open-ended questions that cause pupils to think but have no correct answers.

These are the questions that stimulate creative thinking and imagination. For example, What would the United States be like today if King George III's government had acquiesced to the American colonists' demands?

4. Evaluative questions: questions in which students pass judgment on some action. For example, Do you think that President Jackson was wise to take his stand against the Bank of the United States? Which position on the role of the Federal Government was more defensible, Hamilton's or Jefferson's?[4]

> Prepare an example of
>   a. a cognitive memory question
>   b. a convergent question
>   c. a divergent question
>   d. an evaluative question.

As these categories illustrate, different types of questions elicit different responee. You should be careful to ask questions that will further the instructional goals you want to achieve. Sometimes the appropriate question to ask involves cognitive memory; sometimes convergent; sometimes divergent; and sometimes evaluative.

> Which of the sample questions in Table 11–1 are cognitive memory? convergent? divergent? evaluative?
>
> Prepare sample questions for each of the Bloom categories.
>
> Prepare a question that would fit each of the purposes listed at the beginning of the chapter.

---

[4] James J. Gallagher and Mary Jane Aschner, "A Preliminary Report of Analyses of Classroom Interaction," *The Merrill-Palmer Quarterly of Behavior and Development* (July, 1963), **9**:183–194.

Skillful teachers can aim their questions so that they bring out whichever category of Bloom's Taxonomy of Cognitive Goals they wish, as Table 11–1 shows.

Four Basic Criteria

For questions to be effective, try to ask them so that they measure up to four basic criteria. (Although in this context we are dealing only with oral classroom questions, these criteria, plus a few additional rules, also apply to written test and examination questions.) These four criteria are:

1. *A successful question asks something definite in simple, clear, straightforward English that the student can understand.* Therefore be careful to avoid ambiguity, confusing construction, double questions, parenthetical remarks and other verbiage that might cause the student to lose the point of the question.

Try to word the question so as to get at a definite point consistent with the goal of the lesson. As a rule, vague generalities are usually not valuable in furthering the learning that the lesson is trying to promote. This criterion does not rule out general questions, however. Often questions calling for general answers are needed to open up the students' thinking, but these questions, too, should be worded so that students can perceive what you are driving at. Vague, poorly thought-out questions tend to evoke fuzzy irrelevancies rather than to advance good thinking on the topic at hand.

2. *A good question is challenging and thought provoking.* A main purpose of questioning is to stimulate learning. A good question challenges students to think. Questions that can be answered by merely repeating some fact from a book can never be as stimulating as thought questions. In fact, as often as not, they are not stimulating at all, although sometimes they are necessary.

3. *The good question is adapted to the age, abilities,*

TABLE 11.1

Sample Question	Goal Category	Sample Question	Goal Category
1. Knowledge		which would you expect to reach London first, everything else being equal?	
What is the principle ingredient in the air we breathe?	1.1 Knowledge of specifics.	*4. Analysis*	
What steps would you have to take to become a licensed operator?	1.2 Knowledge of ways and means of dealing with specifics.	Which part of the argument we have just read is fact and which is opinion?	4.1 Analysis of elements.
What is the correct form for presenting a motion before a meeting?		What propaganda devices can you find in this automobile advertisement?	
What is the basic principle behind the operations of a free market?	1.3 Knowledge of universals and abstractions in a field.	Does the conclusion that Senator X made logically follow from the facts he presented?	4.2 Analysis of relationships.
2. Comprehension		In this poem what devices has the author used to build up the characters of the principal antagonists?	4.3 Analysis of organizational principles
In your own words, what does "laissez-faire" economy mean?	2.1 Translation.	*5. Synthesis*	
What does it mean to say that to the victor belong the spoils?		Describe the procedure you used and the results you observed in your experiment.	5.1 Production of a unique communication.
In what ways are the Democratic and Republican positions on support for the military budget similar?	2.2 Interpretation.	How would you go about determining the composition of this unknown chemical?	5.2 Production of a plan or a proposed set of operations.
If the use of electrical energy continues to increase at the present rate, what will be the demand for electrical energy in A.D. 2000?	2.3 Extrapolation.	You have heard the description of the situation. What might be the causes of this situation?	5.3 Derivation of a set of abstract relations.
3. Application		*6. Evaluation*	
If you measure the pressure in your barometer at the foot of a mountain and then measure it again at the summit of the mountain, what difference in the reading would you expect?	3. Application.	In what way is the argument presented illogical?	6.1 Judgment in terms of internal evidence.
If one of two sailing vessels leaving New York at the same time en route to London took a route following the Gulf Stream and one kept consistently south of the Gulf Stream,		Does the theory that organically grown foods are more healthful than other foods conform to what we know of the chemical composition of these foods? Explain.[5]	6.2 Judgment in terms of external criticism.

[5] See Frances P. Hunkins, *Questioning Strategies and Techniques* (Boston: Allyn and Bacon, 1972) for other illustrations of various types of questions.

and interests of the students to whom it is addressed. There is no great point in embarrassing or frustrating students by asking them questions they cannot answer. Neither is there much point in allowing bright youths to slide along on easy questions without stretching their intellects. Moreover, you can harness the interests of various students by asking them questions that appeal to their special interests. For instance, the 4-H club boy who raises stock could contribute greatly to a social studies unit on the country's resources or a general science unit on conservation. He might even be able to make a considerable contribution concerning "the lowing herd [which] winds slowly o'er the lea."

4. *The good question is also appropriate to its purpose.* You must be able to use all the types of questions—cognitive memory, convergent, divergent, evaluative—when the occasion calls for them. Sometimes your questions should be closed-ended and sometimes open-ended.

When facts are needed, closed-ended, cognitive-memory, fact questions are needed. At other times you ought to ask questions that will converge students' thinking on a certain point. Sometimes you should ask wide-ranging questions that open up students' imagination. A good question is one that serves its methodological purposes. The good teacher is one who knows how and when to use all types of questions.

It has been said that a question should be couched in language considerably easier than the students' reading level. Why? Why not?

Of what value is a question answerable in one word?

Suppose that one of your purposes is to stimulate the students' thinking. How can this be done by questioning? Just how would you word the question? Prepare some examples and try them out.

Techniques of Good Questioning

Planning Your Questions

From the foregoing account it seems evident that questioning requires skill and preparation. Good questioners usually carefully brief themselves on the subject under discussion and prepare key questions in advance. Although some teachers seem to be able to ask well-worded questions at the spur of the moment, to do so is quite unusual. If you prepare your key questions in advance, you will probably be more successful. Write them out. They'll probably be clearer and better worded if you do.

In preparing key questions you should consider

1. The teaching objectives.
2. What you want the questions to do. (Well-prepared key questions should give the lesson structure and direction.)
3. The kinds of questions that will best do the job.
4. The desirability of using questions that are in the affective domain.
5. The range of objectives covered by your questions. (Unless one plans one's questions in advance, it is too easy to become involved in minutiae and irrelevancies rather than in significant learning. That is why it is wise to write key questions into one's lesson plans.)
6. The intellectual development of the learners. (Questions that are too difficult or too abstract will lead only to frustration—not learning.)

Asking the Questions

The notion of the teacher as a grand inquisitor attempting to catch the recalcitrant student should be foreign to the modern classroom. Questioning should be thought of as a technique by which to teach—not just to see how much the student knows. Inquisitions are out of place in the classroom.

Many of your questions should be quite informal as you try to help individuals and groups with their various assignments. Questions frequently may be addressed to the entire class, of course, but often they should be addressed to an individual student or a small group. As a matter of fact, in a lively class the students may ask most of the questions.

You should ask your questions in a pleasant, friendly, easy, conversational manner. If you can maintain an atmosphere of easy informality without sacrificing decorum, so much the better. You should always ask your questions in a fashion that indicates that you expect a reasonable answer. If the student does not know the answer, or cannot contribute at the moment, there is no point in teasing him about it. Exhortations to think will not bring back a forgotten lesson. Such exhortations may not be necessary if one takes care to word questions clearly and specifically, to ask them logically and sequentially, to vary them according to difficulty and complexity, to adapt them to students' abilities, to base higher-level questions on lower-level questions, and to allow students sufficient time to think of the answers.

When using questions in a whole-class situation, usually you should first ask the question, wait for the class to think about it, and then ask someone for an answer. In this way everyone has a chance to consider the question before anyone tries to answer it. There is little use in asking thought questions if you don't give the pupils time to think about them.

This technique has another merit in its favor. When you ask the question first, no one knows who is going to be asked. This helps to keep the students alert. When you call on a student before asking the question, other members of the class may heave a sigh of relief and not bother to listen to the question.

As usual, there are exceptions to the rule. When you call on an inattentive student, it is sometimes better to call out the name first and then the question. In this way you may recapture wandering attention and bring the wanderer back to work. Similarly, it is often best to name a slow or shy boy or girl first so that the student will know what

is coming and be able to prepare for the ordeal.

Another technique that may help keep a class attentive is to refrain from repeating questions. If for some legitimate reason the student did not understand or hear, then of course to repeat the question is only fair. But when the cause is inattention, move on to someone else. This rule also applies to repeating answers. Repeating answers merely wastes time and encourages inattention. If you want to reinforce the learning, it is better to come back to the matter in some other way than to repeat answers.

Distributing the questions about the class also helps keep the students alert. However, you should not resort to any mechanical system for doing this. Youngsters soon catch on to these devices. The old system, for instance, of going around the class in alphabetical order, row by row, is sure death to student attention.

The best way to direct student attention to questions is to ask really interesting, thought-provoking questions. Leading questions, questions that give away answers, one-word-answer questions, and the like have the seeds of boredom in them. Avoid overusing them, for they have killed many a potentially good class.

Wait Time

Most teachers do not allow students much time for thought. One study reported that the average amount of time teachers allowed students for their answers was only one second. If a student had not answered by then, the teacher either "repeated or rephrased the question, asked another question, or called on another student."[6]

Giving students more time to think about their answers may increase both student learning and class participation. Waiting several seconds for an

---

[6] M. B. Rowe, "Wait-Time and Reward as Instructional Variables," *Journal of Research on Science Teaching* (1974), **11**:81–94. Cited by William W. Wilen, *Questioning Skills for Teachers* (Washington, DC: National Education Association, 1982), p. 18.

answer has several benefits. According to Rowe, teachers who increased their wait time to from three to five seconds achieved the following results: (1) increased length of student responses; (2) increased number of unsolicited appropriate responses; (3) decreased number of failures to respond; (4) increased student confidence in responding; (5) increased speculative thinking; (6) decreased teacher-centered teaching, increased student-student interaction; (7) more student-provided evidence preceding or following inference statements; (8) increased number of student questions; (9) increased contributions of slow students; (10) increased variety of student structuring, soliciting, and reacting moves.

Rowe also found that teachers developed greater response flexibility, changed the number and kind of questions they used, and tended to wait longer for responses from more capable students.[7] Perhaps if you learn to count to five before closing off answers to unanswered questions, your teaching will become more effective. If you do use this technique, be sure to tell the students that you plan to give them more time to think up answers. Then launch the technique gradually.[8]

Handling Student Answers

In order to create an atmosphere of friendly cooperation, in which the students feel free to do their best, even if their best is none too good, you should accept every sincere response appreciatively. Immature thinking and lack of knowledge are not serious faults. If students were mature and knew all the answers, we should not need schools. Students should be allowed to make mistakes without fear of embarrassment, but they should not be encouraged to do careless work. When a boy does not answers to the best of his ability, follow

up with other questions that will shake him out of his complacency. Usually that will make your point. The practice of following students' answers, grade book in hand—so common in the standard recitation—has little to recommend it, although some students seem to be motivated by it.

Similarly you should insist that the students make themselves understood. An answer that is not clear is not a good answer. If the student fails to make a point, ask for more detail. Each answer should be a complete thought unit—although not necessarily a sentence. If you throw incomplete thoughts back at the students, the students will probably soon learn to answer more clearly. Do not let yourself get bogged down on English grammar, however. The emphasis should be on ideas. Teachers must avoid sacrificing thinking to the niceties of academic English, even though they should strive to develop skill in correct, effective English expression.

Although one should listen appreciatively to all sincere answers, only the good ones should be approved. When an answer is not satisfactory, the student should learn why it is incorrect and how to improve it. Any portion of an answer that is correct should be recognized, of course, but any part of an answer that is incorrect should be corrected. You can do this by pointing out the error yourself or by throwing the question open for discussion by other students. In either case, in order to maintain a positive classroom atmosphere, this should be done tactfully.

Sometimes you can use an incorrect answer as the basis for a discussion or investigation that may clear up a difficult concept. Skillful teachers often use incorrect answers as springboards for other questions, as in the Socratic technique. Such capitalization on mistakes can be achieved by asking other students to comment on the previously given answer or by asking additional questions that will yield a correct or more thorough understanding. These are often called probing questions.

If a question is answered well, express approval. This does not mean that you need be effusive about

---

[7] Ibid.

[8] L. B. Gambrell, "Think-time: Implications for Reading Instruction," *Reading Teacher* (November, 1980), **34**:143–146.

it. For some answers a friendly "That's right" is quite enough. Other questions, designed to bring out major points, need to be given more emphasis. This can be done by using such questions as a basis for further discussion.

At times the best response to the students may be to use nonquestioning techniques such as declarative statements, reflective statements, state-of-the-mind remarks, invitations to elaborate, or just plain silence. The uses of these techniques are discussed in Chapter 12.

Occasionally, a question brings forth no response other than blank stares from the entire class. In such cases the chances are that you have skipped some steps. Perhaps you can get the desired response by breaking the question down into component parts or by backtracking a bit and asking questions that will provide background for the baffling original question. At other times the whole difficulty may be in the wording of the question. When such is the case, restating the question may clear up the problem.

What are the faults of the questioning techniques of teachers you have observed? How can you avoid these faults?

Prepare a list of principles to observe in questioning. Check yourself by these principles in a classroom situation. How well do you do?

The Use of Thought Questions

If you aspire to high-order teaching, you will want to use thought-provoking questions. Although thought questions are not really difficult to use, to use them well requires a little extra skill and preparation. It is so easy to fall into the trap of asking cut-and-dried questions on what it says in the book! Therefore to avoid this temptation toward the easy but uninspiring practice, use thought questions until it becomes second nature. Learn to use

open-ended, divergent, or evaluative questions at every opportune moment. Challenge students to consider what they have said or believe. Build on their contributions. Ask them to comment on each other's answers—not in a carping or criticizing manner, but in the spirit of sharing ideas, opinions, and thinking. "Do you agree with John on that, Mary?" "Do you feel this argument would hold in such and such a case, John?" If you ask questions of this sort, obviously you cannot limit yourself to questions with pat answers. You ought to ask at least some questions whose answers are not in the book. The best thought questions may have *no correct* answers. It is thinking that you are trying to promote, not set conclusions. Try to insist on valid logical reasoning. Make the students show their evidence, point out why the evidence supports their position and defend their reasoning.

However, before you go too far in this way, you should make sure that the students have facts to think with. Use techniques like the following to give them a base for informed thinking.

a. Ask fact questions first and then follow up with thought questions.

b. Use some sort of springboard presentation,[9] oral or written, that presents the background information before you spring your thought-provoking, follow-up questions.

c. Use good summary questions that will ensure that all students have the necessary background to lead to your thought questions.

d. Incorporate the necessary facts in the question itself.

e. Give the students fact sheets that they can consult as they try to think through suitable answers to your challenging questions.

f. Similarly, let students consult their texts before and during the questioning.

g. Give the students the facts before you ask the question. Put them on the blackboard, use an

---

[9] A springboard is any type of presentation that one can use to launch a discussion or inquiry lesson. Springboards are discussed more fully in Chapter 13.

overhead projector, simply tell them the facts or let them use their texts.

At times students do not take kindly to the use of high-level questioning at first. They may much prefer the low-level qustions they have become used to in daily recitations over the past years. But if higher-level learning is to occur, students must develop positive attitudes toward higher-level questions. Perhaps you can develop more positive attitudes by encouraging a more congenial climate and using nonquestion alternatives. It is usually helpful to make the change from an emphasis on low-order questions to a greater emphasis on higher-order cognitive questions gradual.

Perhaps incorporating real "perplexity questions" into your lessons may make the transition to high-level questioning more acceptable. Perplexity questions are real questions that the questioners do not know the answers to although they would like to. Dillon suggests the following technique to encourage the use of student perplexity questions.

1. Have all the students make up four questions for which they know the answers.
2. In addition have them make up another question on a matter that perplexes them.
3. Let them ask questions of each other reserving the ones that perplex them until the teacher is quite sure the students understand the basic subject matter fairly well.[10]

Students should be encouraged to bring up real, relevant questions whenever they feel perplexed by the lesson or subject matter.

Finally, encourage the students to share each other's thinking by questioning other students. Your goal is to establish a friendly, courteous give-and-take in which the students examine the issues and debate the evidence without acrimony so that individuals may make their own decisions as rationally as they can. Good use of thought questions leads

to true discussion, rather than question-answer inquisitorial teaching.

Probing Questions and Clarifying Responses

Many thought-provoking questions are probing questions by which the teacher hopes to dig more deeply into the matter at hand, thus giving students a clearer and more correct understanding. A clarifying response is a probing question by which the teacher hopes to persuade a student to reconsider and think through a statement, belief or value. The idea is to challenge students to look at their own behavior or ideas and to clarify them in their own minds by thinking out implications and ramifications. The clarifying response is especially useful for helping students clarify their values and beliefs.

The technique for the clarifying response is a simple one. Once a student has expressed an opinion or belief, you ask such questions as, "How did you arrive at such a belief? Is that belief based on solid evidence or hearsay? Give an example of what you mean. Should everyone believe that? What would be the result if they did? What are the implications of that belief?" In short, ask any question at all that would cause a self-examination of the student's belief or value. Because the whole idea is to help students to clarify their own thinking, do not force students to come to set conclusions. Sometimes the best type of clarifying response is merely to repeat the student's response or to say "You mean you believe . . ." without further comment.

Use probing questions in the cognitive domain to dig out facts, follow up statements and in general to clarify students' understanding. Thus, for instance, if a person states that it is essential in a nation for everyone to speak the same language, you might ask about Switzerland. Again you might ask students to explain meanings, to think of implications, to develop reasons why such and such is so. Often probing questions can be raised to move

[10] J. T. Dillon, *Teaching and the Art of Questioning.* Fastback 194 (Bloomington, IN: Phi Delta Kappa Educational Foundation, 1983), pp. 13–17.

the class from lower-level to higher-level thinking. Probably when you receive an answer that needs to be followed up by probing questions, it is best to move to another student for the follow-up question, while at other times you may prefer to ask the same student a few follow-up questions. Beware, however, of becoming involved in a dyadic conversation that leaves out the rest of the class. Again the goal is to develop critical thinking, not just a right answer.

Pick a chapter from a textbook or topic for a course you might teach. Develop a number of thought-provoking questions that call for high-order thinking. Try to think of thought-provoking follow-ups that you might use to bring out the thought you are seeking. Try the questions and the follow-up tactics on some of your colleagues.

Prepare a series of thought-provoking questions of both the divergent and convergent type to use with a specific open-text recitation lesson.

Handling Student Questions

You should encourage students to ask questions. If the students leave class with inquiring minds, you will have accomplished much. But how does one encourage student questions? By welcoming them! If you encourage a free, permissive atmosphere in which youngsters know that they and their opinions will be respected, you can expect student questions to increase. Certainly they will if the material studied is interesting and important to them. If you will only ask yourself what the youngsters may want to know before you plan the lesson, you can increase the chances of your material's being interesting and important.

Not all student questions are as important as others. Some questions are so important that if the class is interested it would be wise to depart from the agenda and consider the question in detail, even if it is not exactly pertinent. Others are of little importance and can be answered very briefly. Some questions are so trivial that they have no place in the class at all. If the student asking the trivial or irrelevant question is sincere, answer the question, but briefly. Explain that class time is scarce, that class goals are important, and that there is little time for the trivial. In case the student is not satisfied by a brief answer in class, arrange to go into the matter more deeply in private sometimes later when the discussion would not interrupt the progress of the class. Then be sure to follow up your promise and discuss the question with the student at your earliest opportunity.

At times it is best to turn a question over to some other member of the class or to the class as a whole for discussion. In fact, there seems to be no reason why students should not ask each other questions directly as long as they are pertinent to the discussion and asked courteously. In "good" classes this practice is often encouraged.

Occasionally, you will be asked questions you cannot answer. In that case you should promptly admit your inability. Perhaps another member of the class does know. If not, you can either find out yourself or ask someone to find out for you. If the latter choice is made, be sure to look up the answer too. Thus you can check to be sure that the student reports back correctly.

Listening

Lectures, recitations and questioning techniques hang upon what students hear as much as on what anyone says.

The importance of skill in listening can hardly be overemphasized. As Frank Steeves says

> Most of the time of pupils in typical classes is given to speaking and listening, especially to listening. All other pupils listen while one pupil asks a question.

All listen while the teacher discusses the question. They continue to listen while another pupil adds a comment. Even the most active discussions are largely a time of listening. If nine pupils engage in a forty-five minute discussion and each speaks an equal amount of time, each will speak for five minutes. But each will listen for forty minutes. What each *learns* from the discussion period will not be from what he said during his five minutes but from what he was able to hear during the forty minutes.[11]

Perhaps Steeves has somewhat overstated his case. Not all students listen when another student is talking, and as often as not, the students who do listen do not listen effectively. One of the more interesting experiments one can perform in class is to have each student report his version of what was said in a report or discussion or what you have just said in your lecture. The difference between what a student thinks another person said, and what that person meant to say can be startling. Another similar technique is in a discussion to require students to summarize what the preceding speaker said before they make their own contributions. That students need to learn how to listen well will be self-evident.

Alert teachers find many opportunities to give students assignments that will help them to learn to listen. For example, listen to the radio or television and report exactly what the President said in his State of the Union address, or, more simply, what did the actors really say in the commercial advertising Product Y? Similarly you might ask students to pick the central idea out of a short speech played on the record player. A variation of this same technique is for the students to pick out the principal arguments and show how a speaker's subordinate arguments supported his main thesis. Students can also analyze what they listen to—separating fact from opinion and information from propaganda as well as major points from minor

points or even major points from folderol or window dressing. Students who are taught to anticipate what the speaker will probably say next learn to be alert listeners. Students can also build alertness by noting new technical words in what they hear or by trying to identify the feelings an oral reading expresses.

Students need much practice in such listening skills. Homework and classroom assignments such as those mentioned in these paragraphs will help them learn to listen more attentively, to hear more correctly, and to evaluate what they hear. Direct instruction and practice in listening skills are necessities.

Develop some techniques for helping students learn to listen to your lectures and talks.

Prepare a lecture in which you take particular care to point out with elocutionary aids the points students should hear.

Practice and Review

Sometimes one can learn something quite thoroughly as the result of a powerful, vivid experience. Unfortunately, such impressive experiences are rare in the classroom. More often the learning must be renewed through drill, practice, or review.

The differences in these words are largely differences of connotation. Drill ordinarily connotes emphasis on unthinking, meaningless repetition, whereas practice seems to connote more purposeful, varied repetition. Review implies a second look at what has been learned once before. By implication it is often thought of as less intense than drill or practice. For our purposes in this book there seems to be little merit in drawing distinctions between drill and practice. We use the word *practice* to denote repetition of both sorts.

[11] Frank L. Steeves, *Fundamentals of Teaching in Secondary Schools* (New York: Odyssey Press, 1962), pp. 177–178.

The Value of Repetition

Repetition is necessary in school learning for several purposes. One of them is to reinforce retention of what has been learned. To be sure that students do not forget, learning must be renewed often, much more frequently than is necessary for immediate recall. This extra renewal is called overlearning. Overlearning is essential in memorization, in making behavior automatic, and in creating desirable habits. One major purpose of practice is to provide the overlearning necessary for retention.

Another reason for practice is to develop skill. Great concert pianists practice their selections again and again to improve their renditions. As they practice, they may try to play more accurately or with more feeling; they may experiment with the tempo or they may vary their technique. But they always hope to improve their playing. So it is with the learning of all skills. No one can repeat anything exactly. Because when we practice we vary our behavior, practice makes it possible for us to improve.

Practice can also increase one's understanding. As one repeats and renews the learning, the concepts may become much clearer. Just as actors and actresses find that with numerous repetitions of a role they discover new insight into the character they are portraying, so one may acquire new understanding by restudying a topic. This clarification can be done only if the repetition is meaningful, purposeful and varied. New skills and new concepts seldom result from dull, dry, aimless repetition.

Practice and Drill

Making Practice Meaningful

In one sense one does not learn through drill or practice. Practice merely consolidates, clarifies, and emphasizes what one has already learned.[12]

---
[12] This, too, is learning, of course.

Therefore, before practice sessions start, the students should understand what they are doing and how to do it. Repeating meaningless words or actions is wasteful. When one knows what copper sulphate is, or when one understands the meaning of the verb, this is the time to overlearn $CuSO_4$ = copper sulphate, or to conjugate the verb *amare*.

Repetition is usually more meaningful in context. Students often find it difficult to understand just what they are doing when the material to be learned is isolated from its context. Therefore, practice should occur in as real a setting as possible. For instance, to practice foreign words in sentences and in conversation is probably more effective than to practice them in isolated lists.

Practicing by wholes rather than by parts also makes practice more meaningful. In practicing something very difficult or involved, one may need to practice the difficult parts separately, but, in general, one should practice the whole thing. Then, because no part is learned at the expense of the others, the learning becomes a unit. For example, in practicing the crawl a girl may need to concentrate on her kick or her breathing separately; but she must also practice the entire stroke if she wishes to swim well. Or in memorizing a passage, one can usually learn most efficiently by the whole or part-whole method. If the selection to be memorized is short, one should memorize the whole thing at once, but if the selection is long, one should divide it into meaningful divisions, each of which can be learned separately. One might learn a sonnet as a whole, but a longer poem stanza by stanza.

For similar reasons practice seems to be most successful when it is spread over many different types of activities in many classes. Making practice part of the regular classwork rather than relegating it to special practice sessions tends to make practice and the skills or knowledge to be practiced more meaningful. This procedure also tends to give to the practice its proper proportion and emphasis. When they use special practice sessions as a means of teaching particular skills or knowledge, teachers tend to treat the practice itself as the end of the instruction. Such distortion of the teaching-learning process may lead to confusion.

Motivating Practice Sessions

Because of its very nature practice needs to be well motivated and occur under some pressure. The pressure should not be onerous, but it should be heavy enough to be felt so that the student will strive to improve. Lackadaisical practice is wasteful practice.

The hunger to learn is probably the most desirable motive, but it does not always seem to be present in students. Sometimes one needs to use devices designed to make practice more attractive. The use of games, either individual or competitive, often serves the purpose admirably. Occasionally, someone objects to using competitive games in the classroom. However, if you take care to make them fun for all and to eliminate petty glory-seeking, such games have a place. Individual games that can be used include such things as anagrams, authors, crossword puzzles, and other puzzles of all sorts. These can be played as "solitaire"; but some of them can be competitive as well. Group games such as charades or "baseball" and "basketball" games in which the questions take the place of base hits and field goals are also effective. In fact, almost every parlor game can be adapted for classroom use.

In utilizing such games, you should be careful to include only the pertinent and important. Be particularly wary of quiz games using student-developed questions. Students too often search for the trivial and the obscure. Games which feature such questions help very little and should be avoided. Also avoid games which eliminate those who make errors. The old-fashioned spelling bee is not very useful because the people who need the practice most are eliminated first.

Using the Principle of Spaced Learning

Partly because of motivation factors, learning is usually more efficient over a period of time with rather frequent breaks then when it is concentrated in long, continuous practice sessions. This phenomenon, known as the principle of spaced learning, seems to operate because of several reasons. One

of them is that a person can keep motivation and effort at a high level only for a short time before tiring. Short practice periods interspersed with rest periods make it easier for learners to perform at or near top level, thus giving them maximum benefit from the practice. Also, the shortness of the practice sessions, plus the opportunities for rest, prevents the pupils from developing incorrect habits by practicing when overtired. Another reason for the spacing of practice is that the intervals of rest between practice give the learners a chance to forget their mistakes before they go on to the next practice session. Because after each rest period the students concentrate anew on learning correctly, spaced learning tends to reinforce correct learning and to cause mistakes to drop out.

As the learning becomes more firmly entrenched, the practice periods should become shorter and the intervals longer because not so much time is needed to renew the learning. This also helps to keep the practice from becoming deadly.

Eliminating Unnecessary Drudgery

Practice can be dreadfully boring, as we all know. To keep it from becoming so, the teacher should eliminate as much unnecessary work as possible. If the exercise is to punctuate a paragraph, to copy the entire paragraph is pointless. Indicating the words preceding the punctuation should be enough. It is better still to mimeograph the paragraph and have students punctuate directly on the mimeographed sheet.

For this very reason practice or drill should not be used unnecessarily. Teachers need to bear down on some things but not on others. If they emphasize the drill aspect too much, they run the risk of making the class unnecessarily boring. *Hard practice should be reserved for important learning which needs to be habitualized or to be retained a long time.* In other words, one should concentrate practice on whatever is most important. Also, since memorizing is at best a dreary pastime, teachers should not demand that students memorize things that they need not remember. There are quite enough things a person should know by heart without loading students up with unnecessary memorization.[13]

When Drill Is Needed

In spite of the warning in the previous sections, teachers should not expect to eliminate all rote learning from their teaching. Some facts and abilities simply must be developed by direct attack and repetition. Among these are such things as idiomatic expressions, conjugations, chemical formulas, and mathematical facts. Historical dates provide an excellent example of such facts. Most dates in history can be taught by always associating the event with the date during the discussion. Other techniques, such as making time lines and time charts, are also available and valuable. However, in order to have a skeleton on which to hang historical events, students must learn key dates. These key dates must be taught directly once the students have learned their significance. To ensure that students learn them and retain them, a few minutes at the beginning or end of the period might well be given to practice on key dates several times a week.

Individualizing Practice

If practice is to be really valuable to students, it should be individualized. To find a practice exercise valuable and important to every teenager in your class is virtually impossible. Almost invariably some of the students will have mastered the skill to the point where it would be better for them to move on to something else. On the other hand, other students probably do not understand well enough so that they can truly benefit from the practice at all. So, except for such things as marching drill and similar mass group exercises, group practice should be used sparingly. Instead, practice should be tailor-made for each student.

To individualize practice is easier than it sounds. Since practice ordinarily consists of experiences designed to strengthen learning that has already been acquired, you can leave much of the teaching to the students themselves. By providing self-administering and self-correcting materials and arranging situations in which pairs and small groups can work together correcting and helping each other, you can make it possible for each student to be largely self-directing.

For this reason, diagnosis, particularly self-diagnosis, is an important aid to effective practice. As students realize their weaknesses, they are more likely to see the necessity for practice. Then, if their practice is rewarded by visible progress, they may willingly redouble their efforts. Nothing is so encouraging as success.

An example of such a practice technique was used in the teaching of ninth-grade grammar. In this class the teacher supplied the students with a multitude of exercises designed to give practice in each of the areas studied in grammar.[14] Before studying each grammatical topic, the students took a pretest. If they scored very high in the pretest, they could skip that topic and go on to another; if they did not, they practiced the exercises for that topic until they thought they had mastered the material. As they finished each exercise they corrected their own work, sometimes consulting a teacher or a neighbor about why such and such was so. When they thought they were ready, they tried another mastery test. When they had demonstrated by the test scores that they were the master of that topic, they were allowed to move on to the next one. Of course, the teacher administered the tests and was available to help and guide the students with their practice. The result was a busy class in which individual students worked on the exercises that most concerned them.[15]

---

[13] By this we do not imply that students should never have an opportunity to learn a poem by heart for the pure pleasure of knowing it.

[14] Mostly by cutting up old discarded grammar texts.

[15] You will recognize this as another variation on the continuous progress approach.

How might one adapt a spelling bee to give everyone plenty of practice?

How can one avoid the poor attitudes that often accompany drill?

Why is it recommended that practice should be under some pressure?

Make up some self-correcting, individualized practice material for a topic you might teach.

Review

Review differs somewhat from practice and drill. It does not require drill techniques. What it does require is reteaching. Instead of drill activities one should use such activities as these:

1. Summarizing what has been taught.
2. Having students summarize or outline the essentials that were taught.
3. Reteaching the lesson in a different context.
4. Having students build questions to ask each other about content to be reviewed.
5. Utilizing quiz games such as jeopardy.
6. Dramatization, role playing, or simulating the content to be reviewed.
7. Building open-ended discussion around the main points of the content to be reviewed.
8. Using broad questioning techniques to get students to think about and apply the information in the lesson.
9. Doing problems based on the content to be reviewed.
10. Allowing students to build questions for a test on the subject.
11. Using the content to be reviewed in practical situations or applying it to other situations.
12. Building time lines, charts, tables, diagrams, and so on, that bring out the relationships and important points in the content to be reviewed.

Teachers should review frequently. Some teachers make it a habit to end each class with a review of the main concepts taught that day; others start each class with a review of what has gone before. Almost all do some reviewing at the end of each unit and term, but reviewing should not be limited to the end of the unit or lesson. Rather it should be used anytime that loose ends need to be tied together or students' thoughts need to be regrouped or reorganized. By its use one can drive points home, make learning stick, bind ideas together, and clarify relationships among past, present, and future learning.

Writing

Students need much more opportunity to learn to write than they have in most classrooms. Learning to write well takes practice, and more practice, under guidance. Therefore teachers of all subjects, not just English, should give students many opportunities to write.

Writing under supervision implies that whatever the student writes will be read and evaluated by the teacher. It does not mean, however, that the teacher should be supercritical. As in oral expression, what is important is the idea being expressed and the mode of expression. Students should learn to express themselves clearly and logically. Good attempts should be rewarded. The red pencil should be used sparingly. At times grammatical errors may be safely ignored, but good writing should *always* be rewarded—without fail. Reinforce the positive every chance you get.

Good writers revise. Secondary school students and some college students never seem to have heard of the word. You should insist that first drafts be reworked into final drafts before papers are ultimately submitted as "contributions to the course." And final drafts should always be proofread. Teachers who insist that students take back sloppy work for revision and proofreading are doing both themselves and the students a favor.

During the draft stages much good can come

from students' reading and commenting on each other's papers in pairs or small groups. The criticism of a friend or colleague can be really helpful. It has the advantage of being free from the threat of a mark. Therefore consultation among writers should be welcome. Perhaps students might act as editorial readers such as those used by publishing houses.[16] Perhaps also they might copyedit each other's drafts. Another technique that may prove helpful is for the students to set up their own guidelines for acceptable themes and other compositions.

One of the major difficulties when writing a paper for a class is to find something to write about. In English classes students frequently complain that finding something worthwhile to write about is more difficult than writing. Teachers would do well to provide students with as many acceptable suggestions as they can. In English classes, particularly, teachers should consider correlating their theme writing with assignments in other classes. Students could then combine their work for two classes. Thus the student who is studying the Reconstruction period for a history class could write an English composition on an aspect of the Reconstruction.

Letter exchanges can be an interesting combination of writing practice and learning the subject matter of the writer. In one class students from an urban New Jersey "ghetto" wrote letters explaining why they, as Separatists living in Holland, thought they ought to emigrate to America. These letters were then exchanged and some read to the class by the recipients who wrote back to tell the writers what they might be getting into in the wilds of North America. Another technique useful in English and social studies, and sometimes in other areas, is for the teacher to read a brief, action-packed account which she has written of some real

or imaginary happening and then ask the students to write an ending that would fit the circumstances. Teachers have had great success with student written and edited classroom magazines and newspapers. Just to ditto students' compositions and distribute them to other members of the class can be motivating. Essay test questions and essays the students evaluate themselves have also proved effective. So have such trick games as writing roulette.

In this game, at a command, each person starts to write a story. Then on signal the writing stops, the papers are collected, mixed up, and redistributed at random. At a signal the students read the stories they have received and add to them until told to stop again. This process is repeated two or three times. Then the final versions are collected and as many as possible read orally to the class. Such games are good for persons having difficulty with their reading and writing skills because they combine practice in reading, writing, and oral reading.

When dealing with students who have academic difficulty, it pays to keep compositions short, but you should require more ambitious essays, compositions, term papers, and imaginative pieces from advanced students. This is the time when, if ever, youths are poetic, imaginative, creative and eager to express themselves—even though they may be short of academic skill. Give them a chance to be heard and praised.

Prepare a series of topics that your students might write about in one of your courses. Devise a plan or strategy for giving students practice in writing.

Summary

Active student involvement in the learning process is essential in teaching. In American schools the students' role is liable to be completely passive too

[16] Readers are experts who go over manuscripts before they are published to suggest to the writer ways in which he might improve the book before it goes to press. They point out passages that do not make sense, errors in fact, things that were left out, places that seem illogical, and so on. The writer can accept or reject the readers' suggestions as he sees fit.

much of the time. Student-teacher interaction analysis techniques can help us bring student and teacher involvement in the learning to a proper balance.

The lecture is among the most important of teaching techniques. Although its use has been severely criticized, it has a place in today's schools; it should, however, not be the teacher's mainstay. Short, informal teacher talks are much more effective for most purposes. If one desires quality teaching, other methods involving group process, inquiry, problem solving, and the higher mental processes are often more effective. However, at times, the lecture is the only appropriate method. In such situations you should follow the rules laid down by our best speech makers: Make it short, lively, and to the point. Tell them what you are going to tell them, tell them, tell them what you told them.

Recitation, as commonly practiced in our schools, is obsolete. Teachers who care about learning should replace it with methods that encourage understanding and the use of the higher mental processes. Thought-provoking questioning and open-book recitations are examples of the types of methods that might be used instead.

Questioning is one of the oldest and most dependable tactics. Its uses are legion and range from the checking of memory and understanding to the bringing about of higher learning. Unfortunately, of the four categories of questions suggested by Gallagher and Aschner, most teachers are content to concentrate on memory questions and neglect convergent, divergent, and evaluative questions. Yet it is quite possible, after a little practice, to phrase questions that would cover each category in the Bloom taxonomy.

Good questions are clear, simple, straightforward, challenging, thought-provoking, adapted to the students to whom they are addressed and suitable for the purpose for which they are being used. If your questions are to meet these criteria, you probably will have to write out your key questions in advance. To get the most out of your questioning, you probably should ask questions of individuals

rather than the whole class. The best technique is to ask the question first and then call on a specific person to answer it, to refrain from repeating questions and to distribute the questions evenly and randomly among the class members.

Student answers should be handled courteously. Support all honest attempts to answer, even when the students do not come up with the "right" answer, but do not allow pupil misunderstanding and error to go uncorrected. Students should also be encouraged to ask questions. The best classes are full of student questions and comments. Clarifying responses are most useful for starting students' thought processes.

Practice makes perfect. Secondary school classes should allow plenty of opportunity for the repetition and review necessary to drive learning home. To be most effective, practice should be meaningful, varied, and as free from boredom as possible. To eliminate drudgery and to make practice efficient, one should individualize practice exercises and activities as much as possible after carefully diagnosing the needs of the individual students.

Additional Reading

Broawell, Martin M. *The Lecture Method of Introduction.* Englewood Cliffs, NJ: Educational Technology Publications, 1980.

Devine, Thomas G. "Listening in the Classroom," in *Teaching Study Skills: A Guide for Teachers.* Boston: Allyn and Bacon, 1981.

———. *Listening Skills Schoolwide: Activities and Programs.* Urbana, IL: ERIC Clearinghouse on Reading and Communications Skills, 1982.

Dillon, J. T. *Teaching and the Art of Questioning,* Fastback 194. Bloomington, IN: Phi Delta Kappa Educational Foundation, 1983.

Friedman, Paul G. *Listening Processes: Attention, Understanding, Evaluation.* Washington, DC: National Education Association, 1983.

Gage, N. L., and David C. Berliner. *Educational Psychology*, 3rd ed. Boston: Houghton Mifflin, 1984, Chap. 19.

Hunkins, Francis P. *Involving Students in Questioning.* Boston: Allyn and Bacon, 1976.

Hyman, Ronald T. *Strategic Questioning.* Englewood Cliffs, NJ: Prentice-Hall, 1979.

Judy, Stephen N., and Susan J. Judy. *The Teaching of Writing.* New York: Wiley, 1981.

McLeish, John. "The Lecture Method," in N. L. Gage, ed. *The Psychology of Teaching Methods*, The Seventy-fifth Yearbook of the Society for the Study of Education. Chicago: University of Chicago Press, 1976, Chap. 8.

Orlich, Donald C. et al. *Teaching Strategies: A Guide to Better Instruction*, 2nd ed. Lexington, MA: Heath, 1985, Part VI, Chap. 6.

Sadker, M., and D. Sadker, in James M. Cooper, ed. *Teaching Skills: A Handbook.* Lexington, MA: Heath, 1977.

Sudman, S., and N. M. Bradburn. *Asking Questions.* San Francisco, CA: Jossey-Bass, 1982.

Tchudi, Stephen N., and Margie C. Huerta. *Teaching Writing in the Content Areas.* Washington, DC: National Education Association, 1983.

————., and Joanne M. Yates. *Teaching Writing in the Content Areas: Senior High School.* Washington, DC: National Education Association, 1983.

Wilen, William W. *Questioning Skills for Teachers.* Washington, DC: National Education Association, 1982.

Wolvin, Andrew D., and Carolyn Gwynn Coakley. *Listening Instruction.* Washington, DC: National Education Association, 1979.

12

Group and Discussion Methods

Overview

Open communication and a supportive atmosphere are essential for good discussion. The success of discussions also depends upon teachers' skillful use of questions and careful staging of the classroom situation in order to promote free flow of ideas and thinking. That is one reason why it is necessary for teachers to prepare carefully for discussion lessons. Well done, they often pay off by arousing interest, molding attitudes, and encouraging thinking. In this chapter we point out techniques for making your discussions work. We also show ways to conduct the more formal types of discussions which may be used very effectively to involve students in high-level consideration of controversial and multisided matters. Finally we examine small group and committee approaches—strategies that, although difficult to conduct well, have many uses. Effective teaching of small groups requires attention to detail and constant supervision while at the same time permitting students freedom to carry out their own initiative.

Discussion

Characteristics of a Good Discussion

A discussion is not just a bull session or a rap session. Rather, it is a purposeful conversation proceeding toward some goal with a minimum of rambling and bickering. For a discussion to be successful, the participants need sufficient background to know what they are talking about and to base their arguments on fact. Moreover, the topic must be discussable. The equation $a^2 + b^2 = c^2$ is a fact and so is not a subject for discussion, although perhaps one might discuss its implications.

A discussion is a conversation, not a monologue or a series of questions. In a really effective discussion, everyone should participate, although it is not always necessary for each person to talk. People can participate in different ways. Sometimes they also participate who only sit and listen. In general, however, one can assume that in a discussion the more people who participate actively the better. Discussion is not another name for lecture or recitation.

A really successful discussion is not only purposeful; it also achieves its purpose. If it is at all possible, the discussion should lead to some sort of conclusion. Certainly, even if no conclusion is reached, it should always culminate in some sort of summing up. Sometimes the summary may have to include a minority report.

Although discussions should be purposeful and

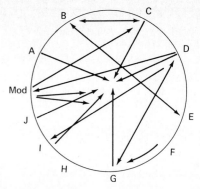

FIGURE 12–1
Satisfactory Patterns of Discussion Flow. Moderator's questions have elicited general responses and exchanges between students. (Arrows to center indicate a statement or questions addressed to the entire group rather than to an individual.)

conclusive, true discussions are not vehicles for expressing the teacher's point of view or devices by which to win support for a particular position (although they can be very effectively used for converting people to a view). In a true discussion all the members of the group think for themselves, and all have a chance to express an opinion, no matter how unpopular the position may be. At best it is informal, but it is always serious. Humor, of course,

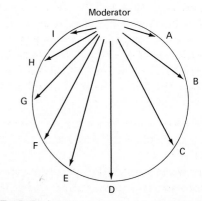

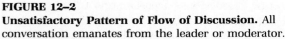

FIGURE 12–2
Unsatisfactory Pattern of Flow of Discussion. All conversation emanates from the leader or moderator.

is welcome, but frivolity is not. Although the group members remain courteous at all times, there is no formal hierarchy of membership. The chairman is merely a moderator, who supervises rather than directs the conversation. The flow of conversation should travel around the group almost at random (Figure 12–1).

Discussions that consist of questions asked by the leaders and answered by the students without considerable side interchange among the students are not really discussions at all (Figure 12–2).

Advantages of True Discussions

Teachers who handle true discussions well find them to be effective. As compared to the lecture, for instance, the discussion seems to impart to the students better skills in thinking and clearer understandings, and it is more likely to effect changes in attitude; the lecture, however, may have the edge as far as conveying information is concerned. The discussion process—including, as it does, defending, applying, modifying, explaining, and reworking one's ideas—gives students the opportunity to develop concepts with deep personal meaning. Concepts developed in this way are more likely to stick with students than concepts developed by more static strategies. In addition, this process is more effective in shaping attitudes, ideals, and appreciations than the more static teaching strategies are. Discussions are also useful as a medium for training students in communications skills and in building positive social attitudes and a sense of belongingness. Their major contribution, however, is

---

What is a discussion? How does it differ from a recitation?

What values do discussions have? For what purposes are they best suited? What sort of things can best be learned through discussion?

What makes a good discussion?

---

the opportunity they give students to practice thinking—to look at their own ideas, to formulate and apply principles, and to face up to immediate feedback from their peers. The discussion is an excellent tool by which to develop creative thinking.

Conducting Discussions

The Role of the Leader

Active, purposeful leadership can make the difference between a successful and unsuccessful discussion. Effective discussion leaders see to it that the discussion starts smoothly by introducing the topic succinctly but clearly so that everyone understands what is to be discussed and the purpose of the discussion, and by posing provocative opening questions or statements. Then they keep the discussion moving by encouraging all to take part and by tactfully bottling up any monologists. They try to keep the discussion from wandering off into unproductive byways by clearing up errors of fact or judgment and by recalling the group to the question at hand when they digress. They summarize from time to time and help the group members evaluate their progress so as to be sure that everyone understands what has been said and so that no one is left behind. Sometimes they suggest next steps and guide the conversation into new or different paths and cut off unproductive side issues and overlong prolongation of the argument. They keep track of the time to be sure that the group can accomplish its task in the time allotted and finally, when all has been said and done, they try to tie together all the ideas, conclusions and generalizations in a final summary.

In spite of the importance of the leadership role, discussion leaders should not dominate discussions, for a discussion should be an opportunity for participants to share ideas. Effective leaders try to see that the ideas of all participants are treated with respect and keep the participants' discussion open so that the truth—or at least notions about truth—may come out. At the same time, they do not turn the discussion over to the group and let it do as it pleases. Laissez-faire leadership seldom leads to profitable discussions. Rather they seek to create an atmosphere in which participants feel free to speak and think freely without fear of embarrassment, but in which all the energies of the group are kept pointed toward the goal.

An ideal discussion leader would possess such qualities as

- Evident interest in the topic at hand.
- A sense of humor.
- A sense of seriousness.
- An interest in and respect for the opinions of others.
- The ability to suppress his own opinions.
- A nonjudgmental attitude and bearing.
- An accepting and encouraging manner.

Although it may seem that this list calls for paragons, many teachers have trained students to be excellent discussion leaders. Figure 12–3 is an observational form that Schmuck and Schmuck suggest secondary school students use to rank student discussion leaders.

FIGURE 12–3
Observation Sheet for Goal-Directed Leadership
(Secondary) (Richard A. Schmuck and Patricia A. Schmuck, *Group Processes in the Classroom* [Dubuque, IA: Brown, 1971], p. 48.)

	Task Functions	Time 1	2	3	4	5
1.	Initiating: proposing tasks or goals; defining a group problem; suggesting a procedure for solving a problem; suggesting other ideas for consideration.					
2.	Information or opinion seeking: requesting facts on the problem; seeking relevant information; asking for suggestions and ideas.					
3.	Information or opinion giving: offering facts; providing relevant information; stating a belief; giving suggestions or ideas.					
4.	Clarifying or elaborating: interpreting or reflecting ideas or suggestions; clearing up confusion; indicating alternatives and issues before the group; giving examples.					
5.	Summarizing: pulling related ideas together; restating suggestions after the group has discussed them.					
6.	Consensus testing: sending up "trial balloons" to see if group is nearing a conclusion; checking with group to see how much agreement has been reached.					
	Social Emotional Functions					
7.	Encouraging: being friendly, warm and responsive to others; accepting others and their contributions; listening; showing regard for others by giving them an opportunity or recognition.					
8.	Expressing group feelings: sensing feeling, mood, relationships within the group; sharing his own feelings with other members.					
9.	Harmonizing: attempting to reconcile disagreements; reducing tension through "pouring oil on troubled waters"; getting people to explore their differences.					
10.	Compromising: offering to compromise his own position, ideas, or status; admitting error; disciplining himself to help maintain the group.					
11.	Gate-keeping: seeing that others have a chance to speak; keeping the discussion a group discussion rather than a 1-, 2-, or 3-way conversation.					
12.	Setting standards: expressing standards that will help group to achieve; applying standards in evaluating group functioning and production.					

The Role of the Recorder

Designating someone to act as a recorder or secretary can be helpful in most group discussions. The job of the recorder is to keep a record of the important points and decisions made during the discussion. From time to time at the request of the leader the recorder may help clarify the course of the discussion, resolve conflicts and confusion, and put wandering discussions back on track by summarizing what has been said.

The recorder's main task is to keep the record of the discussion. Because this task is a difficult one for many boys and girls, you should take special pains to help the student recorder. Usually in classroom discussions verbatim transcripts of the discussion are not desirable. Instead, the group needs to have an account of the major positions taken and the conclusions reached.

One method that will help ensure good recording by beginners is to have the recorder keep his record on the chalkboard. This technique makes it possible for all the participants to see the notes and also permits the teacher to coach the recorder if the need arises. Similarly an overhead projector can be used with the added advantage that the notes recorded on the transparency can be saved for future reference or for reprojecting. In any case you should be prepared to help the recorder keep good notes and keep notes yourself in order to supplement any lapses of the student recorder.

The Role of the Participants

The ability to speak and listen well as participants in group discussions is a rather difficult skill that relatively few adults have truly mastered. When speaking, participants should try to be clear and precise. Although it is difficult to do so during a lively discussion, they should try to organize what they say before they say it so that they can make points more easily. In this respect they should learn that their presentations will be more successful if they speak clearly and simply without affectation.

A simply worded direct argument in which one makes one's points one by one in a simple linear order is usually much more likely to be understood than more complicated approaches. The simple technique of taping a discussion and asking students to listen to themselves and try to arrange the ideas they thought they were presenting into a logical outline sometimes helps students understand the advantages of direct simple organization.

One danger of placing great emphasis on the way students present their opinions is that they may forget to listen to the discussion. Many persons, even participants in television debates and panels, are guilty of being so busy thinking about what they want to say that they never listen to the other participants or to the questions asked them. To train students to listen, some teachers ask each student to repeat the germ of the last speaker's comments before adding his own.

The Role of the Teacher

In discussions, as in other methods, your role as teacher is to prepare, execute, and follow up. However, in the discussion your role during the execution phase should be *subdued*. The bulk of the discussion should be the students' own. Even so, you will probably find that conducting the discussion is hard work for the teacher.

Before the discussion begins, you the teacher must see to it that everyone is properly prepared. During the class's first experiences with real discussion you will have to act as moderator or chairman. At all times you will need to act as supervisor and observer. In these roles you must see to it that the problem to be discussed is properly defined and delimited; furnish information when it is required, set guidelines, see to it that gross errors do not remain unchallenged, pose questions, reflect the content and feeling of the comments made, relate the comments to one another and to the central topic, in general keep the discussion moving on the right track, and finally provide a follow-up. On the occasions that you act as moderator, you will have to do all of these jobs yourself directly. When a student is moderator, you will have to do most of them by indirection. Sometimes a hint to the moderator or recorder will suffice. Sometimes you may have to stop the discussion and restart it. However, the more unobtrusively you can do the job, the better.

Most important, during the discussion you should assume the role of a consultant who is always available as a resource person or advisor for whatever contingency might arise. In discussions, perhaps more than in other strategies, the teacher acts as the servant rather than the master of the group.

Preparing for a Discussion

Students often think of discussions as easy periods, but really discussions are quite difficult to carry out. Both teachers and students must be well prepared for discussion classes if they are to be successful—perhaps they need to be better prepared for discussion classes than for any other type of class.

During the period of preparation you can make sure that students understand exactly what the point at issue is to be and what their roles in the discussion are. Early in the year you may find it desirable to do some direct teaching concerning the how and why of carrying on discussions.

Starting the Discussion

Not only must you, the teacher, be well briefed on the topic to be discussed, but you need a plan for the conducting of the discussion. In the plan, you should include provisions for getting the discussion started and questions for possible use. You should also be prepared with possible conclusions.

Starting a discussion may be something of a strain. It may take a little persuasion, or some special introductory activity. Before starting, try to arrange the group in a homey, informal fashion. As a general rule, the more pleasant the atmosphere

the better chance the discussion has of being successful. If possible, the students should be seated so that they can see each other. In actual practice a circle seems to be the best seating arrangement for a discussion, although any other arrangement that brings the participants face to face will do.

Be sure the students understand what it is they are to discuss, the procedure they will use in discussing it and how long they have for the discussion. Sometimes the introductory portion of the discussion needs to be devoted to clarifying the issues. Presenting the topic to be discussed as a problem sometimes makes the clarifying and launching of the discussion easier.

To get a discussion off to a good start, make use of some activity that will develop interest among the participants. People need an opportunity to think and react before they can discuss anything sensibly. Consequently, it helps to have the discussion develop out of some other activity. Buzz sessions—groups of four to six people who discuss the question for four to six minutes—sometimes help to get the discussion under way. Another common device is to start the discussion with a short introductory talk or to have someone throw some challenging questions (prepared in advance) at the group. A test, quiz, or pretest can sometimes be used to stimulate a brisk discussion.

In any case you should provide an opening statement of some sort to orient the group and establish the ground rules for the discussion. Other ways to stimulate discussion include

- The introduction of a specific case or problem.
- Role playing.
- Films.
- Filmstrips.
- Exhibits.
- Pictures.
- Visitors.
- News items.
- Tape recordings.
- Demonstrations.
- Staged incidents.

- Provocative questions, especially questions emphasizing *how, why,* and *what if?*

Whatever tactic is used to get the discussion going, it should be only long enough to arouse interest and point the direction of the conversation. The discussion should follow immediately. Tomorrow may be too late. Once the mood has been lost, to reestablish it may be impossible.

No matter how dramatic or exciting an initiatory activity may seem, you must be prepared for the response to be negative or for the discussants to start off in directions you never dreamed of. Have a few spare tricks up your sleeve in case of need. Teachers must be prepared for such contingencies in order to save both their own and student led discussions.

What can the leader do to start a discussion when the group seems reluctant to participate? Can you suggest at least five approaches which may help the discussion get started?

How would you arrange the physical setting to encourage discussion? Suppose you wished to use the chalkboard in connection with the discussion. Would that change your decision?

Guiding the Discussion

Once the discussion is started, you must keep it moving briskly in the right direction. Skillful questioning and keeping an outline of the most important points on the chalkboard will help maintain the tempo and hold the group to the topic. So will being sure that all the students know and accept the problem under discussion. Should the group digress, you can redirect it by restating the question, although the group should be allowed to pursue a digression if it seems to have promise. Occasionally groups that have become lost and cannot agree can be helped by a minute of silent consideration of the problem, an impromptu buzz session, or role playing.

Skillful Questioning. One key to successfully guiding the discussion is the skillful use of questions. The leader's role is to draw students out and to keep the conversation moving in the direction it should go. To draw students out ask open-ended, broad, thought-provoking questions. Divergent questions are much more likely to be successful than convergent ones. Evaluative questions are likely to be most valuable of all. Usually you should throw questions out for anyone who wishes to pick them up. Sometimes, however—in order to involve a new participant, to start things moving, to reengage someone's wandering attention, or perhaps even to forestall still another comment by a monopolizer, for instance—it may be better to address your questions to specific individuals.

To involve more students, you should bounce the questions around. Asking students to comment on other students' answers may be effective. Questions such as "Do you agree with Mary, Susie?", "What would you do in such a situation?", and "If you had your druthers, which would you prefer?" tend to keep the conversation going and tend to free students' ideas. When leading a discussion, you should seldom answer questions or express an opinion except in the case of a direct question about a fact. Even then it is better to ask if anyone else can provide the information requested.

Alternative Nonquestions. All too often teachers' questions stifle discussion. By their very nature the questions tend to turn the discussion into a two-way exchange between the teacher and a student. To stimulate discussion and to encourage wide participation teachers should make optimum use of what Dillon calls alternative nonquestioning techniques.[1] Let us look at a few of these "nonquestioning" techniques.

Sometimes the teacher's best technique is to keep silent. Teachers usually talk too much. Often when the discussion falters for a bit, if the teacher would

---

[1] J. T. Dillon, *Teaching and the Art of Questioning* (Bloomington, IN: Phi Delta Kappa Educational Foundation, 1983).

keep quiet, the students would pick up the thread and start embroidering it. Nature abhors vacuums and people abhor empty silence, so you can almost always depend on someone's saying something just to fill in the void. Moments of silence also give students a chance to consider what has been said, and to reformulate their thoughts and arguments. Remember Rowe's suggestion in Chapter 11 that a teacher count up to five before picking up on an unanswered question. This practice works just as well if not better in discussion situations.

When a discussion bogs down because students are unsure of facts or unclear on points, a simple declarative sentence may clear the air and start things moving again. In many situations trying to clear misconceptions and misunderstandings by questioning procedures becomes too inquisitorial. A short explanatory sentence may clarify the point without putting any onus on anyone. It also provides a basis for further comment by the students. Questions call for an answer, but declarative sentences may provide a point of departure or a foundation for further thought. Remember, however, the statements should be short. A discussion is no place for a speech from the podium.

A student's statement can open up discussion and lead to clearer explanations. Asking students to explain what they mean is likely to be fruitless. Restating what you understood the student to say may be profitable. Statements like "If I understand you, you believe that . . ." "I take it you think that . . . ," "So you maintain that . . ." encourage students to clarify their positions, develop their meaning in more detail, and, in general, to participate more fully. This technique is particularly useful when it seems that the students' ideas are not well formed.

If you do not understand what a student means, it is important to let the student know your reaction. In such cases you may say something like "I am sorry, but I do not understand what you are getting at," or "I am not sure I understand what you mean." Another type of reply is to say "I wonder if what you say applies to such and such situa-

tion," or "I wonder if that (what you described) would really make a difference."

Invitations to elaborate on an expressed idea may be more effective than probing questions in discussions. Invitations to elaborate seem to work best when presented obliquely. "That sounds like a great idea; would you like to tell us more about it?" "That's interesting, I'd like to hear more of your feelings about it." If the student takes up your invitation to expand, it will not only help the discussion, it may make the speaker's thought clearer to himself and to the rest of the class. Usually class members are more attentive when students express their ideas and feelings than when students merely respond to questions.

Students should be encouraged to ask questions. If confused students ask questions, perhaps the confusion can be cleared up. Probably the best way to encourage student questions is to answer them. Avoid answering questions with counterquestions however. Particularly encourage student-student exchanges. Students are more willing to ask questions of other students than of teachers. They are also more willing to give detailed full answers to other students' questions than to their teachers.[2]

Creating a Supportive Atmosphere.   You should strive for a supportive atmosphere, accepting all contributions graciously, even when they are not very helpful. To this end, refrain from expressing your approval or disapproval of the comments of the participants. Try to ensure that all are heard with equal respect.

On the other hand, you must not let error pass unchallenged. Always challenge inconsistencies, faulty logic, and superficialities. By using skillful questions you can get the students to see their own ideas and those of their colleagues clearly. To help them clarify their thinking, ask them to explain why they said what they said and believe what they believe. In this way and by skillful questioning, you can get the students to look beyond their state-

---

[2] Ibid.

ments and see the causes and consequences of their beliefs. Dare them to prove their statements and cite their authorities. When confusion is rife, try to clarify the situation by asking such questions as

• Just what does that term mean?
• Exactly what is the issue facing us?

Keeping on Track. One of the most difficult problems you must face when leading a discussion is that of keeping the discussion on the track. Usually you can bring the group back into focus by asking a question that deals directly with the topic at hand. Other times you may have to point out that "I think that we are forgetting the point of our discussion." Sometimes you may have to stop to reorient the group by some technique.

From time to time, you should draw the threads together by summarizing or by asking the recorder to summarize. This gives the group a chance to stop and look at its progress, to see how it stands, and perhaps to decide in which direction to proceed. To bring out these values, you may include any or all of the following:

1. A résumé of the major points made so far.
2. A review of the facts and evidence presented.
3. A synopsis of what has been accomplished and what remains to be finished.
4. A restatement of any conclusions that have been made.
5. An analysis of the course or conduct of the discussion up to this point.

Whatever the gist of the summary, it should be brief, well organized, and to the point. Too many or too long summaries may break up the thread of the discussion and so do more harm than good. Also harmful are summaries that do not represent the thinking of all the group. The final summary at the end of the discussion should pull together all the important ideas and conclusions. To be sure that all points of view are presented fairly, it is often advantageous to elicit the aid of other partici-

pants is developing the summary. To note these ideas and conclusions on the chalkboard for all to see will aid to emphasize their importance and to clarify their meaning.

Although a good summary is essential for the ending of a discussion, it should not end the consideration of the topic. A suitable follow-up activity that drives home the importance of the things learned or leads into the next activity can increase the value of almost any discussion.

> What can be done about discussions that seem to get nowhere?
> What can you do with students who monopolize the discussion?

Evaluating the Discussion

The value of discussion will ordinarily increase as the students learn how to carry on discussions and gain experience. Good discussion techniques must be learned and practiced. If we take stock of ourselves and our discussion from time to time, progress in those skills can be expected. Frequently self-evaluations will help to improve discussion skills. Having the group members check a form as simple as the following can be of considerable value.

1. Did the group discussion do what it set out to do?
2. In what way did we fall short?
3. Did we get off the topic?
4. Did everyone participate?
5. Did anyone monopolize the conversation?

Students' self-evaluation of their discussions can often be enhanced by letting them listen to taped recordings of the discussions. For evaluating a taped discussion the use of a list of criteria similar to that just mentioned or the one prepared by the A.S.C.D. (Association for Supervision and Curriculum Development) can be of great help (Figure 12–4). In spite of its obvious value, the tape recording

Each Group Member and the Discussion Leader in Particular
_____ Helps decide on specific problems and ways of working as a group
_____ Contributes ideas and suggestions related to the problem
_____ Listens to what other members say and seeks helpful ideas and insights
_____ Requests clarification when needed
_____ Observes the group process and makes suggestions
_____ Assumes various roles as needed
_____ Helps group get acquainted
_____ Helps group establish ground rules
_____ Reports results of preconference planning for work of group
_____ Helps group proceed with planning and deciding
_____ Calls on group to clarify, analyze, and summarize problems and suggested solutions
_____ Draws out the "timid soul" and keeps the dominant person from monopolizing
_____ Knows particular contributions which different persons can make
_____ Assists the recorder
_____ Summarizes the thinking of the group as needed.

The Recorder
_____ Consults with the group concerning the kind of record that is developing as the discussion moves forward
_____ Keeps a record of the main problems, issues, ideas, facts, and decisions as they appear in discussion

_____ Summarizes the group discussion upon request
_____ Requests clarification when his notes are unclear
_____ Prepares resolutions and other final reports with other designated members of the group
_____ Attends any scheduled clearinghouse or intergroup sharing committee sessions
_____ Prepares final group report and is responsible for getting it to proper clearinghouse.

Each Group Member
Pays attention to the way the group:
_____ States its goals clearly
_____ Permits participation to be easily and widely spread
_____ Keeps its discussion clear
_____ Assumes leadership responsibility
_____ Uses its resources
_____ Progresses toward its goals
_____ Revises its goals as necessary
_____ Participates in evaluation of the group process
_____ Reports to the group if asked regarding observations on the group process.

Group Members as Resource Persons
Every member of a discussion group is responsible for:
_____ Supplying information or other material to the group when requested, or when the discussion seems to call for it
_____ Citing his own experience freely when it is relevant
_____ Assisting the leader in moving toward the achievement of group goals.

FIGURE 12–4
The A.S.C.D. Checklist (Association for Supervision and Curriculum Development, *1954 Convention Program*, Washington, DC: the Association, a department of the National Education Association, 1954, pp. 54–55. Adapted by the 1954 Committee on Conference Orientation and Evaluation from material prepared for the 1950 Convention Program by J. Cecil Parker, University of California, Berkeley.)

of group discussions may present something of a problem. To record a large group discussion with an ordinary school tape recorder can be very difficult. For recording, the group needs to be seated in a circle with each person as close to a microphone as possible. More than one microphone will probably be needed. In small groups, the microphone can be passed from speaker to speaker, but in most class discussions this technique is too cumbersome to be practicable. Another danger is the temptation to play the recording too long or too often. Running through a tape recording may be advantageous for training in group discussion, but overdone it can become a pernicious time-waster. Only parts of the tape should be rerun to illustrate good or poor portions of the discussion, or to reinforce the report of what happened.

Sometimes, in order to evaluate the group's discussion, one of the members is asked to act as an observer. The observer's job is to watch the group

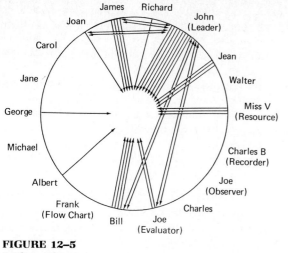

FIGURE 12–5
A Flow Chart.

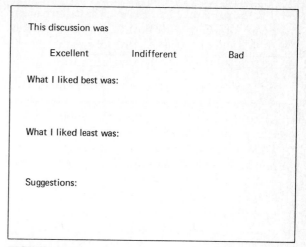

FIGURE 12–7
Discussion Rating Form.

as the discussion progresses and to evaluate and report on their performance. When evaluating, the observer may use as a guide such criteria as those mentioned in the preceding list.

The comments of the observer on the progress of the discussion and the participation of the group members are also an effective means of making overtalkative or noncooperative persons aware of their faults. Frequently the students will respond

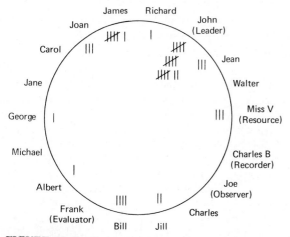

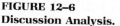

FIGURE 12–6
Discussion Analysis.

more positively to criticism from one of their peers acting as observer than from the teacher.

A flow chart such as the one which appears as Figure 12–5 can be of great help in evaluating the discussion. Another way of recording the progress of the group discussion is for the evaluator to place a tally alongside a speaker's name each time he speaks (see Figure 12–6). Grambs, Carr, and Fitch recommend an alternative to this method. In this system the evaluator uses evaluative marks

— if the contribution detracts from the discussion;

+ if the contribution adds to the discussion;

0 if the contribution neither adds nor detracts;

? if the contribution is a question.[3]

Perhaps the most effective techniques are discussions about the discussion in which pupils examine their own techniques and free reaction sheets in which pupils anonymously and briefly state their reactions favorable or unfavorable, and tell why they feel as they do. Simple rating forms such as the one illustrated as Figure 12–7 are also useful.

---

[3] Jean D. Grambs, John C. Carr and Robert M. Fitch. *Modern Methods in Secondary Education,* 3rd ed. (New York: Holt, 1970), pp. 200–201.

The evaluations may be more honest if reaction sheets or rating forms are turned in to a student committee charged with assessing the success of the activity rather than handed in to the teacher.

Make a simple rating scale with which to evaluate a group discussion.

What does the flow chart (Figure 12–5) tell you about the participating group?

Would flow charts be helpful in high school classes? How would you use them?

Examine the A.S.C.D. criteria for discussion groups. How can they be used in a secondary school class?

How can student leaders, recorders, and resource persons be used in secondary school classes?

Discussion and Thinking

Group discussion can be used as a thinking tool. In fact, our democracy is based on the premise that problems can be thought out and solved through the group process. Evidently, properly used, group discussion is a method that frees creative power in ways no other method can.[4] When a group freely discusses a problem that is real to its members, their combined thinking utilizes many skills, insights, and backgrounds. For the discussion to be a thinking process, however, the topic must seem important to the discussants, and the discussion both free and at the same time disciplined and orderly. Think of what a high school group could do with topics such as the following ones (which happen to be the first two topics of several included in an article on discussion in English classes) in an open, supportive discussion.

1. Discuss objects or areas of human relations in which inventors, customs, or public policy has been highly uncreative, inflexible, or unadaptable. Have students suggest alterations for the betterment of the individual or society.
2. Have students throw a critical, yet creative eye on their own school to identify problems in school life which are not being adequately recognized or met. E.g., evaluate effectiveness of student government, cocurricular program, assemblies; discuss overall needs in the school's program which could be improved for benefit of incoming freshmen.[5]

The procedures in a discussion that is designed to encourage problem solving are just the same as in any other discussion—after all, group discussions should be exercises in group thinking. Seldom does the thinking of the group proceed toward the solution of the problem in strictly logical fashion. However, the discussion should generally follow the steps in the usual pattern of the problem-solving process. As outlined by Burton, Kimball, and Wing, those steps as adapted for group thinking are

1. Discover the existence of a problem of concern that seems to be solvable by group methods, that is, by consensus.
2. Define the problem through group examination and discussion.
3. Analyze the problem to find what are the facts and circumstances to be faced.
4. Attempt to find solutions to the problem. (This is likely to be a long process involving much discussion, data gathering, consulting of outside sources, and so on. In the process the group draws tentative conclusions, conducts straw votes, reviews and summarizes as it works toward consensus.)
5. Make and test conclusions until it finally comes to a decision.[6]

---

[4] William H. Burton, Roland B. Kimball, and Richard L. Wing, *Education for Effective Thinking* (New York: Appleton, 1960), p. 327.

[5] Gladys Veidemanis, "A Curriculum View of Classroom Discussion," *English Journal* (January, 1962), **51**:21–25.

[6] Adapted from Burton, Kimball, and Wing, op. cit., p. 328.

The great value of discussion in problem solving is that it opens up the process to so many ideas. Narrow, stereotypic thinking is difficult to maintain when one is bombarded by the "differing values, biases, levels of insight," standards, conclusions, and beliefs of others. Free discussion brings these differences out in the open. It thus not only forces discussants to put their own values and beliefs on the line for examination but also forces them to consider beliefs and values that are new and different.

Discussion and Value Clarification

Value-clarifying discussions are much like problem-solving discussions. Their purpose is not didactic but to enhance understanding. Like problem-solving discussions, they require that the students have freedom to think without teacher pressure. When conducting value clarification discussions, you must be nonjudgmental and accepting. Refrain from questions that force students to take certain positions. Never come down hard and inform students that their values are wrong. Value-clarifying discussions are always open ended. They have no correct solutions or conclusions. In the words of Raths, Harmin, and Simon

> Thus in this discussion a teacher who is concerned that students develop an intelligent and viable relationship with their worlds, that is, develop clear values, (1) helps them to examine alternatives and consequences in issues, (2) does not tell them, directly or indirectly, what is "right" for all persons and for all times, (3) is candid about his own values but insists that they not be blindly adopted by others, (4) sometimes limits behavior that he considers ill advised, but never limits the right to believe or the right to behave differently in other circumstances, and (5) points to the importance of the individual making his own choices and considering the implications for his own life.[7]

---

[7] Louis E. Raths, Merrill Harmin, Sidney B. Simon, *Values and Teaching* (Columbus, OH: Merrill, 1966), p. 115.

Keep your value-clarifying discussion short. The minute they start to lag, cut them off. As springboards for value-clarifying discussions Raths, Harmin, and Simon recommend the use of provocative questions, pictures without captions, scenes from plays or movies, editorials, song lyrics, election literature, letters to the editor, advertising, cartoons, comic strips, news broadcasts, and the like. Anything that presents value judgment or possible conflict in value will usually bring on a strong discussion. Given the chance, once students know that their opinions and concerns will be taken seriously, they will bring in all the springboard material one needs.

Think up topics that are excellent for discussion in the subject you teach.

How would you use value-clarifying discussion? Do you feel that value clarification should be completely open ended? Why? Why not?

Panels and Debates

Panels, symposia, debates, and jury trials combine audience activities with the give-and-take of the discussion. They are useful in large-class activities when more informal whole-class or small-group discussions would not be feasible. Activities of this sort mentioned in the literature include

- *The round table*—a quite informal group, usually five or fewer participants, who sit around a table and converse among themselves and with the audience.
- *The panel*—a fairly informal setting in which four to six participants with a chairman discuss a topic among themselves, and then there is a give-and-take with the class. Each participant makes an opening statement, but there are no speeches.

- *The forum*—a type of panel approach in which a panel gives and takes with the audience
- *The symposium*—a more formal setting in which the participants present speeches representing different positions and then open up for questions from the floor.
- *The debate*—a very formal approach consisting of set speeches by participants of two opposing teams and a rebuttal by each participant.
- *The British debate*—a somewhat less formal approach in which principal presentations are given by spokesmen of each side and then the floor is opened for comment and questions from members of each side alternately.
- *The jury trial*—approach in which the class simulates a courtroom.

In general, the procedures for conducting all of these techniques are pretty much the same. As a matter of fact, many people use the terms so loosely that one can never be quite sure exactly what *panel*, for instance, means in any given conversation, and truly the techniques are so similar that distinctions may be superfluous. In any event, any of them is likely to be more interesting if it involves questions and discussions from members of the class other than the panelists. It is good policy to schedule either a time for general discussion or a question-and-answer period no matter what the type of presentation.

When to Use Panels and Debates

As we have said, panels, debates, and trials are useful for spicing up and personalizing large classes. These techniques need not be limited to large classes alone, however. Panels and symposia make excellent springboards for discussion in any group. Teachers also find them useful

1. As culminating activities.
2. As methods of presenting committee reports.
   a. Each member of the committee becomes a panelist, or

b. Representatives of various committees who have studied different areas or taken different positions make up the panelists.
3. As a way to get differing points of view on the floor. This technique is particularly useful when discussing controversial issues. Students representing differing points of view make up the panels and present their arguments.
4. As a way to present the findings of student research.
5. As a way to give classes a change of pace.

Conducting Panels, Symposia, Round Tables, and Forums

All discussions are best when the students discuss matters really important to them. For this reason, if for no other, it is wise to involve students in the selection of the topics to be discussed when setting up a panel.

Most student panelists need help as they prepare for their panels. They should do at least part of their preparation in class during some sort of supervised study period so that the teacher can oversee the development of their presentations. It is a good policy for the teacher to require the panelists to present their plans for their presentation for approval a day or so before the panel is to occur. The procedures for preparing for panels, symposia, debates, and so on, are much the same as they would be for any other committee project, report, or research study.

Before the panel or symposium begins, you should carefully brief the students on the procedures to be followed. If there are to be initial presentations, the order of presentation should be arranged and time limits set. Usually these details can best be arranged by the students themselves in an informal planning meeting under your guidance. There needs to be no rehearsal although when the discussion format requires set speeches, students should be encouraged to rehearse their speeches.

After the formal portion of the discussion has ended, as we have noted there should be an open discussion or a question-and-answer period in which everyone may participate. This should be followed by a summary of important points by the chairman. In addition you will usually find it advisable to follow up and tie up loose ends. If lack of time becomes a factor, the summary and follow-up can become review activities for another day.

In order to encourage students other than the panelists to benefit from formal discussions, you may take such steps as

- Requiring students to take notes on the formal presentations and discussion.
- Asking students to summarize the major points and different positions. (Summaries may be oral, written, or even perhaps quizzes.)
- Asking students to evaluate the logic and accuracy of the arguments of the panelists. (Students should not criticize the panelists' rhetorical skill, however.)

Just as in more informal discussions, the chairman can make a great difference in the success of a panel. At first perhaps you should chair the discussion yourself, but once students have developed some skill with the medium, students can be the chairmen. Among the duties the chairman performs are these:

1. *Make the introduction.* Announce the topic, map out the procedure to be followed, prepare the audience by setting mood, filling in necessary background, and explaining the purpose.
2. *Control the conduct of the panel.* Introduce the participants. Stop them when their time is up. Moderate give-and-take within the panel. Sum up when necessary. Redirect flow of discussion if it bogs down.
3. *Moderate the question, answer, and discussion period with the audience.* To get audience participation, sometimes it is wise to have some questions planted. Students can be assigned to make up questions as homework. (If you do assign

questions as homework, collect them whether they were asked during the discussion or not.) In this role the chairman must solicit questions, accept and refer questions in such a way as to encourage more participation, and again sum up and redirect discussion as necessary.
4. *Close the discussion.* Sum up. Tie up loose ends. Thank the panelists and audience participants.

Conducting Debate

Debate is the most formal of the discussion procedures. It requires that there be (1) a formal question to be debated, e.g., *Resolved:* That all television broadcasting stations be owned and operated by the federal government; (2) two teams of debaters, one to argue for the resolution, one to argue against it; and (3) a formal procedure for debating the issue.

Debate Procedure

1. Each of the two teams consists of two or three debators.
2. A moderator introduces the topic and the speakers. After the formal debate has ended the moderator may conduct an open discussion in which members of the audience express their views and perhaps ask questions.
3. A timekeeper times the speeches, warns the speakers when their time is growing short, and stops them when their time has run out. Ordinarily the procedure is for the timekeeper to stand to mark the beginning of the warning period and to call the time when the time has run out.
4. Each team member makes a formal presentation. This presentation is to be no longer than a fixed number of minutes (decided well in advance of the debate).
5. Each team member makes a rebuttal to counter the arguments of the other team. Again the time is limited to a prearranged number of minutes.
6. The order of presentations and rebuttals runs:

First speaker pro.
First speaker con.
Second speaker pro.
Second speaker con.
First rebuttal pro.
First rebuttal con.
Second rebuttal pro.
Second rebuttal con.

7. After the formal debate has ended it is possible to open a general discussion.
8. If one wishes, one may select student or faculty judges who can decide on the basis of a check sheet which side argued more skillfully.

Advantages and Disadvantages

The use of the formal debate is advantageous because it

1. Provides an opportunity for study in depth.
2. Can arouse interest.
3. Shows two sides of an issue.
4. Brings controversy into sharper focus.

On the other hand the formal debate has several serious drawbacks. It

1. Emphasizes dichotomous (black or white) thinking.
2. Involves too few students.
3. Tends to emphasize fluency in debate and winning at the expense of attempting to get at the truth of the matter.

Conducting British-Style Debate

The British-style debate is more useful for most classes than the ordinary formal debate because it opens up the discussion to more participants. The procedure for conducting the British-style debate is simple.

1. Select question or proposition to be debated.
2. Divide the class into two teams, one for the proposition, the other against it.
3. Select two principal speakers for each team.

4. Have the principal speaker of each team present his argument in a five-minute talk.
5. Have the second speaker for each team present his argument in a three-minute talk.
6. Throw the question open to comments, questions, and answers from the other team members. In order to keep things fair, alternate between members of the pro and con teams.
7. Let one member of each team summarize its case. Often the summarizer is the first speaker, but if a third principal speaker does the summarizing, it makes for better class participation.
8. Follow up with general discussion.

Jury-Trial Technique

Another debate technique that is excellent because it can involve a large number of the class in active participation is the jury trial. In this technique the class simulates courtroom procedures to discuss an issue or problem. The procedure seems to be a simple one, but it requires careful preparation if it is to go smoothly.

1. Select an issue or problem to debate. It adds interest if one of the students can act as a defendant.
2. Select lawyers, researchers, and witnesses for both sides. These groups can be as large as you wish, but if they are too large, they become cumbersome. The teacher can act as judge, or better yet, some responsible student can be named for that position. Another student should be selected court stenographer, or recorder, to keep a record of what transpires. All members of the class who are not lawyers, researchers, witnesses, or court officials are the jury. (If you want to do it up brown, you can select someone to be clerk of the court, bailiff, and so on, to give the courtroom verisimilitude.)
3. All students should research the problem. The lawyers and witnesses should get the facts from their own research and from that of other class members.

4. Conduct the trial.
   a. The lawyers open up with their arguments.
   b. Witnesses present their evidence.
   c. Lawyers question and cross-examine.
   d. Lawyers from each side sum up. Each should point out how the evidence favors his side.
   e. The judge sums up and points out errors in the arguments, fallacies, misstatements of fact, and so on.
   f. The class, acting as the jury, votes on which side won the argument.

Think of other techniques you might use to get the nonpanelists to prepare for the panel.

What would you do to ensure that the non-panelist members pay attention and participate in the lesson?

Which type of panel or debate do you prefer? Which seems to be most effective? Why? When would you use formal debate techniques? British debate techniques? Jury trials?

Think of several topics in your subject field that lend themselves to the jury-trial technique. How would you conduct jury trials for these topics?

Speech

Although most classroom time is spent in talking, teachers do relatively little to help students learn to speak correctly and effectively. The ubiquitous television talk shows with their inarticulate celebrities who bury their thoughts in "you know," testify to the ineffectiveness of the teaching of speech in American and British schools.

Since talk is the principal ingredient in classes in all subjects, all teachers must accept the responsibility for teaching students to speak well. Students need lots of chances to talk under supervision. Oral activities, such as discussing, telling stories, reporting, chairing groups, and participating in dramatizations can, and probably should, be part of every course. When conducting these oral activities, encourage students to use colorful, correct, effective language. To accomplish this purpose you should work on oral vocabulary building just as you should work on written vocabulary building. The techniques used for building written vocabularies can be used equally well for building oral vocabularies. You should also work to eliminate lazy speech habits such as the overuse of slang and the meaningless repetition of phrases like "you know," "I mean," and so on.

Being overcritical and picayunish in correcting the mistakes students make in speaking will not help you teach the students to speak effectively. You will be much more likely to succeed if you set a good example, and give students clear rules to follow. As far as you reasonably can, be a model of the effective speaker of good English. However, you do not have to carry the whole load yourself. Tapes, recordings, and moving pictures can be used to provide examples of good speaking. Tape recordings of the students' speaking are also effective. They show students their strengths and weaknesses as well as adding a motivating factor. Sometimes just hearing and seeing oneself on a videotape is enough to encourage one to phenomenal efforts to learn to speak more effectively—particularly after having had an opportunity to compare one's speech with that of an admired expert speaker.

Oral reading is another helpful technique to use for teaching students to speak well. The oral reading techniques discussed in the section on reading may be used successfully in the teaching of speech. Choral speaking, reciting or reading poetry, speech-making, and dramatization are also useful. Probably they should be used more frequently than they are.

When you use such techniques aim them at improving speech skills and subject-matter goals. The content of the exercises is important, but in our concern for content we should not lose sight of the importance of learning to speak well.

Small Groups and Committees

Quite often teachers divide classes into small groups. Among the various types of small groups commonly found are work groups, or committees, discussion groups, buzz groups, ability groups, and interest groups. As often as not, a specific small group is a combination of two or more of these types. A committee, for instance, may also be an interest or ability group. Small groups are used frequently because they are useful for many purposes.

1. Small groups allow for individual instruction and help provide for the many differences in pupils by allowing them to participate in different roles and on different committees.
2. Small-group work promotes effective learning.
   a. Small groups seem to be more successful in problem solving than individuals are.
   b. Small-group techniques tend to develop critical discrimination.
   c. Small groups provide a wide range of information.
   d. Small groups provide opportunities for depth study and wide coverage.
   e. Small groups provide opportunities to develop research and study skills.
3. Small groups provide pupils with opportunities to learn social skills and to develop good social attitudes as a result of the give-and-take.
4. Small groups can help develop leadership ability.
5. Small groups can help develop self-reliance and self-direction.
6. Small groups add variety and interest to classes.
   a. They make it possible to match method with purpose.
   b. They give a change of pace.
   c. They provide release from the tedium of the ordinary class and give pupils an opportunity to work off their energy through active participation.[8]

To Launch Small-Group Work

When students are not familiar with small-group work and lack the social skills necessary to make group work successful, one should begin working with them slowly. Perhaps the best method is to start off by forming small transitory committees to perform definite tasks, e.g., the bulletin board committee, the lab-cleanup committee, the committee in charge of handing out the material for students to work with, and so on. The use of buzz groups is another approach often used by teachers to introduce small-group techniques to their students.

Buzz Groups

Buzz groups are small groups of about a half dozen students who discuss freely and informally for about a half dozen minutes. Because of these characteristics—six people meeting for six minutes—buzz groups are sometimes called 6 × 6 groups.[9] Buzz groups are transitory groups called together for a specific immediate purpose. As soon as its mission is accomplished, the group is dissolved.

Buzz groups are extremely useful because they can prevent classes from centering around the teacher or a small group of dominant (or even domineering) students. They are often used

- To launch large group discussion.
- To reformulate the objectives and background ideas of a discussion that has broken down.
- To decide what to do next.
- To brainstorm.
- To set up rules.
- To exchange ideas and experiences.
- To formulate questions and problems for investigation.

---

[8] Leonard H. Clark, *Teaching Social Studies in Secondary Schools: A Handbook* (New York: Macmillan, 1973), p. 95.

[9] 6 × 6 comes from army jargon for a six-wheeled vehicle with six-wheel drive. In a buzz group all the wheels are drive wheels.

- To formulate questions and problems as a basis for group discussion, to put to guest speakers or panelists, and so on.
- To bring out and speak frankly about controversies and differences.
- To draw out students.
- To share rapidly learning gleaned from such experiences as homework, plays, films, and so on.
- To provide for expression of quick reaction to issues.

To Conduct Buzz Groups

Buzz groups are relatively easy to organize and run. They do have to be planned, however, or they may blow up. Impromptu buzz groups organized on the spur of the moment to solve some classroom exigency (e.g., a disastrous discussion) may work well in experienced classes, but wise teachers keep impromptu buzz groups to a minimum.

Selection of the members of a buzz group is usually done by some simple informal somewhat arbitrary means. Among the methods used successfully are

1. By the seating plan (e.g., the first four persons in this row, the six students sitting in the first three seats in rows 1 and 2).
2. By the alphabet.
3. By counting off (1, 2, 3, 4, 5, 6. 1, 2, 3, 4, 5, 6).
4. By a lottery using numbered cards. (All who draw number 1 are in group one.)
5. By virtue of the teacher's knowledge of the students' talents, interests, background, and so on. (There may be times when one wishes to make special provisions based on these characteristics, but usually buzz groups work for such short periods of time that it seems hardly worth the effort.)

Each buzz group should have at least three but no more than six members.

To prepare students for the buzz group take care that the mission for the group is clear and simple. Then make sure that everyone understands the mis-

sion and knows what to do. Time limits should be set explicitly. It is better that the time limits be too short than too long. Six minutes is usually about right. If the students need more time, you can extend the time. Each group needs a leader and a recorder or secretary. The choice of leader and secretary is not crucial because of the shortness of the buzz group's life.

Follow Up the Buzz Session

At the end of the buzz session the group may report its conclusions in some fashion. When group reports are expected, you should make sure that students know just what the reporting procedure will be before they start working. A common method of reporting is for each group to appoint a representative to a panel that discusses the buzz sessions. When this is done, a recorder may keep an account of the major suggestions on the chalkboard or overhead projector. Oftentimes it is better to omit the group reports and let the class move from buzz group sessions to a whole-class discussion without any intermediate steps.

The Working Committee

The Value of Committees

Working committees have a specific task to perform. Although committee groups are not supposed to be ability groups, the teacher should at once recognize that committees do help provide for individual differences in ability and interest. For example, let us suppose a class is studying family life. The class might form one committee to investigate the family life of animals, another to survey adolescent-parent relationships, still another to investigate family life in a polygamous society. In such an assignment students might be able to work on the topic that seems the most interesting. Within the committee, students should be allocated different tasks depending upon the committee's needs and the students' interests and abilities. Thus, using committees makes it possible for students to assume various degrees of responsibility and to tackle tasks of varying difficulty, as well as to study things interesting to them.

In addition to providing for differences in individuals, teaching via committees has several other values. It allows more students to participate actively than do the class recitation techniques, thus helping students develop skills of leadership, communication, socialization, cooperation, and thinking. Skillfully used it can be instrumental in teaching students how to search out, evaluate, and report on scholarly information. Furthermore, by its very nature committee membership should help students accept and carry out roles that will be theirs in adult life, for one skill, as important as it is rare in adult life, is that of organizing and carrying out effective committee work. It also makes it possible to combine teaching in-depth with wide coverage. Each committee can delve deeply into its area and then share its findings with the rest of the class.

Selecting the Committee

Ideally, a committee should consist of from four to seven members. Whenever a classroom committee grows to include eight or more members it should probably be broken into smaller committees or subcommittees. Committee members can be chosen in many ways. Sometimes you should choose the committee members yourself to suit your own purposes. As a general rule, however, it is probably wise to honor student preferences whenever possible.

In every class, students tend to form natural groups and follow natural leaders. As a rule, it is advantageous to make use of these natural groups and natural leaders when forming committees. In this respect the use of sociograms can be particularly helpful.

Whereas forming committees according to natural group lines may be advantageous, several other requirements must also be considered. Among

them are the nature of the committee's task and interests of the students. One reason for having student committees is to allow students to work at tasks that seem important to them. You should see to it, insofar as possible, that each student works on the committee in which he is most interested. Furthermore, each committee calls for members with different abilities. In choosing committee members, provision should be made for these various abilities.

Whenever possible, committees should be made up of volunteers. This is not always feasible, of course, but you may be able to approach this idea more closely if all the students make two or three choices in writing rather than volunteering orally. Making choices in writing allows the more timid to volunteer without embarrassment. Even so you, or a student steering committee working under your guidance, will have to make some committee assignments. In either case you should take care to see that the membership of each committee meets the criteria noted above.

No matter how the group members are selected, you should keep a record of the committee memberships and committee assignments. Such a record will give you an insight into the relationship of the students in the class. Also, this record will give you the information you need to be sure that all students have opportunities to participate to the fullest and to be sure that no one is neglected.

Determining the Committee Procedures

Every committee should have a specific mission to perform, and the committee members should have a clear understanding of what this mission is before they start to work. This task may be assigned to the committee or be the result of group planning. In any case, the work of each committee should further the plan worked out for the entire class.

Usually it is more satisfactory to use cooperative group planning than teacher assignments when establishing committee goals and tasks. Even when the task is teacher-assigned the committee will have to talk over the assignment and map out a plan for attacking it. In general, committee planning follows a procedure something like the following.

1. One of the first things to be done is to appoint or elect a chairman to lead the committee and a recorder to keep a record of what is done.
2. Next the students discuss their mission and its objectives. In their discussion they consider such questions as What might we do? What must we do? Exactly what will we do? How will we do it? and How do we report what we have done?
3. Then they work out in detail the subordinate problems and tasks and prepare an outline of how they intend to proceed. In this discussion they must find out what they will need to work with and what is available.
4. Finally they divide the tasks among the committee members and make provisions for sharing the results of their individual endeavors. For instance, the committee may ask one student to be responsible for securing certain material and another to be responsible for looking up a specific item of information. In the laying out of the work tasks a form similar to that in Figure 12–8 can be most useful.

As soon as this planning is finished, the students work together to complete their task. If this procedure is to succeed, the students must have a clear understanding of the procedures they can use as well as the mission they are supposed to accomplish. Frequently, the students will find that their original plan was not realistic. You the teacher should keep alert to detect problems as they may develop. On some occasions it will be necessary to stop and start over. Open-ended questioning may cut off deficiencies in planning before the problems develop. Even though you may see faults in the proposals early in the planning, you should be careful not to interfere too quickly. Too much interference may stop the students from thinking for themselves. Usually it is better to let students find their own solutions without undue interference or too pointed suggestions. After all, people learn from mistakes, it is said. However, you should certainly do everything in your power to keep the committee from ending in abject failure.

Helping Student Committees

Committees usually require a great deal of teacher guidance. Inexperienced boys and girls will need much help in determining how they should go about completing their work. They need help in determining their goals, the procedures for fulfilling these goals, and ways of reporting the fruit of their labor to the total group. In advising them, act as a consultant, not as a dictator. Point out alternatives open to the students and the dangers inherent in some lines of approach to the problem. Since boys and girls, like adults, are likely to take the line of least resistance and stick to the tried and true, you should take special care to make students aware of different approaches to committee work.

Tips for Committee Work

Among the procedures that you may find helpful in carrying out committee work are

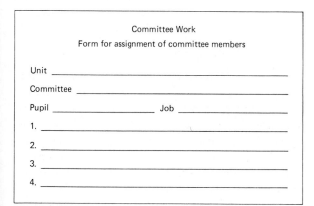

Committee Work
Form for assignment of committee members

Unit _____

Committee _____

Pupil _____ Job _____

1. _____
2. _____
3. _____
4. _____

FIGURE 12–8
Committee Assignment Form

1. Teach students how to work in committees before they start working on their own.

2. Discuss committee work and committee procedures with the entire class before they break into committees.

3. Be sure that the committees set up a reasonable time schedule.

4. Check on all groups frequently. Make sure that everyone has a job to do, knows what the job is and how to do it, and is doing it.

5. Check to be sure everyone is certain what the objective is.

6. Help groups as necessary. Use provocative questioning rather than direct suggestions. Point out alternatives. Let them make their own decisions.

7. Provide access to necessary materials. Help students find what they need. A little coaching in library skills may go a long way here.

8. Keep a log of what goes on. In it include committee assignments, committee members, tasks assigned, tasks completed, leadership responsibilites, and the like.

9. Keep a schedule of jobs showing when they are due for completion.

10. Ask for progress reports.

11. If a committee gets stuck, (a) recommend that the members reconsider their objective (perhaps they should change it); (b) get them to consider the strategies and tactics they have used (maybe there are others that might be better); and (c) use Socratic questioning with them to get them to see what they are doing wrong (if possible, let them find out for themselves, but sometimes you may have to tell them what to do).

12. If a group's discipline breaks down, (a) find out what the trouble is; (b) work with students who need help; (c) try role playing; and (d) talk over the problem with the group.

13. If a student causes trouble, (a) talk things over with him; (b) try to clarify his objectives, tasks, and strategies; (c) let him try a new role or a new group; (d) try role playing; and (e) if all else fails, take direct disciplinary action.

14. If a student is shy, (a) encourage him all you can; (b) do not push him; (c) help him to avoid getting into embarrassing situations; (d) make frequent evaluations and checks; and (e) see to it that his contributions are recognized.

Observe your college classes. Do they ever include small group work? Do you see instances when they might be improved by the use of buzz groups and committee work?

Pick a topic for a course you might teach. What types of committee work or what committee assignments would you suggest for this topic?

How much do you think committees should be self-directing?

You find that a committee does not seem to be producing. What would you do to find and correct the trouble?

The Committee Report

Usually after the committee has accomplished its work, it should report to the class in one way or another. An oral report to the class is a common practice. Unfortunately, oral reports can become deadly, particularly if the class must listen to several of them, one following the other. To relieve the class from boredom try to space the reports between other activities and to see to it that committees report in other different ways. According to Louise Hock, among the many possible ways to report are

Dramatic Presentations
  original plays
  role playing
  skits
  parodies of radio or television programs or movies
  monologues
Panel Type of Discussions
  panels
  forums
  debates
  round-table sessions
  town meetings

Written Materials
   newspapers
   notebooks
   scrapbooks
   duplicated material
   creative writing—poems, stories, plays, songs
Visual Depictions
   slides
   maps
   pictures
   graphs
   posters
   models
   exhibits
   murals
   bulletin board displays
Others
   tape recordings
   action projects—open house for parents, party, presentation to P.T.A. or civic groups.[10]

Evaluation of Committee Work

Students can evaluate the effectiveness of committee work as well as anyone else. Self-rating scales, such as those described in the section on the evaluating of discussion, are excellent. So are discussions in which the students analyze their performance and list the things that they did well and did not do well. More formal reports, such as those shown as Figure 12–9 and Figure 12–10, are also effective. Grambs, Carr, and Fitch recommend the form shown as Figure 12–10.

The Teacher's Role

Obviously, then, your role in small-group committee work is very sensitive. You must encourage the students to work on their own initiative, but at the same time see to it that their work is productive. At all times everyone must understand that you are in charge of the class no matter how much freedom you allow the students. You must oversee and approve student plans and procedures. You

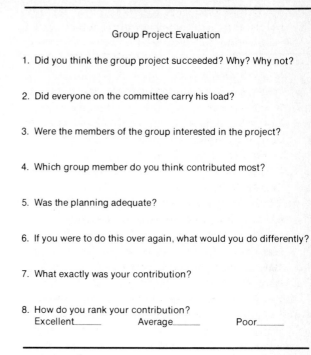

Group Project Evaluation

1. Did you think the group project succeeded? Why? Why not?

2. Did everyone on the committee carry his load?

3. Were the members of the group interested in the project?

4. Which group member do you think contributed most?

5. Was the planning adequate?

6. If you were to do this over again, what would you do differently?

7. What exactly was your contribution?

8. How do you rank your contribution?
Excellent_____   Average_____   Poor_____

FIGURE 12–9
An Evaluation Form.

will have to be sure that committee work is properly scheduled and coordinated with other class activities. In this respect, you should note that it is poor practice to try to do all the instruction by means of small groups and committees. It is seldom

	Effort	Leadership	Quality of work	Cooperation
Joe				
Jane				
etc.				
etc.				
etc.				
etc.				
etc.				

FIGURE 12–10
Group Evaluation Form. (John D. Grambs, John C. Carr, and Robert M. Fitch, *Modern Methods in Secondary Education* [New York: Holt, Rinehart and Winston, Publishers, 1970], p. 202.)

---

[10] Louise E. Hock, *Using Committees in the Classroom* (New York: Holt, 1958), p. 32.

desirable to give more than two or three consecutive days to small group or committee work. Rather, such work should be intermixed with other whole-class and individual activities of various sorts.

You must also be sure that the students have suitable materials readily available for their use. At times this duty will require you to make arrangements with the library. At other times, it will mean that you must collect material yourself. Occasionally it will mean that you must steer the committee off in some other direction because there is no way to provide them with the material they need. A good procedure may be to require students to establish the availability of resources themselves before the committee is allowed to commit itself to any particular problem or course of action. Obviously, teaching by committees requires you to have great knowledge of the content to be covered and the resources available in the area. For this reason, a good resource unit or curriculum guide can be of tremendous assistance.

Following Up Committee Work

Teaching by small groups and committees requires follow-up. Student reports may do much to tie things together, but by their very nature they tend to leave learning fragmented. The teacher's follow-up is needed to fill in gaps, smooth out rough spots, tie up loose ends, show relationships, and drive home important concepts. Without adequate follow-up the learning of the committee members may stop dead in a frustrating *cul de sac*. All too often teachers' neglect of the follow-up brings the students up to the door of understanding and leaves them standing there at the threshold so near to and yet so far from real learning.

Special-Interest Groups

When one divides the class into small, special-interest groups, the procedures are similar to those for conducting committee work.

1. First make the assignment clear to the students and ensure that they have the things they need to work with. If feasible, the group may plan its own procedures. Specialized study guides or learning packets may be extremely useful at this point.
2. If it is a group venture, for example, a group project, see to it that students know what their roles are and that all the necessary jobs are being done. You may have to appoint students to do certain missions. Check to be sure they know how to do what they are supposed to do.
3. Then see to it that they get to work. As the students go about their tasks, supervise them, checking to be sure that they are profiting from what they are doing, guiding and helping as seems necessary, and even teaching directly when it seems desirable.
4. After the group has finished its work, check up on the students' results, evaluating, correcting, reteaching and generally following up as necessary.

Give examples of how the various reporting techniques Hock lists might be used in your classes. Can you think of any other technique that you might use? Which reporting technique do you personally favor?

Do you see any advantage to using the formal report forms for evaluating committee work? What?

Too often committees are made up of one or two persons who do all the work and the other committee members who let them. How would you proceed to see to it that committee members all chip in to do their share of the committee work? How would you see to it that committees do not waste their time in unproductive activity and goofing off?

Some Caveats

In spite of the many advantages of using small-group work, sometimes small groups fail. Usually there is a pedagogical reason for such failures. Perhaps the most common is inadequate preparation of the group by the teacher. The goal of the groups and the role of the workers may not be sufficiently defined. It is most important to establish what is to be done and the procedure to be followed before the group begins. One also must make sure that the students know how to do what they are supposed to do and have the material they need to do it with.

Sometimes the failure is the result of the assignment; the task assigned to the group may not be the kind of job that can be done by a group. Perhaps it is too complicated, perhaps too simple, perhaps it is something that should be done by individual study or projects.

Sometimes the failures are caused by bad groups in which the students do not get along with each other or in which the members are not capable of performing the task required. Consequently teachers need to be careful when selecting group members.

Sometimes the students have just not learned to work together as a group. The young people who come to our classes may or may not have learned to work in groups in earlier grades. Many have excellent group skills; many do not. It may be necessary to work with these students before they will become ready to carry out small-group assignments successfully.

Lack of student motivation can make any approach fail. You should do everything you can to make small-group activities enticing. In every case, group work should center as much as possible around student concerns and ideas. Students work best when a project is their own, so involve them with the planning. The more relevant a project is to the students' lives and concerns, the more likely they are to work on it.

> Observe classes that have been divided into small groups.
> Are the students clear about what they should be doing?
> Are all participating?
> Is someone in charge?
> Does the group process seem to be productive and efficient?

Summary

Because of the characteristics of classroom groups, some of the most effective teaching is group teaching, that is, teaching by and through groups and group methods. By using committee work and discussion, teachers can quite often increase their teaching efficiency. This type of teaching is frequently effective in changing attitudes, ideals, and appreciation. It is particularly useful in raising learning above the verbalizing level. Thus, group methods often lead to thorough, permanent learning. Teaching by group methods takes considerable time and effort, but the results are usually worth it.

A discussion is not a monologue, a question-and-answer period, or a bull session. Rather, it is a controlled conversation in which participants pool their thoughts on a topic or problem in a purposeful, orderly way. The discussion leader's task is to lead the group into fruitful dialogue without dominating the participants or allowing them to meander. In this task the aid of a good recorder is extremely desirable. Observers can help the group to learn how to discuss matters more effectively. Formal discussion techniques are often not as useful as informal discussions, but techniques such as the British debate and the jury system can be used, often with telling results, for getting students to examine, to think about, and to analyze critical issues and problems.

Teaching via committees has become quite popular. It is an effective means of providing for individual differences and laboratory experiences as well as involving students in action learning. Well done, teaching via committees helps to build a classroom climate that is supportive of learning. The membership of student committees may be determined in several ways, but when feasible, the teacher should take advantage of natural student leadership and groups. Although student committee members should do the bulk of their own planning and research, the teacher must always be ready in the background with necessary help and guidance. Sharing the results of the committee work with the rest of the class can be a particular problem. The teacher should place considerable stress on lively, original reporting and serious, careful class follow-up of committee work.

Additional Reading

Gage, N. L., *Educational Psychology.* 3rd ed. Boston: Houghton Mifflin, 1984, Chap. 20.

Gall, Meredith D., and Joyce P. Gall. "The Discussion Method," in N. L. Gage, ed., *The Psychology of Teaching Methods,* The Seventy-fifth Yearbook of the Society of Education. Chicago: University of Chicago Press, 1976, Chap. 6.

Hill, William Fawcett. *Learning Through Discussion: Guide for Leaders and Members of Discussion Groups.* Beverly Hills, CA: Sage Publications, 1969.

Hock, Louise. *Group Discussion.* New York: Holt, 1961.

Howes, Virgil M. *Informal Teaching in the Open Classroom.* New York: Macmillan, 1974.

Johnson, David W., et al. *Circles of Learning: Cooperation in the Classroom.* Alexandria, VA: Association for Supervision and Curriculum Development, 1984.

Orlich, Donald C., et al. *Teaching Strategies: A Guide to Better Instruction,* 2nd ed. Lexington, MA: Heath, 1985, Part 7.

Schmuck, Richard A., and Patricia A. Schmuck. *Group Processes in the Classroom.* Dubuque, IA: Brown, 1971.

Shaw, Marvin E. *Group Dynamics: The Psychology of Small Group Behavior,* 2nd ed. LaJolla, CA: Learning Resources, 1976.

Stanford, Gene. *Developing Effective Classroom Groups: A Practical Guide for Teachers.* New York: Hart, 1977.

Weil, Marsha, and Bruce Joyce. *Social Models of Teaching: Expanding Your Teaching Repertoire.* Englewood Cliffs, NJ: Prentice-Hall, 1978.

Inquiry and Discovery Teaching

Overview

One of the oldest principles of teaching is that learners must do their own learning and develop their own understandings, skills, and attitudes, and that therefore the teacher's job is not so much to impart knowledge as to help and guide the students as they discover the meanings, practice the skills, and undergo the experiences that will shape their learning. This notion is the basis for the discovery or inquiry approach to teaching. In this approach teachers try to actively involve students in the learning process. Among the techniques teachers may use to encourage discovery or inquiry learning are skillful questioning, discussions, problem solving, springboards, and case studies—to name only a few. These strategies and techniques are attractive because they have high motivating value and help students to develop intellectual skills, including skill in thinking rationally, seeing relationships, understanding processes, and building values and attitudes. As a rule, inquiry or discovery strategies can be depended on to build firm concepts and deep understandings.

Nevertheless, this approach does not preclude the teacher's presentation of information to students. For students to rediscover and re-create all knowledge would be most inefficient. The principal point in discovery teaching is rather to provide many instances for students to draw inferences from data by using logical thinking, inductive or deductive, as the case may be. The more realistic and down to earth the inquiry learning, the better, of course. That is why community-involvement activities, simulation, and role-playing activities and real problems are so effective.

In this chapter we investigate a number of methods of learning via inquiry and discovery.

Inquiry Teaching

In teaching by inquiry, or discovery strategies, you should assume the role of guide rather than dictator. As a guide to student learning, try to raise problem issues and questions that will pique the students' interest and call for further investigation. Encourage the students to pursue these matters and guide them in their investigations, helping them to clarify the issues, the facts, and their own thinking as well as to draw reasonable conclusions. Then carry the students a step or two further by inducing them to test their conclusions and generalizations and apply them to other situations.

A major aim of inquiry teaching is to stimulate independent resourceful thinking. To that end use such tactics as

- Checking the students' data-gathering techniques.
- Asking thought questions.
- Asking for interpretations, explanations, and hypotheses.
- Questioning the interpretations, explanations, and hypotheses that the students arrive at.
- Asking students to draw conclusions from their data and information.
- Asking students to apply their principles and conclusions to other situations.
- Asking students to check their thinking and their logic.
- Confronting students with problems, contradictions, fallacies, implications, value assumptions, value conflicts, and other factors that may call for reassessment of their thinking and positions.

In carrying out these tactics it is extremely important to keep the climate supportive. Students must be encouraged to think even though sometimes the conclusions they draw may be somewhat bizarre. To encourage thinking try

- To accentuate the positive.
- To encourage students by showing approval and by providing clues.
- To accept for examination all legitimate hypotheses and means by which students attempt to arrive at truth.
- To encourage the exchange and discussion of ideas.
- To create an open atmosphere in which students feel free to contribute and to analyze the various ideas, interpretations, and logical processes.

In short, try to foster an atmosphere of earnest thinking, free debate, open discussion, and, above all, freedom for the students to try to think things out without fear of reprisal for errors in reasoning.

This teaching method can be very effective. However, when teaching middle school students you should remember that few students can really understand abstract learning until they are twelve or thirteen, and many are not ready for this type of learning until they are older.

The Socratic Method

In the fifth century B.C., Socrates, the great Athenian teacher, used the art of questioning so successfully that to this day we still speak of the Socratic method. Socrates' strategy was to ask his pupils a series of leading questions that gradually snarled them up to the point where they had to look carefully at their own ideas and to think rigorously for themselves. In several ways his technique foreshadowed the most progressive teaching of the most ardent progressivists. Socratic discussions were informal dialogues taking place in a natural, easy, pleasant environment. The motivation of the students was natural and spontaneous although sometimes Socrates had to go to considerable lengths to ignite his students' intrinsic interest. In his dialogues Socrates tried to aid students to develop ideas. He did not impose his own notions on the students. Rather, he encouraged the students to develop their own conclusions and to draw their own inferences. Of course, Socrates usually had preconceived notions about what the final learning should be and carefully aimed his questions so that the students would arrive at the conclusions desired. Still his questions were open-ended. The students were free to go wherever the facts led them.

Many teachers have tried to adapt the Socratic method to the modern secondary school. In some cases it has proved to be quite successful. However, it must be remembered that as Socrates used the method it required a one-to-one relationship between the student and the teacher. Some teachers have adapted it for ordinary class use by asking questions first of one student and then of another, moving about the class slowly. This technique may work well, but it is difficult because the essence of the Socratic technique is to build question on question in a logical fashion so that each question leads the student a step further toward the understanding sought. When you spread the questions around the classroom, you may find it difficult to build up the sequence desired and to keep all the students with the argument. Sometimes you may be able to make use of the Socratic method by directing all the questions at one student—at least for several minutes—while the other students look on. This is the way Socrates did it. When the topic is interesting enough this technique can be quite successful and even exciting, but in the long run the Socratic technique works best in small-group sessions, seminars, and tutorial sessions with individual students.

To conduct a class by the Socratic technique

1. Pose a problem to the class.
2. Ask the students a series of probing questions that will cause them to examine critically the problem and their solution to the problem. The main thrust of the questioning and the key questions must be planned in advance so that the questioning will proceed logically. To think of good probing questions on the spur of the moment is too difficult.

Controlled or Guided Discussion

The controlled or guided discussion is a variation of the Socratic discussion frequently advocated by proponents of discovery or inquiry teaching. It consists simply of (1) providing the students with information by means of lecture, reading, film, or some other expository device and then (2) by the use of probing questions, as in the Socratic method, guiding the students to derive principles and draw generalizations from the material presented. This method differs from a true discussion in that it is teacher-centered with the teacher doing most of the questioning, and from true inquiry in that the principles and generalizations to be arrived at by the students have been decided by the teacher in advance. The controlled discussion is not ordinarily an open-ended method of teaching, although there is no reason why it should not be.

Springboard Techniques

A springboard is any type of presentation that can be used as a jumping-off point for a discussion, research project, or inquiry activity. Springboards serve both as sources of information and as motivating devices. They give the students something to work on and some reason for working on it. One use of the springboard can be seen in the controlled discussion technique that was explained earlier in this chapter. Moving pictures, still pictures, playlets, role playing, models, textbook selections, and anecdotes are only a few examples of what can be used for springboards. Anything that lends itself to such questions as Why? So what? How can this be true? or If this is so, then what? can be used as a springboard. Usually the teacher must follow up the springboard with questions that will bring out ideas, relationships, or conclusions to be discovered, analyzed, or evaluated. A really effective springboard is so stimulating that the students are eager to investigate without further prompting. Parables, contrived incidents, and value sheets are examples of springboards.

The method of the parable used in Biblical times is really a kind of controlled discussion. To employ this type of approach, relate an incident or story and then use it as a springboard, asking probing questions until your students see, from their own thinking, the principle you wish to get across. As used by the great teachers of yore the point of the parable often was definite and obvious, but the parable can be used to introduce open-ended debate and discussion as well.

Contrived incidents are simply exciting incidents realistically staged by the teacher to get students to react and think. To all appearances the incidents are real until the teacher and players let the class in on the secret. For example, a couple of students might come into the class and start a loud argument with each other about a controversial issue. Then on a signal they would stop the argument and the teacher launch a discussion on the merits and demerits of the proposition under discussion. Role playing techniques may be used in the same way.

Read *Meno* by Plato. Here Socrates describes his theory of teaching and illustrates his techniques. What do you see as the virtues of Socrates' basic strategy? Do you see faults?

Basically a controlled discussion is an attempt to adapt the Socratic technique to large groups. Build a plan for conducting a controlled-discussion lesson for a course you might teach.

How open-ended do you think a controlled discussion ought to be? For what purposes are controlled discussions best suited? For which open discussions?

What sort of activities could you use for springboards in your courses? Give some specific examples. The controlled discussion is one type of activity you can initiate by a springboard. Can you think of examples of other types of activities? Give specific examples.

What is the difference between the use of a springboard and set induction?

Value sheets consist of a presentation of an issue, a situation, or an incident followed by a series of questions focused on the values raised by the presentation. The presentation may be made by a short statement or anecdote written on the value sheet itself or by some other springboard technique such as a role playing, tape recording, videotape, or story. The technique is for the students to study the presentation and then answer the value sheet questions in writing. Since these questions deal with the values aroused by the springboard incident or statement, they have no right answers—only the personal opinions of the individual students. You can then use one of the following procedures as a follow up.

1. Have a class discussion on the questions and answers in the value sheet.
2. Have small-group discussions on the value sheets.
3. Read certain selections from the value sheets without comment or identifying the writer.
4. Have the students turn all the value sheets over

to a committee that will analyze them and present to the group the various positions taken by the students in the class.

Reaction sheets are the same as value sheets except that the questions asked may cover a wider range. They may have to do with beliefs, attitudes, logic, reasoning, morals, judgment—in fact any type of question that will get the students thinking. They may be followed up in any of the ways that value sheets are, or they may be made the basis for vigorous intellectual inquiry.

The Problem-Solving Approach

Perhaps problem solving should not be called a teaching technique. Rather it is a general strategy in which one can use many different techniques and tactics. Many theorists feel it to be the most effective of all teaching strategies. It has been used successfully both as an individual and as a group activity. The solving of problems through group activity recently has been used extensively in teaching and in the world of business and research.

Whether a problem is solved by an individual or a group, the general technique is about the same. Perhaps this explains in part the popularity of problem solving. It seems to be a natural way to learn.

In a sense, problem solving is a sophisticated form of trial-and-error learning. It provides people a chance to learn from their successes and failures. Furthermore, because it provides for the students' becoming really involved in their learning, it may lead to real understanding in a way that memorization and drill seldom can. A brief review of the steps will show how actively the student participates in learning through problem solving. The steps are

1. The learner becomes aware of the problem.
2. The learner defines and delimits the problem.
3. The learner gathers evidence that may help solve the problem.
4. The learner forms a hypothesis of what the solution to the problem is.

5. The learner tests the hypothesis.
6. The learner successfully solves the problem or repeats steps 3, 4, and 5, or 4 and 5, until the problem is solved, or gives up.[1]

Selecting the Problem

Although problem solving is a natural way to learn, students, as a general rule, do not just naturally become expert in the techniques of problem solving. This is particularly true when the class attempts to solve problems by group techniques.

In the first place, students need help in finding suitable problems. Sometimes you may find it necessary to suggest problems or to suggest areas in which students may seek problems. When suggesting a problem to a group, it may be better to propose the problem directly, or you may prefer to set the stage in such a way that the problem will suggest itself to the students.

For instance, in a social studies class the teacher introduced a problem by telling of the number of people in the country who do not vote. She cited figures showing the lightness of the voting in the local municipal election. This led to a discussion of why citizens do not exercise their franchise. From this discussion the students developed two problems: the first, what causes the apathy of our citizens? and the second, what can be done to get people to vote at the city elections? In another class the teacher launched a group problem by asking the following question: How does a plant get its food? After a short discussion the group set out to find the answer to the problem.

No matter what the source of their problem, the students will probably need guidance in the selection of a suitable one, for, left alone, even the most experienced adolescent, or group of adolescents, may flounder. Sometimes they can find no problem at all; sometimes they select problems not suitable to the course; sometimes they select problems whose solution requires materials and equipment

---

[1] Based on the analysis of the thought process by John Dewey.

beyond the school's resources; sometimes they select problems too big and unyielding, and blithely
set out to solve in a weekend problems their elders
have struggled with for centuries. In view of these
considerations, you and your students should cooperatively test the problems to be selected against
such criteria as: Is this problem pertinent? Is the
necessary material available? Can it be completed
in the time allotted?

Prepare a complete list of questions you feel
should be considered in testing whether a problem should be selected or not.

Prepare a list of eight or ten problems that
boys and girls might attempt in the study of a
topic in a course in your field of major interest.
Where might you advise boys and girls to search
for suitable problems for such a topic?

"To be worthwhile, problems should be real
and have real solutions." Explain. Do you agree?
How are such problems created and carried
through to a conclusion?

Why is it often claimed that all secondary
school learning should be of the problem-solving
variety?

Defining the Problem

Once the problem has been selected, one must
help the students clarify and define the problem.
You can do this by means of questions and suggestions. The important thing here is to get the problem sharply defined so that the students know exactly what they want to find out. Beginning
teachers sometimes neglect this step. When they
do, students find it difficult to know exactly what
they are expected to do. This is, of course, a handicap in solving any problem.

Let us suppose that the problem selected has
been Why does an airplane fly? The problem here
is quickly and easily defined, for it is obvious to
all that we are to find what it is that keeps an
airplane up in the air. Yet, even in such an easily

defined problem, you may have to make it clear
to some students that this problem does not refer
to helicopters or to rockets.

Searching for Clues

Once the students have defined their problem,
they should start to look for clues for their solution.
This involves amassing data upon which to base
a hypothesis. Here you can be of great help to them.
You can point out areas in which to look for clues.
You can provide the necessary materials, or see
to it that they are available. You can provide references. You can acquaint the students with the tools
by which one can gather data.

Even in the solving of group problems, the gathering of evidence may best be done by individuals
or small groups. After a period of individual searching for information, the group can meet to pool
the data gained and to attempt to find a solution
to the problem.

For instance, if the problem were to prepare a
menu suitable for a week's camping trip for a group
of teenagers, the individual students might gather
the information necessary for solving this problem.
Once they had in their possession information concerning what the ingredients of a healthful,
well-balanced diet are, what foods contain these
ingredients, and any other pertinent data, they
might attempt to build suitable menus individually.
The final menu could be made during a class discussion using the individual suggestions.

An excellent way to handle such discussions is
to have an individual or group present a solution
to the class and then let the class review the proposal and suggest improvements. Before conclud-
ing that the problem has been solved, the students
should test the menu to be sure it meets the criteria
for a healthful, well-balanced camp menu.

Solving the Problem

Preparing the menu in the foregoing example
was really an example of setting up and testing a
hypothesis. Each individual menu prepared was

a hypothetical solution to the problem. These solutions were tested by the students until they found one that met the requirements of a healthful, well-balanced diet. When they found such a menu, the problem was solved.

At this stage of solving a problem, boys and girls often need assistance. Many students find it difficult to think of tentative solutions. To help them, Hart suggests that you

1. Focus on the type of answer they are looking for—"how will they know when we have solved the problem?" Doing so often helps them to define the problem and approach needed for finding a solution.
2. Consider a variety of approaches so as not to be saddled with a possibly unproductive one too early.
3. Examine and evaluate all available data carefully.
4. When a problem is complex, study each of its aspects thoroughly then leave it to gestate for a while.[2]

Although you should be careful not to solve the problem for your students, you can help them in these processes by pointing out relationships, by asking pointed questions, and by using other similar techniques.

Similarly, you can help the students test their proposed solutions. Unless students establish appropriate criteria by which to judge the worth of a solution, they may think they have a problem solved when they really have not. Consequently, you should help the students set up criteria that will tell them whether or not the problem has actually been solved and help them check their solutions against the criteria. Without this aid students often arrive at very poor solutions to their problems.

---

[2] Leslie A. Hart, "The Incredible Brain, How Does It Solve Problems? Is Logic a National Problem?" *National Association of Secondary School Principals Bulletin* (January, 1983), **67**:36–41.

Select a problem that a student might attempt in one of your classes. Where might the student look for clues? What materials should be available to the student? What tools of research might be needed to gather the necessary data? What skills would the student need? How could you prepare yourself to help a student gather the data for this problem?

The Case-Study Method

Case studies are special cases of the problem-solving technique in which the students study individual cases representative of a type of institution, issue, problem situation or the like in order to draw conclusions about the type as a whole. Case studies are useful because they not only give students insights into knotty problems, but also they give them opportunities for study in depth. The latter result is particularly important since at present much secondary school learning is superficial.

The procedures for conducting case studies are relatively simple, but their execution is difficult. Briefly, the steps in the procedure are

1. Select a topic to study.
2. Provide the pupils the wherewithal to study. They should have material that allows them to explore the problem in depth. Some of the newer texts and curriculum programs on the market provide such materials. Frequently you and your students will have to gather it for yourselves. Usually the material will be reading matter to study, but films, pictures, tapes, laboratory experiments, and the like, may be more useful. For many social studies and science topics fieldwork is the best resource. For instance, in one middle school the students closely studied the flora and fauna of a small patch of the Jersey swamp which made up part of their science laboratory to see if they could establish certain ecological relationships.

3. The students then study the case. Before they begin their investigations, you should introduce them to the problem or issue at hand, point out the goals and questions to consider, and establish the ground rules. Sometimes this orientation can be done by group-planning techniques. As students proceed with their investigations, they will find study guides very helpful. Some of the newer books and curriculum programs have developed useful study guides. If such are available, you should use them; otherwise you should probably develop guides of your own.

4. Follow up with a discussion in which the students share their findings and conclusions. Role playing, panels, symposia, and similar methods of presentation are often effective at this stage. Any technique that helps students examine their own thinking and conclusions will do.

> What advantage do you see to using the case-study approach? What technique would you use to generalize knowledge learned in a study of a case? Is it better to spend time studying a case in detail so as to build full concepts or is it better to teach these concepts quickly by expository approaches?

The Project

A Definition

A project is a natural, lifelike learning activity involving investigation and solving of problems by an individual or small group. Ideally it should consist of a task in which a student sets out to attain some definite goal of real personal value. Projects frequently involve the use and manipulation of physical materials and result in tangible products.

A classic example of such a project may be found in the agriculture projects in which students conduct farming enterprises such as raising a calf or a crop. The building and selling of a house and the installation of a solar- or wind-powered energy system by vocational education students are other examples of practical projects of the classic type. A less ambitious project in an academic class might be making a scrapbook anthology for an English class or an illustrated history of the life of the honeybee for a science class.

Selecting the Project

Ideally, the students should plan, execute, and evaluate the entire project themselves. Even so, your role is important. You must help and guide the students. One of the more important ways you can guide them is in selecting a suitable project. Perhaps you will find it necessary to provide a list of possible projects from which students can choose. Or you might suggest readings in which the students might find project ideas. Occasionally, you may be able to stimulate ideas for projects by a discussion or by a teacher talk about what others have done, or by a demonstration of former projects. An interesting device is to have members of previous classes act as consultants and tell the class about some of the projects completed in past years. Sometimes students formulate projects completely on their own. Then you need only to approve the plans they form.

In any case, you should approve a project before the student attempts it, for selecting projects requires sound judgment. The following criteria may help in selecting useful projects.

1. *The project should consist of real learning activities.* Unless one is careful, projects sometimes turn out to be mere busywork. An example of a project that was little more than busywork was a notebook for an English class that consisted of biographies of authors copied from the appendix of the English textbook. Teachers should guard against this danger by continually asking themselves, "What learning will result from this project?"

2. *The project should be pertinent to the course.* Because of their very nature, projects often in-

clude materials and activities from other subjects. Consequently, there is a constant danger
that the project may get out of the field completely.
3. *The learning to be gained from a project should
be worth the time spent on it.* Not only must
the length of time be considered, but one must
also decide whether the learning might be
gained more economically in another way.
4. *The necessary materials and equipment must
be available at reasonable cost.*

Conducting the Project

Once the project has been selected and approved,
the student is ready to proceed with it. As in any
other activity, you will find it necessary to help
and guide the students as the latter attempt to carry
out their plans. However, the students can carry
a great deal of responsibility for executing them.
They are also in a particularly good position to
evaluate their own progress and its results. Consequently, you should allow the student to accept a
good share of this responsibility. Although you
should always be ready to help, you should be careful not to be so solicitous that you stifle the initiative
and ingenuity of any student.

One of the best examples of the project is one
that took place in a science class in a Vermont
school some time ago. In this class, the students
were attempting to study the stars, although they
had no telescope. One day, during a laboratory session, a boy asked if it might be possible to build
a telescope. The teacher answered that it could be
done although it would be difficult. A conference
followed and the boy, with some friends, decided
to attempt to build a telescope as a project. The
first thing that they had to do was to find out how
to construct a telescope, i.e., they had to find out
how a telescope works, what materials are necessary for making one, and how these materials can
be put together. Once they had acquired this information, the boys decided on the kind of telescope
they wished to build and gathered the necessary

materials. Then they put it together. Hours of work
and seemingly insolvable problems were part of
this project, but finally the boys assembled a usable
telescope. After they got through using it, they presented the telescope to the school for use in science
classes.

This project has all the essentials of a good project. The result was well worth the effort; it was
realistic and lifelike; it consisted of problem-solving
situations; and it was conceived, planned, and executed by the students under the guidance of the
teacher.

Research Projects

Independent research projects are true inquiry
strategies. Students at all levels can profitably conduct independent research activities, but ordinarily
the academically talented students are more likely
to enjoy and profit from independent study. Students who do not find research activities in keeping
with their endowment and temperament should
be excused from them. These students, however,
may make good contributions to group projects.

Research projects may be individual or group
projects. Research projects that involve the whole
class seem to be very successful at the secondary
school level. In either case the process is the same
as that of any other problem solving.

1. Decide exactly what it is that one is to try to
find out.
2. Determine the problem so that it is manageable
in the time available and with the materials and
personnel available.
3. Decide on what tasks must be done to get the
data necessary and who will do each job.
4. Gather the materials and equipment necessary.
5. Perform the data-gathering tasks.
6. Review and analyze the data gathered.
7. Draw conclusions and generalizations from the
data gathered.
8. Report the findings and conclusions.

> How might you use individual projects in your class? Group projects? Why is it sometimes said that directions for students may be too explicit?
>
> How could you use projects as a means of individualizing classes? How much freedom can you allow talented students in the conducting of research projects? How would you organize a class to carry out a research project?

Techniques for Teaching Controversial Issues

Some of the content suited for teaching by inquiry and discovery techniques may be controversial. It is not the purpose of classroom instruction to solve controversial issues, but rather to give students an opportunity to become acquainted with the issues, the facts (where they are known), the different positions taken by the various sides and the arguments supporting the points of view. Above all, it gives the students a chance to learn how to deal with controversy as objectively and wisely as possible. In teaching controversial issues the emphasis should be not so much on the content as on the process.

Selecting the Controversial Issue

Sometimes the study of controversial issues sheds more heat than light. Community feelings run high on many issues. Because controversial issues can be so touchy, teachers should be careful when they select controversial issues for class use. We recommend that before you decide whether or not to include a controversial issue in a course, you should consider such questions as these.

1. Is the topic pertinent to your teaching goals?
2. Is it worth taking the trouble? Is it important and timely? Is it of concern to all rather than to only a few individuals?
3. Do you yourself know enough and are you skillful enough to handle the question?
4. Are the students mature enough for rational consideration of the issue? Do they have sufficient background?
5. Can you make enough material available so that students can get a fair picture of the various sides of the issue?
6. Do you have time enough to consider the issue adequately?
7. Is the issue too emotion-ridden? Some issues may be too hot to handle. It may be better to omit topics than to disrupt the class and the community.

Once you have decided to tackle a certain controversial issue, you have your work cut out for you. In order to see to it that all procedes smoothly and fairly, you must keep on top of the topic with all the teaching skill, tact, sensitivity, and common sense you possess. First, you must be sure to acquire all the necessary clearances from your supervisors, especially if there seems to be the slightest possibility that the issue will cause an uproar in the community. Then you must be sure that all the necessary materials for looking up the facts and points of view are available. All sides should be fairly represented. If there is to be a classroom discussion of the controversial issue, you must be sure that both you and the students have the background necessary for reasonable discussion. Too often discussions of controversial issues are the airing of thoughtless prejudices. In the discussion, or study, students should have an opportunity to consider all points of view fairly. No student should be cut out simply because of an unpopular point of view. On the other hand, no one should be given more attention than deserved. The teacher cannot allow errors in fact or logic to go unchallenged either.

In pursuing controversial issues, you should allow students to reach their own conclusions. Avoid influencing them to take one side or another. Particularly be careful not to force your own position on the students either directly or indirectly. Nevertheless, you do have the right, and perhaps the responsibility, to let students know where you stand so that they will be aware of your biases. You can keep from overinfluencing students by warning them that there are no right answers and by holding back your own position until the end of the discussion.

Sometimes discussions of controversial issues get rather heated. To eliminate this problem set up guidelines before the discussion starts. For example,

- All arguments must be supported by authority.
- Everyone must have a chance to be heard.
- All opinions must be considered respectfully and seriously.
- No name calling or personalities will be allowed.
- There will be no direct dyadic argument. (To eliminate arguments the rules might specify that at least two students must speak before a student can speak again, that no one can speak unless he is recognized by the chair, or that no one can make speeches.)

Some Useful Strategies and Tactics

Among the strategies commonly used in the study of controversial issues are

- Debate.
- Panel discussion.
- Dramatics.
- Role playing.
- Simulation.
- Research techniques, e.g., open-ended problem solving.
- Interview.
- Committee work.
- The case-study approach.

Here are some strategies and tactics that have proven successful:

- When an issue is extremely hot locally, study the problem as it has appeared at some other time or as it appears in some other place.
- Use techniques such as clarifying responses, value sheets, value discussions, probing questions, application of logical principles to one's argument, and requests for definition.
- Present unpopular positions yourself. Play the devil's advocate when students can see only one side of the question. Introduce different positions that the students have not considered. Often student thinking on controversial issues becomes polarized between two opposite positions when really there are many other positions one might take. When you present a position say something like "Some people take the position that. . . ." or "Some people believe that. . . ."
- Use fact-opinion tables as in Figure 13–1. Have the class recorder fill out the table as the points are discussed. (One can use a chalkboard, an overhead projector, or even a chart for this purpose).
- Have students argue against their own beliefs. This practice may clarify their thinking and reveal the position of other people.
- Insist that students check on the sources of information and the meaning of words. After all, lots of arguments have no real factual basis. Try to get students to get at the facts underlying emotional arguments.

FIGURE 13–1
Fact–Opinion Table

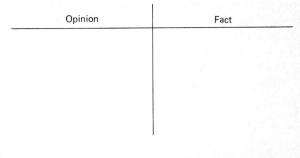

Opinion	Fact

Role Playing and Simulation Games

Role Playing

Role playing and simulation are both useful for making complicated matters clear to students. By definition role playing (or sociodrama) is an unrehearsed dramatization in which the players try to act out what they would do and how they would feel in a certain situation.[3] Role playing is particularly useful in clarifying the motivation and feelings of others.

For instance, in order to teach how prejudice affects both the prejudiced and the prejudiced against, a group in a social studies class attempted to portray the feelings of a pair of boys who were rejected from a fraternity because of their religious beliefs. The players presented two scenes: the first, the discussion of the candidates at the fraternity just prior to the voting; the second, the scene in which the boys were notified of their rejection. In each of these scenes the players attempted to show the emotions of the characters they portrayed. They particularly emphasized how the boys felt after the rejection. Three different casts portrayed these scenes. After the presentations the entire class discussed the justice of the decision and the probable effect of the incident on the persons concerned.

Another example of role playing is an attempt to make the feelings of the American colonists more real to the students. In this class the players represented a group of colonists discussing the news of the stamp tax. The loyalist tried to show the reason for the tax, but the others shouted him down. From role playing of this sort it is hoped that the students will come to understand the tenor of the times being studied.

---

[3] The role playing we are describing is the sociodrama. Psychodramas, which are designed to give insight into psychological aspects of human behavior, are beyond the scope of this book.

Use role playing to

a. clarify attitudes and concepts;
b. demonstrate attitudes and concepts;
c. deepen understanding of social situations;
d. prepare for a real situation (for example, rehearsing the teaching of a lesson with a group of colleagues or practicing interview techniques before going out to be interviewed);
e. plan and try out strategies for attacking problems;
f. test hypothetical solutions of problems;
g. practice leadership and other social skills.

Limitations of Role Playing

In spite of its many virtues, when you use role playing, you should be aware of and guard against its dangers and limitations.

1. Students do not always take role playing seriously. They often think of it as entertainment. As a result of this frivolous attitude, they tend to "ham" up their roles and turn the role playing into a farce instead of a learning experience. Try to avert such behavior by skillful briefing and careful selection of players.
2. Unless students are well prepared, the role playing may become superficial and result in stereotypical thinking. Role players must know the facts and background of both the characters and the situation and the courses of action open to them. To avoid stereotyping, repeat the role playing with different players and encourage individual interpretations of the roles. If the members of your group do not show signs of creativity and imagination, it may be wise to go easy on role-playing activities until the group's imagination has grown. You can encourage the development of both creativity and imagination by providing a variety of activities in a supportive atmosphere. Dramatic presentations and simulations may prove good avenues to imaginative, creative role playing.
3. Role playing is a time-consuming activity. Be

sure to allow enough time for ample briefing, replaying and reinterpretations as needed, and a thorough follow up.

4. Role playing is dependent on an atmosphere supporting free discussion and inquiry. It is a group activity and all should be involved. Therefore you should avoid even the semblance of dictating the conditions and interpretations of the scenes to be portrayed.

5. Unless students know the role players well, they are inclined to mistake the characteristics the players assume in their roles for real-life qualities. So that no one role will become associated with any particular player, try to have students play a number of different types of roles.

Staging the Role Playing

Preparing for Role Playing.   Although role playing is usually done without script or rehearsal, it does require preparation. In the first place the students must understand the situation being presented. For this reason, the situation to be role played should be a simple one. If the situation is too complex, the role playing will probably fail. A situation involving two to four characters will probably be most effective. Once a situation that the students can readily comprehend has been selected, you must carefully brief both the players and the rest of the class to be sure that they do understand it. Not only must you see to it that all the players understand the situation but also that they realize the purpose of the role playing and their parts in it. For this reason, you should spend some time discussing the roles with the players. So that the rest of the class will be prepared to be a receptive audience, you should also brief them on the purpose of the drama and what they should look for as the role playing unfolds. Because of the tendency for students to think of role playing as entertainment, you should make every effort in your briefing to ensure that they realize the role playing is serious business.

Selecting the Cast.   As one can readily see, role playing requires serious effort on the part of each role player. For this reason select the players carefully—if possible, from volunteers. Sometimes selecting the cast is complicated by the fact that the most eager volunteers seem quite incapable of carrying out the roles. Consequently, it is not wise to commit oneself too heartily to the use of volunteers only.

At times you will have to find understudies for the cast. A helpful procedure is to select several casts and have several presentations. This practice may offset poor presentations, give depth to the understanding of the class as a result of the difference in presentation and interpretation of the roles, and offset tendencies toward sterotypical thinking.

Playing Roles.   Because quite often the role players become extremely nervous, they may need help and encouragement. Rehearsing the first few lines and preparing a general plan for the development of the role playing may help the participants play their roles more confidently. On the other hand, too much planning may stifle its spontaneity and straitjacket the role player's interpretation. Similarly a warm-up period may be helpful, but overdone it may take the life out of the actual role playing.

Most role playing is quite loose. Consequently, there is always a danger that inexperienced role players may lose sight of their roles. Carefully selecting the role players and thoroughly explaining their roles to them should minimize this danger. Sometimes, however, these precautions are not sufficient. On such an occasion, if a player does get badly out of character, stop the production and reorient the players. It is better to interrupt the production than to present false information to the class.

Follow Up.   If the students are to benefit from the role playing, it must be followed up. A discussion period following the role playing can be the most worthwhile part of the entire lesson. Sometimes role playing a situation up to a critical point and then stopping the role playing to discuss what might or should happen next can be very effective. In any case, the students should discuss and analyze the action and interpret its significance. In the discussion the participants might explain just what they hoped to do and how they felt during the role playing. Finally, this discussion should end in a summary or perhaps the formulation of some generalization. Do not insist that the students come to a definite conclusion, however. It may be much better to leave the discussion of the role playing open-ended.

Frequently it is helpful, after a period of analysis and discussion, for a second group of students to role play the situation so that other interpretations can be seen.

Dyadic Role Playing

Role playing may be too complex a technique for inexperienced young people to handle effectively and seriously. Zeleny and Gross[4] suggest that teachers use dyadic role playing, i.e., role playing in which only two players participate, to give students experience before they attempt to role play more complex situations. Dyadic role playing, like other role playing, helps students to understand problems and situations better and to develop empathy for people in other situations. Because only two players participate, dyadic role playing is simpler and results in learning that might be difficult to achieve in a more complex situation.

To conduct dyadic role playing, first select two opposing positions or statuses, e.g., management versus labor, and help the students acquire the necessary background so that they understand and identify with the different positions and statuses.

---

[4] Leslie D. Zeleny and Richard E. Gross, "Dyadic Role Playing of Controversial Issues," *Social Education* (December, 1960), **24**:354–358.

Once the students have been well briefed, divide the class into pairs (dyads). In each pair one student should represent one position and one the other. Then all the pairs role play the situation simultaneously. When their role playing is finished, they should reverse their positions and role play the situation again. After each person has played both roles, the pairs evaluate what they have done. In this evaluation they may discuss how well each side was presented, whether they had all the information they needed, or what the role playing showed them. If it seems that the pairs might have done better with more information, perhaps they should find out the necessary information, and replay the roles. Finally the dyadic role playing can be followed up by a general discussion or some other suitable follow-up. Sometimes the follow-up should consist of having a dyad that did particularly well role play before the entire class. Or perhaps two students whose work seems promising can be formed into a new dyad for a class presentation. In either case, the role playing should be followed up by class discussion.

What should the teacher do if a student seems to be badly misinterpreting the assigned role?

What purposes may a sociodrama serve?

What sort of material is best suited to a sociodrama?

How would you try to keep role playing from being treated as a joke?

Simulation Games

Simulation games combine role playing and problem solving. In a simulation exercise students play roles as though they were really executing a real life situation. By acting out roles as though they were real, the students, it is hoped, will learn to understand the important factors in the real situation and learn either how to behave in the real situation or how persons in such situations must behave. Simulations differ from sociodramas and psychodramas in that although the role playing responses are impromptu, the roles of the actors and the scenarios are carefully drafted. Essentially simulation entails two things:

1. That students be assigned to perform definite roles requiring certain types of action which they must perform in a fairly well-defined situation.
2. That the students be confronted with simulations of real life situations in which they must take necessary action just as the character whose role they are taking would have to. As a rule, whatever action is taken leads to new incidents that require new action. In these situations the actors are not free to act in any way they please, but rather must stay in character and keep their actions within the limits prescribed by the realities of the situation being simulated. The technique is the outgrowth of the war games in which army commandants fought mock battles and has since been adopted by business, governmental, and other agencies that prepare people for important situations that they must face in the future. Consequently, the actions and scenarios should be as realistic as possible.

Good simulation games are available through reputable educational publishers and suppliers. An outline showing how to prepare a scenario can be found in Chapter 19. But, unless one builds the scenario carefully, it is usually better to use a professionally written one. A slipshod, hastily put together scenario may do more harm than good. Nevertheless making up their own simulation scenario can be an excellent exercise for students. Mapping out the scenario and delineating the role can provide much learning in depth.

The overall procedure for conducting simulations is quite simple.

1. Make ready any props, equipment, or material that will be needed in the simulation.

2. Introduce the simulation. Explain
   a. The reason for it.
   b. How it is played.
3. Assign students to roles. (Usually it is best for the teacher to assign roles in accordance with the students' potential as role players. Calling for volunteers is also a good method but may result in very poor casting. Sometimes the roles are described on cards that the students draw. If the simulation requires anything but the simplest role playing, drawing cards may be disastrous. Giving each player a card bearing a description of the role selected for him may be advantageous, however.)
4. Once the students understand the simulation and know their roles in it, then conduct the simulation. In doing so follow the scenario to the letter. You may take on the role of umpire, referee, scorekeeper, or consultant yourself or delegate such tasks to designated students, if the occasion warrants it.
5. Follow up the simulation by discussion or similar activities in which the students draw inferences and make generalizations from the simulated activity.

> Simulations are among the most powerful of modern teaching strategies. Why?
>
> Why would it be necessary to work out a scenario for use in a driver-training or flight-training simulation?

Community Involvement Activities

Field Trips

Particularly vivid learning experiences sometimes result from going out into the community. One of the most common devices used for extending the classroom into the community is the field trip. This method is a time-honored one, having been used with great success for centuries. Field trips can take many forms. A nature walk is a field trip. A visit to the museum is a field trip. So is a period spent on the athletic field searching for specimens of insects.

Conducting a field trip is much the same as conducting any other instructional activity. The students must be introduced to it, they must be briefed on what to look for, and the activity should be followed up. However, field trips do present certain special considerations such as scheduling, permissions, transportation, expense, and control.

Before planning the trip, it is a good policy to make the trip yourself, if possible, to see whether it would be worthwhile for the students and how it can be made most productive. You must arrange the details at the place to be visited. Many museums, factories, and other places of interest provide their own tour services. If they do, you must be sure to let the proper persons know the purpose of the visit and what the students should see. You must also arrange for the necessary permissions, schedule changes, transportation, and so forth. Students can often help considerably in the planning and arranging of a field trip. However, you should be careful to double- and triple-check yourself on the details. You must also double-check to be sure that everyone has a mission to perform on the field trip. The trip should not be a joy ride or an outing but a real learning experience.

What are the advantages of taking students on field trips? What are the disadvantages?

Why must field trips be planned? What particularly must be considered in the planning? To what extent and in what ways can the students participate in planning and carrying out the plans?

Many field trips are not worth the time, trouble, and expense. How can you ensure that your field trips are not merely outings?

Resource People

Undoubtedly the most important resource of a community is its people. Even in a poor rural community the number of people who have special knowledge and talent that they can share effectively with a class is amazing. Often these persons can bring to a class new authority, new interest, new information, and a new point of view. Among the people who might be good resource persons are town, county, state, or federal government employees, hobbyists, travelers, businesspeople, college teachers, specialists, clergymen, and people from other lands. Alumni, and parents and relatives of the students are frequently available and usually interested in visiting the schools. A certain chemistry teacher aroused class interest by featuring a visit by a metallurgist from a local brass mill. A source we sometimes forget is the other teachers and school officials of our own or neighboring school systems.

Resource persons can be used for many purposes. They can provide students with help in specialized projects. Resource persons can also provide information not otherwise readily available. Who would know more about soil conservation in your county than the local Soil Conservation Service agent?

Resource persons are frequently used as speakers. Before inviting a layperson to speak to the class, you should check to be sure that there is a reasonable chance for the success of the activity. Quite often one can find out a lot about potential speakers from other teachers and friends. In any case, you should visit them and talk to them about their respective subjects. In your conversation you can probably determine whether a person is the type who understands and can get along with young people. You can also probably determine whether an individual can speak at the young people's level. If a woman's field is engineering and she discusses jet engines only in the language of the professional engineer, she will not contribute much to the class.

When inviting individuals to speak, you should

brief them carefully on what they are to talk about and the purpose of the talk. A suitable agreement should be made concerning the length of the talk, the asking of questions, visual aids, and so forth. It is wise to remind the speaker of these agreements, the time, place, and topic in a letter of confirmation. The letter should be written diplomatically. Perhaps as good a form as any is to state the agreements as you understand them and ask speakers if they concur. You can also remind them of these commitments when you introduce them to the class.

The public announcement that they are to speak for ten minutes and then answer questions often has a desirable effect on long-winded, rambling guests. Such precautions may seem far-fetched but they are sometimes necessary. It is most discouraging to have a speaker talk for forty minutes of a forty-five-minute period without letting the students ask one of the questions they have prepared.

You should also prepare the students for the meeting. As with other instructional aids, they should know what to expect and what to look for. Quite often, making up questions they would like answered is good preparation for listening to the speech and for the discussion period after the speech. Student questions may also be given to the speaker as a guide for his speech.

As a rule, speakers cannot be counted on to hold the attention of a class for a whole period. The guest appearance is usually much more successful if the formal speaking is kept quite short and the bulk of the program devoted to discussion and student questions. Sometimes it is more rewarding to bring in resource persons to act as consultants for pupil discussion groups or as experts in a "Meet the Press" sort of panel.

Studying the Community

A field trip is one way to study an aspect of the community. There are other ways, of course. One of them is to read and study. A surprisingly large amount of printed information is available about almost every community. This material may include reports of the federal, state, and local governments; releases by the Chamber of Commerce and similar agencies; stories in the local press; advertising and promotional literature from local concerns; publications of local civic and fraternal organizations; and, sometimes, articles in state and national publications. Unpublished material can sometimes be used to advantage. A student in a New England community was allowed to use old school records to write an historical account of the founding of the local school system in the early nineteenth century.

Community Surveys

One of the most interesting ways to study a community is to do a survey. Well planned, a survey can bring students face to face with the realities in the community. Poorly planned, it can result in erroneous learning and angry parents. Therefore every community survey should be prepared thoroughly and planned carefully. Take care that the topic is not one to upset the townspeople. After all, there are so many important potential topics that there is little point in selecting one that will cause a furor. Before the students begin, make sure that they are well versed in the topic to be investigated and the techniques they are to use. A poorly prepared survey is seldom worth the students' effort.

Gathering and interpreting the data of the survey can be troublesome. The actual gathering of the data may be done in many ways. Among them are the interview, the questionnaire, observation, and combinations of these and other techniques. Planning for the use of these techniques should be done carefully so that the time of the respondents is not wasted and the data gathered are really useful. The interpretation of the data should be approached with even more caution. One should set up criteria to differentiate between important and unimportant data and between meaningful and meaningless data. Moreover, one should set up criteria to determine the meaning of the data. This can often be done by inspection, but in some classes one may wish to apply simple statistical procedures. High school students can learn to use these procedures readily. Information concerning their use may be found in any textbook on educational measurement or statistics. Many of the newer high school mathematics texts discuss these procedures as well.

You and your students may be tempted to make public the results of the survey. In most cases the temptation should be resisted, and the survey should be reported to the class only. If it seems desirable to make the report public, consult your administrative superior before doing anything. As a rule, the report should be made public only if it is outstanding and if its public release will enhance the relationship that exists between the school and the community.

Students who plan to use questionnaires or opinionnaires need plenty of help in planning them. The following suggestions may be helpful.

1. Determine *exactly* what you want to know. Include only those things that you cannot learn from other sources with reasonable ease.
2. Write the questions as clearly as possible. Try them out on other students and teachers before you send them to the respondents. Beware of ambiguities. Be sure to explain any terms that may be misinterpreted.
3. Make the questions easy to answer. Where it is possible, use checklists or multiple-choice items. In any case be sure to leave a place for the respondents to make comments if they want to. At the secondary school level questionnaire writers should avoid using forced choice items.
4. Set up a system for the respondents' answers that will make your tabulating and interpreting of the data as easy as possible.

Interview Techniques

Another common method by which to study a community is to interview its prominent citizens and knowledgeable old timers. This method is not always fruitful because many persons find interview techniques difficult. If students are to apply it in a community study, they should be properly instructed in how to carry out a successful interview. Provide demonstrations of good interview techniques, and the students should practice on themselves before practicing on adults. Of course adults, particularly important adults, will make allowances for the errors of students who interview them. Nevertheless, you will want students to make a good impression on the people interviewed. For this reason, if no other, the students should be well rehearsed in their roles before leaving for the interview. In order that the students actually ask the questions they should ask in the interviews, they should write out their questions beforehand.

In surveys it is particularly important that each respondent be asked the same questions in the same way. For that reason the use of a form such as the following is recommended.

My name is _____. My class is doing a survey about student participation. I will be speaking to many students in your school and other schools. I would like to ask you a few questions.
A. Do you often discuss school issues with
   1. Friends?
   2. Class officers?
   3. School officials?
B. Have you ever attended a meeting (church, school board, union, etc.) in which school policy was discussed?
C. Have you ever taken an active part regarding school issues, such as writing a letter or presenting a petition?[5]

This type of form is advantageous because the interviewer needs only to check off the responses. In any case, the interviewers should be trained to write down the answers to their questions immediately and not to depend on their memories for anything.

---

[5] Thomas S. Popkewitz, *How to Study Political Participation*, How to Do It Series No. 27 (Washington, DC: National Council for the Social Studies, 1974), p. 5.

Observation Techniques

Still another excellent method to use in studying the community is observation. The familiar device of keeping a record of the foods students eat, so often used in health, hygiene, biology, and home economics classes, is an example of this type of study. Counting the number of cars that do not come to a full stop at a stop sign is another. Ordinarily, for observation to be successful, the students need to be well briefed in what they are looking for. They need to have criteria by which to objectify their observation and some system of recording it. Usually a checklist, or rating scale, or similar form is helpful to observers both for recording and for objectifying the observations. Since accurate observation is rather difficult, students who engage in such techniques should be instructed in their use. Quite often practice sessions will be beneficial.

Community Service and Action Learning

One evening in a suburban city a group of teenagers went from house to house ringing doorbells. They were social studies students conducting a campaign to inform voters of the issues in the coming elections and to persuade them to vote. Such service projects are another effective way to extend the classroom into the community. Quite often such activities get at objectives that the more usual classroom activities fail to reach. The techniques for preparing students for community study are equally efficacious in preparing them for a service project. Lately projects in which students go out into the community to learn by actual participation have been called "action learning," a particularly apt description of what goes on.

Securing Administrative Approval

Community service projects, surveys, field trips, and the like can lead to complications if they are not carefully managed. Projects of this sort have been known to upset school-community relations. For that reason you should always secure the advice and consent of your administrative and supervisory superiors before attempting such activities. In communities where the climate of opinion is not right, these activities may have to be foregone. The administration may find it necessary to withhold permission for other reasons also. Perhaps the proposal would interfere with other activities or classes; perhaps the timing would not be propitious; perhaps the community has had a surfeit of school surveys or service projects; perhaps the budget would not stand the expense. The final decision about whether the activity should or should not be attempted is the administrator's responsibility.

What might be a community service project suitable for use in your community? If you were to attempt to use this project, what preparations and precautions would you take?

In your own circle of friends and relatives, how many of them have special skills and knowledges which they might share with secondary school students? How might you use the resources of these people in a secondary school class?

Summary

Inquiry teaching consists of any strategy in which students attempt to seek information and to draw from it their own generalizations and conclusions. Most inquiry strategies involve problem solving. In general, the problem-solving method used in schools follows the steps outlined by Dewey as the act of a complete thought. These steps include selecting and defining a problem, gathering data, making hypotheses, and testing conclusions. Students need help in carrying out each of these steps. It should be noted that this technique is not the only way of solving problems nor is it always necessary for one to follow the steps in order. The main objective is to seek and discover knowledge for one-self. Among the problem-solving strategies are the case study method, value sheets, and various kinds of projects. Ideally a project should consist of a task that the students set for themselves and then carry through to completion under the teacher's guidance. It should both have intrinsic value to the students and be pertinent to the teacher's educational goals. Sometimes the projects are group projects, but whether group or individual, each project should be realistic, lifelike, and of innate value to the students, and it should be conceived, planned, and executed by the students under the teacher's guidance.

Discovery teaching consists of teaching in which students draw their own conclusions from information that they may have gleaned themselves or that teachers or others may have provided them. The famous Socratic discussion and its modern counterpart, the controlled discussion, are good examples of discovery teaching. The Socratic method, which is characterized by the logical development of concepts through open-ended, thought-provoking leading questions, is chiefly useful in teaching individuals or small classes. The controlled discussion has been developed for using Socratic techniques with full-size classes. Springboard approaches are especially good for use in discovery teaching. They have been used since ancient times in the parable method and in more modern versions such as the value sheet.

Inquiry and discovery teaching sometimes involve controversial issues. Since controversial issues are by definition controversial, teachers should treat them as open-ended and try to see to it that all sides of any issue studied are properly represented.

Field trips, community surveys, and community service projects are time-proven ways to utilize the community for instruction. Community activities should be planned and followed through very carefully to ensure that each activity is worthwhile and to save the school from embarrassment. In activities of this sort the teacher must always bear in mind

their possible effect on school-community relations. Therefore, it is especially important that all such activities be cleared with all the authorities concerned.

One of the most powerful of the methods, when properly used, is role playing, which consists basically of trying to put oneself in the place of someone else and to act out his point of view. In order to be effective, role playing must be an unrehearsed, spontaneous attempt to analyze and understand real problem situations. Simulation games are a type of role playing. The purpose of role playing and simulation is quite different from that of the many other types of dramatic presentations that may be included in the classroom. These other types should be rehearsed as carefully as the time permits in order to be effective.

Additional Reading

Aronstein, Laurence W., and Edward G. Olsen. *Action Learning: Student Community Service Project.* Washington, DC: Association for Supervision and Curriculum Development, 1974.

Frankel, Jack R. *How to Teach About Values: An Analytic Approach.* Englewood Cliffs, NJ: Prentice-Hall, 1977.

Grambs, Jean D., and John C. Carr. *Modern Methods in Secondary Education,* 4th ed. New York: Holt, 1979, Chap. 9.

Heitzmann, Wm. Ray. *Educational Games and Simulation, What Research Says to the Teacher.* Washington, DC: National Education Association, 1974.

Hersh, Richard H., John P. Miller, and Glen D. Fielding. *Models of Moral Education: An Appraisal.* New York: Longman, 1980.

Hoover, Kenneth H. *The Professional Teacher's Handbook: A Guide for Improving Instruction in Today's Middle and Secondary Schools,* 2nd ed.

Boston: Allyn and Bacon, 1976, Chaps. 10, 14, 27, 28, 29.

Kurfman, Dana G., ed. *Developing Decision-Making Skills,* Forty-seventh Yearbook of the National Council for the Social Studies. Washington, DC: National Council for the Social Studies, 1977.

Orlich, Donald C., et al. *Teaching Strategies: A Guide to Better Instruction,* 2nd ed. Lexington, MA: Heath, 1985, Parts 8–9.

Raths, Louis E. *Teaching for Thinking.* Columbus, OH: Merrill, 1973.

Raths, Louis E., Merrill Harmin, and Sidney Simon. *Values and Teaching,* 2nd ed. Columbus, OH: Merrill, 1978.

Seidner, Constance J. "Teaching with Simulations and Games," in N. L. Gage, ed. *The Psychology of Teaching Methods,* The Seventy-fifth Yearbook of the National Society for the Study of Education. Chicago: University of Chicago Press, 1976, Chap. VII.

Shaftel, Fannie, and George Shaftel. *Role Playing for Social Values.* Englewood Cliffs, NJ: Prentice-Hall, 1968.

Shulman, Lee S., and Evan R. Kesslar, eds. *Learning by Discovery.* Chicago: Rand McNally, 1966.

Thompson, John F. *Using Role Playing in the Classroom,* Fastback 114. Bloomington, IN: Phi Delta Kappa Educational Foundation, 1978.

Zeleny, Leslie D. *How to Use Sociodrama: Practical Exercises in Role Interpretation,* How to Do It Series No. 20. Washington, DC: National Council for the Social Studies, 1964.

14

Reading

Overview

All secondary school teachers, no matter what subject they teach, must face up to the necessity of teaching reading in their classes.

Reading is a difficult skill that takes years to master. For most of us it is a skill we must continue to learn well into our adult lives. Even then, none of us reads as well as we might. Undoubtedly most of your best students will not have mastered all the skills they need to become efficient, effective readers and some of your students will be truly disabled readers. If they are ever to become efficient readers and gain the most they can from your courses, someone must teach them how to read the content of your courses. That someone is you.

Reading skills should be taught functionally. Therefore, you as a middle or secondary school teacher must teach reading skills in your regular content courses. Content courses provide a milieu in which students can both learn and apply reading skills. Besides, learning to use these skills while reading material they must study anyway gives students a reason for trying them. Furthermore, when the teaching of the reading skills succeeds, the content reading will also be successful and students will be rewarded with feelings of satisfaction rather than frustration and failure. Thus we see that teaching reading skills in the content courses accomplishes several goals at once. After all, have not we already learned that to practice in context is usually much more effective than to practice out of context?

To be successful in teaching reading to students in your content area, you should address yourself to questions such as the following.

1. What reading and study skills are necessary for success in my study area?
2. How can these skills best be taught?
3. When should they be taught?
4. What are the best techniques for teaching them?
5. What are the best materials for teaching them?[1]

In this chapter, after a quick look at the reading problem in middle and high schools, we shall try to address these questions insofar as they concern teaching students vocabulary and reading comprehension in the content areas.

---

[1] M. J. Weiss, in Joseph F. Brunner, John J. Campbell, *Participating in Secondary Reading: A Practical Approach,* © 1978, pp. xv, 60. Reprinted by permission of Prentice-Hall, Inc., Englewood Cliffs, NJ.

The Reading Problem

As a rule, content-area textbooks are not easy reading—not even for good readers. They present new concepts in a jargon new to the students. Both the new ideas and the new language are essential parts of the discipline to be studied, for in each discipline new words are used to express new concepts, or old concepts that have acquired new names, and familiar words have taken on new meanings. Note the differences in vocabulary load of five content fields when categorized according to Roget's *Thesaurus* as reported in the May, 1979 *NASSP Curriculum Report* (Figure 14–1). Evidently history and mathematics are written in quite different dialects.

Not only do the fields use different vocabularies, they require different reading strategies. Reading a page of an algebra text is different from reading a page of a novel! In addition, reading in certain disciplines requires specialized skills. Reading in history or geography requires some fluency with maps; mathematics reading assumes the ability to read equations. The only person competent and available to teach these special skills is the specialized subject matter teacher concerned.

When you teach your students how to read and study the subject matter in your courses, you should center your teaching on your content, not on reading. Use regular classroom texts and ancillary readings. Select your lesson content for subject-matter objectives, not reading objectives. Adapt your teaching of reading skills to your content objectives. Teach the reading skills students need for learning a particular kind of content when you teach that content. Keep special lessons in reading to a minimum and even then aim the reading lesson at the content of the unit under study. Remember, you are a content specialist, and reading is one of the tools for teaching your content.

In spite of what we have said, the skills of reading do not differ so much from grade to grade and subject to subject as you may think. The differences are not so much differences in kind as differences

FIGURE 14–1
Percentages of Textbook
Vocabulary by Content Field
(*NASSP Curriculum Report*,
"Making an Impact by . . .
Reading in the Content Fields"
[May, 1979, **8**:4].)

	Abstract Relation	Space	Physics	Matter	Sensa-tion	Intellect	Volition	Affec-tions
Biology	15	14	5	52	4	2	8	1
Business	35	5	3	3	0	11	40	4
History	8	8	0	8	0	4	54	18
Math	64	14	0	0	1	14	7	1
Physics	38	22	28	2	4	3	2	0

in degree. As the students move up the ladder from grade five to grade twelve, their skills should become stronger and more sophisticated. Similarly in the content fields, it is not so much that one uses different skills as that one must emphasize different skills. Consequently, students will not come to you completely unskilled. What you must do is to take the students where you find them, teach them how to choose correct approaches to use, and how to carry out the skills needed for these approaches.

Thus while you must teach students to read, you do not have to be a reading specialist. Your task is to help students learn to read the content of your field. You are not responsible for determining the causes of reading disabilities, interpreting standardized reading tests, measuring students' reading potential, and the other esoteric business peculiar to the reading field. If you note where students are deficient in reading and take steps to overcome their faults, you will meet most contingencies. When you suspect something to be radically wrong, call for the specialist.

Reading in the Middle School

If you teach in a middle school, your job for teaching reading skills is somewhat more complicated than it would be if you teach at the senior high school level (assuming, of course, that the middle school teachers have done their job and the

students are well prepared for the high school). At this level you must teach both the basic reading skills and the study of the discipline. Because some boys and girls have learned to read quite well in the earlier grades, do not assume that they no longer need instruction in basic reading. All middle schoolers need instruction in all reading and study skills. They particularly need instruction in the connective prefixes, suffixes and technical vocabulary of the discipline. To prepare your middle school students for their high school courses, read several high school textbooks in your field carefully and use them as a source of vocabulary connectives and the like in your own courses.[2]

Reading in the High School

The high school reading program should be somewhat different from that of the middle or junior high school. It should provide remedial help, reteaching and review of the basic reading skills. (There probably is not a single college student who would not benefit from help in at least one of the reading skills.) Since this is the educational level when academicians take over, you should be ready to help students master the jargon of the discipline and find the meaning of esoteric academic writing.

---

[2] R. Baird Shuman, *Strategies in Teaching Reading: Secondary* (Washington, D C: National Education Association, 1978), Chap. 10 has been the source of many of the ideas in this paragraph.

You should also give your students considerable experience in reading at the higher levels of comprehension. Students should learn to detect an author's mood and purpose, to read independently, to read critically, to adjust their reading speed, and the various other techniques of the mature reader and scholar.

These tasks are all complicated by the great divergence in abilities in high school students. Somehow, the high school program must be individualized so that individual students will get the instruction and help they need at their different stages of development.

In what ways would you expect the teaching of the reading component of your subject in the middle school to differ from that of the senior high school?

What reading skills should you particularly emphasize in teaching your subject?

Can you think of any procedures you might use when teaching your courses to provide for the differences in reading skills among your students?

Look through a high school textbook in your field, noting the connective words and technical vocabulary that seem peculiar to the field and essential for middle school students to learn as preparation for high school courses in the field.

Vocabulary Building

As we have already pointed out, every discipline has its own jargon. The number of new words and old words with new meanings in most content field courses is staggering. It has been said, for instance, there is more new vocabulary to learn in a first course in high school biology than in a first course in high school French. Be that as it may, for your

teaching to be successful, you must teach the vocabulary of the field. Unfortunately, to do this job right takes much time and great effort. There just is not time enough to teach all the new words thoroughly. Therefore, you will have to concentrate on teaching the words that seem most important in view of the goals of the unit and the background of the students. Fortunately your students will not need to master every new word to understand what they read. If they can understand the important words, they can probably figure out other words well enough to grasp the gist of their reading. If you divide your class into small reading groups, as many reading specialists recommend, usually someone in the group will be able to figure out the meaning of most words. Besides, in a pinch you can explain difficult words or the students can turn to the dictionary. All of this means, of course, that you must be careful that the words you select to teach are truly the key words.

In order to ensure that your students' vocabularies are adequate for the job at hand, you should introduce the study of the key words early in the course. Certainly you will want to introduce the key technical words in a unit before you get into the unit. At this point you probably will want to teach the words deductively by definition and by drill. Later as the class moves into the unit, you would do well to help students use word-analysis skills to figure out the unfamiliar words they encounter in their reading.

Connectives

You should give particular care to teaching students to use qualifying and transitional words, for these words set up the relationships in sentences and paragraphs. For example, words like *thus, therefore, consequently, since, resulting,* and so on, indicate cause and effect; words like *on the other hand, however, in spite of, as well as, or, but, yet, similarly, even though,* indicate comparison or contrast; words like *before, after, later, earlier, latest,* indicate time order; and words like *first, second, then, finally, in the beginning, next,* indicate sequence. Point out these words to your students and discuss their significance in the paragraphs and longer selections they read. Connective words cause a particular problem. They tend to differ from subject to subject. Look up lists of the connective words for your subject, or make your own list by noting the most common connectives you find in high school textbooks.

Perhaps the best approach for teaching connectives is to run over the most common ones at the beginning of the course and then to study them more carefully as the course continues. Use drill techniques to drive home both the meaning of connectives and their particular uses in your content area. Give the students writing assignments that focus on connectives. In addition, insist that your students identify the connectives and discuss their significance as the unit goes along. Use exercises in which you scramble the sentences from a paragraph in your textbook and then have the students, by using the connecting words as clues, put them in correct order, or exercises in which you underline the connecting words and ask the students to substitute other connectives for the underlined words without changing the meaning of the paragraph.[3]

Developing Word Power

Because students in middle and high schools face a much larger vocabulary than that with which their elementary school texts have made them familiar, they need to know how to decipher new and unfamiliar words. That is to say that they need skill in the use of phonetical and structural analysis and the use of context clues. Even though instruc-

tion in all of these skills is part of their elementary school instruction, boys and girls need additional instruction and practice before they become independent readers. As a rule, however, most elementary school children acquire a fair amount of skill in working out how a word *sounds.* So at the middle school and high school levels we can concentrate our efforts on working out what the words *mean.* That is what Dean Donald D. Durrell calls "developing word power."

You can help students to build word power in three ways: by using content clues, by word analyses, and by using dictionaries, glossaries, and similar reference works. Give your students direct instruction and plenty of practice in each of these skills.

Using Context Clues

Unless you are different from most of us, when you run into a new word in your reading, you try to figure out its meaning from the variety of clues found in almost every paragraph. Only as a last resort do you go to the dictionary or glossary. Even when you do look up the word in the dictionary, you find it necessary to use these clues to ascertain the correct meaning for the context.

There are a number of context clues ready to be used in everything one reads. Among them are such syntactical clues as the ending *ed,* which probably indicates a verb, or *ly* which usually indicates an adverb, or *ist* which usually indicates a person who does or is something. Markers such as capital letters, articles, auxiliary verbs, and prepositions are also keys to the function of words as is the position of a word in a sentence.

Other clues are semantic. The way a word is used in a sentence, or its relationship with other words, gives the reader a broad hint to its meaning, if not the meaning itself. For instance,

1. The word may summarize several statements.
2. The word may be a synonym for another word in the paragraph.

[3] Joseph F. Brunner and John J. Campbell, *Participating in Secondary Reading: A Practical Approach* (Englewood Cliffs, N J: Prentice-Hall, 1978), pp. 140–141.

3. The word may be in opposition to a known word or phrase.
4. The word may be an antonym of a known word.
5. The word may make a comparison with a known word.
6. The word may make a contrast with a known word.
7. The word may reflect a mood or situation described in the text.
8. The word may refer to a situation or condition with which the reader has had experience.
9. The word is one with which the reader has had previous contact in another form or context.
10. The word is explained or defined by the author.

Students should also learn to look out for such aids as marginal notes, parenthetical definitions, headings, footnotes and formal definitions set off by such signals as commas, i.e., e.g., and the like.[4] Point out to students how to use these context clues and give them opportunities to use them. Usually, however, it will be difficult to provide exercises that can be used successfully with a large number of students. These skills should primarily be learned in the context of one's ordinary reading. When students run up against hard words, they can apply these skills to them. Exercises in which students individually spot words they don't know, as in the example by Elkins cited later in this chapter in the section on oral reading, are useful for this purpose.

Structural Analysis of Words

You should also introduce exercises in word analysis. Insofar as possible, you should make structural analysis a functional part of your study of the course content, but at first you will undoubtedly

---

Note how the context brings out the meaning in each of the following sentences.

1. Jake is a *pugapoo.* His mother was a cute little black poodle, his father a feisty, sandy-haired pug.
2. He was a *rock hound* who loved to wander through the desert hunting for interesting rocks and semiprecious stones.
3. The *gemologist,* an expert when it comes to fashioning jewelry out of native gem stones, welcomed us to his shop.
4. The *savannah,* a flat grassy plain, stretches from here to there.
5. All of a sudden he came to the edge of the hill and saw before him the *savannah* stretching flat and lush all the way from the foot of the hill to the sea.
6. They did not *quail,* but fought on bravely and staunchly.
7. He was a true hero—a *Lochinvar* out of the west.
8. *Orcs* are nasty, despicable, foul-mouthed, foul-breathed, dirty, murderous goblins.
9. He drove forward about a *league,* five miles in our reckoning.
10. In Europe the most popular game is *association football* which we call soccer.
11. Each element has its own pattern or fingerprint of colors it gives out. We call this fingerprint of colors its *spectrum.*
12. The imprisonment was not *oppressive.* We had airy cells, good food, chances for recreation, but no chance for escape. The guerrillas wanted us to be in good shape when time came to trade us for their leader.

have to teach your students what these skills are and how to use them.

Prefixes. In the middle school you will have to teach the fifteen most frequently used prefixes and how they can change a word's meaning. These

---

[4] Harold L. Herber, *Teaching Reading in Content Areas,* 2nd ed. (Englewood Cliffs, NJ: Prentice-Hall, 1978).

> Examine a few high school textbooks. What aids do you find for teaching the vocabulary? Do you find many words that seem difficult for normal students? For slow students? For you?
>
> Pick a chapter from a high school text. What seem to be the key words? Prepare a plan for making sure that the students understand these words. Would you plan to teach them deductively, by giving the students the definitions before starting the chapter or helping the students to puzzle out the meanings via word-power techniques as they go along?

prefixes are *ab* (from), *ad* (to), *be* (by), *com* (with), *de* (from), *dis* (apart), *en* (in), *ex* (out), *in* (into), *in* (not), *pre* (before), *pro* (in front of), *re* (back), *sub* (under), and *un* (not).[5]

You may have to reteach or review them in your high school classes. Shuman recommends that these prefixes be put up on the board as a semipermanent exhibit during the time that you are teaching prefixes and word analysis.[6] Use exercises in which students take apart and put together words. For example, ask students to make as many words as possible by adding different prefixes to *part* (apart, depart, impart), or *form* (conform, deform, inform, reform), or *press* (express, impress, depress, repress, prepress, suppress, unpress, compress). Point out to the students that when we combine word parts we sometimes alter them to make them easier to pronounce. Exercises that feature plenty of action and give-and-take are especially fruitful. For example, the fifteen prefixes might be printed on large cards and given to fifteen youngsters. Other youngsters would have cards on which are printed words like *ignition, visit, jointed, come, necessary,* etc. Each student would try to find another student with whose word he might combine.

This is a good spelling exercise as well as a fine lesson in the uses of prefixes and suffixes.[7]

Don't limit yourself to just the fifteen or so most common prefixes, however. Other prefixes may be fully as useful in your teaching. As Bamman points out, a student who understand the *trans* of *transparent* has already won half the battle of understanding *translucent.*[8] Similar instruction is needed to help students identify words made up of two other words. Similarly one might use games in which contestants shuffle cards, spin wheels, and the like, in a contest to see who can put together the most words by combining prefixes with stems.

Suffixes. Students can learn to use suffixes in much the same way as prefixes. Such study will not only help them to put together word meanings but also will help them learn the parts of speech and grammatical functions of words. One exercise you might use is to have the students see what changes they can make in words by adding suffixes, e.g., *govern* (governor, government, governess, governmental) or *complete* (completion, completely).[9] Bamman, Hogan, and Greene list two similar techniques that have been used very successfully for developing skill in using both prefixes and suffixes, and also recognizing derived forms.

1. Select a root form and build a "family" of words, substituting and adding various prefixes and suffixes. Call attention to the fact that the meaning of the root form *does not change:*

voice	*convocation*
vocal	*vocation*
vocabulary	*avocation*
invoke	*provoke*
evoke	*vociferous*

[5] Russell G. Stauffer, "A Study of Prefixes in the Thorndike List to Establish a List of Prefixes That Should Be Taught in the Elementary School," *Journal of Educational Research* (February 1942), 35:453–458.

[6] Shuman, *op. cit.,* p. 84.

[7] Ibid.

[8] Henry A. Bamman, Ursula Hogan, and Charles E. Greene, *Reading Instruction in the Secondary School* (New York: McKay, 1961), p. 196.

[9] Lists of suffixes can be found in such references as Francis Nelson, *Structure of American English* (New York: Ronald, 1958) or James Sledd, *Short Introduction to English Grammar* (Glenview, IL: Scott Foresman, 1959).

2. Select a derived form and examine its components, calling attention to the meaning of each part. Ask the students to name other words which contain the components:

philo*sophy*	theo*sophy*
phil anthropist	pan*the* ism
mis*anthropy*	*Pan* American
mis ogamist	anti-*American*
big*amist*	*ant* agonist
bi sect	

Skill in this sort of word analysis is necessary in developing good meaningful science vocabularies since much of the nomenclature in scientific classification is a matter of considering roots with suitable prefixes and suffixes, for example, lepidoptera, hymenoptera, hemiptera, and homoptera are classes of insects whose wings (*ptera*) are scale (*lepido*), membrane (*hymen*), half (*hemi*), or all the same texture (*homo*).[10]

Roots. Similarly students should learn to use roots in word analysis. Since studying the use of roots is more difficult than prefixes and suffixes, it is best to postpone their study until the high school and preferably after the students have had some contact with foreign languages. A knowledge of them can add greatly to the deciphering of difficult words in esoteric content.

Syllabication. Another technique of structural analysis that can be used to bring out the meaning of compound words is to break words into syllables. Understanding of syllabication is essential for word-attack skill. Boys and girls who can recognize syllables control knowledge that shows them how to break up words into components, and so to look at their various parts. Syllabication also gives students a key to pronunciation and so directly to meaning. Teach this skill by making ample use of the dictionary and instruction on determining which syllables to stress. Much of this teaching must of course be done orally. Hearing the syllables may be as important to the student as seeing them.

Make up several exercises to use to develop skill in the use of prefixes and suffixes. You ought to be able to concoct several varieties of games for spicing up such exercises. If you are short of ideas, watch some of the television game shows.

Using the Dictionary

The dictionary habit is probably the best aid to good vocabulary development. Encourage each student to acquire a paperback dictionary and to use it. In addition, make sure the students know how to use the dictionary. Among the skills one must teach, according to Evelyn Jan Tausch, are the following.

> The secondary student should be able to recognize alphabetical sequence, use guide words, identify root words in both inflected and derived forms, select the definition that fits the context, and realize the differing purposes of comma and semi-colon as used in dictionary meanings. He should be capable of using the pronunciation key, the etymology key, and responding correctly to the accent mark. He should know that geographical and biographical information can be located in some dictionaries and understand also the limited nature of this information so that he uses it appropriately.[11]

Once students become familiar with the dictionary, one can feel that they are well on their way to literacy.

In spite of these needs, the content classroom is not really the place for dictionary drill. As we have stated earlier, most of us use the dictionary as a last resort when puzzled or to confirm (we hope) what we have already guessed. So why

---

[10] Henry A. Bamman, ''Reading in Science and Mathematics,'' in *Reading Instruction in Secondary Schools*, Perspectives in Reading No. 2 (Newark, DE: International Reading Association, 1964), p. 64.

[11] Evelyn Jan Tausch, ''Teaching Developmental Reading in the Secondary School'' in *Reading Instruction in Secondary Schools*, Perspectives in Reading No. 2, op. cit. p. 52. By permission.

should not the students? Insist that students use the dictionary. As they do, point out to them how to use it efficiently, so that they will become skillful in its use. But also insist that they try to dig out the meaning of a word by using context clues and analysis techniques and then use the dictionary to check their conclusions.

What we have just said does not preclude the use of dictionary exercises in the initial stage of a unit. When you have a list of key words, it does no harm at all to have the pupils look up the key words in the dictionary before they start reading. Again, here is a time to teach the skills of using the dictionary. They should use these skills often enough in the initiatory exercises of a unit and during the course of reading for the use of the dictionary to become second nature. However, remember you are teaching your content field and its vocabulary. Dictionary skills should be a means, not an end, in your courses.

Introducing New Words

You should take particular care when introducing the new vocabulary in the new lesson. Quite frequently boys and girls cannot match any reality to key words in their lessons, even though they can pronounce them. If students are to read these words with any understanding at all, you must see to it that the words are well explained before the students begin reading them. In this process, emphasize relationships and be sure that the students become familiar with the words both orally and visually. When there are too many words in an assignment to be taught thoroughly, or when the students seem familiar with the words orally but not visually, it may help to put the list of words on the board and then run through the list slowly, pronouncing the words carefully and explaining their meaning. Important technical words should be taught much more carefully, of course, before the students start to read the content.

Larry Nook, a teacher at Wingate High School

in New York City, introduces units by new word lessons in which he "preteaches difficult words." In this process, he lists the words on the blackboard and then asks the students three questions for each word.

1. Read the word.
2. Can you see another word in this word?
3. Who knows the meaning of this word?

In this way he combines elements of word analysis with definition of the word, and some assurance that the students will know the words when they begin their reading.[12]

Reinforcement

Students do not master words until they have used them in different contexts and situations. You should, therefore, provide opportunities for students to repeat using their new vocabulary so as to reinforce their learning. See to it that the important words are used again and again in class discussions and assignments, in guides, overviews, and exercises. The common practice in vocabulary building of having students keep notebooks in which they compile a glossary of terms can be helpful. If you use this technique, see to it that the students do not merely copy words and definitions in their notebooks. This practice usually amounts to little more than transferring the word from one page to another. What we want to do is transfer the words into the student's mind. Consequently, exercises that force the student to use the word in context and really to learn its meaning are preferable. Defining a word in one's own words is a difficult feat which sometimes serves these purposes admirably. Similarly, acting out words is sometimes

---

[12] Larry Nook, "Systematic Approach to Vocabulary Building" in Robert L. Schain, David R. Keefer, and Ethel Howard, eds., *Developing Reading Skills Through Subject Areas* (Brooklyn, NY: The Wingate High School Press, 1976).

a pleasant way to bring out the meaning. So are games and exercises in which one tries to find the closest synonyms, crossword puzzles, bubble-grams, anagrams, acrostics and other puzzles, and matching games and exercises. Of course, discussion of words and their meaning is always helpful.

When strange new words come up, writing them on the board and discussing them impresses their meaning on the students' minds. So does keeping a "words to remember" list on the chalkboard or bulletin board. At times it may be wise to stop to give a lesson on the meaning of special words— or ordinary words with special meanings. Sometimes vocabulary study can be made more interesting and meaningful by teaching the history of the words. Genealogical charts showing the words' etymology can make interesting subjects for student bulletin boards. So can cartoons showing how suffixes and prefixes change the meaning of words.

Organizers

Herber recommends the use of graphic organizers as a means to organizing word study and developing an understanding of the concepts and relationships in the unit. He also recommends that students develop graphic organizers of their own as post-reading activities.

The following is an example of how one might prepare such an organizer.

1. Prepare a list of words that seem to you to be the most important in your unit. Include both new and old words.
2. Arrange the words into a diagram that shows the relationships among the ideas to be taught in the unit. Add and delete words as necessary to make the diagram clear and accurate.
3. Put your diagram on the board at the first class of the unit. As you do so, explain the words and tell why you placed them in this pattern. Try to get as much class participation as you can. Be sure that you and the students discuss

the reasons for the placement of all the words, and relationships among the words and ideas they express.

4. At opportune moments in your teaching refer to the diagram. Sketch portions of it on the board, project the diagram via the overhead projector, or give out copies of the diagram to the students so that they can study their arrangements as you discuss them. Have the students contribute to the discussion of the meanings of the words and the relationships of the concepts they represent.[13]

Presumably this type of organizer will direct the students toward the key concepts and the relationships to be studied and learned.

Would your approach for introducing new words to excellent readers be different from that for introducing new words to poor readers? Explain the different strategies you would use.

How can a teacher make a vocabulary notebook into a worthwhile learning experience?

Make up a graphic organizer for the reading in this section of the text.

Developing Reading Comprehension

Teachers in the elementary grades spend great effort teaching students the skills necessary to decipher the words they encounter on the printed page. On the whole, they are quite successful. At the middle and secondary school levels, teachers should turn their attention to building skill in comprehension. Evidently this emphasis is sorely needed. Wil-

---

[13] Herber, op. cit., pp. 147–149.

liam G. Perry[14] tells us that out of one thousand five hundred Harvard and Radcliffe freshmen assigned to read a certain chapter in a history book, only one in one hundred was able to glean the sense of the chapter well enough to write a short statement on what the chapter was about. *Ninety-nine per cent of these Harvard and Radcliffe freshmen had not learned to read for comprehension well enough in their twelve years of college preparation to complete this simple task.*

Theorists disagree concerning what makes up skill in reading comprehension. Niles, however, says that there are "three skills, or abilities, which . . . clearly differentiate between the reader who comprehends well and the reader who does not."[15] These skills are "(1) the ability to observe and to use the various and varied relationships of ideas," for example, time, listing, comparison-contrast, cause and effect, "(2) the ability to read with adjustment to conscious purpose, and (3) the ability to make full use of the substantial backlog of real and vicarious experience which almost every reader, even the beginner, possesses." Certainly to become a successful reader one should develop skill in finding the main idea of what one has read. Also it would seem essential to sharpen one's ability in spotting the details by which the author supports the main idea. Finally, one must work at improving the ability to recognize the patterns in which the ideas and supporting details are organized. Good reading consists of understanding an author's main ideas as well as the supporting details.

Readers may comprehend at any of three levels. The first or lowest level is the literal level. At this level readers are able to comprehend what the author has said. The second level is the interpretive level. At this level readers are able to understand what the author meant. The third and perhaps highest level is the applied level. At this level readers can apply the author's meaning to new or different situations.[16] These are approximately the same levels Gray had in mind when he spoke of reading the lines, reading between the lines, and reading beyond the lines. It behooves us teachers to help students learn to read well enough so that they can comprehend what they read at all three of these levels.

In view of these diagnoses it seems probable that you should concentrate your efforts when teaching reading in your content courses, on

- teaching students to read with purpose;
- teaching students to read at the three levels of comprehension;
- teaching students to find the main ideas in what they have read;
- teaching students to spot the supporting details;
- teaching students to identify the organizational patterns of the selection;
- teaching students to use what they already know;
- teaching students to adjust their reading to their purpose;
- teaching students to think about what they read.

Teaching Students to Read with Purpose

Perhaps the first thing to remember when you teach reading in content courses is that your primary objective is to teach the content. Therefore, for each lesson and unit you teach you should adjust your reading instruction to your content objectives. In short, in the words of Herber, "content determines process."[17]

Importance of the Assignment

Strangely enough the first step in teaching students to read for a purpose is to give them a pur-

---

[14] William G. Perry, Jr., "Students' Use and Misuse of Reading Skills: A Report to the Faculty," *Harvard Educational Review* (Summer, 1959), **29:**193–200; cited in Olive S. Niles, Improvement of Basic Comprehension Skills: An Attainable Goal in Secondary Schools, A Scott Foresman Monograph on Education (Glenview, IL: Scott, Foresman, 1964), p. 4.

[15] Niles, op. cit., p. 5.

[16] Herber, op. cit., Chap. 3.

[17] Herber, op. cit., Chap. 7.

pose for reading. This means that you should pay attention to the way you make your assignments. It also means that you must take advantage of students' intrinsic motivation and provide them with extrinsic motivation. Many of your students' reading and study problems will disappear if you really take the time to prepare them for their reading assignment when you make the assignment.

Stimulating Interest

When it comes to reading for a purpose, interest makes, if not all the difference, at least a good share of it. You would do well to try to sell reading about your subject to your students. Read interesting passages aloud to them. If you can, jazz up your reading to make it exciting. Converse with them about what you have read. Bring interesting books to class and talk about them. Try to have as great a variety of reading as you can because adolescents' interests are varied and changeable. Set up a classroom library. Let the students pick out the books for the library and bring in books that they think would be interesting to the class. Prepare displays of books and book covers. Set up an area for browsing. Have the students tell about the books and selections they recommend. Set up a reference file of 4×6 cards bearing student recommendations and criticisms. (If other students have found a book good, wonderful; if they have found it boring, or hard reading, a fair warning is most desirable.) In short, try to make things to read easily accessible. Most of us who love to read developed the habit by picking up readily available books and reading them. Don't forget, reading for fun is reading for purpose too.

One way to stimulate student interest is to show them that they already know quite a bit about the subject and that they can use what they already know. Consequently, if you use the students' own ideas and information as one basis for your lesson, it is bound to be more interesting than if it is all esoteric and academic. Start a discussion about the topic at hand, see how many words about the topic

students can think of, have students relate experiences pertinent to the lesson, or have students elaborate on something you tell them. The more you encourage them to use their own ideas and the more you use their ideas and knowledge in your lessons, the more likely they are to read and study your lessons.

You can also use student prediction to arouse interest and persuade students to read. You might, for instance, give the students a list of statements about the topic of the selection to be read and ask them whether they think the selection will agree with these statements or not. Then have the students read the selection to see whether or not their predictions were right. Follow up with discussion during which the students prove that the author's position did or did not agree with their predictions. Note that in such a discussion nothing is a matter of opinion, but strictly a matter of what the text says or means.[18]

Teaching the Three Levels of Comprehension

In content teaching you must teach students to read at all three of the comprehension levels: literal, interpretive and applied. First use a discussion or questioning technique that brings out just what it is the author said. It is probably more effective to ask the questions before the students start their reading. In this way you will alert the students to the task and help them arrive at a literal understanding of the piece to be read. Then, after the students have completed reading the assigned selection, you and the students should discuss it, first at the literal level and then at the interpretive and applied levels.

The truncated study guide appearing as Figure 14–2 is an example of a study guide designed to help students learn at the three levels of comprehension. To use such a study guide the students

---

[18] Ibid.

FIGURE 14–2
A Sample Study Guide.

Level One
DIRECTIONS: First read these statements. Then read the selection* that follows. As you read check the statements that say what the author said.

1. Robert L. Thorndike believes that reading comprehension is a unitary ability.
2. Some people believe that reading comprehension is a general skill; others think it is made up of a number of specific skills.

Level Two
DIRECTIONS: Check the statements that tell what the selection means. Be sure that you can show information in the selection that backs up your choice.

6. Frederick Daly's theory of reading comprehension is the same as Robert L. Thorndike's.
7. Thorndike's theory implies that students should think about what they read.

Level Three
DIRECTIONS: Check the statements that use both your own ideas and ideas in the reading selection. Be able to justify your answer.

10. We should include reading in the content areas in high schools.
11. High school teachers in English, history, and mathematics should help students learn how to read in their content courses.

* (In this sample study guide the selection and items 4, 5, 8, 9, and 12 have been omitted to save space.)

---

should (1) read the Level I items, (2) read the selection, (3) discuss the Level I items, (4) answer and discuss the Level II items, (5) answer and discuss the Level III items. In classes in which the students greatly range in reading ability, you may want to assign some students items at the literal level, others items at the interpretive level, and still to others items at the applied (applicative) level or combinations of levels; for example, literal and interpretive, or interpretive and applied, or all three levels. Students' responses to the items at the different levels can be incorporated into class discussion. In this way you can provide for individual differences in student ability and still involve the entire class in a group activity.

Teaching Students to Locate the Main Idea and Supporting Details

You should also place considerable stress on teaching students how to locate the main idea of a selection, and how to detect the supporting de-

tails and their relationship to the main idea. Students should be enticed into studying each of these at the three levels of comprehension. Use questions such as, "What seems to you to be the main idea of this selection? Point out the sentence or sentences that tell you that this is the main idea. What arguments does the author use to justify his main idea?" Use the regular textbook for such practice exercises. The following are only a few of many possibilities. Ask the student to read a paragraph and then tell what it means. Explain the meaning of key words and key sentences, paragraph leads, and topic sentences, and give the student practice in finding them. As soon as the student has learned to get the meaning out of paragraphs, repeat with sections and later with chapters. Exercises of this sort can be made more interesting by using, among other things, games in which one attempts to reproduce the author's outline, by dramatizing the main ideas of a selection, and by boiling down a paragraph or section into a telegram. Sometimes these activities should be made to include the entire class. However, boys and girls who have mastered these skills and use them well should not be required to do the same exercises as students who have not yet learned them. The teacher can expect to find both good students and poor ones among those who need help in these skills.

Teaching the Organizational Patterns

Textbook authors shape concepts by the way they organize their main ideas and supporting ideas. You should, therefore, see to it that the students can detect the pattern of organization in the material they read.

As a rule, paragraphs follow one or the other of four types of organizational patterns:

- Comparison or contrast
- Cause and effect
- Time sequence
- Simple listing.[19]

Of course not all paragraphs fall into any one of the categories. Some authors seem not to follow any organization pattern. Others may mix several types of organization patterns into a complex combination pattern. Still, you should help your students learn to recognize these patterns and to use them as aids for deciphering the meaning of the selections they read.

When identifying the patterns of reading selections, students should make use of the directional words and connectives that the author uses. These words not only give clues to the pattern the author is using but they also hint about the importance of the reading matter. Exercises in which students pick out directional words and tell how they change the meaning of paragraphs are useful means for familiarizing students with these signposts.

One approach to teaching organizational patterns that you might use is to start off by having students run through the selection quickly to identify the pattern the author used. Next have the students read the selection carefully to explore its meaning. Then do exercises in which the students identify the elements of the pattern, that is, the causes and effects, comparisons or contrasts, time order or items in a simple listing, and finally discuss the exercise.

If, before they read the selection, you give students study guide questions such as the following, it will help them to comprehend the patterns and their significance as they read.

- The author lists three causes for the beginning of the war. They are _____, _____, _____.

- The author mentions three events in the paragraph; which occurred first, which second, and which last?

Then, after the reading, the discussion will automatically bring out the pattern and clinch the meaning. Remember, your goal is not to cause students to identify the pattern as cause and effect; rather it is for the students to see what the causes and their effects were. When you use this sort of approach, you should be careful to start off with simple, straightforward paragraphs and then proceed slowly to more complex paragraphs and to paragraphs that combine patterns or paragraphs with unclear patterns.

Teaching Students to Utilize What They Know

In order to motivate students, to give them confidence and to help them acquire an ability that Niles says differentiates between good and poor comprehension, try to build on the prior experiences, knowledge and skills students bring with them when they come to your classroom. For this purpose, use discussions in which students draw on

[19] Olive Niles, ''Organization Perceived,'' in Harold L. Herber, ed., *Developing Study Skills in Secondary School* (Newark, DE.: International Reading Association, 1965), p. 60.

their own experience to set the stage for the reading or to clarify what they have read. Encourage students to draw upon what they already know to establish the meanings of sentences and strange words. Certainly the girl who works at the checkout counter at a supermarket has some inkling about prices, inflation, and other notions found in economics texts. Capitalize on these knowledges. Point out the relationships. Let her tell you what is happening to the prices. Then, when she reads about inflation and its causes it will mean something to her. If students discuss such things before their reading, it will help them understand much more than if you conduct a question and answer session after they have tried to read the assignment.

One of the most troublesome causes of student inability to comprehend what they read is that they do not see the relationships between what they are reading and what they have read before. You should, therefore, take great pains to show how the parts of the course fit together. In your discussions and study guides, point out those relations. When you start a new unit, review salient points of the old unit and discuss their implications for the new one. Start students thinking along the lines, "If that is what happened in that chapter, what might we expect in this one?" Then as the students progress through their new content, force them

to think about the relation of what they are reading to what they have already learned. Presumably as they begin to see the organization of the course and the relationships among the various items of information, concepts, and generalizations, the course content will start to make more sense to them. In addition, it will help them to learn to develop new learning out of past knowledge.

Teaching Students to Adjust Their Reading Speed

Good readers adapt their reading speed to what they are reading and their purpose in reading it. Poor readers tend to read everything at about the same rate. Classroom teachers, then, should concentrate on helping students learn how to adapt their reading attack to the situation. Most reading in science and mathematics, for instance, requires slow, careful study. So does studying the rule book in the physical education class, but reading in mathematics classes seldom calls for skimming or scanning, while in physical education classes one might well want to use these skills frequently to spot rules applicable to specific situations.

Lord Bacon wrote, "Some books are to be tasted, others to be swallowed, and some few to be chewed and digested." Teach students to look for the signposts that indicate the importance and the import of paragraphs, sections and chapters. Show them how to use both external and internal clues. Let them practice with directional words that tell one whether to speed up or slow down. Have group discussion in which students decide what they should concentrate their reading on and what can be treated more lightly. Give your students direct instruction in determining what works should be scanned, skimmed, read, or studied. Point out criteria that indicate the appropriate approach. For instance, it can be said that, in general, reference works are designed to be scanned; fiction and some supplementary reading may deserve only to be skimmed; and most textbooks must be studied.

Practice building study guides for reading selections from textbooks in your field in which you help students to

1. read at each of the three levels of comprehension;
2. locate the main ideas and supporting details of the selection;
3. understand the organizational details of the selection;
4. capitalize on what they already know when reading the selection;
5. see how the selection fits in with preceding parts of the course.

Boys and girls can learn how to use such criteria through class discussion and by application of the criteria to various books. They may even develop their own criteria in a group discussion.

Although most of this chapter is devoted to the chewing and digesting of reading, perhaps we should spend a few moments discussing tasting, that is, skimming, for skimming allows one to sample, to skip the old and become familiar with the new, to concentrate on the pertinent and to brush over the irrelevant.

In the first place, in order to skim one needs to know enough about the subject at hand to recognize the pertinent and novel when one sees them. Then one can glance through the preface and table of contents of a book to see what the book is about. If it seems as though the book may prove useful, the reader can then scan the book, reading the headings, introductory paragraphs, chapter summaries, and sampling the opening, middle, and final paragraphs. If a topic seems provocative, one can read it carefully. Sometimes it will be necessary to go back to read a previous section, but doing this will do no harm because one is still reading only what is most essential or interesting.

To teach boys and girls to skim books effectively, teachers should first teach the techniques involved directly, and then follow up this teaching with practice. An example of practice useful for this purpose follows.

1. In a class discussion decide what the class would like to learn from the chapter.
2. Let each student skim the chapter to see what it has to say on these points.
3. Discuss what the class has found in the chapter.

Teaching Students to Read Critically

Evaluating What One Reads

"All that glitters is not gold," and all that is printed is neither true nor good. Unfortunately, many young people seem to have considerably

---

Examine selections having to do with a topic you might teach. Devise specific strategies you might use to stimulate pupils to read these selections with interest.

How does one determine when to skim and when to read carefully?

Can you think of any exercise games that one might use to teach skimming?

Of what importance is the ability to skim in mathematics, in social studies, in science?

---

more respect for the written word than is warranted. Many high school students believe because it is "in the book." Often these students become sadly confused when they find that what the book says is not necessarily true. Teachers should take it upon themselves to ensure that their students learn to read critically and to evaluate what they read.

How does one teach students to evaluate what they read? One technique is to give the students plenty of practice. When students read several texts on a topic, they soon become aware of the differences of opinion that exist. So perhaps the first step is to give students different readings about the various topics, to consider carefully the differences of opinion, and to discuss why these differences exist.

Another step in evaluating one's reading is to try to establish the difference between fact and fancy. Early in life students should learn that some things are fact and some are fiction. Teachers can teach students how to determine the difference between fact and opinion by asking them such questions as, Is that so? How do you know? How can you check? Is this true or does the writer merely think so?

In their attempts to distinguish fact from fancy, students also should look for signs of bias in the writer. Assignments asking them to check their reading for such things as sensationalizing, emotionality, easy sweeping statements, disregard for facts, and loaded words will help familiarize the students with some of the signs of bias. Another check is to examine the writer's documentation. If one finds references only to old works or works that are in dispute, perhaps the writer has not documented the work carefully. The writer who argues from anecdotes should also be distrusted. Single, isolated cases introduced into the content with the implication that they are typical are often false documentation.

Arguing from anecdote is only one example of writing that violates the rules of logic. When teaching students to evaluate their reading, teachers should teach them to apply the tests of logic to all they read. A technique useful in introducing the application of the rules of logic is to discuss violations of logic in their reading or in television materials. For instance, a television commercial implies that one gasoline is better than another because it is made in a refinery that can make its entire product 100 plus octane gas. Why does this not make good sense? Or again, one reads that a certain athlete smokes Bippos. Is this any reason why anyone else should? What does he know about it? Material of this sort can be used to teach the more obvious breaches of logic. As students become familiar with these errors, they can apply these tests to magazine articles and other readings.

Students should also be wary of polemics, propaganda devices, and other attempts to persuade. Newspaper "Letters to the Editor" and editorials often provide excellent examples of political polemics that lend themselves to classroom instruction in critical reading. Examples of such slanted material can be found in almost any newspaper any day. Teachers can utilize them by giving students individual study assignments or by projecting them via the opaque projector or, after making a transparency, the overhead projector. In either case the teacher might ask the students to analyze the selections and to answer such questions as, Are they logical? Is the presentation just? If not, why not? Can you find instances of loaded words and other propaganda devices?

Exercises of this sort and others that the teacher may devise should help give students skill in evaluating. Moreover, they can be expected to encourage a questioning attitude in the students. It is hoped that after such teaching they will not swallow things, but will read with an active awareness of the snares of misinformation and poor logic, and also be inclined to test any idea before gulping it down.

Stylistic Criticism

Reading critically also includes being alert to style and skill in writing. Does the style serve the thought? Is it appropriate? Does the writing bring out or obscure the meaning? Does it bring out or obscure the feelings? Is the language used symbolic? If so, how is the symbolism used? What does it mean? Are the methods of presentation effective? Any reading that brings out the answers to such questions is critical reading.

So also is any reading that results in the students' questioning or actively thinking about the values or implications of what they read. Especially important is the reading experience that helps to make the student react creatively—by drawing an illustration, by acting out a scene, by being the catalyst for making up an original poem, story, or ballet. Teachers should provide for such reactions by giving the students plenty of opportunity to evaluate, question, discuss, and think about what they read to encourage creative responses of all sorts.

Study Guides for Critical Reading

Study guides are useful for teaching critical reading. Perhaps, particularly with unskilled readers, you will want to use three-level guides such as the truncated example we have already given you. On the other hand, you may wish to concentrate entirely on the thinking and reasoning if you are quite sure that the student understands the author's meaning. In any case, if the students are unskilled

Examine a local newspaper. Find examples of bias, coloring, non sequiturs, propaganda devices, and misrepresentation of facts. Can you find similar inaccuracies, unsubstantiated opinions, and signs of bias in high school and middle school texts? What would you do to help students be aware that all reading, even textbooks, should be viewed critically?

readers, it is usually better to use checklists rather than questions in your guide.

Using Textbooks

Textbooks are the most common information source used in our classrooms. As a teaching tool, the ordinary textbook may be somewhat flawed. It is most probably dull. It represents only one viewpoint, one style of presentation. It is likely to be over the students' heads and to leave out basic information, essential if a newcomer is to understand the field, because the author assumes that *everyone knows that*. Often it is bland, noncontroversial, and spineless, carefully avoiding anything and everything that would stimulate young readers to experiment with new ideas and to think for themselves. And worst of all, it is more than likely too difficult for most of the students to read without great effort.

These faults notwithstanding, the textbook is a most useful tool, if we use it well. If it presents only one point of view, we must find a way to present other viewpoints; if it is dull, we must supply spice; if it is obscure, we must make it plain; if it omits essential information, we must supply another source that will furnish the missing data; and if the text is difficult to read, we must help the students master its language, vocabulary, style, and organization patterns. And finally, if the students will not read the textbook, as opposed to

can not read it, you must find some way to entice them.

Teaching Students to Use the Textbook

Teachers are often surprised because students find reading their textbooks difficult. You should not be surprised because no doubt you find some of your own college texts difficult. Since textbooks are written, usually, in the jargon of the discipline and present new information and introduce new concepts, it would be strange if they were easy reading. Further, since reading ability and level of text difficulty are both a combination of a number of skills and types of reading, it is only natural that most students will have some trouble with some portions of the text, if not with others, no matter how well they read. When you consider that many boys and girls have never mastered the skills needed to use a text most effectively and efficiently, it is not surprising that so many people have trouble getting the meat from the textbook's dry bones. Therefore, don't expect what you have no right to expect. Instead of wailing that the "kids can't read" the text, show them how to do it. After all, that is what teachers are paid to do.[20]

The Author's Aids to Learning

When you give out a new text, you ought to point out the aids to learning that the author has put into the text to help students study it. There are many of them. You might check through your college texts to see what aids to learning the authors have included in them. Among them you may find tables of contents, prefaces, chapter summaries, chapter introductions, chapter headings and subheadings, problems to be solved, charts, graphs, illustrations, signpost sentences, indexes, glossaries, and footnotes. Teach your students to use those devices to organize their reading and thinking, to

[20] Herber, op. cit., p. 17.

set up goals for studying, to separate the important concepts from the forgettable detail, and to see how the various ideas presented in the text are related to each other.

Table of Contents and Preface

The preface of a book usually gives the rationale and purpose of the book, and the table of contents an outline of its organization. It is, therefore, not a bad idea to start off the use of a new text by discussing its preface and table of contents. First, you could give a short introduction in which you point out what prefaces are for, and then you and the students read the preface together and discuss what it says and its implications. You might center your discussion around such questions as

- What does the author say is the purpose of the book?
- Does it have any special features?
- Are there suggestions for using it?
- Does it seem like a good book for our purposes?

Next, you and the students should examine the table of contents to see what the book contains. In your examination you might show them how the parts of the book relate to each other; point out how earlier chapters give background for later chapters; help them discover the scope and sequence of the book and its various chapters; have them find what the author considers the major topics and the minor supporting topics; and practice spotting where selected topics and information are located according to the table of contents. Sometimes it is helpful to have students compare the table of contents of their textbooks with those of other textbooks, criticize them, and decide which table of contents is most useful. This, of course, implies that the students should discuss how to use the table of contents to their advantage. As an example of how to profit from such a study, Brunner and Campbell cite an exercise used by a content area teacher for a text having a very skimpy table of contents.

1. A general discussion of the course content using the table of contents as a guide.
2. Division of the material by students, with teacher guidance into units.
3. Assignment of a group of students to each unit. These students were given the task of expanding the table of contents to include the major topic headings within each chapter.
4. Presentation to the class by other groups of students of suggestions for using the appendix, glossary, and index.
5. Issuance of the expanded table of contents to each student. These new outlines were used for the remainder of the year as guides.
6. Teaching students how to use book parts by their peers.[21]

Similarly you might use the table of contents to orient students to chapters or units of study and to set unit goals. For instance, you might have students discuss

- How does the unit fit into the overall structure of the book or course?
- How do the chapters or parts of the chapters fit into the complete unit?
- What are the major topics and subtopics?
- In view of the outline presented in the table of contents, what would be the best way to organize your approach to studying this unit?

Index and Glossary

Similar exercises may be used to introduce the index and glossary, until you are sure that the students not only know how to use them but have acquired the habit. This, of course, means recurrent practice sessions. In each unit the students should have plenty of opportunities to look up things in the index. More than occasionally you will find that the students have difficulty in using the index because they do not know the alphabet. For these students, special instruction and practice are necessary.

[21] Brunner and Campbell, op. cit., p. 60.

Go through the preface and table of contents of several middle or secondary school textbooks in your field. In what ways do you think they are helpful?

What other "aids to learning" have the authors included in these texts? Do they seem to be helpful?

A good type of practice for students having trouble with alphabetizing consists of scrambling the words from a page in the dictionary and asking the students to put them in correct order. If the words are on cards it makes it easier and saves time while being fully as effective. Students can also make their own lists and test other students. In such cases the students should first demonstrate their own ability to arrange lists properly before testing their peers. You may have to teach directly how to find such things as "questioning, techniques of" and items that do not appear under the expected category but are listed in another. In so doing you should not only show students the basic techniques, but use exercises in which the students practice selecting key words, finding the reference in the index, turning to synonyms when they do not find the original key words, spotting major topics and subheadings, and using cross-references.

If your text contains a glossary, students should learn to use it and do so as part of every unit. Use exercises in which students check out such things as pronunciation and syllabication as well as the meaning of important words. If the book has no glossary, have the students make up their own with their own definitions. Perhaps they should do so anyway as part of their vocabulary study.

Appendices

Many texts have appendices. Social studies texts often include documents as appendices; mathematics and science texts, tables; and so on. During the first lesson on the book you should point out the appendices and explain what they are and how to use them. Then at the earliest opportunity you should use an appendix as an integral part of a lesson or unit. When you do so, discuss with the students again what appendices are, their purpose and how to make the most use of them.

Chapters and Their Parts

In most textbooks the chapters are divided into major and minor heads which represent the author's outline of the chapter. Teach your students the significance of the various headings so that they will be able to separate major topics from supporting detail. Exercises in which the students reproduce the author's outline as set out by the headings should be helpful. Perhaps you might run off a list of the headings in the order they appear in the text and have the students identify which headings are major; which are subheads; which are sub-subheads; and the like.

Similarly, the students should be taught to make the most of the chapter introductions, the summaries, and any marginal notes. Authors put these into their books to be pointers and reinforcers. Help students use them for the purpose they were intended. Before the students read the chapter, let them check each of these devices and then formulate questions of their own concerning what they might learn from the chapter and from the sections. Continued practice with this sort of activity should help create a habit of reading with an inquisitive, open mind.

Typographical Clues

Authors also use a number of typographical clues to point out important facts and ideas. Italics, bold-face type, underlining, parentheses, quotation marks, colored print, and the like are writers' signposts. Teach your students to use them. Perhaps you should take time in an early unit to teach their use directly. Go over several pages of the text, and point out the typographical clues and their uses.

Then have students spot the clues on other pages and discuss their significance. Then make a point to have the students notice and use them in the ordinary course of succeeding units and lessons.

Pictures, Cartoons, Diagrams

As a rule, when authors and publishers go to the trouble and expense of putting pictures, cartoons, and diagrams in their textbooks, they do so to make the book more usable. In other words, they hope the illustrations will illustrate what they want to say—not just make the book prettier. So use them in your lessons. It is not too much to spend an entire lesson on analyzing and interpreting a single picture or diagram. Ask the students to study the picture and its caption and then tell you what they see in it. In your discussion students should consider the import of the picture as a whole and also explain and interpret its various details and their significance to content matter at hand.

For example, Lesson 2 of Jack Abramowitz' *World History Study Lessons*, Unit 1[22] includes several pictures. One shows reconstructions of three kinds of "early men," another a picture of an Old Stone Age cave drawing, a third an illustrated time line, and a fourth a picture of a man making stone tools. These pictures have intrinsic interest and teaching value, but could not the teacher capitalize on these pictures by calling the students attention to the features that mark the differences between the various species of *Homo,* or better yet, let the students spot the differences in characteristics from the pictures themselves? From there could not one go on to see where these various men seem to fit into our time line and which ones might be the artists of the stone caves and the makers of stone tools? Incidentally, this type of teaching can frequently be quite successful with students who ordinarily do not succeed well in book learning.

[22] (Chicago: Follett, 1962).

Maps

When your textbook contains maps, you should feature map study in the appropriate lessons and units. If you do so, you will undoubtedly have to spend some time working on map reading skills. Most boys and girls who enter the middle schools have only the skimpiest knowledge of map reading—at least partly because many map reading skills are too sophisticated for elementary school youngsters. Many middle school and high school young people are not much better off, and among adults map reading seems to have become a lost art. Yet ability to read maps is absolutely essential in the study of history, geography, current events, and often helpful in literature, composition, and other fields.[23]

In any case, if you use maps, you will have to spend much time teaching and reteaching map reading skills such as the use of terms, reading the legend, using scale, finding direction, using latitude and longitude and other grid systems, reading elevation, recognizing key symbols, and the like. Insofar as possible, this instruction should be tied to your content lesson; for example, if you are studying the Northwest Territory, teach the map skills necessary for that unit on maps of the Northwest Territory. As you teach, refer to the maps frequently. Make it a rule never to describe a place in your lesson without placing it on the map. Point it out yourself, or have students point it out and, if appropriate, have the students develop concepts about the lay of the land at that spot by studying its location on the map.

Use exercises such as the following.

- If a family decided to move to Oregon by way of the Oregon Trail, how many miles would it have to drive its carts after leaving Independence?

[23] J. R. R. Tolkien is reported to have said that it is impossible to write a story such as *The Lord of the Rings* unless you have first prepared a map. Certainly close attention to its maps is indispensable if one wishes to follow and understand the details of that story's plot.

- What kinds of terrain would it pass through?
- If you were a native of New Jersey in 1790 what route would you take to get to New Orleans?

Graphs and Tables

You will find it necessary to teach the use of graphs and tables in much the same way as one teaches maps. Usually when authors put graphs and tables into their books they are presenting the crux of the matter in abbreviated form. Yet students tend to skip graphs and tables because they do not know how to use them. This is too bad, because not only can graphs clarify complex ideas and obscure points but they are usually simple to read, certainly simpler than a lot of verbiage, once you know how. Ordinarily you can best teach the use of graphs and tables in the usual units of your courses rather than by introducing a separate unit on the topic. In your regular classwork you can ask questions that require the pupils to refer to graphs or tables. Sometimes the questions can be student-made. Techniques such as the following will probably make the teaching of charts and graphs more effective.

1. Give definite assignments that involve the reading and interpreting of charts, graphs, and other aids from time to time. These assignments should not be special lessons on the use of charts and graphs (although sometimes they may be required). Rather, the teacher should point out important features and their significance in regular lessons as the class goes along.
2. Ask students to use charts and graphs to point out ideas and to support conclusions.
3. Do some direct teaching in the reading and interpretation of graphs. Once this is done the students can make comparisons and inferences from graphs.
4. Use the overhead projector. You can project grid lines onto the chalkboard and then build the chart or graph on the board. You can also project charts and graphs as ordinary visual aids.

> How much time should a biology teacher take to teach students how to use the parts of the biology textbook?
>
> Build some exercise games you might use to help students better understand a text in your field.
>
> Take a picture from a text you might use. How does it illustrate the ideas set forth in the text? What would you expect students to see in it?
>
> Set up an exercise in which students interpret a graph.
>
> Outline a plan for teaching students how to use the "aids to teaching" contained in a middle or high school text in your field.

Matching Reading Levels

The Book's Reading Level

The reading level of the reading matter you use should be compatible with the reading level of the students. Even though strongly motivated readers may manage to cope with reading matter well over their supposed reading level, usually too difficult reading assignments lead only to frustration.

To determine the reading level of a text, the first thing to do is to check the teacher's manual or teacher's edition. If these do not give the reading levels, then you can turn to a readability formula such as the Fry formula. This formula, by analyzing the vocabulary and sentence structure used in a book, estimates the reading difficulty of the book in terms of grade level.

To use the Fry formula

1. Determine the average number of syllables in three one hundred-word selections taken one from the beginning, one from the middle, and one from the ending parts of the book.
2. Determine the average number of sentences in the three one hundred-word selections.

FIGURE 14–3
Fry Readability Graph. (Edward Fry, "A Readability Formula that Saves Time," *Journal of Reading* [April, 1968], **11**:587.)

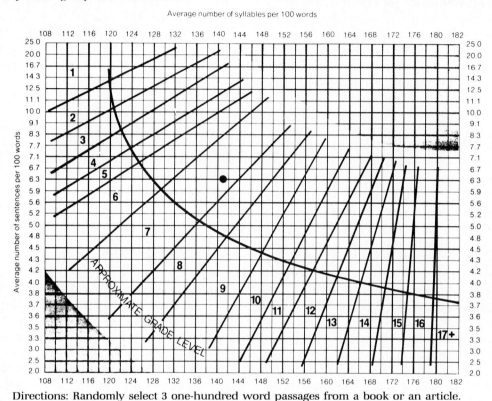

Directions: Randomly select 3 one-hundred word passages from a book or an article. Plot average number of syllables and average number of sentences per 100 words on graph to determine the grade level of the material. Choose more passages per book if great variability is observed and conclude that the book has uneven readability. Few books will fall in gray area but when they do grade level scores are invalid. Count proper nouns, numerals and initializations as words. Count a syllable for each symbol. For example: "1945" is 1 word and 4 syllables, and "IRA" is 1 word and 3 syllables.

3. Plot the two values on the Fry readability graph (Figure 14–3). Their intersection will give you an estimate of the text's reading level at the 50 per cent to 75 per cent comprehension level.[24]

Unfortunately, estimates of reading level gained by formulas of this type apply only to the technical difficulty of the reading matter. They do not take into consideration its conceptual difficulty.[25] Therefore, you must take into account such things as the prior experience of your students with the subject matter, the number of new ideas introduced, the abstraction of the ideas, and the author's use

---

[24] Edward Fry, "Readability Formula That Saves Time," *Journal of Reading* (April 1968), **11**:587.

[25] They may also be misleading. Complex ideas may be stated in simple sentences, and longer, seemingly more complex sentences may make complex ideas easier to understand.

of external and internal clues. These criteria are, of course, all subjective.

In the final analysis, estimating the difficulty of a book is primarily a matter of using your best judgment. We recommend that you first find the technical difficulty of the book by the use of a formula and raise or lower your estimate in accordance with your judgment of its conceptual difficulty.

The Student's Reading Level

Just because the formula tells you that a book is at the seventh-grade reading level, it does not mean that the book is suitable for your seventh-graders. Some seventh-graders read much above grade level and others are almost illiterate. Therefore you need to find out the students' reading levels.

To find the levels at which students are reading, you can use the standardized tests given as part of the school testing program. Probably you should leave analysis and diagnosis via such instruments to reading and guidance specialists. Do not take reading levels scores obtained from the testing program as gospel, however. Your course may require different vocabulary and reading skills than those tested. Short answer and multiple-choice questions do not call for the same skills as sustained reading and studying, for instance. Besides, some of your students may have been nervous and scored too low while others may have been lucky and scored too high.

Evidently, test scores or no test scores, you will have to rely on your own resources to tell you whether or not your reading matter is too difficult for your students. Two informal tests that you might use are the silent reading inventory and the oral reading inventory. To conduct the silent reading inventory, have your students read silently four or five pages of a book at their supposed grade level and administer a ten-question test on the information given on those pages. Presumably students who score above 90 per cent in the test are

independent readers at that grade level, those who score between 75–89 per cent are reading at the instructional grade level, and all who score below 75 per cent are reading below grade level. To carry out the oral reading inventory, simply have the student read a one hundred-word passage from the book orally. All students who can read 95 per cent or more of the words are reading at grade level or above; all who cannot read 95 per cent of the words are reading below grade level and need help.

Probably the simplest way to find whether or not a book is too difficult for individual students is to have the students first read it aloud to you and then tell you what they have read. If a student can read passages aloud without much stumbling and can explain their gist reasonably well, you can assume that the book is not too difficult for that student.

Another technique that seems to be becoming increasingly popular is the CLOZE procedure. Although authorities seem to differ on the best way to carry out this procedure, we recommend using the following technique. From your textbook select several typical passages so that you will have a total of 400–415 words or so. Delete every eighth word in the passage except for words in the first and last sentences, and proper names, numbers, and initial words in sentences. It will be helpful if you eliminate fifty words. Duplicate the passages with ten to fifteen space blanks replacing the eliminated words. Pass out these "mutilated" readings to the pupils. Ask them to fill in the blanks with the most appropriate words they can think of. Collect the papers. Score them by counting all the words that are the exact words in the original text,[26] and dividing the number of correct responses by the number of possibles. (Fifty blanks makes the division very easy.)

$$\text{Score} = \frac{\text{Number of correct responses}}{\text{Number of possibles}}$$

---

[26] Some persons recommend that only exact words be counted; others would allow exact synonyms. We suggest that you not count synonyms or verbs of differing tense, etc.

You can assume that students who score better than 50 per cent can read the book quite well, students who score between 40 and 50 per cent can read the book at the instructional level, and students who score below 40 per cent will probably find the book frustrating.

Try to apply the Fry formula to textbooks.

Prepare a CLOZE test for the text. If possible, try it on a middle- or high school-aged youth.

How can one determine the suitability of a book's reading level for a particular student?

Prepare a list of readings for students of different reading levels for a topic in a course you might teach.

Multiple Readings

Sometimes instruction can be more profitable if one uses several readings rather than a single textbook. Students read at different rates, with different abilities and interests, and with different backgrounds. No single text can cope with all these differences. When a teacher adopts a single text the class is limited to a single point of view, a single reading level, and a single style.

The use of several readings has the advantage of making it possible for students to read material suited to their abilities and needs. If a boy is attempting to learn the contribution of Samuel Gompers to the labor movement, it matters little whether he searches for his information in the *Encyclopaedia Americana*, a biography of Gompers, or a history of the labor movement, as long as he learns it as efficiently and effectively as he can. Since this is true, the teacher can help boys and girls pick books to study that are most suitable for their abilities and which may appeal to their interests. It is very difficult to provide adequately for individual differences if one limits the readings to one text only.

Another important possibility that presents itself in using many readings is the opportunity to read original sources. Textbooks often tell about things superficially. In many instances this treatment is justified because of the limitations of time and space, but certainly the student should be allowed to meet some of the originals face to face. The use of many readings makes this easily possible, especially now that much first-rate material is available in paperback.

Some teachers find it difficult to organize courses when many readings are used. If a teacher uses unit, individualized, and laboratory procedures, this difficulty should be reduced. Another solution to this problem is to adopt one textbook as a basic reader and to supplement it with other readings. Still another is to divide the class into reading groups. When done well, individualizing reading probably gives the most satisfactory results.

Individualizing Reading

Individualized reading is based upon the assumption that students can acquire much the same information and concepts even though they may not read the same books or articles. Thus in the study of Ancient Man students with low reading ability might read such easy reading material as the Abramowitz pamphlet *World History Study Lessons*, whereas others read such difficult and esoteric material as the final chapter of Von Koenigswald's *The Evolution of Man*. Others might be reading in such varied works as Chapters 2 and 3 of Van Loon's *The Story of Mankind*, Ashley Montagu's *Man: His First Million Years*, a *National Geographic* magazine article, or the Dell Visual paperback *Prehistory*. Or they might be reading the first unit "Days before History," in Hartman and Saunders' text *Builders of the Old World*, or Chapter I of Black's textbook *Our World History*.

In any unit, just what the students read does not matter so much as that the students achieve the unit objectives; thus there is no need, ordinarily, for students to all read the same selections. When in a unit one uses the multiple-reading approach, even though the students are reading different texts, the teacher's assignment directs them toward the same instructional objectives. For instance, an assignment might require the readers of Von Koenigswald to find out how early men and women developed their culture and what their first tools were like.[27] Similar questions might be asked of the students reading the Abramowitz material or of those reading Ashley Montagu, while students reading the *National Geographic* magazine might be asked to search for information about life among the ice-age people—their eating habits, hunting techniques, and tools and weapons. The teacher could present the questions to the students orally when giving the assignments or in conferences while they are working. Perhaps a better way would be to prepare a dittoed or mimeographed study guide that would list the questions that the students ought to look for and suggest readings in which the answers might be located. Students could use these guides both to direct their study and as reference lists from which to select their reading.

When conducting individualized reading, you should guide students to select reading suitable to their reading ability, interests, background, and academic needs. In so far as possible, try to match the reading level of the selection with the reading level of the reader. Do not, however, bar students from reading or attempting selections that they might enjoy and profit from just because the selection seems too hard or too easy. Students should be allowed to try difficult assignments. If they find they have bitten off more than they can chew, let them change to something easier. Good readers should be encouraged to read challenging material, but should not be rebuffed because they pick something easy. After all, sometimes the easiest, simplest reading is the best. Common interests and purposes may cause considerable overlap in the reading of able and less able students.

Why do authorities often condemn the use of only one text in the classroom? What is your position on this question?

What advantages does the use of multiple readings have in the subject you wish to teach? What disadvantages? How would you use such a technique in the study of mathematics?

If the students in your class do not all read the same readings, how can you ensure that they all have an opportunity to acquire the important learnings?

Book Reports and Supplementary Reading

Reading reports can be useful in all courses. They can be especially helpful in multitext courses.

Many teachers use formal book reports for collateral readings. In high school honors sections quite frequently the students are required to write formal critical essays or book reviews. For bright, inter-

---

Name of student: _____ Date: _____

Name of Book: _____

Author: _____

Summary of the book:

Critical Comment:

FIGURE 14–4
Book Report Card.

---

[27] Presumably most of the very earliest inventions having to do with food and clothing were made by women.

FIGURE 14–5
Book Report. (Used in Lawrence
High School, Lawrence, Kansas.)

HISTORY
BOOK REPORT

Hour_____

Name _____ When book was read_____
Name of book _____
Author (s) _____ Type of Book_____

Setting of story:
   Where did it take place? _____
   When did it take place? _____
Briefly tell what the book is about: _____
_____
_____
_____
_____
_____
_____
_____
_____

What do you think was the author's aim in writing this book? _____
_____

What about the book was of most interest to you? _____
_____

What is your opinion of this book? Where is the book weak? Strong?
_____
_____
_____

ested students this practice is commendable, but for the average student the accent should be placed on reading rather than reporting. A simple book-report form such as the card illustrated in Figure 14–4 or the simple form appearing as Figure 14–5 should suffice admirably.

Would you be inclined to use the short, informal book report or the more formal book report approach? Why? Would you use both approaches? If so, for what purposes would you use each type? How would you evaluate them?

Oral Reading

Oral reading has many uses. For one, it is an excellent diagnostic tool as we have already seen. For another, it makes it possible for students to learn from one another. It gives the nonreaders a means for learning the content and entering into a discussion; it helps them learn their reading skills as they follow along reading silently, while another student or the teacher reads orally. Further, it has a motivation factor. Some students, even ones who cannot read well, love to read aloud to the class. Sometimes reading orally, or listening to someone else read orally, is more interesting and meaningful than reading silently—especially when the selection to be read is dramatic or poetic. People seldom fully appreciate dramatic works or lyric poetry until they've heard them read aloud well—even if they are reading to themselves. Probably, therefore, there should be daily oral reading in English classes—when teachers or students illustrate points, bring out the effect, savor the flavor, point up the meaning, or just read for fun—and frequent oral reading in other classes. Often a selection gains much meaning when it is well read orally.

To help students learn to read better orally, provide models for them to hear. Play records and tapes for them to listen to and pattern after. Let the students follow the text while these professionals read to them. Let the students record their own reading of the text and then compare their tape (cassette) with that of the professional expert. Give them opportunities to read and act out parts in playlets, historical sketches, and the like. Again, giving the students an opportunity to compare their renditions with those of experts may be beneficial.

Read to your students from time to time both to give pleasure and to facilitate learning. By reading to your students you can create interest, give meaning to difficult passages, foster appreciation, and provide a model for students' reading—and be sure the selection is read correctly—providing of course that you read well. Practice reading orally until you are adept. In the early normal schools and teachers' colleges, prospective teachers studied public speaking, elocution, and oral reading as essential tools of the profession. You would do well to emulate the practice. Read selected important portions of the text to students as they follow along. Bring in documents, incidents, dramatic pieces, pertinent anecdotes, relevant humor, and read them to students. Don't be afraid to ham it up, if necessary. True, you weren't hired to be an entertainer, but a little entertainment does not hurt at appropriate moments. Try starting off an interesting reading assignment by reading it aloud to the class and then turning it over to them to finish

on their own. Record part of the text on a cassette and then let them read as they play the cassette.

Oral reading should not be synonymous with sight reading. To prepare for each oral reading, the student should first read through the selection silently and consider how best to phrase it, where to place the emphasis, and how to pronounce strange and difficult words. In this preparation it is often helpful for the students to underline the thought units in the selection as an aid to improving the phrasing. The oral reading practice may be even more effective if the students read pieces they have written themselves, either singly or in group projects. Then, if possible, the students should record their reading and listen to themselves. In this way they can gain clues of what they should do to improve their phrasing, emphasis and cadence. Sometimes the oral reading practice can best be done in pairs. An example of such dyadic reading in which the use of the first five minutes of each core class was routinely used for "oral reading in duets" is reported by Deborah Elkins.[28]

> There are times when children can share something with only one other classmate. This became evident in one routine procedure which teachers found very fruitful—the use of the first five minutes of every core session for oral reading in "duets." Each child had an outside reading book on his own level, whether it was on the Westward Movement or fantasies for young children or an adventure story. In the adventure-story sequence children were trying to come to some conclusion about what constituted adventure. Did you have to risk your life? Was there adventure in everyday life? Was the same experience adventure for everyone? A standard homework assignment was reading from that book every night. Each child had a mimeographed chart on which he made certain entries.
>
> Then he prepared the paragraph he liked best for reading to his classmate. After reading to his classmate he entered two or three words in the proper column,

---

[28] Deborah Elkins, *Reading Improvement in the Junior High School* (New York: Bureau of Publications, Teachers College, Columbia University, 1963), p. 41.

words he would like to be able to recognize more readily. This work was begun as soon as the children entered the classroom, even while the teacher was on hall duty. Any questions were referred to the teacher. As soon as the teacher returned he circulated around the room, listening, advising, noting progress, making comments of encouragement on the charts wherever this was warranted. In other words, at the start of each day, every child had a chance to read aloud and be heard, and the time consumed was only five minutes.

It is recommended that there be daily oral reading in English classes. Should there be oral reading in other classes such as science, mathematics, industrial arts, and business education? If so, for what purpose? How would you organize it?

Do you agree that oral reading should be used as a means for the building of clear concepts? Why, or why not? If you do, how would you conduct oral reading for this purpose?

Summary

In spite of many changes, reading remains the heart of the secondary school curriculum. Therefore, every teacher should be a teacher of reading. Although reading specialists may teach remedial programs and courses for slow learners, subject-matter teachers must assume responsibility for developmental reading in their subjects.

Selecting the proper reading material is essential. Probably no one text can ever be adequate. To utilize many readings in their classes and to develop techniques for individualizing instruction would usually be more satisfactory. For this reason, full use of the library and the development of classroom libraries is essential.

Ordinarily the reading selection should be matched to the reader's skill. To find the reading level of a book, use formulas such as that of Frye. To determine the student's reading skill, use such techniques as the CLOZE procedure or the silent or oral inventory.

Boys and girls must be taught how to use books effectively and efficiently. They need to know how and when to skim, how and when to read closely, and how to use the aids provided by the author and publisher. Subject teachers must also help students to develop their vocabularies and to read for comprehension. Part of their job is to point out new words and ideas and to suggest methods by which the students can get the most from their reading. But most important of all is their obligation to teach students to read critically with open minds. For students to learn to evaluate what they read is perhaps just as important as their learning to read with understanding.

Oral reading has been neglected in the secondary schools. If students are to be asked to read orally, they should be taught how. On the other hand, teachers must be wary of fads that cause us to emphasize the wrong objectives in our teaching. A recent example is the fad for speed reading. Going through a book quickly is not always a valid goal. Rather, the students should learn to adapt their reading attack to the material to be read.

Additional Reading

Bechtel, Judith, and Bettie Franzblau. *Reading in the Science Classroom.* Washington, DC: National Education Association, 1980.

Bristow, Page S., and Alan E. Farstrup. *Reading in Health/Physical Education/Recreation Classes.* Washington, DC: National Education Association, 1981.

Brunner, Joseph F., and John J. Campbell. *Participation in Secondary Reading: A Practical Approach.* Englewood Cliffs, NJ: Prentice-Hall, 1978.

Bullock, Terry L., and Karl D. Hesse. *Reading in*

the Social Studies Classroom. Washington, DC: National Education Association, 1981.

Burnmeister, Lou E. *Reading Strategies for Middle and Secondary School Teachers*, 2nd ed. Reading, MA: Addison-Wesley, 1978.

Cunningham, James W., Patricia M. Cunningham, and Sharon V. Arthur. *Middle and Secondary School Reading*. New York: Longman, 1981.

Dillner, Martha H., and Joanne P. Olsen. *Personalizing Reading Instruction in Middle Junior and Senior High Schools*, 2nd ed. New York: Macmillan, 1982.

Harker, W. John, ed. *Classroom Strategies for Secondary Reading*. Newark, DE: International Reading Association, 1977.

Herber, Harold L. *Teaching Reading in Content Areas*, 2nd ed. Englewood Cliffs, NJ: Prentice-Hall, 1978.

Hill, Walter R. *Secondary School Reading: Process, Program, Procedure*. Boston: Allyn and Bacon, 1979.

Hodges, Richard E. *Improving Spelling and Vocabulary in the Secondary School*. Urbana, IL: Clearing House on Reading and Communication Skills / National Council of Teachers of English, 1982.

Manning, Maryann Murphy, and Gary L. Manning. *Reading Instruction in the Middle School*. Washington, DC: National Education Association, 1979.

Mikulecky, Larry, and Rita Hough. *Reading in Business Education Classroom*. Washington, DC: National Education Association, 1980.

Purves, Alan C., and Olive Niles. *Becoming Readers in a Complex Society*, Eighty-third Yearbook of the National Society for the Study of Education, Part I. Chicago: University of Chicago Press, 1984.

Robinson, H. Alan. *Teaching Reading and Study Strategies: The Content Areas*. Boston: Allyn and Bacon, 1975.

Roe, Betty, and Barbara D. Stoodt. *Secondary School Reading Instruction: The Content Areas*, 2nd ed. Boston: Houghton Mifflin, 1983.

Shuman, R. Baird. *Strategies in Teaching Reading: Secondary*. Washington, DC: National Education Association, 1978.

Smith, Cyrus F., Jr., and Henry S. Kepner, Jr. *Reading in the Mathematics Classroom*. Washington, DC: National Education Association, 1981.

Thomas, Ellen Lamar, and H. Allan Robinson. *Improving Reading in Every Class*, abridged 2nd ed. Boston: Allyn and Bacon, 1977.

15

Guiding Student Learning

Overview

One of the reasons that students do not learn better in our classes is that we never show them how. Academic skills are not innate. Nor are they easy, as any college student faced with term papers and exam week knows.

Often one hears that students do not have the basic skills, and sometimes they do not, but that does not relieve you from teaching the content of your courses. If the students have not mastered the skills they need, you will have to teach them. Otherwise you will be wasting your effort, their time, and the taxpayers' money. It does no good to complain that they should have learned these things in the lower grades. They didn't, so you must teach them now.

Actually, teaching the academic skills is not as difficult as it may seem. Even the so-called nonreaders and academically disabled students have picked up quite a lot of knowledge in the earlier grades and in their out-of-school experiences. Perhaps they would have picked up more if teachers had been more careful to show them how. We hope that by studying this chapter you will be able to show them how. If we are successful, you will have become familiar with techniques that you can use to

1. Improve students' study techniques.
2. Build up students' skill in taking and using notes.
3. Teach students how to cope with tests.
4. Make your assignments expedite learning.
5. Help with the homework problem.
6. Conduct supervised study.

Improving Students' Study Habits

Some students seem to think that studying is the same as reading. This is not the case. Study includes all those activities that have to do with learning through planned effort. Thus, not only reading but notetaking at lectures, preparation of papers, library work, reference work, problem solving, intensive reading, and skimming should all be considered study activities. They all are techniques that boys and girls need to learn before they can become efficient students.

When teachers first became aroused to the fact that boys and girls needed help in learning how to study, they developed rules for study as guides for the students. Among the admonitions often included in such rules are the following.

1. **Plan your studying.** Make a schedule and stick to it. Have a definite place to work. Make your studying routine and part of your routine.
2. **Start off immediately.** Have your material ready before you sit down to work. Be sure you understand the assignment before you begin it.
3. **Space your learning.** Take two- to three-minute breaks. If possible, take your rests at natural breaks in the material you are studying. Try to master one lesson or selection before moving on to the next.
4. **Study actively.** Develop an interest in what you are studying. Try to find out something. React to the readings. Ask yourself questions. Recite. Work out examples. Illustrate principles. Apply your learning as soon as possible.
5. **Vary your study technique** to suit the subject and your purpose. Learn materials in the form you expect to use them.
6. **Avoid rote memorization.** Memorize those things you need to memorize by the meaningful techniques of logical memory.
7. **Evaluate your own work and study habits.** Try to improve faulty habits. Try to increase your vocabulary; look up words you do not know. Make use of the aids provided in your books. Do not skip headings, marginal notes, questions,

Use this list to evaluate your own study habits. Which of the "rules for study" do you find most useful in your own studying? Are there any that do not seem to work for you? How many of them have you really tried faithfully? If your study habits diverge sharply from those suggested by these rules, maybe you should consider revamping your study procedures. Are there other procedures that you feel seem to work effectively for you?

Pick out several of the rules you consider important and try to devise activities that would make these rules become part of the students' behavior.

prefatory remarks, tables of contents, charts, and graphs. Use them. Take full notes but do not attempt to rewrite the text.

8. Check your work and proofread your papers before handing them in.

On the whole, the advice in these suggestions is good, although we must remember that what is good for the goose is not necessarily good for gander and that, as in everything else, we all have our little idiosyncrasies when it comes to studying.

Teaching How to Study

You can expect little success in developing students' study skills unless you teach these skills directly and give students considerable practice with them in the classroom. In some schools a course in how to study is provided. Such courses may be helpful, but they do not relieve you of the responsibility for teaching study skills. Why not? For one thing, different subjects require different study techniques if study is to be effective. Consequently, in each of your courses, you should try to teach study techniques proper to your course to any youngster who has not mastered them. Furthermore, learning how to study comes only from practicing good techniques, and where else can students practice but in their ordinary courses? Thus every teacher is responsible for teaching students how to study for each course. Among the skills with which the students may need help are

1. How to read for information.
2. How to analyze a problem.
3. How to plan for study.
4. How to review.
5. How to evaluate materials.
6. How to use charts, graphs, and other audiovisual aids.
7. How to take notes.
8. How to concentrate.

9. How to analyze.
10. How to outline.
11. How use the library.
12. How to build an adequate vocabulary both general and specialized.

Learning to Study Independently

Because many teachers do not realize that boys and girls must be taught how to use reading as a tool for studying, many students progress through the elementary, middle, and secondary grades without ever learning how to study or how to extricate the meat from a reading selection. Therefore you should take special care to make sure that your students learn how to read and study independently. Use the following technique to start poor readers toward independent reading and studying. Later, when the students have acquired some skill in independent reading, you can move up to directed reading lessons and then finally to the more sophisticated SQ3R system described in later sections.

A General Study Plan for Poor Readers

When teaching poor readers beginning study skills, we recommend that you

First. Analyze the content to be read to see what principal ideas and supporting concepts and information it presents. If your conception of the lesson or unit indicates principal ideas, concepts or information not in the reading, then you must change your conception or provide the knowledge in some other way.

Second. Decide just what you expect the students to learn from the reading.

Third. Prepare the students for their reading. Try to provide motivation; show through discussion or some other technique how the reading relates to previous lessons or students' experiences in and out of school; go over the vocabulary making sure that students can match meanings with the important key words; give your students clear directions on how to read the assignment; and try to set up in the students' minds an anticipation of something desirable to be found in the reading. Probably these directions can be given and the purpose set through discussion and a study guide that shows the students what to do and how to do it. These study guides are probably most effective when they give the students statements or matching exercises that present students alternatives from which they can choose correct solutions rather than questions. (See Figure 15–1 for an example.) This type of guide makes it possible to run through the process of the comprehension skill in a supportive situation when a series of questions would just cause them to founder. In effect the guide puts students in a position where they simulate the skill rather than perform it, because it eliminates the need for the students' finding the solution to the items completely on their own.

Fourth. Walk the students through the reading in a group situation. Probably it is best to divide the class into random groups that read and discuss the selection together.

Fifth. Follow up with class discussion, questions, and testing as desired. Use this time to clinch the content learning and clarify the principles, concepts and information that were to be learned.

You can use this plan at any or all of the three levels of comprehension. All one has to do is to set a goal for the lesson and build a study guide and study procedures accordingly. Once the students have mastered the comprehension skills with the guides, you can gradually remove the guides and allow them to read independently according to the Direct Reading Activity plan or SQ3R plan described in the following sections.

Step 1. Which of the following statements do you believe to be true? Check them in column I.

I   II

    Most snakes are dangerous to humans.
    Snakes can swallow food bigger than their normal mouth opening.
    Snakes smell through their tongues.
    Snakes eat live animals.
    Usually snakes are full grown by the time they are three years old.

Step 2. Read the selection below. In Column II check the statements that are true according to the selection. How well did your beliefs agree with the facts stated in the selection?

[Selection omitted to save space.]

Step 3. Each of the following items occurs in the selection. Number the items in the order in which they appear in the paragraph.
_____ Snakes are reptiles.
_____ Snakes have large scales on their bellies.
_____ There are 36 kinds of poisonous snakes in the United States.
_____ Snakes' eyelids do not move.
_____ Snakes have small hooked teeth.
_____ There are 250 kinds of snakes in the United States.

FIGURE 15–1
Example of a Study Guide Suitable for Use with Poor Readers.

Directed–Reading Lesson

For students who do read but have not yet learned to direct themselves, one can use the directed-reading lesson. This technique is designed to teach students how to study and how to comprehend and retain what they read. Basically the method consists of five steps.

1. Prepare the students by going over new vocabulary and ideas and reviewing old material and experiences so that they can see the relationships between the new and the old.

2. Have students skim the selection and look at pictures, headings, and so on.
3. Help students formulate questions about the selection to be read, for instance:
   a. What should a student try to find out when studying the selection?
   b. Is this the kind of selection that must be studied carefully?
   c. How does this selection connect with other lessons studied in the past?
Three or four questions are quite enough. Too many questions may confuse and discourage the students. The questions should be student-made rather than teacher-made, if at all possible.
4. Let the students read the selection to themselves.
5. Discuss the reading. By using questions, help the students see the relationships among the facts presented and also relationships to what has been learned previously.[1]

Reading in Questions

An open, inquisitive mind is necessary for productive studying. Because of the need to encourage this frame of mind the following procedure is recommended for studying a chapter or similar reading, once the learner has become self directing.

1. Survey the chapter.
2. Determine what one can expect to learn in the chapter. State as questions or a question outline.
3. Read the chapter to find the answers to the questions.
4. Evaluate what has been read.
5. Apply the information to specific situations or problems.
6. Review by asking oneself the original questions.
7. Reread quickly (skim).

The heart of the method just discussed is asking oneself questions before, during, and after one's

reading. Teachers should encourage such self-questioning in their students. At first, however, the teacher may need to do the questioning directly, either orally or by means of a study guide. If the reading were to be about the prehistoric men mentioned in the preceding chapter, for instance, one might ask the students to look for the answer to such questions as

- The author implies that prehistoric humans were probably just as smart as modern people. What evidence do you find to support that statement?
- What does the author think of prehistoric art? Do you agree with him?
- In what respect do prehistoric people's achievements seem to foreshadow those of modern humans?
- If you were to pick the one general idea as the main idea presented in this selection, what would it be?

Another technique that may be useful for developing searching attitudes in students is to develop the questions together in a discussion before starting on the readings. Such a discussion might be launched by the teacher's asking a question like "What do you think you want to find out from this reading?" or "What do you think that the reading might tell you?" In the case of the prehistoric men again, students might want to know about such things as

- What did prehistoric people eat?
- How did they get their food?
- Where did they live?
- Did they believe in God?
- What did they wear?
- What did they do for recreation?

As such questions are developed in class discussion they could be put on the board by a student recorder. Then, if one wishes, these questions could be made into a formal list or study guide. (Figure 15–2.) In some instances at least, it would probably be better to let individual students adapt these questions to their own use, each one taking as many,

[1] Leonard H. Clark, *Teaching Social Studies in Secondary Schools: A Handbook* (New York: Macmillan, 1973), p. 122.

FIGURE 15–2
Sample Study Guide. (*Twelfth-Grade Philosophy, Cheltenham, Pennsylvania.*)

Factors in the consideration of Means and Ends.

1. Can necessity create its own law?
2. Can "ends" be judged without previous standards of judgment?
3. Who decides, or how is it decided, that an "end" is good?
4. Are the "means" employed toward marking an "end" good?
5. When is necessity "real," when is it "imagined"?
6. Can we separate "means" from "ends"?
7. Are the "means" to be judged before or after the "ends" are achieved?
8. Is the question of the "end justifying the means" equally true for both individuals and states?
9. Do the means determine the ends?
10. Does the pinch of necessity preclude any national consideration of means?
11. How do we consider degrees of "necessity"?
12. How can we determine whether some ends are better than others?
13. Are certain types of "means" and "ends" peculiar to specific aspects of society?
14. Are certain "means" improper, criminal, etc., even when they are not employed?
15. Can means and ends ever be considered amoral?
16. Is law a fact only when it can be enforced?
17. Can evil means ever be employed toward a good end?
18. How can we evaluate abstract ends?
19. How is the concept of what constitutes an end to be reached?
20. Can ends exist independent of the individual?

---

or as few, as seems desirable for their own questions, adding other questions if they wish.

Another approach would be for the students to write down what they expected to learn from the reading. Their lists would be used as the basis for class discussion, or could be checked over by the teacher for approval and possible additional suggestions, before beginning the reading. This approach is good when students' reading is individualized. Ordinarily, students should get the teacher's approval of their questions before they start reading. It is not wise, however, to hold up a student who is ready to read just because the teacher has not had time to approve the student's questions. When that student is ready to go, let him or her proceed under temporary clearance. The checking can come later. In determining the questions to be asked the student can benefit much from knowing how to use the guides and aids put in the text by the author.

The questions asked should not be just questions of fact. Instead put emphasis on relationships: Why? How? So what? Of what importance is this? What's the point? These are the kinds of questions that will bring out ideas. Aim the questions at the big ideas, not the details. Perhaps the first main question in every list should be "What was the idea the author wanted to get across?" And probably the second question should be "What details did the author use to try to get this idea across to the reader?" These same questions should be asked in the students' tests also, because it is by test questions that students determine what learning the teacher really values.

Questions are most useful for developing study skills only when they are asked *before* the student starts reading. One of the reasons that students do not learn to comprehend better is that neither they nor their teacher think to ask the questions beforehand. Asking questions afterward will merely tell whether or not one has understood; it will not help students develop skill in comprehending. The time for the reader to be active and alert is during the reading.

One way to help students read in questions is to give them study guides that point out to them what they should read, what they should learn, how they should learn it and so on.

SQ3R

For the purpose of simplification and for mnemonic purposes these study procedures are often called SQ3R. These letters stand for Survey, Question, Read, Recite, and Review. Skill in these procedures must be developed by direct instruction and much supervised practice in the middle school years.

Learning to Budget Time

In your discussions with your students you should help them learn how to budget their time. Discuss with them just what they do with their time during any twenty-four-hour period. An interesting exercise is for students to make graphs of the time they spend at different activities each day. You should also encourage students to arrange for regular times and places for study. If your discussions are frank and fruitful you may find that some students truly have neither the time nor the place for home study. In such cases teachers may be able to help the student find time to study in school or in class. The discussions should also include the importance of learning good study habits and provide clues by which students may improve their

Pick a selection from a textbook you might use in one of your middle or high school classes. Set up a lesson for teaching this selection following the general plan for teaching poor readers with a suitable study guide. Prepare another plan following the directed reading lesson technique for this or another selection.

If you are not familiar with the SQ3R (i.e., reading in questions) technique, practice using it as you study your college courses. Most people find it helpful and you should become expert at it so you can be a proficient guide and model for your students.

use of time. Do not forget: efficient learning does not come naturally; it must be learned.

The Students' Responsibility for Learning

In addition to trying to teach your students how to learn well, you must also work to convince the students to accept the responsibilities of learning. Every student should learn quickly that there is no royal road to learning. Teachers should show the students how to attack their assignments, but they should not deprive them of their initiative. The idea is to start them off, to encourage them, and to guide them—not to baby them. Perhaps you should conduct a group discussion in which students consider how they would study the material if there were no teacher, then formulate the attack, and work it out under your guidance. This method has the advantage of helping the students find their way under their own initiative yet with the security of the teacher's presence in case of need.

Using a Graded Sequence

No matter what methods are used to teach study skills, the material taught should be graded according to complexity and difficulty. Study skills are both difficult and complex. For this reason, they should be taught in sequence; the easier skills should precede the more difficult ones, the simple should precede the complex. The teaching of how to read for information previously cited serves as an excellent example of this point. Here the teacher first teaches the student how to extract the meaning from a sentence. This having been mastered, one proceeds to teach how to get the meaning from a paragraph. From there one goes on to getting the meaning from a section, a chapter, and finally the entire book.

Building more complex skills on simple study skills is a must. To do this successfully requires the cooperative effort of the teachers in the various grade levels, and the teacher's careful diagnosis of each student's present level of proficiency.

> In what ways could teachers of various grade levels cooperate in the teaching of study skills in your field?
>
> In what ways is the studying of algebra different from studying social studies? From home economics? What skills may be used in studying these courses? Do the necessary skills vary from topic to topic within the fields? How?

Teaching Students to Take Notes

Outlining

Without any doubt being able to outline well is one of the most valuable skills a student can have and teachers in all subjects can help to be sure that students master it. To teach the students to outline correctly, the National Association of Secondary School Principals has recommended the fol-

lowing techniques which have been well proven over the years.[2]

1. Use easy materials and short selections in teaching pupils the mechanics of outlining. The following steps may be followed in teaching pupils to make outlines.
   a. Teacher and pupils working together select the main topics.
   b. Pupils, unaided, select the main topics.
   c. Teacher and pupils select the main topics, leaving space for subheads. Teacher and pupils then fill in these subtopics.
   d. Main topics are selected by the teachers and pupils and are written on the blackboard. Pupils then fill in the subtopics unaided.
   e. Pupils write the main topics and subheads without help.
   f. Pupils organize, in outline form, data gathered from many sources.
2. Train pupils to find the main topics and to place them in outline form. Use books with paragraph headings.
   a. Have pupils read the paragraphs and discuss the headings. Suggest other possible headings and have pupils decide why the author selected the headings he used.
   b. Match a given list of paragraph headings with numbered paragraphs.
   c. Have pupils read a paragraph with this question in mind, "What is the main idea in this paragraph?" Write a number of suggested answers on the blackboard. Choose the best one.
3. Provide practice in filling in subtopics.
   a. The teacher writes the main topics on the board or uses a text that has the main headings. Teacher and pupils then fill in the subheads.
   b. Have pupils skim other articles for more information and read carefully when additional material which is suitable for subheads is found. Add

---

[2] "Teaching Essential Reading Skills," Reprinted by permission from the Bulletin of the National Association of Secondary-School Principals (February 1950). Copyright: Washington, DC. Based on "How to Teach Pupils to Outline," *Teachers' Guide to Child Development in the Intermediate Grades.* Prepared under the direction of the California State Curriculum Commission. Sacramento: California State Department of Education, 1936, pp. 294–295.

these new subheads. Do the same for new main topics.

    c. When pupils have gathered sufficient data, have them reread the complete outline and, if necessary, rearrange the order of the topics.

4. Give instructions in making a standard outline form. Many secondary school pupils do not know how to make an outline. Emphasize the fact that in a correct outline there must always be more than one item in the series under any subdivision. If there is an "a" there must also be a "b"; if there is a "1" there must also be a "2," etc. . . .

5. Have pupils use this outline form in preparing and giving oral reports.

6. To develop ability to draw valid conclusions, have pupils use facts and ideas which have been organized in outline form, not only as a basis for an oral report or as an exercise in outlining a chapter, but also as the basis for drawing conclusions. To check pupils' ability to make outlines, prepare lessons based on the following suggestions.

    a. List main points and subpoints consecutively. Have pupils copy these, indenting to show subordination of subtopics and writing correct numbers and letters in front of each point.

    b. List main topics and subtopics in mixed order and have pupils rearrange and number them.

    c. List main topics with Roman numerals. List subtopics (all one value) with Arabic numerals. Have pupils organize subpoints under correct main points.

    d. Present short paragraphs of well-organized material and have pupils write main topics and specified number of subtopics.

    e. Present part of a skeleton outline and have students complete it.

    f. Have pupils outline a problem without assistance. Class discussion is valuable in checking a lesson of this type.

Lecture Notes

Use similar techniques to teach students to take notes from lectures. During early lectures it is wise to provide a skeleton outline which students are to fill in with subheads and details. During the mid-dle and early secondary school years you should stop to point out where you are on the outline from time to time to be sure that everyone is with you. Later this help may not be necessary. As the students become more skillful in taking lecture notes the outline skeleton should gradually diminish until at last it finally disappears. After lectures in which students have taken notes following their own version of the outline, you would do well to project your outline on the screen so that the students can compare their version with yours. Also, try to give students plenty of clues to the structure of the lectures as you go on. Such helps as *firstly's, secondly's,* and so on, will not only help to keep the inexperienced lecture-note taker on the track but may help keep you on it also. Skeleton outlines, dittoed or projected on the blackboard, are also excellent for this purpose. Lecturers who wander are difficult for any note takers—for beginners they are impossible!

Train students to be on the lookout for such word clues as the *firstly's* and *secondly's* we just mentioned, *most important, the real cause, finally,* and so on. These are the same signal words that we have noted in the section on reading comprehension. Students should also be coached to look out for such other signals as repetition of certain points again and again, changes in the lecturer's tone of voice, gestures and points noted in the summary and introductory remarks. All of these are clues that point out what the lecturer thinks to be important and should find their way into the students' lecture notes.

Reading Notes

Notes in which the students record their reactions to chapters, sections, and passages are greatly helpful, for they cause students to think about what they have read. Outlines consisting of questions with their answers have the additional advantage of highlighting the salient points. Students can also benefit from writing summaries of what they find to be important in the various chapters they read. Such notetaking makes students active participants in their reading. All too often students, unless they use reaction notetaking or summary techniques, can read and outline sections of a book without turning on their minds at all.

Coordinating Lecture and Reading Notes

If one keeps lecture notes on the lefthand side pages of one's notebook and the reading notes on the righthand side, it is possible to set up a coordinated system of notes that should be very helpful when reviewing and studying the notes. And the notes should be reviewed and studied! Teach your students to review their notes as soon as possible after they have written them. The quicker one reviews and studies one's notes the more effective they will be. If one waits too long, it becomes a case of relearning rather than reinforcing what one has learned. Besides, stale notes have a habit of becoming almost meaningless.

Teaching Students to Take Tests

The number of students who do not know how to prepare for and to take tests is amazing, especially when one considers the importance of tests in school life. Experience shows that instruction in preparing for and taking tests can make substantial improvement in students' test scores. Grambs and her associates recommend that the following procedures be taught to students in order to prepare them for taking tests.

  1. Before the test
     Review.
     Re-read.
     Relax.
     Rest.

  2. Take the test with a calm realistic attitude. Be on time. Take the proper materials with you.
  3. Survey the entire test before you begin. Make notes if permitted.
  4. Do the easiest questions first. Skip anything that is difficult until you have completed all other items.
  5. During the test, stop periodically (if it is long) and relax; close your eyes, breathe deeply, consciously work to relieve tension.[3]

Did any teacher ever take time to teach you how to take reading and lecture notes when you were in middle and high school? If so, how did that teacher proceed? Did it help? If not, how did you learn to take notes well? Or did you?

Ordinarily it is best to teach study skills as an integral part of the content. How could you do it in a course you might teach? Could you use the procedure recommended by Brunner and Campbell?

Evaluate the procedures for test taking recommended by Grambs and her associates.

Assignments

Good assignments are absolutely essential for both motivating and guiding learning. It has often been said that boys and girls usually would be quite willing to do their schoolwork if they could only figure out what the teacher wanted them to do and how to do it. There is more than a germ of truth in this statement. Most of us have been in classes in which we did not know what to do. This fault is all too common. If you find your students are not doing their assignments but instead are saying, "I did not know, I had no book," and the like, you should check your directions. Often the fault lies

---

[3] Jean D. Grambs and John C. Carr, *Modern Methods in Secondary Education*, 4th ed. (New York: Holt, 1979), p. 325.

in the assignment. If you hope to keep students working, you must be sure the assignments are definite, the directions clear, and the materials available.

Purposes

In the past the assignment has been almost synonymous with homework. In many classrooms, even today, the assignment consists of a hurried shout at the end of the period—often drowned out by the clamor of the bell and the scuffling of feet eager to be on their way. Today one should think of a good assignment in a different way. An assignment is a job to be done, whether at home or in class. It may be assigned by the teacher or arrived at through the cooperative effort of both teacher and students. No matter who prepares the assignment it should serve the following purposes.

1. Set the direction of study and outline the scope of the task.
2. Motivate the students and prepare them for the task.
3. Help the learners to the means for accomplishing the task, that is, establish possible methods and materials. If necessary show them how.
4. Adapt the tasks to the needs of the various students.

Thus the assignment is an essential factor in motivation and a basic part of any lesson. Let us look at these functions briefly.

To Set the Direction and the Scope of the Task

It is almost impossible to do anything unless one knows what to do. The purpose of the assignment is to make each student's task clear and definite. Some teachers tell the students just what is to be done. Others develop the task cooperatively with the group. Whichever method you use, however, try to make sure that each and every student knows exactly what to do. In case of a problem, for instance, make sure that the students understand the problem, that the problem is well enough defined to be manageable, and that the students know how to go about solving it.

To this end, the assignment must be clear and definite. Probably it is best to give it to the students in writing. Short assignments may be placed on the chalkboard. A wise practice is to reserve a specific spot on the chalkboard for assignments and to always write the daily assignment on that spot. Longer assignments should be duplicated. Written assignments minimize students' forgetting what it is they were going to do. Also, setting the assignment down in writing helps to lessen chances for misunderstandings—both on the part of the student and the teacher—of what the task is.

To Prepare the Students for the Job to Be Done

This preparation includes supplying the background material the students need before starting the new task and providing for adequate motivation. Since the assignment determines what is to be done, it is particularly important to make sure that the students know why they should do this job and why it is worth doing.

To Point Out How to Do It

Although teachers should avoid spoonfeeding the students, they should also be sure the students know how to go about carrying out the task. If it is a job of studying through reading, for instance, the key words should be pointed out, and suggestions concerning what to look for should be made. In other words, the teacher should try to make sure that the students know how to use the methods and materials available to them.

To Provide Every Student with an Appropriate Task

It is hard to prove any subject is truly essential except as it meets the needs of youngsters. If this is true, any assignment that places subject matter above the individual differences of the youngsters is of doubtful validity.

The Marks of a Good Assignment

What, then, are the marks of a good assignment? The following list will suggest some criteria for evaluating an assignment.

1. Is it worthwhile?
2. Does it seem worthwhile to the student? In other words, does it capitalize on pupil interest or create student interest?
3. Is it clear?
4. Is it definite?
5. Does it provide for the differences in students— i.e., their different aptitudes, abilities, and interests?
6. Is it reasonable as far as length and difficulty are concerned?
7. Does it show the student how to go about it? Does it suggest methods and materials that may be used profitably?
8. Does it provide the student with the background necessary for completing the assignment satisfactorily, e.g., vocabulary?

Use these criteria to judge assignments given in your college courses.

Do your college assignments perform the functions assignments should perform? If they fail, in what ways do they fail?

A student teacher's assignment to his United States history class was, "Read pages 184–297 for tomorrow." In what way is this assignment deficient?

Making the Assignment

In order to make an assignment effective, take time to develop it sufficiently. Even a short assignment may require ten minutes for its presentation.

For longer assignments the use of one or more entire periods is not unusual. In fact, to develop properly a long-term assignment or a unit assignment in less than a period is virtually impossible, particularly if the assignment is developed by the teacher and class cooperatively. Beware of giving an assignment at the last minute just as the bell is going to ring (or has started to ring). Students seldom take such assignments seriously. They cannot listen to orders carefully in the last minute rush. There is not time for them to digest the assignment, to ask questions, or to make notes, or for you to give the students direction, to clarify what is to be done, and to motivate the students. Last-minute assignments are almost always disasters.

It matters little whether the assignment is developed at the beginning, middle, or end of a period as long as you allow time enough to do the job properly and make sure that the assignment fits into that spot naturally. To be most effective, the presenting of the assignment should probably immediately precede the task to be done. Homework assignments should be presented at the propitious moment in the lesson when the content of the lesson is most suitable as a background for making the assignment.

Teaching Study Skills in the Assignment

Although teachers often neglect it, the assignment offers a golden opportunity for teaching study skills. It gives the teacher and the students an opportunity to discuss the materials and sources available, the use of the materials, the relative merits of various study techniques and procedures, and the ways to carry out these techniques and procedures.

The reverse side of the assignment coin can also be used to improve study skills. After an assignment has been completed, the students can learn about study skills and their efficiency by discussing the methods different students used to study the assignment and the relative success of the various methods.

Organizers

Advance organizers are introductions to the unit or content to be learned. Their purpose is to give the learners a structure to build on as they learn— or in the words of their inventor, "an educational scaffolding for the stable incorporation and retention of the more detailed and differentiated material that follows."[4] This organizer may be either written or visual. It may consist of a short exposition that provides students with the information that they need to tackle the new learning (an expository organizer), or it may show students graphically the relationship of what they have already learned with what they are to learn (graphic organizer). In either case it should line out in general abstract terms principles on which the students can hang the facts and concepts they will learn, and in general help them see the meaning and relationship of the new subject matter to be learned.

According to Richard E. Mayer, organizers usually have the following characteristics:

> (1) Short set of verbal or visual information, (2) Presented prior to learning a larger body of to-be-learned information, (3) Containing no specific content from the to-be-learned information, (4) Providing a means of generating the logical relationships among the elements in the to-be-learned information, (5) Influencing the learner's encoding process. The manner in which an organizer influences encoding may serve either of two functions: to provide a new general organization as an assimilative context that would not have normally been present, or to activate a general organization from the learner's existing knowledge that would not have normally been used to assimilate the new material.[5]

Mayer goes on to say that "existing research seems to suggest that subject areas that might be most influenced by organizers are topics in mathematics and science."[6]

Organizers presented as diagrams, models, or illustrations are especially helpful for alerting students to the relationships and structure in the content they are about to study. For the teaching of reading in the content subject, Herber recommends the use of "graphic organizers" that give students a "structural overview" of what they are to read and study.[7]

Study Guides and Learning Packets

Study guides and learning packets may serve somewhat the same purpose. Basically they are usually duplicated materials that outline to the students what they are to study; ask questions that will point up what to study; suggest problems that will initiate students' thinking; and provide exercises that will build up concepts, show relationships and generally identify and pull together the ideas, skills, and attitudes that are the instructional goals.[8]

Homework

Educational reformers of the 1980s make much of the benefits of homework. Among the virtues cited are:

1. Homework promotes self-discipline.
2. Homework lengthens the amount of time students spend in learning activities.
3. Homework fosters student initiative, independence, and responsibility.
4. Homework reinforces classroom learning.
5. Homework brings home and school together.
6. Homework provides opportunities for providing for and capitalizing on individual differences.

---

[4] David P. Ausubel, *Educational Psychology: A Cognitive View* (New York: Holt, 1968), p. 148.

[5] Richard E. Mayer, "Can Advance Organizers Influence Meaningful Learning?" *Review of Educational Research* (Spring, 1979), **49**:382.

---

[6] Ibid.

[7] Graphic organizers are discussed in Chapter 14.

[8] See Chapter 10.

Research indicates that probably some of the faith these reformers put in homework is justified. Properly conducted homework activities can make schooling more effective. In mathematics, for instance, research studies indicate that boys and girls who are required to do homework seem to do better on tests than those who are not so required. Similar results have been found in studies for eighth-graders in English and social studies. The catch, however, is that the homework should be properly conducted. Otherwise it can become a waste of time and retard learning.

What Kind of Homework?

Homework assignments may be of several types. One type calls for reading and studying new or old material. Another type calls for the completion of written work to be handed in. Still another type consists of solving problems, working on projects, or performing other tasks that cannot be done well in school, for example, the surveying of a portion of the community. In general, these types of homework assignments can be broken down into three categories: preparation activities, extension of classroom learning activities, and practice and drill activities.

Preparation Activities. By far the largest number of assignments at present seems to consist solely of exhortations to read certain pages in the textbook in preparation for the next day's recitation. All too often preparation activities of this sort fail because the teacher does not give the students proper direction. Reading for tomorrow is not much help if you do not know what to look for and focus on. If teachers spent more care in using the procedure outlined in the sections on making assignments when making homework reading assignments, they would be more successful. Also although reading the text can make excellent homework assignments, teachers tend to overwork it. The list of other types of activities that could make homework interesting as well as informative is almost endless and includes the following:

- Individualized instruction.
- Collateral reading.
- Field trips.
- Preparing a demonstration.
- Projects.
- Committee assignments.
- Observation.
- Radio listening.
- Newspaper study.
- Attending meetings, hearings, and so on.
- Notebook work.
- Problems.
- Library work.
- Interviews.
- Television viewing.
- Reading magazines.
- Use of community resources.
- Watching films.
- Preparing oral reports.

There seems to be no excuse for not having a variety of preparatory homework experiences.

Extension Activities. In general, however, homework is more suitable for reinforcing or extending old learning. The homework should consist of activities that students can do on their own. It should be a logical extension of the classroom work that they can do without supervision or teacher assistance. The learning of new techniques and new materials is usually best done in class situations where the teacher can guide the students and thus guard them from learning the new techniques or new concepts incorrectly. Moreover, assignments of new materials for study at home usually place too much emphasis on memorizing as opposed to understanding or thinking. *That is why homework assignments that carry on some activity started in class often result in better learning,* particularly when the activities are the kinds that require library or laboratory work such as digging out information from several sources and analyzing and identifying or defining problems. Furthermore, students are less likely to be forgetful when the homework stems out of, or continues, an activity they are already working on and is tailored to their interests or needs. Homework never should be just something added on or, even worse, a punishment. It is more likely to be profitable if it extends the learning by applying it to new conditions or situations, requiring students to use their imagination and creative thought, stressing student initiative, individualizing assignments to fit students' talents and interests, and allowing students to plan new projects and to use what they have learned to break new ground. Further investigating a problem that has been launched during class discussion or digging up arguments pro or con for class discussion of controversial issues are examples of the most rewarding type of homework activities. Long-term projects and activities, particularly activities that require independent work, creative thought, original thought, and individual research and study, can be excellent for extending classroom learning, particularly of bright, interested students. With proper encouragement and sufficient variety and recognition of student interests, homework can be an avenue for developing permanent interests that carry over into adult life or even become careers.

Practice Activities.   In some studies such as mathematics, homework most commonly consists of practice activities. However, this approach is not always the most fruitful. To practice activities of a skill after one has learned the basic technique is excellent, but not if the practice is merely repetition for repetition's sake. Moreover, bright students tend to get the knack quickly and then either quit or suffer through the remaining exercises without learning anything more while other students soon get bored and frustrated and give up. That is one reason why it is better to arrange exercises in order of difficulty. Thus slower students, for instance, who have success with the easier problems in the beginning of the assignment, are encouraged to keep on trying.

A Judicious Mix.   It is probably best not to become overcommitted to any one type of homework. A judicious mix of several types is probably the best approach. In algebra, for instance, "spiral approach" homework assignments that combine some "review exercises, some exploratory exercises designed to set the stage for future work, and the current assignment" seem to work best.[9]

Making Homework Assignments

In general, the rules for making assignments spelled out earlier in the chapter apply to all types of assignments. Perhaps homework assignments require more care than other assignments, for you will not be there to straighten out student misunderstandings and to help students when they get stuck.

In the first place it is most important that students be motivated well. Homework that carries strong student motivation goes along satisfactorily. Homework for which students are not well motivated would be better done in school under supervision. The importance of homework needs to be carefully spelled out to the students. General explanations of the role of homework should be part of one's classroom management techniques. Passing on such explanations to the students' parents via letter or handouts may give good returns on your investment of time and effort.

Second, the homework assignment must be very clear. Ordinary daily homework assignments may not need detailed explanations but you should make sure that every student knows the purpose of the assignment, how it ties into what has been done before, and what will happen later. As with any other assignment, you should plan with the students how to attack the assignment and teach whatever skills the students need. This all can be done individually, in small groups or in large groups as the occasion demands.

Third, the homework should match the abilities, talents, and maturity levels of the students. Homework that is too difficult for students frustrates

---

[9] Donald J. Dessard, "Algebra," in *Classroom Ideas from Research in Secondary School Mathematics* (Reston, VA: National Council of Teachers of Mathematics, 1983), p. 9.

them; homework that is too easy bores them. Since students' abilities differ, these facts imply that homework should be at least somewhat individualized.

Students who are having difficulty with the subject, who have schedule problems, who have missed school, who have skipped classwork because of distractions of various kinds, who have special interests or special talents, or who are involved in community and school activities will not all benefit optimally from the same homework assignment. So, insofar as possible, you should adjust students' homework to fit their individual needs, abilities, aptitudes, and interests. Long-term or unit assignments that allow students to select homework activities from a number of options are excellent because they allow for differences in students. Probably the day for exhortations for everyone to read such and such pages and do exercises x, y, and z in the text for tomorrow should soon become a thing of the past.

Homework should not be used as a substitute for independent study, however. Homework can develop independence, but independent study is something else again. Independent study should be done in the classroom, in the resource center, and at home as a total strategy. It is not a tactic to be added on to ordinary teaching as homework.

Fourth, be sure that your homework assignments consist of activities the students can do on their own. If the students cannot complete the assignment without help, do not assign it as homework.

Fifth, when feasible, spread assignments over a period of time. Assignments that distribute the homework over several days seem to result in better learning than those that mass everything into a simple daily assignment. Longer-term assignments can also be used advantageously as we have seen.

How Much Homework?

How much homework should you assign? The answer to this question depends upon your school, your subject and your students. Perhaps your school administration will have established some sort of policy concerning homework. If so, you must conform. Should the policy be a poor one, you might work for its improvement, but under no circumstances should you flout it.

If your school has no policy concerning homework, you should probably fall in line with the school tradition, if any. In any case, try to make sure that students are neither overburdened nor underworked. Often a good unit assignment takes care of this problem automatically. At any rate, by giving long-term assignments you give the students an opportunity to adjust their work so that they can avoid being overburdened by simultaneous major assignments in several courses. Therefore, even if you do not use the unit approach, it may be wise to give out homework assignments for a week or more ahead. Almost invariably, it is more satisfactory to give assignments in writing to prevent confusion, misunderstanding, and the need for repeating the assignment. (A homework announcement section on the chalkboard can be a great help.)

In making decisions about how much homework to give, you might want to consider the following points.

1. We suggest that the daily homework load (study periods plus home study) of all courses combined should be
   None in grades five and six.
   One to two hours in grades seven and eight.
   Two to three hours in grades nine and ten.
   Three hours in grades eleven and twelve.
   In planning homework assignments do not forget that there are more important things than homework in adolescent life.
2. The amount of time available for study during the school day and for a reasonable period after school hours divided by the number of daily classes the student must prepare for represents a fair estimate of the amount of time available for homework for any one class.
3. To avoid excessive homework assignments it is suggested that teachers in grades seven and eight stagger their assignments, e.g., science and math on Monday and Wednesday, English and social

studies on Tuesday and Thursday, and no homework on Friday. (The value of giving assignments to be done over the weekend is dubious.) In the senior high school grades homework time can be equally divided among the various courses. At all levels due allowance should be made for major assignments and tests. (As a rule college-preparatory classes seem to have more homework than other classes do.)

4. The amount of time it takes a student to do assignments depends upon the student. An assignment that one student can do well in thirty minutes may take another student much more than an hour. For this reason, if no other, individualize homework assignments as much as possible.

5. In some classes and schools, students do not do their homework. In such cases it is futile to assign it. Instead, use supervised study and laboratory teaching and try to build up the attitudes and ideals that will cause the students to want to study in out-of-class hours. Important ingredients in this process are the introduction of assignments that seem to be worth doing and positive reinforcement when students attempt to do the assignments.

6. From time to time check on the length of time your assignments are taking. In addition to asking students how long an assignment took them, check by giving pupils sample homework assignments to do during class periods so as to see how long it takes pupils to complete them.

At this point a word of warning may be in order. There seems to have been a tendency for some high school teachers to illustrate how tough they are and what high standards they hold by piling great amounts of homework on their students. Unreasonably long assignments have no place in the secondary school for several reasons. The first is that *the emphasis should be on quality rather than quantity.* Homework should enrich the classroom study. Avoid homework assignments that are merely more of the same. The more real and signifi-

cant the homework, the better. At least some of the time students should get out into the community to where the action is. Perhaps they can participate in the action; at least they can witness it. Assignments that are too long often force students to do less than their best, because there is just not enough time for them to do everything well. In addition, overdoses of homework can deprive students of the social and physical activities they need if they are to develop into well-balanced individuals. It is not necessary for a teacher to be an ogre in order to have high standards.

Evaluating Homework

Evaluating written homework presents several peculiar problems. One of them is that the written homework turned in is not always the work of the student, but that of his friends or relatives. Although teachers may condemn it as cheating, for parents to help their children with homework, and for friends to share their work with each other is an accepted part of our American culture which no one else, certainly not the students nor their parents, feels to be particularly dishonest. Because of this undoubted fact, teachers should assign written homework mainly as practice material from which the students may learn whether someone helps them or not. Homework should not count much in making up a student's mark. Rather the

---

Look back at your high school days. Was the homework load reasonable? Did you have too much to do? Too little? Did you always know what to do and how to do it? Did your teachers take time to get you in the proper set? Did they follow up?

A teacher of English says he corrects homework papers carefully about every fifth assignment. The other assignments he merely checks to see if the work has been done. Is this practice proper? Defend your answer.

marks should be based upon papers and tests done during class. Nevertheless, even though written homework should not carry much weight in one's grading, it should always be checked. Unchecked written homework may serve only to grind errone-ous techniques and incorrect concepts into stu-dents' minds. Recognition of good work serves to stimulate student self-esteem, interest, and effort.

Supervised Study

Many teachers set aside class time in which stu-dents study their homework and other assign-ments. This practice has several advantages. It en-sures that everyone has time to do some studying. It gives you a chance to guide students toward good study habits. It also gives you a chance to guide students in their studying—to see that they get off on the right foot, using the proper procedures and so on. In order to be sure that students get a proper start, when giving students difficult assignments in new work, it is probably always wise to start with a supervised study session before sending them to do the assignment on their own. A short period of supervised study may eliminate student mistakes and make it unnecessary for you to reteach and the students to unlearn.

To prepare for supervised study periods you should establish with the students the purpose of the study assignment and why they should make the effort to study it. This step may not be an easy one. Students seldom see any *real* reason for study-ing assignments even when teachers think them essential. Therefore you should stretch your talents to make clear the relevance and importance of the learning to the students. You should also point out, or better yet help the students establish, what spe-cifically should be learned. Teacher and student questions might include What important points should we look for? How does the new learning relate to what has gone before? and What would you as a student or anyone else want to know about this lesson? Then, the motivation for studying the lesson having been established, you can help stu-dents with such details as setting up their own study goals, time schedules, and methods of attack-ing the subject.

During the supervised study session, be it ten minutes at the beginning or end of the class period or an entire period, you should supervise the stu-dents' studying. During this supervision you can and should observe individual study habits, keep track of each student's progress, and be alert for misunderstandings, poor techniques, and other dif-ficulties that may arise. Sometimes it will be evident that the entire class does not understand how to proceed or is taking a wrong track. In such in-stances you should stop everyone, call attention to the difficulty, and correct misapprehensions. However, occasions of this sort should be rare. The teacher who frequently interrupts the students when they are studying does more harm than good.

As you circulate around the classroom, talk with the students about their progress. Ask students how things are going, but go further than that. Some-times students don't know when things are going badly. Other times they may be unwilling to admit that they are having trouble. A little probing may give you a more realistic picture of the students' progress.

In so far as you can, individualize. As you observe you can find opportunities to differentiate assign-ments by giving different students work at different levels or by finding things that will appeal to stu-dents' peculiar interests or purposes or will help them resolve their difficulties.

Supervised study is such an important technique that you should always include supervised study in your planning. The amount of supervised study will vary according to the lesson or unit, its aims and contents. Some days no supervised study will be needed. At other times proper planning requires that an entire period or even longer be given over to supervised study. As we have seen a supervised-study period is an opportunity both for the student to study under guidance and for the teacher to su-pervise and guide study. Although this can best be done in the regular class, to a lesser extent it can also be done in study halls. Unfortunately, in some schools study halls are looked upon as merely a means for storing students who have no class at the time. This is hardly efficient. Supervised-study periods need real supervision. Merely to sit and watch the students should not be the function of the teacher in a supervised-study period. If keeping order in the study hall is to be the sole function, the school would do better to hire a policeman for this duty.

Students who attend schools with well run resource centers[10] have an advantage over other students. Teachers and aides who work in resource centers usually go out of their way to help students find and use the materials they need to complete their assignments and to become independent learners.

How can you use supervised study periods to develop the study skills essential for success in your subject field?

How would you go about individualizing homework in your classes?

Visit a secondary or middle school departmental resource center if there is one available. How would you try to capitalize on its resources if you were teaching in the school?

Summary

Most secondary school boys and girls need to be taught how to study. The teachers of the various subjects are responsible for seeing that each student learns how to study his discipline. To this end each teacher will have to show students how to perform such scholarly skills as analyzing problems, taking notes, and picking the meat out of lectures. Much of this teaching can be done in giving the assignment.

If students are ever to become scholars, they must learn to study independently. To develop this skill it is first necessary to develop basic skills and confidence in reading independently, and then move to more sophisticated techniques such as the directed reading lesson technique and the SQ3R method. In the initial stages, simple study guides are helpful, but in later stages students should be able to provide their own reading questions.

Students also need to learn how to carry out their learning assignments. For this purpose you will need to provide them both with plenty of freedom to use their own initiative and plenty of guidance. It is helpful if the students can develop these skills in a graded sequence while studying under supervision. In order for students to learn to get the most out of their classes and their reading, teach them how to take careful notes. Reaction notes and a system for coordinating class and lecture notes by using alternate pages of one's notebook are recommended. You will also find that teaching students how to prepare for tests and how to take tests will usually pay off in improved test scores.

Teachers should pay much more attention to giving their assignments than they usually do. Since students can not study effectively unless their assignments are clear to them, teachers should be sure that the assignments:

- set the direction and scope of the task.
- prepare the students for the job to be done.
- point how to do what is to be done.
- provide every student with an appropriate task.

To carry out these goals, the teacher may need to go into great detail when making the assignment. It may be necessary for the teacher to take time to teach study skills, to discuss objectives, to issue study guides and organizers, and to familiarize students with the materials to be used.

Homework is a problem. One seldom knows how much and what kind of homework will be best.

---

[10] Otherwise called learning or materials centers.

There is no virtue in giving too much homework. Some of the problems of how much homework to give can be solved by means of unit assignments in writing. Probably the best kind of homework is that which reinforces old learning or which follows up work which has been well started in class. Giving brand-new work for homework may result in incorrect learning which must be untaught in class later. This is one reason why supervised study in class time may be more suitable. Because of the tendency of friends and parents to share in the homework process, you should not place too much weight on it in evaluating the student. Still, written homework should always be checked.

LaConte, Ronald T. *Homework As a Learning Experience, What Research Says to the Teacher.* Washington, DC: National Education Association, 1981.

Martin, Robert J. *Teaching Through Encouragement. Techniques to Help Students Learn.* Englewood Cliffs, NJ: Prentice-Hall, 1980.

Robinson, H. Alan. *Teaching Reading and Study Strategies: The Content Areas.* Boston: Allyn and Bacon, 1975.

Snider, Jean. *How to Study in High School.* Providence, RI: Jamestown Publishers, 1983.

Zifferbaltt, S. M. *Improving Study and Homework Behaviors.* Champaign, IL: Research Press, 1970.

Additional Reading

Devine, Thomas G. *Teaching Study Skills: A Guide to Teachers.* Boston: Allyn and Bacon, 1981.

Dobbin, John. *How to Take a Test.* Princeton, NJ: Educational Testing Service, 1982.

16

Provisions for Individual Differences

Overview

All humans differ from each other. No two people are the same. We differ in a multitude of ways—in physical makeup, in interests, in ability, in apti-

tude, in home background, in experience, in prior training, in social skill, in ideals, in attitudes, in needs, in vocational goals, and so on ad infinitum. This is an inescapable fact of human nature—a fact fraught with profound implications for the teacher. Because of these difficulties, to treat individuals as though everyone were alike simply will not work. Somehow, some way, we teachers must adapt our teaching to the individual differences in students.

Not only are students different, but they all learn according to their own styles. No two persons ever learn exactly the same concepts from any learning situation. Nor do any two persons ever develop exactly the same method and degree of efficiency. Our learning is always shaped by our interests, our physical and psychic makeup, our past experiences and our goals for the future. We should capitalize on these differences and make them a way to further learning.

In other words, insofar as possible, schooling should be individualized. Curricula, courses, and lessons should be built in ways that allow students to adopt different goals, to study different content, to learn by different media and methods, to progress at different rates, and to be judged by different criteria—in accordance with their own specific needs, ambitions, and talents.

In this chapter we describe some of the procedures and devices that administrators and teachers use in their attempts to cope with the problems caused by individual differences and the need to individualize instruction. As you read the chapter, try to think how you would take advantage of the various administrative provisions for individual differences. Then consider how you would use the various teaching techniques described. Be sure that you understand how to make a differentiated assignment and how to conduct such techniques for individualizing instruction as laboratory teaching, special help, self-instructional techniques, projects, and continuous-progress schemes. You should also

> Observe the members of your own class. In what ways do they seem similar? In what different?
>
> If possible, visit a middle school class or senior high school class. What evidence of individual differences do you find?

consider what you could do to match your teaching to the different types of students you might find in your classes. For instance, consider to what extent and in what ways you would adapt your teaching approaches for classes of slow or gifted students, or of students with different social class or ethnic backgrounds.

Administrative Provisions for Differences in Students

For a long time school administrators have been trying, with rather indifferent success, to find answers for the instructional problems caused by individual differences. Most of the procedures that they have inaugurated to meet this problem have been based upon selecting or categorizing students. Recently, however, some schools have been moving toward attempting to provide for individual differences by making their curriculum organization flexible. Although none of these procedures or devices really solves the problem of individual student differences, they may reduce the scope of the problem somewhat by reducing the heterogeneity of the groups with which the teacher must deal.

Tracks and Streams

To group students according to interest or ability is common practice in secondary and elementary schools both in the United States and abroad. American high schools usually offer several curricula based, supposedly, on the goals of the students. Thus we find a typical high school offering such varied curricula as college preparatory curricula for those students planning to go to college, secretarial curricula for students planning to become office workers, vocational agriculture curricula for students who plan to become farmers, and general curricula for students having no particular plans for the future.

The track or stream is another administrative device for reducing the range of heterogeneity in classrooms. Usually tracks or streams are curricular sequences based upon students' ability in the area. Thus the mathematics program for a school might be divided into four tracks, the first for talented mathematics students, the second for ordinary college preparatory students, the third for noncollege preparatory students, and the fourth for slow learners.

Homogeneous Grouping

Homogeneous groups are similar to tracks or streams except that they are not planned curricular sequences, but merely groupings of students made up for the year or term only. They may be based on similarities of student interests, educational objectives, or demonstrated academic ability. Most homogeneous groups, however, are based on academic ability. By such grouping administrators hope to make it possible for teachers to teach more effectively and to adapt the curriculum to the varying needs of all the students.

Administrative grouping of students is not a direct responsibility of classroom teachers, but it does affect them and their teaching. The basic implication for you is that you should adapt your material and methods so that you will be teaching the content best suited for each class in the way best suited for that class. Simply watering down the academic course for slower students or speeding it up for gifted ones will not suffice. Some comments on how to adapt your teaching to the group will follow in a later section.

One danger that comes from homogeneous grouping, tracking, and streaming is that teachers may get the idea that the groups are really homogeneous. They are not; no group of people is. All that can be done in grouping students is to reduce the range of one or another characteristic or group of

associated characteristics. In a high-ability group the students may all be of relatively high ability, but they will differ in many other ways—in interests, in ambitions, in motivation, in goals, in personality, in aggressiveness, and so on. They even differ in intelligence and ability. Look at the IQ range of the students of a "good" college preparatory class in a New Jersey high school listed in Table 16–1. Although there is some doubt about the validity and meaning of IQ scores, these scores indicate that the range of intelligence in this "good" class extends from slightly above normal to very bright. If you teach ability-grouped classes you will have problems of providing for individual differences just as other teachers do.

Theoretically, homogeneous grouping should make it easier for the teacher to accomplish this task. In practice, however, all too often homogeneous grouping results in the short changing of the less academically inclined students. Such classes for "slow students" may have a deleterious effect on the students' personalities. The students learn that they are not as good as other people. Consequently their levels of aspiration become low. They do not try because they know that teachers do not expect much from them. Their teachers do not try because they feel it to be useless. So we

TABLE 16.1
IQ's of a Homogeneous College Preparatory Tenth-Grade Class

James	136	David	125
Craig	135	Gerald	124
Charlene	135	Peggy	124
Sally	134	Bruce	123
Michelle	133	Jim	123
Judy	133	Margaret	123
Susan	131	Richard	122
Steve	130	Betty	121
Prudence	130	Christine	120
Tim	128	Guy	119
Gail	128	George	118
Joan	126	Wayne	116
Joanna	126	Neil	109

find that the students who need most to be challenged to try their best are not challenged at all. Furthermore, they are deprived of the help and example of their more successful peers. Students learn from each other. Nonacademically inclined students profit intellectually from being with the academically inclined; academically inclined students can profit socially and sometimes intellectually from being with the nonacademically inclined.

Electives and Minicourses

Perhaps the most common way to provide for students' differences in interest and objectives is to make some of the courses in the curriculum elective. Some schools have introduced elective minicourses in order to give students more opportunities to find course offerings suitable to their needs and interests than they can find in the standard curriculum. Minicourses are short courses of anywhere from a few weeks to a full quarter term in length which may or may not be given for credit and may or may not allow much student participation in planning. For electives and minicourses to be really valuable as tools for individualizing instruction, there should be a large enough choice of courses to allow students to find congenial courses.

Other Administrative Techniques

In addition to plans involving grouping, administrators utilize various promotion schemes to provide for individual differences. Among them are the old-fashioned practice of permitting talented students to skip grades and making students who fail repeat grades or courses, and the more recent movement toward continuous promotion and ungraded schools. Similarly, a number of plans to make the secondary school day more flexible have been introduced. Some of these give a large portion of the school day over to independent study. Learning centers to which students may go to study in-

dependently under guidance have become quite common in some areas. In some schools the introduction of teacher aides has made it easier to provide guidance for independent and individualized study. The use of aides can relieve the teachers from some of the busy work so that they can give more time to working with small groups and individuals. Undoubtedly all of these plans have merit. They should make providing for the differences in individual students easier and more effective. But they will not relieve teachers of the responsibility for providing for individual differences within classes.

In the ensuing pages we indicate some ways in which teachers can take advantage of individual differences within the classroom and make the instruction more profitable. This discussion is predicated on the assumption that adequate provisions for individual differences must be based upon thorough knowledge of the abilities, interests, ambitions, problems, and other characteristics of the student.

How could one prevent a caste system from developing as a result of homogeneous grouping of class sections throughout the school?

Examine a high school honors class. What range interests, abilities, life goals, and academic backgrounds do you find?

Examine a minicourse program. In what ways does it provide for individual differences that a traditional program cannot? Or does it?

Matching Teaching Styles to Learning Styles

One of the most important of these considerations is the student's individual learning style. Learning styles really make a difference in how well students learn. For instance, research indicates that field-independent students do better work in low-structured inductive learning situations whereas field-dependent students do better in highly structured deductive classes. Therefore try to match teaching and learning styles as much as feasible.

Doing so is complicated by the fact that there are many cognitive styles. The answer to this problem, according to the *Learning Styles Network Newsletter*, is to identify a student's learning style by some valid instrument and then attempt to match it with a corresponding teaching style. If that teaching style does not seem to work, then review your decision and try another one.[1] Another approach is to use several teaching styles over a period of time so that in the long run each student will meet a teaching style congruous with his learning style at least part of the time. In any case you should probably try as best you can to individualize your instruction and match teaching and learning styles systematically.

Examine yourself. What sort of classroom situation do you find most congenial? In what type of class do you do your best work? If your teachers had been more conscious of your learning style, would your classes have been more profitable? Observe your friends. How do their learning styles differ? Under what conditions do they seem to learn best?

Differentiating Assignments

The Differentiated Assignment

The first instructional procedure for coping with the problem of individual differences that we discuss is the differentiated assignment. A differentiated assignment is a class assignment that allows different students to do different things during the time covered by the assignment. Many types of these assignments can be made. Sometimes the differentiated assignment is long, covering a period of several weeks. However, it can also be very short.

Differentiating the Length or Difficulty of the Assignment

Teachers often arrange their assignments so that slow learners will not have to do quite as much as their more able colleagues. In the sample assignment following, the teacher attempted to do this by assigning group 3, the fast group, considerably more work than group 1, the slow group. In a mathematics class she might have assigned five problems to the slow students, eight problems to the average students, and ten problems to the fast students. In the sample assignment the work assigned to the groups also varies in difficulty. Group 3 is reading in what the teacher considers a "hard" eighth-grade book; group 2, an "easy" eighth-grade book; and group 1, a sixth-grade book. All are studying about the same thing but at different levels of difficulty. In a mathematics class the teacher could have assigned more difficult problems to the better students.

An Example of a Short Differentiated Assignment

GROUP 1

Reading Assignment *Your Country and Mine,* pages 36–41:

1. Form into assigned groups.
2. Select one member to serve on each committee:
   a. Bulletin Board.
   b. *Who's Who in American History.*

---

[1] *Learning Styles Network Newsletter* (Winter, 1982), **3**:2.

3. Choose one of the following assignments:
   a. Write a story about Daniel Boone.
   b. Draw a picture of Boonesborough in its early days.
   c. Draw a map showing how Daniel Boone got to Boonesborough (page 43).

GROUP 2

Reading Assignment *Your Country's Story*, pages 160–163:

1. Form into assigned groups.
2. Select one member for each of the following committees:
   a. Bulletin Board.
   b. *Who's Who in American History.*
3. Choose one of the following assignments:
   a. Make a report on the nature and characteristics of the Indians as seen by the early settlers in Kentucky and Tennessee.
   b. Make a map showing the different routes to the West.
   c. Write a report telling why the Ohio Valley was so attractive to early settlers.

GROUP 3

Reading Assignment *This Is America's Story*, pages 223–231:

1. Form into assigned groups.
2. Select one member for each committee:
   a. Bulletin Board.
   b. *Who's Who in American History.*
3. Choose one of the following assignments:
   a. Prepare a short report on the history of political parties in the United States.
   b. Make a report on Hamilton's policies in solving this country's financial problems.
   c. Write a short report explaining why Jefferson and Hamilton had different views on many things.
4. Answer completely Check-Up Questions 1–3 (page 227) and 1–4 (page 231).
5. Give a brief account of the Northwest Territory and of its importance in the development of the West.

Differentiating the Type of Work

Another approach is to differentiate the type of work various students do, thus allowing for their varying interests and abilities. Students who think best with their hands could be allowed to create with them, whereas bright, academically-interested students might be encouraged to undertake minor research problems. Similarly, students who are interested in current affairs might become specialists and keep the class up-to-date on the stock market or on the situation in the Middle East; artistically inclined students might form a committee to keep the bulletin board attractive and up-to-date; and scientifically minded students might be given reading assignments different from those given to literary types. Give students opportunities to try different types of assignments, however. By skillfully using the students' interests and abilities, you may be able to enlist their enthusiastic cooperation and encourage them to learn more than occurs in dull, humdrum, lockstep classes.

Accepting Different Signs of Achievement

In order to capitalize on different abilities and interests, you should not only allow students to engage in different sorts of learning activity, but you should also accept different signs of growth when estimating and evaluating the academic progress of students. For example, writing essays and answering test questions are not the only ways to show one's understanding of the antebellum South. Many other media are available. Artistic youngsters might produce illustrations of life in the South; a young draftsman might draw a layout of a plantation; a beginning gourmet might investigate the menus of the era; a student interested in fashions might run up a costume appropriate to the period; a young engineer might construct a cotton gin; a young choreographer might score and dance a ballet in the *Gone with the Wind* motif; a poet might contribute some lyric poetry, perhaps an ode or two. In such cases you should evaluate your students' academic success on the basis of the growth and progress they make toward the prescribed goals through these media. Certainly a student who works toward the learning objectives by performing a well-conceived and executed original dance number deserves to be recognized more than a student who does a miserably sloppy research paper.

Examine the sample differentiated assignment. How successful do you think this assignment would be?

How would you go about preparing a differentiated assignment for a course in your major field?

It has been said, "We should not have a standard; we should have standards." What do you think this means? Is it advisable to require one student to do more or better work than another? How would you go about implementing the statement?

Grouping within the Classroom

Teaching is usually easier when the range of differences among students in a group is kept relatively small. Just as school administrators use homogeneous groupings throughout entire schools, teachers can group their students homogeneously within their classes. This grouping can be accomplished in several ways, such as

1. Placing the slow achievers in one group, the average achievers in another, and the rapid achievers in a third.
2. Placing students into groups according to their interests.
3. Placing students with similar interests and similar goals together in a committee to solve a particular problem or to do some sort of research.
4. Placing students into groups according to special needs.

Certain critics have objected to the use of ability groups within the class for several reasons. One objection is that many experienced high school teachers claim that to teach more than one group in the same room is impossible or too difficult. Yet anyone who has watched a skillful teacher conduct a one-room school or a primary room knows that this is not so. Teaching several groups at once is hard work, but then, all good teaching is hard work. Actually, using groups is often easier than attempting to teach the unready something they cannot learn or the uninterested something they will not learn.

As we have already seen, another serious objection is that ability grouping may label some students as inferior. Although the danger does exist, ability grouping within classes is probably not as dangerous as one might expect. The students usually know where the strengths and weaknesses of their classmates lie and recognize which ones are good students, which ones hate to study, which ones are social butterflies, which ones are wallflowers, which ones are sports-oriented, and so on.

Nevertheless these dangers are real ones. We must not allow a caste system to develop in any classroom. The danger may be avoided by seeing to it that the membership of the groups changes frequently, that many types of groups and committees are used so that no student is always in the same group, and that each student has ample opportunities to work both as an individual and as a member of the entire class. To divide a class into three or four ability groups and to keep these groups together constantly for an entire term is malpractice. Instead, center small groups, or committees around the changing interests, problems, or needs of the students. Evidently, in reading

---

If you were to divide your class into groups, what basis for grouping would you use? How would you go about grouping the class? How long would you keep the same groups?

---

groups at least, both bright and gifted students make better progress in mixed, randomly selected groups than in ability groups.[2]

Individualizing Instruction

A differentiated assignment does not really individualize instruction. It merely reduces the problem of individual differences somewhat. If instruction is to meet the needs of individual students, ways must be found for individualizing assignments and instruction. At first glance this task seems to be insuperably difficult, but on closer analysis it is not as overwhelming a task as one might fear.

Acceleration and Enrichment

One way to help brilliant students make the most of their talents is to let them proceed through the course more rapidly than their classmates. In a certain Latin class the teacher arranged the classwork so that the brilliant students could do most of the work independently at their own speed without waiting for slower classmates to catch up. One girl completed one year's work early in April and was well into the next year's work by the end of June. The teacher had made this acceleration possible by preparing units for the entire year in advance. When the student had completed one unit, she went right on to the next one.

In such teaching, since the accelerated student will finish the regular coursework before the end of the school year, you will need to provide additional work for the student. In the example cited, the student went on to units in the next year's work. In other instances one might prefer that the student study more deeply certain aspects of the present

course or aspects of the course ordinarily omitted because of lack of time. This we call enrichment.

Once your students have started to work individually, you must run frequent checks on their progress to be sure that all is going well and to provide help, direction, and redirection as needed. To be sure that the students do have sufficient guidance, it is good to make up a schedule of conferences with them. In addition, you should make yourself available to the students. When a boy or girl needs help, you should be ready to provide it immediately.

Continuous Progress Plans

The Latin teacher's plan for accelerating brilliant students was really a form of the continuous progress plan. Basically continuous progress plans consist of dividing the coursework into short steps, levels or modules, and allowing the students to advance from step to step as they become ready. Even in schools organized into traditional grades and courses, teachers can organize their own courses for continuous progress. Briefly the procedure is

1. Divide the course into units (commonly called modules).
2. Prepare an instructional package for each unit. (These are also called learning modules, learning activity packets, self-instructional units or instructional modules.) Each instructional packet should include
    A diagnostic pretest.
    Behavioral objectives.
    A study guide giving directions and suggestions for study, including required and optional activities—exercises, problems, questions, projects.
    Progress tests.
    Final mastery test.
    Materials for study.
3. Give students the pretest of the appropriate unit. Excuse students who do very well from complet-

---

[2] See Chapter 12 for information on teaching by means of committees and small groups, and Chapter 14 for use of groups in reading.

ing the unit; use the results for diagnosis and
guidance. In some courses this step may be omitted.

4. Let the students work on the unit independently,
following the directions included in the study
guide in the instructional packet. Students may
take progress tests and engage in other activities
as they go along.

5. When students seem ready, let them take the
final mastery test. Students who meet your criteria are deemed to have met the objective and
go on to another unit. Those who do not pass
must do remedial work until they can meet the
criteria.

In a true continuous progress course, some students will move through the units easily whereas
others will take longer than the normal time to
finish the units. In conducting such courses, it is
wise to remember that speed is not always a virtue.
The student who proceeds through the units slowly
but thoroughly may be more able than the star
who flips through them at great speed.

To conduct a course of the continuous-progress
type requires constant supervision and guidance.
You must be constantly available and watchful to
prevent students from having to stand around waiting for help or from struggling through work they
do not understand. Whenever possible, utilize
small-group instruction techniques to help students
who are at the same point in the module or who
are encountering the same problems. However, the
purpose for using learning packets in these courses
is to give you a better opportunity for giving students individual attention as much as it is to break
the regimentation of the standard recitation.

Other suggestions for teaching continuous progress courses and self-instructional units or modules
are,

1. Be flexible. Vary the module requirements for
various persons as the situation requires.

2. Use bulletin boards, tapes, interviews, guest
speakers, simulation games, and the like to add
spark to the modules.

3. Be sure to have whole group activities once a
week or so. Discussions in which students apply
what they have learned are good.

4. Let persons who finish modules become consultants who help other students who find the
work troublesome.

5. Have students rework lessons that they do incorrectly. (This suggestion implies that you must
be constantly checking to be sure that students
are doing the work correctly.)

6. Use incentives to keep students working.
   a. Check their work frequently. Praise and reward each forward step.
   b. Reward students with free time, quest time,
   etc.
   c. Make some units optional, some required.
   d. Utilize the contract procedure in which individuals agree that they will do certain things
   in exchange for certain rewards.
   e. Have students report to you when they finish
   a lesson. Make a chart and check off the lessons completed.
   f. Have students report to a "review committee" before reporting that a lesson or unit
   is completed. This committee should be com-
   posed of two or three students who have
   completed their work. The "review committee" should screen students who need more
   help before they take the final test for a unit
   or lesson.

7. Pair students with reading difficulties with a
"study partner" who is a stronger reader. This
person could help the slow reader with his
module.

8. Do not expect everyone to be on the same lesson
or module at the same time.

Completely Differentiating the Work

At times it is desirable to assign to certain students work that is entirely different from that of
the rest of the class. An example of this is the case
of Pete, a brilliant tenth-grader who had been doing

poor work in his English class. Upon examining the situation, the teacher realized that the boy was finding the assignments too easy. He was bored. To remedy this, the teacher excused the boy from the regular assignment and substituted one she herself had had in college. Rising to this bait, the boy accomplished this assignment in a fashion acceptable for any college introductory literature course. By substituting an entirely different assignment, the teacher was able to inspire this boy to do work well beyond the level of his grade. This is an excellent way to help a gifted youth. If a girl is competent in grammar and knows to perfection the parts of speech the class is presently studying, she should be studying something else. Why not put her to work on a problem in literature, or something else worthwhile? It does not matter particularly what the student does as long as it results in the learning desired. Similarly less able students may be favorably motivated by receiving assignments that catch a special personal interest.

Conducting the Class As a Laboratory

A profitable way to provide for individual differences is to conduct the class as a laboratory. Here the students can work on their various tasks individually or in small groups under the teacher's guidance. In such a laboratory a committee might

What practical problems arise from allowing a student to go to the next year's work? How might these problems be minimized?

In the example cited, the accelerated students worked individually almost entirely. Is this a good practice? How might one accelerate students in a class without making the work entirely individual?

How would you go about setting up a classroom laboratory in a course you might teach? How could you use a classroom laboratory?

be working in one corner of the room preparing a dramatization, in another corner another group might be preparing a report. At their desks individual students might be working on research projects. Others might be reading required or optional readings. In the rear of the class a student might be putting the finishing touches on a model to be presented and explained to the class. Around the teacher's desk another group might be working with the teacher in planning a group project.

As the students work at their tasks, you should help and guide them. Among the many things you can do to help them are

1. Observe students to diagnose poor study habits.
2. Show students where to find information.
3. Show students how to use the tools of learning.
4. Clarify assignments.
5. Show the students how to get the meat out of their studying.
6. Help students form goals for study.
7. Help students summarize.
8. Point out errors and incorrect procedures.
9. Suggest methods for attacking problems.

Laboratory classes of this sort allow the freedom necessary for different students to work at a variety of tasks at speeds suitable for them. To a lesser degree supervised study periods in which the students work on their assignments under the teacher's supervision and guidance can provide the same freedom.

Other Individualized Instruction Schemes

Whatever approach you use, you must somehow find time to work separately with individual students. This does not usually take as much time as one might think. Many students need a minimum of guidance. If they are provided with clear instructions they can often work alone for considerable periods.

Special Help

The most common type of individualized instruction is the special help given to certain students. Teachers have always helped boys and girls who were having trouble with their studies through extra help after school, during conferences, in study halls, and in class. No matter what method of teaching is used, you will need to provide special help for some students.

Not only do students having trouble with their studies need special help; students who are doing well need it also. Everyone at times needs encouragement, criticism, discipline, correction, and inspiration. Taking time to look over students' papers, to compliment them on their progress, and to point out possible ways for improvement can be beneficial for both the most successful and the least successful students.

Nevertheless, in spite of the value of special help, it alone cannot meet the demands of individual differences. Stronger measures are needed. Insofar as possible you should provide individual instruction designed for the individual students to be instructed. Such provision can usually be made most easily within the framework of the classroom laboratory, the differentiated assignment, the unit approach, or the learning packet. In the following paragraphs we discuss some techniques that can be used for individual instruction within such plans.

Self-instructional Devices

The availability of self-instructional devices and materials has made individualizing instruction in ordinary-size classes much easier than in the past. The most spectacular of these devices are the many different sorts of machines now on the market. One of the most versatile of these is the tape or cassette recorder.

For example, in a certain English class one of the major concerns was the improvement of oral language skills. Each student was given a cassette

recording tape to use during the semester. Every student learned how to run the tape recorder and could, if he so desired, use the tape during out-of-class hours. On the tape each student could record conversations, class discussions, oral reports, and practice material. The recordings were criticized both by the students and the teacher. Students noted their own errors and worked on them individually. They also practiced by themselves on material provided by the instructor until they thought they had improved enough to record their voices again and to listen to the playback. The other work of the class was largely individualized, so that students could use the tape recorder whenever they were ready. In this way the students were able to see their errors, and with the teacher's aid set up a program for improvement. Thus they were able to see their progress and to judge whether they had improved enough to go on to other work. The teacher felt that the class improved much more than if he had tried to teach these skills directly and had made the criticisms himself.

Tape recorders can also present other types of lessons to individuals or small groups. Before a class, for instance, you might dictate to a machine a lesson with instructions for individual self-instruction. Then during the class you could turn the student over to the tape recorder and its pretaped lesson for a time. One teacher prepared a tape recording of an account of the religious life of primitive humans. This tape also includes a short introduction to tell what the tape is about and to direct the student's attention to important points and a short follow up to reemphasize these points. Individual students or small groups can put on earphones and work on this lesson without bothering anyone else in the class. Whenever they run into difficulty, they simply turn back the tape and replay the bothersome section without disrupting anyone else's progress.

Similar lessons have been worked out for use on eight-millimeter, self-loading, individual-viewing motion picture projectors. Sometimes two-by-two slides can be arranged in lessons for individual use by teachers who do not have desired filmstrips available. Students can follow the slide sequence on dittoed commentary sheets. Preferably such slide sequences should be presented in trays for automatic or semiautomatic projection. If such are not available and one must use a single-shot machine, one should be sure the slides are numbered in proper order and that the top righthand corner is marked so that the student can tell which way to insert the slides into the machine. With a little ingenuity, regular 16mm projectors can be used in the same way, if prethreaded.

Teaching machines that use automated teaching programs and computer-assisted instruction are the most exotic of all the auto-instructional devices. The self-instructional features of the programs and machines make it possible for students to work through programs as rapidly or as slowly as seems most desirable, and to pursue different topics or themes at the same time.

Some computer programs can be most useful for individualizing instruction because they make it possible to program a separate course of instruction for every student. In such instruction via computer, each student's performance at any instant determines what the next step in the instructional sequence will be. So because Boy A's responses to the computer's tutoring differ from those of Boy B, the computer can and will give him a different sequence of instructional episodes even if both boys are studying the same topic in the same period. Teaching machines and programed texts can do the same thing, but without the aid of the computer, they are less proficient.

Other self-instructional materials one can purchase or make include self-administering and self-correcting drill and practice materials. Usually self-correcting materials can be used only for teaching information and skills; the self-correcting format cannot be adapted easily for instruction in the higher mental processes. Even so, such materials can help free the teacher from much busywork so that he can give more time to helping individual students learn at higher levels.

You can also use dittoed or mimeographed study guides, learning activity packets and contracts to individualize your teaching. Use general guides as a basis for laboratory teaching and special guides for students engaged in different activities. Study guides, learning activity packets, and contracts make it possible for students to proceed at their own pace or on work different from that of other students without having to wait for special oral directions from the teacher who may be busy working with someone else. Similar study and activity guides can be recorded on tape for students whose reading level is not up to their understanding level.

The use of self-instructional materials does not free the teacher from the necessity of selecting the material, preparing the student and setting for instruction, and guiding or supervising the instruction—including helping students with their difficulties and following up the teaching as well as evaluating the students' progress. The teaching task remains the same, but the use of these techniques and devices does make it possible to spend more time with individuals and to develop the higher goals of instruction that so often are neglected.

Individual and Group Projects

Both individual and group projects as described in Chapter 13 are useful for individualizing instruction. Since the basis of the project is that it be selected, planned, and carried out by the student because of some intrinsic value to him, the individual project is one of the techniques best suited for developing and capitalizing on individual interests and abilities.

Independent Study

Noar says that bright students should do a lot of independent study on their own "without constant supervision, without the threat or reward of marks."[3] Probably this is the sort of opportunity

---

[3] Gertrude Noar, *Individualized Instruction* (New York: Wiley, 1972), pp. 66–67.

that should be extended to all students on occasion. After all, one of the major goals of schooling is to help students to learn to work independently. Independent study is good for motivation. It may lead to better control. It should not, however, be the only method used to teach anyone.

To conduct independent study well requires considerable skill. It is important to give students the right amount of support, help, and leadership without stifling their ideas and initiative. The students must be guided into selecting independent study appropriate to their individual abilities, experience, interests, and goals. Students tend to bite off more than they can chew. In the beginning of the independent study it is good to arrive at a rather definite understanding of just what is to be accomplished and how it is to be done. These can be written down. Learning packets and study guides are excellent for this purpose. So are quest proposals. In these proposals the students state what they would like to do, how they propose to do it, and what products they will produce as evidence of successful completion of the quest. See Figure 16–1 for a sample quest proposal.

Use of Free Periods

Occasionally, students may be given free periods in which they are permitted to follow their own

---

How can a teacher find material to suit the varying reading levels of his students on a limited school budget?

How can different types of work areas within a classroom help to provide for individual differences? How can they be used?

How can self-correcting material be used in providing for individual differences?

How can self-evaluation of a student's progress be used to motivate him?

How would you organize your class to use self-instructional devices, quest proposals, and individualized units effectively and efficiently?

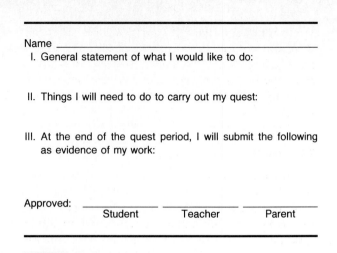

Name _____

I. General statement of what I would like to do:

II. Things I will need to do to carry out my quest:

III. At the end of the quest period, I will submit the following as evidence of my work:

Approved: _____ _____ _____
                 Student   Teacher   Parent

FIGURE 16–1
A Sample Quest Proposal

interests as much as possible. The activities of such a free period should be limited to those that are suitable to the classroom and to the subject. Such periods are usually more appropriate for reading and literature than for other subjects, although this does not need to be so. They are often instrumental in forming new tastes in reading, art, music, and other areas, and often open new vistas of appreciation to the student. They also have the additional advantage of giving the teacher opportunities to help students who need individual attention.

Finding Time for Individual Instruction

Participation in Planning and Evaluation

To provide properly for individual instruction takes time. One of the keys to finding the necessary time is to allow the students to take a greater share in the responsibility for their own studies. *Adolescent boys and girls, particularly the brilliant ones, are quite capable of planning, directing, and evaluating their own work, particularly if they have study guides to help them.* If you allow them to do so, you can not only help them to acquire skill in self-direction but also free yourself for individual and small-group work. Moreover, the use of student planning and evaluation makes it possible for students to map out individual plans suitable to their needs.

The Use of Student Help

Boys and girls often help each other. Usually this help is quite effective for adolescents frequently learn more readily from their peers. Take advantage of this fact by asking students who have mastered a skill or concept to coach other students who are having difficulty. If done carefully this technique can be quite beneficial. It gives teachers some assistance so that they can find time for more individual teaching; it teaches youngsters how to share their talents and how to communicate their ideas to others; it helps foster the idea of service; and it helps both the tutor and the tutored learn the subject more thoroughly.

How can students help each other? How can such help be used to provide for individual differences?

How can a teacher of a large class find time to work and confer with individual students? List occasions when the teacher might consult with pupils informally.

Need for Variety of Materials

Providing for individual differences requires a wealth of instructional materials. It goes without saying that one cannot expect every member of the class to be interested in the same thing. Materials too easy for bright students may be so difficult that they may frustrate the slow students. Consequently, you should provide readings, and other materials, suitable to the various levels and interests

found in the class and make sure they are available when individuals need them.

Remedial Teaching

Teaching designed specifically for boys and girls who have not achieved desired goals is called remedial teaching. Many teachers seem to think there is something esoteric about remedial teaching. There is not. Remedial teaching is merely good teaching concentrated directly on the student and his needs. Usually it is more effective than ordinary teaching only because it is more thorough and more carefully designed to remedy a specific need.

Some teachers seem to feel that remedial teaching should be reserved for extraordinary students and for remedial classes. Nothing could be further from the truth. Every youth needs remedial teaching at one time or another. To provide remedial teaching in each unit is relatively easy to do if evaluation is continuous and the teacher concentrates on the youth rather than on the subject matter.

In the regular class remedial teaching ordinarily consists of reteaching those things that boys and girls have not learned. For instance, if the boys and girls in a class that should already have studied the fulcrum do not seem to understand what it is, the lesson should probably be repeated for all. If only a few persons did not get it, they should probably be retaught in a special group. If it becomes evident that just one boy missed it, he should be retaught individually. To reteach in this fashion may mean spending several days with the entire class on the missed learning, or revamping the next unit to include this learning again, or it may entail no more than just a few minutes of review and explanation, or a short conference with one student.

The following illustration serves as an example of remedial teaching in the regular classroom. In going over the test papers from one of her mathematics classes, the teacher noted that one of her students was having considerable difficulty with the problems. An analysis of his papers showed that the student was neglecting to convert all the parts of the problem to the same terms. At the next class meeting the teacher pointed out to the student the error he was making. She then quizzed the boy to see that he understood how to convert from one unit to the other and assigned to him several special problems by which to practice the technique directly.

Of what value can self-correcting exercises be in remedial teaching? In what ways is remedial teaching different from regular teaching? How can practice materials be utilized in remedial teaching?

Can you give examples of the need for remedial teaching of brilliant youth from your own experience? How should this type of remedial teaching best be handled?

Supposing about one third of your class missed an essential part of the last unit. You estimate that it would take about two days to reteach it properly. What would you do?

Teaching Slow Learners

Slow learners need careful teaching. To them ordinary middle and secondary school classes are a history of discouragement and frustration. Being slow they do not have time to learn the essentials of one lesson before the class moves on to the next one. Consequently they keep dropping "behinder and behinder" until they are hopelessly buried in the debris of not-yet-learned information, concepts and skills. Yet, if you will take the time to explain carefully, repair unlearned skills and background, and adapt the material to be learned, you may be

able to turn slow learners around and get them moving forward.

Therefore, take time with them. Present new work slowly. Take more and shorter steps. Usually they know quite a bit more than they seem to, but in the process of drawing them out you must avoid shortcuts, teach the details, give plenty of individual attention and help them with their study skills. Do not assume that they already know anything until you have checked it out.

All this means that you must be careful to diagnose the students' strengths and weaknesses so that you can capitalize on the strengths, shore up the weaknesses, and fill in the lacking background information and skills.

When teaching slow learners, keep your emphasis on the developmental rather than the remedial. Remedial work is necessary, of course, but you will be more effective if you focus on teaching your subject. Use remedial teaching as a means to teaching the subject rather than as an end in itself. Do not give simply a watered-down version of the academic course (watered-down courses are seldom good for anyone), but do keep the course down to earth, emphasizing basic principles and specifics. Also see to it that the students get a chance to practice the skills of clear, critical thinking in practical, realistic situations. In short, *for your slow learners, try to make the course work simple, practical, realistic and meaningful.*

Therefore you should make judicious use of audiovisual aids. Watching demonstrations, observing phenomena, looking at motion pictures, making collections, and building exhibits and models are all examples of concrete, tangible activities that can help slow students learn. Be sure, however, that these activities are kept simple and clearly explained.

Poor learners need plenty of instruction. In giving explanations, go into detail. Use plenty of illustrations. Keep your language as simple and direct as possible. Be sure the students know the meaning of the words you use; write them on the board. Again, it would be wise to be thorough and to avoid shortcuts, for with these students shortcuts will more than likely turn out to be short circuits. Because slow learners may find it difficult to transfer their learning, be careful to point out the implications of each lesson in some detail.

Your teaching strategies and instructional materials for slow learners should be simple, easy, but adult. Shorter essays, problems and simplified texts, and readings will make your classes more effective if they do not seem babyish. The importance of making sure that what is being taught is mature enough for the students can not be too heavily emphasized. One young teacher of remedial mathematics in a central city high school found that he could not make any headway until he disguised the basic arithmetic he was trying to teach as algebra. When the students worked on the algebra, they began to learn addition and subtraction and also to attend class more regularly (although still continuing to absent themselves from other classes). To walk the tightrope between the too simple and the too complex is often quite hazardous.

Realistic activities help motivate slow learners and make transfer of learning relatively easy. Sometimes these slow students may find it difficult to see the relevance of many mathematics problems, but when the problem has to do with the cost of purchasing, financing, and maintaining a particular car the pertinence of the mathematics involved may become both obvious and interesting to them. So also in English classes letter writing to real people can make composition more realistic. A class newspaper may help students see the importance of their schoolwork. Similarly, the presentation of an assembly or the preparation of an exhibit can be used to make the learning process real.

Above all, you should try to use strategies that build up the slow students' confidence and attract their interest. To catch their interest, try to tie the classwork to their personal lives; give them opportunities to use what they have learned out of school in your classes, and also have them apply what they learn in your classes in the real world. To build up their confidence, teach well-structured les-sons and units made up of a variety of relatively short activities with plenty of time for supervised study in which you give help and guidance; form in-class groups, committees, and other opportunities for students to compare notes and learn from each other; and finally give frequent summaries and reviews. But do not teach pap. These students need to be challenged and to achieve successes doing real learning tasks. Recognition of their successes is most important and may lead to real improvement.

Mainstreaming the Handicapped

Federal law requires that insofar as it is suitable, physically handicapped youths should be taught in regular classrooms and insofar as possible in the same manner as other students. However, you will have to make special provisions for their disabilities and adjust your teaching to their individual educational plans. These plans, which are required by law, have been constructed by teams of specialists, classroom teachers, and parents. You must carry out the portions of the plan that affect your own class to the best of your ability so that the handicapped youths will receive maximum benefit from your teaching and from associating with the other students in your classroom.

The Children of Poverty

The children of the poor are frequently lumped together with slow learners in teachers' thinking. This is unfortunate, because the range of native intelligence is just as great in urban ghettos or rural slums as it is in the affluent suburbs. Many poor youths are truly talented, but, because of the disadvantages that accompany poverty, they may find schools and schooling difficult. Because of these problems and disadvantages, these students need and deserve special consideration.

Children of poverty do not ordinarily like school. In the first place, their experience has taught them that school is one humiliation and failure after another. In their eyes, school is just one more example of the unfairness of society. Seldom do they see much point in striving to learn what is taught. Most of the curriculum seems irrelevant to their lives—past, present, or future. Even though they may see value in the three Rs, science, and information that will keep them from being cheated, they are not likely to see great value in history, literature, and the like. More often than is necessary they do badly in them and as a result drop out of school.

Because many students from urban and rural slums enter into our secondary schools with only meager academic competencies and small expectations, to teach them successfully is liable to be difficult—so difficult that many teachers despair and give up and so compound the students' troubles. Fortunately these youths frequently have much more potential than surface appearances indicate. They deserve more from their schools than faint-hearted teaching. The following paragraphs include ten suggestions that may make the task easier.

First, often the handicap that is holding back a deprived youth may be the inability to read well. Sometimes simply adjusting the reading level of the material to be studied may make the difference between student learning and student frustration. In any case make every effort to bring the students' reading abilities up to par as quickly as possible. Until this objective has been achieved, teachers should try to find easy reading material suitable for the age and interest levels of secondary school students who have difficulty reading. (Certain metropolitan newspapers are written for adult readership at quite low reading levels, for instance.) In addition, the teachers should try to utilize nonreading activities that will lead to the desired learning.

Second, the work laid out for these students should be realistic. Forget about covering the subject and concentrate on teaching well. The best procedure seems to be to pick a theme or topic and divide it into short segments. In teaching these segments seek out much feedback in order to be sure that the students learn the essentials of each segment before they move on to the next one. Because attendance of poor students is likely to be sporadic, teachers should try to individualize their assignments so that students can pick up where they left off and move through the course in an orderly fashion even when they have been absent excessively.

Third, in giving assignments, directions should be clear and explicit. Teachers can often help students tremendously if they will only show them how to study. This is especially true when teaching children from poverty-stricken environments. You should be ready to teach them all sorts of skills that are usually presumed to be part of a normal secondary school student's equipment, for example, how to ask questions, how to study, how to take notes, or how to read.

Assignments should not only be realistic in length and difficulty, they should also be realistic with respect to the experience, needs, and expectations of the students. Students from poverty areas need a curriculum that seems valuable to them and is close enough to their own lives to have meaning. They would profit from learning from people at home and in the community. They need to learn about themselves.

Fourth, try to capitalize on their interests and point out the practical value of what is to be learned. Take advantage of their belief in the usefulness of the fundamentals, the vocational, and the scientific. Utilize the boys' masculinity. Let them read the sports page, science fiction, or anything else that will get them started. This is no time for intellectual snobbery.

A discussion that is centered on topics with which the students have some firsthand familiarity can be a lively, informative, thought-provoking learning experience. Thus when at Jersey City's

Snyder High School one of the "difficult" classes discussed ways to improve the city, the students had an opportunity not only to express themselves in full discussion, but also to think seriously about problems of some importance to themselves personally. When all is said and done, poor adolescents, like other students, manufacture their own concepts. They will build them most effectively if they learn by means that emphasize thinking and creativity.

This illustration points up the fact that classes for "deprived" youth should be interesting, relevant, and active. Role playing and dramatic presentations are often very successful. In Central High School, Newark, N. J., for instance, a black studies class, noted for its high rate of absenteeism, showed an amazing amount of potential talent when it rehearsed, read, and videotaped a short play. At least one student who was believed to be a nonreader showed that she could not only read but read dramatically when the occasion seemed worthwhile.

Other teachers have achieved good results from having students create a class book out of their own writing. A junior high school teacher in an extremely difficult slum area uses student-designed and -executed bulletin boards and displays very effectively. Classes that feature games are usually popular as well as classes that make use of the various media. Classes that utilize a variety of materials are always likely to be more interesting than textbook recitations. Probably books should always be thought as aids to learning. Certainly they should not be the be-all and end-all of instruction in classes in which students do not read well.

Fifth, it is also important to make sure that each student has real success. Everyone needs the feeling that comes from succeeding in doing something worthwhile. Poor adolescents do not have such feelings in school often enough. One way to provide them with the opportunity to experience such feelings is to encourage students to help each other with troublesome assignments and to work together in teams. Such arrangements provide students with allies and coworkers with whom they can share both the work and the responsibility.

Because they are not alone in the learning endeavor, they can look to other students for support and so the fear of failure or of appearing foolish is not so pressing. Frequently students learn better from other students, and as a result both the helper and the one being helped are rewarded with a feeling of success and importance.

Sixth, physical activities are very useful in classes of lower socioeconomic status students. Acting out scenes or role playing can sometimes be very effective, particularly in teaching history or interpreting literature. The tendency of students from the lower socioeconomic classes to be physically oriented also makes it likely that they will take favorably to teaching machines and other gadgetry. In any case teachers should give the students plenty of chances to learn by doing, for such activities will ordinarily be much more successful than lecturing and other primarily verbal techniques.

Seventh, from the preceding paragraphs one can readily see that students from poverty areas, just as other students, benefit from taking the responsibility for charting and conducting their own learning activities. We teachers tend to do too much for students when we should encourage them to do things themselves. Since poor people tend to be dependent on others, one should be especially careful to avoid this fault when teaching them. In so far as possible, one should try to involve students in the planning and executing of the lessons. If one starts with something familiar to them, they are usually competent enough to take a large share in the decision making if they have a little help and guidance.

Eighth, poor adolescents need to have opportunities to create and to learn to think. Problem-solving activities that are consistent with the ability levels and experience of the students seem to be excellent for these students. Taba and Elkins suggest the following sequence as one way of developing skill in thinking with deprived students.

1. Find out by written work and open discussion what the concepts, feelings, and skills of students are.
2. Read a story or two for analysis of the ideas one wishes to consider.

3. Let the students work out these points in small groups with the help of books.
4. Discuss, analyze, compare these points in class.
5. Apply the new broader view to look at their own family situation.[4]

Ninth, open-ended questions and discussions can also be used with good results. To make them most effective teachers should learn to conduct discussions as conversations. The ordinary teacher-centered discussion is liable to be more like an inquisition than a conversation. That is too bad, because it tends to stop students from thinking.

Tenth, the teacher must respect both the students and their culture. Accept the students as persons and let them know by your behavior that you are on their side. Sometimes, because of unfortunate past experiences, the students will need a great deal of convincing. Try to overcome the hostility by deeds not words. Don't talk down to the students. Don't be condescending. Don't demean yourself. Tend to your teaching and concentrate on getting the material across. If you convince the students that you respect them and are trying your best to teach them, you may find that their hostility will be replaced by loyalty and respect.

Ethnic Groups

The United States is a land of many cultures. Your classes may be made up of Blacks, Hispanics, Native Americans, Chinese, WASPS, or representatives of other ethnic or racial groups, each having its own culture.

All of these cultures are rich, but each is different. These differences may be difficult to understand unless you take steps to learn about them and to respect them. As quickly as you can, learn about

---

[4] Hilda Taba and Deborah Elkins, *Teaching Strategies for the Culturally Disadvantaged* (Chicago: Rand McNally, 1966), p. 204.

Examine some of the textbooks for middle school courses in your field. Are there any reasons why they would be unsatisfactory for educationally disadvantaged students?

What could you do to help students from a non-English speaking background?

Are there any things you could do to combat directly the deterrents to school learning that result from poor living conditions or antiintellectual home environments?

---

the cultures from which your students spring. Make yourself aware of their values, taboos, and mores, and adapt your teaching strategies and techniques to them. In doing so remember that individuals in ethnic groups differ from each other. Avoid making unwarranted generalizations because of students' race or language. Social-economic status, place of origin, religion, and so on all have their influence on individual beliefs, values, and notions about correct behavior. Class differences are as great in minority ethnic and racial groups as in the WASP society.

Whenever feasible, you should try to incorporate ethnic materials to bolster your teaching, help students come to grips with the pluralism of modern American society and to eliminate racial and ethnic bias. In most up-to-date school systems the curriculum builders have provided curriculum materials for teachers' use. The point is to use such materials judiciously so as to eliminate ethnic bias and stereotyping. In every course students should have opportunities to become proud of their roots and to make the most of their talents.

You should also make yourself familiar with the language of the groups. If your students are Spanish speaking, learn basic Spanish. If they speak the argot of the ghetto, learn it. Don't worry so much about the words students use and the ways they express themselves as about the ideas they are expressing. Let them use their own idioms without carping on grammar, syntax, and the like. Do, however, try to help them master the skills of standard

English. Your own instruction should be in excellent but simple standard English.

Otherwise your basic strategies for teaching culturally different students should not differ greatly from good teaching of any other students.

Eliminating Sexual Bias

Over the years for various reasons stereotypes concerning the roles and abilities of men and women have become common. The result has been hardship for both boys and girls. Therefore, take care that neither your teaching techniques nor your teaching materials reflect sexual bias or stereotyping. Your own good judgment should be sufficient to guide you in this aspect of your teaching.

The Gifted and Talented

Gifted and talented students are those students who show themselves to be capable of high performance in such areas as

- General intellectual ability.
- Specific academic aptitude.
- Creative and productive thinking.
- Leadership ability.
- Visual and performing arts.[5]

In general we can say that the gifted students are students who have considerable potential in one of these areas and that the talented are these who have built on this potential and demonstrated achievement in one or more of the areas.

A student's giftedness may be limited to only one of these categories, but is more likely to spread across several of them. A student who is gifted in one area may or may not be gifted in another. To identify gifted students one can take advantage of aptitude and achievement test scores. However these scores are not entirely dependable. One should also take advantage of other students' opinions, anecdotal information, autobiographical and biographical information, and particularly observation of the quality of students' work and of their thinking. Oftentimes observation will show you that a student who does not perform exceptionally well in your classes is really smart after all. One should especially be on the lookout for creative students. Those students who are adept at sensing problems or gaps in information, forming ideas or hypotheses, testing and modifying these hypotheses, and communications,[6] too often go unrecognized in our schools.

Strategies and Approaches

In order to realize their potentials, gifted and talented students need special teaching and programs. Proper teaching environments can build talent, but improper teaching can squelch it. So give your gifted students the opportunities to stretch their talents by attempting high-level assignments. Let them study complex units and materials, engage in action-oriented, thought-provoking learning experiences, and undertake optional activities suited to their individual proclivities. Individual and small group investigations of real problems may be especially fruitful, for students of talent need challenge and high, but reasonable, goals to keep from becoming intellectually lazy drifters. Where the ordinary youth may be satisfied to read about the westward movement in a text, the brilliant student could be

[5] Sidney Marland, *Education of the Gifted and Talented:* Report to the Congress of the United States by the U.S. Commissioner of Education (Washington, DC: U.S. Office of Education, 1972), p. 2.

[6] E. Paul Torrance, *Creativity in the Classroom, What Research Says to the Teacher* (Washington, DC: National Education Association, 1977), p. 6.

reading *The Oregon Trail*. When studying World War II, the brilliant student might try to reconcile the accounts given by Sir Winston Churchill, General Eisenhower, and others. In metalworking the academically brilliant youth might, in addition to doing fine work, study such topics as metallurgy, the metal trades, the economics of metals, and the effect of metals on history.

In addition to attempting assignments of a high order, talented students should meet high standards of workmanship. They can do choice work; you must see to it that they do. Do not accept careless, poorly written, or poorly executed work from talented students. To do so engrains in them slothfulness and mediocrity.

Furthermore, bright students can accept considerable responsibility for their own direction. They should have experience in planning and evaluating their own work. Since they are potential leaders, they need the experience in planning, organizing, making decisions, and carrying out plans. Moreover, they should have opportunities for leadership and service in their classes.

Sometimes attempting to hold brilliant students to standards higher than those of their classmates may backfire. Some bright students may resent having to do better work than other students. With bright students this pitfall usually can be avoided by appealing to their pride, by attempting to convince them that the assignments are really worthwhile, and by making the assignments exciting and challenging rather than drudgery. Some teachers provide opportunities for recognition of the brilliant students in their testing by adding additional difficult extra questions at the end of the test making it possible for a student to get more than 100 per cent of the questions on the test. This device has been somewhat successful. However, the threat of marks is usually of little value. Talented students can earn good marks without half trying. To get the most from these students the teacher must call upon more genuine motives. Usually this is not hard to do since the talented youth almost always enjoys challenging tasks.

Reading for the Gifted

Ordinary high school textbooks seldom meet the needs of academically gifted students. This lack can be filled in many ways: students can read their assignments from college texts, primary sources, original writings, or other works. Much use can be made of individualized reading to supplement or substitute for the ordinary assignments. In many courses the students can profitably choose their own reading with only a little guidance. Often they will profit from reading several selections on a topic. A good technique is for each student to make a list of proposed readings, and submit it to the teacher before beginning to work. Another method is to give the gifted students study guides with suggested problems for investigation and a list of suitable, pertinent readings. Learning packets are good if they provide enough challenge.

Not only should gifted students read widely, they should also read critically. Unfortunately many gifted youths never learn the more advanced skills of critical reading. Teachers of gifted students must provide them with direct instruction in critical reading skills and plenty of practice if these students are to ever make full use of their potentials.

Research and Depth Study

Not only should the subject matter for brilliant students deal with generalizations and abstractions, but the students themselves should have a chance to develop their own generalizations. Memorizing facts and other information is not enough for students with good minds. They should find things out for themselves. In science their laboratory work could include real problems. In literature they could write some real criticism. In music they could perform and compose. Their school projects could be actual scholarly research projects, or, at least, the study of a topic in depth. By studying in this manner, students would not only be able to master basic facts and skills but also move on to the creation of new concepts by making logical inferences from the information available. The topics to be studied can be closely allied with the course syllabus or range far from it.

The Seminar Approach

Small seminar classes of bright students are excellent devices for utilizing the impact of depth study. One type of seminar consists of a member's presenting a paper on a topic as a basis for group discussion. Another type consists of general discussion on topics all have studied in some detail. In either case the students are encouraged to bring all their knowledge and skill to bear on the problem in a penetrating, logical analysis. In such discussions the interchange must be free and open. No rules, except those of logical analysis and courtesy, should bar the way. The purpose of the seminar is to encourage hard, incisive examination of carefully researched material.

Creative Students

The routine, conformist, unimaginative nature of so many middle and high school classes can be stifling to creative adolescents. Your classes should provide plenty of opportunities for creative behavior for these students. They should have lots of inquiry, creative research, and other problem-solving activities. In all classes these students should be encouraged to venture forth on their intellectual wings without fear of reprisal. Respect their unusual questions, show that you value their ideas, provide them opportunities to learn for themselves, and give them credit for self-initiated learning. Above all, let them figure things out, discover ideas and concepts, and find their own answers to problems without threat of immediate evaluation and correction. In short, plan learning experiences that will stimulate and foster creativity. Not everyone should be forced into the same rut all the time.

What can be done to provide brilliant students with work sufficiently challenging?

A teacher complained that her bright students were not working up to capacity because she could not make them do more work than ordinary students. What would you suggest that the teacher do to help keep the bright students working up to capacity?

In some schools teachers use the services of brilliant students in teaching the less brilliant. What is your estimate of this practice?

How would you attempt to catch the interest of a brilliant student who was obviously bored in one of your classes?

How would you go about to tempt brilliant students into doing considerably more and harder work than other students?

Summary

Every student is different from every other one, and so each one's education should be different if one is going to benefit from it optimally. These differences cause many pedagogical problems. On the other hand, they also offer the teachers levers by which to make their teaching more effective.

Insofar as possible, schooling should be individualized. Secondary school administrators have attempted to provide for the individual differences by organizational devices. Among these devices have been such things as tracks and streams, homogeneous grouping, electives, minicourses, acceleration of the brilliant, and ungraded schools. None of these plans has been able to provide the complete answer to the problem. Even when the administrative devices are successful, they can cope with only part of the problem. As in all other instructional matters, the final solution must be worked out by individual teachers.

Luckily teachers have at their disposal many techniques for coping with individual differences in students. They may differentiate their assignments by varying the difficulty, length, or type of work from student to student. They may find it desirable to group their students within the classes according to need, interest, or abilities, or to partially differentiate the work through individual or group projects. Sometimes they may find it advantageous to allow some students to move through courses more quickly, or more slowly, than other students, or to encourage some students to enrich their learning by going into topics more deeply than other students do.

Individualizing instruction is not as difficult as teachers fear, and it is necessary. One way to meet this need is by conducting the class as a laboratory. In laboratory periods many students can proceed with a minimum of guidance while the teacher helps students who need assistance. Particularly valuable as means of freeing teachers' time for those who need help are the many self-instructional devices which help students teach themselves. Among these devices are computers, teaching machines and programs as well as older devices like self-administering and self-correcting practice material. Dittoed or tape-recorded study and activity guides and learning packets can be extremely helpful and should be used. Combined with the laboratory approach they are especially effective. The same comment is true of the contract plan, independent study, and continuous progress, all of which require a laboratory atmosphere plus some system of helping and guiding students as they work independently or in groups. Free periods in which students are allowed to follow their own bents are also useful.

Finding time for individual instruction is difficult, but when teachers give students more time to participate in the planning and evaluating of their own studying, they can free a lot of time without slighting any students. Also teachers can make time by encouraging students to help each other.

If one provides well for individual differences one must expect to have to evaluate students' learning on new bases because students will not learn the same things in the same way. As a corollary, one must also expect to use a variety of materials. Not only will many readings be required, but also materials for many other kinds of activities.

Remedial instruction is one method of providing for individual differences. Basically it consists of finding where a student's learning is weak and then aiming instruction at curing the weakness. It may be in the form of small-group or individual instruction of bright, average, or poor students.

Teaching slow learners requires much skill and patience. Careful diagnosis of each student is necessary if students are to receive the kind of help they need. This diagnostic activity is particularly important because poor learning is often the result of insufficiencies in the student's earlier education. In general, the curriculum for poor learners should be simple, practical, realistic, and meaningful. Teaching methods should emphasize concrete, simple activities with sufficient practice and review to make the learning stick. The materials of instruction used ordinarily should be less verbal than in other classes. Reading material should be short and easy, but not childish. Consequently, teachers may find it necessary to develop their own materials.

Low socioeconomic status youth often have many of the problems of slow learners because of gaps and differences in their backgrounds. However, there has been a tendency to underestimate the potential of these youth. Their academic failures are more often failures of the school and the community than student failures. In dealing with them one must treat them with the respect they deserve. As a rule, they tend to accept authoritarian classes whose orientation is physical, practical, and realistic.

The key to teaching gifted, talented and creative youths is to urge them forward and not to hold them back. Since they enjoy the abstract and like to learn, the gifted students need plenty of opportunities to exercise their minds. In doing so they can accept a great amount of the responsibility for directing and evaluating their own learnings if the teacher gives them adequate guidance.

Additional Reading

Banks, James A. *Teaching Strategies for Ethnic Studies,* 2nd ed. Boston: Allyn and Bacon, 1979.

Brockman, Ellen Mary, ed. *Teaching Handicapped Students Mathematics.* Washington, DC: National Education Association, 1981.

Charles, C. M. *Individualizing Instruction,* 2nd ed. St. Louis, MO: C. V. Mosby, 1980.

Correll, Marsha M. *Teaching the Gifted and Talented,* Fastback 119. Bloomington, IN: Phi Delta Kappa Educational Foundation, 1978.

Corrick, Marshall, ed. *Teaching Handicapped Students Science.* Washington, DC: National Education Association, 1981.

Dunn, Rita, and Kenneth Dunn. *Teaching Students Through Their Individual Learning Styles: A Practical Approach.* Reston, VA: Reston Publishing, 1978.

Fenstermacher, Gary D., and John I. Goodlad. *Individual Differences and the Common Curriculum,* Eighty-second Yearbook of the National Society for the Study of Education, Part I. Chicago: University of Chicago Press, 1983.

Fox, Lynn H., and William G. Durden. *Educating Verbally Gifted Youth,* Fastback 176. Bloomington, IN: Phi Delta Kappa Educational Foundation, 1982.

Friedman, Paul G. *Teaching the Gifted and Talented Oral Communication and Leadership.* Washington, DC: National Education Association, 1980.

Gage, N. L., and David C. Berliner. *Educational Psychology,* 3rd ed. Boston: Houghton Mifflin, 1984, Chap. 21.

George, Paul, and Gordon Lawrence. *Handbook for Middle School Teaching.* Glenview, IL: Scott Foresman, 1982.

George, William C., and Kevin G. Bartkovich. *Teaching the Gifted and Talented in the Mathematics Classroom.* Washington, DC: National Education Association, 1980.

Hasazi, Susan E., Paul D. Rice, and Robert York. *Mainstreaming: Merging Regular and Special Education,* Fastback 124. Bloomington, IN: Phi Delta Kappa Educational Foundation, 1979.

Otto, Wayne, and Richard J. Smith. *Corrective and Remedial Teaching,* 3rd ed. Boston: Houghton Mifflin, 1980.

Palomaki, Jane, ed. *Teaching Handicapped Students Vocational Education.* Washington, DC: National Education Association, 1981.

Passow, A. Harry, ed. *The Gifted and the Talented: Their Education and Development,* The Seventy-eighth Yearbook of the National Society for the Study of Education, Part I. Chicago: University of Chicago Press, 1979, Chaps. 1, 2, 11, 18.

Plowman, Paul D. *Teaching the Gifted and Talented in the Social Studies Classroom.* Washington, DC: National Education Association, 1980.

Price, Jane. *Teaching Handicapped Students English.* Washington, DC: National Education Association, 1981.

Roice, G. Robert, ed. *Teaching Handicapped Students Physical Education.* Washington, DC: National Education Association, 1981.

Romey, William D. *Teaching the Gifted and Talented in the Science Classroom.* Washington, DC: National Education Association, 1980.

Shaw, Terry, ed. *Teaching Handicapped Students Social Studies.* Washington, DC: National Education Association, 1981.

Stephens, Thomas M. et al. *Teaching Mainstreamed Students.* New York: Wiley, 1982.

Tannenbaum, Abraham J. *Gifted Children, Psychological and Educational Perspectives.* New York: Macmillan, 1982.

Tuttle, Frederick B. *Gifted and Talented Students, What Research Says to the Teacher,* revised ed. Washington, DC: National Education Association, 1983.

Warger, Cynthia L., Loviak E. Aldinger, and Kathy A. Okum, *Mainstreaming in the Secondary*

School: The Role of the Regular Teacher. Bloomington, IN: Phi Delta Kappa Educational Foundation, 1983.

Wehlage, Gary G. *Effective Programs for the Marginal High School Student*, Fastback 191. Bloomington, IN: Phi Delta Kappa Educational Foundation, 1983.

West, William D. *Teaching the Gifted and Talented in the English Classroom. Washington, DC: National Education Association, 1980.*

Wright, Jill D. *Teaching the Gifted and Talented in the Middle School.* Washington, DC: National Education Association, 1983.

17

Classroom Evaluation

Overview

We teachers are like the navigators of ships at sea. In order to know which way to go, we need to know where we are. Therefore, like the navigator who must keep a running record of the ship's approximate position and make frequent checks to fix its exact position, we must continually appraise and reappraise our positions. Otherwise how would we know in what direction to aim our course? We call this appraisal and reapparaisal of the teaching-learning situation *evaluation*.

Evaluation has many purposes. Teachers use it as a basis for school marks, reporting to parents, and promotion. Administrators use it as a basis for categorizing students into groups. Guidance counselors use it as a basis for student advisement. Students use it as a basis for mapping out their own programs. Parents, school officials, and teachers use it as a basis for curriculum revision. But its most important role is its use in the teaching-learning process itself because

1. It gives the teachers the feedback they need in order to know what the students have learned and what to do next.
2. It gives the students the feedback they need in order to profit from their successes and failures.
3. It helps teachers to understand the students, their abilities, and their needs. Therefore it is the essential element in diagnosis.
4. It is important in motivating students.

In this chapter, after a short look at the theoretical aspects, we discuss the procedures and techniques by which you can carry out the assessment of the students' progress in units and courses, and the selection, construction, and use of measuring devices and techniques. At the conclusion of the chapter, you should be able to build an evaluation plan for a unit or course, select or construct measuring instruments or procedures appropriate for the learning you wish to evaluate, use these instruments and procedures properly, and evaluate their usefulness and accuracy.

As you read the chapter, note that *evaluation is not testing, but making a judgment;* that in teaching, evaluation is based on measurements; that it must conform to the instructional goals if it is to be valid; that there are many different kinds of measuring devices and procedures; that you should be careful to pick the ones appropriate to your objectives; that whatever measuring instruments you use should be valid, reliable, objective, and usable; that the instruments must be carefully constructed; and that all this care may be wasted unless the instruments are carefully administered and scored so as to provide feedback that both you and the students can use as a basis for the next steps in their learning.

Background

Defining Evaluation

The word *evaluate* means to put a value on or assign worth to something. It includes a quantitative and/or a qualitative description (that is, a measurement or assessment) plus a value judgment.

The essential element in evaluation is judgment. This is the quality that makes it different from measurement or assessment. When one measures or assesses a situation, one merely describes the situation; when one evaluates a situation, one judges its value.

For example, let us suppose that we give the students a test and find that Susie's score was 70. This information in itself does not tell us much of anything. Is 70 good or bad? It depends. If 70 represents the highest score of all the students of our school, we may decide that it is very good; if it represents the lowest score, we may decide that it is pretty bad; but if it is the lowest score, but the best effort of the slowest student, we may decide that it is not so bad at that. Evaluation, then, is the judgment or interpretation that one draws from the information at hand. Valid evaluations depend on accurate measurements and assessments.

Consequently, evaluation of students' progress must be a two-step process. In the first step, one must gather the pertinent data for an assessment of the students' status. For this purpose we use the tools and techniques of educational measurement to estimate both the quantity and quality of the students' learning and other pertinent factors. Then, once these estimates or assessments have been made, the second step is to use the information to make reasoned judgments concerning the merits and inadequacies of our students and programs in light of our instructional objectives.

A Word of Caution

You should not expect too much of the evaluation process. All evaluation is subject to some error, although careful design and execution will reduce the chance of error. Measurements are only approximations at best. In education they can never be precise; sometimes they are wildly inaccurate. No matter what types of instruments are used, they are subject to numerous limitations. There is always some error in sampling. There is always some error inherent in the instrument itself (e.g., true-false tests encourage guessing); there is always some error in the process of administering and scoring (e.g., scoring of essay tests is often greatly inconsistent); there is always some error in our interpretation of the results. Therefore you should never accept an educational measurement or evaluation as conclusive unless it is supported by a sufficient amount of other confirmative data. Because of these limitations and the resultant need to support our attempts at measurement with other data, it has become quite common to use the term *assessment* instead of *measurement*.

Recently there has been considerable criticism of the use of tests and measurements in both the popular and professional press. Look up some of these articles. How much should we test? Should promotion and graduation depend on test scores? Should high school diplomas be granted only to those who pass a state test? Should test scores be used to evaluate curricula, teaching, and teacher salaries? How can you both gain the benefit that assessment can provide and avoid the pitfalls of overdependence on tests and measurements and drawing conclusions from erroneous data? (See Chapter 7 and later sections of this chapter on interpretation of scores.)

What is the difference between measurement and evaluation?

What can test results be used for? What are the most valid uses of test scores?

Evaluation in Units and Courses

Objectives and Evaluation

When assessing student progress in units and courses, the first step is to prepare sound instructional objectives. As we stated earlier, evaluation consists of making reasoned judgments in light of the instructional objectives. This implies of course that teachers should be certain that the evaluative data they use are pertinent to their objectives. All too many educational decisions are based on data that are irrelevant to the problem at hand. This fault can be avoided by using clear, specific instructional objectives as a basis for both one's instruction and one's evaluation. In general, specific criterion-referenced behavioral objectives are the most useful types of objectives for the evaluator.[1]

Preparing an Evaluation Plan

The second step in evaluating the unit or course is to set up a plan for evaluation. To be sure that the evaluation includes all the essential aspects and utilizes proper measurement techniques, you should make your plan for evaluating the unit or course before you start to teach it. This evaluation plan should ensure (1) that the instruments used assess the progress made toward achieving each and every objective in proportion to its importance, and (2) that the proper types of instruments are used to assess the progress being made. To make an evaluation plan, simply list your objectives and note the procedures you will use to measure the attainment of these objectives and the weight you will give each in the total assessment. This plan is sometimes called a table of specifications. A form

[1] See Chapter 8 for descriptions and examples of specific objectives.

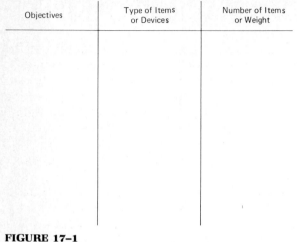

Objectives	Type of Items or Devices	Number of Items or Weight

FIGURE 17–1
Evaluation Plan.

for planning your evaluation appears as Figure 17–1.

Selecting the *Right* Instrument

The third step is to select or construct the instruments and procedures by which you will carry out your plan. This step is complicated by the fact that there are so many devices and procedures for assessing student progress. The ubiquitous pencil-and-paper tests are of course the most commonly used. Some teachers use hardly anything else. They are not, however, always the most useful for they often fail to give us the information we most need. By their very nature, paper-and-pencil tests are more likely to test knowing-about than knowing, verbalizations rather than the ability to do, or platitudes rather than changes in attitude or behavior. Rating scales, checklists, self-reporting devices, questionnaires, anecdotal reports, behavior logs, and sociometric devices may be more useful for your purposes than tests. Each measuring device and test item you use should be carefully selected to do a particular job and matched to the type of job it can do best.

Summative, Formative, or Diagnostic Evaluation

Authorities in the field[2] have divided evaluation into three types: summative evaluation, formative evaluation and diagnostic evaluation. Summative evaluation is the sort of evaluation we perform at the end of a course or unit in order to grade the students and to judge our own teaching success. Formative evaluation is the type of evaluation we perform as we go on in order to decide how well we are doing and what we need to do next. Formative tests are usually sharper in focus than summative tests and less useful for grading students. Diagnostic evaluation tends to combine elements of the other two. At the beginning of courses and units, diagnostic evaluation uses the techniques of summative evaluation to determine where students should be placed (e.g., fast, middle, or slow groups). During the courses and units, diagnostic evaluation uses the techniques of formative evaluation to discover the causes of students' difficulty. In most of your teaching, diagnostic and formative evaluation will converge.

It is most important that you select the proper types of instruments for the type of evaluation appropriate for your aim. Ordinarily the instruments in diagnostic and formative evaluation should be criterion-referenced whereas those used for summative evaluation should be norm-referenced, for instance. (These terms are explained in a later section.) Ordinarily unit assessments should be formative and summative evaluation should be reserved for final examinations and the like.

Criteria for a Good Measuring Device

No matter what type of measuring device you select, you want it to be a good one. Therefore, you should consider four criteria.

[2] E.g., Benjamin S. Bloom, J. Thomas Hastings, and George F. Madaus, *Evaluation to Improve Learning* (New York: McGraw-Hill, 1981).

1. How valid is it?
2. How reliable is it?
3. How objective is it?
4. How usable is it?

Validity. The most important of these criteria is validity, that is, the extent to which the device measures what it is supposed to measure. A measuring device that is not valid is worthless. Validity is dependent on several things. In the first place, the instrument must be suitable to the nature of what is to be measured. A paper-and-pencil test would hardly be a valid measure of a baseball player's ability to bat, for instance. Furthermore, the instrument must measure all the significant aspects of what is to be measured in an amount proportional to their importance. If, in testing batting ability, one tested the batter's stance, but not his hitting, the test would give a false result because of poor sampling. Moreover, to be valid the test must also discriminate. In testing batting ability, of what use is a test that does not differentiate between the good batters and the poor batters?[3]

Curriculum validity is a particularly important criterion in establishing the worth of achievement tests. Curriculum validity indicates the extent to which a test measures what was supposed to be taught in the course. Without it, an achievement test cannot be valid. When the items of an achievement test are concerned with learning that was not part of the course, the test will give incorrect results because of its lack of curriculum validity. Commercial achievement tests sometimes give an inaccurate picture of the achievement of students in a particular school because the curriculum of the school may differ from that for which the commercial test was designed. In the ordinary classroom situation curriculum validity is determined by examining the instrument to be sure (1) that it does test for the specific goals of the unit or course

and (2) that it gives each goal approximately the same weight that the unit or course plan calls for.[4]

Reliability. A second test of the worth of an evaluative device is reliability. An instrument is reliable if it can be trusted to give the same results when it is repeated or when different forms are used. In other words, a reliable instrument is consistent and dependable. When a test is reliable one can be sure that its measurement is fairly accurate because chance errors and other inconsistencies have been largely eliminated. Just as a steel measuring tape is less likely to be stretched out of shape than a cloth tape or a fine laboratory scale is likely to be more dependable than a bathroom scale, a reliable test is less likely to be affected by irrelevant or chance factors than an unreliable one.

Statistical methods are used to determine coefficients of reliability for standardized tests, but techniques of this sort are not really suitable for use with teacher-built tests and other classroom instruments. One can make teacher-built tests fairly reliable by (1) making the tests as long as one reasonably can (so that chance errors will tend to cancel each other out), (2) scoring the test as objectively as possible (so that the number of inconsistencies in scoring will be reduced), (3) writing the items and directions as carefully as possible (so that students will not make irrelevant errors because of ambiguities, misunderstood directions, and so on), and (4) administering the test as carefully as possible (so that error will not be introduced by nonstandard conditions such as distracting noise, lack of time, and so on). Careful preparation, administration, and objective scoring help to improve the reliability of other instruments also.

---

[3] In criterion-referenced testing, a test would discriminate if it ascertained which students met the criterion and which did not.

[4] Perhaps one should make a distinction between content validity and curriculum validity. A standardized test, which gives a good sample of the subject matter of the discipline but not the subject matter of the discipline as taught in a particular school, would have content validity. A test that reflects the subject matter as taught in a particular school's curriculum would have curriculum validity. (A test with content validity might point out where the curriculum in a particular school is lacking). Sometimes the terms are used interchangeably, as we have done.

Validity and reliability are not totally independent. Reliability refers to consistency, and an instrument that is not consistent certainly cannot be counted on to give truthful information. Therefore to be valid, an instrument must be reliable. But a reliable instrument may not necessarily be valid. It can give one wrong information consistently. Consequently, to measure progress toward certain high-level objectives, an essay test with fairly low potential reliability, but reasonably high potential validity, may be a better risk than an objective test with much higher potential reliability, but lower potential validity.

Objectivity.   Another criterion of a good instrument is objectivity. By objectivity educators mean that the personality of the scorer does not affect the scoring of the test. Thus a truly objective test will be scored in exactly the same way by every scorer. For this reason objectivity in an instrument helps make the scoring fair and the instrument reliable. As long as validity is not sacrificed, the more objective the instrument the better. However, a valid instrument may be a good instrument even though it is not objective, whereas an objective instrument that is not valid is always worthless.

Usability.   A fourth criterion of a good evaluative device is its usability. Obviously a two-hour test is not suitable for a forty-minute class period. Everything else being equal, teachers should avoid instruments that are hard to administer, difficult to score, and expensive.

Carrying Out the Plan

The fourth step is to teach the unit or course and carry out your evaluation plan. In this step you must pay particular attention to properly using, administering, and scoring the evaluative devices and procedures. We learn more about this in later sections.

> What are the most important criteria for judging the worth of a test? Rate these criteria in order of importance. Why did you choose that order? When would you use an objective test? Apply these criteria to a test in one of your college courses.

Tools for Assessment

We now turn to a discussion of the construction and use of various measurement instruments. First we discuss observational methods, including evidences of the students' work, then move on to self-reporting techniques, and finally testing.

Observation and Sampling Work

Observation and examination of work samples are perhaps the most common bases for judging the behavior of another person. Through its use an alert teacher, properly trained, can often find clues to the causes for a student's behavior. This technique, although as old as humanity, unfortunately has several limitations. Observers are notoriously unreliable; students behave differently when they know they are being observed. However, to a degree, these limitations can be reduced by careful observation. A helpful technique is to determine in advance what to look for and how to look for it. Another is to set up a checklist, rating scale, or some other written guide to help objectify one's observations. In any case it is helpful to record your impressions soon after your observation.

Rating Scales

Rating scales are especially helpful in judging skills, procedures, and personal social behavior. Rating scales can also be used to help objectify the evaluation of products of the student's work, such as a lampshade made in an industrial arts class or a composition or theme done in an English class. Such devices have the advantage of showing the student an analysis of the rater's evaluation and also of preventing the rater from being unduly influenced by any one aspect of the work being evaluated.

In using such tools, the final evaluation can be made dependent upon a numerical score. However, one must always remember that often, as in the case of literary and art works and other creative activities, evaluation cannot be safely reduced to numbers. To avoid culs-de-sac, the rater should allow for the possibility that sometimes a single characteristic may outweigh all others and that some items may be completely inapplicable.

Preparing a Rating Scale. Rating scales and checklists are easy to build and to use. To make a rating scale, merely decide what characteristic you wish to rate. Then arrange a scale for each of these characteristics. Since a five-point scale is about all a rater can handle, there is little point in making finer distinctions. In any case, do not use more than seven or fewer than three categories. If each point of the scale is labeled, the rating is easier.

To illustrate this process, suppose we wish to build a scale to use as a guide for judging the excellence of some posters that students have prepared. First we must decide what to consider in judging the posters. Let us say that among other things we wish to include neatness, lettering, eye appeal, and design. We then provide a rating scale similar to the one in Figure 17–2. In this rating scale, the gradations are indicated by descriptive words encompassing the gamut from best to worst. These descriptions help make the teacher ratings somewhat more objective than they might be otherwise.

Another type of rating scale is shown in Figure 17–3. In this rating scale five equals the highest rating and one the lowest. "NA" means "not applicable." The scale is used by circling the number desired. Still another plan is simply to list the characteristics you think important and then rate them according to a code such as * + √ − 0 as in Figure 17–4.

In preparing the characteristics to be rated in the scale, be sure that each is significant. Sometimes

FIGURE 17–2
Rating Scale for Posters.

Design					
	Crystalline beautiful perfect	Clear well-balanced pleasing	Mediocre	Confusing poorly balanced crowded	Hodgepodge

Neatness					
	Meticulous	Excellent	Average	Fair	Sloppy

Lettering					
	Superior	Excellent	Average	Fair	Poor

Eye Appeal					
	Overwhelming	Intriguing	Catchy	Dull	Insipid

(Circle number indicating rating. Code: 5, highest; 1, lowest;
NA, not applicable)
1. Originality
                5 4 3 2 1 NA
2. Clearness
                5 4 3 2 1 NA
                        * * *
11. Spelling
                5 4 3 2 1 NA
12. Sentence structure
                5 4 3 2 1 NA

FIGURE 17–3
Rating Scale for Written Work.

some of the characteristics included in rating scales really do not make any real difference. Be sure also that each characteristic is clearly and precisely specified so that the rater knows exactly what to rate. Sometimes in order to make the characteristics clear, it will be necessary to break them into components. Characteristics that are too broad are difficult to rate fairly because one time the rater may emphasize one aspect and another time, another aspect. Be sure also that the characteristics to be rated are readily observable. It is helpful to the rater if the scale allows for ratings between categories, e.g., in Figure 17–2 the rater may feel that the lettering should be rated better than average but not quite excellent. The rater should also be allowed to skip any of the characteristics that seem not applicable.

(Place rating in parenthesis. Key: * Excellent; +Very Good; √Average; −Less than Average; 0 Poor)
1. Original   ( )
2. Clear   ( )
                 * * *
11. Spelling   ( )
12. Sentence structure   ( )

FIGURE 17–4
Simplified Rating Scale for Written Work.

Using Rating Scales. Even though using rating scales is relatively easy, there are a few caveats that raters should be aware of. One is the danger of halo effect. Raters frequently rate students with good reputation higher than they rate students of lesser reputation even when their performance is the same. Similarly, raters tend to rate certain categories higher (or lower) than they should because associated characteristics were rated high (or low). This tendency is called the logical error. Another source of error is the common tendency to rate all students in much the same way. Some raters rate everyone high; some raters rate everyone low; and some raters rate everyone average. Yielding to such tendencies reduces the effectiveness of the rating scale and makes it difficult to separate the good guys from the bad guys.

Checklists

Checklists differ from rating scales in that they only indicate the presence or absence of characteristics. They are most useful in the evaluating of products and procedures. They can also be used to gather evidence concerning students' progress toward specific objectives. They cannot be used to measure personal-social growth, however.

In building checklists one should include only characteristics whose presence or absence is significant. Otherwise checklists are prepared in much the same way as rating scales, and the same procedures and precautions apply except, of course, that one provides a place for checking presence or absence of the characteristic instead of a scale.

For instance, in evaluating some plastic letter openers that the students had made in an industrial

---

Is it really possible to objectify observations? Explain.

Compare the various types of rating scales and checklists given above. What are the strong points and weak points of each? Why?

Check each item if the letter opener is up to standard in this particular:
( ) 1. The blade is properly shaped.
( ) 2. All saw marks are removed.
( ) 3. The plastic is free from warping and pitting.

FIGURE 17–5
Checklist for Plastic Letter Opener—General Shop I.

art class, the teacher might make up a checklist such as the one in Figure 17–5. Checking the applicable items only, the list will give the teacher a firm basis for evaluating the product.

In the device presented in Figure 17–6 used for rating the speech of college students preparing for teaching, spaces are left blank so that the rater can either check or make some comment for each of the various items.

The Ranking Method

Another simple procedure for rating students' skills and accomplishments is the rank-order method. In this procedure the rater simply ranks the students or products from best to worst, or most to least. For instance, one might rank a set of themes from most original to least original, or a group of posters from most eye-appealing to least eye-appealing.

In using the rank-order method it is usually best to start at the ends and rank toward the middle.

Another procedure is to sort the students or products into five groups, e.g., best, better than average, average, less than average, least. This procedure is commonly used by teachers grading essays, essay-test questions, or projects. Usually this procedure involves considerable reshuffling among the groups before the final grouping is arrived at. If one wishes, then the students and projects within each group can be rearranged in rank order until one has a ranking from top to bottom of the entire group. As one can see, this last step is time consuming and cumbersome. Usually in the ordinary classroom it is unnecessary; ranking into five groups will suffice for most classroom purposes.

Rank-order methods have the advantage of ensuring that raters do not rate everyone high or low or average as they tend to do when using rating scales. However, they do not describe behavior as well as some other types of measurements and are meaningful only in the group ranked. The student who places lowest in a high-honors group may be doing very well indeed.

Themes, Notebooks, Homework, and Recitation

Of course, themes, homework, papers, and oral recitations are also evidence of student progress. They should be checked carefully. A good rule is never to assign anything that is not going to be

FIGURE 17–6
Speech Qualification Rating Sheet.

	Explanation	Reading	Questioning
Poised	____	____	____
Direct	____	____	____
Animated	____	____	____
Distinct	____	____	____
Audible	____	____	____
Fluent	____	____	____
Clear (ver)	____	____	____
(vis)	____	____	____
Pronunciation	____	____	____
RECOMMENDATION			

checked by someone. Practice material, however, need not always be checked by the teacher. Sometimes students can check their own and each other's work quite effectively.

In order to provide an objective basis for evaluating written work, teachers can utilize rating scales, checklists, and standards. A checklist for use in correcting themes might include such items as

- Does the student develop his thought logically?
- Is the central idea clearly expressed?
- Does the student document his facts?
- And so on.

Sometimes a simple set of standards to use as guidelines is all the teacher needs as he corrects the students' writing. In the case just mentioned, the standards might include such items as

- The theme clearly expresses a central idea.
- Everything in the theme presented as fact must be documented.
- The writer develops his thoughts logically.
- And so on.

Obviously such standards could be used to make up the items in a checklist.

In any case, both writing exercises and learning devices should be used mainly as aids to instruction. The emphasis should be on diagnosis, practice, and learning rather than on rating.

What would be the best way to test a student's honesty? Ability to swim? Appreciation of a poem? Freedom from prejudices? Understanding that "all men are created equal, with certain inalienable rights"? What do your answers imply as far as a testing program is concerned?

Self-evaluation Techniques

The most important purpose of evaluation is to help guide students to educational goals. The person most concerned in any teaching-learning situation is the student. *If evaluation is to be fully effective and the students are to set their goals correctly, they should participate in evaluating their own progress.*

Student self-evaluation can help students by

a. making the instructional objectives clear to them;
b. showing each student how well he has progressed;
c. showing each student his strengths and weaknesses;
d. developing self-evaluative skills;
e. creating an attitude toward objective self-evaluation.

For example, an evaluation technique used in an English class is to have the students criticize both their own themes and those of other students. Since the primary goal is clarity, the teacher asks the students to read each other's themes and point out what is not clear to them. Then the teacher, or on occasion another student, tells the writer where to find a discussion of the particular error in the text or the supplementary readings. Sometimes she gives the pupils self-correcting exercises to help remedy their faults. Ordinarily, the students work on these exercises independently until they think they have conquered the problem. Since the students know these exercises are not to be counted into their marks, they feel no need to cheat. The teacher feels that the students learn much more efficiently than they would have if she corrected each paper herself and doled out marks.

In another school the members of the class divided into groups each of which developed a plan for a utopian society. The student teacher holding this class devised a rating scale (Figure 17–7) by which the class members rated each group's plan for its utopia and its class presentation.

Students can keep anecdotal reports and behavior logs to measure their own work. For instance, a student working on a project can keep a daily log or diary of his progress and a record of his successes and difficulties. In a unit a student might

Category	Excellent	Good	Average	Fair	Poor	Comments
Believability: Might you want to see this place? Does it exist? Can it?						
Appeal: Are you ready to jump up and join this society?						
Justice: Are the laws plausible? Fair?						
Group Participation: Did each member of the panel seem important?						
Preparation: Did they know what they wanted to say?						
Presentation: Could you follow the logic?						

FIGURE 17–7
Creation of a Utopian Society.

submit short reports on herself at the culmination of different aspects of the work and estimate the worth of her product and the benefits she has gained from the activity. In many classes students keep records and report "The Things I Have Done During This Unit." These reports can be free-response papers in which the students simply list what they have accomplished, or more sophisticated papers in which the students evaluate their accomplishments. Some teachers prepare a list of things the students might do and let the students check the things they have done. In some cases students check off things as they do them; in others they complete the checklist at the end of the unit. Students can also keep profiles of what they have done. Such records as activity checklists and profiles (see Figure 17–8) are especially useful in individualized classes.

The use of cameras and tape recorders may make it easier for students to judge their own progress. They also make it possible for teachers to analyze students' actions, to diagnose errors, and to measure progress. Teachers can also use these devices to show students how well they are getting on and what their faults and strengths are. Motion pictures

are commonly used by coaches and physical education directors for these purposes. Similarly, tape recorders are often used in speech classes and in the evaluation of discussions, panels, and other group activities.

Students may also participate in the evlauation of their own work through conferences with the teacher. In these conferences students have an opportunity to ask the teacher for help on difficult points, while the teacher has an opportunity to evaluate their work, to point out errors, to offer encouragement, and to make diagnoses. The con-

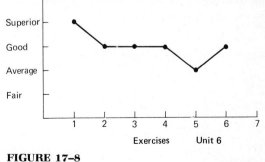

FIGURE 17–8
Profile.

ferences need not be formal. A few words at the teacher's desk or at a student's work station may serve just as well as a full-dress interview. In fact, the more informal the conference, the more valuable it is likely to be.

What steps would you take to help ensure that students' self-evaluations are honest and objective?

Of what value would a preassessment, self-evaluative exercise be?

What might you do to eliminate or minimize feelings of embarrassment and resentment when students evaluate each others' work?

Tests

Not only are there many different types of measuring techniques, there are many types of tests to choose from as well.

Informal and Standardized Tests

Most classroom tests are informal tests of achievement in the cognitive and psychomotor domains. Although there is increased effort by teachers to gather information about the progress of students in the affective domain, most attempts to gain such information must be done by the use of observational and self-report techniques.[5] As a rule, formal standardized tests are used only on special occasions for special purposes.

Mastery, Survey, or Diagnostic Tests

Classroom tests may be either mastery, survey, or diagnostic in nature.[6] The mastery test is designed to determine whether or not students have achieved a minimum standard. It does not attempt

to compare the worth of various students' performance. The survey test is designed to find the differences in students' achievement as an indicator of their general ability in the area being tested. It is used to compare students' scores so as to give them grades. The diagnostic test is used to find where students' abilities and disabilities lie. Although the differences among the different types of tests tend to blur in ordinary classroom testing, if you bear the differences in mind when you are making out your test plans, your testing should be more effective.

Criterion-Referenced Versus Norm-Referenced Tests

Well-built mastery and diagnostic tests are criterion-referenced. Survey tests are more often norm-referenced. The difference between them is that in criterion-referenced tests the student's performance on the test is rated against a set standard while in norm-referenced tests the student's performance is rated against the performance of other students i.e., the norm of the group. Criterion-referenced tests are therefore more likely to be based on the achievement of definite objectives. Because of this fact, they ordinarily do not provide the spread in scores one needs when assigning grades. Even so, they are probably of more real value for use in the classroom than achievement tests of the survey type are.

Speed Versus Power Tests

No matter what the test type, except in unusual cases, classroom tests should be power tests, not speed tests. Therefore when building and administering a classroom test, the teacher should try to ensure that all students have plenty of time to do their best on every part of the test. Hurried test situations are grossly unfair to the thorough and methodical student. They also tend to defeat the purpose of testing. One never can be sure whether students did not answer the later portions of the test because of lack of knowledge or lack of time.

---

[5] Rating scales, checklists, rankings, anecdotal reports, behavioral logs, guess-who tests, sociometric techniques and so on.

[6] Mastery tests are formative tests; survey test, summative.

Objective Versus Essay Tests

In uninformed circles there is quite a bit of debate about the relative merit of objective and essay tests. Such debate is fruitless. Each type of test has merits and each has limitations. The good test builder does not depend entirely on one or the other, but rather uses each for the purposes for which it is best fitted.

In several ways and for certain purposes objective tests are better than essay tests. With them it is much easier to provide an adequate sampling. Furthermore, since objective test items limit the student's choice, the answers do not wander from

TABLE 17.1

Comparative Advantages of Objective and Essay Tests

	Objective Test	Essay Test
Learning outcomes measured	Is efficient for measuring knowledge of facts. Some types (e.g., multiple-choice) can also measure understanding, thinking skills, and other complex outcomes. Inefficient or inappropriate for measuring ability to select and organize ideas, writing abilities, and some types of problem-solving skills.	Is inefficient for measuring knowledge of facts. Can measure understanding, thinking skills, and other complex learning outcomes (especially useful where originality of response is desired). Appropriate for measuring ability to select and organize ideas, writing abilities, and problem-solving skills requiring originality.
Preparation of questions	A relatively large number of questions is needed for a test. Preparation is difficult and time-consuming.	Only a few questions are needed for a test. Preparation is relatively easy (but more difficult than generally assumed).
Sampling of course content	Provides an extensive sampling of course content because of the large number of questions that can be included in a test.	Sampling of course content is usually limited because of the small number of questions that can be included in a test.
Control of pupil's response	Complete structuring of task limits pupil to type of response called for. Prevents bluffing and avoids influence of writing skill, though selection-type items are subject to guessing.	Freedom to respond in own words enables bluffing and writing skill to influence the score, though guessing is minimized.
Scoring	Objective scoring that is quick, easy, and consistent.	Subjective scoring that is slow, difficult, and inconsistent.
Influence on learning	Usually encourages pupil to develop a comprehensive knowledge of specific facts and the ability to make fine discriminations among them. Can encourage the development of understanding, thinking skills, and other complex outcomes if properly constructed.	Encourages pupils to concentrate on larger units of subject matter, with special emphasis on the ability to organize, integrate, and express ideas effectively. May encourage poor writing habits if time pressure is a factor (it almost always is).
Reliability	High reliability is possible and is typically obtained with well-constructed tests.	Reliability is typically low, primarily because of inconsistent scoring.

Norman E. Gronlund, *Measurement and Evaluation in Teaching*, 5th ed., (New York: Macmillan, 1985), p. 131.

the point in the way essay answers sometimes do. Also, they are not as likely to include irrelevant material or to be affected by environmental conditions. For these reasons objective tests are often more reliable than essay tests. In addition, they are easier to score. In fact, the scoring is often so easy that it may be farmed out to clerks or other nonprofessionals. Moreover, the use of keys and automatic scoring devices can make the objective test really objective. It is only when the scorer departs from the key that the test becomes subjective. Objective tests have the additional advantage of being less time-consuming than essay tests. As a matter of fact, objective tests can often do in a single period more than an essay test can do in a double period.

In spite of their virtues objective-type tests have many serious faults. In the first place, good objective-test items are difficult to write. Even in carefully built tests some items are liable to be ambiguous or to contain clues that may give away the answers. Second, to test high-level learning with this type of test is difficult. Although objective-test items can test the ability to organize, the ability to use what has been learned, the ability to show relationships, and the ability to evaluate, such items are extremely difficult to build and frequently even more difficult to key. Consequently objective-type tests often test only isolated facts with a resultant emphasis on verbalism rather than true understanding.

The essay item has several distinct advantages over the objective-test item for testing certain types of learning. Because in the essay test each student must create an answer from memory or imagination, it usually tests a higher level of knowledge than do the run-of-the-mill objective tests. It can also test the ability to organize, to use materials, to show relationships, to apply knowledge, and to write—abilities that are not easily tested by objective-test items. Furthermore, students seem to put more effort into studying for essay tests.

In spite of its virtues, the essay test has many innate faults. First, the validity of an essay test is liable to be low. This lack of validity stems from the fact that in essay testing it is very difficult to get an adequate sample of the students' knowledge of what was to be learned. Have you never taken an essay test in which the professor demanded you write essays on the topics you felt least sure of and never asked a word about the areas in which you felt letter perfect?

Irrelevancies are likely to enter into the essay item. The validity and reliability of the test are lowered by the tendency of some students to wander off the subject, to shoot the bull, and to speak in vague generalities. The reliability of essay tests is also lowered by the tendency of the scorers to mistake skill in expression, style, glibness, handwriting, neatness, and other irrelevant qualities for knowledge of what was to be learned. Scoring essay test items, when done properly, is a slow, difficult process. This greatly reduces the test's usability.

Because essay-test items are prone to these faults—low objectivity, low reliability, and low usability—you should use them with discrimination. As a rule, you should use the essay test when you wish to test a high level of recall or in which you wish to test the ability to organize material, to apply what has been learned, to evaluate, to show relationships, and to write well. In determining whether or not to use such items, you should also consider whether or not essays instead of essay tests might not be a better measure. When students have time to sit and develop their thoughts in a theme or essay, they usually demonstrate their abilities more accurately than in the rush of an examination. Table 17–1 shows a comparison of the advantages and limitations of these two types of tests.

Problem-Situation Tests

Teachers do not always have an opportunity to observe how students act in real situations. To fill this lack, the problem-situation test has been developed. In this type of test the examiner confronts the student with a problem situation. The test is to see what the student will do. For example, a common procedure in an automechanics course is to give the student a motor that will not run and say "Find out what the trouble is." Similarly, in a class in which one is attempting to teach students how to conduct a meeting according to Robert's Rules of Order, the teacher might set up a meeting and see how well various members preside.

To set up real-life situations of this type may be quite difficult. However, teachers can create pencil-and-paper problem-situation tests to serve the same purpose. To observe every member of a class chairing a meeting might be much too time consuming. So one might do better to devise a paper-and-pencil problem-situation test as a substitute for the real thing. Such a test might consist of questions like this one.

You are senior class president. You have just called to order a special meeting of the class to discuss the class trip, the senior ball, commencement activities, and the class gift. What should the order of business be for this meeting?

In the case of a broken engine, the teacher might devise a problem-situation test with questions like this one.

A farmer's tractor will not start. What steps would you take to find out what the matter is with the motor?

The items used in a problem-situation test may be either the essay or objective type. Usually, however, some type of free recall item is better than an item that suggests possible solutions to the problem.

What criteria would you use in deciding whether or not to use an essay or objective test for a specific unit?

What advantages does the use of performance testing have over the ordinary essay or objective test?

Objective-type tests are not always objective. Why not? Why might a truly objective test in composition be a bad test?

Can you think of any instance when you should use a speed test in a course you might teach? How can you eliminate the chance for a power test's accidentally becoming a speed test?

Most of the tests you use in your classes should be mastery or diagnostic. Why? When would you use survey tests?

In another section we spoke of summative and formative evaluations. Into which of these categories would you ordinarily place mastery tests, diagnostic tests, survey tests, and criterion-referenced tests?

Classroom Tests

Building the Classroom Test

General Rules for Test Construction

When you build a test, you should follow the following general procedure.

1. Determine what the specific instructional objectives of the unit are going to be. Define these objectives as specific student behavior.
2. Outline the subject content to be included.
3. Draw up an evaluation plan that will show the objectives and the number or weight of test items (or other measuring devices) to be given to each area (as in Figure 17–1). As you build

your evaluation plan, remember that some objectives are best served by performance tests, some by essay tests, some by objective tests, some by observation, and some by samples of work and the like. In your evaluation plan, try to match the objectives with the most suitable types of testing devices. Note that steps 1, 2, and 3 of this procedure should be completed before the teaching of the unit begins. The evaluation plan should influence instruction as well as evaluation.

4. Build the test items in accordance with the table of specifications.
   a. Select the test items.
   b. Arrange the items.
   c. Write the directions.
   d. Publish the test.

As you prepare the test and test items, bear in mind the following rules of thumb for test design.

1. All teaching objectives should be tested in proportion to their importance. If some objectives are overstressed, understressed, or omitted, the test will not be valid.

2. In survey tests you should include both items easy enough for the slowest students and difficult enough to challenge the brightest students. Doing so will give you the data to determine which students have done well and which poorly—an aid when it comes to assigning marks. In mastery tests it is not necessary to include difficult items—just include items that show whether or not the person has reached the standard. In either case put some easy items at the beginning of the test so that students will not become disheartened and give up.

3. Use only a few types of items. Too many different kinds of items tend to confuse the students and result in accidental errors. Especially do not use both objective- and essay-type items in the same test. To do so not only confuses students, but increases the possibility that stu-

dents will not do well because of misjudging the time.

4. Place all items of the same type together so as not to confuse the students.

5. Arrange the items from the easiest to the most difficult to encourage the less brilliant or slower students to keep on and not become discouraged.

6. Make directions, format and wording crystal clear. This is no time for trick questions or obscurity. A test should not be a joke or a puzzle. Tricky, obscure questions spoil the test's reliability.

7. To be sure each test item is valid, fit it to the objective it is testing. If it does not call for the type of behavior that the objective calls for, it is not adequate. Because it is easier to write memory questions than questions calling for higher mental processes, almost everyone overuses memory questions. Be on your guard. *If your objectives call for use of the higher mental processes, use items that call for the higher mental processes.*

8. Be sure that the test provides the students with all the information and material the students need in order to complete each item. Every time a person has to ask for information, clarification, or materials, your test becomes less reliable.

9. Be sure to write the items clearly and simply in language the students can read easily. If the reading level is too high, the test results will be worthless.

10. Try to avoid the score's being affected by such irrelevancies as students' writing ability, glibness, reading skill, and quickness. Everyone should have a chance to do well on the test. The only criterion for success on the test should be how well the students have learned the things they were supposed to have learned. The test items should be constructed so that it is easy for students to demonstrate what they have learned.

11. Aim several test items at each objective, other-

wise a chance error may give you a false assessment of the student's achievement of that objective.

12. Try to make the test a learning exercise. Write the items so that they "contribute to improved teaching-learning practice."[7]

Of what value are the objectives of a lesson or unit when one is devising a test?

Why is it sometimes stated that there is no such thing as an objective test?

In constructing a teacher-built test, what procedure would you follow? Outline what you would do step by step.

Building an Objective Test

The procedures outlined for constructing tests in general apply specifically to the building of objective tests. Although further discussion of such matters as arranging of items, directions for the test, length of the test, and reproduction of the test would be redundant, there are so many different types of objective-test items that it is important to consider the uses, merits and demerits, and writing of each of the various types. Many teachers do not use the most productive types of objective-test items. With a little study and practice you should be able to become familiar with, and relatively expert in, writing the more sophisticated objective-test items.

Alternative-Response Items. Perhaps the most familiar type of objective-test item is the alternative-response item, in which the student has a choice between two possible responses, for example, true-false or yes-no. Some examples are

Circle the correct answer (or underline the correct answer).

---

[7] Gronlund, op. cit., p. 144.

True-False   1. Milton was a sense realist.
Right-Wrong   2. Reliability is the degree to which the test agrees with itself.

Yes-No   3. Most early scientific discoveries were made by university professors.

Were-Were not   4. Girls _____ allowed to attend school beyond elementary level in Colonial New England.

Forward-Rearward   5. The clutch lever of the Bell and Howell projector must be in the _____ position before it will run.

This type of item can be found in many forms. An interesting variation is the following in which the student must identify synonymous words.

In the following, write S in the space provided if the words are essentially the same; write D if they are different.

( ) 1. reliability-consistency
( ) 2. scoring-grading
( ) 3. measure-evaluate
( ) 4. norm-average.

The most common type of alternative-response item is the true-false item. True-false items have had great popularity. Although they can be useful to find if students can discriminate fact from opinion, cause from effect, valid generalizations from invalid ones, or cases in which there is a clear dichotomy, as a rule multiple-choice items are preferable.

Although true-false items seem to be easy to write, actually this ease is quite illusory. To make true-false items free from ambiguity or irrelevant clues is really difficult for most statements are neither true, nor false, but "iffy." Taking precautions such as the following may help one produce successful true-false tests.

- Avoid broad, general statements. (They are too difficult to key true or false.)
- Avoid trivia. (Trivia obscure the major ideas.)
- Avoid negative statements. (They confuse students.)
- Limit each true-false item to only one central idea. (More than one idea confuses the issue; you cannot tell to which idea a student was responding.)
- Make the test reasonably long. (Short true-false tests are unreliable.)
- Avoid such words as *usual* and *always*. (They give away the answer.)
- Try to have a 60–40 per cent ratio of true and false statements. A test should never be made up entirely of true or false statements.
- Avoid any pattern of true-false responses. Scatter the true and false items haphazardly throughout the test.

Checklist Items.   Checklist items are much like alternative response items. Usually these items consist of fairly long lists from which the pupil checks the items which apply. In the following example the list might well consist of ten items.

Check the duties of the local board of education that appear in the following list.
_____ 1. Hire teachers.
_____ 2. Adopt school budget.
_____ 3. Select superintendent.
_____ 4. Etc.

Matching Items.   Another common type of objective test is the matching test. Again we find several variations of the basic form which consists of two unequal columns of items to be matched as shown at the top of the second column.

On the line to the left of each score listed in column I write the letter from column II of the phrase or statement that accurately describes in whole or in part that type of score. Each statement in column II may be used once, more than once, or not at all.

I	II
_____ 1. z score	a. Has a mean of 50 and a standard deviation of 10.
_____ 2. T score	
_____ 3. Stanine score	b. Its units are equal to one half a standard deviation.
_____ 4. Percentile score	
_____ 5. Deviation IQ score	c. Is computed by a ratio formula.
	d. Gives scores in plus or minus qualities.
	e. Gives scores in fractions.
	f. Has a mean of 100.
	g. Has a median of 50.

Teachers sometimes overuse matching items because they seem to be easy to write. Once again appearances are deceiving. To make good matching items you must be sure that the content of the stimuli (left-hand column) is homogeneous and that there are several plausible responses for each stimulus. Otherwise students can guess the correct answers by elimination. The column should not be too long, however. Five to eight stimuli and a few more responses are quite sufficient. To cut down on guessing by elimination always put in more responses than stimuli, and tell students that they may use each response once, more than once, or not at all. The directions should also clearly state what the basis for matching is to be. It is particularly important that the entire item appear on the same page. Students are likely to make accidental errors if they have to turn the page back and forth in the search for correct answers.

Matching items have only limited usefulness. They can be used for little other than the measurement of rote memorization, facts, and simple associations. For most purposes multiple-choice items are preferable.

Multiple-Choice Items.   Multiple-choice items have the advantage of being relatively free from guessing if four or more alternative responses are used and if reasonable care is used in picking the incorrect responses. However, if these distracters (i.e., incorrect answers) do not seem reasonable, they can easily give the answer away. Following are two examples of multiple-choice questions.

Select the best answer and write its letter in the space in the margin.

_____ The U.S. Secretary of Education is
   a. elected by the people.
   b. elected by the Senate.
   c. appointed by the President with the approval of the Senate.
   d. elected by the House of Representatives.

Underline the right answer (or circle or cross out the right answer).
Which was the first college established?
a. Brown
b. Columbia
c. Harvard
d. Princeton
e. Yale

The multiple-choice test question is probably the most versatile type of test item in the teacher's repertory. It can be used to measure both simple memory and many of the complex higher mental processes, although it is difficult to write multiple-choice items that measure problem-solving ability. As a general rule, multiple-choice items that call for "best answers" are more useful for measuring higher learnings than ones that call for correct answers. These latter are most useful for measuring knowledge of fact.

Multiple-choice items are relatively easy to write if one keeps the following guidelines in mind.

1. Write the stem of the multiple-choice question as a direct question. Then, if there seems to be some reason for doing so, it may be changed to an incomplete statement; but often a direct question plus a list of alternative answers makes the best multiple-choice item. Probably the best way to make up a list of alternatives is to use the stem as a short-answer item and then pick distracters from the incorrect answers.
2. Be sure the items are clearly written. Beware of purple prose and heavy vocabulary loads.
3. Be sure that the alternatives all seem plausible, but that there is one, and only one, correct response. All responses should be independent and mutually exclusive.
4. Be sure that the stem presents a clear, meaningful central problem. Beware of irrelevancies and window dressing.
5. Include in the stem as much of the item as possible. In so far as possible the stem should include all words that would be repeated in the alternatives.
6. Avoid use of the negative except when it is absolutely essential. It is seldom important for students to know what was the "least important," the "poorest reason," or the "principle that does not apply." Besides negatives tend to confuse students. Particularly beware of double negatives.
7. Be sure that the item is grammatically correct and free from rote verbal associations, grammatical inconsistencies, correct responses that are longer (or shorter) than the other alternatives, and other extraneous clues. As far as possible list alternatives in random, numerical, or alphabetical order.
8. Avoid using "none of the above" or "all of the above." (if for no other reason than it seems that the test writer has run out of ideas).

Category or Identification Items. A variation of the multiple-choice item that differs in substance as well as form is the category or identification item. Usually these are used with long lists. For example,

Mark the items that result from action of the sympathetic nervous system, S; those which result from action of the parasympathetic nervous system, P; if neither of these systems controls an item, mark it X.

( ) 1. Increases heartbeat.
( ) 2. Dilates pupils of eyes.
( ) 3. Increases sweating.
( ) 4. Checks flow of saliva.
( ) 5. Etc.

Organization and Evaluation Items. Skillfully made organization and evaluation items can test a high level of learning and the ability to use knowledge. Items that require the students to organize are especially useful in testing higher learning. The following item in which the students are asked to place a list of events in chronological sequence requires more than mere verbalization on the part of the student. In writing such items beware of making the list too long because then the item becomes a puzzle rather than a test item and may cause students to make accidental mistakes.

Place the following in chronological order by numbering the first event 1, the second event 2, and so on.

_____ The Declaration of Independence.
_____ The Articles of Confederation.
_____ The battle of Lexington.
_____ Washington's assumption of command of the Continental Army.

Items that ask students to evaluate and rate practices can not only test knowledge, but can also test the ability to draw fine distinctions. Questions of this sort are excellent for getting at the higher mental processes.

Rate the following techniques according to the following scheme: G, good; D, doubtful; X, poor. Place your responses in the parentheses.
( ) a. Encouraging students by accepting, at least tentatively, all answers to oral questions that can be used at all.
( ) b. Scolding students whenever they are unable to answer oral questions.
    And so on

Situation-Test Items. Situation items also demand that the students be able to use their knowledge. In this example the students must know how to do an item analysis in order to answer correctly.

What does the following item analysis tell you about the items in the test? Put your answers in the space below.

STUDENTS			ITEMS				TOTAL SCORE
	1	2	3	4	5	6	
John	+	0	0	+	0	+	111
Mary	+	+	0	+	0	+	109
Susan	+	+	0	+	0	0	100
Mike	+	+	0	+	0	+	96
Don	+	0	+	+	0	+	94
Harry	+	0	0	+	0	0	60
George	+	0	+	0	0	+	58
Anne	+	0	+	+	0	0	57
Tom	+	0	+	0	0	0	42
Sally	+	0	+	0	0	0	40

1. Item 1 _____
2. Item 2 _____
3. Item 3 _____
4. Item 4 _____
5. Item 5 _____
6. Item 6 _____

Interpretive Items. Interpretive items consist of an introductory statement and a series of questions that ask the student to interpret the data in the introductory presentation. The introductory material may be presented by a picture, graph, chart, formula, statistical table, film, or recording as well as an expository statement. The individual test items are ordinarily multiple-choice or alternative-response items. Short-answer items are sometimes used, but they are harder to key and score. In any case the items should require analysis or interpretation of the introductory material. This type of item, like all others that test higher learnings, is difficult to construct. The introductory material should be brief and clear and lend itself to interpretation or analysis. Usually it will have to be revised several times before it is satisfactory.

The following is an example of a free-response interpretive item.

The two pie graphs presented here show the per cent of the world's gold possessed by various countries in December 1913 and June 1931. Study the graphs and then answer the questions in the place provided.

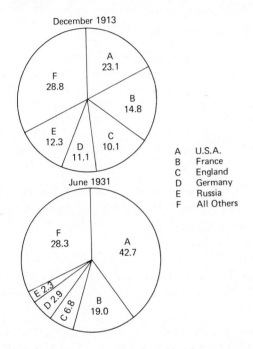

December 1913

A 23.1
B 14.8
C 10.1
D 11.1
E 12.3
F 28.8

A U.S.A.
B France
C England
D Germany
E Russia
F All Others

June 1931

F 28.3
A 42.7
E 2.3
D 2.9
C 6.8
B 19.0

1. Which of the countries possessed the most gold in 1913? _____
2. Which European country had the biggest increase in gold supply between 1913 and 1931?
   _____
3. Which of the countries listed had the smallest supply in 1931? _____
4. What two countries held 60 per cent of the world's gold supply in 1931? _____
5. In which year was the gold more equally distributed? _____

The item could be turned into several multiple-choice interpretation items quite easily as in the following examples.

Which of the countries listed possessed the most gold in 1913?   ( )
a. England; b. France; c. Germany; d. Russia.

Which European country had the largest increase in gold supply between 1913 and 1931?   ( )
a. England; b. France; c. Germany;
d. Russia.

Free-Response Items. Strictly speaking free-response items are not objective-type items. Because they are free response, their answers are open to considerable interpretation. Frequently their scoring must be quite subjective. In fact, short-answer items may be considerably closer to being short-essay items than they are to being objective-type items. Usually both completion- and short-answer items are included in tests that are basically objective type, however.

Free-response items that provide the students with no suggested responses can test a high level of learning. The most common representative of this type of item in objective tests is the completion item. In the completion item the student merely places the correct answer in the blank.

Fill in the blanks.
1. The first permanent secondary school in this country was founded by _____.
2. The Committee of Ten recommended that the elementary schools be limited to grades _____ through _____.

To make scoring easier, teachers often require that the answers to the completion questions be placed in an answer column.

Place the answers in the blanks in the space provided in the margin.
——1. The student body of the average American high school numbers approximately _____ pupils per school.
——2. A stanine is equal to _____ of a standard deviation.

When using completion items, you should be wary of ambiguous questions and unexpected correct responses. Good completion items that call for more than isolated, pinpointed facts are difficult to build. In order to avoid these faults, you should try to word the item so that only one answer can be correct and so that the students know just what type of answer is expected. To be sure that the students can decipher the item, you probably should never allow more than one or two blanks in any one completion item, also make sure that blanks represent only key words, and that they are placed near the end of the sentence so that the students will not have to waste time figuring out what is being asked. The best procedure for writing completion items seems to be to write the item as a short-answer question and then turn it into a completion item if it seems desirable.

Sometimes teachers are tempted to use phrases and sentences copied from the book as completion items. This practice is undesirable. It encourages rote learning and usually results in items that are hard to key because of unexpected correct answers.

Short-Answer Items. Short-answer questions are exactly what the name implies, questions that can be answered in a word or phrase. They are extremely useful, but, as with completion questions, it is difficult to write the items so that they will rule out undesirable responses. When writing short-answer items you must be especially careful to be sure each student knows what is expected. Indicate in the directions, or in the wording of the item, how long and how detailed the answer should be. As in the completion item the wording should make only one correct answer possible. Here are a couple of examples of short-answer test items.

Each of the following can be answered by a single word or phrase. Place the answer to each of the following questions in the space provided.

_____ 1. In an algebra test a boy scored exactly one standard deviation below the mean. What is his T score?

_____ 2. What do Crow and Crow consider to be the best size for a local school board?

For what may the various types of test items be best used? Criticize the items used as illustrations. In what ways might they be improved?

What are the characteristics of a good objective-test item?

Building an Essay Test

Although designing an essay test is much like designing an objective test because of the time factor, the problem of adequate sampling becomes extremely important. As a rule of thumb, one should use many short essay items rather than a few long ones.

Here are some other rules of thumb to keep in mind when constructing essay tests.

1. Limit the questions to something the student can answer adequately in the allotted time and be sure each question is worded so that the student realizes these limits.
2. Be sure the sample is adequate and that the test will actually show how well the students have acquired the learning products that were the goals.
3. Be sure each question tests specific products and that the information necessary for the correct answer was included in the course.
4. Be specific. Be sure each question indicates just what the student is to write about. To do this, it may be necessary to write several sentences explaining the question. Avoid "discuss" questions. They are too vague and general.
5. Decide what the standards are for scoring the answers before you commit yourself to any question.
6. Be clear.

Building Criterion-Referenced Tests

The basic difference between criterion-referenced and other tests is that in criterion-referenced tests, e.g., diagnostic and mastery tests, it is most important that the test items clearly measure the degree to which the objectives have been achieved. This requirement means that the objective must be clearly stated, preferably in terms of terminal behavior. It also means that the criterion test must be narrowed in scope so that it can measure the achievement accurately. Survey tests give us general information; criterion-referenced tests should be quite specific.

Briefly, the basic procedures for building criterion-referenced tests are

1. Define the specific objectives in detail, as criterion-referenced behavioral objectives. Be sure to include in the objectives the standard that will be considered acceptable.
2. Build test items that will show whether or not these standards have been attained.
   a. Be sure each objective is tested in proportion to its importance. An evaluation plan made in advance will help you give the test the proper balance.
   b. Have several items for each objective.
   c. Use items that show whether the students can actually perform the required behavior.
3. Arrange the items into a test.

Assessing Attitudes, Ideals, and Appreciations

To test attitudes, ideals, and appreciations by means of paper-and-pencil tests is more difficult. Students are likely to give the answer you want rather than what they really believe. For instance, one of the attitudes that might be an objective in a unit is: In international affairs, as well as private affairs, one should deal justly with all. If, to test this attitude, you should ask, "Should the United States respect the rights of other nations?" the clever students would answer "Yes," because they think that is the answer you expect. However, if you should pose for discussion a problem in which the United States can gain an advantage by violating the rights of a small nation, you might learn individuals' true attitudes by observing their reaction to the problem. Other methods of getting at attitudes

are observation, rating scales, checklists, questionnaires, and analysis of papers.

Administering and Scoring Teacher-built Tests

Giving the Test

Both essay and objective tests must be administered carefully. Once the test and key have been prepared, the next thing to do is to check the test to be sure it contains no errors. Little slips in typing may cause items to turn out quite differently from what was intended. You should also note any directions that may be unclear and any items that need to be explained. A good way to spot unclear items and directions is to ask another teacher to read the test critically.

If possible, any errors or obscurities should be corrected before you take the test to class. Announcing and correcting errors in class take valuable time away from the test itself, and there is usually someone who misses the correction and is thus penalized. Since correcting the test before class is not always possible, you may have to explain items and procedures to the class orally. If so, you should do so before the test begins. In addition you should write the explanation or correction on the chalkboard, so the students can refer to it as the test progresses and thus will not be penalized if they forget or miss the announcement. Interrupting the test to make announcements is a poor practice because it breaks up the students' train of thought.

To avoid distracting the students once the test has started, be sure that all the students have everything they need before the test begins. It is important that the students check to see that each one of them has a good copy of the complete test. Even the most carefully prepared test may have poorly mimeographed, blank, or missing pages, so you should have extra copies of the test to substitute for defective ones. If this checking is completed before the test starts, it will eliminate confusion and interruptions during the test itself. Confusion and delay may also be minimized by setting up a routine for distributing and collecting the tests.

The physical condition of the classroom makes a difference in the test situation. Comfortable students can do their best work, uncomfortable students often cannot, so pay attention to the light, heat, and ventilation, and if possible, prevent any noises, interruptions, or other distractions. Common practice when giving standardized tests is to post a notice. "TESTING; PLEASE DO NOT DISTURB." There is no reason why such a practice should not be used for teacher-built achievement tests also. Many teachers are guilty of carrying on conversations with students or other teachers during a test. Some leave the classroom doors open while other classes are moving in the corridors. Such disturbances may distract the students and reduce the reliability of the test.

Scoring the Essay Test

After the test has been given, it must be scored. Ordinarily, the test should be scored immediately. Otherwise it becomes difficult to capitalize on the test's motivational and diagnostic aspects.

Essay tests are notoriously hard to score. To score them objectively is almost impossible. However, you must try to score them as objectively as you can. This is no easy task, but the following procedure can somewhat reduce the difficulty.

1. Before giving the test, answer each question yourself. (*Sometimes you will not want to use the item after you try to answer it!*) Note all the acceptable points and the relative importance of each. If you wish, give each point a numerical value or weight. This is the key.
2. After the test has been given, read the first essay question in each of the papers and assign scores on the basis of the key. If a student has mentioned an acceptable point not in the key, add the point to the key and reread the papers already scored to be sure that everyone gets credit for the point.
3. After completing the first question in all of the

papers, repeat the process with the second question. It is much easier to read one question in all of the papers at once because you can concentrate on that one question.

Scoring the Objective Test

The objective test is considerably easier to score than the essay test. The questions lend themselves to easy automatic scoring. In fact, scoring such questions is often so automatic that they can be scored more profitably by a clerk, student, or machine than by the teacher.

Using a Key.   As in the essay test, the key should be made out before the test is given. A good method is to indicate the acceptable answers as the test is being made out. Then you should let the test sit for a day or so, after which you should retest yourself to see whether you still believe that the answers are acceptable. If they are, you are ready to make the key. One of the easiest methods of making a key, if the test is arranged so that the responses are in a column, is simply to take an extra copy of the test and fill in all the responses correctly. The key can be placed against the test and the answers compared. Often, it is easier to cut off the text of the test so that the key will be a strip that can be laid along either side of the answers on the test being corrected. This makes it easier to correct answers listed on the left side of the page if the scorer is right-handed. Some teachers find it easier to score by simply checking all correct items, that is, items that agree with the key. Others prefer to mark the wrong answers. Of course, if one intends to correct for guessing, one must indicate both right and wrong items. Example:

key	test
a	(a) John Smith was: (a) an explorer, (b) a merchant, (c) an admiral, (d) a general.
c	(a) Pocahontas married: (a) John Smith, (b) Myles Standish, (c) John Rolfe, (d) John Winthrop.

Using a Mask. Another common type of key is the mask. Masks are stiff pieces of paper or cardboard that, when placed over the test, cover up all the incorrect responses and allow only the correct responses to appear. They can be made easily. Just cover the test with the paper and then make holes in the mask where the correct answer should appear. With this type of key all the scorer needs to do is to mark correct all answers that show through the mask.

Example:

TEST

---

1. a b c d John Smith was (a) an explorer, (b) a merchant, (c) an admiral, (d) a general.
2. a b c d Pocahontas married (a) John Smith, (b) Myles Standish, (c) John Rolfe, (d) John Winthrop.

MASK

---

1. O
2.   O

Correcting for Guessing. Since in testing one is attempting to determine progress toward desired learning products, one should not conduct a guessing contest. When items have fewer than four responses, students can guess the answers relatively easily. Consequently, some teachers correct for guessing when scoring items with fewer than four responses. This is easily done. The formula is

$$S = R - \frac{W}{C - 1}$$

when S is the corrected score, R is the number of correct responses, W the number of incorrect responses, and C the number of choices provided for each item. Substituting in the formula we find that for alternate-answer items the formula becomes Rights minus Wrongs.

$$S = R - \frac{W}{(2-1)} \quad \text{or} \quad S = R - W$$

For items having three choices we find that the formula becomes Rights minus ½ Wrongs.

$$S = R - \frac{W}{(3-1)} \quad \text{or} \quad S = R - \frac{W}{2}$$

These are the only two instances in which the formula is used.

Many teachers and writers in the field of measurement prefer not to use the correction formula at all. They feel that the correction is not worth the trouble because it seldom changes the relative rating of the students. Besides, students do not understand it very well and do not like it. In addition it may introduce additional errors in measurement caused by students' attitudes.

Perhaps the best answer to the problem is to use items with at least four choices as much as possible. If it is necessary or advisable to use alternate-answer questions, the teacher should probably make the test long enough to accommodate several items directed at each learning product. This will tend to compensate for guessing without using the formula.

Evaluating Teacher–Built Tests

Much of the evaluation of a test can be done before it is given. The most important criterion of a test's worth is, of course, its validity. Does it test what it was supposed to test? Perhaps the easiest and best way to check the validity of a teacher-built achievement test is by inspection. Do the items test the goals of the course? Does the test cover the various goals in proper proportion? Other questions you should ask yourself are: Is it free from catch questions and ambiguous items? Is the physical format correct? Are questions of the same type grouped together? Are the test items arranged from easy to difficult? Is the test free from format blunders such as matching items that go over the page? In other words, is it valid, reliable, objective, and usable?

After the test has been given, it can be evaluated more fully. Things that can be checked are

1. Length.
2. Directions.
3. Item discrimination.
4. Difficulty of items.
5. Clearness.
6. Balance.

Analyzing Test Items. An analysis of the test items can be very helpful in evaluating a test. The procedure for such an analysis is quite simple. On a sheet of graph paper list the students' names on the stub at the left, and items of the test in the heading. We are interested only in the upper and lower quarters, but it is best to list all the students in rank order because the chart can also be used for diagnosis. By using plus (+) and minus (−) signs, indicate whether each of the students answered each of the items correctly or incorrectly, as in the following chart.

Upper Quarter

	1	2	3	4	5	6	7	and so on
Jerry	+	+	+	−	−	+	−	
John	+	+	+	+	−	+	−	
Sally	−	−	+	+	−	+	−	

Lower Quarter

Mike	+	−	−	−	−	+	−
Susy	+	−	+	−	−	−	+
Tom	−	−	−	+	−	−	+
George	+	−	−	+	−	−	+

By studying this chart one can learn how well the items discriminated and how difficult they were. The chart also gives clues to items that are not well written, are ambiguous, or were not learned.

An achievement test of the survey type should have some items that very few people can answer and some that almost everyone can answer. The first are needed to find out who the high achievers are; the second, to encourage the low achievers. Ordinarily, most items should be answered correctly by about half of the students. An item that is answered correctly by fewer than 20 per cent

of the students may well be a bad item. One should examine it to see if it is not too difficult, if it tests any of the objectives, if it is pertinent to the course, or if it is poorly written. On the other hand, if the item is answered correctly by more than 80 per cent of the students, one should check to see if it is too easy or if the wording gives the answer away. These criteria hold for all tests in which the scores of students are compared with each other but not for mastery tests and diagnostic tests, as we shall see.

By comparing the answers of the upper-quarter students with those of the lower-quarter students, one can find other things that help to evaluate the items. If the upper quarter of the students answered an item correctly and the lower quarter of the students answered it incorrectly, the item discriminates between them. If both upper-quarter and lower-quarter students answered the question equally well, it does not discriminate. If an item is answered correctly more frequently by the lower-quarter students than the upper-quarter students, something is very wrong indeed. Perhaps the key is wrong, or perhaps the item needs to be rewritten.

Analysis of Criterion-Referenced Tests. Much of what we have just told you does not really apply to mastery and diagnostic tests. Such tests should be criterion referenced. If they are, the items will tell whether or not individual students know or can do what they were supposed to have learned. Therefore there is no need to spread the scores. If the unit has been well taught, it is quite possible that 80 per cent of the students will have got all of the items right. Thus in a criterion-referenced test, an item that 80 per cent of the students get right may indicate not that an item was too easy, but that the criterion has been achieved. We thus see that the discrimination and difficulty factors are largely irrelevant for this type of test. The touchstone in such tests is the objective. If the items show whether or not the objective has been attained, they are good items. For instance, in one college one of the physical education requirements is to demonstrate the ability to swim two lengths of the pool. The test for this requirement is for the students to swim the length of the pool and back. Either they can do it or they cannot. How well they swim, how fast they swim, and how much farther they can swim are all irrelevant.

Some questions you might ask yourself when checking on one of your criterion-referenced tests are

1. Are there at least two items aimed at every single one of the teaching objectives without exception?
2. Is each item suitable to the objective at which it is pointed, i.e., does it call for the action and performance standards called for by the objective?
3. Is every item pointed at an objective?
4. Is the test free from give-away items, catch questions, poor wording, ambiguity, and similar faults that all types of tests are likely to be heir to?
5. Do students who get one of the items aimed at an objective also get the others? In other words, are the results of the items consistent?
6. Are there any items consistently missed by the better students?
7. Is each item clearly written at a suitable reading level and free from words and expressions students may not understand?
8. Is the test free from scoring difficulties? If several people score it, do they all come out with the same score?
9. Do students who do well in class also do well on the test?
10. Is the test usable? Is it relatively easy to administer? To score? To take?

Diagnostic Item Analysis

After the test has been given and scored, what does it tell us? If the test items have been aimed at specific objectives, an analysis of the items can give us the information fairly easily. All the teacher needs to do is to see how well each student re-

TABLE 17.2
An Item Analysis

Item		A	B	C	D	E	F	G	H	I	J	K
Obj. I	1	✓	✓	✓		✓	✓	✓	✓	✓	✓	✓
	2	✓	✓	✓		✓				✓		
	3	✓		✓				✓				
	4	✓	✓	✓		✓	✓	✓			✓	
Obj. II	5											
	6	✓			✓							✓
	7											
	8						✓					
Obj. III	9	✓	✓	✓	✓		✓	✓		✓	✓	✓
	10	✓		✓	✓	✓		✓		✓	✓	✓
	11		✓	✓	✓			✓				
	12	✓	✓	✓	✓	✓	✓	✓		✓		✓

sponded to the items designed to test the various objectives. Table 17–2 is an example of an item analysis of this sort.

A quick look at this table shows us that none of the students seems to have attained the second objective very well. Also it seems that although students D and K have mastered the third objective quite well, neither of them has done very well with the first or second objective. Pupil H, on the other hand, does not seem to have done well on any of the three objectives. Obviously the teacher would do well to give additional instruction to the entire class on objective 2 and individual or small-group instruction to certain people in the other areas.

Standardized Tests, Scales, and Inventories

Although the teacher-built test will always remain the mainstay in the teacher's tool kit, standardized tests are important supplementary measuring devices. In general, there are three basic types: achievement tests, personality and character tests, and aptitude and intelligence tests. They differ from teacher-built tests in that they are carefully built to provide a common unit of measurement just as the yardstick provides a common measure for length. To this end, the procedures for administering, scoring, and interpreting the tests have been standardized so that the results may be compared all over the country.

Kinds of Standardized Tests

The standardized achievement test is a most useful tool. It comes in two basic types: (1) that which shows strengths and weaknesses of students as a basis for diagnosis and (2) that which shows the status of individual students as compared with boys and girls throughout the nation. Standardized tests are useful for these purposes, but they are not valuable for determining achievement in any particular course or for evaluating the effectiveness of any particular teacher's teaching. In the first place, they rarely measure exactly what was taught in the course. Second, since standardized tests are liable to emphasize facts rather than understandings, abilities, attitudes, and skills, they frequently fail to indicate achievement in the most important aspects of the students' learning. Moreover, if a course or course sequence differs markedly in content from the courses in the schools that were used for standardizing the test, the latter will not measure the true achievement of the students or report accurately how their achievement compares with that of other students. In spite of these shortcomings, they can be excellent tools for diagnosing academic abilities and the effectiveness of school programs.

Personality and character tests are also important tools for the teacher. They can be a source of vivid insights in the diagnostic process. One of the most effective is the problem inventory. These inventories are intended to provide a means for identifying the personal problems of individual students. Similarly, information concerning students' aptitudes, vocational leanings, attitudes, interests and the like may be gleaned from inventories, scales and tests designed for these purposes. Inventories, tests and scales of these sorts are ordinarily given and interpreted by guidance personnel who make the results available to the teachers. Not only is the administering of such instruments usually a sensitive task, but often interpreting their results requires professional skills that few beginning teachers have mastered. Nevertheless they can give you considerable guidance as you lay out your strategies for teaching individual boys and girls. The data gathered by such instruments are usually included in the students' cumulative records.

In this connection we should probably issue a warning about the overenthusiastic acceptance of information gathered by instruments designed to find students' aptitudes and other potentials. Scores of tests and other instruments should never be taken at face value; too many uncontrolled and uncontrollable variables may have influenced the score. For instance, the IQ can be a useful tool, but it can also be a delusion; it is not an infallible indicator of an individual's ability to learn. Good intellectual potential may be hidden by low IQ scores. Poor reading ability, lack of motivation, cultural differences, language problems, poor teaching in earlier grades, poor test conditions, and poorly designed intelligence tests are all factors that may result in false IQs. In spite of efforts to avoid injustices, some intelligence tests are notorious in their unfairness to persons whose culture or class is "different." In judging the potential of any youngster, it is wise never to depend on any one criterion—particularly a single test score.

Selecting a Standardized Test

Standardized tests should be selected with care. There are many of them. Some are excellent, others are not. In searching for a suitable test, the teacher can receive considerable help from such sources as curriculum laboratories and test files maintained by local and state departments of education and by colleges and universities. Textbooks on tests and measurements often list and criticize tests both in the text and appendixes. Catalogs of the various test publishing houses tell what they have to offer. Critical analyses may be found in such works as *The Mental Measurement Yearbooks,* compiled under the editorship of O. K. Buros, and *Tests in Education* by Philip Levy and Harvey Goldstein. New tests are frequently listed in such journals as the *Education Index, Psychological Abstracts, Review of Educational Research,* and *Educational and Psychological Measurement.* Textbooks in specific methods courses often discuss standardized achievement tests in the field with which they are concerned.

These references will usually provide considerable information about the test's content, validity, reliability, and usability. By using these references it should be relatively easy to eliminate the instruments that are patently not appropriate for one's purpose and thus narrow down the number that one should examine most carefully in making the final selection.

In the final selection the test buyer should carefully consult sample copies of the test and its manual. (Any test that lacks a manual should be viewed with particular caution.) The first thing one should check for is the validity of the test. Is it designed to do what you wish it to do? If it is an achievement test, does it fit in with the philosophy and objectives of the school and courses concerned? How was the validity established? From what type of population were the norms derived? If the population was greatly different from the type of class you have, the test will not be valid for your group. How were the items selected? Does a careful, logical, and psychological analysis of the test and its manual indicate that the items measure what they purport to measure?

If the test is valid, then one may go on to check the test's reliability and usability. In so doing, the

teacher should bear in mind that a test bearing a reliability coefficient of less than .70 is probably a bad risk, and that ease in administering, scoring, and interpreting can lighten what is at best a difficult job.

Administering a Standardized Test

Any standardized test worth its salt will give clear, detailed directions for the administering of the test. Teachers should follow these directions exactly. Failure to do so may give false scores. As much as possible, standardized tests should be treated as routine classroom activities. A great to-do about the giving of a standardized test may cause tensions and upset the purpose of the test. Particularly reprehensible is coaching students for the test. A standardized test is a sampling. If boys and girls are coached on the sample, the test will be much in error and it will be impossible to find out what the test might have told you. The only sure way to give a test a chance to do what you wish it to do is to administer it exactly as the manual prescribes.

If you were to select a standardized test to measure the achievement of students in one of your classes, how would you go about it?

What three qualities would you have to check?

Where does cost appear in your answer?

How would you find out if a standardized achievement test was valid in your situation?

In what ways might poor administering of a standardized test upset the test results?

Summary

If we are to keep from drifting aimlessly, we need to determine where we are and where we should go. This process is evaluation. It differs from measurement in that it involves judgment of worth, whereas measurement merely describes the student's status. Many devices can be used to measure the status of the learning of boys and girls. We should use more of these devices than we ordinarily do, but evaluations can be made only by the evaluator himself. Consequently, goals and standards must be established to give the evaluator touchstones against which to compare the value of what he is judging.

But the purpose of evaluation is not merely to determine a student's worth. Evaluation should be the basis for determining what comes next, or where do we go from here. Evaluation can also be useful as a basis for remedial action or as a basis for deciding whether retention or promotion will be better for a student. Evaluation is a concomitant of good teaching.

Evaluation instruments stand or fall on the basis of their validity. If an instrument is reliable, objective, and usable, so much the better. But one that is not valid is worthless. The key to test building is to choose items that will ascertain whether or not the students have attained the teaching objectives. Consequently, you should aim your items at specific goals.

Although teachers tend to use test scores as the basis for a large share of their evaluations, they have many other tools and devices for evaluation available to them. Among them are rating scales, checklists, behavior logs, anecdotal reports, problem-situation tests, themes, notebooks, other written work, homework, class recitation and participation, and various sociometric devices. Students can profitably take on some of the responsibility for their own work. Self-report forms and rating scales make pupil self-evaluation easier and more profitable.

A test is a systematic procedure for measuring behavior. Classroom tests determine how much and how well students have learned. They are used as a basis for grading and motivating students and for planning and review. There are many types of tests. Most classroom tests are informal tests of cognitive or psychomotor achievement. They may be survey, diagnostic, or mastery in nature. Norm-referenced classroom tests are better as a basis for marking, but criterion-referenced tests are more useful for most classroom purposes. Both essay-test items and objective-test items have good and bad points. For many purposes the objective-test item when well written is the better of the two. However, it is the purpose of the test that should determine the type of item used rather than some notion about the innate worth of objective- or essay-test items.

To build a classroom test, one should follow these procedures: (1) define the objectives; (2) outline the content to be tested; (3) draw up a table of specifications; and (4) construct test items to meet the specifications. In designing the test itself one should make sure that all objectives are tested in proportion to their importance, that there are at least some relatively easy items included so that students will not become quickly discouraged, that only a few types of items are used in the test, that all items of the same type are placed together, that the items are arranged from easiest to most difficult, that the items are appropriate for their purpose and for the sophistication of the students, and that the test provides the students with clear directions and the information and materials they need for completing it. Classroom tests are designed not as jokes or puzzles, but to find out how well the students have learned what it was hoped they would learn.

There are many types of objective-test items. Each type has its merits, and each has its faults. Probably the most useful of them all is the multiple-choice item. However, teachers should be careful to use each type of item to do only the type of thing it is designed to do. Organization and evaluation items, situation items, and interpretation items are excellent for testing higher intellectual learnings and are not used as much as they should be.

Free-response items include completion items, short-answer items, and essay items. They can test a high level of recall but are much more difficult to write than one might expect. Essay tests are also difficult to design, although, again, few people realize it. In designing an essay test one should be sure to (1) limit the number and scope of questions to the time allotted for the test; (2) sample the teaching objectives adequately; (3) test specific learning products that were in the course; (4) write items that specify what answers are called for; (5) write "correct" answers to the items before you decide whether or not to use them; and last and most important, (6) be clear.

In designing criterion-referenced tests there are only two major steps: (1) determine the objectives; and (2) build items that test those objectives adequately. These steps are basically those outlined earlier as the general procedure for test construction.

Tests should be carefully administered, scored, and interpreted. In so far as possible, scoring should be objective. It is extremely good policy, once a test has been given, to analyze it and save those items that have proven to be good for use another time. Item analyses may be very useful for this purpose.

Standardized tests are also a source of information useful in the diagnostic process. Standardized tests come in all shapes and sizes. Some are very good and some very bad. Before using them one should check out their worth carefully. For this purpose references like Buros' *Mental Measurement Yearbook* can be most helpful. The administration of a standardized test can make the difference between obtaining good data and misinformation; therefore the tests should be given exactly as the test's manual prescribes. Any variation from the prescribed procedure may invalidate the test.

Additional Reading

Bloom, Benjamin S., George F. Madaus, and J. Thomas Hastings. *Evaluation to Improve Learning.* New York: McGraw-Hill, 1981.

Ebel, Robert L. *Essentials of Educational Measurement,* 3rd ed. Englewood Cliffs, NJ: Prentice-Hall, 1981.

Gronlund, Norman E. *Measurement and Evaluation in Education,* 5th ed. New York: Macmillan, 1985.

————. *Preparing Criterion-Referenced Tests for Classroom Instruction.* New York: Macmillan, 1973.

————. *Stating Objectives for the Classroom,* 3rd ed. New York: Macmillan, 1985.

Hopkins, Charles D., and Richard L. Antes. *Classroom Measurement and Evaluation,* 2nd ed. Itasca, IL: F.E. Peacock, 1984.

Making the Classroom Test, 2nd ed. Princeton, NJ: Educational Testing Service, 1963.

Mehrens, William, and Irving J. Lehmann. *Measurement and Evaluation in Education and Psychology,* 3rd ed. New York: Holt, 1984.

Multiple Choice Questions: A Close Look. Princeton, NJ: Educational Testing Service, 1963.

Weiner, Elliot A., and Barbara J. Stewart. *Assessing Individuals: Psychological and Educational Tests and Measurements.* Boston: Little, Brown, 1984.

Wilhelms, Fred T., ed. *Evaluation as Feedback and Guide.* Washington, DC: Association for Supervision and Curriculum Development, 1967.

13

Marking and Reporting to Parents

Overview

Marks, or grades,[1] hold an extremely high position in schools. They are used as a basis for reporting student progress to parents and to other interested

persons and as a basis for promotion, graduation, and honors. Teachers frequently use marks as a means of motivating students to greater effort. Guidance personnel use marks in guiding boys and girls for college entrance or employment. College admission officers and prospective employers use student marks as one basis of their decision making.

Nonetheless, for the past fifty years or so, marks and marking systems have been the target for much criticism. In spite of this dissatisfaction with marks and marking systems, no one has yet come up with

---

[1] In pedagogical literature marks and grades are used synonymously. In this book we use the word *marks* to denote the results of evaluation, and *grades* to denote class levels (as in ninth grade, tenth grade, and so on.)

an alternative system acceptable to everyone. Therefore you should become familiar with the marking systems available and know how to use them in ways that are both fair and effective. As you read this chapter, try to develop a personal philosophy concerning marks and marking and their use in reporting student progress to parents and as a basis for promotion. Although your philosophy will be a personal matter, it should be based on an understanding of the marking systems and their alternatives and the techniques for determining marks for tests, classwork, papers, units and courses.

Marks and Marking

To determine marks, most school systems use a system based on a five-point scale. The most common version is the A B C D F scale. Variations of this scale use the numbers 1 2 3 4 5 or the terms "Superior," "Above Average," "Average," "Below Average," and "Unsatisfactory." Some schools use a scale based on 100 per cent, whereas others merely indicate the work to be passing or failing, or in some cases outstanding, passing, or failing.

Criticism of Marking Systems

Unfortunately the five-point scale has never been completely satisfactory in any of its variations for at least five reasons.

First. Marks seldom give a clear picture of a student's achievement or progress. For example, if someone says that Johnny received an A in ninth-grade social studies, what does that tell you? Does it mean he worked hard or that he is a bright loafer? Does it mean that he has mastered some particular bit of subject matter, or does it mean he has a charming personality?

Letter and percentage marks do not give the an-swers to such questions. They do not show what skills, concepts, attitudes, appreciations, or ideals the students have learned. They do not tell us students' strengths or weaknesses in a subject, nor do they tell how much they have progressed. For instance, because of her excellence in literature, reading, grammar, or written composition, Sally receives an A in English. However, she may be quite poor in conversational skill. The mark of A, therefore, hides the fact that she is deficient in one area of English. Such a marking system is of little value to anyone who really wants to know much about a student's real progress in school. Still, it does predict fairly well students' continued success in a subject and does give a rough index of teachers' estimate of their overall success in a course.

Even as an indication of the teacher's estimate of a student's achievement, marks are not always very valuable. Teachers' marks are often influenced by extraneous matters such as sex, effort, extracurricular activities, neatness, school behavior, attitudes, and attendance. Obviously, such inconsistencies may result in many inequities. In fact, marks may give more misinformation than information.

Particularly futile are marking systems that attempt to give precise marks. No human being can make the fine distinctions in the schoolwork of students that the percentage system requires. Neither have we been able to develop testing instruments capable of such fine distinctions. Since the data on which student marks are based are so rough, the computing of percentage marks hardly seems worth the trouble.

Second. The ordinary school marking system does not adequately allow for individual differences in students. Students have differences in aptitudes, abilities and backgrounds. All the efforts in the world will not make a true expert out of the aptitudeless. We cannot all become president, no matter how much we try.

Third. In spite of our high hopes, experience in the adult world does not show a high correlation between school marks and later worldly success.

Fourth. Adult life is competitive, although perhaps not nearly as competitive as some critics claim. Even so, the school marking system is not a good training system for the competition in adult life. In the real world of adulthood, the rules are quite different from those in schools. In schools students must compete with everyone, while we adults have some choice about our competition. We do not compete with people not in our league.

Fifth. Perhaps the more valid argument for using letter or percentage marks is that they have a certain motivational effect, particularly with the better students. Even this effect, however, may be illusory. If marks really motivated effectively, would not fewer students fail?

As a matter of fact, sometimes marks have a very poor motivational effect. Altogether too often the mark rather than the learning becomes the major goal. In such circumstances the students concentrate on getting marks rather than on learning. The result often is cheating, cramming, electing easy courses, and expending only enough energy to pass. Frequently they cause unsuccessful students to give up trying. Nevertheless percentage and letter marks and grades are commonly used throughout the United States and other countries. They have the strength of familiarity and tradition behind them. Because parents and other lay people grew up with them and think they understand them, they prefer such marking systems.

> Of what value are marks? Do they serve the purposes to which they pretend? If they do, how do they do it?
>
> What do you think of competitive marking? What value does it have? What weaknesses?
>
> For what purposes should marks be used?

Marking Tests

At best, assigning marks is a difficult task. In the following paragraphs several ways to do this job will be suggested. However, you must remember that no procedure can relieve you of the responsibility for making decisions, some of which will be difficult.

Teachers may assign marks on the basis of either some set standard or a relative scale. The old-fashioned tests in which students had to have 90 per cent or better of the items right in order to achieve an A, 80 to 90 per cent of the test right for a B, 70 to 80 per cent for a C, and 60 to 70 per cent for a D furnish one example of the use of an arbitrary standard for marking. Another example is the more modern criterion-referenced, or mastery, test that requires a student to answer eight problems out of ten correctly in order to pass. In relative scales, the students' marks depend upon the relationship of their scores or their performance to the scores or performance of other students in the group. Marking on the curve is an example of the relative scale technique.

Marking on the Curve

According to the theory of the normal curve, which is based on the laws of chance, any continuous variable will be distributed according to a perfectly smooth bell-shaped curve (Figure 18–1), if no factors are present to throw things off balance. Thus, according to the laws of chance, in a large group marks should tend to fall according to the normal curve. In other words, letter marks would, according to this theory, be distributed about as follows: A, 7 per cent; B, 23 per cent; C, 40 per

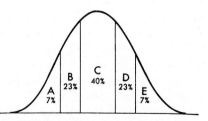

FIGURE 18–1
The Normal Curve of Probability.

cent; D, 23 per cent; E (or F), 7 per cent. Just what the exact percentages should be is debatable.

Unfortunately this theory seldom applies to ordinary classes, for talent in a single class is almost never distributed normally. This is especially true in the high school. Because of the selection process caused by the dropping out of so many of the slower and less motivated students at sixteen or so, the distribution of marks in high school classes should vary considerably from the normal curve. The marks of twelfth-graders on the whole, for instance, probably should be closer to A, 15 per cent; B, 25 per cent; C, 40 per cent; D, 15 per cent; E (or F), 5 per cent, than a "normal" distribution. When one considers the other factors that may be operating (for instance, ability grouping, selective curriculum tracks, and so on), it seems obvious that the curve in any single class will probably be far from normal. In an honors section the proper distribution of marks might be 40 per cent, A; 60 per cent, B; in an advanced section, 25 per cent, A; 50 per cent, B; 25 per cent, C; in a slow section, 50 per cent, C; 30 per cent, D; 20 per cent, F; and so on.

Further, few classes are large enough to warrant using the normal curve. In order for the theory of the normal curve to operate, one needs at least several hundred pupils to be marked against the same criteria. To use the normal curve as a basis for marks in a smaller group may lead to errors in marking. Therefore, when marking, teachers must depend largely upon their own judgment. Statistical procedures such as using the normal curve are seldom worth the effort.

Finally, the ordinary classroom teacher-built test is seldom designed so as to give a normal distribution. In his investigations, Terwilliger[2] found that classroom tests are usually skewed negatively, that is, the marks tend to fall on the low side. For all of these reasons, then, it is most unwise to base A B C D F class marks on the normal curve.

Besides, the practice can lead to behavioral and motivational problems. Since marking on a curve almost always dooms some students to failure, it frequently causes these students to adopt such avoidance techniques as not trying, having low levels of aspiration, giving up, and exhibiting other inappropriate behavior.[3]

Relative-Growth Groups

Blount and Klausmeier recommend the use of a simple relative growth scale instead of marks or grades. According to this system, instead of reporting marks or grades, the teacher would use the highest, lowest, or middle third (or quarter) of the class. For example, a teacher might report a student's standing in various areas to be

Speaking: In the highest third of the class.
Listening: In the middle third of the class.
Reading: In the lowest third of the class.
Spelling: In the lowest third of the class.
Composition: In the lowest third of the class.[4]

Comparative groups of this sort can be used for reporting test results or student standings at the end of the marking period.

Although the relative-growth groups can be quite useful, students and parents have become so mark-oriented that they do not always willingly accept this practice.

Standard Scores and Percentiles

Some authorities believe that the marks of the future will be either standard scores or stanine scores.[5]

The standard score most useful for use in mark-

---

[2] James S. Terwilliger, *Assigning Grades to Students* (Glenview, IL.: Scott, Foresman, 1971), pp. 77–78.

[3] Robert F. Biehler and Jack Snowman, *Psychology Applied to Teaching*, fourth ed. (Boston: Houghton Mifflin, 1982), p. 386.

[4] Nathan S. Blount and Herbert S. Klausmeier, *Teaching in Secondary School*, 3rd ed. (New York: Harper & Row, 1968), pp. 430–431.

[5] Standard scores, stanine scores, and T scores have been discussed in Chapter 7.

ing classroom tests and exercises is the T score, or Z score. To compute a T score or Z score use the formula

$$\text{T score} = 10\,\frac{(X - M)}{SD} + 50$$

where

> X = any raw score
> M = arithmetic mean of raw scores
> SD = standard deviation of raw scores.[6]

To compute approximate stanine scores use the following procedure.

1. Find the standard deviation of the raw scores.
2. Find the mean of the raw scores.
3. Measure ¼ standard deviation down from the mean and ¼ standard deviation up from the mean. This will establish the limits of stanine 5.
4. Find the limits of the other stanines by measur-

---

[6] The terms T score and Z score both refer to scores derived by the formula

$$\text{T score} = 50 + 10\,\frac{(X - M)}{SD}.$$

Some authorities call any set of scores derived from these scores T scores. Others use the term T score to refer only to normalized scores, and the term Z score to any score derived from the formula

$$\text{Z score} = 50 + 10\,\frac{(X - M)}{SD}.$$

To save time and computation, when one has a small distribution and a fairly normal curve, find the approximation of the standard deviation (SD) by dividing the range of the raw scores by 4. If the extremes of the distribution deviate from the normal, divide the range between the 10th and 90th percentiles by 4.

Although the statistical procedures suggested here give only approximations, they are quite accurate enough for most class marks. See works on statistics and tests and measurements for computing by accurate procedures. Shortcut statistics methods can be found in Merle W. Tate and Richard C. Clelland, *Non Parametric and Shortcut Statistics* (Danville, IL.: The Interstate Printers and Publishers, 1957); Paul B. Diederich, *Shortcut Statistics for Teacher-Made Tests.* Evaluation and Advisory Series No. 5 (Princeton, NJ: Educational Testing Service, 1960); and Paul B. Diederich, "Pinhead Statistics," in Fred T. Wilhelms, ed., *Evaluation as Feedback and Guide* (Washington, DC: Association for Supervision and Curriculum Development, 1967).

ing down or up ½ standard deviation for each stanine.

Thus if the standard deviation of the raw scores is 6 and the mean 40, the stanines would be

1	0–29	6	42–44
2	30–32	7	45–47
3	33–35	8	48–50
4	36–38	9	50+
5	39–41 (38.5–41.5)		

Test results may also be reported as percentiles. However there is a danger that students and parents may confuse percentiles with per cents and so misunderstand.

Raw Scores

Another effective procedure is to give results of objective tests in raw scores, telling the students the range of the scores and the range of the relative-growth groups. By comparing their scores, high school students soon realize how they stand in comparison with their classmates. If the scores are accompanied by comments such as, "I think you have missed the point of . . . , and should reread it," or "You did not provide enough illustrations," or "You have not differentiated between major and minor points," and so on, the students can learn how they stand in relation to their own potential and the standards of the course. Conferences also help make these points clear. This procedure is probably the fairest of all marking sytems. It also has the advantage of being the procedure least likely to be misused by beginners.

Assigning Marks

Assigning Marks to Tests

Both the raw-score plan and the relative-growth plan avoid giving actual marks to tests. Experts in the field of measurement feel that

1	<u>83</u>	A
	78	
	77	
	76	
	74	
9	73	B
	70	
	68	
	68	
	<u>68</u>	
	65	
	64	
	63	
	62	
	59	
12	58	C
	58	
	57	
	56	
	54	
	53	
	<u>53</u>	
2	50	D
	<u>48</u>	
1	40	F

FIGURE 18–2
Distribution of Test Scores and Assigned Letter Grades.

Teachers should consider these instruments [e.g., quizzes, tests, homework assignments, term papers, laboratory exercises, etc.] as data-collection devices that yield numerical results which will subsequently provide a basis for value judgments concerning individual students. Scoring procedures, however crude, should be devised so that the results of all classroom measurement can be recorded in quantitative terms. Grades (e.g., A, B, C, D, F) should *not* be assigned every time measurement occurs but, instead, should be withheld until official reports are required.[7]

However, if one must give marks, the only satisfactory solution seems to be to establish certain criteria for each mark and then mark on the basis of those criteria. Thus, for a fifty-item test, you might

set up the following criteria: 46–50, A; 41–45, B; 36–40, C; 31–35, D; and 0–30, F.

A less satisfactory approach is to base test marks on a distribution scheme such as

A = 10 per cent of pupils tested.
B = 25 per cent.
C = 45 per cent.
D = 15 per cent.
F = 5 per cent.

In this method one simply finds the raw score of the tests, lists them from highest to lowest, and then apportions the letter grades according to the proportions selected—taking advantage of the natural breaks wherever possible. Thus in the example in Figure 18–2 in a class of 25, the teacher assigned 1 A, 9 Bs, 12 Cs, 2 Ds, and 1 F. These marks do not quite correspond to the distribution scheme, but they are close enough given the nature of the distribution of the raw scores. The decreed distribution should not be held sacred. When the raw scores cluster together in an obviously skewed distribution, one should not hold rigidly to the distribution. In marking tests, teachers should remember

---

What procedure would you use to grade an objective test if your school used the five-letter system of marking? Would you use a different procedure for marking an essay test? If so, what?

Why do authorities generally condemn the percentage system of grading tests? What is your own opinion?

What are z scores, T scores, and Z scores? What are the good and bad points of z scores, T scores, and Z scores? How would you use them marking tests?

In a certain school the school policy holds that students' marks should approximate the normal curve. A teacher of an honors section found that all fifteen students did exceptionally well on a test. Would a mark of A for each student be justified?

---

[7] Terwilliger, op. cit., p. 23.

that the purposes of tests are primarily to evaluate student progress and to diagnose student learning rather than to give marks. Further, in such schemes the distributions of marks are quite arbitrary and are subject to the limitations of any set distribution scheme. Some students, no matter how they try, will get low marks, so they soon learn not to try.[8] To mark on the basis of set criteria is much more satisfactory.

Assigning Marks to Compositions and Other Creative Work

Compositions and other creative work are difficult to mark. Perhaps the following technique used by a veteran teacher of English is as good as any in marking original written work:

First, he selects a comfortable chair with plenty of floor space around him. Then he reads each paper carefully, making notes as he reads them. On the basis of this reading he judges whether the paper is "Superior," "Excellent," "Average," "Fair," or "Poor." Then, without placing any mark on the paper, he places it on a portion of the floor designated for papers of that category. After reading all the papers, he places them into piles according to their categories and lets them lie fallow for a while. Later, refreshed, he rereads each paper in each group to test his previous judgment, and moves from pile to pile those papers that he believes he has rated too high or too low. He then assigns marks to the papers in the piles. He could have just as easily assigned them to relative-growth groups or even assigned them point scores. Although this technique is not foolproof, with a little ingenuity it can be adapted for marking various types of original work.

Another method is to rate each paper according to each of various qualities such as originality, expression, mechanics, and so on. Rating scales and checklists are particularly useful for this purpose.

The ratings produced by these procedures can be converted into point scores if one desires.[9]

Term and Course Marks

Purpose of Term Marks

As we have already seen, the more one reads about marks and marking, the more one is tempted to believe that there can be no such thing as a fair mark or marking system. Yet marks seem to be necessary.

1. To inform pupils, parents, and other interested persons such as teachers, prospective employers, and college admissions officers of the pupil's achievement in his secondary school work.
2. To motivate pupils by giving them feedback on their progress.
3. To identify the strengths and weaknesses of pupils.
4. To inform those concerned of the progress or achievement of pupils in comparison with other pupils.
5. As a basis for guiding the pupils in their choice of courses, activities, curriculum, and career.
6. As a basis for promotion, grouping, graduation, honors, college entrance, and eligibility for certain awards, activities, or programs.
7. To show parents and others the objectives of the school.
8. To indicate pupils' personal social development.[10]

Criteria for Marks and Marking Systems

To carry out their purposes, marks and marking systems should meet the following criteria.

1. Marks should indicate the attainment of definite worthwhile goals. These goals should be well defined, or the marks themselves will become the goals.

---

[8] Biehler and Snowman, op. cit.

[9] See Chap. 17 for information on the use of rating devices.
[10] William L. Wrinkle, *Improving Marking and Reporting Practices* (New York: Holt, Rinehart and Winston, Inc.), pp. 31–32. Copyright 1947. Reproduced by permission.

2. Marks should be easily understood by students and parents.
3. Marks should be as objective as possible.
4. Marks should be free from bias and the influence of other irrelevant considerations.
5. Marks should be based on an abundance of evidence.
6. Students should be informed in advance what will be counted in computing the mark.
7. The method used to compute the marks should be objective and statistically valid.
8. Marks for achievement and personal social development should be separated.
9. Marks should be based on positive evidence.
10. Marks should be used as means to an end. They should not be ends in themselves. Overemphasis on marks distorts the teaching-learning process.

Bases for Term Marks

Term marks should be based on the teacher's best estimate of the student's achievement in the course. No basis other than achievement is valid for granting subject marks. Because of the nature of education and educational measurement, no teacher can be completely objective or accurate in determining student achievement. The best one can do is to gather all the evidence one can find and then make a judgment. But effort, attendance, and classroom behavior should not be included in the course mark. That such things should be noted and reported to school officials, guidance persons, new teachers, and parents is axiomatic, but they should be reported as separate entities not as part of a course mark. *A course mark should be an index of achievement in a course, nothing less.* That is why Oliva and Scrafford recommend that one should give three types of marks:

(1) A subject matter achievement grade determined competitively in relation to the performance of pupils at a particular grade level; (2) information concerning the relationship of the pupils' attainment and ability; and (3) information concerning personal traits, social skills, and study habits.[11]

Some teachers and theoreticians have proposed the theory that students should be marked on the amount of progress they have made during a year. On the face of it, progress is an admirable criterion for marking. However, if marks are to be an index of the student's level of achievement, then a mark based solely on the amount of progress made during the period may be misleading, as the following case demonstrates.

When they arrived at the first class of their drawing course, Joan already had great—almost professional—skill in drawing, while Anne had no skill whatsoever. After a year in class, Joan has progressed comparatively little, although she can still draw much better than anyone else in the class. Anne, however, has become interested in drawing and has made swift progress. She is now slightly better than the average pupil in the class, although still not nearly as good as Joan. How should one mark the two girls? If one bases the marks on progress, then Anne should get the higher mark, but this would lead to the ridiculous situation of giving the higher mark to the less skilled student. To be fair and to give a reasonably accurate picture in a mark the criterion should be achievement rather than progress.

Other teachers and experts seem to feel that students' marks should be related to native ability. Thus a boy who did the very best he could would be marked A, whereas one who did not come up to his promise would be marked less. Again the

> Suppose you are an eleventh-grade English teacher. What should you wish to know about a boy coming to you from the tenth grade? Would the fact that he got a B help you? If not, what information would be more helpful?

[11] Peter F. Oliva and Ralph A. Scrafford, *Teaching in a Modern Secondary School* (Columbus, OH: Merrill, 1965), p. 186.

system can lead us into ridiculous situations in which an ignoramus whose best turns out to be very little would receive a higher mark than a brilliant student who does infinitely better work without half trying.

Determining Term Marks

Combining Unit Marks. A way to determine term marks for a course is to give the students marks for each unit. The final mark can be computed by taking an average of the units, making due allowance for those units that may be more important than others.

Some schools require that marks be recorded and reported as percentages. This presents a problem to the conscientious teacher because percentage scores often require judgments finer than the human mind can make. However, such scores may be approximated by assigning values to the unit marks. For instance, if the passing grade is 70 per cent, then the teacher can assign the following values: A, 95 per cent; B, 87 per cent; C, 80 per cent; D, 73 per cent; F, 65 per cent or less, if you wish. To attempt to give finer evaluations for the various units may be merely deceiving oneself and one's clientele.

Other methods for determining term marks are discussed in succeeding paragraphs. These methods can also be used to establish unit marks.

Total-Performance Scores. Another highly recommended system of calculating term marks is to rank the students according to their total-performance scores. To use this system you should record a point score for each and every activity to be reflected in the course mark and then total all of the activity scores (tests, quizzes, themes, papers, class recitations, and so on). Once you have computed the total scores for every student, assign marks to the individual students using as a basis some such scheme as

Top 15 per cent of the pupils   A
Next 20 per cent of the pupils   B
Next 45 per cent of the pupils   C

Next 15 per cent of the pupils   D
Bottom 5 per cent of the pupils   F.

This technique can also be used for computing unit marks. The per cent of students in each category would be an arbitrary decision based on your estimate of the ability of the class as a whole. It would be patently unfair to use the same per cent breakdown for an honors group as for a class of low achievers. If natural breaks occur, it is usually better to use these breaks as cutoff points rather than to hew strictly to the per cent scheme. The total performance score technique is perhaps the fairest of all the methods we shall discuss.

A Method for Computing Final Term and Unit Marks. When a teacher has given marks to students as the class moved on through the course, the following procedure for combining the marks into a final mark works quite well.

Decide what weight is to be given to each mark. (This should have been done in your evaluation plan.) For instance, if we should plan to base our marks on daily work, 25 per cent; papers and themes, 50 per cent; tests, 25 per cent, we could follow the following procedure:

1. Change the letter marks to numerical values: A = 4; B = 3; C = 2; D = 1; F = 0.
2. Combine the daily marks by averaging. For instance, supposing a girl had earned the following daily marks, A, B, B, A, C, A, D, we would use the following computation to find her average score;

$$
\begin{array}{rl}
A = & 4 \\
B = & 3 \\
B = & 3 \\
A = & 4 \\
C = & 2 \\
A = & 4 \\
D = & \underline{1} \\
& 21 : 7 = 3.00
\end{array}
$$

3. Average the marks on the themes and papers. For purposes of illustration let us assume that there are three themes and one major paper, and that the paper is equivalent to three themes, and that the student received a mark of A on one theme and marks of B on the other themes and the major paper.

First Theme	A	4	4
Second Theme	B	3	3
Third Theme	B	3	3
Major Paper	B	3×3	9
			$\overline{19 : 6 = 3.17}$

(Note that the major paper is counted as three themes and so the divisor is 6).

4. Combine the test scores: in this case just one test.

$$A = 4$$

5. Combine the averages:

Daily Work	3.00	3.00
Themes & Papers	3.17×2	6.34
Test	4	4.00
		$\overline{13.34 : 4 = 3.34}$

(Note that since our original plan was to weigh the mark on the basis of daily work 25 per cent, themes and papers are given twice the weight of the other items and so the divisor is 4).

Final score is 3.34 or B.

To Build Multiclass Norms. When the content for different sections of a course is much the same, it is quite possible to combine the score distribution of the sections or of classes taught in successive years into performance norms. To make this plan feasible, the measurement for the course must be planned so that the possible number of points that can be earned is the same in all sections. Usually this means that the teacher or teachers must use the same or comparable tests and assignments in all sections and score and weigh the tests and assignments in the same way. To make the norms the teachers simply combine the score distribution of the sections into one distribution. Marks can be assigned from the combined raw scores, e.g., top 10 per cent, A; next 25 per cent, B; next 45 per cent, C; next 15 per cent, D; and last 5 per cent, F. Standard scores or stanine scores could be combined in the same manner.[12]

To Combine Standard Scores. To combine scores recorded as standard scores is quite easy. If, for instance, the daily marks were to count 50 per cent; quizzes, 25 per cent; and tests, 25 per cent; and the marks were recorded as T scores, the computation of a student's mark would follow the pattern:

Daily work	*Quizzes*	*Test*
55	50	52
71	65	52
63	65	
59	$\overline{180 : 3 = 60}$	
68		
64		
60		
65		
60		
$\overline{565 : 9 = 62.78}$		

Daily work	$62.78 \times 2 =$	125.56
Quizzes	$=$	60
Test	$=$	52
		$\overline{237.56}$

Students' letter marks could then be determined by the position of the total scores in the total distribution. If, for instance, a student's score fell in the

---

[12] See Terwilliger, op. cit., Chap. 6, for instructions by which to build norms based on standard scores.

TO PARENTS OF: _____

MATH TEACHER: _____

Please call the Math Teacher if you have any questions or would like a personal conference.	DECIMAL UNIT					
	BASIC DEVELOPMENT OF DECIMALS	ADDITION AND SUBTRACTION	MULTIPLICATION	DIVISION	ADVANCED TOPICS IN DECIMALS	PROBLEM SOLVING
PROGRESS						
Test results indicate:						
1. Significant Growth						
2. Reasonable Growth						
3. Little or No Growth						
Progress was hindered by frequent absence from class.						
I believe more growth has taken place than the test data indicate.						
SKILL DEVELOPMENT						
Is at an introductory stage.						
Demonstrates an understanding of the process and is working toward mastery.						
Has demonstrated mastery of the skills involved.						
No work was assigned because:						
1. The pre-test indicated previous mastery.						
2. Work in other topics was deemed more important.						

COMMENTS REGARDING THE STUDENT AS A LEARNER

_____ Demonstrates conscientious effort.

_____ Demonstrates reasonable effort.

_____ Does not seem to be making a reasonable effort.

_____ Makes a real attempt to learn from assigned work.

_____ Views work as a task to be completed rather than a means of learning.

_____ Persists even if understanding does not come immediately.

_____ Is willing to settle for incomplete understanding.

_____ Tends to seek help prematurely.

_____ Seeks help effectively.

_____ Seems unwilling to seek help.

_____ Uses resources to gather information.

_____ Draws conclusions based on well-organized data.

_____ Demonstrates a willingness to test conclusions.

_____ Effectively seeks alternate or additional assignments.

_____ Demonstrates a willingness to evaluate his or her work and set objectives to correct weaknesses.

COMMENTS REGARDING STUDENT AS A CLASS MEMBER

_____ Generally cooperates with class.

_____ Distracts other members of the class.

_____ Contributes positively to class welfare.

_____ Is easily distracted.

FIGURE 18–3
Interim Report, Mathematics, West Hartford, Conn.

middle 45 per cent of the total scores, the letter grade would probably be C.

Teacher's Responsibility for the Grade

You will notice that in each of the examples no matter how much computation the teacher did, in the end the mark was based on the teacher's best judgment. Measuring techniques may make the basis for the judgment more objective, but they cannot make marking an automatic process.

Marks in Attitude, Citizenship, Behavior, Effort

Most report cards call for the reporting of social-personal qualities as well as subject marks. Sometimes these marks are broken into categories as in the West Hartford Schools (Figure 18–3) or sometimes all the categories are lumped under the heading Attitudes or Citizenship as in Woodbridge Township (Figure 18–4a and Figure 18–4b). The teacher's basis for making such marks is usually observation sometimes bolstered with inferences

							YEAR		**CR.**							**YEAR**		**CR.**

Fords Junior High School

Woodbridge Township,

GRADE 7–8   WOODBRIDGE, NEW JERSEY   19____ 19____

JUNIOR HIGH SCHOOL

NAME_____   GRADE_____   HOMEROOM_____

		1	2	3	4	YEAR M	A	CR.			1	2	3	4	YEAR M	A	CR.
ENGLISH	M								COMMERCE	M							
	A									A							
PHYS. ED.	M									M							
	A									A							
HYGIENE	M								ART	M							
	A									A							
LANGUAGE	M								VOCAL MUSIC	M							
	A									A							
	M								INSTR. MUSIC	M							
	A									A							
SOCIAL SC.	M								COOKING	M							
	A									A							
	M								SEWING	M							
	A									A							
SCIENCE	M								WOODSHOP	M							
	A									A							
	M								METAL SHOP	M							
	A									A							
MATH.	M									M							
	A									A							
ABSENT									TARDY								

FIGURE 18–4a

Report Card Used in Woodbridge Township Junior High Schools, Woodbridge, N.J.

M = Academic mark

A = Attitude mark

CR = Credit

WOODBRIDGE TOWNSHIP JUNIOR HIGH SCHOOLS

Woodbridge, New Jersey

Grade 7-8

REPORT CARD

SIGNIFICANCE OF MARKS

Academic
(Designated by M)

A = Superior

B = Good

C = Average

D = Poor

I = Incomplete

X = Probation
(Parental Conference
Required)

F = Failure

Academic marks are based
on subject matter
achievement only.

Attitude
(Designated by A)

O = Outstanding
(Above Average)

S = Satisfactory

U = Unsatisfactory

Attitude marks are based
on behavior, effort, and
citizenship.

Two period marks of F in achievement constitute
failure in that subject for the year.

Parents should recognize that good attendance has
a positive effect on student achievement.

_____ Principal

Parents are requested to study this report carefully,
sign, and return it immediately.

1. _____

2. _____

3. _____

4. _____

FIGURE 18–4b
Reverse Side, Woodbridge Township Junior High School Report Card,
Woodbridge, N.J.

from the student's schoolwork, behavior, or sometimes sociometric devices. These marks should be made out more carefully than they usually are. Probably the best method to use is to rate all students as average at the beginning of the marking period; raise the marks of those students whose attitude, effort, or behavior is excellent; or lower the marks for those students whose behavior, attitude, or effort is bad.

Criterion-Referenced Marking Systems

The methods for deriving term marks already described have all been based upon normative or relative marking. In some schools we now find a movement toward criterion-referenced marking systems. Such systems base marks on an absolute or arbitrary standard or set of standards. Students who achieve the standard succeed; those who do not, fail. Those who achieve the standard for C, get C; those who do not, do not. How well others do is irrelevant. For example, let us suppose that you give a 65-item mastery test for which you have determined that each student must answer 55 items correctly to pass. Since the criterion set is 55 items, if of the thirty students in the class twenty-eight get from 55 to 65 items correct, they pass, and if the other two students get 54 items correct, they fail. If it were the other way around and of the thirty students twenty-eight scored in the 50–54 range, and two scored in the 55 plus range, then the twenty-eight would fail and the two would pass.[13] Similarly, you could set up standards for letter marks, e.g., A = 63 and above; B = 60–62; C = 55–59; D = 51–54; F = 50 or below. The per cent correct marking system, so common in the past, is theoretically based on absolute standards (e.g., 90 per cent and above, A; 80–89 per cent, B; 70–79 per cent, C; 60–69 per cent, D; 59 per cent and below, F). In reality teachers seldom keep to the absolute standards, but rather base the per cent

on the students' standing instead of basing the students' standing on the per cent. In fact, criterion-referenced tests or marks based on absolute standards do not work well in most courses as presently organized because there are no real criteria or standards by which to gauge the marking.

Criterion-referenced testing is most useful for mastery situations in which the student proceeds through a sequence of modules or units on a continuous-progress plan. In such a system the criterion-referenced marking could be based on a go no-go or pass–fail system. To carry out the system

1. The teacher, or higher authority, sets up a series of behavioral objectives which the student must achieve.
2. The teacher, or other authority, devises instruments that will measure whether or not the students can perform the behavior required.
3. If the students perform the behavior as required, they pass. If they do not, they do not pass. In a modulated continuous progress course, students who do not pass should be allowed to go back, restudy, and then try again.

For example, the objective may be that the student will be able to type forty words per minute without making more than one error per minute. If the students meet this standard, they have met the requirement and may go on. Although we have spoken of criterion-referenced system marking in terms of pass-fail, there is no reason that the same sort of criteria cannot be set up for other letter marks, i.e., for a C the student must be able to type Y words per minute and for a B, Z words per minute. Such standards are easiest to establish in skill subjects, but they can be built for other subjects too as the discussion of behavioral objectives in Chapter 8 shows. Creating worthwhile behavioral objectives in some subjects (e.g., literature and most of the social studies areas) may be extremely difficult, however.

In some schools the mark in a criterion-referenced system simply acknowledges that the student has achieved the objective. The student or teacher

---

[13] Few teachers would have enough gumption to let these disastrous results stand, however.

might simply record that a unit has been completed satisfactorily on such and such a day. In some systems the student fills in a square on a bar graph whenever a unit has been satisfactorily completed (Figure 18–5), or the teacher may record and initial the date the student satisfactorily completed the unit. These marks may be turned into letter marks representing student progress or combined with other factors to give letter marks, as in the Wilde Lake High School, Howard County, Maryland, Progress Report (Figure 18–6).

In reporting to parents, the criterion-referenced or continuous-progress marking system may simply indicate the units completed, but it usually provides other information concerning student progress as in the Bishop Carroll High School report shown as Figure 18–7 and the West Hartford report shown as Figure 18–3.

In some schools a judgment concerning how well the students did the work or to what degree they had reached the objective is recorded as the mark. This type of mark can be given in otherwise criterion-referenced programs. Thus in the Plant Junior

High School in West Hartford, Connecticut, the student understanding of each social studies unit and tool skill studied was marked on an achievement scale of "Considerable," "Adequate," or "Inadequate." (Figure 18–8)

Combination Marking Systems

Perhaps the most satisfactory marking system would be a combination of the normative and criterion-referenced systems.[14] Terwilliger recommends that passing or failing should be determined by the use of absolute criteria. He suggests that every student be required to take a test referenced to minimal instructional objectives. On this test (which could be a performance exercise) the student must achieve the minimum score determined before the administering of the test—usually at least 80 per cent of the possible score. Higher marks such as A, B, or C would be figured on the same basis as in any normative marking system.

> Which of the various marking systems described seems the fairest? Why?
>
> Which marking system would you rather use? Why?
>
> Which is preferable, a criterion-referenced marking system or a normative marking system?

Reporting to Parents

The Right to Know

All parents have the right to know how their children are progressing in school. In fact, they probably are obligated to know whether they want

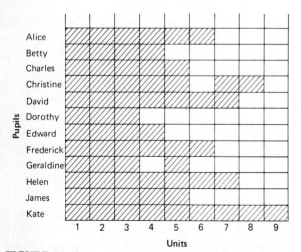

FIGURE 18–5
Bar Graph Recording Pupil Progress. (*Note:* Some pupils have skipped units. Some teachers record progress on such a chart by dating and initialing the proper square when the pupil has satisfactorily completed a unit.)

[14] Terwilliger, op. cit., pp. 97–99.

PROGRESS REPORT 19____

WILDE LAKE HIGH SCHOOL
HOWARD COUNTY, MARYLAND

PAGE _____ OF _____

CHRONOLOGICAL
GRADE LEVEL _____

ACADEMIC
GRADE LEVEL _____

STUDENT: _____

ADVISOR: _____

MARKING OPTIONS

A = EXCELLENCE
B = GOOD
C = SATISFACTORY
I = INCOMPLETE

Academic Grade Level is determined by number of credits earned.

Grade Level	Credits Earned
9	0.00 – 3.75
10	4.00 – 8.75
11	9.00 – 13.75
12	14.00 – up

THE STUDENT'S MARK IN EACH SEGMENT IS DETERMINED BY THE QUALITY OF HIS WORK.

SEGMENT NUMBERS CORRESPOND TO THE NUMBERS ON THE COURSE DESCRIPTION.

STANDARDIZED TEST SCORES WHICH REFLECT THE STUDENT'S STANDING IN RELATIONSHIP TO OTHER STUDENTS WILL BE REPORTED BY THE ADVISOR AT APPROPRIATE TIMES DURING THE SCHOOL YEAR.

ATTENDANCE	1	2	3	4
CUMULATIVE DAYS PRESENT				
CUMULATIVE DAYS ABSENT				
CUMULATIVE DAYS TARDY				

Course: _____ Date Ent _____
Evaluating Teacher: _____
_____ Segments = _____ Credit   Date Dropped: _____
Final Mark: _____ Cr. Earned _____   Continued Next Year
Date: _____   Yes   No   (Circle)

SEGMENT	1	2	3	4	5	6	7	8	9	10	11	12	13	14	15	16	17	18	19	20
MARK																				

COMMENTS: (REPORT 1)   Check PROGRESS   Sat.   Unsat.
COMMENTS: (REPORT 2)
COMMENTS: (REPORT 3)
COMMENTS: (REPORT 4)

Course: _____ Date Ent _____
Evaluating Teacher: _____
_____ Segments = _____ Credit   Date Dropped: _____
Final Mark: _____ Cr. Earned _____   Continued Next Year
Date: _____   Yes   No   (Circle)

SEGMENT	1	2	3	4	5	6	7	8	9	10	11	12	13	14	15	16	17	18	19	20
MARK																				

COMMENTS: (REPORT 1)   Check PROGRESS   Sat.   Unsat.
COMMENTS: (REPORT 2)
COMMENTS: (REPORT 3)
COMMENTS: (REPORT 4)

Course: _____ Date Ent _____
Evaluating Teacher: _____
_____ Segments = _____ Credit   Date Dropped: _____
Final Mark: _____ Cr. Earned _____   Continued Next Year
Date: _____   Yes   No   (Circle)

SEGMENT	1	2	3	4	5	6	7	8	9	10	11	12	13	14	15	16	17	18	19	20
MARK																				

COMMENTS: (REPORT 1)   Check PROGRESS   Sat.   Unsat.
COMMENTS: (REPORT 2)
COMMENTS: (REPORT 3)
COMMENTS: (REPORT 4)

Course: _____ Date Ent _____
Evaluating Teacher: _____
_____ Segments = _____ Credit   Date Dropped: _____
Final Mark: _____ Cr. Earned _____   Continued Next Year
Date: _____   Yes   No   (Circle)

SEGMENT	1	2	3	4	5	6	7	8	9	10	11	12	13	14	15	16	17	18	19	20
MARK																				

COMMENTS: (REPORT 1)   Check PROGRESS   Sat.   Unsat.
COMMENTS: (REPORT 2)
COMMENTS: (REPORT 3)
COMMENTS: (REPORT 4)

Course: _____ Date Ent _____
Evaluating Teacher: _____
_____ Segments = _____ Credit   Date Dropped: _____
Final Mark: _____ Cr. Earned _____   Continued Next Year
Date: _____   Yes   No   (Circle)

SEGMENT	1	2	3	4	5	6	7	8	9	10	11	12	13	14	15	16	17	18	19	20
MARK																				

COMMENTS: (REPORT 1)   Check PROGRESS   Sat.   Unsat.
COMMENTS: (REPORT 2)
COMMENTS: (REPORT 3)
COMMENTS: (REPORT 4)

Course: _____ Date Ent _____
Evaluating Teacher: _____
_____ Segments = _____ Credit   Date Dropped: _____
Final Mark: _____ Cr. Earned _____   Continued Next Year
Date: _____   Yes   No   (Circle)

SEGMENT	1	2	3	4	5	6	7	8	9	10	11	12	13	14	15	16	17	18	19	20
MARK																				

COMMENTS: (REPORT 1)   Check PROGRESS   Sat.   Unsat.
COMMENTS: (REPORT 2)
COMMENTS: (REPORT 3)
COMMENTS: (REPORT 4)

FIGURE 18–6
Progress Report Wilde Lake High School, Howard County, Maryland.

Date: October ____

End of October Report

The school year is now well underway. The purpose of this assessment is to ensure that you have made a good start. By now an effort should have been made in all subjects so that you have a clear idea about difficulty, length, or special features.

	COURSE	CREDIT VALUE	UNITS in COURSE	UNITS to DATE	COMPLETED SINCE LAST REPORT			UNITS TO BE COMPLETED BY End of DECEMBER	
					UNITS	CREDITS	FINAL MARK	NEW	TOTAL
1									
2									
3									
4									
5									
6									
7									
8									
9									
10									
11									
12									
	TOTALS								

_____ instructional days since last report, _____ DAYS absent, _____ TIMES late

Student Comments:

PROGRESS: ☐ EXCELLENT ☐ SATISFACTORY ☐ UNSATISFACTORY _____
Student signature

T-A Comments:

_____
T-A signature

Parent Comments:

_____
Parent signature

FIGURE 18–7
Excerpt from 1984–85 Student Progress Report, Bishop Carroll High School, Calgary, Alberta.

to or not. Following is a list of what parents should know about the progress of their children in school.

1. How well is the student progressing in each subject?
2. How does the student's progress compare with that of other boys and girls of the same age and class?
3. What are the student's potentialities? Is the student developing any particular talents or interests?
4. Is the student's progress up to potential?
5. What specific difficulties does the student have, if any?
6. In what has the student done well?
7. How does the student behave in school?
8. How does the student get along with other students? With teachers?
9. Is there any way the parent can help the student?
10. Is there any way the parent can help the teachers?

Such information should be passed on to the parent at regular intervals in some fashion or other for many reasons. In the first place, it is through this reporting that the school can fulfill its responsibilities of telling parents of their children's status in school. Second, it gives the school an opportunity to enlist parents' help in educating their child. Third, it gives the school an opportunity to explain its program to the parents and to solicit their understanding and assistance.

Report Cards

By far the most common medium for reporting to parents is the report card. The report card is a vital link in the teacher's relationship with students and parents. Improper marking can upset students' morale and destroy home relationships. However, if a mark is consistent with what has been going on in class, the students will usually accept it with-

out question. So will most parents if they are forewarned. Therefore, one must be careful in making out report cards. Quite often the school provides definite instructions for preparing them. When this is done, you should follow the instructions exactly. If instructions are not available, you should be sure to find out from a supervisor or experienced teacher just what the procedures are. It is always better to find out before a disaster than afterward.

Several report cards have been included in this chapter (Figure 18–3 through 18–8). Note the difference in procedure. Note what is included on each card. Criticize the cards. Which do you think is most satisfactory? Attempt to fill out the report for some youth. Doing so may point out several things you had not thought of. Which do you prefer? Why?

Look at the report card files in your curriculum library or resource center. Consider the merits of the various student progress cards and marking systems.

Supplementary Reports

Many schools find the report card alone insufficient as a basis for reporting student progress, even when some information over and above marks is supplied to parents. To meet this need, several schools issue supplementary progress reports from time to time. Preparing these reports may be the responsibility of the classroom teacher, the homeroom teacher, or guidance personnel. More often than not, supplementary reports take the form of warnings of possible failure or reports of unsatisfactory progress. In a few school systems such reports are sent on other occasions, for example, to notify the parent that the student is doing well. These reports may be made as notes to parents, warning slips, checklists, conferences, and letter of commendation.

TO PARENTS OF _____

SOCIAL STUDIES TEACHER: _____

SOCIAL STUDIES PROGRAM	PUPIL ACHIEVEMENT		
	Considerable	Adequate	Inadequate
I. Units Taught Pupil understanding of the unit was judged according to test scores, projects, participation in class activities and teacher observation.			
1.			
2.			
3			
II. Social Studies Tool Skills Pupils practiced the following skills during the marking period:			
III. Pupil As A Learner This section refers to pupil progress toward becoming an independent and effective learner.*			
1. Skills a. Asks appropriate questions			
b. Finds necessary information			
c. Organizes information logically			
d. Develops answers to questions			
e. Evaluates own work			
2. Attitudes Toward Learning a. Seems eager to ask questions			
b. Promptly and freely collects information			
c. Readily organizes data			
d. Enthusiastically develops answers to questions			
e. Willingly evaluates own work.			

Topic   IV. Independent Study (where applicable)
Teacher Comments:
_____

V. Teacher Comments (optional)

_____

*A more detailed explanation of section III will accompany this form the first time it
 is distributed during the school year.

FIGURE 18–8
Social Studies Report, Plant Junior High School, West Hartford, Conn.

Letters to Parents

Letters to parents are of two types: (1) routine letters used as reports to parents in addition to, or in place of, report cards; and (2) letters for special occasions—requests to see the parent, invitations to class functions, letters notifying the parent about the student's work, and letters calling the parent's attention to some abnormality in the child's behavior.

Letters to parents—no matter what their purpose—should be carefully written. They should always be correct as to form and style. Errors in spelling, composition, grammar, and sentence structure should be avoided at all costs. Errors that might never be noticed in the letter of a lawyer, doctor, or dentist may be very embarrassing if made by a teacher. This is particularly true in the so-called better neighborhoods. Teachers should not take offense at parents' expecting high standards in English usage. It is the price of being a teacher. "Teachers *should* know, you know."

Letters used as progress reports should be short and to the point. Unless one is careful, such letters soon become stereotyped. If possible, each letter should be a personal message to the parents, but even a stereotyped letter is better than one that is not clear. In writing to parents, you should remember that parents may not be familiar with the professional jargon of teachers. Consequently, you should attempt to write in clear, idiomatic everyday English.

In writing such letters it is usually best to start and end on a pleasant note. A frequent recommendation is always to commence by reporting something favorable about the student and ending in an optimistic vein. This is sound advice. However, the effort to be pleasant must not outweigh truthfulness. Parents are entitled to an accurate report that reflects the teacher's best judgment concerning the child. Sometimes teachers are so careful not to hurt the parents' feelings and so eager to establish amicable relations that they fail to point out the student's failings. This is not fair to the parents. While you should not be tactless, you should let the parents know the facts about the child. The best rule is to decide what you wish the parent to know and then say it simply and pleasantly.

The body of the report should estimate the progress of the student, as accurately as possible. This estimate should indicate the student's progress in relation to his ability and also in relation to the normal achievement for students at that grade level. It should point out the student's strong and weak points, and show where he needs help. The report should not be limited to achievement in subject matter alone, but should also provide information concerning the student's social behavior and other aspects of school life. At times, you will wish to ask the parent for cooperation in some specific way. Certainly you should always ask the parent for comments.

When writing a letter to a parent, be brief, clear, pleasant, honest, and factual. An example of a homeroom teacher's letter to a ninth-grader's parents follows.

Dear Mr. and Mrs. Smith:

Joan's teachers have reported to me the results of her first quarter's work. They are quite satisfactory except for algebra, in which she is experiencing some difficulty. Her difficulty seems to be caused by a lack of understanding of mathematical principles. Mr. Courtney, her algebra teacher, feels that she should have extra help in his course. In all other respects, Joan seems to be making an excellent start this year.

If you have any suggestions or comments to make about Joan's school work, we should welcome them. Also, we should very much like to have you visit our school whenever it is convenient for you.

Cordially yours,
Jennie Jones

Conferences with Parents

Parent-teacher conferences are an increasingly popular method of reporting student progress to parents. This procedure has many advantages. It allows the teacher and the parent to discuss the student face-to-face. The conference should serve to create better understanding between parents and teachers and to prevent the parental misunderstandings that sometimes result from teachers' letters and report forms. The conference gives the parent an opportunity to ask questions and to make suggestions. It also gives the teacher an opportunity to solicit additional information from the parent and to suggest ways in which the parent can cooperate to improve the child's work.

Conferences can be very helpful as supplements to the written reports of student progress to parents. It is doubtful whether they should be the sole medium for reporting, although some elementary schools rely almost wholly upon them. In secondary schools, conferences are more likely to be arranged to meet certain definite problems.

Some suggestions for conducting parent-teacher conferences follow.

1. Plan what you wish to say and how you wish to conduct the conference. Do not make a fetish of your plan, but do try to keep to the purpose of the conference at least. If possible, keep the conference moving. On the other hand do not rush the parent. In your planning allow enough time to talk things over thoroughly and leisurely.

2. Be pleasant, courteous, tactful, and patient. Remember that the visit to the school may be upsetting to parents. Listen to them and try to understand their point of view. Remember that they have much information that is valuable to you. Let them tell it to you. When they are running hot, keep cool and let them talk it out. However, do not be obsequious. One does not need to agree with a parent to be polite. If the parents are severely critical of the school, arrange a conference with the principal or someone else in authority. Remember at all times that a conference is serious business and should be conducted with care and dignity.

3. Be clear and specific. Try to be sure that parents understand you. Use simple English and avoid technical terms. Make specific points and back

them up with specific examples. Avoid vague, unsubstantiated generalizations which may lead to misunderstanding. Summarizing at critical points during the conference and at its end may help eliminate confusion and ensure a common understanding of what has transpired.

4. Avoid criticizing other teachers and school officials. First, it is unethical. Second, it will surely hurt your standing with your colleagues. Third, it will probably cause the parent to form a poor impression of you.

5. Solicit the parents' cooperation. The school is as much theirs as it is yours, and they have as much stake in its success as you do. Their interest in their own children is presumably greater than yours. Many parents would be eager to help if they only knew how. On the other hand, beware of making suggestions which might be construed as an intrusion on the parents' privacy, home life or social life. If any suggestions of this sort need to be made, you should be sure that your suggestions are constructive and that the parents are ready to act upon them. Frequently the better part of discretion is to leave

---

Marks quite often become a bone of contention between parents and the school. Why? How can this be avoided?

In a conference the parent strongly criticizes the school administration or another teacher. You wholeheartedly agree with the parent. What should you do?

Compare the merits and faults of the following as a means of reporting to parents:

     letter marks
     percentage marks
     pass-fail marks
     letters to parents
     conferences with parents
     descriptive marks.

Which would be the most informative? Which would you rather receive if you were a parent?

such suggestions to guidance personnel, an administrator or a supervisor.

6. After the conference note down what has been said, what suggestions have been made, and what conclusions have been reached. This should be done as soon as possible lest some of the information be forgotten.

7. Ordinarily there should be some follow-up on every teacher-parent conference.

Promotion

Continuous Progress

Most logically promotion should be based on readiness. Students should progress through their course work in orderly fashion, staying with a particular course or unit only long enough to learn the material well and then moving on. In other words, the students should be promoted when they are ready. Promotion based on readiness is called continuous progress.

Unfortunately, the secondary school is seldom organized in a manner suitable for continuous progress. The difficulty preventing continuous promotions is that our schools are graded. At the end of a year the students must go on to the next grade, ready or not, or repeat their present grade. This system makes little sense. It forces students to repeat material they have already learned, or forces them ahead to more difficult material they are not ready for.[15]

Setting Standards for Promotion

Although most secondary schools are not organized for continuous promotion, the principles behind it do apply to promotion in general. The basic

criterion for deciding if students should be promoted is whether or not they are ready to profit from the next higher course in the subject. Even when the students do not intend to go on to the next course, the principle still holds in general, although perhaps it need not be applied quite so stringently. *In other words, teachers should have standards of minimum achievement for their courses, and these standards should represent what the students must know or be able to do before they go on to the next course.* In some states and districts these standards may be mandated by stated promotion policies.

Social Promotion

Although one should ordinarily promote only those students who are ready, on occasion students are promoted whether they are ready or not. This practice is called social promotion. On occasion, it is justified. The old practice of keeping sixteen-year-old youths in third-grade classes was cruel. An example of a well-justified social promotion follows.

A junior high school boy was reading well below his grade level. Although evidently of at least normal intelligence, he was quite incapable of doing junior high school work. The boy also suffered from an acute speech defect and certain other emotional problems. The school psychiatrist examined the boy and recommended a social promotion as a means of helping him find himself.

In this case the promotion was justified. *But automatic promotions are never justified!* Too often the young people are promoted to free the classrooms

---

[15] See Chapter 9 for a description of how continuous progress plans are organized and conducted.

To what extent can one apply the principle of continuous progress in the ordinary secondary school? To what extent should it be applied?

Do you agree that social promotion was justified in the example given in the preceding section?

and because of a mistaken attempt to be democratic. Except in cases such as the one just noted, students should be required to meet minimum standards before they move on.

Two Considerations

Although teachers should maintain standards, these standards should be flexible. The fact that a girl has not mastered the material of a course may not be sufficient reason for keeping her back. On the other hand, her having spent a year in a classroom is not sufficient reason for promoting her either. Some students should repeat courses. Each problem of promotion should be decided on its own merits. In applying promotion standards to a particular case, one should bear in mind two main questions: (1) How will the decision affect the student concerned? and (2) How will the decision affect the other students? Probably the final criterion should be: Which would benefit the student more, repeating the course or moving on?

To Pass or Not to Pass

Deciding if a student should pass or fail often calls for difficult decisions. To illustrate the complexity of the problem let us consider the following situation. In your Algebra I class you have a boy who has done poor work. It is your considered opinion that he is just not a mathematician. He is unable to do the work, no matter how hard he tries—and he seems to have tried very hard. He and his family are determined that he go on to college and insist that he continue with mathematics. Presumably, if he passes Algebra I, he will try Algebra II for which he is definitely not ready. What should you do? What would be best for the boy? To pass and attempt Algebra II? To fail and to repeat Algebra I? Is there some other way out? What about the effect on the other students? What information do you need and what must you consider to answer this problem intelligently?

As you can see, if you try to think this problem

through, it probably has no truly satisfactory answer. Even though we have stated categorically that when students have not been able to achieve the minimum standard they shall not pass, is this perhaps not a case where justice should be tempered with mercy? Fortunately, many schools help the teacher in making this decision by establishing quite definite school policies concerning promotion. When they do, the teacher should try to follow the policy. Other schools have no formal policy, although there may be an informal one. Even if there is no policy at all, the principal can advise one on what to do. Even so, the decision of whether or not to promote must be made by the teacher. In spite of statistics and theory, in the end all decisions concerning marks and marking come down to teacher judgment.

An exception to this rule would be when the state or district mandates a specific score on a state- or district-run minimum competency test as a requirement for graduation or promotion. In such cases the state or local law or regulation must prevail.

Summary

Parents have the right to know how well their children are doing in school, and teachers have a duty to keep the parents informed. For many years teachers have used marks to meet this obligation. Although many parents, students, and teachers do not realize it, marks, unfortunately, do not inform anyone of much of anything. Moreover, present-day marking systems tend to emphasize the mark rather than the learning. About the only value they have is a certain amount of incentive value, and even that seems to be overrated.

As teachers have come to recognize these facts, they have made numerous attempts to create better methods of evaluating and reporting students' progress. So far none of these attempts has been completely successful. Probably what is needed is a system that explains in writing what students can or cannot do and how well they are doing in relation to the standard for the group and to their own potentialities. In reporting to parents and students, such devices should undoubtedly be supplemented by conferences. Modern systems of reporting to parents seem to be moving in that direction. However, in many cases they still have a long distance to go. In the meantime, we shall have to do the best we can with what we have.

Promotion has always been a problem for the conscientious teacher. Promotion should be based on readiness, but this principle of continuous progress is not readily feasible in the middle and secondary schools as now organized.

There is no truly satisfactory answer to the problem of promotion. The final decision, however, should rest with the teacher. This decision should be based on what is best for the student and for the other students in the class and school and on state or district promotion policy.

Additional Reading

Bellanca, James A. *Grading.* Washington, DC: National Education Association, 1977.

Bloom, Benjamin S., George F. Madaus, and J. Thomas Hastings. *Evaluation to Improve Learning.* New York: McGraw-Hill, 1981.

Grambs, Jean D., and John C. Carr. *Modern Methods in Secondary Education.* New York: Holt, 1979.

Gronlund, Norman E. *Improving Marking and Reporting in Classroom Instruction.* New York: Macmillan, 1974.

Simon, Sidney B., and James A. Bellanca, eds. *Degrading the Grading Myths: A Primer of Alternatives to Grades and Marks.* Washington, DC: Association for Supervision and Curriculum Development, 1976.

Terwilliger, James S. *Assigning Grades to Students.* Glenview, IL: Scott Foresman, 1971.

19

Teaching Tools

Overview

Mark Hopkins, it is said, could conduct a school merely by sitting on one end of a log. Most teachers need more to work with than that. In fact, for most teachers the more they have available, the better they can teach. This chapter discusses some of the tools and materials that are available and how they may be used to aid instruction.

Among the tools are audiovisual media, television, printed and duplicated materials, and teaching machines and programs, including computer-assisted instruction. Some of these materials are sophisticated and costly, but most of them are surprisingly easy to use and quite inexpensive to obtain, if one uses a little ingenuity. The important thing is to use them to give variety and point to your classes, for they can ward off the humdrum and sharpen students' learning of the concepts, skills, and attitudes that are your objectives.

In this chapter we discuss some of the characteristics of these teaching tools, and point out some of the ways they can help you make your teaching more effective.

Audiovisual Media

Uses of Audiovisual Media

Although no longer fashionable, the term *audiovisual aids* is appropriate because it describes just what instructional materials are—aids to teaching and learning. Instructional aids cannot substitute for real teaching, however. They have an entirely different role; a powerful role, it is true, but a role in support of teaching. If you think of them and use them as teaching tools, you will not go far wrong.

Audiovisual materials can help make ideas and concepts clear. As an earlier chapter points out, verbalism is one of the banes of the American secondary school. Audiovisual media can help raise learning from verbalism to true understanding. The words "rubber bogey buffer bumper" may mean little to you, but if you should see a picture or model of one or watch one in operation in a moving picture, the words would probably become meaningful.

Audiovisual instructional media can also make learning interesting and vivid. A Chinese proverb tells us that one picture is worth a thousand words. Whether or not this is true, good audiovisual materials have eye and ear appeal. By snaring our attention they make learning more effective. They can

be invaluable in promoting motivation and retention.

Making the Most of the Medium

In a suburban school a beginning teacher surprised her supervisor by asking, "Is it all right to use filmstrips for my American history class?" "Of course," he replied, "Why not?" "Well," she said, "I tried one last week and the class gave me a lot of trouble. They seemed to think the filmstrip was kid stuff and they acted up something terrible." Yet that same day the supervisor had visited a class—supposedly a class of the most difficult youngsters in the school—where the teacher, who was using a filmstrip in science, had excellent interest and attention. The difference seemed to be that one teacher expected the filmstrip to teach itself; the other was really teaching with the filmstrip as an aid.

Audiovisual aids need skillful teaching to make them effective. Just like any other instructional activity, audiovisual aids should be selected because they seem best suited for that point in the lesson. And, as with any other activity, the teacher must prepare the class for the audiovisual activity, guide the class through it, and follow-up after its completion.

Selecting the Audiovisual Material

In selecting the audiovisual aid, you should consider, in addition to its suitability, such things as visibility, clearness, level of understanding, ease of

---

Why is it impossible to substitute audiovisual media for good teaching? Is this statement true of programed and computer-based teaching? Why, or why not?

In a certain school the eighth-grade team always presents moving pictures to all its students on Friday afternoon. Criticize this practice.

presentation, and availability of material. To be sure that the aid is effective and appropriate, if it is at all possible, try it out before using it with the class. This is particularly important in selecting films, filmstrips, and recordings and in presenting demonstrations. Sometimes films and recordings seem to have little resemblance to their descriptions in the catalog, and a demonstration that does not come off is literally worse than useless.

Planning to Use the Materials

Once you have previewed the audiovisual material, you are in a position to plan how to make the best use of it. In this process you should (1) spell out the objectives that the material will best serve, (2) note the important terms or ideas presented in the audiovisual material, (3) identify any words or ideas that may cause students difficulty without some preliminary explanation, and then (4) make up your plan for introducing, presenting and following up the audiovisual material. For instance, in introducing and presenting a filmclip you may plan to (a) give a short explanation of the source and setting of the filmclip, (b) play the clip through quickly without stopping or commenting, and (c) play the clip again, stopping and analyzing the action in detail. Or you might decide to play it through and discuss it. You might also decide to stop and analyze the action from time to time in the first run through. The choice is yours, but you should choose your approach beforehand, not blunder into it.

Preparing for the Audiovisual Activity

To get the most out of any activity, you must prepare the students for it. Do so by introducing the audiovisual material. Sometimes a short sentence identifying the aid and its purpose will suffice. At other times, it would be better to spend considerable time discussing the purpose of the activity and suggesting how the students can get the most from it. The introduction to a moving picture or a filmstrip, or a recording, should point out its purpose and suggest points that students should watch for in their viewing or listening.

Not only must you prepare the students for the activity, you must also prepare the activity itself. Nothing can be more embarrassing or more disruptive than movies that do not move, demonstrations that do not demonstrate and similar audiovisual fiascos. *Competent teachers check the little things.* Do you have chalk? Are there extra fuses? Can everyone see the poster? Will the machine run? Do we have all the transparencies and are they all in the correct order? Be careful about the details. More than one class has been upset by the lack of a piece of chalk or an extension cord.

Guiding Students Through Audiovisual Activities

Instead of relieving you of your responsibility for guiding students' learning, the use of the audiovisual materials gives you an opportunity to make your guidance more fruitful. So that the students get the most from the audiovisual aid, point out what to look for and listen for. Often it may be necessary to explain to the students what they are seeing or hearing. To do this, you might be wise to provide the students with a list of questions or a study guide to direct their attention to salient points (see Figure 19–1). On other occasions you should stop to discuss vital relationships on the spot.

Following Up Audiovisual Activities

In spite of the appeal and vividness of audiovisual media, they cannot prevent some students from misunderstanding or missing part of the instruction. You must follow up the audiovisual activity to bridge the gaps and to clear up misunderstand-

FIGURE 19–1
Listening Questions for *The Phoenician Traders* Record.

(These questions are illustrative of the type of questions one might use in a special study guide for use with a record. They represent different levels and types of questions. In using such study guides one must guard against merely mechanical exercises.)

1. What seems to be the major business of the Phoenicians?
2. What seems to be the relationship between Tyre and Carthage?
3. What can you learn about the trade routes of the Phoenicians?
4. What was life like on a caravan?
5. What can you note about Phoenician ships and seamanship?
6. What did you learn about Phoenician trade? How did they carry it on? How did they keep accurate accounts and so on? In what way did they trade?
7. How nearly accurate is the reconstruction of Phonenician life? If you do not know, how can you find out?
8. Prepare a list of questions that would emphasize or bring about the important idea expressed in this recording.

ings. Follow-up also renews the learning and thus increases retention. Furthermore, it has motivational aspects. One danger in using films, filmstrips, television, and radio is that students sometimes think of these activities as recreational, and so give scant attention to them. If you follow up activities featuring audiovisual aids with discussion, review, practice, and testing, you can usually correct this misapprehension and also point up and drive home the learning desired. Students must realize that a film presentation in your class is not just a movie, but a lesson for which they are responsible.

Suppose you order a film from an audiovisual center and when it arrives it turns out not to be what you had expected. What would you do?

If you were to order a film for a class in your field, what criteria would you use in your selection?

Select an audiovisual aid that you might use in one of your courses. What would you have to do to introduce it properly? What would you do to clinch the learning from this audiovisual material?

Kinds of Audiovisual Materials

Chalkboards

Now that we have discussed the proper use of audiovisual material in general, let us consider some of them in particular. Perhaps the most commonplace of all teaching tools is the old-fashioned blackboard or its brighter modern counterpart, the chalkboard. This device is so omnipresent that many of us fail to think of it as an audiovisual aid at all; yet most teachers would be hard put if they had no chalkboards available.

The first point in the use of the chalkboard is that people cannot learn much from a visual aid they cannot see. It is important to write legibly, to use portions of the board within the students' range of vision, to write large, and to stand out of the students' line of sight. In passing, one might add that pointers are useful tools. They do not obstruct the view nearly as much as an arm, a shoulder, or a back.

A second point is that a neat, orderly board aids learning, whereas a cluttered board can be distracting. To get the best out of a chalkboard, it should be neat and orderly with plenty of blank space so that the material to be learned or studied will stand out.

To achieve a neat, uncluttered appearance, and to reduce distractions, you should erase anything that you no longer need as soon as you are through with it. Too many chalkboards look like attics—full of old junk. If you must put something on the board before it is needed, cover it up, if feasible. You can pull down a map over it, or cover it with wrapping paper taped to the board with masking tape. Dramatically uncovering the material during a lecture is an excellent way to drive home a point.

To make important ideas stand out, you can use underlining, color, and boxes for emphasis. Use stickmen, diagrams, diagrammatic maps, and rough drawings to illustrate and clarify points.

When drawing on the board, use stencils, patterns, or projected images to make drawing easier and more accurate. By projecting maps, pictures and exercises on the chalkboard you can make it possible for students to write comments, add details, fill in blanks, and so on, right on the chalkboard.

Flannel Boards, Felt Boards, Hook–and–Loop Boards, and Magnetic Boards

Flannel boards, felt boards, hook-and-loop boards and magnetic boards can be used in much the same way as the chalkboard. You can construct your own flannel board quickly by stretching a piece of flannel across a board of the desired size and tacking it down securely. Signs, pictures, letters and the like can be stuck on the flannel if their backs are covered with strips of sandpaper or felt. Magnetic boards can be constructed quickly out of a sheet of iron or steel on which material can be displayed by means of magnets. Families use such magnetic boards in the kitchen or family area to remind each other of things they ought not to forget. Their use can be just as effective in the classroom. Hook-and-loop boards are made of the same type of material as Velcro fasteners and can be purchased. They are used extensively by professional speakers and sales representatives, among others.

These devices have certain advantages over the chalkboard. They are more dramatic. Because they lend themselves to techniques that utilize immediacy and drama, it has been estimated that they are 50 per cent more effective than chalkboards. Furthermore, they save teachers time and effort because the material used on them can be prepared in advance and can be saved from year to year. With devices such as the ones just mentioned, the technique is to prepare the materials ahead of time and then magically stick them onto the board at the propitious moments in the class presentation. Thus as you make each point in a lesson, you can slap the appropriate word, caption, picture, or what have you onto the flannel board to drive the point home.

Bulletin Boards

Well used, bulletin boards can be effective teaching tools. They can motivate, interpret, supplement and reinforce one's lessons. They should be always kept up-to-date and aimed at the current lessons. They should not be used simply to dress up the classroom.

To make a bulletin board effective requires planning. In order to capture the students' interest and direct it toward a salient point, try to arrange each bulletin board and display so that the observer's eye automatically travels toward the center of interest around which the display is focused. One can facilitate this focus by keeping the board or display free from extraneous material, by centering the most significant portion of the display, and by using lines, real or imaginary, to direct the attention from the subordinate items to the central items. In addition, titles and captions are extremely helpful in putting the central idea across. It is also a good idea to have plenty of white space. Crowding materials on a board makes it unattractive and confusing. In the use of bulletin boards, neatness and attractiveness are extremely important. Here especially you should strive for an uncluttered look.

Bulletin boards are more effective if they are arranged simply and tastefully. Collages and psychedelic displays can be fun, but they are more likely to obscure the idea than to point it up.

Bulletin boards should be as exciting as possible. For this purpose you can utilize ideas from magazine, newspaper, and television advertising. Use eye catchers of various sorts—color, three-dimensional objects, variety, humor, lines of momentum—to enliven the board. Another way to add spice is to combine the bulletin board with a table display. To do this set the table directly in front of the bulletin board. Colored strings from the table to the bulletin board can be used to tie the two displays together. Given a little help students can come up with exciting displays on their own.

Charts, Posters, Maps, Graphs, and Overlays

The principles applicable to the use of chalkboards, bulletin boards, and flannel boards generally apply to the use of charts, posters, maps, and graphs. Again simplicity, clarity, and dramatic impact are the keystones. In the use of charts, as with chalkboards, it is wise to cover material prepared for display later in the lesson. When this is not done, students are liable to pay more attention to aids planned for later use than to the lesson in progress. This procedure can be made even more effective by covering the different sections of a chart or display in such a way that one can uncover one section at a time as it is needed. With a little imagination you can make the procedure highly vivid and dramatic. You can get the same effect with an overhead projector by gradually uncovering the transparency or by adding flip-ons. Another variation is the flip chart, which consists of a large pad of sheets that can be flipped over out of the way to reveal new material as the class proceeds.

Among the charts you may use in your classes are maps and graphs. Although techniques for teaching with maps and graphs are the same as for other types of charts, you should be sure to teach the language and symbols of graphs and maps

to the students who do not understand, or they will be worthless.

Overlays can make charts and maps more effective. An overlay is simply a sheet of transparent material that can be laid over the map or chart so that one can write on it without injuring it. Good ones have been made out of old plastic tablecloth covers, plastic drop cloths, and the like. Individual overlays may be used with the maps and charts in books and magazines. The overlay may be preprinted or developed as the class moves along by writing on the plastic with a china marking pencil (grease pencil), or with a felt-tipped marking pen.

Observe the board work of your teachers and fellow students. What makes it effective? What keeps it from being more effective?

What advantages can you see in the flannel or hook-and-loop board over an ordinary blackboard? Why is this type of board often used in television commercials or sales meetings rather than the chalkboard?

Go around the school. Look at bulletin boards and other displays. What techniques have been used to make them effective? What could you do to make them more effective?

Using Projectors

Many types of projection equipment are available. Among them are opaque projectors, slide projectors, filmstrip projectors, overhead projectors, microprojectors, as well as the ubiquitous motion picture projectors. These machines can bring to the entire class experiences that would otherwise be impossible, or possible only on an individual basis, or at great cost. For example, if you wish to show English money to a social studies class, you could project the images of various English coins on a screen by means of an opaque projector (if you have some coins). This technique allows everyone to see the coins without interrupting the presentation, something impossible if the coins are passed around. Or, if you wish to show students what actually happens during the making of steel, you could show them a film or filmstrip. Sometimes such techniques can make clear to students things that they could not see in a real field trip.

The Opaque Projector. Even though the opaque projector requires almost complete darkness to be effective and even then may be difficult to focus and rather awkward to use, it is an extremely valuable tool. It will project on the screen the image of opaque surfaces that are too small for all students to see readily from their seats and it will do so in color. With it a teacher can project not only realia such as the coins mentioned previously, but also pictures and pages from books, pamphlets, and magazines. It can also be used to enlarge maps and the like by projecting them on a suitable surface for copying; to project students' work for evaluation, correction, or exhibit; and as a basis for student reports.

The Overhead Projector. Overhead projectors are also extremely useful and versatile. It is not too much to say that there should be one in every classroom. They can be used in lighted classrooms without darkening the room, thus allowing students to take notes or do other activities not possible in darkened classrooms. Some teachers, for instance, use overhead projection to present quiz questions rather than mimeographing them or writing them on the chalkboard. Moreover, they are so constructed that you can write, draw, and point things out from the front of the room without turning your back on the class and obstructing the students' lines of sight.

The versatility of the overhead projector makes it particularly valuable. Not only are the transparencies easy to make, but they can be prepared in advance and used over and over, thus avoiding the tedious job of copying material on the chalkboard and tying up the board with "Do Not Erase" signs. In addition, transparencies can be placed on top

of one another so as to present information in almost any combination one desires. Further, the overhead projector can be used effectively for on-the-spot recording and illustrating. Such characteristics are valuable for making teaching more effective and at the same time reducing the amount of tedious busywork which sometimes interferes with more important teaching tasks.

> What advantage does projecting a picture via the opaque projector have over showing the picture itself by passing it around or holding it up in front of the class?
>
> What advantage does the overhead projector have over the chalkboard? The bulletin board?

Slide and Filmstrip Projectors. Slide projectors and filmstrip projectors can be discussed simultaneously because the two are often combined into one machine. After all, a filmstrip is little more than a series of slides joined together on a strip of film. The filmstrip has the advantage of having been put together by an expert in a ready-made sequence. Slides are more versatile, but using them requires more careful planning by the teacher. Just one slide out of order or upside down can throw a well-conceived lesson out of step.

Some filmstrips come with recorded commentary and sound effects. Although these are usually quite impressive, you may prefer to provide your own commentary as the filmstrip progresses. If you wish, you can prerecord your own commentary and sound effects and synchronize them to a filmstrip or to a series of slides. Utilizing sound with slides is usually enhanced by the use of an automatic projector. If you can influence the choice of slide projectors, you would do well to insist on a projector that will operate both manually and automatically.

Filmstrip and 2 x 2 slide projectors are small enough and simple enough to operate for small-group or individual use. For individual or small-group viewing, the image can be thrown onto a sheet of cardboard no larger than the projector itself. It seems surprising that more teachers do not take advantage of this capability of the filmstrip and slide projectors.

Microprojection. The number of students who never see what it is they are supposed to see through the microscope is probably astronomical. The microprojector can eliminate for practical purposes much of this difficulty by enlarging and projecting the image in the microscope's field onto a screen so that all the students can see the image and so that the teacher can point out salient features to everyone at once. Another technique that gives much the same result is to take pictures of the slide through the microscope. This technique is not difficult. It is merely a matter of screwing a compatible camera to the microscope and taking pictures by means of the optics of the microscope. The resulting 2 x 2 slides can be projected on a screen. In much the same way transparencies for overhead projection can be made with a Polaroid camera.

Preparing such materials takes time, but almost always they are worth the effort. In many instances much of the preparation of such aids can be done by students, thus giving them valuable learning experiences and saving time for the teacher.

Moving Picture Films

To be effective, motion pictures must be selected with care, previewed, introduced, and followed up. Remember, a darkened classroom is an excellent place for older students to sleep and for younger students to commit mischief.

Presenting the Film. Before presenting a film, you should prepare the setting and the equipment. Check the equipment, for the motion picture projector can be a particularly cranky machine. Run a little of the film before the presentation to be sure all is working well. Sometimes repositioning

the projector and screen in the room may make the image on light-struck screens more visible. Then when the setting and equipment are ready, alert the students to what they are to see and learn. Make sure they realize that viewing the film is a job to be done, not recreation.

Once you have started the film, keep quiet. Do not try to outshout the sound track. Students cannot listen both to you and the film at the same time. If you absolutely must explain something, stop the film before you speak; but you will usually be more effective if you make your comments before or after the viewing. In this respect, the silent film has an advantage over the sound film.

In the past the use of the motion picture in the classroom has been plagued by two distinct disadvantages. One was that the projection was designed solely for large-group instruction; the other that the films had to be shown in darkened classrooms. Neither condition needs to obtain any longer. New self-threading individual eight millimeter projection devices make motion picture projection a means for providing for individual differences, and new rear projection arrangements allow moving picture projection in lighted rooms. Increased use of these devices can make motion picture projection considerably more effective.

> What misconceptions are liable to rise from the use of aids such as the moving pictures? How can these be avoided?
> What steps should you as a teacher go through before presenting a film to a class?

Moving Picture Production. With modern equipment production of one's own moving pictures has become relatively easy. With help students can carry out the tasks necessary for completing interesting, productive films. If you are interested in producing films you should consult your school audiovisual or media-center director, and such books as Kemp's *Planning and Producing*

Audio-Visual Materials[1] and technical manuals on the subject.

Pictures and Specimens

Pictures of all sorts are available for classroom use. Especially useful are the pictures in textbooks. In addition, you should collect as many pictures as you can. Not only are the pictures useful aids, but collecting them can be fun. Specimens and other realia having to do with one's subject can be equally valuable and are likewise fun to collect. In fact, numerous teachers have developed picture and specimen collecting into lifetime hobbies.

In selecting pictures for classroom use, consider such questions as

1. Does it fit the purpose?
2. Is it relevant and important to the lesson?
3. Is it accurate and authentic?
4. Can its point be easily understood?
5. Is it interesting?
6. Is the size, quality, color, such as to make it easily visible?

No particular technique is necessary in the use of these materials. However, you of course should remember to point out whatever the students are to learn from the aid. Here it is probably more productive to ask questions than to pontificate. Use pictures as springboards for class discussion or for further study and research. Oftentimes an entire lesson can be built around a single picture or specimen. However, avoid exhibiting pictures or specimens just because you have them. Although showing students a collection may be splendid fun, even for the students, you should make sure that the material is pertinent and effective before using precious class time on it.

Another practice to avoid is passing pictures and other materials around the room so that students may look at them while the lecture, recitation, or

discussion continues. Students cannot pay attention to two things at once. While students are examining the audiovisual aid they cannot concentrate on the lesson. A much better practice is to utilize the opaque projector to throw an image of the picture or object on the screen where all can see it at once. Another alternative is to display or to pass the material around during a laboratory or work session when it is less liable to disrupt the learning process.

Models and Replicas

Models, replicas, and sand tables also make admirable audiovisual materials, and students can help in constructing them. In using student help in building aids of any sort, teachers should be wary of two dangerous faults: one, that students may spend so much time creating the aid that they neglect the things they can learn from it; and two, that inaccurate models may give students erroneous concepts. You should be particularly on guard against incorrect proportions, historical anachronisms, and other details that can mislead students. Whenever it is necessary to distort in order to be effective, as is often the case in preparing three-dimensional maps, for instance, be sure to warn the students of the inaccuracies.

Audio Tapes and Records

The ability of modern technology to capture outside events and transport them into the classroom is a boon teachers should exploit to the hilt. Through the use of the tape recorder and record player, you can bring to the class the voice of an eminent mathematician discussing mathematical theory, a famous actor reading an ancient or modern play, a diplomat discussing foreign policy or a symphony orchestra playing Rimski-Korsakov. By audio and video recording you can capture class presentations, student speech habits, and the like, as a basis for analysis, evaluation, and as an aid to improvement. Prerecorded instructions, lessons,

---

[1] Jerrold E. Kemp, *Planning and Producing Audio-Visual Materials*, 4th ed. (New York: Harper & Row, 1980).

and study guides can be very effective in providing for individual differences.

What audiovisual aids are available to you personally? What aids can you create? How could you use them? Survey the situation. You will undoubtedly find a wealth of material you had not thought of before. Consider such things as pictures, moving pictures, slides, microprojectors, chalkboards, bulletin boards, charts, graphs, diagrams, demonstrations, schematic representations, opaque projectors, records, tapes, models, maps, globes, filmstrips, radio, television, felt boards, overhead projectors, tachistoscopes, displays, exhibits, aquaria, terraria, stereopticon slides, sand tables, and realia.

How can realia be used? Is the real object, if available, always the best aid to learning? Justify your answer.

If you have not done so, videotape yourself as you teach a mini lesson.

Multimedia

Various media can and should be used to reinforce each other. Teachers use mixed media naturally, when, for instance, they use pictures to illustrate a lecture. But teaching can be made more effective by consciously utilizing multimedia presentations to make the learning process more interesting and to drive home understanding.

You can mix media by using them sequentially or simultaneously. Thus in a geography class, you might move through a carefully planned sequence involving the use of several media, e.g., a map, a pictorial representation, a model, and a film. In each step of this sequence the new medium would build upon the learning brought about by the preceding medium. Or it might be more effective to present the media simultaneously. Thus you might teach the geography lesson by presenting a picture, model, and contour map of the terrain simultaneously, moving back and forth from one to another of the media comparing and analyzing as you build up the concept. Examples of simultaneous presentations using two screens suggested by Haney and Ullmer include the following uses:

1. To hold an overview shot or complete picture on one screen, such as a laboratory experiment arrangement, while moving to a series of detailed close-up pictures on the other.
2. To show two pictures side by side for comparison, such as two works of art, each on a separate slide.
3. To hold a title of a group classification on one screen, with a series of example pictures on the other screen, providing a sort of visual paragraphing.
4. To show a line drawing or labeled schematic diagram of an object or organism next to an actual photograph.
5. To show three to six different photographs to convey a range of examples; any or all can be changed as desired.
6. To display a picture while showing a series of questions or factual notes on a second screen.[2]

Obviously in multimedia presentations the media to be used must be compatible and complimentary. Unless they work together to bring about one's teaching objectives, there is no point in using them. Misused multimedia presentations can confuse rather than clarify.

Think of at least a half dozen ways you could mix media in teaching your classes.

---

[2] John B. Haney and Eldon J. Ullmer, *Educational Media and the Teacher* (Dubuque, IA: Brown, 1970), p. 102.

Television

Instructional Television

In certain school systems, master teachers teach large numbers of classes simultaneously by means of television. In such classes it is possible to bring to students teaching that they would not otherwise get. Still, television teaching does not relieve the classroom teacher of responsibility for instruction. Even when a master teacher conducts a television lesson, you the classroom teacher still have to go through your standard routine. You must plan, you must select, you must introduce, you must guide, and you must follow up in order to fill in the gaps, correct misunderstandings, and guide the students' learning.

Before the television presentation begins, see to it that everything is ready. Students can benefit from television only if they can see and hear clearly.

To ensure good viewing one needs to observe a few rules of thumb for the physical arrangement of the classroom whether large or small. The following rules are more or less generally accepted by experts in the field.

1. The television sets should have 21- to 24-inch screens and front directional speakers.
2. The sets should be placed so that each student has an unobstructed line of sight.
3. The screen should not be more than thirty feet from any student.
4. The set should be about five and one half feet from the floor (that is, about the same height as the teacher's face).
5. The vertical angle of sight from any pupil to the set should never be more than 30°; the horizontal angle, never more than 45°.
6. The room should be kept lighted so that students can see to take notes.
7. No glare should reflect from the screen. To reduce glare one can
   a. Move the set away from the windows.
   b. Tilt the set downward.
   c. Provide the set with cardboard blinders.

8. The sound should come from front directional speakers. If several sets are in use in one room, it may be better to use the sound from only one set than to have it come from several sources. In large rooms for large-class instruction it may be more satisfactory to run the sound from one set through a public address system.
9. Students should have adequate surface space for writing.
10. To allow for quick, easy transition from the telecast, television classrooms should be fitted out with adequate audiovisual equipment, display space, and filing and storage space.

Also be sure you are familiar with the subject of the lesson and the television teacher's plan. Study the study guide, studio script, and course of study well before the lesson. Gather any materials you may need and have them ready and waiting before the telecast. Also before the telecast starts, brief the students on the lesson—its purpose, what to look for and the like; point out any new vocabulary and fill in any serious voids evident in the presentation.

During a telecast, as classroom teacher, you must continue your role as guide to learning. You should circulate among the students to determine whether they understand and are proceeding correctly. Sometimes you will have to supplement the television teacher's instruction. In work-type lessons you may need to correct and help students. More frequently you will prefer to take notes of student reactions—particularly evidences of lack of understanding or misunderstanding—for use in follow-up activities after the telecast.

The follow up after the television class is fully as important as the class itself. Check the students' learning against the objectives of the lesson. If necessary, reteach or provide additional experiences to enrich and carry forward the learning. Center class discussion around such questions as, What did we learn? Was the learning important? If so, why? If not, why not? What should we do next in view of what we have learned? Since creative activity is so necessary for effective learning and since television lessons are liable to be largely passive, you should consider the desirability of utilizing many projects, discussions, experiments, investigations, writing and similar activities that allow students to engage actively in their own learning.

General Television Programs

When matters of great international or national significance are being telecast, it may be wise to stop other class activities and witness the event. Such activities are well worthwhile, particularly when the telecast is skillfully introduced and followed up.

Telecasts unfortunately usually occur at times which do not allow direct classroom viewing. This difficulty can be circumvented by recording the program and playing significant parts during school hours. Recent advances in videotape technology have made it possible for schools to do their own video recording relatively cheaply. However, much of the material telecast by commercial and educational television stations is copyrighted and may not be available for rebroadcast to schools without permission of the copyright holder. Television company officials usually do not object to your taping an evening newscast for use in your class the next day, however.

Another technique is to assign home viewing of telecasts. Because not all students have television sets available to them,[3] it may be necessary to make such assignments selectively, with certain individuals or committees responsible for reporting them. At times, in order to get wider experiences to share in class, it may be wise to ask different students to view the coverage on different channels. As with other assignments, television viewing assignments should be clear so that the students know what to look for and what they are trying to do. The use of a bulletin board to list assignments with attendant problems, questions, and projects has proved successful for many teachers.

Determining how best to use educational and cultural television programs can be something of a problem. Television sections of local newspapers and television magazines carry descriptions of featured programs that you can use as a basis for lesson planning and assignments. Frequently, professional magazines carry study guides for exceptional programs. Sometimes you can secure information about both the proposed scheduling and the content of coming programs in advance by writing to local television stations or to the television networks. When such information is available, classroom activities can be planned around certain television programs, or the planned class sequence can be altered in order to take advantage of exceptional television opportunities.

What seem to you to be the arguments for or against the use of instructional television?

What methods could you take as a classroom teacher to keep television instruction on a personal basis? What could you do as a television teacher?

Printed and Duplicated Materials

Pamphlets and Brochures

A tremendous amount of reading material suitable for classroom use is available for the asking or for a small fee—one particularly rich source be-

---

[3] When father, mother, brother, and sister want to watch the ball game on Channel 7, *Romeo and Juliet* on Channel 13 may not be available to a student even though you have assigned it!

ing the federal and state governmental agencies. The Government Printing Office lists thousands of pamphlets and books for sale, and the various federal agencies distribute great amounts of interesting informative material for the asking. Other sources are large industrial and commercial firms; foreign governments; supragovernmental agencies, such as the United Nations, UNESCO, and NATO; civic organizations, such as the League of Women Voters; and professional organizations, such as the National Education Association.

Workbooks

Many textbook publishers provide workbooks for use by students in secondary and middle school classes. If well written and well used, they can be very helpful. Whatever is true of them can also be said of teacher-prepared exercises.

When properly used, workbooks and duplicated exercises make it possible to allow students to pace themselves and so provide for the differences in students. There is no need for all students to do the same exercise at the same time. As a matter of fact there is no real reason why all students need use the same workbook. It is quite possible to use a workbook designed for use with one text with another one. However, when so doing the teacher should take care to see that the selections used are compatible. When differences between the text and a workbook may cause confusion, a little editing and cutting may make the content match well enough to avoid any serious difficulty.

One of the complaints against workbooks is that they encourage rote learning and discourage creative thought. These criticisms are often justified. Try to select workbooks that present problems, review material, and study guides that elicit much more than simple rote learning.

As with anything else, assignments in workbooks and locally produced materials must be followed up. Reinforcement is probably better if the follow-up is immediate. In some instances good results

can be achieved by providing answer sheets so that the students can check their own work. In other cases the workbook problems lend themselves better to follow-up in classroom discussion or by the teacher's going over the problem in class. *In no case should you leave the workbook work completely unchecked until you can find a propitious moment at some later time to collect and correct it. Do it now!*

Examine several workbooks. Do they seem to encourage independent learning or rote memorizing? Examine teacher-prepared material in the same way. How can these materials be made to encourage independent thought, if they do not?

Duplicated Material

In the better school systems, the teachers seem to provide their students with great amounts of duplicated materials. These materials should be used in just the same way as printed materials of the same type.

Teachers often give such material to the students to keep, or to use up at the time. In a good many cases this practice is desirable. On the other hand, preparing mimeographed or duplicated material costs time and money. There is no reason why duplicated exercises and supplementary reading materials should not be used again and again if one takes precautions. Therefore, you may wish to have the students write their answers to exercises and problems in a notebook, or on a separate sheet of paper, rather than on the materials directly. If you bind the duplicated, supplementary reading matter in some sort of stiff cover, it will be quite durable. Construction paper or manila file folders are excellent for this purpose. Pamphlets made this way will last longer if the copy is stapled to the cover rather than fastened with paper fasteners.

Some schools provide teachers enough secretarial service to prepare stencils and run off everything that teachers can wish for. More usually the job of preparing supplementary materials falls to the teacher. Consequently, as soon as you can, learn how to prepare and run off mimeograph stencils and spirit duplicator masters. Neither the mimeograph machine nor the spirit duplicator is very difficult to operate and the latter is made available for teacher use in the teachers' workrooms of many schools. One merit of the spirit duplicator is that master copies can be made easily by hand. This characteristic makes it a boon for the nonexpert typist and for the teacher who needs to reproduce drawings, figures, and other devices not easily done on a typewriter. This is also true of most office copying machines.

Paperback Books

In order to provide for the differences in interests, needs, and abilities of boys and girls, and to allow the implementation of laboratory and inquiry teaching, every school and classroom should have a well-stocked library. Paperback books can fill this need at relatively small cost.

By buying paperbacks the school library can acquire a great variety of books of all sorts to augment their more permanent collection and to build classroom libraries.

In the classroom paperbacks can supplement or even replace textbook sets. The best thing about paperbacks is that they are inexpensive enough so that students can buy them. In schools that have no classroom libraries students can pool their resources and start their own classroom libraries with paperbacks. More important, teachers should encourage students to build their own personal libraries, and so to become really intimate with books of their own.

When students own their own books, they should mark them up as they read them. Skill in marking up books is an important aid to analytical and inter-pretive reading. All students should have a chance to learn and practice this skill in their own books in school. They should underline and label passages that seem specially significant and worthwhile and note and comment on things that strike them as good or bad, true or false, logical or illogical.

Of course, students should not mark up books that they do not own. Instead, they should learn to write notes to themselves on cards or in a notebook, but it is not quite the same. Learning to mark up books properly is so important that school districts would do well to furnish students with inexpensive paperbacks that the students can mark up to their hearts' content.

By using paperbacks, teachers may make it possible for students to read primary sources rather than secondary or tertiary ones—whole works rather than snippets—and to explore them both extensively and intensively rather than being exposed only to a single textbook account. With inexpensive paperbacks it is much easier to provide students with opportunities to analyze and compare works, a practice that is almost impossible if one uses only the ordinary textbook or anthology.

Newspapers and Magazines

Newspapers and magazines are an ever-ready source of material for every one of the curriculum fields. Teachers in all subjects can encourage students to read newspapers and magazines profitably and make use of pertinent articles to enrich and point up their subject content. Search out the current issues to find articles that bring knowledge in the subject up to date. Use them as a basis for interesting, relevant, and current reading. In addition, newspapers and periodicals can furnish the material for bulletin board displays and other visual aids. Gathering suitable material of this type of display can be delegated to a class committee. Sometimes this committee can combine its efforts with those of the bulletin board committee to search out pertinent material and display it effectively.

Selecting a Textbook

Textbooks are the most commonly used instructional tools in our schools. Obviously they should be selected with care. In some schools the teachers choose the texts for their own classes. In other schools committees of teachers select the texts. Even when texts are selected by state or local district authorities, the teacher may have a choice among various possibilities. Consequently, you should be aware of what makes a good textbook, even though you may have to use texts that have been selected by others. The following questions may serve as a guide.

1. Will the use of this book lead to the attainment of your course objectives?
2. Does the book cover the proper topics with the proper emphases? Is any content omitted?
3. Is the book so arranged and so written that it will enhance student learning?
4. Is the book interesting? Is it readable?
5. Are the topics arranged in a desirable sequence? If not, can the sequence be altered or portions omitted without disrupting the usefulness of the book?
6. Are the concepts presented clearly? Are they adequately developed with sufficient detail or is there a tendency to attempt to jam in too many ideas too compactly?
7. Is the content accurate and accurately presented?
8. Is the book free from bias?
9. Are information and interpretations up to date? What is the copyright date?
10. Is the author competent in the field?
11. Does the author write clearly and well?
12. Is the technical reading level appropriate?
13. Is its conceptual reading level appropriate?
14. Are the vocabulary and language appropriate for the students of the class?[4]

15. Does the book presume background knowledge and experience that the students do not yet have?
16. Does the author make good use of headings, summaries, and similar devices? Are there opportunities for the readers to visualize, generalize, apply, and evaluate the content?
17. Are the table of contents, preface, index, appendices, and glossary adequate?
18. Does the book provide suggestions for use of supplementary materials?
19. Does the book provide a variety of suggestions for stimulating, thought-provoking instructional activities?
20. Are these suggestions sufficiently varied both in level and kind?
21. Are the sources used by the author documented adequately?
22. Is the book well illustrated? Are the illustrations accurate, purposeful, and properly captioned? Are they placed near the text they are designed to illustrate?
23. Does the book have suitable maps, charts, and tables? Are they clear and carefully done? Does the author refrain from trying to cram too much data onto the maps and charts?
24. Is the book well made? Does it seem to be strong and durable?
25. Does the book look good? Is the type clear and readable? Do the pages make a pleasant appearance with enough white space?

[4] See Chapter 14 for a discussion of formulas for finding reading levels of texts and students' reading ability. Chapter 14 also discusses how to teach students to use the textbooks profitably.

Using the criteria listed in this chapter as a basis, review several textbooks in your field. In what ways are they good? In what ways are they bad? If you had a choice which would you adopt?

Examine several texts for courses you may teach. What do you like about them? What do you dislike? How do they measure up to the criteria cited here?

Teaching Machines, Programed Learning, and Computers

The teaching machine differs from the ordinary audiovisual aid in that it actually does some of the teaching. In effect, what the machine does is to present and follow up a series of lessons, that is to say, teaching programs. In this sense the machine is a mechanical tutor that works with the student in a one-to-one relationship, although in reality it is the teaching program that does the actual teaching. The teaching machine, whether it be a complex computer or a simple, programed text, is simply the delivery system. In some circumstances it may well be that a programed textbook may be more effective than the computer. In the jargon of the trade these machines and their attachments, e.g., disc drives and printers, are called "hardware," the programs are called "software," and supporting readings, exercises, and the like are called "courseware."

Characteristics of Teaching Programs

There are two basic types of teaching programs, the linear and the intrinsic programs. Computer-assisted instruction is simply a highly sophisticated form of programing. Well-made programs of every type have the following characteristics.

1. The objectives are clearly defined.

2. The student progresses toward these objectives by means of a carefully planned sequence of steps.

3. The sequence and the items in that sequence have been rigorously tested and revised to ensure that the program does in fact lead to the objective.

4. The student is active; it is he who does the learning.

5. The student assumes the responsibility for learning and sets his own pace.

6. The program provides immediate feedback, so the student knows the results of his activity in one step before he goes on to the next.

Basically, the procedure in both types of programs is the same.

1. The machine or program presents the student with something to learn and then asks him to answer the question or solve a problem.

2. The student attempts to answer the question or solve the problem.

3. The machine (or program) informs the student whether he is correct or not and tells him what to do next.

4. In the case of the linear program, the student moves on to the next item. Linear programs provide no room for error. Instead they consist of easy steps from item to item so that the student will always answer correctly thus reinforcing the correct answer and learning by operant conditioning. In the case of the intrinsic program, the answer to one question determines what the next question or activity will be. If the student makes an error, the program or machine reteaches him and asks him the same or similar question or problem again to determine if the student now understands. In a sense, by his responses the student builds his own program under the machine's guidance as he goes along. With its great versatility, a computer can be programed so that it will be extremely responsive to the student's needs.

Because of its flexibility and because students work on programs alone rather than in groups, programed instruction, especially computer-programed instruction, makes it possible to provide truly individualized programs for the students. In addition, because it can actually teach information and skills, programed instruction can free the teacher from some of the more mundane teaching duties. While students are working on their programs, the teacher can work with other students individually or in small groups. Therefore teachers would do well to use instructional programs and machines as a basis for individualizing instruction, as a medium for teaching students basic skills and information, as a way of providing students the background necessary for discussion, inquiry, and problem-solving activities, and as a means for freeing themselves so that they can give students individual attention and concentrate on higher learnings.

Although programs will teach, you cannot expect to turn the students over to the machine and have it solve all your problems. Even the most sophisticated of systems will require skilled classroom teachers always on the job. They are needed to

1. Guide and supervise the students.
2. Continually check the students' progress.
3. Select suitable programs for individual students and see to it that the students go through these programs correctly.
4. Provide follow-up activities. (Programed activities make good springboards, but teachers must provide the follow-up.)
5. Provide other types of instruction. (Programed teaching should not be overused. Some students find it boring. Besides too much of even a good thing quickly palls.)
6. Evaluate student progress. (Although computers can give and correct tests, teachers apply other criteria and their own best judgment to assess students' progress and strengths.)

Computers

Computers are sweeping the country. In spite of their cost, their use is spreading widely, because of their reputed efficiency as a learning tool.

Evidently this reputation is well earned. Computer-assisted instruction seems to improve student attention, motivation, and time on task. It tends to keep students alert and interested. At least when students are taught by computer, they seem to ask more questions and to talk about their learning more.[5] Computers also seem quite successful in teaching problem solving.

Probably much of the computer's success is because students like instruction by computer. They find that it

gives them a sense of control and power;
allows active learning;
demands interaction;
makes them the decision maker;
allows them to stop and start when ready and motivated;
doesn't get angry;
gives immediate feedback;
provides risk-free simulation;
provides a sense of mastery;
is friendly, patient, and never gives detention.[6]

In any case research seems to indicate "that computer-based education can be an improvement over conventional methods."[7]

Learning about Computers

Computers are complex, sophisticated, powerful tools. They can help teachers wonderfully. But they are only tools. Well used they can make your teaching more profitable, but they cannot relieve you of your teaching responsibilities. It is you who must decide how best to use computers to accomplish your goals, just as you must decide how to incorporate other media into your instructional strategies. Consequently you should make yourself "computer literate" enough not only to use computers skillfully in instruction but also to select good hardware and software, and to be helpful in the development of useful computer-assisted programs and courseware.

To this end you should know how the computer works, the terms and jargon of "computerese," the history of computers and their use, the uses of computers in education, their nonschool uses, and the

---

[5] Mary Alice White, "Synthesis of Research on Electronic Learning," *Educational Researcher* (May, 1983), **40:**11–15.

[6] Doris A. Mathieson, "Computers: From Confusion to Collaboration," *Educational Leadership* (November, 1982), **40:**13–15.

[7] Karen Billings, "Research on School Computing," in M. Tim Grady and Jane D. Gawronski, eds., *Computers in Curriculum and Instruction* (Alexandria, VA: Association for Supervision and Curriculum Development, 1983), p. 13.

relationship between computers and society. In particular you should be well versed in the techniques of problem solving and the use of computers in problem solving. In addition, you should also know something about computer hardware and its potentials and limitations, and how to evaluate and select software. And you should know at least one computer language, probably BASIC for a starter.[8] Most important, you should also know how to use the computer as an instructional tool in the subjects you plan to teach. For instance:

In social studies computers can be useful for individualizing instruction, for presenting materials in graphic form, for constructing graphs and maps, for drill and practice, and for presenting social or moral problems for solution.

In mathematics computers are excellent for use in problem solving. One can use them to set up a problem, to develop the steps for solving it, to carry out the steps, and to see why the solution did or did not work.

In science computers are useful for presenting simulations. With a little coaching students can develop their own simulations.

In business education computers can be used for such computer-assisted activities as problem solving, drill and practice, simulations, and tutoring. They are excellent for building vocabulary and spelling skills. They are also important for teaching special topics—especially topics having to do with computers in business. In teaching special topics computers can be used to introduce the topic, to motivate, to conduct drill and practice, to assess progress, and to follow up.

In English computers are useful for high-level problem solving and drill and practice in grammar, spelling, vocabulary, and the like. Computers can also be used to present literary games and individualized teaching packets.

In any subject area computers can be helpful in developing thinking skills. Computers require students to describe matters appropriately and to arrange them in proper sequence step by step; they give students practice in using problem-solving procedures and in modifying them to fit the circumstances; they help students to develop procedures for attacking and solving new problems.

Computer Capabilities

As the previous section indicates, computers can be used in almost any field to teach subject content and skills, and to develop thinking, problem-solving, and other intellectual skills (Computer-Assisted Instruction), and as a means for assessing student progress, recording results, and prescribing next steps (Computer-Managed Instruction).

Computer-Assisted Instruction. In computer-assisted instruction computers can be used for conducting such strategies and tactics as the following.

Drill and practice: The computer can be used to present practice material to students as individuals or in groups, and give the students immediate feedback concerning their performance.

Tutoring: The computer can be used to present new material to students on a one-to-one basis. It can conduct exercises concerning that material, correct student responses, and then provide follow-up material to strengthen student weaknesses and correct misunderstandings.

Simulation and modeling: The computer can be used to present simulations to the students and as a medium for students to construct their own simulations or models.

Data analysis: The computer can be used to analyze data into its various elements, find significant facts, and present them in tabular, graphic, or other easily understood formats.

Problem solving: The computer can be used to set forth problems, analyze the information, provide trial solutions, and test those solutions.

Independent study: The computer can be used to allow students to pursue certain topics alone. It can be programmed to map out the course of instruction, to present materials, to test the individ-

---

[8] M. Tim Grady and James L. Poirot, "Teacher Competence: What Is Needed," in Grady and Gawronski, op. cit., p. 79.

uals' progress, and to prescribe additional study and activities.

Individualizing instruction: The computer can be used to allow students to progress at their own rates. It can present new materials to students when they are ready so that they will not be held up by slower students and it can allow slower students to proceed more slowly and finish topics difficult for them without penalty. It can permit bright students to venture on new ground that the other students may not be up to. It can also let students pursue individual interests without being fettered by the desires and talents of other group members.

Games: Computer games can be used to add great interest to the class and also to clarify understandings. Frequently they challenge students to attempt and achieve learning that they might otherwise forgo.

Testing and evaluation: Computers can be used to give and score tests, and to analyze test results. They can also be used to evaluate student performance on exercises and other learning activities.

Computer-Managed Instruction. Computers can also be helpful for diagnostic and record-keeping purposes. In computer-managed instruction the computers are used to test and record each student's progress, to diagnose weaknesses, to recommend remedial work if necessary, and to indicate when the student is ready to move on to the next step, and to provide needed additional drill and practice.

For example, in one such program, the course is divided into two week units each centered around behavioral objectives and learning activities designed to lead to those objectives. These learning activities use a variety of teaching materials. The computer is used to diagnose individual student's progress, to give the student feedback, and to prescribe the next steps. By this means each student is able to work toward the objectives on a personally prescribed course on the basis of an objective analysis of progress, strengths, and weaknesses.

In such a program the computer gives an assessment of the students' needs, prescribes an assignment in view of this assessment, gives a followup assessment, prescribes an alternate remedial assignment on the basis of this assessment, and finally certifies the students' mastery of the unit content. Programs of this sort can be used both for individual and small-group instruction.

Planning Computer Activities

How one uses computers in class depends, of course, on the number of computers available. To best utilize problem-solving, drill, practice, and tutorial activities, for instance, you should really have a computer for every user because this type of arrangement allows the learners to control the content and pace their learning.

Computer simulations and gaming activities are best presented via small-group activities. Activities of these sorts can foster cooperation and interpersonal communication. For this type of teaching to be most effective, one needs several computers so that the various groups can each gather around a computer. This will allow the different groups to work on the program at the same time thus permitting them all to discuss the program with each other, to interact, and then to move on to the next step in the sequence. In any case when using simulations and games, the teacher must introduce the program, conduct it, and then follow up with other activities.

If only one computer is available, you are pretty much limited to dividing the class into groups that take turns at the computer, or to large-group activities. Large-group computer activities can be excellent for introducing or summarizing topics. Again, as with other audiovisual presentations, they need to be introduced, followed up, and, in general, included in one's overall strategy.[9]

No matter how one uses the computer, the com-

---

[9] Ken Brumbaugh and Don Rawitsch, *Establishing Instructional Computing: The First Step* (St. Paul, MN: Minnesota Educational Computing Consortium, 1982), pp. 34–35.

puter activities and noncomputer activities should be combined into meaningful integrated lessons and units. In order to integrate computer and noncomputer activities, Brumbaugh and Rawitsch recommend that lessons incorporating computer activities be divided into three steps.

First, an activity to stimulate student interest in the topic.

Second, an activity that covers or conveys specific content, skills, and/or activities.

Third, an activity that summarizes learning or has students apply learning to a new situation.[10]

Only one of these three steps should include computer activity. The other steps should be made up of other types of activities. In this way Brumbaugh and Rawitsch believe one can further well-balanced, well-rounded learning.

Selecting Software

Without the appropriate software any computer is useless. To select appropriate programs, adopt a procedure such as the following.

1. Decide just what you want the program to do.
2. Set up criteria based on your needs and goals.
3. Find out what software is available. Check catalogs, library directories, and so on.
4. Check the reviews.[11]
5. Preview the most promising programs.
6. Check on the reliability and supportiveness of the supplier.
7. Determine what supporting courseware is available.
8. Evaluate the supporting courseware for suitability and quality.

In carrying out this procedure, ask yourself questions such as the following.

---

[10] Ibid., p. 61.

[11] Minnesota Educational Computing Consortium, St. Paul, Minnesota, is highly recommended as a source of information about software, also such journals as *The Computing Teacher* and *Classroom Computer News.*

1. Does the program fit your instructional objectives?
2. Does the program mesh with your content and teaching approaches? Does it aim at important objectives? Are the concepts clearly developed? Are the style, content, and educational philosophy compatible with yours?
3. Is the program motivating? Will it appeal to students? Remember, dull, dry computer programs can be just as ineffectual as any other teaching.
4. Will the program open up students' creativity, imagination, and thinking? Will it encourage logical thought?
5. For whom is the program designed? For individuals? For small groups? For large groups? What ability groups is it aimed at? Can it accomplish a range of ability levels? Is it suitable for the ability levels of your students? Is the reading level suitable? What prerequisites are necessary?
6. For what instructional uses is the program designed? Drill or practice, tutoring, simulation, gaming, problem solving, exposition, demonstration, testing, analysis, instructional management? Do these uses suit your proposed objectives and teaching style?
7. Is the program usable? Are the instructions easy to follow? Are the responses clear and appropriate? Is the screen formatting well done? Does it have adequate support materials? How long does it take to run?
8. Is the program friendly, supportive and encouraging or is it threatening? Does it help students who make errors or does it react harshly? Does it provide for constructed responses? (Some programs provide only "unique responses." These linear programs tell the student if he is right or wrong, and then go on to the next question. These programs may repeat the rule. Programs with constructed responses tell students why they are wrong and may give them clues, or hints, for getting correct answers. Better programs may indicate

steps that students should take to solve their problem. Well done, constructed response programs provide for cognitive skills and for "effective application of skills." These intrinsic programs are the kinds of programs we should buy.)[12]

9. Does the program allow for teacher management? How much teacher supervision is necessary?
10. What does the program cost? Does it seem durable? Will the suppliers give it proper support and backup? Is it worth the expense?

Selecting a Computer

The chances are that as a beginning teacher you will not be asked to pick a computer for your use. Nevertheless you should take it upon yourself to become knowledgeable in the area of computer hardware. Strangely enough the crucial element in computer selection is the software. The computer must be compatible with the computer programs selected for instruction. A computer that will not play the software best suited for your course will not be very serviceable. Therefore the first thing to check is the quality and quantity of the software available. Other points to check are the ease of use, the cost of the computer and supporting hardware and software, the availability and dependability of servicing, what supporting materials and equipment are available, and which of these are necessary or desirable for future expansion of the system.

Videodiscs

Videodiscs are most frequently used in the same manner as moving-picture projectors. As new software is developed, it is becoming a tool of great potential. It can play a program straight through

---

[12] Jay Comras and Jeffrey Zerowin, "The Computer As a Positive Learning Experience," *NASSP Bulletin* (September, 1982), **66**:18–21.

or play it in slow motion, or stop action to hold a frame. Recent improvements make it possible to combine videodiscs with microcomputers so as to produce "interaction learning." This type of learning is the epitome of the branching teaching machine idea. It allows the program to move on when the student answers correctly, but when the student answers incorrectly it immediately analyzes the incorrect response and then selects remediation tactics and materials suitable for the individual under the circumstances.

Look up some computer programs in your field. How could you use them? Do you think they are worth buying? Why, or why not? What courseware would be needed to support each program?

Look at some classroom computers. What software suitable for courses you might teach is available for these computers?

Sources of Teaching Materials

Occasionally, teachers defend dull, humdrum teaching on the grounds that the school administration will not give them adequate materials. Usually such complaints are merely passing the buck, although they may be signs of incompetence; for at the expense of a little ingenuity and initiative, boundless supplies of materials are available to even the poorest schools.

In the first place, materials for learning can be found almost everywhere. Among good sources of information telling where to find and how to use materials of instruction are curriculum guides and resource units, and references such as those listed at the end of the chapter. You can often pick up samples of materials and leads to sources of other materials at teachers' conventions and other professional meetings such as those held by your state teachers' association or the organization of teachers in your field. Teachers' resource centers maintained by college and university schools of education and by the state and county educational departments are also good sources of information about available materials.

> Examine a sample resource unit. Note the amount of material it presents. How could you use such a resource unit for your own teaching?
>
> Similarly examine a number of curriculum guides.

Free and Inexpensive Materials

Much teaching material is free or inexpensive. As pointed out in an earlier section, building a file of pictures is relatively easy, inexpensive, and can be considerable fun. In addition, such a file is so useful that the prospective teacher can hardly afford not to build one. You can start by collecting pictures from periodicals. Picture magazines, such as *National Geographic* or *Smithsonian* are full of potentially useful pictures. So are the special-interest magazines such as those devoted to travel, popular science, and history. You can also obtain pictures from commercial sources such as museums and publishing houses both by purchase and rental. Many libraries have pictures to lend to teachers for short or long periods.

Not only pictures but other materials, such as slides, specimens, souvenirs, models, and the like, are readily available for the asking. Many museums will send such material to schools free of charge. In almost every hamlet in the United States some villager has a collection of interesting materials that could be used with profit in the classroom. Usually any collector will be pleased to show off his collection. Quite often the most avid collectors are other teachers.

Stores, factories, commercial concerns of all sorts are willing, and in some instances anxious, to give samples of raw and processed materials to the schools. Likewise, many firms offer films, slides, filmstrips, and other similar audiovisual materials free upon request. The amount of excellent material available free from local, state, national, and foreign government agencies is almost boundless.

Culling the Material

A word of caution concerning free and inexpensive material is in order. Although much free material is available, some of it is hardly worth cluttering up one's shelves with. Consequently, you should cull the material quite thoroughly. Use criteria such as the following.

1. Will the material really further educational objectives?
2. Is it free from objectionable advertising, propaganda and so on?
3. Is it accurate, honest, free from bias (except where one wishes to illustrate dishonesty and bias, of course)?
4. Is it interesting, colorful, exciting?
5. Does it lend itself to school use?
6. Is it well made?

Writing for Free Material

To get free material all one must do is to write and ask for it. When writing for free material, you should use official school stationery. Your letter should state exactly what you want and why you want it. Many firms like to know just how the material will be used and how many persons will see it. Sometimes teachers ask students to write the letter. Although doing so is excellent practice for the students, some firms will honor only letters from the teacher. Of course, you can sidestep this problem by having the students prepare letters for your signature or by countersigning students' letters.

Classroom Films

Most of the more valuable classroom films are not lent to the school gratis, but are rented from film libraries or district, county, or state resource centers. Your school will probably have a clear policy and procedure about renting films. This policy should be followed to the letter. The critical thing is to order films early. Good films are in demand; a late order may mean that you will have to do without.

Each renting library publishes a catalog of its films. In addition, film companies and other agencies publish catalogs and announcements of films. Hints about useful films can also be found in textbooks, curriculum guides, and resource units. Through these sources teachers can usually find film suitable to their purposes. Perhaps the list of sources at the end of the chapter may help you. In using the list one should note that the list is not limited to films or even to audiovisual material alone.

Television Programs

Information about television programs suitable for classroom use can be obtained in professional journals, such as *Today's Education*, specialized magazines such as *T.V. Guide*, the television sections of newspapers and magazines, and from the television stations and networks themselves.

Since it is almost impossible for any teacher to keep well informed concerning all the television programs that might be potentially useful, it may be wise for you to enlist the aid of the students to scout out and report on programs of value. Many teachers regularly post billings of such programs on the chalkboard or bulletin board. These billings may be enhanced by the adding of commentary and suggested aids for viewing.

Television programs that seem to have no direct bearing on the course of study can sometimes be useful. All television dramas have plots, most of them have music, they all take place in time and space, and so almost any one of them can be used for some purpose in English, social studies, art, or music classes. The ubiquitous wild-western television drama, for instance, can be used in a study of the customs and mores of the times, and to bring home the differences between historical fact and fiction, to illustrate plot structure, or flat versus round characterization, the use of music in the theater, and so on. Particularly useful are the many documentaries and educational programs that commercial television stations use to fill in blank periods during their off hours and that make up much of the bill of fare of public television programs. Instructional television courses telecast for adults are often good sources of enrichment and a means for providing for individual differences. Sometimes they require high-level ability from the viewer, but usually they do not. The public television stations telecasting such programs usually publish program schedules, reading lists, and study materials that can be purchased for a relatively small fee.

Making One's Own Materials

Frequently teachers need to make their own materials, particularly practice materials and study guides. Modern methods of duplicating written and typed materials are easy to use and very versatile. With relatively little effort and ingenuity, you can duplicate exercises, diagrams, reading materials, assignments, study guides, and a multitude of other things. One advantage of building your own material is that you get what you want—not what some professor or merchandiser thinks you want. Against this advantage you must weigh the cost in time and effort. Oftentimes teachers expend great amounts of energy developing materials that are really not worth the effort. Once prepared, useful materials should be shared with other teachers. To hoard valuable teaching materials is wasteful.

An interesting technique used by a social studies

teacher is to tear chapters out of old books and rebind them into pamphlets by stapling them into folders or notebook binders. By this technique she has amassed a considerable library of short articles on many topics pertinent to her social studies courses from discarded textbooks, *National Geographic* magazines, and other books and periodicals at practically no expense. Not only is this a cheap method of securing reading matter, but reducing the books and periodicals to pamphlet form makes a large number of different readings accessible at the same time. The scheme has the additional advantage of cleaning out school closets and family attics.

A certain English teacher collects exercises for punctuation study by having students submit sentences to be punctuated. She collects them until she has a large number of exercises which she reproduces for student use. A science teacher makes a habit of going around to garages and junk shops to pick up old switches and other materials which, with the help of his students, he turns into demonstration equipment for his laboratory. Another sci-

ence teacher allows brilliant boys and girls to prepare microscope slides for class use. An art teacher prepares his own clay for ceramics classes by processing, with the help of his students, clay dug from a bank near a river a few miles from the school.

Other materials that you can make for yourself include springboards, study guides, and instructional learning packets.

Building a Simulation Game

Simulation games have become increasingly popular. So many have come on the market that it seems hardly necessary for teachers to build their own. Yet, homemade simulations are often the best. Even student-built simulations may be very effective. To develop a simulation model

1. Select the process to be simulated.
   a. Determine the specific objectives.
   b. Decide what type of simulation would bring out these objectives.
2. Select a situation.
   a. Historical or current event.
      (1) May give a better understanding of the situation and the problems.
      (2) May be difficult to present because of biases, emotions, or lack of information.
   b. Hypothetical situation.
      (1) Good for demonstrating specific processes, skills, and pressures.
      (2) Likely to involve emotion and bias.
      (3) Easier to control the variables—thus making the simulation simpler and clearer.
3. Research the situation in depth.
4. Develop the essential elements to be replicated.
   a. Try to keep all unessential elements out of the simulation model, for they tend to confuse and obscure the essential elements and complicate the simulation.
   b. Establish the relationships between the various roles (for example, power relationships).
5. Prepare the draft scenario.

These incidents illustrate a few examples of the myriad sources of materials open to the ingenious teacher. What materials could you use for a class of your own? Where might you find these materials? How might you use them?

Does your state, county or university publish a guide to free materials and local resources?

It is none too soon for you to start collecting material for the classes you may sometime teach. If you pick up and save all the pertinent material you can find, you have a start toward becoming a well-equipped teacher.

Examine catalogs to find films and other materials available for use in courses you hope to teach.

Search old magazines and so on to find material suitable for your future classes. It is never too early to start collecting teaching material.

a. Read several other simulations to see how they have been developed. This may give you ideas.
b. Set up some criteria or media for showing relationships.
c. Try to keep the simulation from being too simple or too complicated.
d. Write the draft scenario.
e. Try out the draft scenario.
f. Rewrite the draft scenario.
g. Repeat (e) and (f) until you get a satisfactory draft.
h. Present it to the class.
i. Rewrite it (or junk it).[13]

Homemade Visual Aids

Many visual aids can be made easily by the teacher or the student. We have already described the making of flannel boards, felt boards and magnetic boards and hinted at the possibilities in 35-millimeter photography slides and slide shows.

Filmstrips and Slide Programs. To produce filmstrips is more difficult than to make individual slides. Ordinarily the process involves copying from other slides by means of an expensive adaptation of a 35-millimeter camera. Camera clubs and other local personnel can develop filmstrips and even motion pictures, if they wish.

Fortunately, however, the same effect can be achieved with slides. In fact, individual slides, not being locked into a fixed sequence, may sometimes be preferable to filmstrips. Just arrange the slides into the order you wish to show them, decide what comments you want to make, and then proceed just as though you were showing your friends the pictures of your last vacation trip. If you wish, you can write a formal script to be read as the pictures are shown. With surprisingly little extra effort, you can provide synchronized tape recordings for your slide programs. All you need to do is to write a script with clues, noting when the operator should change slides, and then transcribe the script on a tape recording. Not only is it fairly easy, but it is fun to do. Homemade sound filmstrips of this sort can be used for large-group instruction in an assembly or lecture hall or for individual instruction in the classroom utilizing earphones and a miniature screen. If the necessary equipment is available, you can add a signal to the tape that will activate the slide changer on an automatic slide projector. While this is fun to do, it may not be worth the effort as it tends to lock you into a format that you may later wish to change.

Transparencies. There are many ways to make transparencies for the overhead projector. A number of photocopying or dry copying office machines will make transparencies of printed, typed, or written material or drawings. Preparing transparencies on some of these machines is something of an art. On others all one does is push a button and wait for a few seconds. One can also make transparencies by using a special carbon paper or by using a China marking pencil or India ink. Some popular felt-tipped pens, for example, a Magic Marker, can be used to make transparencies in color. One can also make transparencies directly with a Polaroid camera. With all these sources and acetate sheets so inexpensive (most clear acetate can be used to make transparencies by hand—the machine-made transparencies require specially treated film), there seems to be no reason why one should not have all the transparencies one needs. In order to preserve them and to keep them accessible it is recommended that one frame transparencies and file them. Commercial frames are readily available for transparencies.

Flip-ons, which are simply additional sheets that can be placed on top of another transparency to add further detail or information, are made in ex-

---

[13] Leonard H. Clark, *Teaching Social Studies in Secondary Schools: A Handbook* (New York: Macmillan, 1973), p. 322.

Based on Dale M. Garvey and Sancha K. Garvey, *Simulation, Role Playing and Sociodrama in the Social Studies*, The Emporia State Research Studies (Emporia: Kansas State Teachers College, 1957), 16, no. 2.

actly the same way as other transparencies. If one wishes one can fasten these to the frame of the original transparency with little metallic foil hinges. The use of frames and hinges has the advantage of keeping the transparency and its flip-ons together in proper order.

What sources of audiovisual material are available to you in your community?

What materials are available for use in your college classes? What could you do to make more material available if you were one of the teachers?

Pick a course you might teach and see what audiovisual materials you could develop for it.

The Classroom Library

In order to teach in the way we think one ought to teach, students must have plenty of material to read. To make this supply of reading material readily available, each classroom should be a library. In this classroom library, all sorts of reading material should be readily accessible to the student— periodicals, pamphlets, brochures, and the like, as well as books. For record keeping a self-charging system with students acting as librarians from time to time may suffice. Usually one needs worry little about loss of material if such a system is used.

In addition to the classroom library one should make good use of the town and school libraries. Although it is true that in some communities these libraries are rather scantily supplied, the librarians are almost invariably eager to cooperate with teachers. Teachers should make the most of this opportunity.

Few boys and girls, or men and women for that matter, use libraries well. Although instruction in the use of the library may ordinarily be the English Department's or the librarian's responsibility, the teacher whose students use the library is also responsible to see that students use the library facili-

ties efficiently. A visit to the library early in the year might well increase the efficient use of its facilities by the students.

What skills and information does a student need in order to learn to use the library effectively?

If your school provided no classroom library, what would you do to provide suitable reading materials?

The Community As a Resource

Extending the classroom into the community can make a course exciting and forceful, for every community is a gold mine of resources for teaching. The experiences of the students as they get out into the community are not only a welcome change but also potent learning activities. Similar benefits can also come from bringing the community into a classroom. Lay speakers and consultants, for instance, can add practical expertise, specialized knowledge and reality to your instruction. For this reason every school should have a file of community resources available. Individual teachers sometimes keep such files for use in their own classes, but probably a well-kept central file is more efficient, although you will need to keep additional information applicable to your own classes. A 5x8 card file is most satisfactory for this purpose. In it should be kept such information as

1. Possible field trips.
   a. What is there.
   b. Where is it and how to get there.
   c. Whom to see about arrangements.
   d. Expense involved.
   e. Time required.
   f. Other comments.
2. Resource people, speakers, etc.
   a. Who they are.
   b. How they can help.
   c. Addresses.

  3. Resource material and instructional materials obtainable locally.
     a. What it is.
     b. How to procure it.
     c. Expense involved.
  4. Community groups.
     a. Names and addresses.
     b. Function and purpose.
     c. Type of thing they can help with.
  5. Local businesses, industries, and agencies.
     a. Name
     b. Address.
     c. Key personnel.

Summary

Good teachers can be better teachers when they have plenty of materials to work with. Fortunately, American teachers are blessed with materials galore, although some may have to search a little to find them. Prominent on the list are audiovisual aids—films, pictures, maps, globes, charts, models, graphs, mock-ups, simulations, terrain boards, radio, television, chalkboards, and tack boards. All of them are excellent aids to teaching if they are used well, but they are not miracle drugs. They alone cannot do the job of teaching. The same teaching techniques—introducing, explaining, problem solving, follow-up and evaluation—used in other teaching are also needed to get the most from audiovisual aids. These techniques apply particularly to the presentation of films and filmstrips. In using display devices such as chalkboards, bulletin boards, and the like, it is important to provide for impact. They should be clearly visible and uncluttered, with a clear center of interest and plenty of white space. Both their content and presentation should be as dramatic as possible. For this reason, and because of their better visibility, the use of overhead, opaque, and other projectors is often more effective than other display methods. For the same reason flannel boards are usually more effective than chalkboards.

Recent advances in mass media have created many opportunities for teachers to capitalize on the cinema and television. Teachers who do not utilize these commercial media may be missing opportunities to harness their undoubted appeal to youth. The use of new media, particularly television, film, and tapes, has proved valuable as a means of bringing to the classroom outstanding experiences and personalities not otherwise available. But do not expect miracles of them. Television, film, and recorded presentations like anything else need to be introduced and followed up properly. On their own, they may do nothing; carefully handled they can work wonders. This is, of course, true of all tools.

The teaching program is a sophisticated adaptation of the workbook, utilizing scientific principles. Whether presented by machine, book, computer, or some other means, the program acts as a mechanical tutor that presents and follows up lessons. At the present there are many types of programs, the two major types being the linear and the intrinsic. So far the only really dependable way to judge a program's worth is to try it out with students.

Computers can be used as sophisticated teaching machines. They can be used for drill and practice, tutoring, simulating and modeling, data analyses, problem solving, independent study, individualizing instruction, gaming, and testing and evaluation in all the disciplines. You cannot turn instruction over to the computer, however. You must, with care, combine it with other techniques so as to develop well-balanced knowledge and skills and pick your teaching programs and support materials.

Free or inexpensive reading matter on almost any subject is available from governmental and business agencies. You will probably find it advantageous to make your own dittoed or mimeographed readings, study guides, practice materials, and exercises. When you do, it may be wise to consider methods by which one can preserve homemade materials for reuse.

Paperback books, newspapers and periodicals can be sources of up-to-date, interest-catching content in all middle and secondary school courses. They give students opportunities for wide reading and help develop habits and skills in effective critical and pleasurable reading that they may carry into adult life.

Some audiovisual materials are expensive and hard to get. This is true of other materials also. But this fact should not discourage the teacher. Much material is available for the asking. Much more can be made or improvised. Hints on how to obtain and create such materials can be found in the catalogs, curriculum guides, source units, and periodicals on the subject; many of these materials can be procured by simply writing. Today no teacher has an excuse for not having a supply of suitable materials.

Perhaps the best resource the teacher has is the community itself. It is both a source of subject matter and a source of instructional material and resource persons. Community lay persons can be used as classroom speakers and as consultants and guides.

Additional Reading

Brown, James W., and Shirley N. Brown, eds. *Educational Media Yearbook.* Littleton, CO: Libraries Unlimited, 1983.

———, Richard B. Lewis, and Fred R. Harclerod. *A V Instruction: Technology, Media, and Methods,* 5th ed. New York: McGraw-Hill, 1977.

Bumpass, Donald E. *Selected A V Recipes: Materials, Equipment Use and Maintenance.* Dubuque, IA: Kendal Hunt Publishing, 1981.

Gerlach, Vernon S., and Donald P. Ely. *Teaching & Media,* 2nd ed. Englewood Cliffs, NJ: Prentice Hall, 1980.

Heinrich, Robert, and M. Molenda. *Instructional Media: The New Technologies of Instruction.* New York: Wiley, 1982.

Heitzman, William Ray. *Educational Games and Simulations, What Research Says to the Teacher,* revised ed. Washington, DC: National Education Association, 1983.

Kemp, Jerrold E. *Planning and Producing Audio-Visual Materials,* 4th ed. New York: Harper Row, 1980.

Kinder, James. *Using Instructional Media.* New York: D. Van Nostrand, 1973.

Klein, M. Frances. *About Learning Materials.* Washington, DC: Association for Supervision and Curriculum Development, 1978.

Krepel, Wayne J., and Charles R. DuVall. *Field Trips: A Guide for Planning and Conducting Educational Experiences.* Washington, DC: National Education Association, 1981.

Leifer, Aimee Dorr. "Teaching with Television and Film," in N. L. Gage, ed., *The Psychology of Teaching Method,* The Seventy-fifth Yearbook of the National Society for the Study of Education. Chicago: University of Chicago Press, 1976, Chap. 9.

Locatis, Craig N., and Francis D. Atkinson. *Media and Technology for Education and Training.* Columbus, OH: Charles E. Merrill, 1984.

Potter, Rosemary Lee. *Using Television in the Curriculum,* Fastback 208. Bloomington, IN: Phi Delta Kappa Educational Foundation, 1984.

Simonson, Michael, and Roger P. Volker. *Media Planning and Production.* Columbus, OH: Charles E. Merrill, 1984.

Wegner, Hart. *Teaching with Film,* Fastback 103. Bloomington, IN: Phi Delta Kappa Educational Foundation, 1977.

Williams, Catherine. *The Community as Textbook,* Fastback 64. Bloomington, IN: Phi Delta Kappa Educational Foundation, 1975.

Woodbury, Marda. *Selecting Instructional Materials,* Fastback 110. Bloomington, IN: Phi Delta Kappa Educational Foundation, 1978.

A Sampling of References Listing Sources of Instructional Materials

The American Film Review. St. Davids, PA: The American Educational and Historical Film Center, Eastern Baptist College.

An Annotated Bibliography of Audio-visual Materials Related to Understanding and Teaching the Culturally Disadvantaged. Washington, DC: National Education Association.

Annual Paperbound Book Guide for High Schools. New York: R. R. Bowker.

Aubrey, Ruth H. *Selected Free Materials for Classroom Teachers,* 6th ed. Belmont, CA: Fearon-Pitman, 1978.

Bibliography of Free and Inexpensive Materials for Economic Education. New York: Joint Council on Economic Education.

Civil Aeronautics Administration, *Sources of Free and Low-Cost Materials.* Washington, DC: U. S. Department of Commerce.

Educational Film Guide. New York: H. W. Wilson.

    Educators' Guide to Free Audio and Visual Materials.

    Educators' Guide to Free Films.

    Educators' Guide to Free Film Strips.

    Educators' Guide to Free and Inexpensive Teaching Materials.

    Educators' Guide to Free Social Studies Materials.

    Educators' Guide to Free Teaching Aids.

Educators' Progress Service Publications. Randolph, WI.

Feature Films on 8mm and 16mm. New York: R. R. Bowker.

Film Guide for Music Educators. Washington, DC: Music Educators National Conference.

Free and Inexpensive Learning Materials. Nashville, TN: Division of Surveys and Field Services, George Peabody College for Teachers.

Horn, Robert E. *The Guide to Simulations/Games for Education and Training,* 3rd ed. Cranford, NJ: Didactic Systems, 1977.

Index to Multi-Ethnic Teaching Materials and Teaching Resources. Washington, DC: National Education Association.

Materials List for Use by Teachers of Modern Foreign Languages. New York: Modern Foreign Language Association.

National Tape Recording Catalog. Washington, DC: National Education Association.

New Educational Materials. Englewood Cliffs, NJ: Citation Press.

Rufsuold, Margaret. *Guides to Educational Media.* Chicago: American Library Association.

Textbooks in Print. New York: R. R. Bowker.

U. S. Government Films for Educational Use. Washington, DC: Government Printing Office.

U. S. Government Printing Office. Thousands of publications. Catalogs available.

Using Free Materials in the Classroom. Washington, DC: Association for Supervision and Curriculum Development.

A Sampling of Periodicals That Carry Information about Instructional Materials and How to Procure Them

Audio-Visual Guide: The Learning Media Magazine.

Classroom Computer News.

The Computer Teacher.

Educational Technology.

The English Journal.

Journal of Business Education.

Journal of Home Economics.

Journal of Physical Education and Recreation.

Learning.

The Mathematics Teacher.

Media and Methods.
Music Educators' Journal.
School Arts.
The Science Teacher.
Social Education.
Social Studies.

A Sampling of References on the Production and Use of Instructional Materials

Brown, James W., and Richard B. Lewis. *AV Instructional Technology Manual for Independent Study,* 5th ed. New York: McGraw-Hill, 1977.

Bullard, John R., and Calvin E. Mether. *Audio-Visual Fundamentals: Basic Equipment Operation and Simple Materials Production,* 2nd ed. Dubuque, IA: Brown, 1979.

Eastman Kodak Publications. Rochester, N Y.
    Adapting Your Tape Recorder to the Kodak Carousel Programmer, SC-1.
    Applied Color Photography Indoors, E-76.
    Audio-Visual Projection, S-3.
    Basic Copying, AM-2.
    Basic Developing, Printing and Enlarging, AJ-2.
    Color Photography Outdoors, E-75.
    Composition, AC-11.
    Copying, M-1.
    Effective Lecture Slides, S-22.
    Good Color Pictures—Quick and Easy, AE-10.
    Making Black and White Transparencies for Overhead Projection, S-17.
    Planning and Producing Visual Aids, S-13.
    Producing Slides and Filmstrips, S-8.
    Some Sources of 2x2 inch Color Slides.
    Sources of Slides and Filmstrips, S-9.

Green, Lee. *Teaching Tools You Can Make.* Wheaton, IL: Victor, 1978.

Kemp J. E. *Planning and Producing Audio-Visual Materials,* 4th ed. New York: Harper & Row, 1980.

Minor, Edward O. *Handbook for Preparing Visual Media,* 2nd ed. New York: McGraw-Hill, 1978.

————, and Harvey R. Frye. *Techniques for Producing Instructional Media,* 2nd ed. New York: McGraw-Hill, 1977.

Oates, Stanton C. *Audio-Visual Equipment: Self Instructional Manual,* 4th ed. Dubuque, IA: Brown, 1979.

University of Texas at Austin, Instructional Media Center (VIB) Publications, *Designing Instructional Visuals: Theory, Composition, Implementation*

————, *Instructional Display Boards*

————, *The Overhead System: Production, Implementation, and Utilization*

————, *Local Production Techniques*

————, *Production of 2 x 2 Inch Slides*

————, *Lettering Techniques*

————, *Educational Displays and Exhibits*

————, *The Tape Recorder, Revised Edition*

————, *Better Bulletin Boards*

————, *Models for Teaching*

————, *Using Tear Sheets*

————, *Basic Design and Utilization of Instructional Television*

A Sampling of Readings on Computers in Teaching

Brumbaugh, Ken, and Don Rawitsch. *Establishing Instructional Computing: The First Steps.* St. Paul, MN: Minnesota Educational Computing Consortium, 1982.

DeVault, M. Vere. "Computers," in Elizabeth Fennima, ed., *Mathematics Education Research: Implications for the 80s.* Alexandria, VA: Association for Supervision and Curriculum Development, 1981, Chap. 8.

Grady, M. Tim, and Jane D. Gawronski. *Computers in Curriculum and Instruction.* Alexandria, VA: Association for Supervision and Curriculum Development, 1983.

Hofmeister, Alan. *Microcomputer Applications in the Classroom.* New York: Holt, 1984.

Kepner, Henry S., Jr., ed. *Computers in the Classroom.* Washington, DC: National Education Association, 1982.

National Council of Teachers of Mathematics. *Computers in Mathematics Education,* 1984 Yearbook. Reston, VA: National Council of Teachers of Mathematics, 1984.

Roberts, Nancy, et al. *Practical Guide to Computers in Education.* Reading, MA: Addison-Wesley, 1982.

Taylor, Robert P. *The Computer in the School: Tutor, Tool, Tutee.* New York: Teachers College Press, 1980.

Vockel, Edward L., and Robert H. Rivers. *Instructional Computing for Today's Teachers.* New York: Macmillan, 1984, Particularly Chaps. 1–5, 12.

20

The Professional Teacher

Overview

In this last chapter we examine procedures by which one becomes a truly professional teacher. After a brief look at what a professional teacher is, we examine the student teaching or internship experience. It is here that one puts together one's knowledge of teaching theory and methods and begins to develop expertise. This process can be greatly helped if one examines one's teaching by using the techniques of self-evaluation and by soliciting the evaluation of colleagues, teachers, and students. Teachers who do not examine their teaching seldom progress beyond amateurism. This generalization holds true throughout one's professional life. Becoming truly professional is a lifelong task. No one ever masters all the ins and outs of teaching methods and materials and subject matter. Therefore we must all make our professional preparation

431

a matter of lifelong learning. In the latter part of the chapter we discuss some ways to make our professional life more successful.

The Real Pro

The word *professional* has at least two connotations. One connotation refers to the type of work that is done by professional workers; the other connotation is that which is expressed in the common expression "being a real pro," that is to say, a really competent performer.

Although it may be some time before you can become a real pro, you should try to be a thoroughly professional teacher from the day you start teaching. Truly professional teachers give a full measure of professional service. They do a fine job at the highest possible level; they undertake all professional responsibilities willingly; and they carry out to the best of their abilities whatever they undertake. In return, they expect to be paid adequately and treated respectfully.

Above all, professional teachers are proud of their profession, although it is arduous and exacting and has not always been rewarded as well as it should have been.

It will take you a little while to become a real pro. A retired superintendent of schools says that judging from his thirty years of experience in the superintendency, it takes a beginning teacher at least two years to become "worth his salt." Be that as it may, as you gain experience, you will gain competence. If you are successful, you will become an expert on three essentials—your students, your subject and how to teach. You will have mastered a large repertoire of techniques and strategies you can adapt skillfully to whatever type of teaching situation you face and you will have learned to get the most out of your students and to adapt the curriculum to their needs and abilities. In short, you will be a master teacher—a real pro.

Student Teaching and Internship

The first major step in moving from amateur status toward gaining the competencies that mark the real pro is the student-teaching or internship program. This experience is the neophyte's first real opportunity to put educational theory and methods into practice. Simulations, minilessons, and microteaching are all excellent learning opportunities, but they do not match the reality one finds in the internship or student teaching. Even these experiences are not completely real teaching experiences. They are designed to be learning experiences and so are likely to be somewhat artificial.

That student teaching[1] is first and foremost a learning situation cannot be emphasized too much. This is the time for you to master the rudiments of your craft before you have to put your skills on the line in your own classroom. Here is a chance for you to learn from your mistakes without causing harm to the students. Here is the time you can try your wings and find out the strategies, tactics and teaching styles that best suit you. It is a time of trial and error and for growing confidence and beginning expertness. It is not a time of perfection, but of striving for competence.

Some Facts of Life

The following comments, based upon many years of watching student teachers, were written in the hope that they can make your life as a student teacher a little easier and more rewarding. They are not intended to preach; rather, they are intended to point out some pitfalls and ways to avoid them and to suggest ways to make the most of the student-teaching experience.

---

[1] From this point on, we use the term *student teaching* to cover both student teaching and internship in this section.

Becoming Prepared

First you should know that student teaching is a difficult experience requiring a lot of hard work. Do not underestimate its demands. Most students find it to be much more time consuming than any other college work they have had. Students who try to combine full-time student teaching assignments with additional courses or part-time jobs usually find themselves overwhelmed. It is much wiser to concentrate all one's time on the student teaching from the very beginning than to have to drop out later on.

Because student teaching is hard work, you need to find out as much as you can about your assignment as soon as you can—long before the student-teaching period begins. If possible, find out what topics you are to teach and prepare yourself for these topics. Most student teachers do not have perfect command of the content that middle and secondary school students study. For instance, mathematics student teachers seldom are at their best in high school geometry; English student teachers cannot possibly be familiar with all the works students may read; and social studies student teachers are not likely to have recently studied all the history, geography, economics, political science, and sociology they may be called on to teach. *If you are wise, you will use the period before student teaching begins to master the content and think about how to teach it!*

Probably the first thing you should do is to procure the curriculum guide, textbook, and other readings used in each of the courses you are to teach and then master them. In addition it might be wise to study a review book. Such works may give you a basis for organizing units and lessons and ideas for building lessons and tactics. You can also find many ideas in the curriculum guide, question banks, and other materials developed by various school systems and on file in the local or university curriculum library or teacher center. If it is feasible, you should build yourself a resource unit covering each of the areas you will have to teach.

Unless this early preparation is done carefully, you may find yourself having to become an instant expert on something about which you know little or nothing.

Many student teachers who have not taken time to prepare properly find it necessary to spend so much of their time trying to master the content that they never do learn to teach it well.

A Learning Experience

As we have said, student teaching is a learning experience. It is not expected that the student teacher will be a master teacher from the first day. As a matter of fact, few teachers become real masters of the art of teaching in the first few years. If you find that your lessons do not always go as well as you had hoped, do not be surprised. Every beginner makes mistakes. Learn from them! Often teachers who find the first few weeks hard going develop into the best of teachers if they are sensitive and learn as they go along. On the other hand, student teachers who find that things at first go very well should not become overconfident. Many of our poorest teachers are young people who, having had a fair amount of success at first, became overconfident and self-satisfied, and so did not strive to become real pros. As a result, they have remained amateurish ever since.

No Longer Just a Student

Although the student-teaching or internship experience is designed to be a learning experience, you should remember that student teaching is also a job, and the cooperating teacher, and other supervisors, are bosses. Student teachers are expected to toe the mark just as other employees are. If they do not, they may be fired! Looseness or slackness that may get by in ordinary college classes has no place in student teaching.

Because the local cooperating teacher and the college supervisor are your immediate supervisors, they must be pleased and satisfied with your performance. Therefore, carry out their instructions, directions, and suggestions without "ifs," "ands" or "buts." Unfortunately sometimes the instructions, directions, and suggestions of the various supervisors may be incompatible. If this should happen to you go to the college supervisor for help and advice.

Some student teachers worry about the restraints on their behavior during the student-teaching period. In certain ways student teachers are in a peculiarly anomalous situation. They are neophytes learning, and at the same time they are teachers. Therefore student teaching can be quite trying. Some student teachers rebel against the demands of student teaching, which admittedly are great. Some believe that these demands infringe on their rights. However, it is not wise to press one's rights overmuch during one's student teaching because it is doubtful how many rights one really has—at least as far as the cooperating school is concerned. Student teachers are guests of the school and their cooperating teacher. They are in the school mostly on sufferance. The teacher-education institution can only try to persuade the local personnel. It cannot dictate or demand. Consequently, both student teachers and college supervisors must do their best to meet the expectations of the school.

Relations with Supervisors

It is extremely important for you to establish and maintain good relationships with your supervisors. If your student-teaching situation is typical, your immediate supervisor will be the cooperating or critic teacher who has lent you the classes you are practicing on. One of the advantages of student teaching, ordinarily, is that the cooperating teacher is there to give you close supervision, help and support in time of need. Nevertheless such intimate relationships can be trying. They require tact, patience, understanding, and forbearance on the part of both the individuals concerned.

Most cooperating teachers find the student teaching period a bothersome time. Supervision is never an easy assignment. Most cooperating teachers find it more difficult to supervise a student teacher than to teach the classes themselves. Furthermore, many cooperating teachers find student teachers something of a threat to the success of their own teaching. They may fear that the bungling of an inexperienced student teacher may cause the progress of their classes to suffer, their discipline to disintegrate or the class atmosphere to deteriorate. Many a cooperating teacher has had to work extra hard for several weeks in order to whip back into shape a class that has gone sour under a student teacher. For the insecure teacher merely for another adult to be in the room may seem threatening.

Sometimes student teachers commit tactical errors that cause the relationship with their supervisors to fall apart. Let us consider some of the mistakes that supervisors complain about. Some of them seem so obvious that it would seem ridiculous to mention them, but for the fact that they cause so many student teaching failures.

Preparedness. Some student teachers do not prepare well enough. Immediately the students become aware that these student teachers do not know their stuff or what they are trying to do. Once this happens, the student teacher is through. To reestablish the confidence of pupils and supervisors in such cases is a monumental task. Student teachers who must continually improvise are anathema to most supervisors.

Attention to Detail. Some student teachers neglect their duties. If unit plans or lesson plans are due on Friday, supervisors expect them on Friday—not Monday. If attendance is to be taken at the beginning of the period, then supervisors expect it to be taken at the beginning of the period. If the student teacher plans to use audiovisual aids, the supervisor expects the student teacher to make all the arrangements in plenty of time and, insofar as one possibly can, to be sure that all the equipment and materials are ready. Any student teacher who does not attend to details of this sort goes down in the supervisor's book as irresponsible.

Responsibility and Dependability. Being responsible and dependable rate very high with most supervisors. They expect student teachers to do what they are supposed to do or at least try their utmost to do it without alibis or excuses. The quickest way to earn the supervisor's disfavor is to try to alibi one's self out of one's failure to deliver.

Punctuality and Attendance. Supervisors consider tardiness and unnecessary absence as particularly heinous offenses. As a rule they consider them to be inexcusable.

Complaining and Criticizing. In no case should a student teacher criticize the school or the cooperating teacher, so be particularly careful about what you say in conversations with other teachers or other student teachers. Also avoid going to the principal or department head with complaints. When you find that you need to complain or criticize, go to your college supervisor. If any action needs to be taken, let the college supervisor be the one to negotiate with the school personnel concerned. If any onus is to fall on anyone because of disagreements over policy or method, it is better that it fall on the college supervisor than on you.

Conforming to the School's Expectation. To keep relationships pleasant, try to conform to the standards and customs of the school. Drastic departures from the norm in language, dress, appearance, and so on can be upsetting to principals and cooperating teachers. If you find out what is expected of you in these matters early and then live up to these expectations, you will find that things will go more smoothly than if you do not.

In this connection a word about appearance may be in order. How you carry yourself, your expression, your posture and how you dress make a difference in how your pupils and your colleagues will perceive you. Consequently it will behoove you to

be sprightly, attractive, pleasant appearing, and appropriately dressed. Usually it is helpful to conform to the standard and style of dress common to the older teachers. Being a little on the conservative side does not hurt. Some young looking student teachers find it helpful to dress so as to look older. After all, the age difference between college seniors and high school seniors is not great. Anything that accentuates your maturity should help you establish yourself.[2]

Listen! One complaint constantly heard is that student teachers do not listen. Cooperating teachers and college supervisors say they have to repeat instructions or advice over and over again before their student teachers heed them. Sometimes this is because the student teachers do not really listen—perhaps because they are too busy thinking of reasons why they did not do better. If you listen carefully, ask questions to be sure you understand, and then make a sincere effort to follow the advice or instructions, relations with your supervisors will usually be easy and cordial.

Avoid Competing with the Teacher. At all costs avoid any appearance of competing with the cooperating teacher. You are there to learn from the cooperating teacher, and there are very few cooperating teachers you cannot learn from. Consequently you should consult the cooperating teacher before you undertake anything, and then you should follow the advice given to the best of your ability. In this connection, sometimes the students tell student teachers how well the student teachers teach and that they prefer the student teachers to their regular teachers. No matter how flattering this may be, you should pass off such remarks without comment. Do not allow yourself to get in the position of discussing any other teacher's teaching with a student. To do so can lead only to misunderstanding and unhappiness.

---

[2] If nothing more, it may save you from being embarrassingly mistaken for a student.

Show Initiative.   You can raise your stock with your supervisors and cooperating teachers by showing initiative and volunteering to do things before you have to be asked to do them. If you take on arduous tasks willingly and readily, you will endear yourself to your cooperating teacher. Sometimes student teachers feel that they are being used if the cooperating teacher asks them to read papers or to correct tests. Actually you should be glad to do tasks of this sort. Such tasks are an important part of a teacher's job and you should show your mettle here as in other tasks. Also many cooperating teachers feel that you can learn much about the job and that they can learn much about your capabilities by giving you jobs of this sort. In this connection, most cooperating teachers and supervisors expect the student teachers to do their share in cafeteria supervision, extracurricular activities, attendance at PTA, student activities, and all the other additional tasks that make up the teacher's professional life. Principals and department heads find willing participation in these extras by student teachers quite impressive.

> How well do you think you measure up to the expectations listed previously? Where do you think are you strong? Where are you least strong? What do you propose to do to make yourself stronger all around?

The Student-Teaching Experience

When you arrive at your student-teaching assignment, it is expected that you will bring with you certain knowledge and competencies, for example,

- an understanding of the teacher's role and responsibilities;
- a command of the subjects to be taught;
- a basic understanding of the nature of the learner and the learning process;
- a repertory of teaching skills and some competence in them;

- a supply of instructional materials;
- beginning skill in the techniques of evaluation.

If you measure up reasonably well to the standards implied by this list, you should expect your student-teaching experience to be satisfying. If you find yourself very deficient in these competencies and understandings, probably you would be wise not to attempt student teaching until you have brought yourself up to the standard.

Observation

One's student teaching usually starts off with a few days of observation. During this period you should try to learn as much as you can about the school and how it works—its customs, procedures, requirements, and the like. In particular you should become acquainted with the personality and customs of each of the classes you will teach. The more you can learn about the students and the basic situation and routines, e.g., the materials available and the procedures for requisitioning and distributing materials, the better off you will be. It will be especially helpful for you to observe what the students expect from the class and the teacher, what the teacher expects from each student, and how the teacher deals with pupils both as a group and as individuals.

A wise step to take during this period is to learn the names of the students. Sitting down with the seating chart and attempting to match names and faces may pay dividends when you begin to teach the class. If you also learn something about the personalities of the students, it is much easier to create a smooth, personalized atmosphere in the class when you begin to teach.

Beginning to Teach

Most student teachers find their first teaching experience somewhat traumatic. Of course you will be nervous. Probably anyone who is not nervous is not sensitive enough to be a good teacher. To compensate for this nervousness and to build up your confidence, skill, and understanding, you would probably do well to begin your student teaching in small ways—e.g., by taking the roll, acting as assistant teacher, working with a small group, introducing a movie, or attempting similar tasks.

Different Styles and Methods

One beauty of a good student-teaching experience is that it gives the student teacher an opportunity to try out a variety of teaching styles and methods. Seize that opportunity. By trying out a variety of methods you can not only broaden your repertory of teaching skills, but you can also learn which types of approaches are most comfortable to you. The teaching style another teacher finds easy and comfortable may be uncongenial and even disagreeable to you.

Since teaching styles differ, you may find it advantageous to work with two cooperating teachers whose modes of teaching differ. In such a situation you can observe different teaching styles in action and try them under supervision. Sometimes these differences in styles cause conflicts, however. If such should be the case, consult with your college supervisor immediately.

Although you should try various techniques, it is not wise to be too innovative at first. Adolescents, like adults, feel most secure in their established routines. They may not accept new ways of teaching or learning willingly. Further, some cooperating teachers are suspicious of new methods which, they fear, may upset the even tenor of the class. Cooperating teachers, too, sometimes feel threatened by too much change. Therefore the best policy is to introduce innovations slowly. Besides, as a neophyte it is best if you master the tried and true methods the class is used to before you branch out. Sometimes it is necessary to learn to walk before one learns to run.

On the other hand, you should not be too quick to drop an innovative method that does not seem to work. The reason the method does not work may have nothing to do with the method itself. Perhaps your execution was faulty, or you may have rushed the students into it before they were ready, or the technique was ill adapted to the class or situation in which you used it. When a technique falls flat, do not conclude that the method is no good, but rather try to determine why it went wrong. Usually you will find it was because of some ineptness on your part rather than because of a fault in the method itself.

Before you attempt a new approach, talk it over with your cooperating teacher. Sometimes the cooperating teacher may resist your innovation, perhaps because your plan seems flawed; appears to be too great a change from what the class has been doing; requires too much time; does not seem to be suited to the class; or is theoretically incongenial. Student teachers who are progressively oriented, for instance, may find themselves in very conservative situations in which they cannot use the progressive approaches they are so eager to try (or vice versa). In any case, defer to the cooperating teacher's judgment. In cases in which the cooperating teacher objects to your plan because of its progressivism or conservatism, do your best to do it well according to the cooperating teacher's orientation. After all, to become a real pro you must learn how to use both conservative and progressive strategies and techniques. So use this teaching experience to become expert in whatever methods are compatible with the orientation of the cooperating teacher and the school. Later in your own class you can try out other techniques and strategies until you have a complete battery of methods in which you are expert.

Planning in Student Teaching

Planning is crucial in student teaching. When student teachers fail in their teaching it is almost always because they have not planned adequately. Every student teacher needs specific detailed plans. Every single day you should know, and have written down, exactly what you want the students to learn during the lesson, exactly what content will be covered, exactly what methods you plan to use and how you plan to use them, and what materials you need. You should try to anticipate every contingency as best you can. Very little should be left to chance. For that reason key questions, major points to be covered in the summary, and other details should be worked out ahead of time and included in the plan. Once you become experienced, such detailed planning may not be quite so necessary, but you will never outgrow the need to plan thoroughly.

Making Assignments

Frequently student teachers find determining the length and difficulty of assignments bothersome. Here is an area in which the cooperating teacher can help. The wise student teacher follows the cooperating teacher's lead because any quick change from the accustomed length and difficulty may upset the class.

Seeking Help

Old hands are usually very glad to give beginners the benefit of their experience. Usually their advice is good and their opinions valid, although sometimes their suggestions should be listened to politely and then forgotten as quickly as possible. (The old truism that some teachers have twenty years of experience while others have only one year of experience twenty times still holds.) In any event the student teacher would be wise to ask for advice and suggestions. It never hurts a beginner to ask an old hand for help. If for no other reason than that it makes the old hand feel important.

Developing a Time Budget

Many student teachers find themselves overwhelmed by the demands on their time during the student-teaching period. This problem can be alle-

viated somewhat by developing a time budget. By allocating reasonable amounts of time to the different tasks that must be performed during the day before, during, and after school, you may be able to ensure that all the tasks get done reasonably well. In making such a time budget try to be as realistic as you can. If your time budget is too demanding it may be worse than no budget at all.

> Judging from past experience, what types of teaching approaches and methods do you think you would find most congenial?
>
> What in teaching causes you the greatest concern? How do you intend to prepare for it?
>
> If you had your choice, what type of class would you run? Open, closed, or other?
>
> Do you incline to conservative, traditional, or progressive techniques? Why?

Evaluating One's Student Teaching

Your supervisors will evaluate your student teaching from time to time and confer with you on your strengths and weaknesses. In addition, you should evaluate yourself in order to learn from your successes and your mistakes. In this process be critical, but not too critical. Sometimes student teachers demand of themselves more than they have a right to expect. Nevertheless each day you should set aside some time to think about your lessons and try to determine what went well and what poorly and why.

Self-analysis

One of the most satisfactory techniques for self-appraisal is to use a self-analysis form, such as that appearing as Figure 20–1, to assess the effectiveness of one of your best classes daily during the first three weeks of your student teaching and once a week thereafter. If your classroom tests are well built and criterion-referenced, using the techniques described in Chapter 17 to analyze the results should be revealing. However vague general objectives and vague general test items render such analyses worthless.

Student Judgments

The students' reaction to one's teaching is another fairly reliable indicator of its success. Probably the easiest way to find out what students think of your teaching is to observe their reaction to your classes. Apathetic, bored, surly, inattentive, restless classes indicate that the instruction is not going very well. Interested, attentive classes, on the other hand, indicate that you must be doing at least something right.

Another simple way to determine what students think of your teaching is to ask them. Simple questionnaires or rating sheets may be used for this purpose. If the information is to be useful, the ratings should be anonymous. For that reason forms that call for checking rather than handwritten comments are recommended. Even so, free-response questions that ask students to suggest ways instruction can be made more effective or more interesting may be very useful. Students feel flattered to be asked for their opinions and will not feel too threatened to respond honestly in such a format.

Interaction Analysis

In order to get a picture of what your classes are really like, use the interaction analysis techniques explained in Chapter 11, or in the case of discussion classes the flow charts explained in Chapter 12.

Audio and Video Playback

Audio and video recordings can be wonderful tools for studying one's skill in lecturing, questioning, leading a discussion and so on. You can greatly improve your teaching skill by reviewing tapes of your lessons and asking yourself such questions as

- Are my explanations clear?
- Do I speak well and clearly?
- Do I speak in a monotone? Do I slur my words? Do my sentences drop off so that ends are difficult to hear?
- Do I involve everyone in the class or do I direct my teaching only to a few?
- Are my questions clear and unambiguous? Do I use broad or narrow questions?
- Do I dominate class discussion?
- Do I allow certain students to dominate the class? And so on.

Whatever questions you decide to ask yourself, it is wise to concentrate on only a few areas when reviewing a tape of your teaching. If you limit yourself to studying your questioning technique in one session and to studying your discussion technique in another, you may find it easier to pinpoint your merits and deficiencies than if you do not concentrate your observation on a particular technique. Nevertheless generally reviewing the entire lesson can be helpful, particularly if one uses a self-analysis form similar to the one described earlier in this chapter (Figure 20–1).

Make a list of check questions that you might use to evaluate your own teaching.

Sharing with Other Student Teachers

When feasible, it can be very helpful for student teachers to observe each other. By sharing evaluations of each other's work, you can have added input for your self-evaluation. Student teachers who observe each other would do well to be guided by a check list or a rating scale similar to that appearing as Figure 20–1. They can also gather data for interaction analysis. These observations should be followed by free-flowing discussions over coffee

FIGURE 20–1
Self-analysis of a Lesson.

Use this form to analyze the class you thought went best this day.
1. Do you feel good about this class? Why, or why not?
2. In what way was the lesson most successful?
3. If you were to teach this lesson again, what would you do differently? Why?
4. Was your plan adequate? In what ways would you change it?
5. Did you achieve your major objectives?
6. Was the class atmosphere pleasant, productive, and supportive?
7. Were there signs of strain or misbehavior? If so, what do you think was the cause?
8. How much class participation was there?
9. Which students did extremely well?
10. Were there students who did not learn? How might you help them?
11. Were the provisions for motivation adequate?
12. Was the lesson individualized so that students had opportunities to learn something according to their abilities, interests, and needs?
13. Did the students have any opportunities to think?

and Danish or in some other easy social setting. Perhaps the following analyses of the characteristics of successful teachers will help you and your colleagues evaluate each other.

Characteristics of Successful Teachers Summarized

Successful teachers are good classroom managers.

Evidently successful teachers are the ones who most carefully prepare and organize their classes. Their classes are always well planned and businesslike. In them the students know what to do and how to do it. Things move smoothly without unnecessary interruptions, abrupt switches of content or activity, slowdowns, or distractions. These teachers know what is going on. They are able to keep track of and control several activities at once, even when conducting something else. They insist on careful, accurate work. They set deadlines and see to it that students meet those deadlines. They do not accept late or sloppy work. They insist that their students pay attention. They keep their classes work-oriented by constantly monitoring and following up. Assignments are always graded. They keep records. They give students positive encouragement and help. They always know what is going on in their classes. In their classes there is no doubt about who is in charge.

Successful teachers are well organized.

Successful teachers are good organizers. They organize class time efficiently. They are adept at planning and organizing activities and developing new approaches.

Successful teachers encourage time on task.

Successful teachers conduct their classes so that the students spend their time on task. That is to say the students' time is actually spent on productive learning activities rather than on irrelevancies and time-wasting behaviors or activities.

Successful teachers focus their class activities.

Successful teachers focus each class on a common purpose. They require their students to work toward that purpose.

Successful teachers know their stuff.

Successful teachers know and like the subjects they teach. They are masters of their content. Their enthusiasm for the subject field shows. Having both a strong command of the subject matter and a large repertory of teaching skills, they are able to make well-informed snap decisions intuitively.

Successful teachers teach imaginatively.

Successful teachers teach imaginatively. They spice their teaching with variety. When necessary or desirable, they improvise. They are able to work toward several goals concurrently. Their presentations are clear and not humdrum. The classes move on briskly, allowing plenty of time to work on the subject at hand with a minimum amount of wasted time, motion, or effort, and a maximum amount of interest and enjoyment.

Successful teachers know their students.

Successful teachers make it a point to know their students. Because they know their students, they can, and do, match their teaching approaches to the students they teach, adapting questions and other techniques to the abilities of the students. To get the most from each student they adapt their strategies, tactics, and assignments to the cognitive styles, interests, and goals of their different students.

Successful teachers hold high expectations.

Successful teachers expect a lot of their students. Although they try to keep from being too demanding, they do expect students to do their best, and that that best will be productive and respectable. They have faith that the students can do well if they try and they are confident that their students will try. Because they know a lot about their students' characteristics, prior learning, and learning styles, and try to take these traits into consideration in their teaching, these teachers keep their expectations reasonable and their teaching approaches appropriate.

Successful teachers are supportive.

Successful teachers empathize with their students. They acknowledge and praise good student responses, but when the students' responses are not satisfactory, they follow up with probing questions and helpful comments and explanations. In general, they stress positive feedback. Their classroom style is positive and supportive and provides students direction so that they know what to do

and how to do it, and how to use the knowledge once they have learned it.

Successful teachers adapt.

Successful teachers can adapt their teaching to different sorts of teaching-learning situations. They either use flexible teaching styles that encompass a great number of strategies or tactics, or they change teaching style as the situation demands.

Successful teachers use intrinsic control.

Successful teachers utilize intrinsic control. They involve students in class activities, catch their interest, and convince them of the worth of doing well rather than depending on threats and punishment and extrinsic motivation to control student behavior.

Successful teachers match content and tests.

Successful teachers try to match the teaching objectives and goals and their teaching procedures and content to the content of the tests students will take.

Try to remember three most successful teachers you have known in your middle and high school years. What characteristics made them successful in your opinion?

Look over the characteristics of successful teachers carefully. What qualities do you think you have? What do you think you will have to work on most?

Prepare a questionaire that you would be willing to have students rate you on.

The New Job

By the time that you begin your student teaching or internship, you should be thinking about finding a job. Actually you should have started planning for securing a job early in your college career. By now you should have become quite knowledgeable about the job market and be making plans accordingly. If you are headed for a crowded field, perhaps you should reconsider your objectives. As this is being written, the job market for teachers is tight in some areas. There is every reason to believe that this situation will soon change. In the meantime, if a suitable job is not immediately forthcoming, anyone who really wishes to teach should consider enrolling for an advanced degree. Another strategy is to apply for a job as a substitute. Substituting is an excellent way to get experience and to learn the system. It is also a method for getting one foot in the door. Substitute teachers who do well are first in line for permanent teaching positions. Still another choice is to pursue one's education career in business, industry, or government. Such concerns need to employ numbers of people with professional teaching skills for their training and educational programs every year. Because the students in such programs are likely to be well-motivated adults, this type of teaching may be particularly rewarding.

If you have not already done so, carefully study the certification requirements of the state in which you wish to teach. Do this early. To find, at graduation time, that you are deficient in one of the state requirements can be disconcerting. Sometimes a small change in your program can make quite a difference in your certification. For instance, you may have an excellent program mapped out in biology. A glance at the certification requirements may show you that by substituting a course in chemistry for one biology course you can certify for general science as well as biology. Thus a three-hour course may make a tremendous difference in your worth to a potential employer.

You should also bear in mind what courses are offered in typical secondary schools and select college courses that prepare you for them. Although Nordic literature may be an excellent course, it may be that some other course, e.g., a course in writing, would be more helpful to you as a beginning English teacher, and make you more employable.

You should probably also bear in mind that teaching positions often call for subject combinations. Most secondary school social studies departments, for instance, offer courses in sociology, geography, government, economics, and perhaps other social sciences as well as American and European history. Principals and department heads hope to find teachers who can teach several of these areas. A candidate who can teach only sociology may not be of much use to a department, but a sociology major who also has background in U.S. history and economics may be just what the department needs. Similarly a school may not need another full-time French teacher but have great need for someone who can teach both French and English.

Early in your final college year you should get in touch with your college placement service to find out what services it can provide. Usually the placement service is anxious to coach you on ways to find, apply for and obtain jobs. It can also tell you how best to prepare yourself for the jobs that are available. You should also talk over with your education professors such matters as finding job opportunities, writing letters of application, and securing favorable recommendations, job interviews, and the like. The sooner you become knowledgeable in these areas the better chance you have for satisfactory employment.

Where would you like to teach? What courses would you like to teach? What courses will you be able to teach when you finish your college program? For what courses and levels will you be certifiable? What can you do to make yourself most employable?

Getting Started

Most of what we have said about student teaching and internship applies to the first job as well. As soon as you know what you have to teach, start preparing for it. Learn as much as you can about the school, community and students, and work hard to make yourself as expert as you can in the subject field before school starts. Then on the first day of school, try to get your classes off to a good beginning. If you can, use some sort of interest-catching activity that will launch the course. Remember, the initial activity may set the tone for the whole course.[3]

Your success or failure will mostly be determined by your relationship with the students. Pay particular attention to classroom management, control and motivation. If you conduct businesslike, no-nonsense classes in a pleasant, workmanlike atmosphere and show that you are interested in and respect your students as people, you will have progressed a long way toward success. Similarly, if you work hard to set up cordial relations with parents, supervisors, and other teachers and carry your share of the workload faithfully, carefully and ungrudgingly, you will find that your work can be a pleasure. On the whole, school people are pleasant to have for colleagues, if you give them a chance.

Growing in the Profession

Growing Personally

To become a real pro one must combine experience with diligent efforts to learn one's business, and to keep growing both professionally and personally. Try to avoid the ivory tower and get out into the world to do things. Try to keep your mind sharp by interesting yourself in many things and becoming an expert in some one thing. In short, try to develop an interesting wholesome personality and keep alive your intellectual curiosity.

Growing Professionally

Not only must one grow as a person, one must also develop professionally. The first step in growing professionally is to do a good job of teaching.

[3] See Chapter 5.

This means that you must give your heart to your work. Teaching should never be a secondary occupation. A teacher may find it necessary to combine teaching with other work—either part-time work or home-making—but the teacher must not let other work detract from teaching. Your first responsibility is to your students.

Keeping Abreast with Your Field. If one is to teach well, one must keep up with one's subject. Without continued study to keep up one's competence, one's teaching soon becomes dry and dusty. Therefore you will need to keep abreast of the developments in your field. Occasionally, you may need to take refresher courses at a university or college. You should do advanced work in your field and perhaps some original research. During vacations you may be able to get work related to your subject and thus acquire additional experience. No matter how you do it, you must move forward with the growth of your field.

Keeping Up with the Profession. You must also become an expert in the study of your profession. Particularly important are changes in methods and curriculum that affect your specialty. You should continue to study the nature of learning, the theory and practice of teaching, basic philosophical positions, and current experimentation in education. Reading professional periodicals and books, as well as coursework at colleges and universities, is helpful for this purpose.

Experimenting with new techniques or materials will make your teaching more lively and meaningful. Observing your own work and that of others may help you grow considerably, particularly if you continually ask yourself: Why did this technique work? Why was this one unsuccessful? Why did this one succeed in section A and fail in section B? Attempts to find better ways to teach should never cease. They are the only sure way to professional growth.

In order to find better ways of teaching, you should be constantly on the alert for new ideas.

Visit other teachers, talk to them and try to get ideas from them. Try out the material and techniques other teachers have found successful. Visit the teacher conventions and other professional meetings in search of new ideas. A fine source of ideas for teaching is the book exhibit at conventions. But you should do more than make use of the work of others, you should share successful experiences of your own. One way is to write about your experiences for publication in a professional journal. Although you may not think that your work is of interest to others, editors are always anxious to obtain articles that tell what teachers are doing. Moreover, setting down your thoughts in writing may help clarify your own professional thinking.

Membership in Professional Associations. Many teachers get inspiration and help from mem-

berships in professional organizations. Undoubtedly you would find membership in the organization of teachers in your field rewarding. In almost every instance these organizations publish a professional journal that can help you in keeping abreast of developments in your teaching field and the methods of teaching it. For most teachers the meetings of these associations are especially valuable. Here you can meet and share experiences with others who face the same problems you do.

In addition to the professional organization of teachers in your field, you should probably belong to the local teachers' organization and its state and national parent organization. In some communities, you may have a choice between joining the local chapter of the American Federation of Teachers AFL-CIO or the local affiliate of the National Education Association. Which association to join is a choice you must make for yourself. Do not, however, let yourself be rushed into making a decision. Before deciding you should look carefully at the goals and programs of both organizations at the local and national levels. Then make your decision on the basis of what seems best for the profession and for you.

Think through your philosophy of teaching and working. What sort of relations do you hope to set up with your students and colleagues? How would you go about doing it?

What practical advantages may be obtained from maintaining good relationships with the custodial personnel? What would you do to keep up favorable relationships?

How can one keep from becoming a person who merely repeats one year of teaching experience again and again? What do you plan to do in order to grow on the job?

What type of graduate and in-service work would you be most interested in? What would be most helpful to you in view of your goals? Map out a program of advanced study that you think would be suitable for you after you have started teaching.

Look over the professional journals. Which seem to be most useful for your purposes?

Which professional organizations do you think you should join?

Last Words

This chapter begins by stating that one should try to be a professional teacher from the day one starts teaching. That is a rather high standard.

To become a real master of the trade one must be a pretty special person, for really professional teachers are persons of quality—persons with a sense of high commitment and a great faith in the value of what they are doing; persons with great respect for themselves, their students, and learning; and perhaps most importantly persons who care about the students, about themselves, about society, about the content they teach, and about education.

They do their best to help youth develop into self-sufficient, knowledgeable adults who will face the future with a repertoire of skills, attitudes, and knowledge that will make them able to cope with the experiences of an unpredictable and perhaps perilous future.

The task may be difficult and arduous, but it is truly rewarding. No professional life can be more exciting, interesting, or important than that of the master teacher. When master teachers work with young minds, there is never a dull moment. Their influence is great. Through their students they can contribute to the shaping of the community. Teaching is a profession to be proud of. The really professional teacher glories in being able to say, "I am a teacher." There is no greater praise of anyone in any walk of life than for people to say of one, "There goes a master teacher—a real pro."

Additional Reading

Britt, Samuel S., and Daniel C. Walsh. *The Reality of Teaching.* Dubuqe, IA: Kendall-Hunt, 1979.

Emmens, Amy Puett. *After the Lesson Plan: Realities of High School Teaching.* New York: Teachers College Press, 1981.

Gray, Jenny. *Teachers Survival Guide,* 2nd ed. Palo Alto, CA: Fearon, 1976.

———. *Teaching Without Tears,* 2nd ed. Palo Alto, CA: Fearon, 1976.

Henson, Kenneth T. *Secondary Teaching Methods.* Lexington, MA: D. C. Heath, 1981, Chap. 16.

Highet, Gilbert. *The Art of Teaching.* New York: Vintage Books, 1955.

Kelley, James L. *The Successful Teacher: Essays in Secondary School Instruction.* Ames, IA: Iowa State University Press, 1982.

Lorton, Eveleen, et al. *The Teacher's World,* Special Current Issues Publication No. 9. Washington, D C: ERIC Clearinghouse on Teacher Education, 1979.

Ryan, Kevin, et al. *Biting the Apple: Accounts of First Year Teachers.* New York: Longman, 1980.

Travers, Robert M. W., and Jacqueline Dillon. *The Making of a Teacher: A Plan for Professional Self-Development.* New York: Macmillan, 1975.

Troisi, Nicholas F. *Effective Teaching and Student Achievement.* Reston, VA: National Association of Secondary School Principals, 1983.

Stuart, Jesse. *To Teach, To Love.* New York: Penguin, 1973.

Appendix

A Learning Activity Packet*

Instructions for Use of This Packet

This packet is divided into several sections. Each section is designed to aid you in acquiring specific information and skills. The following suggestions will aid you in using this packet.

1. Take time to explore the *whole* packet.
2. Read the rationale and the primary and secondary ideas for this packet. If you've read these you'll know the WHY and the WHAT you'll be studying.
3. There are goals or objectives in each packet you'll use. For each goal there are activities to aid you in achieving the goal. Familiarize yourself with goals and activities.
4. Your assignments while using these packets are given DIRECTLY THROUGH THE ACTIVITIES, so READ CAREFULLY.
5. All assignments resulting from activities completed in reaching the goals or objectives will be recorded by YOU in your personal folder.
6. Remember that you *do not* have to complete all activities. If and when you feel you've fulfilled the goal or objective go on to another.
7. Most of the materials you'll use in working on these packets will be found in the library, the resource center, the audiovisual bank, teacher-led discussions, and your textbook. Be sure you keep your notes from these sources as they will help you later.
8. There are corresponding *Annexes* in the back of the packets to aid you in your study. These annexes include the following: lists of films, tapes, records, and so on; outlines of information and other material. When working with audiovisual materials you select what you need and use them. If what you are looking for is not listed, ask your teacher to help you.
9. At times in the packet you will finish activities and be expected to report to a certain teacher for a small group lecture over certain important topics. If the teacher leading the discussion has only two or three people in a group he will have you sign up and then call on you to come into the discussion later. In the meantime you may go on with another activity.
10. There are self-assessments at the end of each objective. If you can answer the questions and fulfill the goals you are ready to take the unit test. If you can't answer the self-assessment

* By Dennis Caulk, Washington Irving Junior High School, Colorado Springs, Colorado. Reprinted by permission of the author.

questions, review the activities until you can do so.

11. When you have finished the self-assessment and have satisfied yourself that you can answer all questions, report to your teacher for the UNIT TEST. This unit test will evaluate the objectives of the unit as well as the content knowledge you should have acquired while doing the activities.

12. If you have a grade of 76 per cent or better you may go on to the next packet. If, however, you have a grade of 75 per cent or below you *must* complete the recycling activities in the packet before going on.

13. You may move as rapidly as you like through this packet. Remember you only cheat yourself if you don't fulfill the goals as they are set up.

14. If you are having any problems with this packet report to one of the teachers for help. This way, they will aid you early, and straighten out the problem.

15. DO NOT WRITE IN THIS PACKET!

Packet #1 Colonial America and the French and Indian War

Rationale

The chance to earn a living brought many people to the English colonies. In the northern area, New England, people worked at lumbering and fishing. They were also sailors, shippers, and merchants.

Most people in the middle colonies were farmers. They raised wheat and other grains. Because their agriculture produced chiefly grain for flour-making, these middle colonies were called the "bread colonies."

The people in the southern colonies also engaged in agriculture. Southern farmers grew rice, tobacco, indigo, and hemp. Southern farmers often used slaves from Africa to raise their crops.

The chance to earn a living was not the only reason settlers came to the English colonies. Many people came to America because they wanted religious freedom. They wanted to worship God in their own way. In most parts of Europe, they could not. They had to belong to a national church.

Quakers, Catholics, Puritans, and Jews were among the people who came to America for religious reasons. Catholics found refuge in Maryland. Puritans founded Massachusetts. The Quakers first settled Pennsylvania. The idea of free worship came early to America.

Political rights of Englishmen also brought settlers. England allowed the colonists a considerable amount of self-rule, and this also made people want to live in the English colonies.

English colonists had helped fight for their liberties. They fought alongside British soldiers in the wars against France. In 1763, the French lost their lands in North America to England. After that, the colonists did not have to fear attack by the French, or Indian raids from Canada.

Defeating the French had cost England a great deal of money. England needed money for her empty treasury and decided to collect taxes from her colonies. England had placed taxes on the colonists before but, until 1763, she had not tried very hard to collect them. When England did try to seriously collect these taxes, it led to trouble with the colonists.

Primary Idea

The people who came to America to set up colonies did so mainly to have a better way of life.

Secondary Ideas

1. Early colonization in the New World was carried out by the English, French, and Dutch.
2. Three distinct sections developed in the thirteen

colonies. They were the northern or New England colonies, the Middle colonies, and the Southern colonies.

3. Because of geographical conditions each section (New England, Middle, and Southern) had different patterns of living.
4. French settlement in the New World was not based primarily on religion as had been true of English settlement.
5. Rivalry between France and England in Europe led to wars which extended to North America.
6. France was defeated in the French and Indian War and her territorial claims were lost.
7. French influence is still present in North America.

Objective A

You will be able to write a paragraph for at least three (3) of the four reasons explaining why the English came to settle colonies in the New World between 1607 and 1733.

Activity 1

Read section 1 of Chapter 4, page 81, in *This Is America's Story*, or Chapter 4, page 37, in *Adventures in American History*. Also see the filmstrip *England Prepares to Colonize*. Take notes on your reading and viewing.

Activity 2

Make a list of four (4) causes for English colonization in America. Could you write a paragraph summary of each cause?

Activity 3

Make a chart showing the thirteen English Colonies. Use these headings for your chart: *Name of Colony; Date Founded; Who* (leader or group) *Founded It;* and *Reasons for Founding.* Now research and fill in the chart.

Activity 4

With the information you've gathered from activities 2 and 3, write four (4) paragraphs. Each paragraph will describe a reason for English colonization.

Activity 5

Imagine you have been hired by the Pilgrims, Lord Baltimore, or William Penn to make posters to attract settlers to one of the three colonies. Before you make your poster, decide what point or points you want to emphasize, then illustrate these in your poster.

Self-Assessment

At this point, can you write four (4) paragraphs explaining the four main reasons for English colonization, 1607–1733? If not, see your teacher.

Objective B

You will be able to construct an outline or a chart which will give the order of settlement of the New England, the Middle, and the Southern colonies between 1607 and 1733.

Activity 1

Read and take notes on sections 2, 3, 4, and 5 in Chapter 4 of *This Is America's Story*, or review Chapter 4 in *Adventures in American History*. You may group with three (3) other students to go over these notes.

Activity 2

Make a chart or an outline pointing out how the New England, Middle, and Southern colonies were founded. Make sure you get the names under the right heading or sections of colonies. Hint! Activity #3 for objective A may help you in doing this activity.

Activity 3

Write entries in an imaginary diary kept by a boy or girl who went to the New World with (a) the Jamestown settlers in 1607, (b) the Pilgrims in 1620, (c) the Puritans in 1630.

Activity 4

Find pictures showing costumes worn by French, English, Spanish, and Dutch colonists. Show these to the class or prepare a bulletin board display.

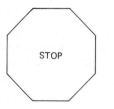

STOP

Take your chart or outline to a teacher and, using it, explain how the three colonial areas were founded.

Objective C

You will be able to fill in the names of the thirteen colonies on a blank map.

Activity 1

Review the activities you've completed for the previous two objectives.

Activity 2

Study the map on page 87 in *This Is America's Story*, or page 50 in *Adventures in American History*. Be sure you can spell correctly the name of each colony.

Activity 3

With a blank outline map of the eastern coast of America fill in the names of the colonies. Your teacher will give you the map.

Activity 4 (optional)

Include on your map for Activity #3 the major topographical features (major rivers, mountain ranges, and so on) of the eastern America colonial area.

Now—Put your name on your map and post it on the bulletin board.

Self-assessment

If you were given a blank map of the thirteen colonies could you fill in the names of the colonies in their right locations?

Objective D

You will be able to write a paper explaining how people lived in the New England, Middle, and Southern colonies.

Activity 1

Read Chapter 5 in *This Is America's Story*, or Chapter 5 in *Adventures in American History*. Also take the time to view those filmstrips in the *English Colonies Series* (see Annex) that interest you. Take notes!!

Activity 2

Using your notes from Activity 1 write a paper of a page or more describing what it was like living in America during the Colonial Period. You should include the following in your paper:

A. the geography of each section
B. the ways of making a living

C. the class structure
D. the educational opportunities
E. religion
F. recreational opportunities
G. types of homes
H. anything else you would like to add

Activity 3 (optional)

Trace the development of freedom of worship in colonial America. Note the established churches, and list as many other denominations or faiths you can find.

Activity 4 (optional)

Compare the educational opportunities in the New England, Middle, and Southern colonies.

Activity 5 (optional)

Write a paper showing comparisons between the life of indentured servants and of slaves in colonial America.

Self-assessment

Could you now write a one to two page report describing the different ways people lived in the New England, Middle, and Southern colonies? If not, go to a teacher for further assistance.

Objective E

You will be able to trace the settlement of the French in the New World and point out in writing or orally how French colonization differed from that of the English.

Activity 1

Read and take notes on Section 1 of Chapter 6 in *This is America's Story* or parts 2 through 4 (pages 29–36) in *Adventures in American History*.

Activity 2

Make a list of the developments that occurred as the French settled in the New World.

Activity 3

With your list from Activity 2 write a comparison between British and French colonization in the New World.

Activity 4

Write or prepare orally a report describing how the French and British went about colonization in different ways.

Activity 5 (optional)

Read Longfellow's "Evangeline" (in your literature book), which deals with the troubles faced by the Acadians. Draw conclusions from your reading and then write a paper naming any similar groups of displaced persons in the world today.

Self-Assessment

Can you trace the settlement of the French in the New World and explain how it differed from English settlement? Can you do this in a one page written paper or a one to two minute oral report?

Objective F

You will be able to write a paper or give an oral report on the French and Indian War, including the causes of the War, the main events, and the results.

Activity 1

Read Sections 2 and 3 in Chapter 6 of *This Is America's Story* or part 5, page 36 in *Adventures in American History*. Also see the film *French and*

Indian War: Seven Years War in America. Be sure you take notes—you'll need them later on.

Activity 2

Make a list of: (a) three (3) reasons why the British and French went to war; (b) three (3) advantages the French had and three (3) the British had in the war; (c) five (5) of the main events of the war, and (d) all of the results you can find that came from the war.

Activity 3

From the lists you made in Activity 2, write a two page summary or prepare a five minute oral report demonstrating your knowledge of the French and Indian War. At this point, turn in your summary, or make an appointment with your teacher for presenting your oral report.

Activity 4 (optional)

By working with two other students, answer the following questions in a panel discussion:

1. What geographical area in North America was the prize which the French and the British wished to hold? Why did both have such ambitions? What were the results of that struggle between the two countries? Name the states that lie within the area today. In what way is it still a prize?
2. How did geography aid the French in protecting Quebec? How did the British overcome this French advantage?
3. Canada today may be called a country of two cultures. What are they and why is this true?
4. Name the large area of land in North America that Spain gained after the French and Indian War. With what other possessions on the continent was it joined?
5. Why was England so eager to gain control of Florida? When?

When you are ready to present your panel discussion, contact one of the teachers.

Self-Assessment

Can you write a two page paper or give a five minute oral report covering the causes, events, and results of the French and Indian War?

Self-assessment

If you can answer the following questions at this time you should report to your teacher for the Unit Test. If, however, you cannot answer the questions review the activities of this packet until you can.

1. Given four (4) reasons for English colonization can you write a paragraph describing each?
2. Can you construct an outline or a chart showing how the New England, the Middle, and the Southern colonies were founded?
3. If you were given a blank map of the thirteen colonies could you fill in the names of the colonies in their right locations?
4. Can you write a one to two page report describing the different ways people lived in the New England, Middle, and Southern colonies?
5. Can you trace the settlement of the French in the New World and explain how it differed from English settlement? Can you do this in a one page written paper or a one to two minute oral report?
6. Can you write a two page paper or give a five minute oral report covering the causes, events, and results of the French and Indian War?

Annex A

Listed here are materials to aid you in the study of this packet. Take advantage of these resources as they will benefit you greatly. These materials are stored in the Audio Visual Resource Bank and are available to you when you need them.

1. *The Beginnings of The American Nation* 209 Filmstrip
2. *Colonial America*   0410   Filmstrip
3. *Earning A Living in the Colonies* 0431   Filmstrip
4. *Eighteenth Century Life in Williamsburg, Virginia*   981   Film 44 min.
5. English Colonies Series—Filmstrips
   a. *England Prepares to Colonize*   1528–0239
   b. *Virginia Colony*   0261–0246
   c. *Other Southern Colonies*   0244–0263
   d. *Colony of Massachusetts*   0267–0237
   e. *Other New England Colonies*   0243–0264
   f. *New York Colony*   0241–0268
   g. *Colonies of Pennsylvania and New Jersey*   0236–0269
   h. *England Conquers New France*   0238–0266
   i. *Occupations and Amusements of the Colonists*   0242
   j. *Social and Cultural Life of the Colonists*   0262–0245
6. *French and Indian War: Seven Year's War in America*   1321   1059   Film-16 minutes
7. *Landing of Pilgrims*   T-179   T-100   Tape 15 minutes.
8. *French Colonization*   1166   Filmstrip

Be sure you check with the *Social Studies Bibliography* for additional resources.

Enrichment Reading from your literature book

1. Bradford and Winslow's "So Goodly a Land."
2. Hawthorne's "The Pine Tree Shillings."

Annex B (Content Outline)

A. The French Colonies
   I. Obstacles to French colonization in North America
      A. Feeling that North America was not as valuable as the West Indies.
      B. Troubles in recruiting colonists
   II. Government and society in the French colonies
      A. Royal governor

B. No self-government
III. French treatment of Indians
   A. Indians were treated well
   B. Indians were allies and a source of furs
   C. Algonquins and Hurons
IV. Slow growth of French colonies
   A. Mistakes in policy and lack of interest
   B. French kings were not as interested in granting New World lands to individuals and to small groups of settlers as were the English kings
B. The Founding of the English Colonies
   I. Rivalry between England and Spain
      A. Sir Francis Drake and defeat of the Spanish Armada (1588)
      B. Expanding English trade throughout the world
      C. Growing English interest in colonization
   II. Motives and Methods of English colonization
      A. English colonies were founded by private enterprise rather than by government
      B. The English allowed religious dissenters to settle in their colonies
      C. The English also allowed settlements to be established for reasons of social necessity (Georgia) and because of western movement from more settled colonies (New Hampshire)
      D. English colonies enjoyed a great deal of local self-government
   III. Making a living in the English colonies
      A. New England colonies
         1. Thin soil, harsh climate, and few natural resources
         2. Lumbering develops (ship building)
         3. Fishing industry grows
         4. Trade (shipping)
      B. The Middle or "Bread" colonies
         1. Rich soil and navigable rivers
         2. Farming
            a. grains
            b. livestock

  3. Some fur trading was done
  4. Trade (shipping)
C. Southern colonies
  1. Plantation system used in agriculture—tide water area
  2. Farming
    a. rice
    b. indigo
    c. tobacco
    d. livestock
  3. Forests
    a. lumber
    b. turpentine
IV. Colonial Society
A. Upper class—superior position by law and custom
  1. Merchants
  2. Clergymen
  3. Large land owners

B. Mobile society—you can move up the ladder, and up the river
C. Indentured servants
  1. Passage given for a promised number of years of service
  2. Wages were higher in America than in England—workers were scarce
V. Effects of the Frontier
A. Leveled the social class barrier
B. Land was abundant and usually free
C. Women became more self-reliant
VI. Widespread prosperity
A. Hardly any paupers or beggars
B. Crime was seen very little
C. Most people were busy all the time (no idle rich)
D. Extra energies spent in improving colonial life (for example: Ben Franklin, Thomas Jefferson)

Index

455